Curves and Surfaces in Geometric Modeling

Theory and Algorithms

The Morgan Kaufmann Series in Computer Graphics and Geometric Modeling

Series Editor, Brian A. Barsky

Curves and Surfaces in Geometric Modeling: Theory and Algorithms
Jean Gallier

Advanced RenderMan: Creating CGI for Motion Pictures
Anthony A. Apodaca and Larry Gritz

Andrew Glassner's Notebook: Recreational Computer Graphics
Andrew S. Glassner

Warping and Morphing of Graphical Objects
Jonas Gomes, Lucia Darsa, Bruno Costa, and Luis Velho

Jim Blinn's Corner: Dirty Pixels
Jim Blinn

Rendering with Radiance: The Art and Science of Lighting Visualization
Greg Ward Larson and Rob Shakespeare

Introduction to Implicit Surfaces
Edited by Jules Bloomenthal

Jim Blinn's Corner: A Trip Down the Graphics Pipeline
Jim Blinn

Interactive Curves and Surfaces: A Multimedia Tutorial on CAGD
Alyn Rockwood and Peter Chambers

Wavelets for Computer Graphics: Theory and Applications
Eric J. Stollnitz, Tony D. DeRose, and David H. Salesin

Principles of Digital Image Synthesis
Andrew S. Glassner

Radiosity & Global Illumination
François X. Sillion and Claude Puech

Knotty: A B-Spline Visualization Program
Jonathan Yen

User Interface Management Systems: Models and Algorithms
Dan R. Olsen, Jr.

Making Them Move: Mechanics, Control, and Animation of Articulated Figures
Edited by Norman I. Badler, Brian A. Barsky, and David Zeltzer

Geometric and Solid Modeling: An Introduction
Christoph M. Hoffmann

An Introduction to Splines for Use in Computer Graphics and Geometric Modeling
Richard H. Bartels, John C. Beatty, and Brian A. Barsky

Curves and Surfaces in Geometric Modeling

Theory and Algorithms

Jean Gallier

University of Pennsylvania

Morgan Kaufmann Publishers
San Francisco, California

Senior Editor   Diane D. Cerra
Director of Production and Manufacturing   Yonie Overton
Production Editor   Cheri Palmer
Editorial Coordinator   Belinda Breyer
Cover Design   Ross Carron Design
Cover Image   Keren Su/Tony Stone Images
Copyeditor   Ken DellaPenta
Proofreader   Jennifer McClain
Text Design, Composition, and Illustration   Windfall Software, using ZzTEX
Indexer   Ty Koontz
Printer   Courier Corporation

Designations used by companies to distinguish their products are often claimed as trademarks or registered trademarks. In all instances where Morgan Kaufmann Publishers is aware of a claim, the product names appear in initial capital or all capital letters. Readers, however, should contact the appropriate companies for more complete information regarding trademarks and registration.

Morgan Kaufmann Publishers
Editorial and Sales Office
340 Pine Street, Sixth Floor
San Francisco, CA 94104-3205
USA
Telephone 415 / 392-2665
Facsimile 415 / 982-2665
Email mkp@mkp.com
WWW http://www.mkp.com

Order toll free 800 / 745-7323

04   03   02   01   00   5   4   3   2   1

Library of Congress Cataloging-in-Publication Data
Gallier, Jean H.
   Curves and surfaces in geometric modeling : theory and algorithms
/ Jean Gallier.
      p.   cm
   Includes bibliographical references and index.
   ISBN 1-55860-599-1
   1. Curves, Algebraic—Data processing.   2. Surfaces—Data
processing.   3. Computer-aided design.   I. Title.
QA567.G28   2000
516.3'52—dc21   99-36401
                                                           CIP

To my new daughter Mia, my wife Anne,
my son Philippe, and my daughter Sylvie

This book is primarily an introduction to geometric concepts and tools needed for solving problems of a geometric nature with a computer. Our main goal is to provide an introduction to the mathematical concepts needed in tackling problems arising notably in computer graphics, geometric modeling, computer vision, and motion planning, just to mention some key areas. Many problems in the above areas require some geometric knowledge, but in our opinion, books dealing with the relevant geometric material are either too theoretical, or else rather specialized and application-oriented. This book is an attempt to fill this gap.

We present a coherent view of geometric methods applicable to many engineering problems at a level that can be understood by a senior undergraduate with a good math background. Thus, this book should be of interest to a wide audience including computer scientists (both students and professionals), mathematicians, and engineers interested in geometric methods (for example, mechanical engineers). In particular, we provide an introduction to affine geometry. This material provides the foundations for the algorithmic treatment of polynomial curves and surfaces, which is a main theme of this book. We present some of the main tools used in computer-aided geometric design (CAGD), but our goal is not to write another text on CAGD. In brief, we are writing about geometric modeling methods in engineering.

We refrained from using the expression "computational geometry" because it has a well-established meaning that does not correspond to what we have in mind. Although we will touch some of the topics covered in computational geometry (for example, triangulations), we are more interested in dealing with curves and surfaces *from an algorithmic point of view*. In this respect, we are flirting with the intuitionist's ideal of doing mathematics from a "constructive" point of view. Such a point of view is of course very relevant to computer science.

This book consists of four parts.

- Part I provides an introduction to affine geometry. This ensures that you are on firm ground to proceed with the rest of the book, in particular the study of curves and surfaces. This is also useful to establish the notation and terminology. If you are proficient in geometry, you may omit this section, or use it by need. On the other hand, if you are totally unfamiliar with this material, you will probably have a hard time with the rest of the book. You are advised to do some extra reading in order to assimilate some basic knowledge of geometry. For example, we highly recommend Berger [5, 6], Pedoe [59], Samuel [69], Hilbert and Cohn-Vossen [42], do Carmo [26], Berger and Gostiaux [7], Böhm and Prautzsch [11], and Tisseron [83].

- Part II deals with an algorithmic treatment of polynomial curves (Bézier curves) and spline curves.

- Part III deals with an algorithmic treatment of polynomial surfaces (Bézier rectangular or triangular surfaces) and spline surfaces. We also include a section on subdivision surfaces, an exciting and active area of research in geometric modeling and animation, as attested by several papers in SIGGRAPH '98, especially the paper by DeRose, Kass, and Truong [24] on the animated character Geri, from the short movie *Geri's Game*.

- Part IV consists of appendices consisting of the basics of linear algebra, certain technical proofs that were omitted earlier, complements of affine geometry, analysis, and differential calculus. This part has been included to make the material of Parts I–III self-contained. Our advice is to use it *by need*!

Our goal is not to write a text on the many specialized and practical CAGD methods. Our main goal is to provide an introduction to the concepts needed in tackling problems arising in computer graphics, geometric modeling, computer vision, and motion planning, just to mention some key areas. As it turns out, one of the most spectacular applications of these concepts is the treatment of curves and surfaces in terms of control points, a tool extensively used in CAGD. This is why many pages are devoted to an algorithmic treatment of curves and surfaces. However, we only provide a cursory coverage of CAGD methods. Luckily, there are excellent texts on CAGD, including Bartels, Beatty, and Barsky [4], Farin [32, 31], Fiorot and Jeannin [35, 36], Risler [68], Hoschek and Lasser [45], and Piegl and Tiller [62]. Similarly, although we cover affine geometry in some detail, we are far from giving a comprehensive treatment of these topics. For such a treatment, we highly recommend Berger [5, 6], Pedoe [59], Tisseron [83], Samuel [69], Dieudonné [25], Sidler [76], and Veblen and Young [85, 86], a great classic. Several sections of this book are inspired by the treatment in one of several of the above texts, and we are happy to thank the authors for providing such inspiration.

Lyle Ramshaw's remarkably elegant and inspirational DEC-SRC report, "Blossoming: A connect-the-dots approach to splines" [65], radically changed our perspective on polynomial curves and surfaces. We have happily and irrevocably adopted the view that the most transparent manner for presenting much of the theory of polynomial curves and surfaces is to stress the multilinear nature (really multiaffine) of these curves and surfaces. This is in complete agreement with de Casteljau's original spirit, but as Ramshaw, we are more explicit in our use of multilinear tools. As you will discover, much of the algorithmic theory of polynomial curves and surfaces is captured by three words: "Polarize, homogenize, tensorize!"

We will be dealing primarily with the following kinds of problems:

- *Approximating a shape (curve or surface).* We will see how this can be done using polynomial curves or surfaces (also called Bézier curves or surfaces) and spline curves or surfaces.

- *Interpolating a set of points, by a curve or a surface.* Again, we will see how this can be done using spline curves or spline surfaces.

- *Drawing a curve or a surface.* The tools and techniques developed for solving the approximation problem will be very useful for solving the other two problems.

The material presented in this book is related to the classical differential geometry of curves and surfaces and to numerical methods in matrix analysis. In fact, it is often possible to reduce problems involving certain splines to solving systems of linear equations. Thus, it is very helpful to be aware of efficient methods for numerical matrix analysis. For further information on these topics, see the excellent texts by Gray [39], Strang [81], and Ciarlet [19]. Strang's beautiful book on applied mathematics is also highly recommended as a general reference [80]. There are other interesting applications of geometry to computer vision, computer graphics, and solid modeling. Some great references are Koenderink [46] and Faugeras [33] for computer vision, Hoffman [43] for solid modeling, and Metaxas [53] for physics-based deformable models.

Novelties

As far as we know, there is no fully developed modern exposition integrating the basic concepts of affine geometry as well as a presentation of curves and surfaces from the algorithmic point of view in terms of control points (in the polynomial case). There is also no reasonably thorough textbook presentation of the main surface subdivision schemes (Doo-Sabin, Catmull-Clark, Loop) and a technical discussion of convergence and smoothness.

New Treatment, New Results

This book provides an introduction to affine geometry. Generally, background material or rather technical proofs are relegated to appendices.

We give an in-depth presentation of polynomial curves and surfaces from an algorithmic point of view. The approach (sometimes called *blossoming*) consists in multilinearizing everything in sight (getting *polar forms*), which leads very naturally to a presentation of polynomial curves and surfaces in terms of control points (Bézier curves and surfaces). We present many algorithms for subdividing and drawing curves and surfaces, all implemented in Mathematica. A clean and elegant presentation of control points is obtained by using a construction for embedding an affine space into a vector space (the so-called hat construction, originating in Berger [5]). We even include an optional chapter (Chapter 11) covering tensors and symmetric tensors to provide an in-depth understanding of the foundations of blossoming and a more conceptual view of the computational material on curves and surfaces. The continuity conditions for spline curves and spline surfaces are expressed in terms of polar forms, which yields both geometric and computational insights into the subtle interaction of knots and de Boor control points.

Subdivision surfaces are the topic of Section 9.4. Subdivision surfaces form an active and promising area of research. They provide an attractive alternative to spline surfaces in modeling applications where the topology of surfaces is rather complex, and where the initial control polyhedron consists of various kinds of faces, not just triangles or rectangles. As far as we know, this is the first textbook presentation of three popular methods due to Doo and Sabin [27, 29, 28], Catmull and Clark [17], and Charles Loop [50]. We discuss Loop's convergence proof in some detail, and for this, we give a crash course on discrete Fourier transforms and (circular) discrete convolutions. A glimpse at subdivision surfaces is given in a new section added to Farin's fourth edition [32]. Subdivision surfaces are also briefly covered in Stollnitz, DeRose, and Salesin [79], but in the context of wavelets and multiresolution representation.

As a general rule, we try to be rigorous, but we always keep the algorithmic nature of the mathematical objects under consideration in the forefront.

Many problems and programming projects are proposed (over 200). Some are routine; some are (very) difficult.

Many Algorithms and Their Implementation

Although one of our main concerns is to be mathematically rigorous, which implies that we give precise definitions and prove almost all of the results in this book, we are primarily interested in the representation and the implementation of concepts and tools used to solve geometric problems. Thus, we devote a great deal of effort to the development and implemention of algorithms to manipulate curves, surfaces, triangulations, and so on. As a matter of fact, we provide Mathematica code for most of the geometric algorithms presented in this book. These algorithms were used to prepare most of the illustrations in this book. We also urge you to write your own algorithms, and we propose many challenging programming projects.

Open Problems

Not only do we present standard material (although sometimes from a fresh point of view), but whenever possible, we state some open problems, thus taking you to the cutting edge of the field. For example, we describe very clearly the problem of finding an efficient way to compute control points for C^k-continuous triangular surface splines. We also discuss some of the problems with the convergence and smoothness of subdivision surface methods.

What Is Not Covered in This Book

Since this book is already quite long, we have omitted rational curves and rational surfaces, and projective geometry. A good reference on these topics is Farin [31]. We are writing a text covering these topics rather extensively (and more). We also have omitted solid modeling techniques, methods for rendering implicit curves and surfaces, the finite-element method, and wavelets. The first two topics are nicely covered in Hoffman [43], a remarkably clear presentation of wavelets is given in Stollnitz, DeRose, and Salesin [79], and a more mathematical presentation in Strang and Truong [82]; and the finite-element method is the subject of so many books that we will not even attempt to mention any references.

Acknowledgments

This book grew out of lecture notes that I wrote while teaching CIS510, "Introduction to Geometric Methods in Computer Science," for the past four years. I wish to thank some students and colleagues for their comments, including Doug DeCarlo, Jaydev Desai, Will Dickinson, Charles Erignac, Hany Farid, Steve Frye, Edith Haber, Andy Hicks, David Jelinek, Ioannis Kakadiaris, Hartmut Liefke, Dimitris Metaxas, Jeff Nimeroff, Rich Pito, Ken Shoemake, Bond-Jay Ting, Deepak Tolani, Dianna Xu, and most of all Raj Iyer, who screened half of the manuscript with a fine-tooth comb. Thanks to Norm Badler, for triggering my interest in geometric modeling, and to Marcel Berger, Chris Croke, Ron Donagi, Gerald Farin, Herman Gluck, and David Harbater, for sharing some of their geometric secrets with me. I also wish to express my deep appreciation to the reviewers of the manuscript, Alain Fournier and Ian Ashdown from the University of British Columbia; Spencer Thomas from the University of Michigan; and Brian Barsky, Series Editor, from the University of California, Berkeley. Finally, many thanks to Eugenio Calabi, for teaching me what I know about differential geometry (and much more!).

CHAPTER 1

Introduction

1.1   Geometric Methods in Engineering

Geometry, what a glorious subject! For centuries, geometry has played a crucial role in the development of many scientific and engineering disciplines, such as astronomy, geodesy, mechanics, ballistics, civil and mechanical engineering, ship building, architecture, and in this century, automobile and aircraft manufacturing, among others. What makes geometry a unique and particularly exciting branch of mathematics is that it is primarily *visual*. You might say that this is only true of geometry up to the end of the nineteenth century, but even when the objects are higher dimensional and very abstract, the intuitions behind these fancy concepts almost always come from shapes that can somehow be visualized. On the other hand, it was discovered at the end of the nineteenth century that there was a danger in relying too much on visual intuition, and that this could lead to wrong results or fallacious arguments. What happened then is that mathematicians started using more algebra and analysis in geometry, in order to put it on firmer ground and to obtain more rigorous proofs. The consequence of the striving for more rigor and the injection of more algebra in geometry is that mathematicians at the beginning of the twentieth century began suppressing geometric intuitions from their proofs. Geometry lost some of its charm and became a rather impenetrable discipline, except for the initiated. It is interesting to observe that most college textbooks of mathematics included a fair amount of geometry up to the '40s. Beginning with the '50s, the amount of geometry decreases to basically disappear in the '70s.

Paradoxically, with the advent of faster computers, starting in the early '60s, automobile and plane manufacturers realized that it was possible to design cars and planes using computer-aided methods. These methods, pioneered by de Casteljau, Bézier, and Ferguson, used geometry. Although not very advanced, the type of geometry used is very elegant. Basically, it is a branch of affine geometry, and it

1

is very useful from the point of view of applications. Thus, there seems to be an interesting turn of events. After being neglected for decades, stimulated by computer science, geometry seems to be making a comeback as a fundamental tool used in manufacturing, computer graphics, computer vision, and motion planning, just to mention some key areas.

We are convinced that geometry will play an important role in computer science and engineering in the years to come. The demand for technology using 3D graphics, virtual reality, animation techniques, and so on, is increasing fast, and it is clear that storing and processing complex images and complex geometric models of shapes (face, limbs, organs, etc.) will be required. We will need to understand better how to *discretize* geometric objects such as curves, surfaces, and volumes. This book represents an attempt at presenting a coherent view of geometric methods used to tackle problems of a geometric nature with a computer. We believe that this can be a great way of learning about curves and surfaces, while having fun. Furthermore, there are plenty of opportunities for applying these methods to real-world problems.

Our main focus is on curves and surfaces, but our point of view is algorithmic. We concentrate on methods for discretizing curves and surfaces in order to store them and display them efficiently. Thus, we focus on polynomial curves defined in terms of control points, since they are the most efficient class of curves and surfaces from the point of view of design and representation. However, in order to gain a deeper understanding of this theory of curves and surfaces, we present the underlying geometric concepts in some detail, in particular, affine geometry. In turn, since this material relies on some algebra and analysis (linear algebra, directional derivatives, etc.), in order to make the book entirely self-contained, we provide some appendices where this background material is presented.

In the next section, we list some problems arising in computer graphics and computer vision that can be tackled using the geometric tools and concepts presented in this book.

1.2 Examples of Problems Using Geometric Modeling

The following is a nonexhaustive listing of several different areas in which geometric methods (using curves and surfaces) play a crucial role:

- Manufacturing

- Medical imaging

- Molecular modeling

- Computational fluid dynamics

- Physical simulation in applied mechanics

- Oceanography, virtual oceans

- Shape reconstruction

- Weather analysis

- Computer graphics (rendering smooth curved shapes)

- Computer animation

- Data compression

- Architecture

- Art (sculpture, 3D images, etc.)

A specific subproblem that often needs to be solved—for example, in manufacturing problems or in medical imaging—is to fit a curve or a surface through a set of data points. For simplicity, let us discuss briefly a curve-fitting problem.

Problem: Given $N + 1$ data points $x_0, \ldots, x_N$ and a sequence of $N + 1$ reals $u_0, \ldots, u_N$, with $u_i < u_{i+1}$ for all i, $0 \leq i \leq N - 1$, find a C^2-continuous curve F, such that $F(u_i) = x_i$, for all i, $0 \leq i \leq N$.

As stated above, the problem is actually underdetermined. Indeed, there are many different types of curves that solve the above problem (defined by Fourier series, Lagrange interpolants, etc.), and we need to be more specific as to what kind of curve we would like to use. In most cases, efficiency is the dominant factor, and it turns out that piecewise polynomial curves are usually the best choice. Even then, the problem is still underdetermined. However, the problem is no longer underdetermined if we specify some "end conditions"—for instance, the tangents at x_0 and x_N. In this case, it can be shown that there is a unique B-spline curve solving the above problem (see Section 6.8). The next figure shows $N + 1 = 8$ data points, and a C^2-continuous spline curve F passing through these points, for a uniform sequence of reals u_i.

Other points $d_{-1}, \ldots, d_8$ are also shown. What happens is that the interpolating B-spline curve is really determined by some sequence of points $d_{-1}, \ldots, d_{N+1}$ called *de Boor control points* (with $d_{-1} = x_0$ and $d_{N+1} = x_N$). Instead of specifying the tangents at x_0 and x_N, we can specify the control points d_0 and d_N. Then, it turns out that $d_1, \ldots, d_{N-1}$ can be computed from $x_0, \ldots, x_N$ (and d_0, d_N) by solving a system of linear equations of the form

$$\begin{pmatrix} 1 & & & & & & \\ \alpha_1 & \beta_1 & \gamma_1 & & & & \\ & \alpha_2 & \beta_2 & \gamma_2 & & 0 & \\ & & & \ddots & & & \\ & 0 & & \alpha_{N-2} & \beta_{N-2} & \gamma_{N-2} & \\ & & & & \alpha_{N-1} & \beta_{N-1} & \gamma_{N-1} \\ & & & & & & 1 \end{pmatrix} \begin{pmatrix} d_0 \\ d_1 \\ d_2 \\ \vdots \\ d_{N-2} \\ d_{N-1} \\ d_N \end{pmatrix} = \begin{pmatrix} r_0 \\ r_1 \\ r_2 \\ \vdots \\ r_{N-2} \\ r_{N-1} \\ r_N \end{pmatrix}$$

where r_0 and r_N may be chosen arbitrarily, the coefficients $\alpha_i, \beta_i, \gamma_i$ are easily computed from the u_j, and $r_i = (u_{i+1} - u_{i-1})x_i$ for $1 \leq i \leq N - 1$ (see Section 6.8).

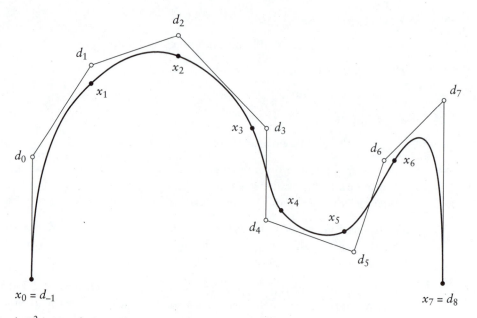

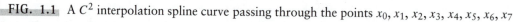

FIG. 1.1 A C^2 interpolation spline curve passing through the points $x_0, x_1, x_2, x_3, x_4, x_5, x_6, x_7$

Figure 1.1 gives an example of an interpolating curve passing through the points $x_0, x_1, \ldots, x_7$.

The previous example suggests that curves can be defined in terms of *control points*. Indeed, specifying curves and surfaces in terms of control points is one of the major techniques used in geometric design. For example, in medical imaging, we may want to find the contour of some organ, say, the heart, given some discrete data. We may do this by fitting a *B*-spline curve through the data points. In computer animation, we may want to have a person move from one location to another, passing through some intermediate locations, in a smooth manner. Again, this problem can be solved using *B*-splines. Many manufacturing problems involve fitting a surface through some data points—for example, automobile design, plane design (wings, fuselage, etc.), engine parts, ship hulls, ski boots, and so on.

We could go on and on with many other examples, but it is now time to review some basics of affine geometry!

PART I

BASICS OF AFFINE GEOMETRY

CHAPTER 2

Basics of Affine Geometry

2.1   Affine Spaces

Geometrically, curves and surfaces are usually considered to be sets of points with some special properties, living in a space consisting of "points." Typically, we are also interested in geometric properties invariant under certain transformations, for example, translations, rotations, projections, and so on. We could model the space of points as a vector space, but this is not very satisfactory for a number of reasons. One reason is that the point corresponding to the zero vector $(\vec{0})$, called the origin, plays a special role, when there is really no reason to have a privileged origin. Another reason is that certain notions, such as parallelism, are handled in an awkward manner. But the deeper reason is that vector spaces and affine spaces really have different geometries. The geometric properties of a vector space are invariant under the group of bijective linear maps, whereas the geometric properties of an affine space are invariant under the group of bijective affine maps, and these two groups are not isomorphic. Roughly speaking, there are more affine maps than linear maps.

Affine spaces provide a better framework for doing geometry. In particular, it is possible to deal with points, curves, surfaces, and so on, in an *intrinsic manner*, that is, independently of any specific choice of a coordinate system. As in physics, this is highly desirable to really understand what's going on. Of course, coordinate systems have to be chosen to finally carry out computations, but you should learn to resist the temptation to resort to coordinate systems until it is really necessary.

Affine spaces are the right framework for dealing with motions, trajectories, and physical forces, among other things. Thus, affine geometry is crucial to a clean presentation of kinematics, dynamics, and other parts of physics (for example, elasticity). After all, a rigid motion is an affine map, but not a linear map in general. Also, given an $m \times n$ matrix A and a vector $b \in \mathbf{R}^m$, the set $U = \{x \in \mathbf{R}^n \mid Ax = b\}$

of solutions of the system $Ax = b$ is an affine space, but not a vector space (linear space) in general. *Use coordinate systems only when needed!*

This chapter proceeds as follows. We take advantage of the fact that almost every affine concept is the counterpart of some concept in linear algebra. We begin by defining affine spaces, stressing the physical interpretation of the definition in terms of points (particles) and vectors (forces). Corresponding to linear combinations of vectors, we define affine combinations of points (barycenters), realizing that we are forced to restrict our attention to families of scalars adding up to 1. Corresponding to linear subspaces, we introduce affine spaces as subsets closed under affine combinations. Then, we characterize affine spaces in terms of certain vector spaces called their directions. This allows us to define a clean notion of parallelism. Next, corresponding to linear independence and bases, we define affine independence and affine frames. We also define convexity. Corresponding to linear maps, we define affine maps as maps preserving affine combinations. We show that every affine map is completely defined by the image of one point and a linear map. We investigate briefly some simple affine maps, the translations and the central dilatations. Certain technical proofs and some complementary material on affine geometry are relegated to Appendix B.

Our presentation of affine geometry is far from being comprehensive, and it is biased towards the algorithmic geometry of curves and surfaces. For more details, see Pedoe [59], Snapper and Troyer [77], Berger [5, 6], Samuel [69], Tisseron [83], and Hilbert and Cohn-Vossen [42].

Suppose we have a particle moving in 3-space and we want to describe the trajectory of this particle. If we look up a good textbook on dynamics, such as Greenwood [40], we find out that the particle is modeled as a point, and that the position of this point x is determined with respect to a "frame" in $\mathbf{R}^3$ by a vector. Curiously, the notion of a frame is rarely defined precisely, but it is easy to infer that a frame is a pair $(O, (\vec{e_1}, \vec{e_2}, \vec{e_3}))$ consisting of an origin O (which is a point) together with a basis of three vectors $(\vec{e_1}, \vec{e_2}, \vec{e_3})$. For example, the standard frame in $\mathbf{R}^3$ has origin $O = (0, 0, 0)$ and the basis of three vectors $\vec{e_1} = (1, 0, 0)$, $\vec{e_2} = (0, 1, 0)$, and $\vec{e_3} = (0, 0, 1)$. The position of a point x is then defined by the "unique vector" from O to x.

But wait a minute, this definition seems to be defining frames and the position of a point without defining what a point is! Well, let us identify points with elements of $\mathbf{R}^3$. If so, given any two points $a = (a_1, a_2, a_3)$ and $b = (b_1, b_2, b_3)$, there is a unique *free vector* denoted $\vec{ab}$ from a to b, the vector $\vec{ab} = (b_1 - a_1, b_2 - a_2, b_3 - a_3)$ (see Figure 2.1). Note that

$$b = a + \vec{ab},$$

addition being understood as addition in $\mathbf{R}^3$. Then, in the standard frame, given a point $x = (x_1, x_2, x_3)$, the position of x is the vector $\vec{Ox} = (x_1, x_2, x_3)$, which coincides with the point itself. In the standard frame, points and vectors are identified.

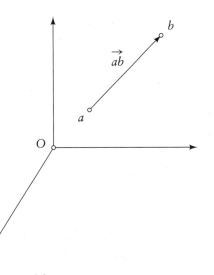

FIG. 2.1 Points and free vectors

What if we pick a frame with a different origin, say, $\Omega = (\omega_1, \omega_2, \omega_3)$, but the same basis vectors $(\vec{e_1}, \vec{e_2}, \vec{e_3})$? This time, the point $x = (x_1, x_2, x_3)$ is defined by two position vectors: $\vec{Ox} = (x_1, x_2, x_3)$ in the frame $(O, (\vec{e_1}, \vec{e_2}, \vec{e_3}))$, and $\vec{\Omega x} = (x_1 - \omega_1, x_2 - \omega_2, x_3 - \omega_3)$ in the frame $(\Omega, (\vec{e_1}, \vec{e_2}, \vec{e_3}))$. This is because

$$\vec{Ox} = \vec{O\Omega} + \vec{\Omega x}$$

and

$$\vec{O\Omega} = (\omega_1, \omega_2, \omega_3).$$

We note that in the second frame $(\Omega, (\vec{e_1}, \vec{e_2}, \vec{e_3}))$, points and position vectors are no longer identified. This gives us evidence that points are not vectors. It may be computationally convenient to deal with points using position vectors, but such a treatment is not frame invariant, which has undesirable effects. Inspired by physics, it is important to define points and properties of points that are frame invariant. An undesirable side effect of the present approach shows up if we attempt to define linear combinations of points. First, let us review the notion of linear combination of vectors. Given two vectors $\vec{u}$ and $\vec{v}$ of coordinates (u_1, u_2, u_3) and (v_1, v_2, v_3) with respect to the basis $(\vec{e_1}, \vec{e_2}, \vec{e_3})$, for any two scalars λ, μ, we can define the linear combination $\lambda\vec{u} + \mu\vec{v}$ as the vector of coordinates

$$(\lambda u_1 + \mu v_1, \lambda u_2 + \mu v_2, \lambda u_3 + \mu v_3).$$

If we choose a different basis $(\vec{e_1}', \vec{e_2}', \vec{e_3}')$ and if the matrix P expressing the vectors $(\vec{e_1}', \vec{e_2}', \vec{e_3}')$ over the basis $(\vec{e_1}, \vec{e_2}, \vec{e_3})$ is

$$P = \begin{pmatrix} a_1 & b_1 & c_1 \\ a_2 & b_2 & c_2 \\ a_3 & b_3 & c_3 \end{pmatrix},$$

which means that the columns of P are the coordinates of the $\vec{e'_j}$ over the basis $(\vec{e_1}, \vec{e_2}, \vec{e_3})$, since

$$u_1\vec{e_1} + u_2\vec{e_2} + u_3\vec{e_3} = u'_1\vec{e'_1} + u'_2\vec{e'_2} + u'_3\vec{e'_3}$$

and

$$v_1\vec{e_1} + v_2\vec{e_2} + v_3\vec{e_3} = v'_1\vec{e'_1} + v'_2\vec{e'_2} + v'_3\vec{e'_3},$$

it is easy to see that the coordinates (u_1, u_2, u_3) and (v_1, v_2, v_3) of $\vec{u}$ and $\vec{v}$ with respect to the basis $(\vec{e_1}, \vec{e_2}, \vec{e_3})$ are given in terms of the coordinates (u'_1, u'_2, u'_3) and (v'_1, v'_2, v'_3) of $\vec{u}$ and $\vec{v}$ with respect to the basis $(\vec{e'_1}, \vec{e'_2}, \vec{e'_3})$ by the matrix equations

$$\begin{pmatrix} u_1 \\ u_2 \\ u_3 \end{pmatrix} = P \begin{pmatrix} u'_1 \\ u'_2 \\ u'_3 \end{pmatrix}$$

and

$$\begin{pmatrix} v_1 \\ v_2 \\ v_3 \end{pmatrix} = P \begin{pmatrix} v'_1 \\ v'_2 \\ v'_3 \end{pmatrix}.$$

From the above, we get

$$\begin{pmatrix} u'_1 \\ u'_2 \\ u'_3 \end{pmatrix} = P^{-1} \begin{pmatrix} u_1 \\ u_2 \\ u_3 \end{pmatrix}$$

and

$$\begin{pmatrix} v'_1 \\ v'_2 \\ v'_3 \end{pmatrix} = P^{-1} \begin{pmatrix} v_1 \\ v_2 \\ v_3 \end{pmatrix},$$

and by linearity, the coordinates

$$(\lambda u'_1 + \mu v'_1, \lambda u'_2 + \mu v'_2, \lambda u'_3 + \mu v'_3)$$

of $\lambda\vec{u} + \mu\vec{v}$ with respect to the basis $(\vec{e'_1}, \vec{e'_2}, \vec{e'_3})$ are given by

$$\begin{pmatrix} \lambda u'_1 + \mu v'_1 \\ \lambda u'_2 + \mu v'_2 \\ \lambda u'_3 + \mu v'_3 \end{pmatrix} = \lambda P^{-1} \begin{pmatrix} u_1 \\ u_2 \\ u_3 \end{pmatrix} + \mu P^{-1} \begin{pmatrix} v_1 \\ v_2 \\ v_3 \end{pmatrix} = P^{-1} \begin{pmatrix} \lambda u_1 + \mu v_1 \\ \lambda u_2 + \mu v_2 \\ \lambda u_3 + \mu v_3 \end{pmatrix}.$$

Everything worked out because the change of basis does not involve a change of origin. On the other hand, if we consider the change of frame from the frame $(O, (\vec{e_1}, \vec{e_2}, \vec{e_3}))$ to the frame $(\Omega, (\vec{e_1}, \vec{e_2}, \vec{e_3}))$, where $\overrightarrow{O\Omega} = (\omega_1, \omega_2, \omega_3)$, given two points a and b of coordinates (a_1, a_2, a_3) and (b_1, b_2, b_3) with respect to the frame $(O, (\vec{e_1}, \vec{e_2}, \vec{e_3}))$ and of coordinates (a'_1, a'_2, a'_3) and (b'_1, b'_2, b'_3) of with respect to the frame $(\Omega, (\vec{e_1}, \vec{e_2}, \vec{e_3}))$, since

$$(a'_1, a'_2, a'_3) = (a_1 - \omega_1, a_2 - \omega_2, a_3 - \omega_3)$$

and

$$(b'_1, b'_2, b'_3) = (b_1 - \omega_1, b_2 - \omega_2, b_3 - \omega_3),$$

the coordinates of $\lambda a + \mu b$ with respect to the frame $(O, (\vec{e_1}, \vec{e_2}, \vec{e_3}))$ are

$$(\lambda a_1 + \mu b_1, \lambda a_2 + \mu b_2, \lambda a_3 + \mu b_3),$$

but the coordinates

$$(\lambda a'_1 + \mu b'_1, \lambda a'_2 + \mu b'_2, \lambda a'_3 + \mu b'_3)$$

of $\lambda a + \mu b$ with respect to the frame $(\Omega, (\vec{e_1}, \vec{e_2}, \vec{e_3}))$ are

$$(\lambda a_1 + \mu b_1 - (\lambda + \mu)\omega_1, \lambda a_2 + \mu b_2 - (\lambda + \mu)\omega_2, \lambda a_3 + \mu b_3 - (\lambda + \mu)\omega_3),$$

which are different from

$$(\lambda a_1 + \mu b_1 - \omega_1, \lambda a_2 + \mu b_2 - \omega_2, \lambda a_3 + \mu b_3 - \omega_3),$$

unless $\lambda + \mu = 1$.

Thus, we discovered a major difference between vectors and points: the notion of linear combination of vectors is basis independent, but the notion of linear combination of points is frame dependent. In order to salvage the notion of linear combination of points, some restriction is needed: the scalar coefficients must add up to 1.

A clean way to handle the problem of frame invariance and to deal with points in a more intrinsic manner is to make a clearer distinction between points and vectors. We duplicate $\mathbf{R}^3$ into two copies, the first copy corresponding to points, where we forget the vector space structure, and the second copy corresponding to free vectors, where the vector space structure is important. Furthermore, we make explicit the important fact that the vector space $\mathbf{R}^3$ acts on the set of points $\mathbf{R}^3$: given any **point** $x = (x_1, x_2, x_3)$ and any **vector** $\vec{v} = (v_1, v_2, v_3)$, we obtain the **point**

$$a + \vec{v} = (a_1 + v_1, a_2 + v_2, a_3 + v_3),$$

which can be thought of as the result of translating a to b using the vector $\vec{v}$. We can imagine that $\vec{v}$ is placed such that its origin coincides with a and that its tip coincides with b. This action $+: \mathbf{R}^3 \times \mathbf{R}^3 \to \mathbf{R}^3$ satisfies some crucial properties. For example,

$$a + \vec{0} = a,$$

$$(a + \vec{u}) + \vec{v} = a + (\vec{u} + \vec{v}),$$

and for any two points a, b, there is a unique free vector $\overrightarrow{ab}$ such that

$$b = a + \overrightarrow{ab}.$$

It turns out that the above properties, although trivial in the case of $\mathbf{R}^3$, are all that is needed to define the abstract notion of affine space (or affine structure). The basic idea is to consider two (distinct) sets E and $\vec{E}$, where E is a set of points (with no structure) and $\vec{E}$ is a vector space (of free vectors) acting on the set E. Intuitively, we can think of the elements of $\vec{E}$ as forces moving the points in E, considered as physical particles. The effect of applying a force (free vector) $\vec{u} \in \vec{E}$ to a point $a \in E$ is a translation. By this, we mean that for every force $\vec{u} \in \vec{E}$, the action of the force $\vec{u}$ is to "move" every point $a \in E$ to the point $a + \vec{u} \in E$ obtained by the translation corresponding to $\vec{u}$ viewed as a vector. Since translations can be composed, it is natural that $\vec{E}$ is a vector space.

For simplicity, it is assumed that all vector spaces under consideration are defined over the field $\mathbf{R}$ of real numbers. It is also assumed that all families of vectors and scalars are finite. The formal definition of an affine space is as follows.

Definition 2.1.1

An affine space *is either the empty set, or a triple* $\langle E, \vec{E}, + \rangle$ *consisting of a nonempty set* E *(of* points*), a vector space* $\vec{E}$ *(of* translations, *or* free vectors*), and an action* $+: E \times \vec{E} \to E$, *satisfying the following conditions:*

(AF1) $a + \vec{0} = a$, *for every* $a \in E$;

(AF2) $(a + \vec{u}) + \vec{v} = a + (\vec{u} + \vec{v})$, *for every* $a \in E$, *and every* $\vec{u}, \vec{v} \in \vec{E}$;

(AF3) *For any two points* $a, b \in E$, *there is a unique* $\vec{u} \in \vec{E}$ *such that* $a + \vec{u} = b$. *The unique vector* $\vec{u} \in \vec{E}$ *such that* $a + \vec{u} = b$ *is denoted as* $\overrightarrow{ab}$, *or sometimes as* $b - a$.

Thus, we also write

$$b = a + \overrightarrow{ab}$$

(or even $b = a + (b - a)$*).*

The dimension *of the affine space* $\langle E, \vec{E}, + \rangle$ *is the dimension* $\dim(\vec{E})$ *of the vector space* $\vec{E}$. *For simplicity, it is denoted as* $\dim(E)$.

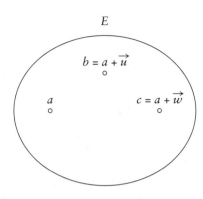

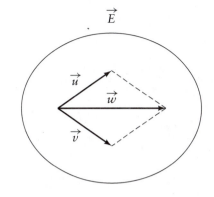

FIG. 2.2 Intuitive picture of an affine space

Note that

$$\overrightarrow{a(a + \vec{v})} = \vec{v}$$

for all $a \in E$ and all $\vec{v} \in \vec{E}$, since

$$\overrightarrow{a(a + \vec{v})}$$

is the unique vector such that

$$a + \vec{v} = a + \overrightarrow{a(a + \vec{v})}.$$

Thus, $b = a + \vec{v}$ is equivalent to $\overrightarrow{ab} = \vec{v}$. Figure 2.2 gives an intuitive picture of an affine space. It is natural to think of all vectors as having the same origin, the null vector.

The axioms defining an affine space $\langle E, \vec{E}, + \rangle$ can be interpreted intuitively as saying that E and $\vec{E}$ are two different ways of looking at the same object, but wearing different sets of glasses, the second set of glasses depending on the choice of an "origin" in E. Indeed, we can choose to look at the points in E, forgetting that every pair (a, b) of points defines a unique vector $\overrightarrow{ab}$ in $\vec{E}$, or we can choose to look at the vectors $\vec{u}$ in $\vec{E}$, forgetting the points in E. Furthermore, if we also pick any point a in E viewed as an *origin* in E, then we can recover all the points in E as the translated points $a + \vec{u}$ for all $\vec{u} \in \vec{E}$. This can be formalized by defining two maps between E and $\vec{E}$.

For every $a \in E$, consider the mapping from $\vec{E}$ to E:

$$\vec{u} \mapsto a + \vec{u},$$

where $\vec{u} \in \vec{E}$, and consider the mapping from E to $\vec{E}$:

$$b \mapsto \overrightarrow{ab},$$

where $b \in E$. The composition of the first mapping with the second is

$$\vec{u} \mapsto a + \vec{u} \mapsto \overrightarrow{a(a + \vec{u})},$$

which, in view of (AF3), yields $\vec{u}$. The composition of the second with the first mapping is

$$b \mapsto \overrightarrow{ab} \mapsto a + \overrightarrow{ab},$$

which, in view of (AF3), yields b. Thus, these compositions are the identity from $\vec{E}$ to $\vec{E}$ and the identity from E to E, and the mappings are both bijections.

When we identify E to $\vec{E}$ via the mapping $b \mapsto \overrightarrow{ab}$, we say that we consider E as the vector space obtained *by taking a as the origin in E*, and we denote it as E_a. Thus, an affine space $\langle E, \vec{E}, + \rangle$ is a way of defining a vector space structure on a set of points E, without making a commitment to a *fixed* origin in E. Nevertheless, as soon as we commit to an origin a in E, we can view E as the vector space E_a. However, we urge you to think of E as a physical set of points and of $\vec{E}$ as a set of forces acting on E, rather than reducing E to some isomorphic copy of $\mathbf{R}^n$. After all, points are points, and not vectors! For notational simplicity, we will often denote an affine space $\langle E, \vec{E}, + \rangle$ as $(E, \vec{E})$, or even as E. The vector space $\vec{E}$ is called the *vector space associated with E*.

You should be careful about the overloading of the addition symbol $+$. Addition is well defined on vectors, as in $\vec{u} + \vec{v}$, the translate $a + \vec{u}$ of a point $a \in E$ by a vector $\vec{u} \in \vec{E}$ is also well defined, but addition of points $a + b$ does *not make sense*. In this respect, the notation $b - a$ for the unique vector $\vec{u}$, such that $b = a + \vec{u}$, is somewhat confusing, since it suggests that points can be subtracted (but not added!). Yet, we will see in Section 10.1 that it is possible to make sense of linear combinations of points, and even mixed linear combinations of points and vectors.

Any vector space $\vec{E}$ has an affine space structure specified by choosing $E = \vec{E}$, and letting $+$ be addition in the vector space $\vec{E}$. We will refer to this affine structure on a vector space as the *canonical (or natural) affine structure on $\vec{E}$*. In particular, the vector space $\mathbf{R}^n$ can be viewed as an affine space denoted as $\mathbf{A}^n$. In order to distinguish between the double role played by members of $\mathbf{R}^n$, points and vectors, we will denote points as row vectors, and vectors as column vectors. Thus, the action of the vector space $\mathbf{R}^n$ over the set $\mathbf{R}^n$ simply viewed as a set of points is given by

$$(a_1, \ldots, a_n) + \begin{pmatrix} u_1 \\ \vdots \\ u_n \end{pmatrix} = (a_1 + u_1, \ldots, a_n + u_n).$$

The affine space $\mathbf{A}^n$ is called the *real affine space of dimension n*. In most cases, we will consider $n = 1, 2, 3$.

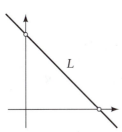

An affine space: the line of equation $x + y - 1 = 0$

2.2   Examples of Affine Spaces

Let us now give an example of an affine space that is not given as a vector space (at least, not in an obvious fashion). Consider the subset L of $\mathbf{A}^2$ consisting of all points (x, y) satisfying the equation

$$x + y - 1 = 0.$$

The set L is the line of slope -1 passing through the points $(1, 0)$ and $(0, 1)$ (see Figure 2.3).

The line L can be made into an official affine space by defining the action $+ : L \times \mathbf{R} \to L$ of $\mathbf{R}$ on L defined such that for every point $(x, 1 - x)$ on L and any $u \in \mathbf{R}$,

$$(x, 1 - x) + u = (x + u, 1 - x - u).$$

It immediately verified that this action makes L into an affine space. For example, for any two points $a = (a_1, 1 - a_1)$ and $b = (b_1, 1 - b_1)$ on L, the unique (vector) $u \in \mathbf{R}$ such that $b = a + u$ is $u = b_1 - a_1$. Note that the vector space $\mathbf{R}$ is isomorphic to the line of equation $x + y = 0$ passing through the origin.

Similarly, consider the subset H of $\mathbf{A}^3$ consisting of all points (x, y, z) satisfying the equation

$$x + y + z - 1 = 0.$$

The set H is the plane passing through the points $(1, 0, 0)$, $(0, 1, 0)$, and $(0, 0, 1)$. The plane H can be made into an official affine space by defining the action $+ : H \times \mathbf{R}^2 \to H$ of $\mathbf{R}^2$ on H defined such that for every point $(x, y, 1 - x - y)$ on H and any $\binom{u}{v} \in \mathbf{R}^2$,

$$(x, y, 1 - x - y) + \begin{pmatrix} u \\ v \end{pmatrix} = (x + u, y + v, 1 - x - u - y - v).$$

For a slightly wilder example, consider the subset P of $\mathbf{A}^3$ consisting of all points (x, y, z) satisfying the equation

$$x^2 + y^2 - z = 0.$$

The set P is paraboloid of revolution, with axis Oz. The surface P can be made into an official affine space by defining the action $+: P \times \mathbf{R}^2 \to P$ of $\mathbf{R}^2$ on P defined such that for every point $(x, y, x^2 + y^2)$ on P and any $\binom{u}{v} \in \mathbf{R}^2$,

$$(x, y, x^2 + y^2) + \binom{u}{v} = (x + u, y + v, (x + u)^2 + (y + v)^2).$$

This should dispell any idea that affine spaces are dull. Affine spaces not already equipped with an obvious vector space structure arise in projective geometry.

2.3   Chasles's Identity

Given any three points $a, b, c \in E$, since $c = a + \vec{ac}$, $b = a + \vec{ab}$, and $c = b + \vec{bc}$, we get

$$c = b + \vec{bc} = (a + \vec{ab}) + \vec{bc} = a + (\vec{ab} + \vec{bc})$$

by (AF2), and thus, by (AF3),

$$\vec{ab} + \vec{bc} = \vec{ac},$$

which is known as *Chasles's identity* (see Figure 2.4).

Since $a = a + \vec{aa}$ and, by (AF1), $a = a + \vec{0}$, by (AF3), we get

$$\vec{aa} = \vec{0}.$$

Thus, letting $a = c$ in Chasles's identity, we get

$$\vec{ba} = -\vec{ab}.$$

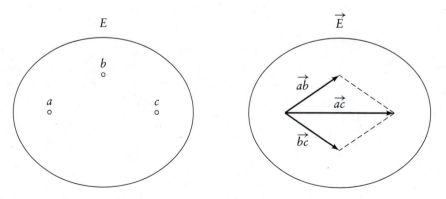

FIG. 2.4 Points and corresponding vectors in affine geometry

Given any four points $a, b, c, d \in E$, since by Chasles's identity

$$\overrightarrow{ab} + \overrightarrow{bc} = \overrightarrow{ad} + \overrightarrow{dc} = \overrightarrow{ac},$$

we have $\overrightarrow{ab} = \overrightarrow{dc}$ iff $\overrightarrow{bc} = \overrightarrow{ad}$ (the *parallelogram law*).

2.4   Affine Combinations, Barycenters

A fundamental concept in linear algebra is that of a linear combination. The corresponding concept in affine geometry is that of an *affine combination*, also called a *barycenter*. However, there is a problem with the naive approach involving a coordinate system, as we saw in Section 2.1. Since this problem is the reason for introducing affine combinations, at the risk of boring certain readers, we give another example showing what goes wrong if we are not careful in defining linear combinations of points. Consider $\mathbf{R}^2$ as an affine space, under its natural coordinate system with origin $O = (0, 0)$ and basis vectors $\binom{1}{0}$ and $\binom{0}{1}$. Given any two points $a = (a_1, a_2)$ and $b = (b_1, b_2)$, it is natural to define the affine combination $\lambda a + \mu b$ as the point of coordinates $(\lambda a_1 + \mu b_1, \lambda a_2 + \mu b_2)$.

Thus, when $a = (-1, -1)$ and $b = (2, 2)$, the point $a + b$ is the point $c = (1, 1)$. However, let us now consider the new coordinate system with respect to the origin $c = (1, 1)$ (and the same basis vectors). (See Figure 2.5.) This time, the coordinates of a are $(-2, -2)$, the coordinates of b are $(1, 1)$, and the point $a + b$ is the point d of coordinates $(-1, -1)$. However, it is clear that the point d is identical to the origin $O = (0, 0)$ of the first coordinate system. Thus, $a + b$ corresponds to two different points depending on which coordinate system is used for its computation!

Thus, some extra condition is needed in order for affine combinations to make sense. It turns out that if the scalars sum up to 1, the definition is intrinsic, as the following lemma shows.

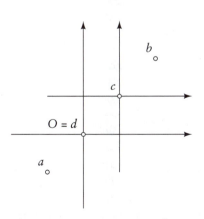

FIG. 2.5 Two coordinate systems in $\mathbf{R}^2$

Lemma 2.4.1

Given an affine space E, let $(a_i)_{i \in I}$ be a family of points in E, and let $(\lambda_i)_{i \in I}$ be a family of scalars. For any two points $a, b \in E$, the following properties hold:

1. If $\sum_{i \in I} \lambda_i = 1$, then

$$a + \sum_{i \in I} \lambda_i \overrightarrow{aa_i} = b + \sum_{i \in I} \lambda_i \overrightarrow{ba_i}.$$

2. If $\sum_{i \in I} \lambda_i = 0$, then

$$\sum_{i \in I} \lambda_i \overrightarrow{aa_i} = \sum_{i \in I} \lambda_i \overrightarrow{ba_i}.$$

Proof: (1) By Chasles's identity (see Section 2.3), we have

$$a + \sum_{i \in I} \lambda_i \overrightarrow{aa_i} = a + \sum_{i \in I} \lambda_i (\overrightarrow{ab} + \overrightarrow{ba_i})$$

$$= a + \left(\sum_{i \in I} \lambda_i\right) \overrightarrow{ab} + \sum_{i \in I} \lambda_i \overrightarrow{ba_i}$$

$$= a + \overrightarrow{ab} + \sum_{i \in I} \lambda_i \overrightarrow{ba_i} \qquad \text{since } \sum_{i \in I} \lambda_i = 1$$

$$= b + \sum_{i \in I} \lambda_i \overrightarrow{ba_i} \qquad \text{since } b = a + \overrightarrow{ab}.$$

(2) We also have

$$\sum_{i \in I} \lambda_i \overrightarrow{aa_i} = \sum_{i \in I} \lambda_i (\overrightarrow{ab} + \overrightarrow{ba_i})$$

$$= \left(\sum_{i \in I} \lambda_i\right) \overrightarrow{ab} + \sum_{i \in I} \lambda_i \overrightarrow{ba_i}$$

$$= \sum_{i \in I} \lambda_i \overrightarrow{ba_i},$$

since $\sum_{i \in I} \lambda_i = 0$. $\blacksquare$

Thus, by Lemma 2.4.1, for any family of points $(a_i)_{i \in I}$ in E, for any family $(\lambda_i)_{i \in I}$ of scalars such that $\sum_{i \in I} \lambda_i = 1$, the point

$$x = a + \sum_{i \in I} \lambda_i \overrightarrow{aa_i}$$

is independent of the choice of the origin $a \in E$. The unique point x is called the *barycenter* (or *barycentric combination*, or *affine combination*) of the points a_i

assigned the weights λ_i, and it is denoted as

$$\sum_{i \in I} \lambda_i a_i.$$

In dealing with barycenters, it is convenient to introduce the notion of a *weighted point*, which is just a pair (a, λ), where $a \in E$ is a point, and $\lambda \in \mathbf{R}$ is a scalar. Then, given a family of weighted points $((a_i, \lambda_i))_{i \in I}$, where $\sum_{i \in I} \lambda_i = 1$, we also say that the point $\sum_{i \in I} \lambda_i a_i$ is the *barycenter of the family of weighted points* $((a_i, \lambda_i))_{i \in I}$. Note that the barycenter x of the family of weighted points $((a_i, \lambda_i))_{i \in I}$ is the unique point such that

$$\overrightarrow{ax} = \sum_{i \in I} \lambda_i \overrightarrow{aa_i} \quad \text{for every } a \in E,$$

and setting $a = x$, the point x is the unique point such that

$$\sum_{i \in I} \lambda_i \overrightarrow{xa_i} = \overrightarrow{0}.$$

In physical terms, the barycenter is the *center of mass* of the family of weighted points $((a_i, \lambda_i))_{i \in I}$ (where the masses have been normalized, so that $\sum_{i \in I} \lambda_i = 1$, and negative masses are allowed).

Remarks: (1) For all $m \geq 2$, it is easy to prove that the barycenter of m weighted points can be obtained by repeated computations of barycenters of two weighted points.

(2) When $\sum_{i \in I} \lambda_i = 0$, the vector $\sum_{i \in I} \lambda_i \overrightarrow{aa_i}$ does not depend on the point a, and we may denote it as $\overrightarrow{\sum_{i \in I} \lambda_i a_i}$. This observation will be used in Section 10.1 to define a vector space in which linear combinations of both points and vectors make sense, regardless of the value of $\sum_{i \in I} \lambda_i$.

Figure 2.6 illustrates the geometric construction of the barycenters g_1 and g_2 of the weighted points $(a, \frac{1}{4})$, $(b, \frac{1}{4})$, and $(c, \frac{1}{2})$, and $(a, -1)$, $(b, 1)$, and $(c, 1)$.

The point g_1 can be constructed geometrically as the middle of the segment joining c to the middle $\frac{1}{2}a + \frac{1}{2}b$ of the segment (a, b), since

$$g_1 = \frac{1}{2}\left(\frac{1}{2}a + \frac{1}{2}b\right) + \frac{1}{2}c.$$

The point g_2 can be constructed geometrically as the point such that the middle $\frac{1}{2}b + \frac{1}{2}c$ of the segment (b, c) is the middle of the segment (a, g_2), since

$$g_2 = -a + 2\left(\frac{1}{2}b + \frac{1}{2}c\right).$$

Later on, we will see that a polynomial curve can be defined as the set of barycenters of a fixed number of points. For example, let (a, b, c, d) be a sequence

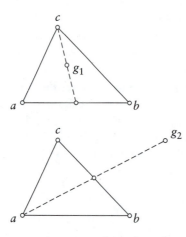

FIG. 2.6 Barycenters, $g_1 = \frac{1}{4}a + \frac{1}{4}b + \frac{1}{2}c$, $g_2 = -a + b + c$

of points in $\mathbf{A}^2$. Observe that

$$(1-t)^3 + 3t(1-t)^2 + 3t^2(1-t) + t^3 = 1,$$

since the sum on the left-hand side is obtained by expanding $(t + (1-t))^3 = 1$ using the binomial formula. Thus,

$$(1-t)^3\,a + 3t(1-t)^2\,b + 3t^2(1-t)\,c + t^3\,d$$

is a well-defined affine combination. Then, we can define the curve $F\colon \mathbf{A} \to \mathbf{A}^2$ such that

$$F(t) = (1-t)^3\,a + 3t(1-t)^2\,b + 3t^2(1-t)\,c + t^3\,d.$$

Such a curve is called a *Bézier curve*, and (a, b, c, d) are called its *control points*. Note that the curve passes through a and d, but generally not through b and c. We will see in the next chapter how any point $F(t)$ on the curve can be constructed using an algorithm performing three affine interpolation steps (the *de Casteljau algorithm*).

2.5   Affine Subspaces

In linear algebra, a (linear) subspace can be characterized as a nonempty subset of a vector space closed under linear combinations. In affine spaces, the notion corresponding to the notion of (linear) subspace is the notion of affine subspace. It is natural to define an affine subspace as a subset of an affine space closed under affine combinations.

Definition 2.5.1

Given an affine space $\langle E, \vec{E}, + \rangle$, a subset V of E is an affine subspace *if for every family of weighted points $((a_i, \lambda_i))_{i \in I}$ in V such that $\sum_{i \in I} \lambda_i = 1$, the barycenter $\sum_{i \in I} \lambda_i a_i$ belongs to V.*

An affine subspace is also called a *flat* by some authors. According to Definition 2.5.1, the empty set is trivially an affine subspace, and every intersection of affine subspaces is an affine subspace.

As an example, consider the subset U of $\mathbf{A}^2$ defined by

$$U = \{(x, y) \in \mathbf{R}^2 \mid ax + by = c\},$$

that is, the set of solutions of the equation

$$ax + by = c,$$

where it is assumed that $a \neq 0$ or $b \neq 0$. Given any m points $(x_i, y_i) \in U$ and any m scalars λ_i such that $\lambda_1 + \cdots + \lambda_m = 1$, we claim that

$$\sum_{i=1}^{m} \lambda_i (x_i, y_i) \in U.$$

Indeed, $(x_i, y_i) \in U$ means that

$$ax_i + by_i = c,$$

and if we multiply both sides of this equation by λ_i and add up the resulting m equations, we get

$$\sum_{i=1}^{m} (\lambda_i a x_i + \lambda_i b y_i) = \sum_{i=1}^{m} \lambda_i c,$$

and since $\lambda_1 + \cdots + \lambda_m = 1$, we get

$$a \left(\sum_{i=1}^{m} \lambda_i x_i \right) + b \left(\sum_{i=1}^{m} \lambda_i y_i \right) = \left(\sum_{i=1}^{m} \lambda_i \right) c = c,$$

which shows that

$$\left(\sum_{i=1}^{m} \lambda_i x_i, \sum_{i=1}^{m} \lambda_i y_i \right) = \sum_{i=1}^{m} \lambda_i (x_i, y_i) \in U.$$

Thus, U is an affine subspace of $\mathbf{A}^2$. In fact, it is just a usual line in $\mathbf{A}^2$.

It turns out that U is closely related to the subset of $\mathbf{R}^2$ defined by

$$\vec{U} = \{(x, y) \in \mathbf{R}^2 \mid ax + by = 0\},$$

that is, the set of solution of the homogeneous equation

$$ax + by = 0$$

obtained by setting the right-hand side of $ax + by = c$ to zero. Indeed, for any m scalars λ_i, the same calculation as above yields

$$\sum_{i=1}^{m} \lambda_i(x_i, y_i) \in \vec{U},$$

this time *without any restriction* on the λ_i, since the right-hand side of the equation is null. Thus, $\vec{U}$ is a subspace of $\mathbf{R}^2$. In fact, $\vec{U}$ is one-dimensional, and it is just a usual line in $\mathbf{R}^2$. This line can be identified with a line passing through the origin of $\mathbf{A}^2$, which is parallel to the line U of equation $ax + by = c$. Now, if (x_0, y_0) is any point in U, we claim that

$$U = (x_0, y_0) + \vec{U},$$

where

$$(x_0, y_0) + \vec{U} = \{(x_0 + u_1, y_0 + u_2) \mid (u_1, u_2) \in \vec{U}\}.$$

First, $(x_0, y_0) + \vec{U} \subseteq U$, since $ax_0 + by_0 = c$ and $au_1 + bu_2 = 0$ for all $(u_1, u_2) \in \vec{U}$. Second, if $(x, y) \in U$, then $ax + by = c$, and since we also have $ax_0 + by_0 = c$, by subtraction, we get

$$a(x - x_0) + b(y - b_0) = 0,$$

which shows that $(x - x_0, y - y_0) \in \vec{U}$, and thus $(x, y) \in (x_0, y_0) + \vec{U}$. Hence, we also have $U \subseteq (x_0, y_0) + \vec{U}$, and $U = (x_0, y_0) + \vec{U}$.

The above example shows that the affine line U defined by the equation

$$ax + by = c$$

is obtained by "translating" the parallel line $\vec{U}$ of equation

$$ax + by = 0$$

passing through the origin (see Figure 2.7). In fact, given any point $(x_0, y_0) \in U$,

$$U = (x_0, y_0) + \vec{U}.$$

More generally, it is easy to prove the following fact. Given any $m \times n$ matrix A and any vector $c \in \mathbf{R}^m$, the subset U of $\mathbf{A}^n$ defined by

$$U = \{x \in \mathbf{R}^n \mid Ax = c\}$$

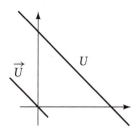

FIG. 2.7 An affine line U and its direction

is an affine subspace of $\mathbf{A}^n$. Furthermore, if we consider the corresponding homogeneous equation $Ax = 0$, the set

$$\overrightarrow{U} = \{x \in \mathbf{R}^n \mid Ax = 0\}$$

is a subspace of $\mathbf{R}^n$, and for any $x_0 \in U$, we have

$$U = x_0 + \overrightarrow{U}.$$

This is a general situation. Affine subspaces can be characterized in terms of subspaces of $\overrightarrow{E}$. Let V be a nonempty subset of E. For every family $(a_1, \ldots, a_n)$ in V, for any family $(\lambda_1, \ldots, \lambda_n)$ of scalars, for every point $a \in V$, observe that for every $x \in E$,

$$x = a + \sum_{i=1}^{n} \lambda_i \overrightarrow{aa_i}$$

is the barycenter of the family of weighted points

$$\left((a_1, \lambda_1), \ldots, (a_n, \lambda_n), \left(a, 1 - \sum_{i=1}^{n} \lambda_i \right) \right),$$

since

$$\sum_{i=1}^{n} \lambda_i + \left(1 - \sum_{i=1}^{n} \lambda_i \right) = 1.$$

Given any point $a \in E$ and any subspace $\overrightarrow{V}$ of $\overrightarrow{E}$, let $a + \overrightarrow{V}$ denote the following subset of E:

$$a + \overrightarrow{V} = \{a + \overrightarrow{v} \mid \overrightarrow{v} \in \overrightarrow{V}\}.$$

Lemma 2.5.2

Let $\langle E, \vec{E}, + \rangle$ be an affine space.

1. *A nonempty subset V of E is an affine subspace iff, for every point $a \in V$, the set*

$$\vec{V_a} = \{\overrightarrow{ax} \mid x \in V\}$$

   is a subspace of $\vec{E}$. Consequently, $V = a + \vec{V_a}$. Furthermore,

$$\vec{V} = \{\overrightarrow{xy} \mid x, y \in V\}$$

   is a subspace of $\vec{E}$ and $\vec{V_a} = \vec{V}$ for all $a \in E$. Thus, $V = a + \vec{V}$.

2. *For any subspace $\vec{V}$ of $\vec{E}$, for any $a \in E$, the set $V = a + \vec{V}$ is an affine subspace.*

Proof: (1) Clearly, $\vec{0} \in \vec{V}$. If V is an affine subspace, then V is closed under barycentric combinations, and by the remark before the lemma, for every $x \in E$,

$$\overrightarrow{ax} = \sum_{i=1}^{n} \lambda_i \overrightarrow{aa_i}$$

iff x is the barycenter

$$\sum_{i=1}^{n} \lambda_i a_i + \left(1 - \sum_{i=1}^{n} \lambda_i\right) a$$

of the family of weighted points $((a_1, \lambda_1), \ldots, (a_n, \lambda_n), (a; 1 - \sum_{i=1}^{n} \lambda_i))$. Then, it is clear that $\vec{V_a}$ is closed under linear combinations, and thus, it is a subspace of $\vec{E}$. Since $\vec{V} = \{\overrightarrow{xy} \mid x, y \in V\}$ and $\vec{V_a} = \{\overrightarrow{ax} \mid x \in V\}$, where $a \in V$, it is clear that $\vec{V_a} \subseteq \vec{V}$. Conversely, since

$$\overrightarrow{xy} = \overrightarrow{ay} - \overrightarrow{ax},$$

and since $\vec{V_a}$ is a subspace of $\vec{E}$, we have $\vec{V} \subseteq \vec{V_a}$. Thus, $\vec{V} = \vec{V_a}$, for every $a \in V$.

(2) If $V = a + \vec{V}$, where $\vec{V}$ is a subspace of $\vec{E}$, then, for every family of weighted points, $((a + \vec{v_i}, \lambda_i))_{1 \le i \le n}$, where $\vec{v_i} \in \vec{V}$, and $\lambda_1 + \cdots + \lambda_n = 1$, the barycenter x being given by

$$x = a + \sum_{i=1}^{n} \lambda_i \overrightarrow{a(a + \vec{v_i})} = a + \sum_{i=1}^{n} \lambda_i \vec{v_i}$$

is in V, since $\vec{V}$ is a subspace of $\vec{E}$. ∎

In particular, when E is the natural affine space associated with a vector space E, Lemma 2.5.2 shows that every affine subspace of E is of the form $\vec{u} + U$, for a subspace U of E. The subspaces of E are the affine subspaces that contain $\vec{0}$.

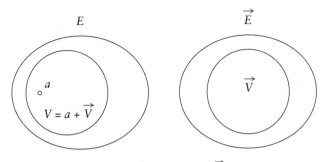

FIG. 2.8 An affine subspace V and its direction $\vec{V}$

The subspace $\vec{V}$ associated with an affine subspace V is called the *direction of V* (see Figure 2.8). It is also clear that the map $+: V \times \vec{V} \to V$ induced by $+: E \times \vec{E} \to E$ confers to $\langle V, \vec{V}, + \rangle$ an affine structure.

By the dimension of the subspace V, we mean the dimension of $\vec{V}$. An affine subspace of dimension 1 is called a *line*, and an affine subspace of dimension 2 is called a *plane*. An affine subspace of codimension 1 is called a *hyperplane* (recall that a subspace F of a vector space E has codimension 1 iff there is some subspace G of dimension 1 such that $E = F \oplus G$, the direct sum of F and G, see Appendix A). We say that two affine subspaces U and V are *parallel* if their directions are identical. Equivalently, since $\vec{U} = \vec{V}$, we have $U = a + \vec{U}$, and $V = b + \vec{U}$, for any $a \in U$ and any $b \in V$, and thus, V is obtained from U by the translation $\overrightarrow{ab}$.

By Lemma 2.5.2, a line is specified by a point $a \in E$ and a nonzero vector $\vec{v} \in \vec{E}$; that is, a line is the set of all points of the form $a + \lambda \vec{u}$, for $\lambda \in \mathbf{R}$. We say that three points a, b, c are *collinear* if the vectors $\overrightarrow{ab}$ and $\overrightarrow{ac}$ are linearly dependent. If two of the points a, b, c are distinct, say, $a \neq b$, then there is a unique $\lambda \in \mathbf{R}$, such that $\overrightarrow{ac} = \lambda \overrightarrow{ab}$, and we define the ratio $\frac{\overrightarrow{ac}}{\overrightarrow{ab}} = \lambda$.

A plane is specified by a point $a \in E$ and two linearly independent vectors $\vec{u}, \vec{v} \in \vec{E}$; that is, a plane is the set of all points of the form $a + \lambda \vec{u} + \mu \vec{v}$, for $\lambda, \mu \in \mathbf{R}$. We say that four points a, b, c, d are *coplanar* if the vectors $\overrightarrow{ab}, \overrightarrow{ac}$, and $\overrightarrow{ad}$ are linearly dependent. Hyperplanes will be characterized a little later.

Lemma 2.5.3

Given an affine space $\langle E, \vec{E}, + \rangle$, for any family $(a_i)_{i \in I}$ of points in E, the set V of barycenters $\sum_{i \in I} \lambda_i a_i$ (where $\sum_{i \in I} \lambda_i = 1$) is the smallest affine subspace containing $(a_i)_{i \in I}$.

Proof: If $(a_i)_{i \in I}$ is empty, then $V = \emptyset$, because of the condition $\sum_{i \in I} \lambda_i = 1$. If $(a_i)_{i \in I}$ is nonempty, then the smallest affine subspace containing $(a_i)_{i \in I}$ must contain the set V of barycenters $\sum_{i \in I} \lambda_i a_i$, and thus, it is enough to show that V is closed under affine combinations, which is immediately verified. ∎

Given a nonempty subset S of E, the smallest affine subspace of E generated by S is often denoted as $\langle S \rangle$. For example, a line specified by two distinct points a and b is denoted as $\langle a, b \rangle$, or even (a, b), and similarly for planes, and so on.

Remark: Since it can be shown that the barycenter of n weighted points can be obtained by repeated computations of barycenters of two weighted points, a nonempty subset V of E is an affine subspace iff for every two points $a, b \in V$, the set V contains all barycentric combinations of a and b. If V contains at least two points, V is an affine subspace iff for any two distinct points $a, b \in V$, the set V contains the line determined by a and b, that is, the set of all points $(1 - \lambda)a + \lambda b$, $\lambda \in \mathbf{R}$.

2.6   Affine Independence and Affine Frames

Corresponding to the notion of linear independence in vector spaces, we have the notion of affine independence. Given a family $(a_i)_{i \in I}$ of points in an affine space E, we will reduce the notion of (affine) independence of these points to the (linear) independence of the families $(\overrightarrow{a_i a_j})_{j \in (I - \{i\})}$ of vectors obtained by choosing any a_i as an origin. First, the following lemma shows that it is sufficient to consider only one of these families.

Lemma 2.6.1

Given an affine space $\langle E, \vec{E}, + \rangle$, let $(a_i)_{i \in I}$ be a family of points in E. If the family $(\overrightarrow{a_i a_j})_{j \in (I - \{i\})}$ is linearly independent for some $i \in I$, then $(\overrightarrow{a_i a_j})_{j \in (I - \{i\})}$ is linearly independent for every $i \in I$.

Proof: Assume that the family $(\overrightarrow{a_i a_j})_{j \in (I - \{i\})}$ is linearly independent for some specific $i \in I$. Let $k \in I$ with $k \neq i$, and assume that there are some scalars $(\lambda_j)_{j \in (I - \{k\})}$ such that

$$\sum_{j \in (I - \{k\})} \lambda_j \overrightarrow{a_k a_j} = \vec{0}.$$

Since

$$\overrightarrow{a_k a_j} = \overrightarrow{a_k a_i} + \overrightarrow{a_i a_j},$$

we have

$$\sum_{j \in (I - \{k\})} \lambda_j \overrightarrow{a_k a_j} = \sum_{j \in (I - \{k\})} \lambda_j \overrightarrow{a_k a_i} + \sum_{j \in (I - \{k\})} \lambda_j \overrightarrow{a_i a_j}$$

$$= \sum_{j \in (I - \{k\})} \lambda_j \overrightarrow{a_k a_i} + \sum_{j \in (I - \{i,k\})} \lambda_j \overrightarrow{a_i a_j}$$

$$= \sum_{j \in (I - \{i,k\})} \lambda_j \overrightarrow{a_i a_j} - \left(\sum_{j \in (I - \{k\})} \lambda_j \right) \overrightarrow{a_i a_k}$$

and thus

$$\sum_{j\in(I-\{i,k\})} \lambda_j \overrightarrow{a_i a_j} - \left(\sum_{j\in(I-\{k\})} \lambda_j\right) \overrightarrow{a_i a_k} = \vec{0}.$$

Since the family $(\overrightarrow{a_i a_j})_{j\in(I-\{i\})}$ is linearly independent, we must have $\lambda_j = 0$ for all $j \in (I - \{i, k\})$ and $\sum_{j\in(I-\{k\})} \lambda_j = 0$, which implies that $\lambda_j = 0$ for all $j \in (I - \{k\})$. ∎

We define affine independence as follows.

Definition 2.6.2

Given an affine space $\langle E, \vec{E}, + \rangle$, a family $(a_i)_{i\in I}$ of points in E is affinely independent if the family $(\overrightarrow{a_i a_j})_{j\in(I-\{i\})}$ is linearly independent for some $i \in I$.

Definition 2.6.2 is reasonable, since by Lemma 2.6.1, the independence of the family $(\overrightarrow{a_i a_j})_{j\in(I-\{i\})}$ does not depend on the choice of a_i. A crucial property of linearly independent vectors $(\vec{u_1}, \ldots, \vec{u_m})$ is that if a vector $\vec{v}$ is a linear combination

$$\vec{v} = \sum_{i=1}^{m} \lambda_i \vec{u_i}$$

of the $\vec{u_i}$, then the λ_i are unique. A similar result holds for affinely independent points.

Lemma 2.6.3

Given an affine space $\langle E, \vec{E}, + \rangle$, let $(a_0, \ldots, a_m)$ be a family of $m + 1$ points in E. Let $x \in E$, and assume that $x = \sum_{i=0}^{m} \lambda_i a_i$, where $\sum_{i=0}^{m} \lambda_i = 1$. Then, the family $(\lambda_0, \ldots, \lambda_m)$ such that $x = \sum_{i=0}^{m} \lambda_i a_i$ is unique iff the family $(\overrightarrow{a_0 a_1}, \ldots, \overrightarrow{a_0 a_m})$ is linearly independent.

Proof: Recall that

$$x = \sum_{i=0}^{m} \lambda_i a_i \quad \text{iff} \quad \overrightarrow{a_0 x} = \sum_{i=1}^{m} \lambda_i \overrightarrow{a_0 a_i},$$

where $\sum_{i=0}^{m} \lambda_i = 1$. However, it is a well-known result of linear algebra that the family $(\lambda_1, \ldots, \lambda_m)$ such that

$$\overrightarrow{a_0 x} = \sum_{i=1}^{m} \lambda_i \overrightarrow{a_0 a_i}$$

is unique iff $(\overrightarrow{a_0 a_1}, \ldots, \overrightarrow{a_0 a_m})$ is linearly independent (for a proof, see Appendix A, Lemma A.1.10). Thus, if $(\overrightarrow{a_0 a_1}, \ldots, \overrightarrow{a_0 a_m})$ is linearly independent, by Lemma A.1.10, $(\lambda_1, \ldots, \lambda_m)$ is unique, and since $\lambda_0 = 1 - \sum_{i=1}^{m} \lambda_i$, λ_0 is also unique. Conversely,

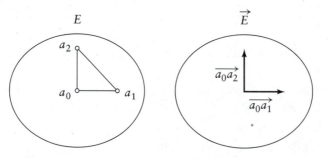

FIG. 2.9 Affine independence and linear independence

the uniqueness of $(\lambda_0, \ldots, \lambda_m)$ such that $x = \sum_{i=0}^{m} \lambda_i a_i$ implies the uniqueness of $(\lambda_1, \ldots, \lambda_m)$ such that

$$\overrightarrow{a_0 x} = \sum_{i=1}^{m} \lambda_i \overrightarrow{a_0 a_i},$$

and by Lemma A.1.10 again, $(\overrightarrow{a_0 a_1}, \ldots, \overrightarrow{a_0 a_m})$ is linearly independent. ∎

Lemma 2.6.3 suggests the notion of affine frame. Affine frames are the affine analogs of bases in vector spaces. Let $\langle E, \vec{E}, + \rangle$ be a nonempty affine space, and let $(a_0, \ldots, a_m)$ be a family of $m + 1$ points in E. The family $(a_0, \ldots, a_m)$ determines the family of m vectors $(\overrightarrow{a_0 a_1}, \ldots, \overrightarrow{a_0 a_m})$ in $\vec{E}$. Conversely, given a point a_0 in E and a family of m vectors $(\vec{u}_1, \ldots, \vec{u}_m)$ in $\vec{E}$, we obtain the family of $m + 1$ points $(a_0, \ldots, a_m)$ in E, where $a_i = a_0 + \vec{u}_i$, $1 \le i \le m$.

Thus, for any $m \ge 1$, it is equivalent to consider a family of $m + 1$ points $(a_0, \ldots, a_m)$ in E, and a pair $(a_0, (\vec{u}_1, \ldots, \vec{u}_m))$, where the $\vec{u}_i$ are vectors in $\vec{E}$. For an example, see Figure 2.9.

When $(\overrightarrow{a_0 a_1}, \ldots, \overrightarrow{a_0 a_m})$ is a basis of $\vec{E}$, then, for every $x \in E$, since $x = a_0 + \overrightarrow{a_0 x}$, there is a unique family $(x_1, \ldots, x_m)$ of scalars, such that

$$x = a_0 + x_1 \overrightarrow{a_0 a_1} + \cdots + x_m \overrightarrow{a_0 a_m}.$$

The scalars $(x_1, \ldots, x_m)$ are coordinates with respect to $(a_0, (\overrightarrow{a_0 a_1}, \ldots, \overrightarrow{a_0 a_m}))$. Since

$$x = a_0 + \sum_{i=1}^{m} x_i \overrightarrow{a_0 a_i} \quad \text{iff} \quad x = \left(1 - \sum_{i=1}^{m} x_i\right) a_0 + \sum_{i=1}^{m} x_i a_i,$$

$x \in E$ can also be expressed uniquely as

$$x = \sum_{i=0}^{m} \lambda_i a_i$$

with $\sum_{i=0}^{m} \lambda_i = 1$, and where $\lambda_0 = 1 - \sum_{i=1}^{m} x_i$, and $\lambda_i = x_i$ for $1 \le i \le m$. The scalars $(\lambda_0, \ldots, \lambda_m)$ are also certain kinds of coordinates with respect to $(a_0, \ldots, a_m)$. All this is summarized in the following definition.

Definition 2.6.4

Given an affine space $\langle E, \vec{E}, + \rangle$, an affine frame with origin a_0 *is a family $(a_0, \ldots, a_m)$ of $m + 1$ points in E such that $(\overrightarrow{a_0 a_1}, \ldots, \overrightarrow{a_0 a_m})$ is a basis of $\vec{E}$. The pair $(a_0, (\overrightarrow{a_0 a_1}, \ldots, \overrightarrow{a_0 a_m}))$ is also called an* affine frame with origin a_0. *Then, every $x \in E$ can be expressed as*

$$x = a_0 + x_1 \overrightarrow{a_0 a_1} + \cdots + x_m \overrightarrow{a_0 a_m}$$

for a unique family $(x_1, \ldots, x_m)$ of scalars, called the coordinates of x with respect to the affine frame $(a_0, (\overrightarrow{a_0 a_1}, \ldots, \overrightarrow{a_0 a_m}))$. *Furthermore, every $x \in E$ can be written as*

$$x = \lambda_0 a_0 + \cdots + \lambda_m a_m$$

for some unique family $(\lambda_0, \ldots, \lambda_m)$ of scalars such that $\lambda_0 + \cdots + \lambda_m = 1$ called the barycentric coordinates of x with respect to the affine frame $(a_0, \ldots, a_m)$.

The coordinates $(x_1, \ldots, x_m)$ and the barycentric coordinates $(\lambda_0, \ldots, \lambda_m)$ are related by the equations $\lambda_0 = 1 - \sum_{i=1}^{m} x_i$ and $\lambda_i = x_i$, for $1 \le i \le m$. An affine frame is called an *affine basis* by some authors. Figure 2.10 shows affine frames for $|I| = 0, 1, 2, 3$.

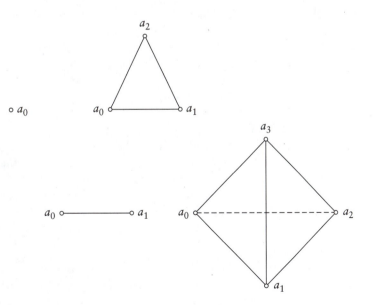

FIG. 2.10 Examples of affine frames

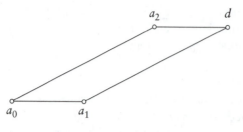

FIG. 2.11 A parallelotope

A family of two points (a, b) in E is affinely independent iff $\overrightarrow{ab} \neq \overrightarrow{0}$, iff $a \neq b$. If $a \neq b$, the affine subspace generated by a and b is the set of all points $(1 - \lambda)a + \lambda b$, which is the unique line passing through a and b. A family of three points (a, b, c) in E is affinely independent iff $\overrightarrow{ab}$ and $\overrightarrow{ac}$ are linearly independent, which means that a, b, and c are not on a same line (they are not collinear). In this case, the affine subspace generated by (a, b, c) is the set of all points $(1 - \lambda - \mu)a + \lambda b + \mu c$, which is the unique plane containing a, b, and c. A family of four points (a, b, c, d) in E is affinely independent iff $\overrightarrow{ab}$, $\overrightarrow{ac}$, and $\overrightarrow{ad}$ are linearly independent, which means that a, b, c, and d are not in a same plane (they are not coplanar). In this case, a, b, c, and d, are the vertices of a tetrahedron.

Given $n + 1$ affinely independent points $(a_0, \ldots, a_n)$ in E, we can consider the set of points $\lambda_0 a_0 + \cdots + \lambda_n a_n$, where $\lambda_0 + \cdots + \lambda_n = 1$ and $\lambda_i \geq 0$ ($\lambda_i \in \mathbf{R}$). Such affine combinations are called *convex combinations*. This set is called the *convex hull* of $(a_0, \ldots, a_n)$ (or *n-simplex spanned by* $(a_0, \ldots, a_n)$). When $n = 1$, we get the line segment between a_0 and a_1, including a_0 and a_1. When $n = 2$, we get the interior of the triangle whose vertices are a_0, a_1, a_2, including boundary points (the edges). When $n = 3$, we get the interior of the tetrahedron whose vertices are a_0, a_1, a_2, a_3, including boundary points (faces and edges). The set

$$\{a_0 + \lambda_1 \overrightarrow{a_0 a_1} + \cdots + \lambda_n \overrightarrow{a_0 a_n} \mid 0 \leq \lambda_i \leq 1 \ (\lambda_i \in \mathbf{R})\},$$

is called the *parallelotope spanned by* $(a_0, \ldots, a_n)$. When E has dimension 2, a parallelotope is also called a *parallelogram*, and when E has dimension 3, a *parallelepiped*. A parallelotope is shown in Figure 2.11: it consists of the points inside of the parallelogram (a_0, a_1, a_2, d), including its boundary.

More generally, we say that a subset V of E is *convex* if for any two points $a, b \in V$, we have $c \in V$ for every point $c = (1 - \lambda)a + \lambda b$, with $0 \leq \lambda \leq 1$ ($\lambda \in \mathbf{R}$).

Points are not vectors!

The following example illustrates why treating points as vectors may cause problems. Let a, b, c be three affinely independent points in $\mathbf{A}^3$. Any point x in the plane (a, b, c) can be expressed as

$$x = \lambda_0 a + \lambda_1 b + \lambda_2 c,$$

where $\lambda_0 + \lambda_1 + \lambda_2 = 1$. How can we compute $\lambda_0, \lambda_1, \lambda_2$? Letting $a = (a_1, a_2, a_3)$, $b = (b_1, b_2, b_3)$, $c = (c_1, c_2, c_3)$, and $x = (x_1, x_2, x_3)$ be the coordinates of a, b, c, x in the standard frame of $\mathbf{A}^3$, it is tempting to solve the system of equations

$$\begin{pmatrix} a_1 & b_1 & c_1 \\ a_2 & b_2 & c_2 \\ a_3 & b_3 & c_3 \end{pmatrix} \begin{pmatrix} \lambda_0 \\ \lambda_1 \\ \lambda_2 \end{pmatrix} = \begin{pmatrix} x_1 \\ x_2 \\ x_3 \end{pmatrix}.$$

However, there is a problem when the origin of the coordinate system belongs to the plane (a, b, c), since in this case, the matrix is not invertible! What we should really be doing is to solve the system

$$\lambda_0 \overrightarrow{Oa} + \lambda_1 \overrightarrow{Ob} + \lambda_2 \overrightarrow{Oc} = \overrightarrow{Ox},$$

where O is any point *not* in the plane (a, b, c). An alternative is to use certain well-chosen cross-products.

It can be shown that barycentric coordinates correspond to various ratios of areas and volumes (see the problems).

2.7   Affine Maps

Corresponding to linear maps, we have the notion of an affine map. An affine map is defined as a map preserving affine combinations.

Definition 2.7.1

Given two affine spaces $\langle E, \vec{E}, + \rangle$ and $\langle E', \vec{E}', +' \rangle$, a function $f: E \to E'$ is an affine map iff for every family $((a_i, \lambda_i))_{i \in I}$ of weighted points in E such that $\sum_{i \in I} \lambda_i = 1$, we have

$$f\left(\sum_{i \in I} \lambda_i a_i \right) = \sum_{i \in I} \lambda_i f(a_i).$$

In other words, f preserves barycenters.

Affine maps can be obtained from linear maps as follows. For simplicity of notation, the same symbol $+$ is used for both affine spaces (instead of using both $+$ and $+'$).

Given any point $a \in E$, any point $b \in E'$, and any linear map $h: \vec{E} \to \vec{E}'$, we claim that the map $f: E \to E'$ defined such that

$$f(a + \vec{v}) = b + h(\vec{v})$$

is an affine map.

Proof: Indeed, for any family $(\lambda_i)_{i \in I}$ of scalars such that $\sum_{i \in I} \lambda_i = 1$, for any family $(\vec{v_i})_{i \in I}$, since

$$\sum_{i\in I}\lambda_i(a+\vec{v_i})=a+\sum_{i\in I}\lambda_i\overrightarrow{a(a+\vec{v_i})}=a+\sum_{i\in I}\lambda_i\vec{v_i},$$

and

$$\sum_{i\in I}\lambda_i(b+h(\vec{v_i}))=b+\sum_{i\in I}\lambda_i\overrightarrow{b(b+h(\vec{v_i}))}=b+\sum_{i\in I}\lambda_i h(\vec{v_i}),$$

we have

$$f\left(\sum_{i\in I}\lambda_i(a+\vec{v_i})\right)=f\left(a+\sum_{i\in I}\lambda_i\vec{v_i}\right)$$

$$=b+h\left(\sum_{i\in I}\lambda_i\vec{v_i}\right)$$

$$=b+\sum_{i\in I}\lambda_i h(\vec{v_i})$$

$$=\sum_{i\in I}\lambda_i(b+h(\vec{v_i}))$$

$$=\sum_{i\in I}\lambda_i f(a+\vec{v_i}).\quad\blacksquare$$

Note that the condition $\sum_{i\in I}\lambda_i=1$ was implicitly used (in a hidden call to Lemma 2.4.1) in deriving that

$$\sum_{i\in I}\lambda_i(a+\vec{v_i})=a+\sum_{i\in I}\lambda_i\vec{v_i}$$

and

$$\sum_{i\in I}\lambda_i(b+h(\vec{v_i}))=b+\sum_{i\in I}\lambda_i h(\vec{v_i}).$$

As a more concrete example, the map

$$\begin{pmatrix}x_1\\x_2\end{pmatrix}\mapsto\begin{pmatrix}1&2\\0&1\end{pmatrix}\begin{pmatrix}x_1\\x_2\end{pmatrix}+\begin{pmatrix}3\\1\end{pmatrix}$$

defines an affine map in $\mathbf{A}^2$. It is a "shear" followed by a translation. The effect of this shear on the square (a,b,c,d) is shown in Figure 2.12. The image of the square (a,b,c,d) is the parallelogram (a',b',c',d').

Let us consider one more example. The map

$$\begin{pmatrix}x_1\\x_2\end{pmatrix}\mapsto\begin{pmatrix}1&1\\1&3\end{pmatrix}\begin{pmatrix}x_1\\x_2\end{pmatrix}+\begin{pmatrix}3\\0\end{pmatrix}$$

is an affine map. Since we can write

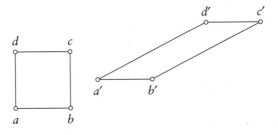

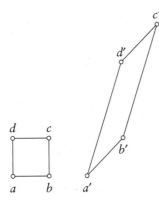

FIG. 2.12 The effect of a shear

FIG. 2.13 The effect of an affine map

$$\begin{pmatrix} 1 & 1 \\ 1 & 3 \end{pmatrix} = \sqrt{2} \begin{pmatrix} \frac{\sqrt{2}}{2} & -\frac{\sqrt{2}}{2} \\ \frac{\sqrt{2}}{2} & \frac{\sqrt{2}}{2} \end{pmatrix} \begin{pmatrix} 1 & 2 \\ 0 & 1 \end{pmatrix},$$

this affine map is the composition of a shear, followed by a rotation of angle $\pi/4$, followed by a magnification of ratio $\sqrt{2}$, followed by a translation. The effect of this map on the square (a, b, c, d) is shown in Figure 2.13. The image of the square $(a, b, c; d)$ is the parallelogram (a', b', c', d').

The following lemma shows the converse of what we just showed. Every affine map is determined by the image of any point and a linear map.

Lemma 2.7.2

Given an affine map $f: E \to E'$, there is a unique linear map $\overrightarrow{f}: \overrightarrow{E} \to \overrightarrow{E'}$, such that

$$f(a + \overrightarrow{v}) = f(a) + \overrightarrow{f}(\overrightarrow{v}),$$

for every $a \in E$ and every $\overrightarrow{v} \in \overrightarrow{E}$.

Proof: The proof is not difficult, but very technical. It can be found in Appendix B, Section B. We simply sketch the main ideas. Let a be any point in E. If a linear map

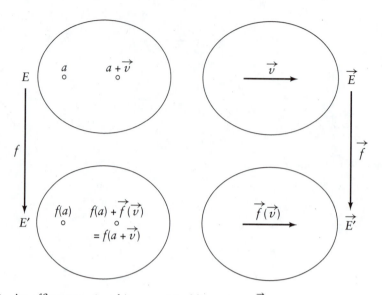

FIG. 2.14 An affine map f and its associated linear map $\overrightarrow{f}$

$\overrightarrow{f}\colon \overrightarrow{E} \to \overrightarrow{E'}$ satisfying the condition of the lemma exists, this map must satisfy the equation

$$\overrightarrow{f}(\overrightarrow{v}) = \overrightarrow{f(a)f(a + \overrightarrow{v})}$$

for every $\overrightarrow{v} \in \overrightarrow{E}$. We then have to check that the map defined in such a way is linear and that its definition does not depend on the choice of $a \in E$. ■

The unique linear map $\overrightarrow{f}\colon \overrightarrow{E} \to \overrightarrow{E'}$ given by Lemma 2.7.2 is called the *linear map associated with the affine map* f (see Figure 2.14).

Note that the condition

$$f(a + \overrightarrow{v}) = f(a) + \overrightarrow{f}(\overrightarrow{v}),$$

for every $a \in E$ and every $\overrightarrow{v} \in \overrightarrow{E}$, can be stated equivalently as

$$f(x) = f(a) + \overrightarrow{f}(\overrightarrow{ax}),$$

or

$$\overrightarrow{f(a)f(x)} = \overrightarrow{f}(\overrightarrow{ax}),$$

for all $a, x \in E$. Lemma 2.7.2 shows that for any affine map $f\colon E \to E'$, there are points $a \in E$, $b \in E'$, and a unique linear map $\overrightarrow{f}\colon \overrightarrow{E} \to \overrightarrow{E'}$, such that

$$f(a + \overrightarrow{v}) = b + \overrightarrow{f}(\overrightarrow{v}),$$

for all $\vec{v} \in \vec{E}$ (just let $b = f(a)$, for any $a \in E$). Affine maps for which $\vec{f}$ is the identity map are called *translations*. Indeed, if $\vec{f} = \text{id}$,

$$f(x) = f(a) + \vec{f}(\overrightarrow{ax})$$

$$= f(a) + \overrightarrow{ax} = x + \overrightarrow{xa} + \overrightarrow{af(a)} + \overrightarrow{ax} = x + \overrightarrow{xa} + \overrightarrow{af(a)} - \overrightarrow{xa} = x + \overrightarrow{af(a)},$$

and so

$$\overrightarrow{xf(x)} = \overrightarrow{af(a)},$$

which shows that f is the translation induced by the vector $\overrightarrow{af(a)}$ (which does not depend on a).

Since an affine map preserves barycenters, and since an affine subspace V is closed under barycentric combinations, the image $f(V)$ of V is an affine subspace in E'. So, for example, the image of a line is a point or a line, the image of a plane is either a point, a line, or a plane.

It is easily verified that the composition of two affine maps is an affine map. Also, given affine maps $f: E \to E'$ and $g: E' \to E''$, we have

$$g\big(f(a + \vec{v})\big) = g\big(f(a) + \vec{f}(\vec{v})\big) = g\big(f(a)\big) + \vec{g}(\vec{f}(\vec{v})),$$

which shows that $\overrightarrow{(g \circ f)} = \vec{g} \circ \vec{f}$. It is easy to show that an affine map $f: E \to E'$ is injective iff $\vec{f}: \vec{E} \to \vec{E'}$ is injective, and that $f: E \to E'$ is surjective iff $\vec{f}: \vec{E} \to \vec{E'}$ is surjective. An affine map $f: E \to E'$ is constant iff $\vec{f}: \vec{E} \to \vec{E'}$ is the null (constant) linear map equal to $\vec{0}$ for all $\vec{v} \in \vec{E}$.

If E is an affine space of dimension m and $(a_0, a_1, \ldots, a_m)$ is an affine frame for E, for any other affine space F, for any sequence $(b_0, b_1, \ldots, b_m)$ of $m + 1$ points in F, there is a unique affine map $f: E \to F$ such that $f(a_i) = b_i$, for $0 \le i \le m$. Indeed, f must be such that

$$f(\lambda_0 a_0 + \cdots + \lambda_m a_m) = \lambda_0 b_0 + \cdots + \lambda_m b_m,$$

where $\lambda_0 + \cdots + \lambda_m = 1$, and this defines a unique affine map on the entire E, since $(a_0, a_1, \ldots, a_m)$ is an affine frame for E. Figure 2.15 illustrates the above result when $m = 2$.

Using affine frames, affine maps can be represented in terms of matrices. We explain how an affine map $f: E \to E$ is represented with respect to a frame $(a_0, \ldots, a_n)$ in E, the more general case where an affine map $f: E \to F$ is represented with respect to two affine frames $(a_0, \ldots, a_n)$ in E and $(b_0, \ldots, b_m)$ in F being analogous. Since

$$f(a_0 + \vec{x}) = f(a_0) + \vec{f}(\vec{x})$$

for all $\vec{x} \in \vec{E}$, we have

$$\overrightarrow{a_0 f(a_0 + \vec{x})} = \overrightarrow{a_0 f(a_0)} + \vec{f}(\vec{x}).$$

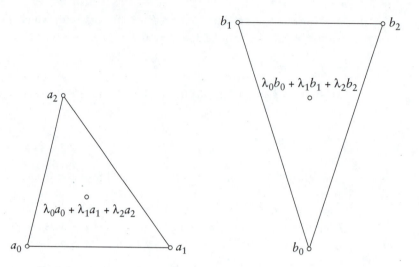

FIG. 2.15 An affine map mapping a_0, a_1, a_2 to b_0, b_1, b_2

Since $\vec{x}$, $\overrightarrow{a_0 f(a_0)}$, and $\overrightarrow{a_0 f(a_0 + \vec{x})}$ can be expressed as

$$\vec{x} = x_1 \overrightarrow{a_0 a_1} + \cdots + x_n \overrightarrow{a_0 a_n},$$

$$\overrightarrow{a_0 f(a_0)} = b_1 \overrightarrow{a_0 a_1} + \cdots + b_n \overrightarrow{a_0 a_n},$$

$$\overrightarrow{a_0 f(a_0 + \vec{x})} = y_1 \overrightarrow{a_0 a_1} + \cdots + y_n \overrightarrow{a_0 a_n},$$

if $A = (a_{i\,j})$ is the $n \times n$ matrix of the linear map $\vec{f}$ over the basis $(\overrightarrow{a_0 a_1}, \ldots, \overrightarrow{a_0 a_n})$, letting x, y, and b denote the column vectors of components $(x_1, \ldots, x_n)$, $(y_1, \ldots, y_n)$, and $(b_1, \ldots, b_n)$,

$$\overrightarrow{a_0 f(a_0 + \vec{x})} = \overrightarrow{a_0 f(a_0)} + \vec{f}(\vec{x})$$

is equivalent to

$$y = Ax + b.$$

Note that $b \neq 0$ unless $f(a_0) = a_0$. Thus, f is generally not a linear transformation, unless it has a *fixed point*; that is, there is a point a_0 such that $f(a_0) = a_0$. The vector b is the "translation part" of the affine map. Affine maps do not always have a fixed point. Obviously, nonnull translations have no fixed point. A less trivial example is given by the affine map

$$\begin{pmatrix} x_1 \\ x_2 \end{pmatrix} \mapsto \begin{pmatrix} 1 & 0 \\ 0 & -1 \end{pmatrix} \begin{pmatrix} x_1 \\ x_2 \end{pmatrix} + \begin{pmatrix} 1 \\ 0 \end{pmatrix}.$$

This map is a reflection about the x-axis followed by a translation along the x-axis. The affine map

$$\begin{pmatrix} x_1 \\ x_2 \end{pmatrix} \mapsto \begin{pmatrix} \frac{1}{4} & -\sqrt{3} \\ \frac{\sqrt{3}}{4} & \frac{1}{4} \end{pmatrix} \begin{pmatrix} x_1 \\ x_2 \end{pmatrix} + \begin{pmatrix} 1 \\ 1 \end{pmatrix}$$

can also be written as

$$\begin{pmatrix} x_1 \\ x_2 \end{pmatrix} \mapsto \begin{pmatrix} 2 & 0 \\ 0 & \frac{1}{2} \end{pmatrix} \begin{pmatrix} \frac{1}{2} & -\frac{\sqrt{3}}{2} \\ \frac{\sqrt{3}}{2} & \frac{1}{2} \end{pmatrix} \begin{pmatrix} x_1 \\ x_2 \end{pmatrix} + \begin{pmatrix} 1 \\ 1 \end{pmatrix}$$

which shows that it is the composition of a rotation of angle $\pi/3$, followed by a stretch (by a factor of 2 along the x-axis, and by a factor of $\frac{1}{2}$ along the y-axis), followed by a translation. It is easy to show that this affine map has a unique fixed point. On the other hand, the affine map

$$\begin{pmatrix} x_1 \\ x_2 \end{pmatrix} \mapsto \begin{pmatrix} \frac{8}{5} & -\frac{6}{5} \\ \frac{3}{10} & \frac{2}{5} \end{pmatrix} \begin{pmatrix} x_1 \\ x_2 \end{pmatrix} + \begin{pmatrix} 1 \\ 1 \end{pmatrix}$$

has no fixed point, even though

$$\begin{pmatrix} \frac{8}{5} & -\frac{6}{5} \\ \frac{3}{10} & \frac{2}{5} \end{pmatrix} = \begin{pmatrix} 2 & 0 \\ 0 & \frac{1}{2} \end{pmatrix} \begin{pmatrix} \frac{4}{5} & -\frac{3}{5} \\ \frac{3}{5} & \frac{4}{5} \end{pmatrix},$$

and the second matrix is a rotation of angle θ such that $\cos\theta = \frac{4}{5}$ and $\sin\theta = \frac{3}{5}$. For more on fixed points of affine maps, see the problems.

There is a useful trick to convert the equation $y = Ax + b$ into what looks like a linear equation. The trick is to consider an $(n+1) \times (n+1)$ matrix. We add 1 as the $(n+1)$th component to the vectors x, y, and b, and form the $(n+1) \times (n+1)$ matrix

$$\begin{pmatrix} A & b \\ 0 & 1 \end{pmatrix}$$

so that $y = Ax + b$ is equivalent to

$$\begin{pmatrix} y \\ 1 \end{pmatrix} = \begin{pmatrix} A & b \\ 0 & 1 \end{pmatrix} \begin{pmatrix} x \\ 1 \end{pmatrix}.$$

This trick is very useful in kinematics and dynamics, where A is a rotation matrix. Such affine maps are called *rigid motions*.

If $f\colon E \to E'$ is a bijective affine map, given any three collinear points a, b, c in E, with $a \neq b$, where, say, $c = (1-\lambda)a + \lambda b$, since f preserves barycenters, we have $f(c) = (1-\lambda)f(a) + \lambda f(b)$, which shows that $f(a), f(b), f(c)$ are collinear in E'. There is a converse to this property, which is simpler to state when the ground field is $K = \mathbf{R}$. The converse states that given any bijective function $f\colon E \to E'$ between two real affine spaces of the same dimension $n \geq 2$, if f maps any three collinear points to collinear points, then f is affine. The proof is rather long (see Berger [5] or Samuel [69]).

Given three collinear points a, b, c, where $a \neq c$, we have $b = (1 - \beta)a + \beta c$ for some unique β, and we define the *ratio of the sequence* a, b, c, as

$$\text{ratio}(a, b, c) = \frac{\beta}{(1 - \beta)} = \frac{\overrightarrow{ab}}{\overrightarrow{bc}},$$

provided that $\beta \neq 1$ (i.e., that $b \neq c$). When $b = c$, we agree that $\text{ratio}(a, b, c) = \infty$. We warn you that other authors define the ratio of a, b, c as

$$-\text{ratio}(a, b, c) = \frac{\overrightarrow{ba}}{\overrightarrow{bc}}.$$

Since affine maps preserve barycenters, it is clear that affine maps preserve the ratio of three points.

2.8 Affine Groups

We now take a quick look at the bijective affine maps. Given an affine space E, the set of affine bijections $f: E \to E$ is clearly a group, called the *affine group of* E, and denoted as $\mathbf{GA}(E)$. Recall that the group of bijective linear maps of the vector space $\overrightarrow{E}$ is denoted as $\mathbf{GL}(\overrightarrow{E})$. Then, the map $f \mapsto \overrightarrow{f}$ defines a group homomorphism $L: \mathbf{GA}(E) \to \mathbf{GL}(\overrightarrow{E})$. The kernel of this map is the set of translations on E.

The subset of all linear maps of the form $\lambda \ \text{id}_{\overrightarrow{E}}$, where $\lambda \in \mathbf{R} - \{0\}$, is a subgroup of $\mathbf{GL}(\overrightarrow{E})$, and is denoted as $\mathbf{R}^* \ \text{id}_{\overrightarrow{E}}$ (where $\lambda \ \text{id}_{\overrightarrow{E}}(\overrightarrow{u}) = \lambda \overrightarrow{u}$, and $\mathbf{R}^* = \mathbf{R} - \{0\}$). The subgroup $\mathbf{DIL}(E) = L^{-1}(\mathbf{R}^* \ \text{id}_{\overrightarrow{E}})$ of $\mathbf{GA}(E)$ is particularly interesting. It turns out that it is the disjoint union of the translations and of the dilatations of ratio $\lambda \neq 1$.

The elements of $\mathbf{DIL}(E)$ are called *affine dilatations*. Given any point $a \in E$, and any scalar $\lambda \in \mathbf{R}$, a *dilatation* (or *central dilatation* or *homothety*) of center a and *ratio* λ is a map $H_{a,\lambda}$ defined such that

$$H_{a,\lambda}(x) = a + \lambda \overrightarrow{ax},$$

for every $x \in E$.

Remark: The terminology does not seem to be universally agreed upon. The terms *affine dilatation* and *central dilatation* are used by Pedoe [59]. Snapper and Troyer use the term *dilation* for an affine dilatation and *magnification* for a central dilatation [77]. Samuel uses *homothety* for a central dilatation, a direct translation of the French "homothétie" [69]. Since dilation is shorter than dilatation and somewhat easier to pronounce, perhaps we should use that!

Observe that $H_{a,\lambda}(a) = a$, and when $\lambda \neq 0$ and $x \neq a$, $H_{a,\lambda}(x)$ is on the line defined by a and x, and is obtained by "scaling" $\overrightarrow{ax}$ by λ.

Figure 2.16 shows the effect of a central dilatation of center d. The triangle (a, b, c) is magnified to the triangle (a', b', c'). Note how every line is mapped to a parallel line.

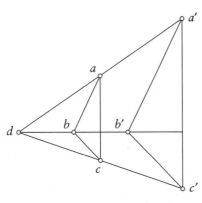

The effect of a central dilatation

When $\lambda = 1$, $H_{a,1}$ is the identity. Note that $\overrightarrow{H_{a,\lambda}} = \lambda \ \mathrm{id}_{\overrightarrow{E}}$. When $\lambda \neq 0$, it is clear that $H_{a,\lambda}$ is an affine bijection. It is immediately verified that

$$H_{a,\lambda} \circ H_{a,\mu} = H_{a,\lambda\mu}.$$

We have the following useful result.

Lemma 2.8.1

Given any affine space E, for any affine bijection $f \in \mathbf{GA}(E)$, if $\overrightarrow{f} = \lambda \ \mathrm{id}_{\overrightarrow{E}}$, for some $\lambda \in \mathbf{R}^*$ with $\lambda \neq 1$, then there is a unique point $c \in E$ such that $f = H_{c,\lambda}$.

Proof: Choose some origin a in E. Since f is affine, we have

$$f(b) = f(a + \overrightarrow{ab}) = f(a) + \lambda\overrightarrow{ab}$$

for all $b \in E$. Thus, there is a point $c \in E$ such that $f(c) = c$ iff

$$c = f(a) + \lambda\overrightarrow{ac},$$

iff

$$\overrightarrow{ac} = \overrightarrow{af(a)} + \lambda\overrightarrow{ac},$$

iff

$$(1 - \lambda)\overrightarrow{ac} = \overrightarrow{af(a)},$$

iff

$$\overrightarrow{ac} = \frac{1}{1 - \lambda} \ \overrightarrow{af(a)},$$

that is,

$$c = \frac{1}{1-\lambda}\, f(a) - \frac{\lambda}{1-\lambda}\, a.$$

Taking this unique point c as the origin, we have $f(b) = c + \lambda \overrightarrow{cb}$ for all $b \in E$, which shows that $f = H_{c,\lambda}$.   ∎

Clearly, if $\overrightarrow{f} = \mathrm{id}_{\overrightarrow{E}}$, the affine map f is a translation. Thus, the group of affine dilatations $\mathbf{DIL}(E)$ is the disjoint union of the translations and of the dilatations of ratio $\lambda \neq 0, 1$. Affine dilatations can be given a purely geometric characterization.

Another point worth mentioning is that affine bijections preserve the ratio of volumes of parallelotopes. Indeed, given any basis $B = (\vec{u}_1, \dots, \vec{u}_m)$ of the vector space $\overrightarrow{E}$ associated with the affine space E, given any $m + 1$ affinely independent points $(a_0, \dots, a_m)$, we can compute the determinant $\det_B(\overrightarrow{a_0 a_1}, \dots, \overrightarrow{a_0 a_m})$ with respect to the basis B. For any bijective affine map $f \colon E \to E$, since

$$\det_B(\overrightarrow{f}(\overrightarrow{a_0 a_1}), \dots, \overrightarrow{f}(\overrightarrow{a_0 a_m})) = \det(\overrightarrow{f})\, \det_B(\overrightarrow{a_0 a_1}, \dots, \overrightarrow{a_0 a_m})$$

and the determinant of a linear map is intrinsic (i.e., only depends on $\overrightarrow{f}$, and not on the particular basis B), we conclude that the ratio

$$\frac{\det_B(\overrightarrow{f}(\overrightarrow{a_0 a_1}), \dots, \overrightarrow{f}(\overrightarrow{a_0 a_m}))}{\det_B(\overrightarrow{a_0 a_1}, \dots, \overrightarrow{a_0 a_m})} = \det(\overrightarrow{f})$$

is independent of the basis B. Since $\det_B(\overrightarrow{a_0 a_1}, \dots, \overrightarrow{a_0 a_m})$ is the volume of the parallelotope spanned by $(a_0, \dots, a_m)$, where the parallelotope spanned by any point a and the vectors $(\vec{u}_1, \dots, \vec{u}_m)$ has unit volume (see Berger [5], Section 9.12), we see that affine bijections preserve the ratio of volumes of parallelotopes. In fact, this ratio is independent of the choice of the parallelotopes of unit volume. In particular, the affine bijections $f \in \mathbf{GA}(E)$ such that $\det(\overrightarrow{f}) = 1$ preserve volumes. These affine maps form a subgroup $\mathbf{SA}(E)$ of $\mathbf{GA}(E)$ called the *special affine group of E*.

2.9   Affine Hyperplanes

We now consider affine forms and affine hyperplanes. In Section 2.5, we observed that the set L of solutions of an equation

$$ax + by = c$$

is an affine subspace of $\mathbf{A}^2$ of dimension 1—in fact, a line (provided that a and b are not both null). It would be equally easy to show that the set P of solutions of an equation

$$ax + by + cz = d$$

is an affine subspace of $\mathbf{A}^3$ of dimension 2—in fact, a plane (provided that a, b, c are not all null). More generally, the set H of solutions of an equation

$$\lambda_1 x_1 + \cdots + \lambda_m x_m = \mu$$

is an affine subspace of $\mathbf{A}^m$, and if $\lambda_1, \ldots, \lambda_m$ are not all null, it turns out that it is a subspace of dimension $m - 1$ called a *hyperplane*.

We can interpret the equation

$$\lambda_1 x_1 + \cdots + \lambda_m x_m = \mu$$

in terms of the map $f: \mathbf{R}^m \to \mathbf{R}$ defined such that

$$f(x_1, \ldots, x_m) = \lambda_1 x_1 + \cdots + \lambda_m x_m - \mu$$

for all $(x_1, \ldots, x_m) \in \mathbf{R}^m$. It is immediately verified that this map is affine, and the set H of solutions of the equation

$$\lambda_1 x_1 + \cdots + \lambda_m x_m = \mu$$

is the *null set*, or *kernel*, of the affine map $f: \mathbf{A}^m \to \mathbf{R}$, in the sense that

$$H = f^{-1}(0) = \{x \in \mathbf{A}^m \mid f(x) = 0\},$$

where $x = (x_1, \ldots, x_m)$.

Thus, it is interesting to consider *affine forms*, which are just affine maps $f: E \to \mathbf{R}$ from an affine space to $\mathbf{R}$. Unlike linear forms f^*, for which Ker f^* is never empty (since it always contains the vector $\vec{0}$), it is possible that $f^{-1}(0) = \emptyset$, for an affine form f. Given an affine map $f: E \to \mathbf{R}$, we also denote $f^{-1}(0)$ as Ker f, and we call it the *kernel* of f. Recall that an (affine) hyperplane is an affine subspace of codimension 1. The relationship between affine hyperplanes and affine forms is given by the following lemma.

Lemma 2.9.1

Let E be an affine space. The following properties hold:

1. *Given any nonconstant affine form $f: E \to \mathbf{R}$, its kernel $H = $ Ker f is a hyperplane.*

2. *For any hyperplane H in E, there is a nonconstant affine form $f: E \to \mathbf{R}$ such that $H = $ Ker f. For any other affine form $g: E \to \mathbf{R}$ such that $H = $ Ker g, there is some $\lambda \in \mathbf{R}$ such that $g = \lambda f$ (with $\lambda \neq 0$).*

3. *Given any hyperplane H in E and any (nonconstant) affine form $f: E \to \mathbf{R}$ such that $H = $ Ker f, every hyperplane H' parallel to H is defined by a nonconstant affine form g such that $g(a) = f(a) - \lambda$, for all $a \in E$, for some $\lambda \in \mathbf{R}$.*

Proof: (1) Since $f: E \to \mathbf{R}$ is nonconstant, by a previous observation, $\vec{f}: \vec{E} \to \mathbf{R}$ is not identically null, and since $\vec{f}$ is a linear form, it is surjective, which implies that

f is surjective. Thus, there is some $a \in E$ such that $f(a) = 0$. Since $f(a + \vec{v}) = \vec{f}(\vec{v})$ for all $\vec{v} \in \vec{E}$, we have $f(a + \vec{v}) = 0$ iff $\vec{f}(\vec{v}) = 0$, and since by Lemma A.5.1, Ker $\vec{f}$ is a hyperplane $\vec{H}$ in $\vec{E}$, clearly, $f^{-1}(0) = a + \vec{H}$ is a hyperplane H in E.

(2) If H is an affine hyperplane, then by Lemma 2.5.2, for any $a \in H$, we have $H = a + \vec{H}$, where $\vec{H}$ is a hyperplane of $\vec{E}$. By Lemma A.5.1, $\vec{H} = \text{Ker } f^*$ for some nonnull linear form f^*, and thus, letting $f : E \to \mathbf{R}$ be the affine form defined such that

$$f(a + \vec{v}) = f^*(\vec{v}),$$

we have $H = f^{-1}(0)$, and f is nonconstant, since f^* is nonnull. The second part of (2) is as in Lemma A.5.1 (3).

(3) This follows easily from the proof of (2) and is left as an exercise. ∎

When E is of dimension n, given an affine frame $(a_0, (\vec{u_1}, \ldots, \vec{u_n}))$ of E with origin a_0, recall from Definition 2.6.4 that every point of E can be expressed uniquely as $x = a_0 + x_1\vec{u_1} + \cdots + x_n\vec{u_n}$, where $(x_1, \ldots, x_n)$ are the *coordinates* of x with respect to the affine frame $(a_0, (\vec{u_1}, \ldots, \vec{u_n}))$.

Also recall that every linear form f^* is such that $f^*(\vec{x}) = \lambda_1 x_1 + \cdots + \lambda_n x_n$, for every $\vec{x} = x_1\vec{u_1} + \cdots + x_n\vec{u_n}$, for some $\lambda_1, \ldots, \lambda_n \in \mathbf{R}$. Since an affine form $f : E \to \mathbf{R}$ satisfies the property $f(a_0 + \vec{x}) = f(a_0) + \vec{f}(\vec{x})$, denoting $f(a_0 + \vec{x})$ as $f(x_1, \ldots, x_n)$, we see that we have

$$f(x_1, \ldots, x_n) = \lambda_1 x_1 + \cdots + \lambda_n x_n + \mu,$$

where $\mu = f(a_0) \in \mathbf{R}$, and $\lambda_1, \ldots, \lambda_n \in \mathbf{R}$. Thus, a hyperplane is the set of points whose coordinates $(x_1, \ldots, x_n)$ satisfy the (affine) equation

$$\lambda_1 x_1 + \cdots + \lambda_n x_n + \mu = 0.$$

We are now ready to study polynomial curves.

Problems

[10 pts]   **1.** Given a triangle (a, b, c), give a geometric construction of the barycenter of the weighted points $(a, 1/4)$, $(b, 1/4)$, and $(c, 1/2)$. Give a geometric construction of the barycenter of the weighted points $(a, 3/2)$, $(b, 3/2)$, and $(c, -2)$.

[20 pts]   **2.** Given a tetrahedron (a, b, c, d), given any two distinct points $x, y \in \{a, b, c, d\}$, let $m_{x,y}$ be the middle of the edge (x, y). Prove that the barycenter g of the weighted points $(a, 1/4)$, $(b, 1/4)$, $(c, 1/4)$, and $(d, 1/4)$ is the common intersection of the line segments $(m_{a,b}, m_{c,d})$, $(m_{a,c}, m_{b,d})$, and $(m_{a,d}, m_{b,c})$. Show that if g_d is the barycenter of the weighted points $(a, 1/3)$, $(b, 1/3)$, $(c, 1/3)$, then g is the barycenter of $(d, 1/4)$ and $(g_d, 3/4)$.

[20 pts]   **3.** Let E be a nonempty set, and $\vec{E}$ a vector space, and assume that there is a function $\Phi : E \times E \to \vec{E}$, such that if we denote $\Phi(a, b)$ as $\vec{ab}$, the following properties hold:

(1) $\vec{ab} + \vec{bc} = \vec{ac}$, for all $a, b, c \in E$.

(2) For every $a \in E$, the map $\Phi_a: E \to \vec{E}$ defined such that for every $b \in E$, $\Phi_a(b) = \vec{ab}$, is a bijection.

Let $\Psi_a: \vec{E} \to E$ be the inverse of $\Phi_a: E \to \vec{E}$.

Prove that the function $+: E \times \vec{E} \to E$ defined such that

$$a + \vec{u} = \Psi_a(\vec{u}),$$

for all $a \in E$ and all $\vec{u} \in \vec{E}$, makes $\langle E, \vec{E}, + \rangle$ into an affine space.

Note: We showed in the text that an affine space $\langle E, \vec{E}, + \rangle$ satisfies the properties stated above. Thus, we obtain an equivalent characterization of affine spaces.

[20 pts] **4.** Given any three points a, b, c in the affine plane $\mathbf{A}^2$, letting (a_1, a_2), (b_1, b_2), and (c_1, c_2) be the coordinates of a, b, c, with respect to the standard affine frame for $\mathbf{A}^2$, prove that a, b, c are collinear iff

$$\begin{vmatrix} a_1 & b_1 & c_1 \\ a_2 & b_2 & c_2 \\ 1 & 1 & 1 \end{vmatrix} = 0,$$

that is, the determinant is null.

Letting (a_0, a_1, a_2), (b_0, b_1, b_2), and (c_0, c_1, c_2) be the barycentric coordinates of a, b, c with respect to the standard affine frame for $\mathbf{A}^2$, prove that a, b, c are collinear iff

$$\begin{vmatrix} a_0 & b_0 & c_0 \\ a_1 & b_1 & c_1 \\ a_2 & b_2 & c_2 \end{vmatrix} = 0.$$

Given any four points a, b, c, d in the affine space $\mathbf{A}^3$, letting (a_1, a_2, a_3), (b_1, b_2, b_3), (c_1, c_2, c_3), and (d_1, d_2, d_3) be the coordinates of a, b, c, d with respect to the standard affine frame for $\mathbf{A}^3$, prove that a, b, c, d are coplanar iff

$$\begin{vmatrix} a_1 & b_1 & c_1 & d_1 \\ a_2 & b_2 & c_2 & d_2 \\ a_3 & b_3 & c_3 & d_3 \\ 1 & 1 & 1 & 1 \end{vmatrix} = 0,$$

that is, the determinant is null.

Letting (a_0, a_1, a_2, a_3), (b_0, b_1, b_2, b_3), (c_0, c_1, c_2, c_3), and (d_0, d_1, d_2, d_3) be the barycentric coordinates of a, b, c, d with respect to the standard affine frame for $\mathbf{A}^3$, prove that a, b, c, d are coplanar iff

$$\begin{vmatrix} a_0 & b_0 & c_0 & d_0 \\ a_1 & b_1 & c_1 & d_1 \\ a_2 & b_2 & c_2 & d_2 \\ a_3 & b_3 & c_3 & d_3 \end{vmatrix} = 0.$$

[10 pts]   5. The function $f : A \to A^3$, given by

$$t \mapsto (t, t^2, t^3),$$

defines what is called a *twisted cubic* curve. Given any four pairwise distinct values t_1, t_2, t_3, t_4, prove that the points $f(t_1)$, $f(t_2)$, $f(t_3)$, and $f(t_4)$ are not coplanar.
Hint: Have you heard of the Vandermonde determinant?

[20 pts]   6. Given any two distinct points a, b in A^2 of barycentric coordinates (a_0, a_1, a_2) and (b_0, b_1, b_2) with respect to any given affine frame (O, i, j), show that the equation of the line $\langle a, b \rangle$ determined by a and b is

$$\begin{vmatrix} a_0 & b_0 & x \\ a_1 & b_1 & y \\ a_2 & b_2 & z \end{vmatrix} = 0,$$

or equivalently

$$(a_1 b_2 - a_2 b_1)x + (a_2 b_0 - a_0 b_2)y + (a_0 b_1 - a_1 b_0)z = 0,$$

where (x, y, z) are the barycentric coordinates of the generic point on the line $\langle a, b \rangle$.
Prove that the equation of a line in barycentric coordinates is of the form

$$ux + vy + wz = 0,$$

where $u \neq v$, or $v \neq w$, or $u \neq w$. Show that two equations

$$ux + vy + wz = 0$$

and

$$u'x + v'y + w'z = 0$$

represent the same line in barycentric coordinates iff $(u', v', w') = \lambda(u, v, w)$ for some $\lambda \in R$ (with $\lambda \neq 0$).
A triple (u, v, w), where $u \neq v$, or $v \neq w$, or $u \neq w$, is called a system of *tangential coordinates* of the line defined by the equation

$$ux + vy + wz = 0.$$

[30 pts]   7. Given two lines D and D' in A^2 defined by tangential coordinates (u, v, w) and (u', v', w') (as defined in Problem 6), let

$$d = \begin{vmatrix} u & v & w \\ u' & v' & w' \\ 1 & 1 & 1 \end{vmatrix} = vw' - wv' + wu' - uw' + uv' - vu'.$$

(a) Prove that D and D' have a unique intersection point iff $d \neq 0$, and that when it exists, the barycentric coordinates of this intersection point are

$$\frac{1}{d}(vw' - wv', \ wu' - uw', \ uv' - vu').$$

(b) Letting (O, i, j) be any affine frame for $\mathbf{A}^2$, recall that when $x + y + z = 0$, for any point a, the vector

$$x\overrightarrow{aO} + y\overrightarrow{ai} + z\overrightarrow{aj}$$

is independent of a and equal to

$$y\overrightarrow{Oi} + z\overrightarrow{Oj} = (y, z).$$

The triple (x, y, z) such that $x + y + z = 0$ is called the *barycentric coordinates* of the vector $y\overrightarrow{Oi} + z\overrightarrow{Oj}$ with respect to the affine frame (O, i, j).

Given any affine frame (O, i, j), prove that for $u \neq v$, or $v \neq w$, or $u \neq w$, the line of equation

$$ux + vy + wz = 0$$

in barycentric coordinates (x, y, z) (where $x + y + z = 1$) has for direction the set of vectors of barycentric coordinates (x, y, z) such that

$$ux + vy + wz = 0$$

(where $x + y + z = 0$).

Prove that D and D' are parallel iff $d = 0$. In this case, if $D \neq D'$, show that the common direction of D and D' is defined by the vector of barycentric coordinates

$$(vw' - wv', \ wu' - uw', \ uv' - vu').$$

(c) Given three lines D, D', and D'', at least two of which are distinct, and defined by tangential coordinates (u, v, w), (u', v', w'), and (u'', v'', w''), prove that D, D', and D'' are parallel or have a unique intersection point iff

$$\begin{vmatrix} u & v & w \\ u' & v' & w' \\ u'' & v'' & w'' \end{vmatrix} = 0.$$

[30 pts] 8. Let (A, B, C) be a triangle in $\mathbf{A}^2$. Let M, N, P be three points, respectively, on the lines BC, CA, and AB of barycentric coordinates $(0, m', m'')$, $(n, 0, n'')$, and $(p, p', 0)$, with respect to the affine frame (A, B, C).

(a) Assuming that $M \neq C$, $N \neq A$, and $P \neq B$, that is, $m'n''p \neq 0$, show that

$$\frac{\overrightarrow{MB}}{\overrightarrow{MC}} \frac{\overrightarrow{NC}}{\overrightarrow{NA}} \frac{\overrightarrow{PA}}{\overrightarrow{PB}} = -\frac{m''np'}{m'n''p}.$$

(b) Prove *Menelaus's theorem*: The points M, N, P are collinear iff

$$m''np' + m'n''p = 0.$$

When $M \neq C$, $N \neq A$, and $P \neq B$, this is equivalent to

$$\frac{\overrightarrow{MB}}{\overrightarrow{MC}} \frac{\overrightarrow{NC}}{\overrightarrow{NA}} \frac{\overrightarrow{PA}}{\overrightarrow{PB}} = 1.$$

(c) Prove *Ceva's theorem:* The lines AM, BN, CP have a unique intersection point or are parallel iff

$$m''np' - m'n''p = 0.$$

When $M \neq C$, $N \neq A$, and $P \neq B$, this is equivalent to

$$\frac{\overrightarrow{MB}}{\overrightarrow{MC}} \frac{\overrightarrow{NC}}{\overrightarrow{NA}} \frac{\overrightarrow{PA}}{\overrightarrow{PB}} = -1.$$

[20 pts]   9. This problem uses notions and results from Problems 6, 7, and 8.

In view of (a) and (b) of Problem 7, it is natural to extend the notion of barycentric coordinates of a point in $\mathbf{A}^2$ as follows. Given any affine frame (a, b, c) in $\mathbf{A}^2$, we will say that the barycentric coordinates (x, y, z) of a point M, where $x + y + z = 1$, are the *normalized* barycentric coordinates of M. Then, any triple (x, y, z) such that $x + y + z \neq 0$ is also called a system of barycentric coordinates for the point of normalized barycentric coordinates

$$\frac{1}{x + y + z} (x, y, z).$$

With this convention, the intersection of the two lines D and D' is either a point or a vector, in both cases of barycentric coordinates

$$(vw' - wv', \ wu' - uw', \ uv' - vu').$$

When the above is a vector, we can think of it as a point at infinity (in the direction of the line defined by that vector).

Let (D_0, D_0'), (D_1, D_1'), and (D_2, D_2') be three pairs of six distinct lines, such that the four lines belonging to any union of two of the above pairs are neither parallel nor concurrent (have a common intersection point). If D_0 and D_0' have a unique intersection point, let M be this point, and if D_0 and D_0' are parallel, let M denote a nonnull vector defining the common direction of D_0 and D_0'. In either case, let (m, m', m'') be the barycentric coordinates of M, as explained at the beginning of the problem. We call M the *intersection* of D_0 and D_0'. Similarly, define $N = (n, n', n'')$ as the intersection of D_1 and D_1', and $P = (p, p', p'')$ as the intersection of D_2 and D_2'.

Prove that

$$\begin{vmatrix} m & n & p \\ m' & n' & p' \\ m'' & n'' & p'' \end{vmatrix} = 0$$

iff either

(i) (D_0, D_0'), (D_1, D_1'), and (D_2, D_2') are pairs of parallel lines, or

(ii) the lines of some pair (D_i, D_i') are parallel, each pair (D_j, D_j') (with $j \neq i$) has a unique intersection point, and these two intersection points are distinct and determine a line parallel to the lines of the pair (D_i, D_i'), or

(iii) each pair (D_i, D_i') $(i = 0, 1, 2)$ has a unique intersection point, and these points M, N, P are distinct and collinear.

[20 pts] **10.** Prove the following version of *Desargues's theorem*. Let A, B, C, A', B', C' be six distinct points of $\mathbf{A}^2$. If no three of these points are collinear, then the lines AA', BB', and CC' are parallel or collinear iff the intersection points M, N, P (in the sense of Problem 7) of the pairs of lines $(BC, B'C')$, $(CA, C'A')$, and $(AB, A'B')$ are collinear in the sense of Problem 9.

[20 pts] **11.** Prove the following version of *Pappus's theorem*. Let D and D' be distinct lines, and let A, B, C and A', B', C' be distinct points, respectively, on D and D'. If these points are all distinct from the intersection of D and D' (if it exists), then the intersection points (in the sense of Problem 7) of the pairs of lines (BC', CB'), (CA', AC'), and (AB', BA') are collinear in the sense of Problem 9.

[30 pts] **12.** The purpose of this problem is to prove *Pascal's theorem* for the nondegenerate conics. In the affine plane $\mathbf{A}^2$, a *conic* is the set of points of coordinates (x, y) such that

$$\alpha x^2 + \beta y^2 + 2\gamma xy + 2\delta x + 2\lambda y + \mu = 0,$$

where $\alpha \neq 0$, or $\beta \neq 0$, or $\gamma \neq 0$. We can write the equation of the conic as

$$(x, y, 1) \begin{pmatrix} \alpha & \gamma & \delta \\ \gamma & \beta & \lambda \\ \delta & \lambda & \mu \end{pmatrix} \begin{pmatrix} x \\ y \\ 1 \end{pmatrix} = 0.$$

If we now use barycentric coordinates (x, y, z) (where $x + y + z = 1$), we can write

$$\begin{pmatrix} x \\ y \\ 1 \end{pmatrix} = \begin{pmatrix} 1 & 0 & 0 \\ 0 & 1 & 0 \\ 1 & 1 & 1 \end{pmatrix} \begin{pmatrix} x \\ y \\ z \end{pmatrix}.$$

Let

$$B = \begin{pmatrix} \alpha & \gamma & \delta \\ \gamma & \beta & \lambda \\ \delta & \lambda & \mu \end{pmatrix}, \qquad C = \begin{pmatrix} 1 & 0 & 0 \\ 0 & 1 & 0 \\ 1 & 1 & 1 \end{pmatrix}, \qquad \text{and} \qquad X = \begin{pmatrix} x \\ y \\ z \end{pmatrix}.$$

(a) Letting $A = C^\top BC$, prove that the equation of the conic becomes

$$X^\top AX = 0.$$

Prove that A is symmetric, that $\det(A) = \det(B)$, and that $X^\top AX$ is homogeneous of degree 2. The equation $X^\top AX = 0$ is called the *homogeneous equation* of the conic.

We say that a conic of homogeneous equation $X^\top AX = 0$ is *nondegenerate* if $\det(A) \neq 0$, and *degenerate* if $\det(A) = 0$. Show that this condition does not depend on the choice of the affine frame.

(b) Given any affine frame (A, B, C), prove that any conic passing through A, B, C has an equation of the form

$$ayz + bxz + cxy = 0.$$

Prove that a conic containing more than one point is degenerate iff it contains three distinct collinear points. In this case, the conic is the union of two lines.

(c) Prove Pascal's theorem. Given any six distinct points A, B, C, A', B', C', if no three of the above points are collinear, then a nondegenerate conic passes through these six points iff the intersection points M, N, P (in the sense of Problem 7) of the pairs of lines (BC', CB'), (CA', AC'), and (AB', BA') are collinear in the sense of Problem 9.

Hint: Use the affine frame (A, B, C), and let (a, a', a''), (b, b', b''), and (c, c', c'') be the barycentric coordinates of A', B', C', respectively, and show that M, N, P have barycentric coordinates $(bc, cb', c''b)$, $(c'a, c'a', c''a')$, $(ab'', a''b', a''b'')$.

[10 pts] **13.** The *centroid* of a triangle (a, b, c) is the barycenter of $(a, \frac{1}{3})$, $(b, \frac{1}{3})$, $(c, \frac{1}{3})$. If an affine map takes the vertices of triangle $\Delta_1 = \{(0, 0), (6, 0), (0, 9)\}$ to the vertices of triangle $\Delta_2 = \{(1, 1), (5, 4), (3, 1)\}$, does it also take the centroid of Δ_1 to the centroid of Δ_2? Justify your answer.

[20 pts] **14.** Let E be an affine space over $\mathbf{R}$, and let $(a_1, \ldots, a_n)$ be any $n \geq 3$ points in E. Let $(\lambda_1, \ldots, \lambda_n)$ be any n scalars in $\mathbf{R}$, with $\lambda_1 + \cdots + \lambda_n = 1$. Show that there must be some i, $1 \leq i \leq n$, such that $\lambda_i \neq 1$. To simplify the notation, assume that $\lambda_1 \neq 1$. Show that the barycenter $\lambda_1 a_1 + \cdots + \lambda_n a_n$ can be obtained by first determining the barycenter b of the $n - 1$ points $a_2, \ldots, a_n$ assigned some appropriate weights, and then the barycenter of a_1 and b assigned the weights λ_1 and $\lambda_2 + \cdots + \lambda_n$. From this, show that the barycenter of any $n \geq 3$ points can be determined by repeated computations of barycenters of two points. Deduce from the above that a nonempty subset V of E is an affine subspace iff whenever V contains any two points $x, y \in V$, then V contains the entire line $(1 - \lambda)x + \lambda y$, $\lambda \in \mathbf{R}$.

[20 pts] **15.** (**Extra Credit**) Assume that K is a field such that $2 = 1 + 1 \neq 0$, and let E be an affine space over K. In the case where $\lambda_1 + \cdots + \lambda_n = 1$ and $\lambda_i = 1$, for $1 \leq i \leq n$ and $n \geq 3$, show that the barycenter $a_1 + a_2 + \cdots + a_n$ can still be computed by repeated computations of barycenters of two points.

Finally, assume that the field K contains at least three elements (thus, there is some $\mu \in K$ such that $\mu \neq 0$ and $\mu \neq 1$, but $2 = 1 + 1 = 0$ is possible). Prove that the barycenter of any $n \geq 3$ points can be determined by repeated computations of barycenters of two points. Prove that a nonempty subset V of E is an affine subspace iff whenever V contains any two points $x, y \in V$, then V contains the entire line $(1 - \lambda)x + \lambda y$, $\lambda \in K$.

Hint: When $2 = 0$, $\lambda_1 + \cdots + \lambda_n = 1$, and $\lambda_i = 1$, for $1 \leq i \leq n$, show that n must be odd, and that the problem reduces to computing the barycenter of three points in two steps involving two barycenters. Since there is some $\mu \in K$ such that $\mu \neq 0$ and $\mu \neq 1$, note that μ^{-1} and $(1 - \mu)^{-1}$ both exist, and use the fact that

$$\frac{-\mu}{1 - \mu} + \frac{1}{1 - \mu} = 1.$$

[20 pts] **16.** (a) Let (a, b, c) be three points in $\mathbf{A}^2$, and assume that (a, b, c) are not collinear. For any point $x \in \mathbf{A}^2$, if $x = \lambda_0 a + \lambda_1 b + \lambda_2 c$, where $(\lambda_0, \lambda_1, \lambda_2)$ are the barycentric coordinates of x with respect to (a, b, c), show that

$$\lambda_0 = \frac{\det(\overrightarrow{xb}, \overrightarrow{bc})}{\det(\overrightarrow{ab}, \overrightarrow{ac})}, \qquad \lambda_1 = \frac{\det(\overrightarrow{ax}, \overrightarrow{ac})}{\det(\overrightarrow{ab}, \overrightarrow{ac})}, \qquad \lambda_2 = \frac{\det(\overrightarrow{ab}, \overrightarrow{ax})}{\det(\overrightarrow{ab}, \overrightarrow{ac})}.$$

Conclude that $\lambda_0, \lambda_1, \lambda_2$ are certain signed ratios of the areas of the triangles (a, b, c), (x, a, b), (x, a, c), and (x, b, c).

(b) Let (a, b, c) be three points in $\mathbf{A}^3$, and assume that (a, b, c) are not collinear. For any point x in the plane determined by (a, b, c), if $x = \lambda_0 a + \lambda_1 b + \lambda_2 c$, where $(\lambda_0, \lambda_1, \lambda_2)$ are the barycentric coordinates of x with respect to (a, b, c), show that

$$\lambda_0 = \frac{\overrightarrow{xb} \times \overrightarrow{bc}}{\overrightarrow{ab} \times \overrightarrow{ac}}, \qquad \lambda_1 = \frac{\overrightarrow{ax} \times \overrightarrow{ac}}{\overrightarrow{ab} \times \overrightarrow{ac}}, \qquad \lambda_2 = \frac{\overrightarrow{ab} \times \overrightarrow{ax}}{\overrightarrow{ab} \times \overrightarrow{ac}}.$$

Given any point O not in the plane of the triangle (a, b, c), prove that

$$\lambda_0 = \frac{\det(\overrightarrow{Ox}, \overrightarrow{Ob}, \overrightarrow{Oc})}{\det(\overrightarrow{Oa}, \overrightarrow{Ob}, \overrightarrow{Oc})}, \qquad \lambda_1 = \frac{\det(\overrightarrow{Oa}, \overrightarrow{Ox}, \overrightarrow{Oc})}{\det(\overrightarrow{Oa}, \overrightarrow{Ob}, \overrightarrow{Oc})}, \qquad \lambda_2 = \frac{\det(\overrightarrow{Oa}, \overrightarrow{Ob}, \overrightarrow{Ox})}{\det(\overrightarrow{Oa}, \overrightarrow{Ob}, \overrightarrow{Oc})}.$$

(c) Let (a, b, c, d) be four points in $\mathbf{A}^3$, and assume that (a, b, c, d) are not coplanar. For any point $x \in \mathbf{A}^3$, if $x = \lambda_0 a + \lambda_1 b + \lambda_2 c + \lambda_3 d$, where $(\lambda_0, \lambda_1, \lambda_2, \lambda_3)$ are the barycentric coordinates of x with respect to (a, b, c, d), show that

$$\lambda_0 = \frac{\det(\overrightarrow{xb}, \overrightarrow{bc}, \overrightarrow{bd})}{\det(\overrightarrow{ab}, \overrightarrow{ac}, \overrightarrow{ad})}, \qquad \lambda_1 = \frac{\det(\overrightarrow{ax}, \overrightarrow{ac}, \overrightarrow{ad})}{\det(\overrightarrow{ab}, \overrightarrow{ac}, \overrightarrow{ad})},$$

$$\lambda_2 = \frac{\det(\overrightarrow{ab}, \overrightarrow{ax}, \overrightarrow{ad})}{\det(\overrightarrow{ab}, \overrightarrow{ac}, \overrightarrow{ad})}, \qquad \lambda_3 = \frac{\det(\overrightarrow{ab}, \overrightarrow{ac}, \overrightarrow{ax})}{\det(\overrightarrow{ab}, \overrightarrow{ac}, \overrightarrow{ad})}.$$

Conclude that $\lambda_0, \lambda_1, \lambda_2, \lambda_3$ are certain signed ratios of the volumes of the five tetrahedra (a, b, c, d), (x, a, b, c), (x, a, b, d), (x, a, c, d), and (x, b, c, d).

(d) Let $(a_0, \ldots, a_m)$ be $m + 1$ points in $\mathbf{A}^m$, and assume that they are affinely independent. For any point $x \in \mathbf{A}^m$, if $x = \lambda_0 a_0 + \cdots + \lambda_m a_m$, where $(\lambda_0, \ldots, \lambda_m)$ are the barycentric coordinates of x with respect to $(a_0, \ldots, a_m)$, show that

$$\lambda_i = \frac{\det(\overrightarrow{a_0 a_1}, \ldots, \overrightarrow{a_0 a_{i-1}}, \overrightarrow{a_0 x}, \overrightarrow{a_0 a_{i+1}}, \ldots, \overrightarrow{a_0 a_m})}{\det(\overrightarrow{a_0 a_1}, \ldots, \overrightarrow{a_0 a_{i-1}}, \overrightarrow{a_0 a_i}, \overrightarrow{a_0 a_{i+1}}, \ldots, \overrightarrow{a_0 a_m})}$$

for every i, $1 \leq i \leq m$, and

$$\lambda_0 = \frac{\det(\overrightarrow{x a_1}, \overrightarrow{a_1 a_2}, \ldots, \overrightarrow{a_1 a_m})}{\det(\overrightarrow{a_0 a_1}, \ldots, \overrightarrow{a_0 a_i}, \ldots, \overrightarrow{a_0 a_m})}.$$

Conclude that λ_i is the signed ratio of the volumes of the simplexes $(a_0, \ldots, x, \ldots, a_m)$ and $(a_0, \ldots, a_i, \ldots, a_m)$, where $0 \leq i \leq m$.

[30 pts] **17.** With respect to the standard affine frame for the plane $\mathbf{A}^2$, consider the three geometric transformations f_1, f_2, f_3 defined by

$$x' = -\frac{1}{4}x - \frac{\sqrt{3}}{4}y + \frac{3}{4}, \qquad y' = \frac{\sqrt{3}}{4}x - \frac{1}{4}y + \frac{\sqrt{3}}{4},$$

$$x' = -\frac{1}{4}x + \frac{\sqrt{3}}{4}y - \frac{3}{4}, \qquad y' = -\frac{\sqrt{3}}{4}x - \frac{1}{4}y + \frac{\sqrt{3}}{4},$$

$$x' = \frac{1}{2}x, \qquad y' = \frac{1}{2}y + \frac{\sqrt{3}}{2}.$$

(a) Prove that these maps are affine. Can you describe geometrically what their action is (rotation, translation, scaling)?

(b) Given any polygonal line L, define the following sequence of polygonal lines:

$$S_0 = L,$$

$$S_{n+1} = f_1(S_n) \cup f_2(S_n) \cup f_3(S_n).$$

Construct S_1 starting from the line segment $L = ((-1, 0), (1, 0))$.

Can you figure out what S_n looks like in general? (You may want to write a computer program.) Do you think that S_n has a limit?

[20 pts] **18.** In the plane $\mathbf{A}^2$, with respect to the standard affine frame, a point of coordinates (x, y) can be represented as the complex number $z = x + iy$. Consider the set of

geometric transformations of the form

$$z \mapsto az + b,$$

where a, b are complex numbers such that $a \neq 0$.

(a) Prove that these maps are affine. Describe what these maps do geometrically.

(b) Prove that the above set of maps is a group under composition.

(c) Consider the set of geometric transformations of the form

$$z \mapsto az + b \quad \text{or} \quad z \mapsto a\bar{z} + b,$$

where a, b are complex numbers such that $a \neq 0$, and where $\bar{z} = x - iy$ if $z = x + iy$. Describe what these maps do geometrically. Prove that these maps are affine and that this set of maps is a group under composition.

[20 pts] **19.** The purpose of this problem is to study certain affine maps of $\mathbf{A}^2$.

(a) Consider affine maps of the form

$$\begin{pmatrix} x_1 \\ x_2 \end{pmatrix} \mapsto \begin{pmatrix} \cos\theta & -\sin\theta \\ \sin\theta & \cos\theta \end{pmatrix} \begin{pmatrix} x_1 \\ x_2 \end{pmatrix} + \begin{pmatrix} b_1 \\ b_2 \end{pmatrix}.$$

Prove that such maps have a unique fixed point c if $\theta \neq 2k\pi$, for all integers k. Show that these are rotations of center c, which means that with respect to a frame with origin c (the unique fixed point), these affine maps are represented by rotation matrices.

(b) Consider affine maps of the form

$$\begin{pmatrix} x_1 \\ x_2 \end{pmatrix} \mapsto \begin{pmatrix} \lambda\cos\theta & -\lambda\sin\theta \\ \mu\sin\theta & \mu\cos\theta \end{pmatrix} \begin{pmatrix} x_1 \\ x_2 \end{pmatrix} + \begin{pmatrix} b_1 \\ b_2 \end{pmatrix}.$$

Prove that such maps have a unique fixed point iff $(\lambda + \mu)\cos\theta \neq 1 + \lambda\mu$. Prove that if $\lambda\mu = 1$ and $\lambda > 0$, there is some angle θ for which either there is no fixed point, or there are infinitely many fixed points.

(c) Prove that the affine map

$$\begin{pmatrix} x_1 \\ x_2 \end{pmatrix} \mapsto \begin{pmatrix} \frac{8}{5} & -\frac{6}{5} \\ \frac{3}{10} & \frac{2}{5} \end{pmatrix} \begin{pmatrix} x_1 \\ x_2 \end{pmatrix} + \begin{pmatrix} 1 \\ 1 \end{pmatrix}$$

has no fixed point.

(d) Prove that an arbitrary affine map

$$\begin{pmatrix} x_1 \\ x_2 \end{pmatrix} \mapsto \begin{pmatrix} a_1 & a_2 \\ a_3 & a_4 \end{pmatrix} \begin{pmatrix} x_1 \\ x_2 \end{pmatrix} + \begin{pmatrix} b_1 \\ b_2 \end{pmatrix}$$

has a unique fixed point iff the matrix

$$\begin{pmatrix} a_1 - 1 & a_2 \\ a_3 & a_4 - 1 \end{pmatrix}$$

is invertible.

[20 pts]   **20.** Let $(E, \vec{E})$ be any affine space of finite dimension. For every affine map $f : E \to E$, let $Fix(f) = \{a \in E \mid f(a) = a\}$ be the set of fixed points of f.

(a) Prove that if $Fix(f) \neq \emptyset$, then $Fix(f)$ is an affine subspace of E such that for every $b \in Fix(f)$,

$$Fix(f) = b + \mathrm{Ker}\,(\vec{f} - \mathrm{id}).$$

(b) Prove that $Fix(f)$ contains a unique fixed point iff

$$\mathrm{Ker}\,(\vec{f} - \mathrm{id}) = \{\vec{0}\},$$

that is, $\vec{f}(\vec{u}) = \vec{u}$ iff $\vec{u} = \vec{0}$.
Hint: Show that

$$\overrightarrow{\Omega f(a)} - \overrightarrow{\Omega a} = \overrightarrow{\Omega f(\Omega)} + \vec{f}(\overrightarrow{\Omega a}) - \overrightarrow{\Omega a},$$

for any two points $\Omega, a \in E$.

[20 pts]   **21.** Let $(c_1, \ldots, c_n)$ be $n \geq 3$ points in $\mathbf{A}^m$ (where $m \geq 2$). Investigate whether there is a closed polygon with n vertices $(a_1, \ldots, a_n)$ such that c_i is the middle of the edge (a_i, a_{i+1}) for every i with $1 \leq i \leq n - 1$, and c_n is the middle of the edge (a_n, a_0).
Hint: The parity (odd or even) of n plays an important role. When n is odd, there is a unique solution, and when n is even, there are no solutions or infinitely many solutions. Clarify under which conditions there are infinitely many solutions.

[20 pts]   **22.** Let a, b, c, be any distinct points in $\mathbf{A}^3$, and assume that they are not collinear. Let H be the plane of equation

$$\alpha x + \beta y + \gamma z + \delta = 0.$$

(a) What is the intersection of the plane H and of the solid triangle determined by a, b, c (the convex hull of a, b, c)?

(b) Give an algorithm to find the intersection of the plane H and of the triangle determined by a, b, c.

[20 pts]   (c) (**Extra Credit**) Implement the above algorithm so that the intersection can be visualized (you may use Maple, Mathematica, Matlab, etc.).

PART II

POLYNOMIAL CURVES
AND SPLINE CURVES

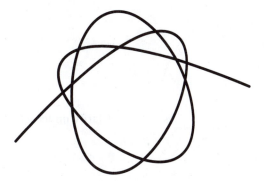

CHAPTER 3

Introduction to the Algorithmic Geometry of Polynomial Curves

3.1   Why Parameterized Polynomial Curves?

In order to be able to design, manipulate, and render curves and surfaces, we have to choose some mathematical model for defining curves and surfaces. The kind of model that we will adopt consists of specifying a curve or surface S in terms of a certain system of equations, which is used to determine which points lie on S and which do not. Given that we adopt such a model, we face a number of questions.

A Single Piece, or Several Pieces Joined Together?

We can model the entire shape S via a single system of equations. This is usually mathematically simpler, and it works well for very simple shapes. But for complex shapes, possibly composite, a combinatorial explosion usually occurs, which makes this approach impractical. Furthermore, such an approach is not modular, and unsuitable to tackle problems for which it may be necessary to modify certain parts and leave the other parts unchanged. Such design problems are usually handled by breaking the curve or surface into simpler pieces, and by specifying how these pieces join together, with some degree of smoothness. In CAGD jargon, we model composite shapes with *splines*. Nevertheless, since composite shapes are decomposed into simpler pieces, it is very important to know how to deal with these simpler building blocks effectively, and we will now concentrate on modeling a single curve or surface. Later on, we will come back to splines.

Parametric or Implicit Model?

Mathematically, when a shape S is modeled by a system of equations, we view these equations as defining a certain function F, and the shape S is viewed either as the range of this function, or as the zero locus of this function (i.e., the set of points that are mapped to "zero" under F). Oversimplifying a bit, the shape S lives in

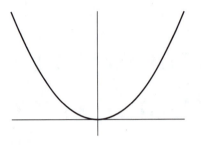

 **FIG. 3.1** A parabola

some *object space* $\mathcal{E}$ of some dimension n (typically, the affine plane $\mathbf{A}^2$, or the 3D affine space $\mathbf{A}^3$), and the shape has some dimension $s \leq n$ ($s = 1$ for a curve, $s = 2$ for a surface). The two models just mentioned define S either in terms of a function $F : P \to \mathcal{E}$, where P is another space called the *parameter space* (typically $P = \mathbf{A}$ for a curve, where $\mathbf{A}$ denotes the affine line, and $P = \mathbf{A}^2$ for a surface, where $\mathbf{A}^2$ denotes the affine plane), or a function $F : \mathcal{E} \to P$, in which case P doesn't have a standard name. In the first case where $F : P \to \mathcal{E}$, we say that we have a *parametric model*, and in the second case where $F : \mathcal{E} \to P$, we say that we have an *implicit model*. Let us examine each model.

In the *parametric model*, a shape S of dimension s specified by a function $F : P \to \mathcal{E}$, where $\mathcal{E}$ is of dimension $n \geq s$, is defined as the *range $F(P)$ of the function F*. Thus, the parameter space P also has dimension $s \leq n$. Every point lying on the shape S is represented as $F(a)$, for some parameter value $a \in P$ (possibly many parameter values). For example, the function $F : \mathbf{A} \to \mathbf{A}^2$ defined such that

$$F_1(t) = 2t + 1,$$
$$F_2(t) = t - 1,$$

represents a straight line in the affine plane. The function $F : \mathbf{A} \to \mathbf{A}^2$ defined such that

$$F_1(t) = 2t,$$
$$F_2(t) = t^2,$$

represents a parabola in the affine plane (see Figure 3.1).

For a fancier example of a space curve, the function $F : \mathbf{A} \to \mathbf{A}^3$ defined such that

$$F_1(t) = t,$$
$$F_2(t) = t^2,$$
$$F_3(t) = t^3,$$

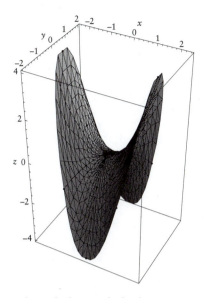

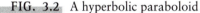
FIG. 3.2 A hyperbolic paraboloid

represents a curve known as a *twisted cubic*, in the 3D affine space $\mathbf{A}^3$. For an example of a surface, the function $F\colon \mathbf{A}^2 \to \mathbf{A}^3$ defined such that

$$F_1(u, v) = u,$$

$$F_2(u, v) = v,$$

$$F_3(u, v) = u^2 - v^2,$$

represents what is known as a *hyperbolic paraboloid* (see Figure 3.2). Roughly speaking, it looks like a saddle (an infinite one!).

The function $F\colon \mathbf{A}^2 \to \mathbf{A}^3$ defined such that

$$F_1(u, v) = u,$$

$$F_2(u, v) = v$$

$$F_3(u, v) = 2u^2 + v^2,$$

represents what is known as an *elliptic paraboloid* (see Figure 3.3).

For a more exotic example, the function $F\colon \mathbf{A}^2 \to \mathbf{A}^3$ defined such that

$$F_1(u, v) = u,$$

$$F_2(u, v) = v,$$

$$F_3(u, v) = u^3 - 3v^2u,$$

represents what is known as a *monkey saddle* (see Figure 3.4).

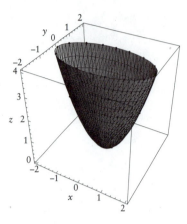

FIG. 3.3 An elliptic paraboloid

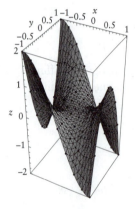

FIG. 3.4 A monkey saddle

In the *implicit model*, a shape S of dimension s specified by a function $F: \mathcal{E} \to P$, where $\mathcal{E}$ is of dimension $n \geq s$, is defined as the *zero locus $F^{-1}(0)$ of the function F*, that is, as the set of zeros of the function F:

$$S = F^{-1}(0) = \{a \mid a \in \mathcal{E},\ F(a) = 0\}.$$

In this case, the space P is a vector space, and it has some dimension $d \geq n - s$. Of course, it is possible that $F^{-1}(0) = \varnothing$. For example, if $F: \mathbf{A}^2 \to \mathbf{A}$ is the function defined such that

$$F(x, y) = x^2 + y^2 + 1,$$

since the equation $x^2 + y^2 = -1$ has no real solutions, F defines the empty curve. In order to avoid such situations, we could assume that our spaces are defined over the field of complex numbers (or more generally, an algebraically closed field). This would have certain mathematical advantages, but does not help us much for visualizing the shape, since we are primarily interested in the real part of shapes (curves and surfaces). Thus, we will make the working assumption that we are only considering functions that define nonempty shapes.

There are some serious problems with such an assumption. For example, it is not clear that it can be decided whether an arbitrary algebraic equation has real solutions or not. These complications are one of the motivations for paying more attention to the parametric model. However, the implicit model is more natural to deal with certain classes of problems, where implicit equations of shapes are directly available.

As a simple example of a curve defined implicitly, the function $F: \mathbf{A}^2 \to \mathbf{A}$ defined such that

$$F(x, y) = 2y - x + 3,$$

for all $x, y \in \mathbf{A}$, defines a straight line (in fact, the same line as defined above parametrically). The function $F: \mathbf{A}^2 \to \mathbf{A}$ defined such that

$$F(x, y) = 4y - x^2,$$

for all $x, y \in \mathbf{A}$, defines the same parabola as the above parametric definition, since we immediately see that $y = x^2/4$ for every point on this parabola. The function $F: \mathbf{A}^2 \to \mathbf{A}$ defined such that

$$F(x, y) = 2x^2 + y^2 - 1,$$

for all $x, y \in \mathbf{A}$, defines an ellipse in the affine plane. Although this is not entirely obvious, the twisted cubic is defined implicitly by the function $F: \mathbf{A}^3 \to \mathbf{A}^2$, defined such that

$$F_1(x, y, z) = y - x^2,$$
$$F_2(x, y, z) = z - xy.$$

The unit sphere is defined implicitly by the function $F: \mathbf{A}^3 \to \mathbf{A}$, defined such that

$$F(x, y, z) = x^2 + y^2 + z^2 - 1.$$

The hyperbolic paraboloid discussed in the parametric model is defined by the function

$$F(x, y, z) = z - x^2 + y^2.$$

The elliptic paraboloid discussed in the parametric model is defined by the function

$$F(x, y, z) = z - 2x^2 - y^2.$$

If P has dimension $d \geq n - s$, instead of saying that S is the zero locus of the function $F: \mathcal{E} \to P$, since the function F corresponds to d scalar-valued functions $(F_1, \ldots, F_d)$, we usually say that S is *defined by the set of equations*

$$F_1 = 0,$$

$$F_2 = 0,$$

$$\vdots$$

$$F_d = 0,$$

or that S is the *zero locus* of the above system of equations. For another familiar example, the unit circle is defined implicitly by the equation

$$x^2 + y^2 - 1 = 0,$$

and it has the parametric representation

$$x = \cos \theta,$$

$$y = \sin \theta.$$

This last example leads us to another major question.

What Class of Functions for F?

Although trigonometric functions are perfectly fine, for computational (algorithmic) reasons, we may want to use a simpler class of functions. Certainly, we should only consider continuous functions that are sufficiently differentiable, to yield shapes that are reasonably smooth. The class of functions definable by polynomials is very well behaved and turns out to be sufficient for most purposes. When polynomials are insufficient, we can turn to the class of functions definable by rational functions (fractions of polynomials), which is sufficient for most computational applications. As a matter of fact, dealing with rational fractions turns out to be largely reduced to dealing with polynomials. From a practical point of view, using polynomials is rarely a restriction (continuous functions on reasonable domains can be approximated by polynomial functions). Thus, we will be dealing with polynomial functions (and rational functions).

In the implicit model, studying shapes S defined by systems of polynomial equations is essentially the prime concern of *algebraic geometry*. This is a fascinating, venerable, and very difficult subject, way beyond the scope of this book. Bold readers are urged to consult Fulton [37] or Harris [41]. In the parametric model, since polynomials are differentiable at any order, studying shapes S defined by systems of parametric polynomials (or rational fractions) is in some sense subsumed by *differential geometry*, another venerable subject. We will make a very modest use of elementary notions of differential geometry, and an even more modest use of very elementary notions of algebraic geometry. In fact, what we use primarily is some elements of multilinear algebra. Having decided that we will use polynomial (or rational) functions, there is one more question.

What Degree for F?

In most practical applications involving many small pieces joined together (splines), the degree $m = 2$ or $m = 3$ is sufficient for the small pieces. However, for a single piece, the degree could be quite high. In general, the choice of degree depends on how many pieces are involved and how complex each piece is.

Because the study of shapes modeled as zero loci of polynomial equations is quite difficult, we will focus primarily on the study of shapes modeled parametrically. There are other advantages in dealing with the parametric model. For example, it is easier to "carve out" portions of the shape, by simply considering subsets of the parameter space. Also, the function $F: P \to \mathcal{E}$ provides immediate access to points on the shape S: every parameter value $a \in P$ yields a point $F(a)$ lying on the shape S. This is not so for the implicit model, where the function $F: \mathcal{E} \to P$ does not provide immediate access to points in S. Given a point $b \in \mathcal{E}$, to determine whether $b \in S$ usually requires solving a system of algebraic equations, which may be very difficult. Nevertheless, given a parametric definition $F: P \to \mathcal{E}$ for a shape S, it is often useful to find an implicit definition $G: \mathcal{E} \to P$ for S. In the case where F is given by rational functions, it can be shown that it is always possible to find an algebraic implicit definition G for S.[1] This is called *implicitization* and is done using the algebraic concept of a *resultant*.

It should be noted that it is not always possible to go from an implicit algebraic definition $G: \mathcal{E} \to P$ for S to a parametric algebraic definition $F: P \to \mathcal{E}$ for S. The discrepancy shows up for $m = 2$ for polynomial functions, and for $m = 3$ for rational functions.

It should also be noted that if we consider parametric curves $F: \mathbf{A} \to \mathcal{E}$ defined by functions that are more general than polynomial or rational functions, for example, functions that are only continuous, then some unexpected objects show up as the traces of curves. For example, Peano and Hilbert (among others) showed that there are *space-filling curves*, that is, continuous curves $F: [0, 1] \to \mathbf{A}^2$ whose trace is the entire unit square (including its interior)! See the problems. This is a good motivation for assuming that the functions F are sufficiently differentiable. Polynomials certainly qualify!

Before we launch into our study of parametric curves, we believe that it may be useful to review briefly what kind of plane curves are defined in the implicit model,

---

1. Actually, as we shall see very soon, there are some subtleties regarding over which field we view the curves or surfaces as being defined.

that is, what sort of curves are defined by polynomial equations $f(x, y) = 0$, where $f(x, y)$ is a polynomial in x, y, with real coefficients, of total degree $m \leq 2$.

For $m = 1$, we have the equation

$$ax + by + c = 0,$$

which defines a straight line. It is very easy to see that straight lines are also definable in the parametric model.

The general curve of degree 2 is defined by an equation of the form

$$ax^2 + bxy + cy^2 + dx + ey + f = 0.$$

Such an equation defines a (plane) *conic* (because it is the curve obtained by intersecting a circular cone with a plane). Except for some degenerate cases, the conics can be classified in three types (after some suitable change of coordinates):

- *Parabolas*, of equation

  $$y^2 = 4ax.$$

- *Ellipses*, of equation

  $$\frac{x^2}{a^2} + \frac{y^2}{b^2} = 1.$$

  (Without loss of generality, we can assume $a \geq b$.)

- *Hyperbolas*, of equation

  $$\frac{x^2}{a^2} - \frac{y^2}{b^2} = 1.$$

The above definitions are algebraic. It is possible to give more geometric characterizations of the conics, and we briefly mention the classical bifocal definition.

Let us begin with the parabola. The point F of coordinates $(a, 0)$ is called the *focus* of the parabola, and the line D of equation $x = -a$ (parallel to the y-axis) is called the *directrix* of the parabola. For any point M in the plane, if H is the intersection of the perpendicular through M to D, then the parabola of equation $y^2 = 4ax$ is the set of points in the plane such that $\|MH\| = \|MF\|$.[2]

For example, the parabola of equation

$$y^2 = 4x$$

has focus $F = (1, 0)$, and directrix D of equation $x = -1$ (see Figure 3.5).

In the case of an ellipse, since we are assuming that $a \geq b$, let $c = \sqrt{a^2 - b^2}$ (so that $a^2 = b^2 + c^2$). Let F and F' be the points of coordinates $(-c, 0)$ and $(c, 0)$. Each

---

2. The above definition of the conics assumes a Euclidean structure on the affine plane, and $\|AB\|$ denotes the Euclidean length of the line segment AB.

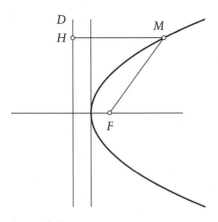

FIG. 3.5 A parabola

of F, F' is a *focus* of the ellipse. Then, the ellipse defined by

$$\frac{x^2}{a^2} + \frac{y^2}{b^2} = 1$$

is the set of points in the plane such that $\|MF\| + \|MF'\| = 2a$ (note that $c \leq a$). This is the "gardener's definition" of an ellipse. Indeed, you can take a string, make two knots at distance $2a$ from each other, and drive a nail through each knot in such a way that the nails are positioned on the foci F and F'. Then, using a stick, you can draw the ellipse, on the ground, by moving the stick along the string (perpendicular to the ground) in such a way that the string is kept stiff.

For example, the ellipse

$$\frac{x^2}{25} + \frac{y^2}{9} = 1$$

is such that $a = 5$, $b = 3$, and thus $c = \sqrt{a^2 - b^2} = \sqrt{25 - 9} = \sqrt{16} = 4$. The foci are $F = (-4, 0)$ and $F' = (4, 0)$. (See Figure 3.6.)

The case where $c = 0$, that is, $a = b$, corresponds to a circle.

In the case of a hyperbola, we let $c = \sqrt{a^2 + b^2}$ (so that $c^2 = a^2 + b^2$). Let F and F' be the points of coordinates $(-c, 0)$ and $(c, 0)$. Each of F, F' is a *focus* of the hyperbola. Then, the hyperbola defined by

$$\frac{x^2}{a^2} - \frac{y^2}{b^2} = 1$$

is the set of points in the plane such that $|\, \|MF\| - \|MF'\| \,| = 2a$ (note that $c > a$).

For example, the hyperbola

$$x^2 - y^2 = 1$$

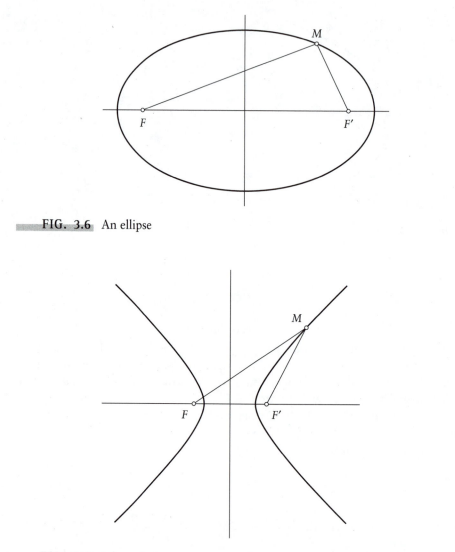

 **FIG. 3.6** An ellipse

FIG. 3.7 A hyperbola

is such that $a = b = 1$, and thus, $c = \sqrt{a^2 + b^2} = \sqrt{1 + 1} = \sqrt{2}$, and the foci are $F = (-\sqrt{2}, 0)$ and $F' = (\sqrt{2}, 0)$. (See Figure 3.7.)

In the case of an ellipse, parabola, or hyperbola (where $c > 0$), the constant

$$e = \frac{c}{a} > 0$$

is called the *eccentricity* of the conic. There is also a monofocal definition of ellipses, parabolas, and hyperbolas, involving the eccentricity. For more details, see standard geometry texts, for example, Berger [5, 6] or Pedoe [59].

We will see very soon that only the parabolas can be defined parametrically using polynomials. On the other hand, all the conics can be defined parametrically using rational fractions.

For $m = 3$, things become a lot tougher! The general curve of degree 3 is defined by an equation of the form

$$\varphi_3(x, y) + \varphi_2(x, y) + \varphi_1(x, y) + \varphi_0 = 0,$$

where each $\varphi_i(x, y)$ is a homogenous polynomial of total degree i, with $i = 1, 2, 3$, and φ_0 is a scalar. The curve defined by such an equation is called a (plane) *cubic*. In general, a plane cubic cannot be defined parametrically using rational functions (and a fortiori, using polynomials). Since we assumed that we are only considering nonempty curves, we can pick any point of the cubic as the origin. In this case $\varphi_0 = 0$, and the equation of the cubic becomes

$$\varphi_3(x, y) + \varphi_2(x, y) + \varphi_1(x, y) = 0.$$

It can be shown that the cubics that have rational representations are characterized by the fact that $\varphi_1(x, y)$ is the null polynomial. We will also characterize those cubics that can be defined parametrically in terms of polynomials.

After these general considerations, it is now time to focus on the parametric model for defining curves, and we begin with a rigorous definition. For reasons that will become clear later on, it is preferable to consider the parameter space **R** as the affine line **A**. Recall that every point $\bar{t} \in \mathbf{A}$ is expressed as $\bar{t} = (1 - t)0 + t1$ in terms of the affine basis $(0, 1)$. A parameterized polynomial curve is defined as follows.

Definition 3.1.1

Given any affine space $\mathcal{E}$ of finite dimension n and any affine frame $(a_0, (\overrightarrow{e_1}, \ldots, \overrightarrow{e_n}))$ for $\mathcal{E}$, a (parameterized) polynomial curve of degree (at most) m is a map $F : \mathbf{A} \to \mathcal{E}$, such that for every $\bar{t} \in \mathbf{A}$,

$$F(\bar{t}) = a_0 + F_1(t)\overrightarrow{e_1} + \cdots + F_n(t)\overrightarrow{e_n},$$

where $\bar{t} = (1 - t)0 + t1$, and every $F_i(X)$ is a polynomial in $\mathbf{R}[X]$ of degree $\leq m$, $1 \leq i \leq n$. Given any affine frame (r, s) for $\mathbf{A}$ with $r < s$, a (parameterized) polynomial curve segment $F[r, s]$ of degree (at most) m is the restriction $F : [r, s] \to \mathcal{E}$ of a polynomial curve $F : \mathbf{A} \to \mathcal{E}$ of degree at most m. The set of points $F(\mathbf{A})$ in $\mathcal{E}$ is called the trace *of the polynomial curve F, and similarly, the set of points $F([r, s])$ in $\mathcal{E}$ is called the* trace *of the polynomial curve segment $F[r, s]$,*

For simplicity of notation, we view $\bar{t} \in \mathbf{A}$ as the real number $t \in \mathbf{R}$, and write $F(t)$ instead of $F(\bar{t})$. Intuitively, a polynomial curve is obtained by bending and twisting the affine line **A** using a polynomial map. It should be noted that if d is the maximum degree of the polynomials $F_1, \ldots, F_n$ defining a polynomial curve F of degree m, then $d \neq m$ is possible, and it is only required that $d \leq m$. This decision, which may seem unusual, will in fact be convenient later on for CAGD applications.

For example, we will need to join curve segments of possibly different degrees, and it will be convenient to "raise" the degree of some of these curve segments to a common degree. Also, in most cases, we are more interested in the trace of a curve than in its actual parametric representation. As a matter of fact, many different parametric representations may yield the same trace, sometimes called the *geometric curve* associated with $F: \mathbf{A} \to \mathcal{E}$.

We will now try to gain some insight into polynomial curves by determining the shape of the traces of plane polynomial curves (curves living in $\mathcal{E} = \mathbf{A}^2$) of degree $m \leq 3$. On the way, we will introduce a major technique of CAGD, *blossoming*.

3.2   Polynomial Curves of Degree 1 and 2

We begin with $m = 1$. A polynomial curve F of degree ≤ 1 is of the form

$$x(t) = F_1(t) = a_1 t + a_0,$$

$$y(t) = F_2(t) = b_1 t + b_0.$$

If both $a_1 = b_1 = 0$, the trace of F reduces to the single point (a_0, b_0). Otherwise, $a_1 \neq 0$ or $b_1 \neq 0$, and we can eliminate t between x and y, getting the implicit equation

$$a_1 y - b_1 x + a_0 b_1 - a_1 b_0 = 0,$$

which is the equation of a straight line.

Let us now consider $m = 2$, that is, quadratic curves. A polynomial curve F of degree ≤ 2 is of the form

$$x(t) = F_1(t) = a_2 t^2 + a_1 t + a_0,$$

$$y(t) = F_2(t) = b_2 t^2 + b_1 t + b_0.$$

Since we already considered the case where $a_2 = b_2 = 0$, let us assume that $a_2 \neq 0$ or $b_2 \neq 0$. We first show that by a change of coordinates (amounting to a rotation), we can always assume that either $a_2 = 0$ (or $b_2 = 0$). If $a_2 \neq 0$ and $b_2 \neq 0$, let $\rho = \sqrt{a_2^2 + b_2^2}$, and consider the matrix R given below:

$$R = \begin{pmatrix} \frac{b_2}{\rho} & -\frac{a_2}{\rho} \\ \frac{a_2}{\rho} & \frac{b_2}{\rho} \end{pmatrix}$$

Under the change of coordinates

$$\begin{pmatrix} x_1 \\ y_1 \end{pmatrix} = R \begin{pmatrix} x \\ y \end{pmatrix},$$

we get

$$x_1(t) = \frac{a_1b_2 - a_2b_1}{\rho}t + \frac{a_0b_2 - a_2b_0}{\rho},$$

$$y_1(t) = \rho t^2 + \frac{a_1a_2 + b_1b_2}{\rho}t + \frac{a_0a_2 + b_0b_2}{\rho}.$$

The effect of this rotation is that the curve now "stands straight up" (since $\rho > 0$). If $a_1b_2 = a_2b_1$, then we have a degenerate case where $x_1(t)$ is equal to a constant and $y_1(t) \geq y_1(t_0)$, with

$$t_0 = -\frac{(a_1a_2 + b_1b_2)}{2\rho^2},$$

which corresponds to a half line. Note that the implicit equation

$$x_1 = \frac{a_0b_2 - a_2b_0}{\rho}$$

gives too much! The above equation yields the entire line, whereas the parametric representation yields the upper half line. Thus, there is a mismatch between the implicit representation and the parametric representation. We will come back to this point later on.

If $a_1b_2 - a_2b_1 \neq 0$, then we can eliminate t between x_1 and y_1. However, before doing so, it is convenient to make a change of parameter, to suppress the term of degree 1 in t in $y_1(t)$, by letting

$$t = u - \frac{(a_1a_2 + b_1b_2)}{2\rho^2}.$$

Then, we have a parametric representation of the form

$$x_1(u - \mu) = au + a_0',$$

$$y_1(u - \mu) = bu^2 + b_0',$$

with $b > 0$.

Finally, we can change coordinates again (a translation), letting

$$X(u) = x_1(u - \mu) - a_0',$$

$$Y(u) = y_1(u - \mu) - b_0',$$

and we get a parametric representation of the form

$$X(u) = au,$$

$$Y(u) = bu^2,$$

with $b > 0$. The corresponding implicit equation is

$$Y = \frac{b}{a^2}X^2.$$

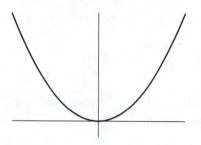

FIG. 3.8 The parabola $x = 2t$, $y = t^2$

This is a parabola, passing through the origin, and having the Y-axis as axis of symmetry. Figure 3.8 shows the parabola defined by the following parametric equations:

$$F_1(t) = 2t,$$

$$F_2(t) = t^2.$$

Intuitively, the previous degenerate case corresponds to $b/a^2 = \infty$.

Conversely, since by an appropriate change of coordinates, every parabola is defined by the implicit equation $Y = aX^2$, every parabola can be defined as the parametric polynomial curve

$$X(u) = u,$$

$$Y(u) = au^2.$$

In summary, the nondegenerate polynomial curves of true degree 2 are the parabolas. Thus, ellipses and hyperbolas are not definable as polynomial curves of degree 2. In fact, it can be shown easily that ellipses and hyperbolas are not definable by polynomial curves of any degree. On the other hand, it will be shown later that the conics (parabolas, ellipses, hyperbolas) are precisely the curves definable as rational curves of degree 2 (parametric definitions involving rational fractions of quadratic polynomials).

Remark: In the degenerate case of a half line, the mismatch between the parametric representation and the implicit representation can be resolved, if we view our curves as the real trace of complex curves. In this case, since every polynomial has roots (possibly complex numbers), the mismatch goes away.

We now show that there is another way of specifying quadratic polynomial curves that yields a very nice geometric algorithm for constructing points on these curves. The general philosophy is to *linearize* (or more exactly, multilinearize) polynomials.

3.3   First Encounter with Polar Forms (Blossoming)

As a warm-up, let us begin with straight lines.

The parametric definition of a straight line $F: A \to A^3$ is of the form

$$x_1(t) = a_1 t + b_1,$$

$$x_2(t) = a_2 t + b_2,$$

$$x_3(t) = a_3 t + b_3.$$

Observe that each function $t \mapsto a_i t + b_i$ is affine, where $i = 1, 2, 3$. Thus, $F: A \to A^3$ is itself an affine map. Given any affine frame (r, s) for A, where $r \neq s$, every $t \in A$ can be written uniquely as $t = (1 - \lambda)r + \lambda s$. In fact, we must have

$$t = (1 - \lambda)r + \lambda s = r + \lambda(s - r),$$

and so,

$$\lambda = \frac{t - r}{s - r}$$

and

$$1 - \lambda = \frac{s - t}{s - r}.$$

Now, since F is affine, we have

$$F(t) = F((1 - \lambda)r + \lambda s)$$

$$= (1 - \lambda)\, F(r) + \lambda\, F(s).$$

This means that $F(t)$ is completely determined by the two points $F(r)$ and $F(s)$ and the ratio of interpolation λ.

Furthermore, since $F(t)$ is the barycenter of $F(r)$ and $F(s)$ assigned the weights $1 - \lambda$ and λ, we know that

$$\overrightarrow{bF(t)} = (1 - \lambda)\overrightarrow{bF(r)} + \lambda\overrightarrow{bF(s)},$$

for every point b, and picking $b = F(r)$, we have

$$\overrightarrow{F(r)F(t)} = \lambda\overrightarrow{F(r)F(s)}.$$

Substituting the value of λ in the above, we have

$$\overrightarrow{F(r)F(t)} = \left(\frac{t - r}{s - r}\right)\overrightarrow{F(r)F(s)},$$

which shows that $F(t)$ is on the line determined by $F(r)$ and $F(s)$, at "$\frac{t-r}{s-r}$ of the way from $F(r)$" (in particular, when $r \leq t \leq s$, $F(t)$ is indeed between $F(r)$ and $F(s)$, at

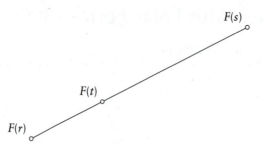

FIG. 3.9 Linear interpolation

"$\frac{t-r}{s-r}$ of the way from $F(r)$"). For example, if $r=0$, $s=1$, and $t=0.25$, then $F(0.25)$ is a fourth of the way from $F(0)$ between $F(0)$ and $F(1)$.

Thus, in the case of an affine map $F: \mathbf{A} \rightarrow \mathbf{A}^3$, given any affine frame (r, s) for $\mathbf{A}$, where $r \neq s$, every point $F(t)$ on the line defined by F is obtained by a single interpolation step

$$F(t) = \left(\frac{s-t}{s-r}\right) F(r) + \left(\frac{t-r}{s-r}\right) F(s),$$

as illustrated in Figure 3.9, where

$$\frac{t-r}{s-r} = \frac{1}{3}.$$

We would like to generalize the idea of determining the point $F(t)$ on the line defined by $F(r)$ and $F(s)$ by an interpolation step, to determining the point $F(t)$ on a polynomial curve F, by several interpolation steps from some (finite) set of given points related to the curve F. For this, it is first necessary to turn the polynomials involved in the definition of F into multiaffine maps, that is, maps that are affine in each of their arguments. We now show how to turn a quadratic polynomial into a biaffine map.

As an example, consider the polynomial

$$F(X) = X^2 + 2X - 3.$$

Observe that the function of two variables

$$f_1(x_1, x_2) = x_1 x_2 + 2x_1 - 3$$

gives us back the polynomial $F(X)$ on the diagonal, in the sense that $F(X) = f_1(X, X)$, for all $X \in \mathbf{R}$, but f_1 is also affine in each of x_1 and x_2. It would be tempting to say that f_1 is linear in each of x_1 and x_2, but this is not true, due to the presence of the term $2x_1$ and of the constant -3, and f_1 is only *biaffine*. Note that

$$f_2(x_1, x_2) = x_1 x_2 + 2x_2 - 3$$

is also biaffine, and $F(X) = f_2(X, X)$, for all $X \in \mathbf{R}$.

It would be nicer if we could find a unique biaffine function f such that $F(X) = f(X, X)$, for all $X \in \mathbf{R}$, and of course, such a function should satisfy some additional property. It turns out that requiring f to be symmetric is just what's needed. We say that a function f of two arguments is *symmetric* iff

$$f(x_1, x_2) = f(x_2, x_1),$$

for all x_1, x_2. To make f_1 (and f_2) symmetric, simply form

$$f(x_1, x_2) = \frac{f_1(x_1, x_2) + f_1(x_2, x_1)}{2} = x_1 x_2 + x_1 + x_2 - 3.$$

The symmetric biaffine function

$$f(x_1, x_2) = x_1 x_2 + x_1 + x_2 - 3$$

is called the (affine) *blossom*, or *polar form*, of F. For an arbitrary polynomial

$$F(X) = aX^2 + bX + c$$

of degree ≤ 2, we obtain a unique symmetric, biaffine map

$$f(x_1, x_2) = ax_1 x_2 + b \frac{x_1 + x_2}{2} + c$$

such that $F(X) = f(X, X)$, for all $X \in \mathbf{R}$, called the polar form, or blossom, of F. Note that the fact that f is symmetric allows us to view the arguments of f as a multiset (the order of the arguments x_1, x_2 is irrelevant).

This is all fine, but what have we gained? What we have gained is that using the fact that a polar form is symmetric and biaffine, we can show that every quadratic curve is completely determined by three points, called *control points*, and that furthermore, there is a nice algorithm for determining any point on the curve from these control points, simply using three linear interpolation steps. Thus, assume for simplicity that we have a quadratic curve $F \colon \mathbf{A} \to \mathbf{A}^3$, given by three quadratic polynomials F_1, F_2, F_3. We can compute their polar forms f_1, f_2, f_3 as we just explained, and we get a symmetric biaffine map $f \colon \mathbf{A}^2 \to \mathbf{A}^3$, such that $F(X) = f(X, X)$, for all $X \in \mathbf{A}$.

Let us pick an affine frame for $\mathbf{A}$, that is, two distinct points $r, s \in \mathbf{A}$ (we can. if we wish, assume that $r < s$, but this is not necessary). As we said already, every $t \in \mathbf{A}$ can be expressed uniquely as a barycentric combination of r and s, say, $t = (1 - \lambda)r + \lambda s$, where $\lambda \in \mathbf{R}$.

Let us compute

$$f(t_1, t_2) = f\big((1 - \lambda_1)r + \lambda_1 s,\ (1 - \lambda_2)r + \lambda_2 s\big).$$

Since f is symmetric and biaffine, we get

$$f(t_1, t_2) = f\big((1 - \lambda_1)r + \lambda_1 s, \ (1 - \lambda_2)r + \lambda_2 s\big)$$

$$= (1 - \lambda_1)\, f(r, \ (1 - \lambda_2)r + \lambda_2 s) + \lambda_1\, f(s, \ (1 - \lambda_2)r + \lambda_2 s)$$

$$= (1 - \lambda_1)(1 - \lambda_2)\, f(r, r)$$

$$+ \big((1 - \lambda_1)\lambda_2 + \lambda_1(1 - \lambda_2)\big)\, f(r, s) + \lambda_1 \lambda_2\, f(s, s).$$

The coefficients of $f(r, r)$, $f(r, s)$, and $f(s, s)$ are obviously symmetric biaffine functions, and they add up to 1, as it is easily verified by expanding the product

$$(1 - \lambda_1 + \lambda_1)(1 - \lambda_2 + \lambda_2) = 1.$$

This had to be expected, since f being biaffine preserves barycentric combinations in each of its arguments.

Since

$$\lambda_i = \frac{t_i - r}{s - r}, \quad \text{for } i = 1, 2,$$

we get

$$f(t_1, t_2) = \left(\frac{s - t_1}{s - r}\right)\left(\frac{s - t_2}{s - r}\right) f(r, r)$$

$$+ \left[\left(\frac{s - t_1}{s - r}\right)\left(\frac{t_2 - r}{s - r}\right) + \left(\frac{t_1 - r}{s - r}\right)\left(\frac{s - t_2}{s - r}\right)\right] f(r, s)$$

$$+ \left(\frac{t_1 - r}{s - r}\right)\left(\frac{t_2 - r}{s - r}\right) f(s, s).$$

Thus, we showed that every symmetric biaffine map $f\colon \mathbf{A}^2 \to \mathbf{A}^3$ is completely determined by the sequence of three points $f(r, r)$, $f(r, s)$, and $f(s, s)$ in $\mathbf{A}^3$, where $r \neq s$ are elements of $\mathbf{A}$.

Conversely, it is clear that given any sequence of three points $a, b, c \in \mathbf{A}^3$, the map

$$(t_1, t_2) \mapsto \left(\frac{s - t_1}{s - r}\right)\left(\frac{s - t_2}{s - r}\right) a$$

$$+ \left[\left(\frac{s - t_1}{s - r}\right)\left(\frac{t_2 - r}{s - r}\right) + \left(\frac{t_1 - r}{s - r}\right)\left(\frac{s - t_2}{s - r}\right)\right] b$$

$$+ \left(\frac{t_1 - r}{s - r}\right)\left(\frac{t_2 - r}{s - r}\right) c$$

is symmetric biaffine, and that $f(r, r) = a$, $f(r, s) = b$, $f(s, s) = c$.

The points $f(r, r)$, $f(r, s)$, and $f(s, s)$, are called *control points*, or *Bézier control points*, and as we shall see, they play a major role in the de Casteljau algorithm and its extensions. If we let $r = 0$ and $s = 1$, then $t_1 = \lambda_1$ and $t_2 = \lambda_2$, and thus, the polynomial function corresponding to $f(t_1, t_2)$ being obtained by letting $t_1 = t_2 = t$, we get

$$F(t) = f(t, t) = (1 - t)^2 \, f(0, 0) + 2(1 - t)t \, f(0, 1) + t^2 \, f(1, 1).$$

The polynomials

$$(1 - t)^2, 2(1 - t)t, t^2$$

are known as the *Bernstein polynomials of degree* 2. Thus, $F(t)$ is also determined by the control points $f(0, 0)$, $f(0, 1)$, and $f(1, 1)$, and the Bernstein polynomials. Incidentally, this also shows that a quadratic curve is necessarily contained in a plane, the plane determined by the control points b_0, b_1, b_2.

However, it is better to observe that the computation of

$$f(t_1, t_2) = f((1 - \lambda_1)r + \lambda_1 s, \ (1 - \lambda_2)r + \lambda_2 s),$$

that we performed above, can be turned into an algorithm, known as the *de Casteljau algorithm*.

3.4   First Encounter with the de Casteljau Algorithm

Let us assume that we have a quadratic polynomial curve F given by its polar form $f: \mathbf{A}^2 \to \mathbf{A}^3$, or equivalently as we just showed, by the three control points $b_0 = f(r, r)$, $b_1 = f(r, s)$, and $b_2 = f(s, s)$. Given any $t \in \mathbf{A}$, we will show how to construct geometrically the point $F(t) = f(t, t)$ on the polynomial curve F. Let $t = (1 - \lambda)r + \lambda s$. Then, $f(t, t)$ is computed as follows:

$$
\begin{array}{cccc}
0 & 1 & 2 \\
f(r, r) & & \\
 & f(r, t) & \\
f(r, s) & & f(t, t) \\
 & f(t, s) & \\
f(s, s) & & \\
\end{array}
$$

The algorithm consists of two stages. During the first stage, we compute the two points

$$f(r, t) = f(r, \ (1 - \lambda)r + \lambda s) = (1 - \lambda)f(r, r) + \lambda f(r, s)$$

and

$$f(t, s) = f((1 - \lambda)r + \lambda s, \ s) = (1 - \lambda)f(r, s) + \lambda f(s, s),$$

by linear interpolation, where $f(r, t)$ is computed from the two control points $f(r, r)$ and $f(r, s)$, and $f(t, s)$ is computed from the two control points $f(r, s)$ and $f(s, s)$, the ratio of interpolation being

$$\lambda = \frac{t - r}{s - r}.$$

Since by symmetry, $f(r, t) = f(t, r)$, during the second stage, we compute the point

$$f(t, t) = f(t, (1 - \lambda)r + \lambda s) = (1 - \lambda)f(t, r) + \lambda f(t, s),$$

from the points $f(t, r)$ and $f(t, s)$ computed during the first stage, the ratio of interpolation also being

$$\lambda = \frac{t - r}{s - r}.$$

Thus, by three linear interpolation steps, we obtain the point $F(t)$ on the curve. Note that the two control points $f(r, r) = F(r)$ and $f(s, s) = F(s)$ are on the curve, but $f(r, s)$ is not. We will give a geometric interpretation of the polar value $f(r, s)$ in a moment.

If $r \leq \lambda \leq s$, then only convex combinations are constructed. Geometrically, the algorithm consists of a diagram consisting of two polylines, the first one consisting of the two line segments

$$(f(r, r), \ f(r, s)) \quad \text{and} \quad (f(r, s), \ f(s, s)),$$

and the second one of the single line segment

$$(f(t, r), \ f(t, s)),$$

with the desired point $f(t, t)$ determined by λ. Each polyline given by the algorithm is called a *shell*, and the resulting diagram is called a *de Casteljau diagram* (see Figure 3.10). The first polyline is also called a *control polygon* of the curve. Note that the shells are nested nicely. Actually, when t is outside $[r, s]$, we still obtain two polylines and a de Casteljau diagram, but the shells are not nicely nested.

Figure 3.11 shows the construction of the point $F(t)$ corresponding to $t = \frac{1}{2}$, on the curve F, for $r = 0$, $s = 1$.

Figure 3.11 also shows the construction of another point on the curve, assuming different control points. The parabola in this figure is actually given by the parametric equations

$$F_1(t) = 2t,$$

$$F_2(t) = -t^2.$$

The polar forms are

$$f_1(t_1, t_2) = t_1 + t_2,$$

$$f_2(t_1, t_2) = -t_1 t_2.$$

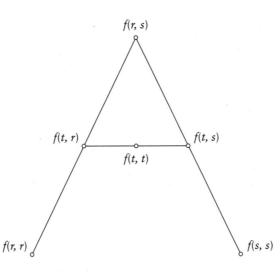

FIG. 3.10 A de Casteljau diagram

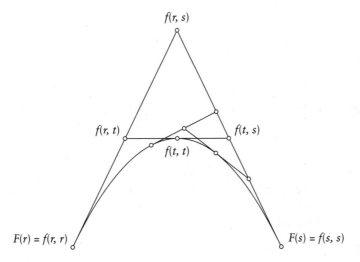

FIG. 3.11 The de Casteljau algorithm

The de Casteljau algorithm can also be applied to compute any polar value $f(t_1, t_2)$:

The only difference is that we use different λs during each of the two stages. During the first stage, we use the scalar λ_1 such that $t_1 = (1 - \lambda_1)r + \lambda_1 s$, to compute the two points

$$f(r, t_1) = f(r, (1 - \lambda_1)r + \lambda_1 s) = (1 - \lambda_1)f(r, r) + \lambda_1 f(r, s)$$

and

$$f(t_1, s) = f((1 - \lambda_1)r + \lambda_1 s, s) = (1 - \lambda_1)f(r, s) + \lambda_1 f(s, s),$$

by linear interpolation, where $f(r, t_1)$ is computed from the two control points $f(r, r)$ and $f(r, s)$, and $f(t_1, s)$ is computed from the two control points $f(r, s)$ and $f(s, s)$, the ratio of interpolation being

$$\lambda_1 = \frac{t_1 - r}{s - r}.$$

During the second stage, we use the scalar λ_2 such that $t_2 = (1 - \lambda_2)r + \lambda_2 s$, to compute

$$f(t_1, t_2) = f(t_1, (1 - \lambda_2)r + \lambda_2 s) = (1 - \lambda_2)f(t_1, r) + \lambda_2 f(t_1, s),$$

from the points $f(t_1, r) = f(r, t_1)$ and $f(t_1, s)$ computed during the first stage, the ratio of interpolation being

$$\lambda_2 = \frac{t_2 - r}{s - r}.$$

Thus, the polar values $f(t_1, t_2)$, also called *blossom values*, can be viewed as meaningful labels for the node of de Casteljau diagrams. It is in this sense that the term "blossom" is used: by forming the blossom of the polynomial function F, some hidden geometric information is revealed. We recommend reading de Casteljau's original presentation in de Casteljau [23].

A nice geometric interpretation of the polar value $f(t_1, t_2)$ can be obtained. For this, we need to look closely at the intersection of two tangents to a parabola. Let us consider the parabola given by

$$x(t) = at,$$

$$y(t) = bt^2.$$

The equation of the tangent to the parabola at $(x(t), y(t))$ is

$$x'(t)(y - y(t)) - y'(t)(x - x(t)) = 0,$$

that is,

$$a(y - bt^2) - 2bt(x - at) = 0,$$

or

$$ay - 2btx + abt^2 = 0.$$

To find the intersection of the two tangents to the parabola corresponding to $t = t_1$ and $t = t_2$, we solve the system of linear equations

$$ay - 2bt_1x + abt_1^2 = 0,$$

$$ay - 2bt_2x + abt_2^2 = 0,$$

and we easily find that

$$x = a\,\frac{t_1 + t_2}{2},$$

$$y = bt_1t_2.$$

Thus, the coordinates of the point of intersection of any two tangents to the parabola are given by the polar forms of the polynomials expressing the coordinates of the parabola. Turning this property around, we can say that the polar form $f(t_1, t_2)$ of the polynomial function defining a parabola gives precisely the intersection point of the two tangents at $F(t_1)$ and $F(t_2)$ to the parabola. There is a natural generalization of this nice geometric interpretation of polar forms to cubic curves, but unfortunately, it does not work in general, and when it does, only for curves not contained in a plane (it involves intersecting the osculating planes at three points on the curve).

The de Casteljau algorithm, in addition to having the nice property that the line determined by $F(r)$ and $f(r, s)$ is the tangent at $F(r)$, and that the line determined by $F(s)$ and $f(r, s)$ is the tangent at $F(s)$, also has the property that the line determined by $f(r, t)$ and $f(s, t)$ is the tangent at $F(t)$ (this will be shown in Section 5.4). Let us give an example of the computation of the control points from the parametric definition of a quadratic curve.

Example: Consider the parabola given by

$$F_1(t) = 2t,$$

$$F_2(t) = t^2.$$

The polar forms of F_1 and F_2 are

$$f_1(t_1, t_2) = t_1 + t_2,$$

$$f_2(t_1, t_2) = t_1t_2.$$

The control points $b_0 = f(0, 0)$, $b_1 = f(0, 1)$, and $b_2 = f(1, 1)$ have coordinates:

$$b_0 = (0, 0),$$

$$b_1 = (1, 0),$$

$$b_2 = (2, 1).$$

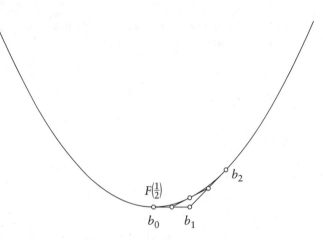

FIG. 3.12 The parabola defined by (b_0, b_1, b_2)

For $t = \frac{1}{2}$, the point $F(\frac{1}{2}) = (1, \frac{1}{4})$ on the parabola, is the middle of the line segment joining the middle of the segment (b_0, b_1) to the middle of the segment (b_1, b_2). (See Figure 3.12.)

Let us now consider $m = 3$, that is, cubic curves.

3.5   Polynomial Curves of Degree 3

A polynomial curve F of degree ≤ 3 is of the form

$$x(t) = F_1(t) = a_3 t^3 + a_2 t^2 + a_1 t + a_0,$$

$$y(t) = F_2(t) = b_3 t^3 + b_2 t^2 + b_1 t + b_0.$$

Since we already considered the case where $a_3 = b_3 = 0$, let us assume that $a_3 \neq 0$ or $b_3 \neq 0$. As in the case of quadratic curves, we first show that by a change of coordinates (amounting to a rotation), we can always assume that either $a_3 = 0$ (or $b_3 = 0$). If $a_3 \neq 0$ and $b_3 \neq 0$, let

$$\rho = \sqrt{a_3^2 + b_3^2},$$

and consider the matrix R given below:

$$R = \begin{pmatrix} \frac{b_3}{\rho} & -\frac{a_3}{\rho} \\ \frac{a_3}{\rho} & \frac{b_3}{\rho} \end{pmatrix}$$

Under the change of coordinates $\begin{pmatrix} x_1 \\ y_1 \end{pmatrix} = R \begin{pmatrix} x \\ y \end{pmatrix}$, we get

$$x_1(t) = \frac{a_2 b_3 - a_3 b_2}{\rho} t^2 + \frac{a_1 b_3 - a_3 b_1}{\rho} t + \frac{a_0 b_3 - a_3 b_0}{\rho},$$

$$y_1(t) = \rho t^3 + \frac{a_2 a_3 + b_2 b_3}{\rho} t^2 + \frac{a_1 a_3 + b_1 b_3}{\rho} t + \frac{a_0 a_3 + b_0 b_3}{\rho}.$$

The effect of this rotation is that the curve now "stands straight up" (since $\rho > 0$).

Case 1: $a_2 b_3 = a_3 b_2$.

Then we have a degenerate case where $x_1(t)$ is equal to a linear function. If $a_1 b_3 = a_3 b_1$ also holds, then $x_1(t)$ is a constant and $y_1(t)$ can be arbitrary, since its leading term is ρt^3, and we get the straight line

$$X = \frac{a_0 b_3 - a_3 b_0}{\rho}.$$

If $a_1 b_3 - a_3 b_1 \neq 0$, let us assume that $a_1 b_3 - a_3 b_1 > 0$, the other case being similar. Then, we can eliminate t between $x_1(t)$ and $y_1(t)$, and we get an implicit equation of the form

$$y = a' x^3 + b' x^2 + c' x + d',$$

with $a' > 0$. As in the case of quadratic curves, we can suppress the term $b' X^2$ by the change of coordinates

$$x = X - \frac{b'}{3a'}.$$

We get an implicit equation of the form

$$y = a X^3 + b X + c,$$

with $a > 0$. By one more change of coordinates, where $Y = y - c$, we get the implicit equation

$$Y = a X^3 + b X,$$

with $a > 0$. This curve is symmetric with respect to the Y-axis. Its shape will depend on the variations of sign of its derivative

$$Y' = 3a X^2 + b.$$

Also, since $Y'' = 6a X$, and $Y''(0) = 0$, the origin is an inflection point.

If $b > 0$, then $Y'(X)$ is always strictly positive, and $Y(X)$ is strictly increasing with X. It has a flat S-shape, the slope b of the tangent at the origin being positive.

If $b = 0$, then $Y'(0) = 0$, and 0 is a double root of Y', which means that the origin is an inflection point. The curve still has a flat S-shape, and the tangent at the origin is the X-axis.

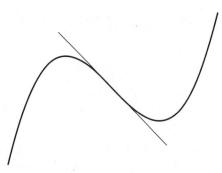

FIG. 3.13 "S-shaped" cubic

If $b < 0$, then $Y'(X)$ has two roots:

$$X_1 = +\sqrt{\frac{-b}{3a}}, \qquad X_2 = -\sqrt{\frac{-b}{3a}}.$$

Then, $Y(X)$ is increasing when X varies from $-\infty$ to X_1, decreasing when X varies from X_1 to X_2, and increasing again when X varies from X_2 to $+\infty$. The curve has an S-shape, the slope b of the tangent at the origin being negative. Figure 3.13 shows the cubic of the implicit equation

$$y = 3x^3 - 3x.$$

In all three cases, note that a line parallel to the Y-axis intersects the curve in a single point. This is the reason why we get a parametric representation.

Case 2: $a_2b_3 - a_3b_2 \neq 0$.

In this case, we say that we have a *nondegenerate cubic* (recall that $\rho > 0$). First, as in the quadratic case, by a change of parameter, we can suppress the term of degree 1 in t in $x_1(t)$, and by a change of coordinates, we can make the constant terms disappear, which yields parametric equations of the form

$$x(t) = F_1(t) = a_2t^2,$$

$$y(t) = F_2(t) = b_3t^3 + b_2t^2 + b_1t,$$

with $b_3 > 0$. We now apply a bijective affine transformation that will suppress the term b_2t^2 in $y(t)$. Consider the matrix S below

$$S = \begin{pmatrix} 1 & 0 \\ -b_2 & a_2 \end{pmatrix}$$

and the change of coordinates

$$\begin{pmatrix} x_1 \\ y_1 \end{pmatrix} = S \begin{pmatrix} x \\ y \end{pmatrix}.$$

We get

$$x_1(t) = a_2 t^2,$$

$$y_1(t) = a_2 t (b_3 t^2 + b_1),$$

with $b_3 > 0$.

We can now eliminate t between $x_1(t)$ and $y_1(t)$ as follows: first, square $y_1(t)$, getting

$$(y_1(t))^2 = a_2^2 t^2 (b_3 t^2 + b_1)^2,$$

and express t^2 in terms of $x_1(t)$ from $x_1(t) = a_2 t^2$, getting the implicit equation

$$(y_1)^2 = a_2 x_1 \left(\frac{b_3}{a_2} x_1 + b_1 \right)^2.$$

In terms of the original coordinates x, y, we have the implicit equation

$$(a_2 y - b_2 x)^2 = a_2 x \left(\frac{b_3}{a_2} x + b_1 \right)^2.$$

In fact, as it will be clearer in a moment, it is preferable to make the change of coordinates (translation)

$$x = X - \frac{b_1 a_2}{b_3},$$

$$y = Y - \frac{b_1 b_2}{b_3},$$

and we get the implicit equation

$$a_2 \left(\frac{a_2}{b_3} Y - \frac{b_2}{b_3} X \right)^2 + \frac{b_1 a_2}{b_3} X^2 = X^3,$$

with $b_3 > 0$. Then, we can show the following lemma.

Lemma 3.5.1

Given any nondegenerate cubic polynomial curve F, that is, any polynomial curve of the form

$$x(t) = F_1(t) = a_2 t^2,$$

$$y(t) = F_2(t) = b_3 t^3 + b_2 t^2 + b_1 t,$$

where $b_3 > 0$, after the translation of the origin given by

$$x = X - \frac{b_1 a_2}{b_3},$$

$$y = Y - \frac{b_1 b_2}{b_3},$$

the trace of F sastifies the implicit equation

$$a_2 \left(\frac{a_2}{b_3} Y - \frac{b_2}{b_3} X \right)^2 + \frac{b_1 a_2}{b_3} X^2 = X^3.$$

Furthermore, if $b_1 \leq 0$, then the curve defined by the above implicit equation is equal to the trace of the polynomial curve F, and when $b_1 > 0$, the curve defined by the above implicit equation, excluding the origin $(X, Y) = (0, 0)$, is equal to the trace of the polynomial curve F. The origin $(X, Y) = (0, 0)$ is called a singular point of the curve defined by the implicit equation.

Proof: It is straightforward and not very informative. We leave it as an exercise. ■

Thus, Lemma 3.5.1 shows that every nondegenerate polynomial cubic is defined by some implicit equation of the form

$$c(aY - bX)^2 + cdX^2 = X^3,$$

with the exception that when $d > 0$, the singular point $(X, Y) = (0, 0)$ must be excluded from the trace of the polynomial curve. The case where $d > 0$ is another illustration of the mismatch between the implicit and the explicit representations of curves. Again, this mismatch can be resolved if we treat these curves as complex curves.

The reason for choosing the origin at the singular point is that if we intersect the trace of the polynomial curve with a line of slope m passing through the singular point, we discover a nice parametric representation of the polynomial curve in terms of the parameter m.

Lemma 3.5.2

For every nondegenerate cubic polynomial curve F, there is some parametric definition G of the form

$$X(m) = c(a\,m - b)^2 + cd,$$

$$Y(m) = m(c(a\,m - b)^2 + cd),$$

such that F and G have the same trace, which is also the set of points on the curve defined by the implicit equation

$$c(aY - bX)^2 + cdX^2 = X^3,$$

excluding the origin $(X, Y) = (0, 0)$, when $d > 0$. Furthermore, unless it is a tangent at the origin to the trace of the polynomial curve F (which only happens when $d \leq 0$), every line of slope m passing through the origin $(X, Y) = (0, 0)$ intersects the trace of the polynomial curve F in a single point other than the singular point $(X, Y) = (0, 0)$. The line $aY - bX = 0$ is an axis of symmetry for the curve, in the sense that for any two points (X, Y_1) and (X, Y_2) such that

$$Y_1 + Y_2 = \frac{2b}{a} X,$$

(X, Y_1) belongs to the trace of F iff (X, Y_2) belongs to the trace of F. The tangent at the point

$$(X, Y) = \left(cd, \ \frac{bcd}{a} \right)$$

of the trace of F (also on the axis of symmetry) is vertical.

Proof: Lemma 3.5.1 shows that every nondegenerate polynomial cubic is defined by some implicit equation of the form

$$c(aY - bX)^2 + cdX^2 = X^3,$$

with the exception that when $d > 0$, the singular point $(X, Y) = (0, 0)$ must be excluded from the trace of the polynomial curve. Since every line of slope m through the origin has the equation $Y = mX$, to find the intersection of this line with the trace of the polynomial curve F, we substitute mX for Y in the implicit equation, getting

$$X^2(c(a\,m - b)^2 + cd - X) = 0.$$

Thus, either $X = 0$, which is a double root, or $c(a\,m - b)^2 + cd - X = 0$. If $X \neq 0$, then

$$X = c(a\,m - b)^2 + cd.$$

Now, we have $c(a\,m - b)^2 + cd = 0$, that is, $(a\,m - b)^2 + d = 0$, iff $d \leq 0$. In this case, the roots of the equation $(a\,m - b)^2 + d = 0$ give us the slopes of the tangent to the trace of F at the origin. Otherwise, we get a unique point

$$X(m) = c(a\,m - b)^2 + cd,$$

$$Y(m) = m(c(a\,m - b)^2 + cd),$$

on the trace of F, distinct from the origin. The fact that the line $aY - bX = 0$ is an axis of symmetry for the curve results from a trivial computation. Since $X(m) = c(a\,m - b)^2 + cd$, we have $X'(m) = 2ac(a\,m - b)$, and thus, $X'(m) = 0$ for $m = b/a$, the slope of the axis of symmetry. This value of m corresponds to the point

$$(X, Y) = \left(cd, \ \frac{bcd}{a}\right)$$

on the trace of F. ∎

We can now specify more precisely what is the shape of the trace of F, by studying the changes of sign of the derivative of $Y(m)$. Since

$$Y(m) = m(c(a\,m - b)^2 + cd) = a^2 cm^3 - 2abc\,m^2 + (b^2 c + cd)m,$$

we have

$$Y'(m) = 3a^2 cm^2 - 4abc\,m + (b^2 c + cd).$$

Let us compute the discriminant Δ of the polynomial $Y'(m)$ to see if it has roots. We have

$$\Delta = 16a^2 b^2 c^2 - 12a^2 c(b^2 c + cd) = 4a^2 c^2 (b^2 - 3d).$$

Thus, $Y'(m)$ has roots iff $b^2 - 3d \geq 0$. Then, we obtain the following classification for the nondegenerate polynomial cubic curves defined by

$$X(m) = c(a\,m - b)^2 + cd,$$

$$Y(m) \Leftarrow m(c(a\,m - b)^2 + cd).$$

3.6   Classification of the Polynomial Cubics

We treat the case where $c > 0$, the case $c < 0$ being similar.

Case 1: $3d > b^2$.

In this case, we must have $d > 0$, which means that the singular point $(X, Y) = (0, 0)$ is not on the trace of the cubic. When $b^2 - 3d < 0$, the polynomial $Y'(m)$ has no roots, and since we assumed $c > 0$, the polynomial $Y'(m)$ is always positive, which means that $Y(m)$ is strictly increasing. We get a kind of "humpy" curve, tangent to the vertical line $X = cd$ at the intersection of this line with the axis of symmetry $aY - bX = 0$, and only intersecting the X-axis for $m = 0$, that is, for

$$X = cd + cb^2.$$

The cubic of equation

$$3(Y - X)^2 + 6X^2 = X^3$$

is shown in Figure 3.14.

Case 2: $b^2 \geq 3d > 0$.

In this case, since $d > 0$, the singular point $(X, Y) = (0, 0)$ is not on the trace of the cubic either. When $b^2 - 3d > 0$, the polynomial $Y'(m)$ has two roots m_1, m_2,

FIG. 3.14 **FIG. 3.14** "Humpy" cubic ($3d > b^2$)

and since we assumed $c > 0$, then $Y(m)$ increases when m varies from $-\infty$ to m_1, decreases when m varies from m_1 to m_2, and increases when m varies from m_2 to $+\infty$. We also get a kind of "humpy" curve, tangent to the vertical line $X = cd$ at the intersection of this line with the axis of symmetry $aY - bX = 0$, and only intersecting the X-axis for $m = 0$, that is, for

$$X = cd + cb^2,$$

but between the two vertical lines $X = cd$ and $X = cd + cb^2$, the curve makes two turns. When $b^2 - 3d = 0$, $Y'(m)$ has a double root $m_0 = 2b/3a$, and $Y'(m)$ is positive except for $m = m_0$. Thus, $Y(m)$ increases when m varies from $-\infty$ to ∞, and there is an inflection point for $m = m_0$. We also get a kind of "humpy" curve. The cubic of equation

$$3(Y - 2X)^2 + 3X^2 = X^3$$

is shown in Figure 3.15.

Case 3: $d = 0$ (a cuspidal cubic).
   In this case, we have $b^2 - 3d > 0$, and $Y'(m)$ has two roots, which are easily computed:

$$m_1 = \frac{b}{3a}, \quad m_2 = \frac{b}{a}.$$

For m_2, we note that $X(m_2) = 0$, $Y(m_2) = 0$, $X'(m_2) = 0$, and $Y'(m_2) = 0$, which means that the origin is a cusp, which belongs to the trace of the cubic. Thus, $Y(t)$ increases as m varies from $-\infty$ to m_1, then $Y(t)$ decreases as m varies from m_1 to m_2,

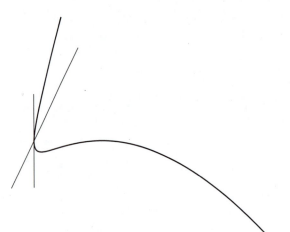

FIG. 3.15 "Humpy" cubic ($b^2 \geq 3d > 0$)

FIG. 3.16 Cuspidal cubic ($d = 0$)

reaching the cusp point, and finally $Y(t)$ increases as m varies from m_2 to $+\infty$. The curve is tangential to the axis $aY - bX = 0$ at the origin (the cusp), and intersects the X-axis only at $X = b^2 c$. The cubic of equation

$$3(Y - X)^2 = X^3$$

is shown in Figure 3.16.

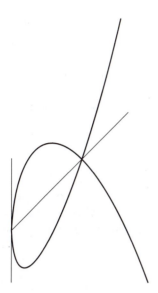

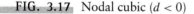
FIG. 3.17 Nodal cubic ($d < 0$)

Case 4: $d < 0$ (a nodal cubic).

In this case, $b^2 - 3d > 0$, and $Y'(m)$ has two roots m_1 and m_2. Furthermore, since $d < 0$, the singular point $(X, Y) = (0, 0)$ belongs to the trace of the cubic. Since $d < 0$, the polynomial $X(m) = c(a\, m - b)^2 + cd$ has two distinct roots, and thus, the cubic is self-intersecting at the singular point $(X, Y) = (0, 0)$. Since we assumed $c > 0$, then $Y(m)$ increases when m varies from $-\infty$ to m_1, decreases when m varies from m_1 to m_2, and increases when m varies from m_2 to $+\infty$. The trace of the cubic is a kind of "loopy curve" in the shape of an α, tangent to the vertical line $X = cd$ at the intersection of this line with the axis of symmetry $aY - bX = 0$, having the origin as a double point. The curve also intersects the X-axis for $m = 0$, that is, for $X = cd + cb^2$. The cubic of equation

$$\frac{3}{4}(Y - X)^2 - 3X^2 = X^3$$

is shown in Figure 3.17.

Observe the progression of the shape of the curve, from "humpy" to "loopy," through "cuspy."

Remark: The implicit equation

$$c(aY - bX)^2 + cdX^2 = X^3$$

of a nondegenerate polynomial cubic (with the exception of the singular point) is of the form

$$\varphi_2(X, Y) = X^3,$$

where $\varphi_2(X, Y)$ is a homogeneous polynomial in X and Y of total degree 2. (In the case of a degenerate cubic of equation $y = aX^3 + bx^2 + cx + d$, the singular point is at infinity. To make this statement precise, projective geometry is needed.) Note that X^3 itself is a homogeneous polynomial in X and Y of degree 3. Using some algebraic geometry, it can be shown that the (nondegenerate) cubics that can be represented by parametric rational curves of degree 3 (i.e., fractions of polynomials of degree ≤ 3) are exactly those cubics whose implicit equation is of the form

$$\varphi_2(X, Y) = \varphi_3(X, Y),$$

where $\varphi_2(X, Y)$ and $\varphi_3(X, Y)$ are homogeneous polynomials in X and Y of total degree 2 and 3, respectively. These cubics have a singular point at the origin. Thus, the polynomial case is obtained in the special case where $\varphi_3(X, Y) = X^3$. Furthermore, there are some cubics that cannot be represented even as rational curves. For example, the cubics defined by the implicit equation

$$Y^2 = X(X - 1)(X - \lambda),$$

where $\lambda \neq 0, 1$, cannot be parameterized rationally. Such cubics are *elliptic curves*. Elliptic curves are a venerable and fascinating topic, but definitely beyond the scope of this book!

Returning to polynomial cubics, inspired by our treatment of quadratic polynomials, we would like to extend blossoming to polynomials of degree 3.

3.7   Second Encounter with Polar Forms (Blossoming)

First, we need to define the polar form (or blossom) of a polynomial of degree 3. Given any polynomial of degree ≤ 3,

$$F(X) = aX^3 + bX^2 + cX + d,$$

the polar form of F is a symmetric triaffine function $f: \mathbf{A}^3 \to \mathbf{A}$—a function that takes the same value for all permutations of x_1, x_2, x_3, that is, such that

$$f(x_1, x_2, x_3) = f(x_2, x_1, x_3)$$
$$= f(x_1, x_3, x_2) = f(x_2, x_3, x_1) = f(x_3, x_1, x_2) = f(x_3, x_2, x_1),$$

which is affine in each argument, and such that

$$F(X) = f(X, X, X),$$

for all $X \in \mathbf{R}$. We easily verify that f must be given by

$$f(x_1, x_2, x_3) = ax_1x_2x_3 + b \, \frac{x_1x_2 + x_1x_3 + x_2x_3}{3} + c \, \frac{x_1 + x_2 + x_3}{3} + d.$$

Then, given a polynomial cubic curve $F: \mathbf{A} \to \mathbf{A}^3$, determined by three polynomials F_1, F_2, F_3 of degree ≤ 3, we can determine their polar forms f_1, f_2, f_3, and we obtain a symmetric triaffine map $f: \mathbf{A}^3 \to \mathbf{A}^3$, such that $F(X) = f(X, X, X)$, for all $X \in \mathbf{A}$. Again, let us pick an affine basis (r, s) in $\mathbf{A}$, with $r \neq s$, and let us compute

$$f(t_1, t_2, t_3) = f((1 - \lambda_1)r + \lambda_1 s, \ (1 - \lambda_2)r + \lambda_2 s, \ (1 - \lambda_3)r + \lambda_3 s).$$

Since f is symmetric and triaffine, we get

$$
\begin{aligned}
f(t_1, t_2, t_3) &= f((1 - \lambda_1)r + \lambda_1 s, \ (1 - \lambda_2)r + \lambda_2 s, \ (1 - \lambda_3)r + \lambda_3 s) \\
&= (1 - \lambda_1)(1 - \lambda_2)(1 - \lambda_3) \, f(r, r, r) \\
&\quad + \big((1 - \lambda_1)(1 - \lambda_2)\lambda_3 + (1 - \lambda_1)\lambda_2(1 - \lambda_3) \\
&\qquad + \lambda_1(1 - \lambda_2)(1 - \lambda_3)\big) \, f(r, r, s) \\
&\quad + \big((1 - \lambda_1)\lambda_2\lambda_3 + \lambda_1(1 - \lambda_2)\lambda_3 + \lambda_1\lambda_2(1 - \lambda_3)\big) \, f(r, s, s) \\
&\quad + \lambda_1\lambda_2\lambda_3 \, f(s, s, s).
\end{aligned}
$$

The coefficients of $f(r, r, r)$, $f(r, r, s)$, $f(r, s, s)$, and $f(s, s, s)$ are obviously symmetric triaffine functions, and they add up to 1, as it is easily verified by expanding the product

$$(1 - \lambda_1 + \lambda_1)(1 - \lambda_2 + \lambda_2)(1 - \lambda_3 + \lambda_3) = 1.$$

Since

$$\lambda_i = \frac{t_i - r}{s - r}, \quad \text{for } i = 1, 2, 3,$$

we get

$$
\begin{aligned}
f(t_1, t_2, t_3) = \ & \left(\frac{s - t_1}{s - r}\right)\left(\frac{s - t_2}{s - r}\right)\left(\frac{s - t_3}{s - r}\right) f(r, r, r) \\
& + \left[\left(\frac{s - t_1}{s - r}\right)\left(\frac{s - t_2}{s - r}\right)\left(\frac{t_3 - r}{s - r}\right) + \left(\frac{s - t_1}{s - r}\right)\left(\frac{t_2 - r}{s - r}\right)\left(\frac{s - t_3}{s - r}\right)\right. \\
& \left. + \left(\frac{t_1 - r}{s - r}\right)\left(\frac{s - t_2}{s - r}\right)\left(\frac{s - t_3}{s - r}\right)\right] f(r, r, s) \\
& + \left[\left(\frac{s - t_1}{s - r}\right)\left(\frac{t_2 - r}{s - r}\right)\left(\frac{t_3 - r}{s - r}\right) + \left(\frac{t_1 - r}{s - r}\right)\left(\frac{s - t_2}{s - r}\right)\left(\frac{t_3 - r}{s - r}\right)\right. \\
& \left. + \left(\frac{t_1 - r}{s - r}\right)\left(\frac{t_2 - r}{s - r}\right)\left(\frac{s - t_3}{s - r}\right)\right] f(r, s, s) \\
& + \left(\frac{t_1 - r}{s - r}\right)\left(\frac{t_2 - r}{s - r}\right)\left(\frac{t_3 - r}{s - r}\right) f(s, s, s).
\end{aligned}
$$

Thus, we showed that every symmetric triaffine map $f: \mathbf{A}^3 \to \mathbf{A}^3$ is completely determined by the sequence of four points $f(r, r, r)$, $f(r, r, s)$, $f(r, s, s)$, and $f(s, s, s)$ in $\mathbf{A}^3$, where $r \neq s$ are elements of $\mathbf{A}$.

Conversely, it is clear that given any sequence of four points $a, b, c, d \in \mathbf{A}^3$, the map

$$(t_1, t_2, t_3) \mapsto \left(\frac{s-t_1}{s-r}\right)\left(\frac{s-t_2}{s-r}\right)\left(\frac{s-t_3}{s-r}\right) a$$

$$+ \left[\left(\frac{s-t_1}{s-r}\right)\left(\frac{s-t_2}{s-r}\right)\left(\frac{t_3-r}{s-r}\right) + \left(\frac{s-t_1}{s-r}\right)\left(\frac{t_2-r}{s-r}\right)\left(\frac{s-t_3}{s-r}\right)\right.$$

$$\left.+ \left(\frac{t_1-r}{s-r}\right)\left(\frac{s-t_2}{s-r}\right)\left(\frac{s-t_3}{s-r}\right)\right] b$$

$$+ \left[\left(\frac{s-t_1}{s-r}\right)\left(\frac{t_2-r}{s-r}\right)\left(\frac{t_3-r}{s-r}\right) + \left(\frac{t_1-r}{s-r}\right)\left(\frac{s-t_2}{s-r}\right)\left(\frac{t_3-r}{s-r}\right)\right.$$

$$\left.+ \left(\frac{t_1-r}{s-r}\right)\left(\frac{t_2-r}{s-r}\right)\left(\frac{s-t_3}{s-r}\right)\right] c$$

$$+ \left(\frac{t_1-r}{s-r}\right)\left(\frac{t_2-r}{s-r}\right)\left(\frac{t_3-r}{s-r}\right) d$$

is symmetric triaffine, and that $f(r, r, r) = a$, $f(r, r, s) = b$, $f(r, s, s) = c$, and $f(s, s, s) = d$.

As in the quadratic case, the points $f(r, r, r)$, $f(r, r, s)$, $f(r, s, s)$, and $f(s, s, s)$ are called *control points*, or *Bézier control points*. They play a major role in the de Casteljau algorithm and its extensions. Note that the polynomial curve defined by f passes through the two points $f(r, r, r)$ and $f(s, s, s)$, but not through the other control points. If we let $r = 0$ and $s = 1$, so that $\lambda_1 = t_1$, $\lambda_2 = t_2$, and $\lambda_3 = t_3$, the polynomial function associated with $f(t_1, t_2, t_3)$ is obtained by letting $t_1 = t_2 = t_3 = t$, and we get

$$F(t) = f(t, t, t)$$

$$= (1-t)^3 f(0, 0, 0) + 3(1-t)^2 t\, f(0, 0, 1) + 3(1-t)t^2 f(0, 1, 1)$$

$$+ t^3 f(1, 1, 1).$$

The polynomials

$$(1-t)^3, 3(1-t)^2 t, 3(1-t)t^2, t^3,$$

are the *Bernstein polynomials of degree 3*. They form a basis of the vector space of polynomials of degree ≤ 3. Thus, the point $F(t)$ on the curve can be expressed in terms of the control points $f(r, r, r)$, $f(r, r, s)$, $f(r, s, s)$, and $f(s, s, s)$, and the Bernstein polynomials. However, it is more useful to extend the de Casteljau algorithm.

It is immediately verified that the above arguments do not depend on the fact that the affine space in which the curves live is $\mathbf{A}^3$, and thus, we will assume any affine space $\mathcal{E}$ of dimension ≥ 2. Summarizing what we have done, we have shown the following result.

Lemma 3.7.1

Given any sequence of four points a, b, c, d in $\mathcal{E}$, there is a unique polynomial curve $F: \mathbf{A} \to \mathcal{E}$ of degree 3, whose polar form $f: \mathbf{A}^3 \to \mathcal{E}$ satisfies the conditions $f(r, r, r) = a$, $f(r, r, s) = b$, $f(r, s, s) = c$, and $f(s, s, s) = d$ (where $r, s \in \mathbf{A}$, $r \neq s$). Furthermore, the polar form f of F is given by the formula

$$
f(t_1, t_2, t_3) = \left(\frac{s - t_1}{s - r}\right) \left(\frac{s - t_2}{s - r}\right) \left(\frac{s - t_3}{s - r}\right) a
$$

$$
+ \left[\left(\frac{s - t_1}{s - r}\right) \left(\frac{s - t_2}{s - r}\right) \left(\frac{t_3 - r}{s - r}\right) + \left(\frac{s - t_1}{s - r}\right) \left(\frac{t_2 - r}{s - r}\right) \left(\frac{s - t_3}{s - r}\right) \right.
$$

$$
\left. + \left(\frac{t_1 - r}{s - r}\right) \left(\frac{s - t_2}{s - r}\right) \left(\frac{s - t_3}{s - r}\right) \right] b
$$

$$
+ \left[\left(\frac{s - t_1}{s - r}\right) \left(\frac{t_2 - r}{s - r}\right) \left(\frac{t_3 - r}{s - r}\right) + \left(\frac{t_1 - r}{s - r}\right) \left(\frac{s - t_2}{s - r}\right) \left(\frac{t_3 - r}{s - r}\right) \right.
$$

$$
\left. + \left(\frac{t_1 - r}{s - r}\right) \left(\frac{t_2 - r}{s - r}\right) \left(\frac{s - t_3}{s - r}\right) \right] c
$$

$$
+ \left(\frac{t_1 - r}{s - r}\right) \left(\frac{t_2 - r}{s - r}\right) \left(\frac{t_3 - r}{s - r}\right) d.
$$

It is easy to generalize the de Casteljau algorithm to polynomial cubic curves.

3.8   Second Encounter with the de Casteljau Algorithm

Let us assume that the cubic curve F is specified by the control points $f(r, r, r) = b_0$, $f(r, r, s) = b_1$, $f(r, s, s) = b_2$, and $f(s, s, s) = b_3$ (where $r, s \in \mathbf{A}$, $r < s$). Given any $t \in [r, s]$, the computation of $F(t)$ can be arranged in a triangular array, as shown below, consisting of three stages:

0	1	2	3
$f(r, r, r)$			
	$f(r, r, t)$		
$f(r, r, s)$		$f(t, t, r)$	
	$f(r, t, s)$		$f(t, t, t)$
$f(r, s, s)$		$f(t, t, s)$	
	$f(t, s, s)$		
$f(s, s, s)$			

The above computation is usually performed for $t \in [r, s]$, but it works just as well for any $t \in A$, even outside $[r, s]$. When t is outside $[r, s]$, we usually say that $F(t) = f(t, t, t)$ is computed by *extrapolation*.

Let us go through the stages of the computation. During the first stage, we compute the three points

$$f(r, r, t) = f(r, r, (1 - \lambda)r + \lambda s) = (1 - \lambda)f(r, r, r) + \lambda f(r, r, s),$$

from $f(r, r, r)$ and $f(r, r, s)$,

$$f(r, t, s) = f(r, (1 - \lambda)r + \lambda s, s) = (1 - \lambda)f(r, r, s) + \lambda f(r, s, s),$$

from $f(r, r, s)$ and $f(r, s, s)$, and

$$f(t, s, s) = f((1 - \lambda)r + \lambda s, s, s) = (1 - \lambda)f(r, s, s) + \lambda f(s, s, s),$$

from $f(r, s, s)$ and $f(s, s, s)$, the ratio of interpolation being

$$\lambda = \frac{t - r}{s - r}.$$

During the second stage, since by symmetry, $f(r, r, t) = f(t, r, r)$ and $f(r, t, s) = f(t, s, r) = f(t, r, s)$, we compute the two points

$$f(t, t, r) = f(t, (1 - \lambda)r + \lambda s, r) = (1 - \lambda)f(t, r, r) + \lambda f(t, s, r),$$

from $f(t, r, r)$ and $f(t, s, r)$, and

$$f(t, t, s) = f(t, (1 - \lambda)r + \lambda s, s) = (1 - \lambda)f(t, r, s) + \lambda f(t, s, s),$$

from $f(t, r, s)$ and $f(t, s, s)$, the ratio of interpolation also being

$$\lambda = \frac{t - r}{s - r}.$$

During the third stage, we compute the point

$$f(t, t, t) = f(t, t, (1 - \lambda)r + \lambda s) = (1 - \lambda)f(t, t, r) + \lambda f(t, t, s),$$

from $f(t, t, r)$ and $f(t, t, s)$, the ratio of interpolation still being

$$\lambda = \frac{t - r}{s - r}.$$

In order to describe the above computation more conveniently as an algorithm, let us denote the control points $b_0 = f(r, r, r), b_1 = f(r, r, s), b_2 = f(r, s, s)$, and $b_3 = f(s, s, s)$ as $b_{0,0}, b_{1,0}, b_{2,0}$, and $b_{3,0}$; and the intermediate points $f(r, r, t), f(r, t, s), f(t, s, s)$ as $b_{0,1}, b_{1,1}, b_{2,1}$, the intermediate points $f(t, t, r), f(t, t, s)$ as $b_{0,2}, b_{1,2}$; and the point $f(t, t, t)$ as $b_{0,3}$. Note that in $b_{i,j}$, the index j denotes the stage of the computation, and $F(t) = b_{0,3}$. Then the triangle representing the computation is as follows:

$$
\begin{array}{cccc}
0 & 1 & 2 & 3 \\
b_0 = b_{0,0} & & & \\
 & b_{0,1} & & \\
b_1 = b_{1,0} & & b_{0,2} & \\
 & b_{1,1} & & b_{0,3} \\
b_2 = b_{2,0} & & b_{1,2} & \\
 & b_{2,1} & & \\
b_3 = b_{3,0} & & &
\end{array}
$$

Then, we have the following inductive formula for computing $b_{i,j}$:

$$
b_{i,j} = \left(\frac{s-t}{s-r}\right) b_{i,j-1} + \left(\frac{t-r}{s-r}\right) b_{i+1,j-1},
$$

where $1 \leq j \leq 3$, and $0 \leq i \leq 3 - j$. We have $F(t) = b_{0,3}$.

As we shall see in Section 5.1, the above formula generalizes to any degree m. When $r \leq t \leq s$, each interpolation step computes a convex combination, and $b_{i,j}$ lies between $b_{i,j-1}$ and $b_{i+1,j-1}$. In this case, geometrically, the algorithm constructs the three polylines

$$(b_0,\ b_1),\ (b_1,\ b_2),\ (b_2,\ b_3)$$
$$(b_{0,1},\ b_{1,1}),\ (b_{1,1},\ b_{2,1})$$
$$(b_{0,2},\ b_{1,2})$$

called *shells*, and with the point $b_{0,3}$, they form the *de Casteljau diagram* (see Figure 3.18).

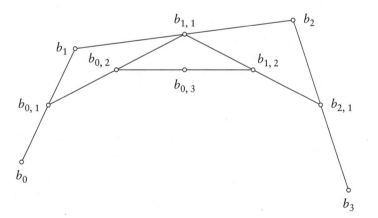

FIG. 3.18   A de Casteljau diagram in the cubic case

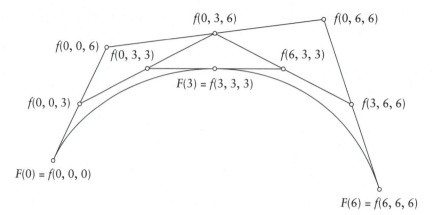

FIG. 3.19 The de Casteljau algorithm for $t = 3$

Note that the shells are nested nicely. The polyline

$$(b_0,\ b_1),\ (b_1,\ b_2),\ (b_2,\ b_3)$$

is also called a *control polygon* of the curve. When λ is outside $[r, s]$, we still obtain three shells and a de Casteljau diagram, but the shells are not nicely nested. Figure 3.19 illustrates the de Casteljau algorithm for computing the point $F(t)$ on a cubic, where $r = 0$ and $s = 6$. This figure shows the construction of the point $F(3)$ corresponding to $t = 3$, on the curve F.

The de Casteljau algorithm also gives some information about some of the tangents to the curve. It will be shown in Section 5.4 that the tangent at b_0 is the line $(b_0,\ b_1)$, the tangent at b_3 is the line $(b_2,\ b_3)$, and the tangent at $F(t)$ is the line $(b_{0,2},\ b_{1,2})$, where $b_{0,2}$ and $b_{1,2}$ are computed during the second stage of the de Casteljau algorithm.

Remark: The above statements only make sense when $b_0 \neq b_1$, $b_2 \neq b_3$, and $b_{0,2} \neq b_{1,2}$. It is possible for some (even all!) of the control points to coincide. The algorithm still computes $f(t, t, t)$ correctly, but the tangents may not be computed as easily as above.

As in the quadratic case, the de Casteljau algorithm can also be used to compute any polar value $f(t_1, t_2, t_3)$ (which is not generally on the curve). All we have to do is to use a different ratio of interpolation λ_j during phase j, given by

$$\lambda_j = \frac{t_j - r}{s - r}.$$

The computation can also be represented as a triangle:

$$
\begin{array}{cccc}
0 & 1 & 2 & 3 \\
f(r,r,r) & & & \\
& f(r,r,t_1) & & \\
f(r,r,s) & & f(t_1,t_2,r) & \\
& f(r,t_1,s) & & f(t_1,t_2,t_3) \\
f(r,s,s) & & f(t_1,t_2,s) & \\
& f(t_1,s,s) & & \\
f(s,s,s) & & &
\end{array}
$$

As above, it is convenient to denote the intermediate points $f(r,r,t_1)$, $f(r,t_1,s)$, $f(t_1,s,s)$ as $b_{0,1}, b_{1,1}, b_{2,1}$; the intermediate points $f(t_1,t_2,r)$, $f(t_1,t_2,s)$ as $b_{0,2}, b_{1,2}$; and the point $f(t_1,t_2,t_3)$ as $b_{0,3}$. Note that in $b_{i,j}$, the index j denotes the stage of the computation, and $f(t_1,t_2,t_3) = b_{0,3}$. Then the triangle representing the computation is as follows:

$$
\begin{array}{cccc}
0 & 1 & 2 & 3 \\
b_0 = b_{0,0} & & & \\
& b_{0,1} & & \\
b_1 = b_{1,0} & & b_{0,2} & \\
& b_{1,1} & & b_{0,3} \\
b_2 = b_{2,0} & & b_{1,2} & \\
& b_{2,1} & & \\
b_3 = b_{3,0} & & &
\end{array}
$$

We also have the following inductive formula for computing $b_{i,j}$:

$$
b_{i,j} = \left(\frac{s - t_j}{s - r}\right) b_{i,j-1} + \left(\frac{t_j - r}{s - r}\right) b_{i+1,j-1},
$$

where $1 \le j \le 3$, and $0 \le i \le 3 - j$. We have $f(t_1, t_2, t_3) = b_{0,3}$.

Thus, there is very little difference between this more general version of the de Casteljau algorithm computing polar values and the version computing the point $F(t)$ on the curve: just use a new ratio of interpolation at each stage. The de Casteljau algorithm enjoys many nice properties that will be studied in Section 5.1.

Let us give a few examples of the computation of polar forms associated with parametric representation of cubics, and computations of the coordinates of control points.

3.9   Examples of Cubics Defined by Control Points

We begin with an example of plane cubics.

Example 1: Consider the plane cubic defined as follows:

$$
F_1(t) = 3t,
$$

$$
F_2(t) = 3t^3 - 3t.
$$

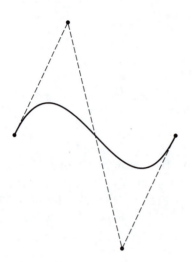

FIG. 3.20 Bézier cubic 1

The polar forms of $F_1(t)$ and $F_2(t)$ are

$$f_1(t_1, t_2, t_3) = t_1 + t_2 + t_3,$$

$$f_2(t_1, t_2, t_3) = 3t_1t_2t_3 - (t_1 + t_2 + t_3).$$

With respect to the affine frame $r = -1, s = 1$, the coordinates of the control points are

$$b_0 = (-3, 0),$$

$$b_1 = (-1, 4),$$

$$b_2 = (1, -4),$$

$$b_3 = (3, 0).$$

The shape of the curve is shown in Figure 3.20. This cubic is an example of a degenerate "S-shaped" cubic.

Example 2: Consider the plane cubic defined as follows:

$$F_1(t) = 3(t - 1)^2 + 6,$$

$$F_2(t) = 3t(t - 1)^2 + 6t.$$

Since

$$F_1(t) = 3t^2 - 6t + 9,$$

$$F_2(t) = 3t^3 - 6t^2 + 9t,$$

we get the polar forms

FIG. 3.21 Bézier cubic 2

$$f_1(t_1, t_2, t_3) = (t_1 t_2 + t_1 t_3 + t_2 t_3) - 2(t_1 + t_2 + t_3) + 9,$$

$$f_2(t_1, t_2, t_3) = 3t_1 t_2 t_3 - 2(t_1 t_2 + t_1 t_3 + t_2 t_3) + 3(t_1 + t_2 + t_3).$$

With respect to the affine frame $r = 0, s = 1$, the coordinates of the control points are

$$b_0 = (9, 0),$$

$$b_1 = (7, 3),$$

$$b_2 = (6, 4),$$

$$b_3 = (6, 6).$$

The shape of the curve is shown in Figure 3.21.

We leave as an exercise to verify that this cubic corresponds to Case 1, where $3d > b^2$. The axis of symmetry is $y = x$.

Example 3: Consider the plane cubic defined as follows:

$$F_1(t) = 3(t - 2)^2 + 3,$$

$$F_2(t) = 3t(t - 2)^2 + 3t.$$

Since

$$F_1(t) = 3t^2 - 12t + 15,$$

$$F_2(t) = 3t^3 - 12t^2 + 15t,$$

we get the polar forms

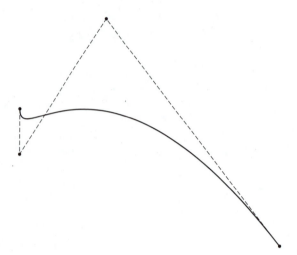

FIG. 3.22 Bézier cubic 3

$$f_1(t_1, t_2, t_3) = (t_1 t_2 + t_1 t_3 + t_2 t_3) - 4(t_1 + t_2 + t_3) + 15,$$

$$f_2(t_1, t_2, t_3) = 3t_1 t_2 t_3 - 4(t_1 t_2 + t_1 t_3 + t_2 t_3) + 5(t_1 + t_2 + t_3).$$

With respect to the affine frame $r = 0, s = 2$, the coordinates of the control points are

$b_0 = (15, 0),$

$b_1 = (7, 10),$

$b_2 = (3, 4),$

$b_3 = (3, 6).$

The shape of the curve is shown in Figure 3.22.

We leave as an exercise to verify that this cubic corresponds to Case 2, where $b^2 \geq 3d > 0$. The axis of symmetry is $y = 2x$. It is interesting to see which control points are obtained with respect to the affine frame $r = 0, s = 1$:

$b_0' = (15, 0),$

$b_1' = (11, 5),$

$b_2' = (8, 6),$

$b_3' = (6, 6).$

The second "hump" of the curve is outside the convex hull of this new control polygon. This shows that it is far from obvious, just by looking at some of the control points, to predict what the shape of the entire curve will be!

Example 4: Consider the plane cubic defined as follows:

$$F_1(t) = 3(t - 1)^2,$$

$$F_2(t) = 3t(t - 1)^2.$$

Since

$$F_1(t) = 3t^2 - 6t + 3,$$

$$F_2(t) = 3t^3 - 6t^2 + 3t,$$

we get the polar forms

$$f_1(t_1, t_2, t_3) = (t_1 t_2 + t_1 t_3 + t_2 t_3) - 2(t_1 + t_2 + t_3) + 3,$$

$$f_2(t_1, t_2, t_3) = 3t_1 t_2 t_3 - 2(t_1 t_2 + t_1 t_3 + t_2 t_3) + (t_1 + t_2 + t_3).$$

With respect to the affine frame $r = 0, s = 2$, the coordinates of the control points are

$$b_0 = (3, 0),$$

$$b_1 = (-1, 2),$$

$$b_2 = (-1, -4),$$

$$b_3 = (3, 6).$$

The shape of the curve is shown in Figure 3.23.

We leave as an exercise to verify that this cubic corresponds to Case 3, where $d = 0$, a cubic with a cusp at the origin. The axis of symmetry is $y = x$. It is interesting to see which control points are obtained with respect to the affine frame $r = 0, s = 1$:

$$b_0' = (3, 0),$$

$$b_1' = (1, 1),$$

$$b_2' = (0, 0),$$

$$b_3' = (0, 0).$$

Thus, $b_2' = b_3'$. This indicates that there is a cusp at the origin.

Example 5: Consider the plane cubic defined as follows:

$$F_1(t) = \frac{3}{4}(t - 1)^2 - 3,$$

$$F_2(t) = \frac{3}{4}t(t - 1)^2 - 3t.$$

Since

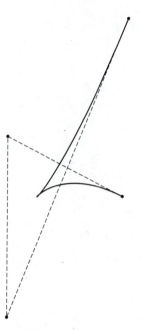

FIG. 3.23 Bézier cubic 4

$$F_1(t) = \frac{3}{4}t^2 - \frac{3}{2}t - \frac{9}{4},$$

$$F_2(t) = \frac{3}{4}t^3 - \frac{3}{2}t^2 - \frac{9}{4}t,$$

we get the polar forms

$$f_1(t_1, t_2, t_3) = \frac{1}{4}(t_1t_2 + t_1t_3 + t_2t_3) - \frac{1}{2}(t_1 + t_2 + t_3) - \frac{9}{4},$$

$$f_2(t_1, t_2, t_3) = \frac{3}{4}t_1t_2t_3 - \frac{1}{2}(t_1t_2 + t_1t_3 + t_2t_3) - \frac{3}{4}(t_1 + t_2 + t_3).$$

With respect to the affine frame $r = -1, s = 3$, the coordinates of the control points are

$$b_0 = (0, 0),$$

$$b_1 = (-4, 4),$$

$$b_2 = (-4, -12),$$

$$b_3 = (0, 0).$$

The shape of the curve is shown in Figure 3.24.

Note that $b_0 = b_3$. We leave as an exercise to verify that this cubic corresponds to Case 4, where $d < 0$, a cubic with a node at the origin. The axis of symmetry is

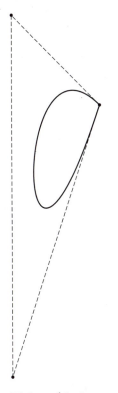

FIG. 3.24 Bézier cubic 5

$y = x$. The two tangents at the origin are $y = -x$ and $y = 3x$ (this explains the choice of $r = -1$ and $s = 3$). Figure 3.25 gives a more global view of the same cubic.

It is interesting to see which control points are obtained with respect to the affine frame $r = 0, s = 1$:

$$b_0' = \left(-\frac{9}{4}, 0\right),$$

$$b_1' = \left(-1, -\frac{3}{4}\right),$$

$$b_2' = (-3, -2),$$

$$b_3' = (-3, -3).$$

As in Example 3, this example shows that it is far from obvious, just by looking at some of the control points, to predict what the shape of the entire curve will be!

The above examples suggest that it may be interesting, and even fun, to investigate which properties of the shape of the control polygon (b_0, b_1, b_2, b_3) determine the nature of the plane cubic that it defines. Try it!

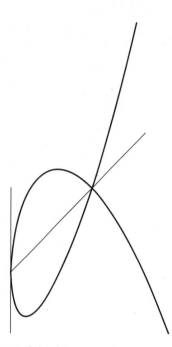

FIG. 3.25 Nodal cubic $(d < 0)$

Challenge: Given a planar control polygon (b_0, b_1, b_2, b_3), is it possible to find the singular point geometrically? Is it possible to find the axis of symmetry geometrically?

Let us consider one more example, this time of a space curve.

Example 6: Consider the cubic, known as a *twisted cubic* (it is not a plane curve), defined as follows:

$$F_1(t) = t,$$

$$F_2(t) = t^2,$$

$$F_3(t) = t^3.$$

We get the polar forms

$$f_1(t_1, t_2, t_3) = \frac{1}{3}(t_1 + t_2 + t_3)$$

$$f_2(t_1, t_2, t_3) = \frac{1}{3}(t_1 t_2 + t_1 t_3 + t_2 t_3)$$

$$f_3(t_1, t_2, t_3) = t_1 t_2 t_3.$$

With respect to the affine frame $r = 0, s = 1$, the coordinates of the control points are

$b_0 = (0, 0, 0)$

$b_1 = \left(\dfrac{1}{3}, 0, 0\right)$

$b_2 = \left(\dfrac{2}{3}, \dfrac{1}{3}, 0\right)$

$b_3 = (1, 1, 1).$

The reader should apply the de Casteljau algorithm to find the point on the twisted cubic corresponding to $t = \frac{1}{2}$. This curve has some very interesting algebraic properties. For example, it is the zero locus (the set of common zeros) of the two polynomials

$y - x^2 = 0,$

$z - xy = 0.$

It can also be shown that any four points on the twisted cubic are affinely independent.

We would like to extend polar forms and the de Casteljau algorithm to polynomial curves of arbitrary degrees (not only $m = 2, 3$), and later on, to rational curves and also to polynomial and rational surfaces. In order to do so, we need to investigate some of the basic properties of multiaffine maps. This is the object of the next two chapters.

Problems

[40 pts] **1.** Write a computer program implementing the de Casteljau algorithm for cubic curves, over some interval $[r, s]$.

You may use Mathematica or any other available software in which graphics primitives are available.

[20 pts] **2.** Consider (in the plane) the cubic curve F defined by the following four control points, assuming that $r = 0$ and $s = 1$:

$b_0 = (6, -6),$

$b_1 = (-6, 10),$

$b_2 = (-6, -10),$

$b_3 = (6, 6).$

Use the de Casteljau algorithm to find the coordinates of the points $F(\frac{1}{3})$, $F(\frac{1}{2})$, and $F(\frac{2}{3})$. Plot the cubic as well as you can.

[30 pts]   **3.** Consider the cubic defined by the equations

$$x(t) = 9p(3t^2 - 1),$$

$$y(t) = 9pt(3t^2 - 1),$$

where p is any scalar.

(a) Find the polar forms of $x(t)$ and $y(t)$. Find the control points with respect to the affine frame $r = -1, s = 1$.

(b) What are the slopes of the tangents at the origin? Give a geometric construction of the tangent to the cubic for $t = 0$. Plot the curve as well as possible (choose some convenient value for p).

Remark: This cubic is known as the *Tchirnhausen cubic*.

[20 pts]   **4.** Consider (in the plane) the cubic curve F defined by the following four control points, assuming that $r = 0$ and $s = 1$:

$$b_0 = (-4, 0),$$

$$b_1 = (-1, 6),$$

$$b_2 = (1, 6),$$

$$b_3 = (4, 0).$$

Give a geometric construction of the point $F(\frac{1}{2})$. Construct the points $F(\frac{1}{4})$ and $F(\frac{3}{4})$. Plot the curve as well as you can.

[25 pts]   **5.** Explain how to treat a parabola as a degenerate cubic. More specifically, given three control points b_0, b_1, b_2 specifying a parabola, determine control points b'_0, b'_1, b'_2, b'_3 yielding the same parabola, viewed as a cubic.

[30 pts]   **6.** (The "four tangents theorem")

(a) Given any sequence (a, b, c, d) of four distinct points on a line, we define the *cross-ratio* $[a, b, c, d]$ of these points as

$$[a, b, c, d] = \frac{\overrightarrow{ca}/\overrightarrow{cb}}{\overrightarrow{da}/\overrightarrow{db}}$$

In any affine space $\mathcal{E}$, given any sequence (a, b, c, d) of four distinct points, such that $c = (1 - \alpha)a + \alpha b$ and $d = (1 - \beta)a + \beta b$, show that

$$[a, b, c, d] = \frac{\alpha}{(1 - \alpha)} \frac{(1 - \beta)}{\beta}.$$

Show that $[a, b, c, d] = -1$ iff

$$\frac{1}{\alpha} + \frac{1}{\beta} = 2.$$

In this case, we say that (a, b, c, d) forms a *harmonic division*.

(b) Given any parabola F defined by some bilinear symmetric affine map $f: \mathbf{A}^2 \to \mathbf{A}^2$, given any four distinct values t_1, t_2, t_3, t_4, consider the four collinear points $(f(t, t_1), f(t, t_2), f(t, t_3), f(t, t_4))$, for any t. Prove that

$$[f(t, t_1), f(t, t_2), f(t, t_3), f(t, t_4)]$$

only depends on t_1, t_2, t_3, t_4.

Given t_1, t_2, find the values of t_3, t_4 such that

$$[f(t, t_1), f(t, t_2), f(t, t_3), f(t, t_4)] = -1.$$

[20 pts] **7.** Prove Lemma 3.5.1.

[30 pts] **8.** Given a plane cubic specified by its control points (b_0, b_1, b_2, b_3), explain what happens when two control points are identical. In particular, consider the following questions:

(a) Does the degree of the curve drop?

(b) Does the curve have a cusp at some control point?

(c) Does the curve have an inflection point at some control point?

(d) Assuming that $\mathbf{A}^2$ is equipped with its usual Euclidean inner product, does the curve have points where the curvature is null?

(e) What happens when three control points are identical? What if the four control points are identical?

[20 pts] **9.** What is the maximum number of intersection points of two plane cubics? Give the control points of two plane cubics that intersect in the maximum number of points.

[20 pts] **10.** Plot the Bernstein polynomials $B_i^3(t)$, $0 \leq i \leq 3$, over $[0, 1]$.

[80 pts] **11.** **Challenge:** Consider the cubic of Problem 3 (except that a new origin is chosen), defined by the equations

$$x(t) = 27pt^2,$$

$$y(t) = 9pt(3t^2 - 1),$$

where p is any scalar. Let F be the point of coordinates $(p, 0)$. Any line D through F intersects the cubic in three points N_1, N_2, N_3.

(a) Let H_i be the foot of the perpendicular from F to the tangent to the cubic at N_i. Prove that H_1, H_2, H_3 belong to the parabola of equation $y^2 = 4px$.

Hint: Consider the following construction. For every point M on the parabola $y^2 = 4px$, let ω be the intersection of the normal at M to the parabola with the mediatrix of the line segment FM, and let N be the symmetric of F with respect to ω. Show that when M varies on the parabola, N varies on the cubic, and that MN is tangent to the cubic at N. It is best to use polar coordinates (with pole $F = (p, 0)$). You can check that you are right if you find that the cubic is defined by

$$x(\theta) = 3p + 6p \frac{\cos \theta}{1 - \cos \theta},$$

$$y(\theta) = 2p \frac{\sin \theta (1 - 2 \cos \theta)}{(1 - \cos \theta)^2}.$$

(b) Prove that the tangents to the cubic at N_1, N_2, N_3 intersect in three points forming an equilateral triangle.

(c) What is the locus of the center of gravity of this triangle?

   Hint: Use the representation in polar coordinates. You may want to use Mathematica to play around with these curves.

CHAPTER 4

Multiaffine Maps and Polar Forms

4.1   Multiaffine Maps

In this chapter, we discuss the representation of certain polynomial maps in terms of multiaffine maps. This has applications to curve and surface design, and more specifically to Bézier curves, splines, and the de Casteljau algorithm, in a form usually called "blossoming." This material is quite old, going back as early as 1879, and it is not very easily accessible. A presentation of the polarization of polynomials can be found in Hermann Weyl's *The Classical Groups* [87] (Chapter 1, pages 4–6), which first appeared in 1939. An equivalent form of polarization is discussed quite extensively in Cartan [16] (Chapter 1, Section 6), in the case of polynomial maps between vector spaces, and some discussion of the affine case can be found in Berger [5] (Chapter 3, Section 3). It should be pointed out that de Casteljau pioneered the approach to polynomial curves and surfaces in terms of polar forms (see de Casteljau [23]). In fact, there is little doubt that the polar approach led him to the discovery of the beautiful algorithm known as the "de Casteljau algorithm."

The chapter proceeds as follows. After a quick review of the binomial and multinomial coefficients, multilinear and multiaffine maps are defined. Next, we prove a generalization of Lemma 2.7.2, characterizing multiaffine maps in terms of multilinear maps. This result is quite technical in nature, but it plays a crucial role in Section 10.1. The proof can be omitted at first reading. Affine polynomial functions and their polar forms are defined. Affine polynomial functions $h: E \to F$ are described explicitly in the case where E has finite dimension, showing that they subsume the usual multivariate polynomial functions. Polynomial curves in polar form are defined, and their characterization in terms of control points and Bernstein polynomials is shown. The uniqueness of the polar form of an affine polynomial function is proved next. It is shown how polynomials in one or several variables are polarized, and the equivalence between polynomials and symmetric multiaffine maps is established. We conclude by showing that the definition of a polynomial curve in polar form is equivalent to the more traditional definition (Definition 3.1.1), and that the Bernstein polynomials of degree $\leq m$ form a basis of the vector space of polynomials of degree $\leq m$.

We first review quickly some elementary combinatorial facts.

For every $n \in \mathbf{N}$, we define $n!$ (read "n factorial") as follows:

$$0! = 1,$$

$$(n + 1)! = (n + 1)n!$$

It is well known that $n!$ is the number of permutations on n elements. For $n \in \mathbf{N}$, and $k \in \mathbf{Z}$, we define $\binom{n}{k}$ (read "n choose k") as follows:

$$\binom{n}{k} = 0, \quad \text{if } k \notin \{0, \ldots, n\},$$

$$\binom{0}{0} = 1,$$

$$\binom{n}{k} = \binom{n-1}{k} + \binom{n-1}{k-1}, \quad \text{if } n \geq 1.$$

It is immediately shown by induction on n that

$$\binom{n}{k} = \frac{n!}{k!(n-k)!},$$

for $0 \leq k \leq n$. Furthermore, when $n \geq 0$, we can prove by induction that $\binom{n}{k}$ is the number of subsets of $\{1, \ldots, n\}$ consisting of k elements. Indeed, when $n = 0$, we have the empty set, which has only one subset, namely, itself. When $n \geq 1$, there are two kinds of subsets of $\{1, \ldots, n\}$ having k elements: those containing 1, and those not containing 1. Now, there are as many subsets of k elements from $\{1, \ldots, n\}$ containing 1 as there are subsets of $k - 1$ elements from $\{2, \ldots, n\}$, namely, $\binom{n-1}{k-1}$, and there are as many subsets of k elements from $\{1, \ldots, n\}$ not containing 1 as there are subsets of k elements from $\{2, \ldots, n\}$, namely, $\binom{n-1}{k}$. Thus, the number of subsets of $\{1, \ldots, n\}$ consisting of k elements is $\binom{n-1}{k} + \binom{n-1}{k-1}$, which is equal to $\binom{n}{k}$. The numbers $\binom{n}{k}$ are also called *binomial coefficients*, because they arise in the expansion of the binomial expression $(a + b)^n$. It is easy to see that

$$\binom{n}{k} = \binom{n}{n-k}.$$

The binomial coefficients can be computed inductively by forming what is usually called *Pascal's triangle*, which is based on the recurrence for $\binom{n}{k}$:

n	$\binom{n}{0}$	$\binom{n}{1}$	$\binom{n}{2}$	$\binom{n}{3}$	$\binom{n}{4}$	$\binom{n}{5}$	$\binom{n}{6}$	$\binom{n}{7}$	$\cdots$
0	1								
1	1	1							
2	1	2	1						
3	1	3	3	1					
4	1	4	6	4	1				
5	1	5	10	10	5	1			
6	1	6	15	20	15	6	1		
7	1	7	21	35	35	21	7	1	
$\vdots$	$\vdots$	$\vdots$	$\vdots$	$\vdots$	$\vdots$	$\vdots$	$\vdots$	$\vdots$	$\ddots$

For any $a, b \in \mathbf{R}$, the following identity holds for all $n \geq 0$:

$$(a+b)^n = \sum_{k=0}^{n} \binom{n}{k} a^k b^{n-k}.$$

The proof is a simple induction. More generally, for any $a_1, \ldots, a_m \in \mathbf{R}$, $m \geq 2$, and $n \geq 0$, we have the identity

$$(a_1 + \cdots + a_m)^n = \sum_{\substack{k_1 + \cdots + k_m = n \\ 0 \leq k_i \leq n}} \frac{n!}{k_1! \cdots k_m!} a_1^{k_1} \cdots a_m^{k_m}.$$

Again, the proof is by induction. The coefficients

$$\frac{n!}{k_1! \cdots k_m!},$$

where $k_1 + \cdots + k_m = n$, are called *multinomial coefficients*, and they are also denoted as

$$\binom{n}{k_1, \ldots, k_m}.$$

We now proceed with multiaffine maps. For the reader's convenience, we recall the definition of a multilinear map. Let $E_1, \ldots, E_m$, and F, be vector spaces over $\mathbf{R}$, where $m \geq 1$.

Definition 4.1.1

A function $f: E_1 \times \ldots \times E_m \to F$ is a multilinear map *(or an m-linear map), iff it is linear in each argument, holding the others fixed. More explicitly, for every i, $1 \leq i \leq m$, for all $\overrightarrow{x_1} \in E_1 \ldots, \overrightarrow{x_{i-1}} \in E_{i-1}, \overrightarrow{x_{i+1}} \in E_{i+1}, \ldots, \overrightarrow{x_m} \in E_m$, for every family $(\overrightarrow{y_j})_{j \in J}$ of vectors in E_i, for every family $(\lambda_j)_{j \in J}$ of scalars,*

$$f(\overrightarrow{x_1}, \ldots, \overrightarrow{x_{i-1}}, \sum_{j \in J} \lambda_j \overrightarrow{y_j}, \overrightarrow{x_{i+1}}, \ldots, \overrightarrow{x_n})$$

$$= \sum_{j \in J} \lambda_j f(\overrightarrow{x_1}, \ldots, \overrightarrow{x_{i-1}}, \overrightarrow{y_j}, \overrightarrow{x_{i+1}}, \ldots, \overrightarrow{x_n}).$$

Having reviewed the definition of a multilinear map, we define multiaffine maps. Let $E_1, \ldots, E_m$, and F, be affine spaces over $\mathbf{R}$, where $m \geq 1$.

Definition 4.1.2

A function $f: E_1 \times \ldots \times E_m \to F$ is a multiaffine map *(or an m-affine map), iff it is affine in each argument, that is, for every i, $1 \leq i \leq m$, for all $a_1 \in E_1, \ldots, a_{i-1} \in E_{i-1}, a_{i+1} \in E_{i+1}, \ldots, a_m \in E_m, a \in E_i$, the map $a \mapsto f(a_1, \ldots, a_{i-1}, a, a_{i+1}, \ldots, a_m)$ is an affine map, that is, iff it preserves barycentric combinations. More explicitly, for every family $(b_j)_{j \in J}$ of points in E_i, for every family $(\lambda_j)_{j \in J}$ of scalars such that $\sum_{j \in J} \lambda_j = 1$, we have*

$$f\left(a_1, \ldots, a_{i-1}, \sum_{j \in J} \lambda_j b_j, a_{i+1}, \ldots, a_m\right) = \sum_{j \in J} \lambda_j f(a_1, \ldots, a_{i-1}, b_j, a_{i+1}, \ldots, a_m).$$

An arbitrary function $f: E^m \to F$ is symmetric *(where E and F are arbitrary sets, not just vector spaces or affine spaces) iff*

$$f(x_{\pi(1)}, \ldots, x_{\pi(m)}) = f(x_1, \ldots, x_m),$$

for every permutation $\pi: \{1, \ldots, m\} \to \{1, \ldots, m\}$.

It is immediately verified that a multilinear map is also a multiaffine map (viewing a vector space as an affine space).

Let us try to gain some intuition for what multilinear maps and multiaffine maps are, in the simple case where $E = \mathbf{A}$ and $F = \mathbf{A}$, the affine line associated with $\mathbf{R}$. Since $\mathbf{R}$ is of dimension 1, every linear form $f: \mathbf{R} \to \mathbf{R}$ must be of the form $x \mapsto \lambda x$, for some $\lambda \in \mathbf{R}$. An affine form $f: \mathbf{A} \to \mathbf{A}$ must be of the form $x \mapsto \lambda_1 x + \lambda_2$, for some $\lambda_1, \lambda_2 \in \mathbf{R}$. A bilinear form $f: \mathbf{R}^2 \to \mathbf{R}$ must be of the form

$$(x_1, x_2) \mapsto \lambda x_1 x_2,$$

for some $\lambda \in \mathbf{R}$, and a little thinking shows that a biaffine form $f: \mathbf{A}^2 \to \mathbf{A}$ must be of the form

$$(x_1, x_2) \mapsto \lambda_1 x_1 x_2 + \lambda_2 x_1 + \lambda_3 x_2 + \lambda_3,$$

for some $\lambda_1, \lambda_2, \lambda_3, \lambda_4 \in \mathbf{R}$. For any $n \geq 2$, an n-linear form $f : \mathbf{R}^n \to \mathbf{R}$ must be of the form

$$(x_1, \ldots, x_n) \mapsto \lambda x_1 \cdots x_n.$$

What about an n-affine form $f : \mathbf{A}^n \to \mathbf{A}$?

The next lemma will show that an n-affine form can be expressed as the sum of $2^n - 1$ k-linear forms, where $1 \leq k \leq n$, plus a constant. Thus, we see that the main difference between multilinear forms and multiaffine forms is that multilinear forms are *homogeneous* in their arguments, whereas multiaffine forms are not, but they are sums of homogeneous forms. A good example of n-affine forms is the elementary symmetric functions. Given n variables $x_1, \ldots, x_n$, for each k, $0 \leq k \leq n$, we define the kth *elementary symmetric function* $\sigma_k(x_1, \ldots, x_n)$, for short, σ_k, as follows:

$$\sigma_0 = 1;$$

$$\sigma_1 = x_1 + \cdots + x_n;$$

$$\sigma_2 = x_1 x_2 + x_1 x_3 + \cdots + x_1 x_n + x_2 x_3 + \cdots + x_{n-1} x_n;$$

$$\sigma_k = \sum_{1 \leq i_1 < \ldots < i_k \leq n} x_{i_1} \cdots x_{i_k};$$

$$\sigma_n = x_1 x_2 \cdots x_n.$$

A concise way to express σ_k is as follows:

$$\sigma_k = \sum_{\substack{I \subseteq \{1, \ldots, n\} \\ |I| = k}} \left(\prod_{i \in I} x_i \right).$$

Note that σ_k consists of a sum of

$$\binom{n}{k} = \frac{n!}{k!(n-k)!}$$

terms of the form $x_{i_1} \cdots x_{i_k}$. As a consequence,

$$\sigma_k(x, x, \ldots, x) = \binom{n}{k} x^k.$$

Clearly, each σ_k is symmetric.

We will prove a generalization of Lemma 2.7.2, characterizing multiaffine maps in terms of multilinear maps. The proof is more complicated than might be expected, but luckily, an adaptation of Cartan's use of "successive differences" allows us to overcome the complications.

In order to understand where the proof of the next lemma comes from, let us consider the special case of a biaffine map $f : E^2 \to F$, where F is a vector space. Because f is biaffine, note that

$$f(a_1 + \vec{v_1}, a_2 + \vec{v_2}) - f(a_1, a_2 + \vec{v_2}) = g(\vec{v_1}, a_2 + \vec{v_2})$$

is a linear map in $\vec{v_1}$, and as a difference of affine maps in $a_2 + \vec{v_2}$, it is affine in $a_2 + \vec{v_2}$. But then, we have

$$g(\vec{v_1}, a_2 + \vec{v_2}) = g(\vec{v_1}, a_2) + h_1(\vec{v_1}, \vec{v_2}),$$

where $h_1(\vec{v_1}, \vec{v_2})$ is linear in $\vec{v_2}$. Thus, we have

$$f(a_1 + \vec{v_1}, a_2 + \vec{v_2}) - f(a_1, a_2 + \vec{v_2}) = f(a_1 + \vec{v_1}, a_2) - f(a_1, a_2) + h_1(\vec{v_1}, \vec{v_2}),$$

that is,

$$f(a_1 + \vec{v_1}, a_2 + \vec{v_2}) = f(a_1, a_2) + h_1(\vec{v_1}, \vec{v_2}) + f(a_1, a_2 + \vec{v_2}) - f(a_1, a_2)$$
$$+ f(a_1 + \vec{v_1}, a_2) - f(a_1, a_2).$$

Since

$$g(\vec{v_1}, a_2 + \vec{v_2}) - g(\vec{v_1}, a_2) = h_1(\vec{v_1}, \vec{v_2}),$$

where both $g(\vec{v_1}, a_2 + \vec{v_2})$ and $g(\vec{v_1}, a_2)$ are linear in $\vec{v_1}$, $h_1(\vec{v_1}, \vec{v_2})$ is also linear in $\vec{v_1}$, and since we already know that $h_1(\vec{v_1}, \vec{v_2})$ is linear in $\vec{v_2}$, then h_1 is bilinear. But $f(a_1, a_2 + \vec{v_2}) - f(a_1, a_2)$ is linear in $\vec{v_2}$, and $f(a_1 + \vec{v_1}, a_2) - f(a_1, a_2)$ is linear in $\vec{v_1}$, which shows that we can write

$$f(a_1 + \vec{v_1}, a_2 + \vec{v_2}) = f(a_1, a_2) + h_1(\vec{v_1}, \vec{v_2}) + h_2(\vec{v_1}) + h_3(\vec{v_2}),$$

where h_1 is bilinear, and h_2 and h_3 are linear. The uniqueness of h_1 is clear, and as a consequence, the uniqueness of h_2 and h_3 follows easily.

The above argument uses the crucial fact that the expression

$$f(a_1 + \vec{v_1}, a_2 + \vec{v_2}) - f(a_1, a_2 + \vec{v_2}) - f(a_1 + \vec{v_1}, a_2) + f(a_1, a_2) = h_1(\vec{v_1}, \vec{v_2}),$$

is bilinear. Thus, we are led to consider differences of the form

$$\Delta_{\vec{v_1}} f(a_1, a_2) = f(a_1 + \vec{v_1}, a_2) - f(a_1, a_2).$$

The slight trick is that if we compute the difference

$$\Delta_{\vec{v_2}} \Delta_{\vec{v_1}} f(a_1, a_2) = \Delta_{\vec{v_1}} f(a_1, a_2 + \vec{v_2}) - \Delta_{\vec{v_1}} f(a_1, a_2),$$

where we incremented the *second* argument instead of the first argument as in the previous step, we get

$$\Delta_{\vec{v_2}} \Delta_{\vec{v_1}} f(a_1, a_2) = f(a_1 + \vec{v_1}, a_2 + \vec{v_2}) - f(a_1, a_2 + \vec{v_2})$$
$$- f(a_1 + \vec{v_1}, a_2) + f(a_1, a_2),$$

which is precisely the bilinear map $h_1(\vec{v_1}, \vec{v_2})$. This idea of using successive differences (where at each step, we move from argument k to argument $k + 1$) will be central to the proof of the next lemma.

Lemma 4.1.3

For every m-affine map $f: E^m \to F$, *there are* $2^m - 1$ *unique multilinear maps* $f_S: \overrightarrow{E}^k \to \overrightarrow{F}$, *where* $S \subseteq \{1, \ldots, m\}$, $k = |S|$, $S \neq \emptyset$, *such that*

$$f(a_1 + \overrightarrow{v_1}, \ldots, a_m + \overrightarrow{v_m}) = f(a_1, \ldots, a_m) + \sum_{\substack{S \subseteq \{1,\ldots,m\}, k=|S| \\ S=\{i_1,\ldots,i_k\}, k \geq 1}} f_S(\overrightarrow{v_{i_1}}, \ldots, \overrightarrow{v_{i_k}}),$$

for all $a_1 \ldots, a_m \in E$, *and all* $\overrightarrow{v_1}, \ldots, \overrightarrow{v_m} \in \overrightarrow{E}$.

Proof: It is extremely technical, and can be found in Appendix B, Section B.1.   ∎

When $f: E^m \to F$ is a symmetric m-affine map, we can obtain a more precise characterization in terms of m symmetric k-linear maps, $1 \leq k \leq m$.

Lemma 4.1.4

For every symmetric m-affine map $f: E^m \to F$, *there are m unique symmetric multilinear maps* $f_k: \overrightarrow{E}^k \to \overrightarrow{F}$, *where* $1 \leq k \leq m$, *such that*

$$f(a_1 + \overrightarrow{v_1}, \ldots, a_m + \overrightarrow{v_m}) = f(a_1, \ldots, a_m) + \sum_{k=1}^{m} \sum_{1 \leq i_1 < \ldots < i_k \leq m} f_k(\overrightarrow{v_{i_1}}, \ldots, \overrightarrow{v_{i_k}}),$$

for all $a_1 \ldots, a_m \in E$, *and all* $\overrightarrow{v_1}, \ldots, \overrightarrow{v_m} \in \overrightarrow{E}$.

Proof: Since f is symmetric, for every k, $1 \leq k \leq m$, for every sequence $\langle i_1 \ldots, i_k \rangle$ and $\langle j_1 \ldots, j_k \rangle$ such that $1 \leq i_1 < \ldots < i_k \leq m$ and $1 \leq j_1 < \ldots < j_k \leq m$, there is a permutation π such that $\pi(i_1) = j_1, \ldots, \pi(i_k) = j_k$, and since

$$f(x_{\pi(1)}, \ldots, x_{\pi(m)}) = f(x_1, \ldots, x_m),$$

by the uniqueness of the sum given by Lemma 4.1.3, we must have

$$f_{\{i_1,\ldots,i_k\}}(\overrightarrow{v_{j_1}}, \ldots, \overrightarrow{v_{j_k}}) = f_{\{j_1,\ldots,j_k\}}(\overrightarrow{v_{j_1}}, \ldots, \overrightarrow{v_{j_k}}),$$

which shows that

$$f_{\{i_1,\ldots,i_k\}} = f_{\{j_1,\ldots,j_k\}},$$

and then that each $f_{\{i_1,\ldots,i_k\}}$ is symmetric, and thus, letting $f_k = f_{\{1,\ldots,k\}}$, we have

$$f(a_1 + \overrightarrow{v_1}, \ldots, a_m + \overrightarrow{v_m}) = f(a_1, \ldots, a_m) + \sum_{k=1}^{m} \sum_{\substack{S \subseteq \{1,\ldots,m\} \\ S=\{i_1,\ldots,i_k\}}} f_k(\overrightarrow{v_{i_1}}, \ldots, \overrightarrow{v_{i_k}}),$$

for all $a_1, \ldots, a_m \in E$, and all $\overrightarrow{v_1}, \ldots, \overrightarrow{v_m} \in \overrightarrow{E}$.   ∎

Thus, a symmetric m-affine map is obtained by making symmetric in $\overrightarrow{v_1}, \ldots, \overrightarrow{v_m}$, the sum $f_m + f_{m-1} + \cdots + f_1$ of m symmetric k-linear maps, $1 \leq k \leq m$. The above lemma shows that it is equivalent to deal with symmetric m-affine maps, or with symmetrized sums $f_m + f_{m-1} + \cdots + f_1$ of symmetric k-linear maps, $1 \le k \le m$. In the next section, we will use multiaffine maps to define generalized polynomial functions from an affine space to another affine space.

4.2   Affine Polynomials and Polar Forms

The beauty and usefulness of symmetric affine maps lies in the fact that these maps can be used to define the notion of a polynomial function from an affine (vector) space E of any dimension to an affine (vector) space F of any dimension. In the special case where $E = \mathbf{A}^n$ and $F = \mathbf{A}$, this notion is actually equivalent to the notion of polynomial function induced by a polynomial in n variables. The added benefit is that we achieve a "multilinearization," and also that we can define (parameterized) "polynomial curves" in a very elegant and convenient manner. Such an approach, sometimes called "blossoming" (a term introduced by Ramshaw, who was among the first to use it in the context of curve and surface representation), also leads to an elegant and effective presentation of the main algorithms used in CAGD, in particular splines.

Definition 4.2.1

Given two affine spaces E and F, an affine polynomial function of polar degree m, *or for short an* affine polynomial of polar degree m, *is a map $h\colon E \to F$, such that there is some symmetric m-affine map $f\colon E^m \to F$, called the m-polar form of h, with*

$$h(a) = f(\underbrace{a, \ldots, a}_{m}),$$

for all $a \in E$. A homogeneous polynomial function of degree m *is a map $h\colon \vec{E} \to \vec{F}$, such that there is some nonnull symmetric m-linear map $f\colon \vec{E^m} \to \vec{F}$, called the polar form of h, with*

$$h(\vec{v}) = f(\underbrace{\vec{v}, \ldots, \vec{v}}_{m}),$$

for all $\vec{v} \in \vec{E}$. A polynomial function of polar degree m *is a map $h\colon \vec{E} \to \vec{F}$, such that there are m symmetric k-linear maps $f_k\colon \vec{E^k} \to \vec{F}$, $1 \le k \le m$, and some $f_0 \in \vec{F}$, with*

$$h(\vec{v}) = f_m(\underbrace{\vec{v}, \ldots, \vec{v}}_{m}) + f_{m-1}(\underbrace{\vec{v}, \ldots, \vec{v}}_{m-1}) + \cdots + f_1(\vec{v}) + f_0,$$

for all $\vec{v} \in \vec{E}$.

The definition of a homogeneous polynomial function of degree m given in Definition 4.2.1 is the definition given by Cartan [16]. The definition of a polynomial function of polar degree m given in Definition 4.2.1 is almost the definition given by Cartan [16], except that we allow any of the multilinear maps f_i to be null, whereas Cartan does not. Thus, instead of defining polynomial maps of degree exactly m (as Cartan does), we define polynomial maps of degree at most m.

For example, if $\vec{E} = \mathbf{R}^n$ and $\vec{F} = \mathbf{R}$, we have the bilinear map $f\colon (\mathbf{R}^n)^2 \to \mathbf{R}$ (called the *inner product*), defined such that

$$f((x_1, \ldots, x_n), (y_1, \ldots, y_n)) = x_1 y_1 + x_2 y_2 + \cdots + x_n y_n.$$

The corresponding polynomial $h\colon \mathbf{R}^n \to \mathbf{R}$, such that

$$h(x_1, \ldots, x_n) = x_1^2 + x_2^2 + \cdots + x_n^2,$$

is a polynomial of total degree 2 in n variables.

However, the triaffine map $f\colon \mathbf{R}^3 \to \mathbf{R}$, defined such that

$$f(x, y, z) = xy + yz + xz,$$

induces the polynomial $h\colon \mathbf{R} \to \mathbf{R}$ such that

$$h(x) = 3x^2,$$

which is of polar degree 3 but a polynomial of degree 2 in x.

We adopt the more inclusive definition of a polynomial function (of polar degree m) because it is more convenient algorithmically, and because it makes the correspondence with multiaffine polar forms nicer. From the point of view of terminology, it is cumbersome to constantly have to say "polar degree" rather than degree, although degree is confusing (and wrong, from the point of view of algebraic geometry). Nevertheless, we will usually allow ourselves this abuse of language, having sufficiently forewarned you.

Clearly, if a map $h\colon \vec{E} \to \vec{F}$ is a polynomial function of polar degree m defined by m symmetric k-linear maps f_k, and by f_0, then f is also defined by the symmetric m-affine map

$$g(\vec{v_1}, \ldots, \vec{v_m}) = \sum_{k=1}^{m} \binom{m}{k}^{-1} \left(\sum_{1 \leq i_1 < \ldots < i_k \leq m} f_k(\vec{v_{i_1}}, \ldots, \vec{v_{i_k}}) \right) + f_0.$$

Conversely, in view of Lemma 4.1.4, if a map $h\colon \vec{E} \to \vec{F}$ is defined by some symmetric m-affine map $f\colon \vec{E^m} \to \vec{F}$, with

$$h(\vec{v}) = f(\vec{v}, \ldots, \vec{v}),$$

for all $\vec{v} \in \vec{E}$, then h is also defined by the m symmetric k-linear maps $g_k = \binom{m}{k} f_k$ and $g_0 = f(\vec{0}, \ldots, \vec{0})$, where $f_m, \ldots, f_1$ are the unique (symmetric) multilinear maps associated with f, and $g_0 = f(\vec{0}, \ldots, \vec{0})$. Thus, a polynomial function h of polar degree m can be defined by a symmetric m-affine map $f: \overrightarrow{E^m} \to \overrightarrow{F}$. This is the definition commonly used by the CAGD community.

Let us see what homogeneous polynomials of degree m are, when $\overrightarrow{E}$ is a vector space of finite dimension n, and $\overrightarrow{F}$ is a vector space (if you are nervous, assume for simplicity that $\overrightarrow{F} = \mathbf{R}$). Let $(\overrightarrow{e_1}, \ldots, \overrightarrow{e_n})$ be a basis of $\overrightarrow{E}$.

Lemma 4.2.2

Given any vector space $\overrightarrow{E}$ of finite dimension n, and any vector space $\overrightarrow{F}$, for any basis $(\overrightarrow{e_1}, \ldots, \overrightarrow{e_n})$ of $\overrightarrow{E}$, for any symmetric multilinear map $f: \overrightarrow{E^m} \to \overrightarrow{F}$, for any m vectors

$$\overrightarrow{v_j} = v_{1,j}\overrightarrow{e_1} + \cdots + v_{n,j}\overrightarrow{e_n} \in \overrightarrow{E},$$

we have

$$f(\overrightarrow{v_1}, \ldots, \overrightarrow{v_m})$$

$$= \sum_{\substack{I_1 \cup \cdots \cup I_n = \{1,\ldots,m\} \\ I_i \cap I_j = \emptyset,\, i \neq j \\ 1 \leq i,j \leq n}} \left(\prod_{i_1 \in I_1} v_{1,i_1} \right) \cdots \left(\prod_{i_n \in I_n} v_{n,i_n} \right) f(\underbrace{\overrightarrow{e_1}, \ldots, \overrightarrow{e_1}}_{|I_1|}, \ldots, \underbrace{\overrightarrow{e_n}, \ldots, \overrightarrow{e_n}}_{|I_n|}),$$

and for any $\overrightarrow{v} \in \overrightarrow{E}$, the homogeneous polynomial function h associated with f is given by

$$h(\overrightarrow{v}) = \sum_{\substack{k_1 + \cdots + k_n = m \\ 0 \leq k_i,\, 1 \leq i \leq n}} \binom{m}{k_1, \ldots, k_n} v_1^{k_1} \cdots v_n^{k_n} f(\underbrace{\overrightarrow{e_1}, \ldots, \overrightarrow{e_1}}_{k_1}, \ldots, \underbrace{\overrightarrow{e_n}, \ldots, \overrightarrow{e_n}}_{k_n}).$$

Proof: By multilinearity of f, we have

$$f(\overrightarrow{v_1}, \ldots, \overrightarrow{v_m}) = \sum_{(i_1,\ldots,i_m) \in \{1,\ldots,n\}^m} v_{i_1,1} \cdots v_{i_m,m} f(\overrightarrow{e_{i_1}}, \ldots, \overrightarrow{e_{i_m}}).$$

Since f is symmetric, we can reorder the basis vector arguments of f, and this amounts to choosing n disjoint sets $I_1, \ldots, I_n$ such that $I_1 \cup \cdots \cup I_n = \{1, \ldots, m\}$, where each I_j specifies which arguments of f are the basis vector $\overrightarrow{e_j}$. Thus, we get

$$f(\overrightarrow{v_1}, \ldots, \overrightarrow{v_m})$$

$$= \sum_{\substack{I_1 \cup \cdots \cup I_n = \{1,\ldots,m\} \\ I_i \cap I_j = \emptyset,\, i \neq j \\ 1 \leq i,j \leq n}} \left(\prod_{i_1 \in I_1} v_{1,i_1} \right) \cdots \left(\prod_{i_n \in I_n} v_{n,i_n} \right) f(\underbrace{\overrightarrow{e_1}, \ldots, \overrightarrow{e_1}}_{|I_1|}, \ldots, \underbrace{\overrightarrow{e_n}, \ldots, \overrightarrow{e_n}}_{|I_n|}).$$

When we calculate $h(\overrightarrow{v}) = f(\underbrace{\overrightarrow{v}, \ldots, \overrightarrow{v}}_{m})$, we get the same product $v_1^{k_1} \cdots v_n^{k_n}$ a multiple number of times, which is the number of ways of choosing n disjoints sets I_j, each of cardinality k_i, where $k_1 + \cdots + k_n = m$, which is precisely $\binom{m}{k_1,\ldots,k_n}$, which explains the second formula. ∎

Thus, Lemma 4.2.2 shows that we can write $h(\vec{v})$ as

$$h(\vec{v}) = \sum_{\substack{k_1+\cdots+k_n=m \\ 0 \le k_i, \, 1 \le i \le n}} v_1^{k_1} \cdots v_n^{k_n} \, c_{k_1,\ldots,k_n},$$

for some "coefficients" $c_{k_1,\ldots,k_n} \in \vec{F}$, which are vectors. When $\vec{F} = \mathbf{R}$, the homogeneous polynomial function h of degree m in n arguments $v_1, \ldots, v_n$ agrees with the notion of a polynomial function defined by a homogeneous polynomial. Indeed, h is the homogeneous polynomial function induced by the homogeneous polynomial of degree m in the variables $X_1, \ldots, X_n$,

$$\sum_{\substack{(k_1,\ldots,k_n), k_j \ge 0 \\ k_1+\cdots+k_n=m}} c_{k_1,\ldots,k_n} X_1^{k_1} \cdots X_n^{k_n}.$$

Thus, when $\vec{E} = \mathbf{R}^n$ and $\vec{F} = \mathbf{R}$, the notion of an (affine) polynomial of polar degree m in n arguments agrees with the notion of a polynomial function induced by a polynomial of degree $\le m$ in n variables $(X_1, \ldots, X_n)$.

Using the characterization of symmetric multiaffine maps given by Lemma 4.1.4 and Lemma 4.2.2, we obtain the following useful characterization of multiaffine maps $f\colon E \to F$, when E is of finite dimension.

Lemma 4.2.3

Given any affine space E of finite dimension n, and any affine space F, for any basis $(\vec{e_1}, \ldots, \vec{e_n})$ of $\vec{E}$, for any symmetric multiaffine map $f\colon E^m \to F$, for any m vectors

$$\vec{v_j} = v_{1,j}\vec{e_1} + \cdots + v_{n,j}\vec{e_n} \in \vec{E},$$

for any points $a_1, \ldots, a_m \in E$, we have

$$f(a_1 + \vec{v_1}, \ldots, a_m + \vec{v_m})$$

$$= b + \sum_{1 \le p \le m} \sum_{\substack{I_1 \cup \cdots \cup I_n = \{1,\ldots,p\} \\ I_i \cap I_j = \emptyset, \, i \ne j \\ 1 \le i, j \le n}} \left(\prod_{i_1 \in I_1} v_{1,i_1} \right) \cdots \left(\prod_{i_n \in I_n} v_{n,i_n} \right) \vec{w}_{|I_1|,\ldots,|I_n|},$$

for some $b \in F$, and some $\vec{w}_{|I_1|,\ldots,|I_n|} \in \vec{F}$, and for any $a \in E$, and $\vec{v} \in \vec{E}$, the affine polynomial function h associated with f is given by

$$h(a + \vec{v}) = b + \sum_{1 \le p \le m} \sum_{\substack{k_1+\cdots+k_n=p \\ 0 \le k_i, \, 1 \le i \le n}} v_1^{k_1} \cdots v_n^{k_n} \, \vec{w}_{k_1,\ldots,k_n},$$

for some $b \in F$, and some $\vec{w}_{k_1,\ldots,k_n} \in \vec{F}$.

Lemma 4.2.3 shows the crucial role played by homogeneous polynomials. We could have taken the form of an affine map given by this lemma as a definition, when E is of finite dimension.

When $\vec{F}$ is a vector space of dimension greater than 1, or an affine space, you should not confuse such polynomial *functions* with the polynomials defined as usual, say, in Lang [47], Artin [1], or Mac Lane and Birkhoff [52]. The standard approach is to define formal polynomials whose coefficients belong to a (commutative) ring. Then, it is shown how a polynomial defines a polynomial function. In the present approach, we define directly certain functions that behave like generalized polynomial functions. Another major difference between the polynomial functions of Definition 4.2.1 and formal polynomials is that formal polynomials can be added and multiplied. Although we can make sense of addition as affine combination in the case of polynomial functions having an affine space as range, multiplication does not make any sense.

Nevertheless, this generalization of the notion of a polynomial function is very fruitful, as the next example will show. Indeed, we can define (parameterized) *polynomial curves in polar form*. Recall that the canonical affine space associated with the field **R** is denoted as **A**, unless confusions arise.

Definition 4.2.4

A *(parameterized)* polynomial curve in polar form of degree m is an affine polynomial map $F : \mathbf{A} \to \mathcal{E}$ of polar degree m, defined by its m-polar form, *which is some symmetric m-affine map $f : \mathbf{A}^m \to \mathcal{E}$, where $\mathbf{A}$ is the real affine line, and $\mathcal{E}$ is any affine space (of dimension at least 2). Given any $r, s \in \mathbf{A}$, with $r < s$, a (parameterized) polynomial curve segment $F([r, s])$ in polar form of degree m is the restriction $F : [r, s] \to \mathcal{E}$ of an affine polynomial curve $F : \mathbf{A} \to \mathcal{E}$ in polar form of degree m. We define the* trace of F as $F(\mathbf{A})$, *and the* trace of $F[r, s]$ as $F([r, s])$.

Typically, the affine space $\mathcal{E}$ is the real affine space $\mathbf{A}^3$ of dimension 3. Definition 4.2.4 is not the standard definition of a parameterized polynomial curve, as given in Section 3.1 (see Definition 3.1.1). However, Definition 4.2.4 turns out to be more general and equivalent to Definition 3.1.1 when $\mathcal{E}$ is of finite dimension, and it is also more convenient for the purpose of designing curves satisfying some simple geometric constraints.

Remark: When defining polynomial curves, it is convenient to denote the polynomial map defining the curve by an uppercase letter, such as $F : \mathbf{A} \to \mathcal{E}$, and the polar form of F by the same but lowercase letter, f. It would then be confusing to denote the affine space that is the range of the maps F and f also as F, and thus, we denote it as $\mathcal{E}$ (or at least, we use a letter different from the letter used to denote the polynomial map defining the curve). Also note that we defined a polynomial curve in polar form of degree at most m, rather than a polynomial curve in polar form of degree exactly m, because an affine polynomial map f of polar degree m may end up being degenerate, in the sense that it could be equivalent to a polynomial map of lower polar degree (the symmetric multilinear maps $f_m, f_{m-1}, \ldots, f_{m-k+1}$ involved in the unique decomposition of f as a sum of multilinear maps may be identically null, in which case, f is also defined by a polynomial map of polar degree $m - k$). For convenience, we will allow ourselves the abuse of language where we abbreviate "polynomial curve in polar form" to "polynomial curve."

Thus, we are led to consider symmetric m-affine maps $f: \mathbf{A}^m \to F$, where F is any affine space, for example, $F = \mathbf{A}^3$.

4.3   Polynomial Curves and Control Points

In Section 3.1, we considered the case of symmetric biaffine functions $f: \mathbf{A}^2 \to \mathbf{A}^3$ and symmetric triaffine functions $f: \mathbf{A}^3 \to \mathbf{A}^3$, and we saw a pattern emerge. Let us now consider the general case of a symmetric m-affine map $f: \mathbf{A}^m \to F$, where F is any affine space. Let us pick an affine basis (r, s) in $\mathbf{A}$, with $r \neq s$, and let us compute

$$f(t_1, \ldots, t_m) = f((1 - \lambda_1)r + \lambda_1 s, \ldots, (1 - \lambda_m)r + \lambda_m s).$$

Since f is symmetric and m-affine, by a simple induction, we get

$$f(t_1, \ldots, t_m) = f((1 - \lambda_1)r + \lambda_1 s, t_2, \ldots, t_m)$$

$$= (1 - \lambda_1)\, f(r, t_2, \ldots, t_m) + \lambda_1\, f(s, t_2, \ldots, t_m)$$

$$= \sum_{k=0}^{m} \sum_{\substack{I \cup J = \{1,\ldots,m\} \\ I \cap J = \emptyset,\, |J| = k}} \prod_{i \in I}(1 - \lambda_i) \prod_{j \in J} \lambda_j\; f(\underbrace{r, \ldots, r}_{m-k},\, \underbrace{s, \ldots, s}_{k}),$$

and since

$$\lambda_i = \frac{t_i - r}{s - r}, \quad \text{for } 1 \leq i \leq m,$$

we get

$$f(t_1, \ldots, t_m) = \sum_{k=0}^{m} \sum_{\substack{I \cup J = \{1,\ldots,m\} \\ I \cap J = \emptyset,\, |J| = k}} \prod_{i \in I}\left(\frac{s - t_i}{s - r}\right) \prod_{j \in J}\left(\frac{t_j - r}{s - r}\right)\; f(\underbrace{r, \ldots, r}_{m-k},\, \underbrace{s, \ldots, s}_{k}).$$

The coefficient

$$p_k(t_1, \ldots, t_m) = \sum_{\substack{I \cup J = \{1,\ldots,m\} \\ I \cap J = \emptyset,\, |J| = k}} \prod_{i \in I}\left(\frac{s - t_i}{s - r}\right) \prod_{j \in J}\left(\frac{t_j - r}{s - r}\right)$$

of

$$f(\underbrace{r, \ldots, r}_{m-k},\, \underbrace{s, \ldots, s}_{k})$$

is obviously a symmetric m-affine function, and these functions add up to 1, as it is easily verified by expanding the product

$$\prod_{i=1}^{i=m} \left(\frac{s-t_i}{s-r} + \frac{t_i-r}{s-r} \right) = 1.$$

Thus, we showed that every symmetric m-affine map $f\colon \mathbf{A}^m \to F$ is completely determined by the sequence of $m+1$ points

$$f(\underbrace{r,\ldots,r}_{m-k},\ \underbrace{s,\ldots,s}_{k}),$$

where $r \neq s$ are elements of $\mathbf{A}$.

Conversely, given any sequence of $m+1$ points $a_0, \ldots, a_m \in F$, the map

$$(t_1, \ldots, t_m) \mapsto \sum_{k=0}^{m} \ \sum_{\substack{I \cup J = \{1,\ldots,m\} \\ I \cap J = \emptyset,\ |J|=k}} \prod_{i \in I} \left(\frac{s-t_i}{s-r} \right) \prod_{j \in J} \left(\frac{t_j-r}{s-r} \right) a_k$$

is symmetric m-affine, and we have

$$f(\underbrace{r,\ldots,r}_{m-k},\ \underbrace{s,\ldots,s}_{k}) = a_k.$$

The points

$$a_k = f(\underbrace{r,\ldots,r}_{m-k},\ \underbrace{s,\ldots,s}_{k})$$

are called *control points*, or *Bézier control points*, and as we have already said several times, they play a major role in the de Casteljau algorithm and its extensions.

The polynomial function associated with f is given by $h(t) = f(t, \ldots, t)$, that is,

$$h(t) = \sum_{k=0}^{m} \binom{m}{k} \left(\frac{s-t}{s-r} \right)^{m-k} \left(\frac{t-r}{s-r} \right)^{k} f(\underbrace{r,\ldots,r}_{m-k},\ \underbrace{s,\ldots,s}_{k}).$$

The polynomials

$$B_k^m[r,s](t) = \binom{m}{k} \left(\frac{s-t}{s-r} \right)^{m-k} \left(\frac{t-r}{s-r} \right)^{k}$$

are the *Bernstein polynomials of degree m over* $[r,s]$. These polynomials form a *partition of unity*:

$$\sum_{k=0}^{m} B_k^m[r,s](t) = 1.$$

This is shown using the binomial expansion formula:

$$\sum_{k=0}^{m} B_k^m[r,s](t) = \sum_{k=0}^{m} \binom{m}{k} \left(\frac{s-t}{s-r}\right)^{m-k} \left(\frac{t-r}{s-r}\right)^{k} = \left(\frac{s-t}{s-r} + \frac{t-r}{s-r}\right)^{m} = 1.$$

For $r = 0$ and $s = 1$, since $t_i = \lambda_i$, some simplifications take place, and the polynomial function h associated with f is given by

$$h(t) = \sum_{k=0}^{m} \binom{m}{k} (1-t)^{m-k} t^k \, f(\underbrace{0,\ldots,0}_{m-k}, \underbrace{1,\ldots,1}_{k}).$$

The polynomials

$$B_k^m(t) = \binom{m}{k} (1-t)^{m-k} t^k$$

are the *Bernstein polynomials of degree m (over $[0,1]$)*. It is not hard to show that they form a basis for the vector space of polynomials of degree $\leq m$. Clearly, we have

$$B_k^m[r,s](t) = B_k^m\left(\frac{t-r}{s-r}\right).$$

Summarizing the above considerations, we show the following lemma.

Lemma 4.3.1

Given any sequence of $m+1$ points $a_0, \ldots, a_m$ in some affine space $\mathcal{E}$, there is a unique polynomial curve $F: A \to \mathcal{E}$ of degree m, whose polar form $f: A^m \to \mathcal{E}$ satisfies the conditions

$$f(\underbrace{r,\ldots,r}_{m-k}, \underbrace{s,\ldots,s}_{k}) = a_k,$$

(where $r, s \in A$, $r \neq s$). Furthermore, the polar form f of F is given by the formula

$$f(t_1, \ldots, t_m) = \sum_{k=0}^{m} \sum_{\substack{I \cup J = \{1,\ldots,m\} \\ I \cap J = \emptyset, \, |J| = k}} \prod_{i \in I} \left(\frac{s - t_i}{s - r}\right) \prod_{j \in J} \left(\frac{t_j - r}{s - r}\right) a_k,$$

and $F(t)$ is given by the formula

$$F(t) = \sum_{k=0}^{m} B_k^m[r,s](t) a_k,$$

where the polynomials

$$B_k^m[r,s](t) = \binom{m}{k} \left(\frac{s-t}{s-r}\right)^{m-k} \left(\frac{t-r}{s-r}\right)^{k}$$

are the Bernstein polynomials of degree m over $[r, s]$.

Of course, we will come back to polynomial curves and the de Casteljau algorithm and its generalizations, but we hope that the above considerations are striking motivations for using polar forms.

4.4 Uniqueness of the Polar Form of an Affine Polynomial Map

Remarkably, we can prove in full generality that the polar form f defining an affine polynomial h of degree m is unique. We could use Cartan's proof in the case of polynomial functions, but we can give a slightly more direct proof that yields an explicit expression for f in terms of h. All the ingredients to prove this result are in Bourbaki [14] (Chapter A.I, Section 8.2, Proposition 2), and [15] (Chapter A.IV, Section 5.4, Proposition 3), but they are deeply buried!

We now prove a general lemma giving the polar form of a polynomial in terms of this polynomial. Before plunging into the proof of Lemma 4.4.1, you may want to verify that for a polynomial $h(X)$ of degree 2, the polar form is given by the identity

$$f(x_1, x_2) = \frac{1}{2}\left[4h\left(\frac{x_1 + x_2}{2}\right) - h(x_1) - h(x_2)\right].$$

You may also want to try working out on your own a formula giving the polar form for a polynomial $h(X)$ of degree 3. Note that when $h(X)$ is a homogeneous polynomial of degree 2, the above identity reduces to the (perhaps more familiar) identity

$$f(x_1, x_2) = \frac{1}{2}\left[h(x_1 + x_2) - h(x_1) - h(x_2)\right],$$

used for passing from a quadratic form to a bilinear form.

Lemma 4.4.1

Given two affine spaces E and F, for any polynomial function h of degree m, the polar form $f\colon E^m \to F$ of h is unique and is given by the following expression:

$$f(a_1, \ldots, a_m) = \frac{1}{m!}\left[\sum_{\substack{H \subseteq \{1,\ldots,m\} \\ k=|H|, k\geq 1}} (-1)^{m-k}\, k^m\, h\left(\frac{\sum_{i\in H} a_i}{k}\right)\right].$$

Proof: It is quite technical, and can be found in Appendix B (Section B.1). ■

It should be noted that Lemma 4.4.1 is very general, since it applies to arbitrary affine spaces, even of infinite dimension (for example, Hilbert spaces). The expression of Lemma 4.4.1 is far from being economical, since it contains $2^m - 1$ terms. In particular cases, it is often possible to reduce the number of terms.

4.5   Polarizing Polynomials in One or Several Variables

We now use Lemma 4.4.1 to show that polynomials in one or several variables are uniquely defined by polar forms that are multiaffine maps. We first show the following simple lemma.

Lemma 4.5.1

1. For every polynomial $p(X) \in \mathbf{R}[X]$, of degree $\leq m$, there is a symmetric m-affine form $f: \mathbf{R}^m \to \mathbf{R}$, such that $p(x) = f(x, x, \ldots, x)$ for all $x \in \mathbf{R}$. If $p(X) \in \mathbf{R}[X]$ is a homogeneous polynomial of degree exactly m, then the symmetric m-affine form f is multilinear.

2. For every polynomial $p(X_1, \ldots, X_n) \in \mathbf{R}[X_1, \ldots, X_n]$, of total degree $\leq m$, there is a symmetric m-affine form $f: (\mathbf{R}^n)^m \to \mathbf{R}$, such that $p(x_1, \ldots, x_n) = f(x, x, \ldots, x)$, for all $x = (x_1, \ldots, x_n) \in \mathbf{R}^n$. If $p(X_1, \ldots, X_n) \in \mathbf{R}[X_1, \ldots, X_n]$ is a homogeneous polynomial of total degree exactly m, then f is a symmetric multilinear map $f: (\mathbf{R}^n)^m \to \mathbf{R}$.

Proof: (1) It is enough to prove it for a monomial of the form X^k, $k \leq m$. Clearly,

$$f(x_1, \ldots, x_m) = \frac{k!(m-k)!}{m!} \sigma_k$$

is a symmetric m-affine form satisfying the lemma (where σ_k is the kth elementary symmetric function, which consists of

$$\binom{m}{k} = \frac{m!}{k!(m-k)!}$$

terms), and when $k = m$, we get a multilinear map.

(2) It is enough to prove it for a homogeneous monomial of the form $X_1^{k_1} \cdots X_n^{k_n}$, where $k_i \geq 0$, and $k_1 + \cdots + k_n = d \leq m$. Let f be defined such that

$$f((x_{1,1}, \ldots, x_{n,1}), \ldots, (x_{1,m}, \ldots, x_{n,m}))$$

$$= \frac{k_1! \cdots k_n!(m-d)!}{m!} \sum_{\substack{I_1 \cup \cdots \cup I_n \subseteq \{1,\ldots,m\} \\ I_i \cap I_j = \emptyset,\, i \neq j,\, |I_j| = k_j}} \left(\prod_{i_1 \in I_1} x_{1,i_1}\right) \cdots \left(\prod_{i_n \in I_n} x_{n,i_n}\right).$$

The idea is to split any subset of $\{1, \ldots, m\}$ consisting of $d \leq m$ elements into n disjoint subsets $I_1, \ldots, I_n$, where I_j is of size k_j (and with $k_1 + \cdots + k_n = d$). There are

$$\frac{m!}{k_1! \cdots k_n!(m-d)!} = \binom{m}{k_1, \ldots, k_n, m-d}$$

such families of n disjoint sets, where $k_1 + \cdots + k_n = d \leq m$. Indeed, this is the number of ways of choosing $n + 1$ disjoint subsets of $\{1, \ldots, m\}$ consisting, respectively, of $k_1, \ldots, k_n$, and $m - d$ elements, where $k_1 + \cdots + k_n = d$. We can also argue as follows: There are $\binom{m}{k_1}$ choices for the first subset I_1 of size k_1, and then $\binom{m-k_1}{k_2}$ choices for the second subset I_2 of size k_2, and so on, and finally,

$$\binom{m - (k_1 + \cdots + k_{n-1})}{k_n}$$

choices for the last subset I_n of size k_n. After some simple arithmetic, the number of such choices is indeed

$$\frac{m!}{k_1! \cdots k_n!(m-d)!} = \binom{m}{k_1, \ldots, k_n, m-d}.$$

It is clear that f is symmetric m-affine in $x_1, \ldots, x_m$, where $x_j = (x_{1,j}, \ldots, x_{n,j})$, and that

$$f(\underbrace{x, \ldots, x}_{m}) = x_1^{k_1} \cdots x_n^{k_n},$$

for all $x = (x_1, \ldots, x_n) \in \mathbf{R}^n$. Also, when $d = m$, it is easy to see that f is multilinear. ∎

As an example, if

$$p(X) = X^3 + 3X^2 + 5X - 1,$$

we get

$$f(x_1, x_2, x_3) = x_1 x_2 x_3 + x_1 x_2 + x_1 x_3 + x_2 x_3 + \frac{5}{3}(x_1 + x_2 + x_3) - 1.$$

When $n = 2$, which corresponds to the case of surfaces, we can give an expression that is easier to understand. Writing $U = X_1$ and $V = X_2$, to minimize the number of subscripts, given the monomial $U^h V^k$, with $h + k = d \leq m$, we get

$$f((u_1, v_1), \ldots, (u_m, v_m)) = \frac{h!k!(m - (h+k))!}{m!} \cdot \sum_{\substack{I \cup J \subseteq \{1, \ldots, m\} \\ I \cap J = \emptyset \\ |I| = h, |J| = k}} \left(\prod_{i \in I} u_i\right) \left(\prod_{j \in J} v_j\right).$$

For a concrete example involving two variables, if

$$p(U, V) = UV + U^2 + V^2,$$

we get

$$f((u_1, v_1), (u_2, v_2)) = \frac{u_1 v_2 + u_2 v_1}{2} + u_1 u_2 + v_1 v_2.$$

We can now prove the following theorem showing a certain equivalence between polynomials and multiaffine maps.

Theorem 4.5.2

There is an equivalence between polynomials in $\mathbf{R}[X_1, \ldots, X_n]$, of total degree $\leq m$, and symmetric m-affine maps $f: (\mathbf{R}^n)^m \to \mathbf{R}$, in the following sense:

1. *If $f: (\mathbf{R}^n)^m \to \mathbf{R}$ is a symmetric m-affine map, then the function $p: \mathbf{R}^n \to \mathbf{R}$, defined such that*

$$p(x_1, \ldots, x_n) = f(x, x, \ldots, x)$$

    for all $x = (x_1, \ldots, x_n) \in \mathbf{R}^n$, is a polynomial (function) corresponding to a unique polynomial $p(X_1, \ldots, X_n) \in \mathbf{R}[X_1, \ldots, X_n]$ of total degree $\leq m$.

2. *For every polynomial $p(X_1, \ldots, X_n) \in \mathbf{R}[X_1, \ldots, X_n]$, of total degree $\leq m$, there is a unique symmetric m-affine map $f: (\mathbf{R}^n)^m \to \mathbf{R}$, such that*

$$p(x_1, \ldots, x_n) = f(x, x, \ldots, x)$$

    for all $x = (x_1, \ldots, x_n) \in \mathbf{R}^n$.

Furthermore, when $p(X_1, \ldots, X_n) \in \mathbf{R}[X_1, \ldots, X_n]$ is a homogeneous polynomial of total degree exactly m, f is a symmetric multilinear map $f: (\mathbf{R}^n)^m \to \mathbf{R}$, and conversely.

Proof: Part (1) is trivial. To prove part (2), observe that the existence of some symmetric m-affine map $f: (\mathbf{R}^n)^m \to \mathbf{R}$ with the desired property is given by Lemma 4.5.1, and the uniqueness of such an f is given by Lemma 4.4.1. ∎

We can now relate the definition of a (parameterized) polynomial curve in polar form of degree (at most) m given in Definition 4.2.4 to the more standard definition (Definition 3.1.1) given in Section 3.1.

First, we show that a standard polynomial curve of degree at most m, in the sense of Definition 3.1.1, is an affine polynomial curve of polar degree m, in the sense of Definition 4.2.4. Indeed, using Lemma 4.5.1, every polynomial $F_i(t)$ corresponds to a unique m-polar form $f_i: \mathbf{R}^m \to \mathbf{R}$, $1 \leq i \leq n$, and the map $f: \mathbf{A}^m \to \mathcal{E}$, defined such that

$$f(t_1, \ldots, t_m) = a_0 + f_1(t_1, \ldots, t_m)\vec{e_1} + \cdots + f_n(t_1, \ldots, t_m)\vec{e_n},$$

is clearly a symmetric affine map such that $F(t) = f(t, \ldots, t)$.

Conversely, when $\mathcal{E}$ is of finite dimension n, we show that an affine polynomial curve of polar degree m, in the sense of Definition 4.2.4, is a standard polynomial curve of degree at most m, in the sense of Definition 3.1.1. Assume that the affine polynomial curve F of polar degree m is defined by a polar form $f: \mathbf{A}^m \to \mathcal{E}$. Let

$r, s \in \mathbf{A}$, with $r < s$. Let us introduce the following abbreviations. We will denote

$$f(\underbrace{r, \ldots, r}_{m-k}, \underbrace{s, \ldots, s}_{k}),$$

as $f(r^{m-k} s^k)$, with

$$f(r^m) = f(\underbrace{r, \ldots, r}_{m})$$

and

$$f(s^m) = f(\underbrace{s, \ldots, s}_{m}).$$

Remark: The abbreviation $f(r^{m-k} s^k)$ can be justified rigorously in terms of symmetric tensor products (see Section 11.1).

By Lemma 4.3.1, the curve F is completely determined by the $m + 1$ points $b_k = f(r^{m-k} s^k)$, $0 \le k \le m$, and in fact, we showed that

$$f(t_1, \ldots, t_m) = \sum_{k=0}^{m} p_k(t_1, \ldots, t_m) \, f(r^{m-k} s^k),$$

where the coefficient

$$p_k(t_1, \ldots, t_m) = \sum_{\substack{I \cup J = \{1, \ldots, m\} \\ I \cap J = \emptyset, |J| = k}} \prod_{i \in I} \left(\frac{s - t_i}{s - r} \right) \prod_{j \in J} \left(\frac{t_j - r}{s - r} \right)$$

of $f(r^{m-k} s^k)$ is a symmetric m-affine function. Thus, if we let $(b_{k,1}, \ldots, b_{k,n})$ denote the coordinates of the point $b_k = f(r^{m-k} s^k)$ over the affine basis $(a_0, (\vec{e_1}, \ldots, \vec{e_n}))$, we have

$$F(t) = f(t, \ldots, t) = b_0 + \sum_{i=1}^{n} \left(\sum_{k=0}^{m} p_k(t, \ldots, t) b_{k,i} \right) \vec{e_i},$$

and since the $p_k(t, \ldots, t)$ are polynomials of degree $\le m$, this shows that F is a standard polynomial curve of degree at most m.

We will see later on how polar forms of polynomials simplify quite considerably the treatment of Bézier curves and splines, among other things.

We conclude this chapter by proving that the Bernstein polynomials $B_0^m(t), \ldots,$ $B_m^m(t)$ also form a basis of the polynomials of degree $\le m$. For this, we express each t^i, $0 \le i \le m$, in terms of the Bernstein polynomials $B_j^m(t)$ (over $[0, 1]$). Recall that the Bernstein polynomials $B_j^m(t)$ form a partition of unity:

$$\sum_{j=0}^{m} B_j^m(t) = 1.$$

Using this identity for $m - i$ (instead of m), where $0 \leq i \leq m$, we have

$$\sum_{j=0}^{m-i} B_j^{m-i}(t) = 1.$$

Multiplying both sides by t^i, we get

$$t^i = \sum_{j=0}^{m-i} t^i B_j^{m-i}(t).$$

However, we know that $B_j^{m-i}(t) = \binom{m-i}{j}(1-t)^{m-i-j}t^j$, and thus,

$$t^i B_j^{m-i}(t) = t^i \binom{m-i}{j}(1-t)^{m-i-j}t^j = \binom{m-i}{j}(1-t)^{m-(i+j)}t^{i+j}.$$

Since $B_{i+j}^m(t) = \binom{m}{i+j}(1-t)^{m-(i+j)}t^{i+j}$, we just have to prove that

$$\binom{m}{i}\binom{m-i}{j} = \binom{m}{i+j}\binom{i+j}{i},$$

to conclude that

$$t^i B_j^{m-i}(t) = \binom{m-i}{j}(1-t)^{m-(i+j)}t^{i+j} = \frac{\binom{i+j}{i}}{\binom{m}{i}} B_{i+j}^m(t).$$

The verification consists in showing that

$$\frac{m!}{(m-i)!i!}\frac{(m-i)!}{(m-(i+j))!j!} = \frac{m!}{(m-(i+j))!(i+j)!}\frac{(i+j)!}{j!i!},$$

which is indeed true! Thus, substituting

$$t^i B_j^{m-i}(t) = \frac{\binom{i+j}{i}}{\binom{m}{i}} B_{i+j}^m(t)$$

in

$$t^i = \sum_{j=0}^{m-i} t^i B_j^{m-i}(t),$$

we get

$$t^i = \sum_{j=0}^{m-i} \frac{\binom{i+j}{i}}{\binom{m}{i}} B_{i+j}^m(t).$$

Since $1, t, t^2, \ldots, t^m$ form a basis of the polynomials of degree $\leq m$, the $m+1$ Bernstein polynomials $B_0^m(t), \ldots, B_m^m(t)$ also form a basis of the polynomials of degree $\leq m$ (since they generate this space, and there are $m+1$ of them).

Problems

[20 pts]   **1.** Prove that for any $a, b \in \mathbf{R}$, the following identity holds for all $n \geq 0$:

$$(a+b)^n = \sum_{k=0}^{n} \binom{n}{k} a^k b^{n-k}.$$

More generally, for any $a_1, \ldots, a_m \in \mathbf{R}$, $m \geq 2$, and $n \geq 0$, prove the identity

$$(a_1 + \cdots + a_m)^n = \sum_{\substack{k_1 + \cdots + k_m = n \\ 0 \leq k_i \leq n}} \frac{n!}{k_1! \cdots k_m!} a_1^{k_1} \cdots a_m^{k_m}.$$

[20 pts]   **2.** Prove the following statement assumed in the proof of Lemma 4.1.3:

$$\Delta_{\overrightarrow{v_m}} \cdots \Delta_{\overrightarrow{v_1}} f(a)$$

$$= \sum_{k=0}^{m} (-1)^{m-k} \sum_{1 \leq i_1 < \ldots < i_k \leq m} f(a_1, \ldots, a_{i_1} + \overrightarrow{v_{i_1}}, \ldots, a_{i_k} + \overrightarrow{v_{i_k}}, \ldots, a_m).$$

[10 pts]   **3.** Show that the Bernstein polynomial

$$B_k^m(t) = \binom{m}{k} (1-t)^{m-k} t^k$$

reaches a maximum for $t = k/m$.

[20 pts]   **4.** Let $F: \mathbf{A} \to \mathcal{E}$ be a polynomial cubic curve. Prove that the polar form $f: \mathbf{A}^3 \to \mathcal{E}$ of F can be expressed as

$$f(u, v, w)$$

$$= \frac{1}{24} \left[27F\left(\frac{u+v+w}{3}\right) - F(u+v-w) - F(u+w-v) - F(v+w-u) \right]$$

[20 pts] 5. Let $F: \mathbf{A} \to \mathcal{E}$ be a polynomial cubic curve. Prove that the polar form $f: \mathbf{A}^3 \to \mathcal{E}$ of F can be expressed as

$$f(u, v, w) = \frac{(w-v)^2 F(u)}{3(w-u)(u-v)} + \frac{(w-u)^2 F(v)}{3(w-v)(v-u)} + \frac{(v-u)^2 F(w)}{3(v-w)(w-u)}.$$

Advice: There is no need to do horrendous calculations. Think hard!

[50 pts] 6. (a) Write a computer program taking a polynomial $F(X)$ of degree n (in one variable X), and returning its m-polar form f, where $n \leq m$. You may use Mathematica or any other language with symbolic facilities.

Estimate the complexity of your algorithm.

(b) Let

$$f_k^m = \frac{1}{\binom{m}{k}} \sum_{\substack{I \subseteq \{1,\ldots,m\} \\ |I|=k}} \left(\prod_{i \in I} t_i \right).$$

and $\sigma_k^m = \binom{m}{k} f_k^m$. Prove the following recurrence equations:

$$\sigma_k^m = \begin{cases} \sigma_k^{m-1} + t_m \sigma_{k-1}^{m-1} & \text{if } 1 \leq k \leq m; \\ 1 & \text{if } k = 0 \text{ and } m \geq 0; \\ 0 & \text{otherwise.} \end{cases}$$

Alternatively, show that f_k^m can be computed directly using the recurrence formula

$$f_k^m = \frac{(m-k)}{m} f_k^{m-1} + \frac{k}{m} t_m f_{k-1}^{m-1},$$

where $1 \leq k \leq m$.

Can you improve the complexity of the algorithm of question (a) if you just want to compute the polar values $f(0^{m-i}, 1^i)$, where $0 \leq i \leq m$?

[20 pts] 7. Plot the Bernstein polynomials $B_i^4(t)$, $0 \leq i \leq 4$, over $[0, 1]$.

[20 pts] 8. Give the matrix expressing the polynomials $1, t, t^2, t^3$ in terms of the Bernstein polynomials $B_0^3(t)$, $B_1^3(t)$, $B_2^3(t)$, $B_3^3(t)$. Show that in general,

$$B_i^m(t) = \sum_{j=i}^{m} (-1)^{j-i} \binom{m}{j} \binom{j}{i} t^j.$$

CHAPTER 5

Polynomial Curves as Bézier Curves

5.1   The de Casteljau Algorithm

In this chapter, the de Casteljau algorithm presented earlier for curves of degree 3 in Section 3.8 is generalized to polynomial curves of arbitrary degree m. The powerful method of subdivision is also discussed extensively. Some programs written in Mathematica illustrate concretely the de Casteljau algorithm and its version using subdivision. In preparation for the discussion of spline curves, the de Boor algorithm is also introduced. Finally, the formulae giving the derivatives of polynomial curves are given, and the conditions for joining polynomial curve segments with C^k-continuity are shown.

We saw in Section 4.3, Lemma 4.3.1, that an affine polynomial curve $F: \mathbf{A} \to \mathcal{E}$ of degree m defined by its m-polar form $f: \mathbf{A}^m \to \mathcal{E}$ is completely determined by the sequence of $m + 1$ points $b_k = f(r^{m-k} s^k)$, where $r, s \in \mathbf{A}$, $r \neq s$, $0 \leq k \leq m$, and we showed that

$$f(t_1, \ldots, t_m) = \sum_{k=0}^{m} p_k(t_1, \ldots, t_m) \, f(r^{m-k} s^k),$$

where the coefficient

$$p_k(t_1, \ldots, t_m) = \sum_{\substack{I \cup J = \{1,\ldots,m\} \\ I \cap J = \emptyset, \, |J| = k}} \prod_{i \in I} \left(\frac{s - t_i}{s - r} \right) \prod_{j \in J} \left(\frac{t_j - r}{s - r} \right)$$

of $f(r^{m-k} s^k)$, is a symmetric m-affine function.

Typically, we are interested in a polynomial curve segment $F([r, s])$. The de Casteljau algorithm gives a geometric iterative method for determining any point $F(t) = f(t, \ldots, t)$ on the curve segment $F([r, s])$, specified by the sequence of its

$m + 1$ *control points,* or *Bézier control points,* $b_0, b_1, \ldots, b_m$, where $b_k = f(r^{m-k} s^k)$. Actually, the de Casteljau algorithm can be used to calculate any point $F(t) = f(t, \ldots, t)$ on the curve F specified by the sequence of control points $b_0, b_1, \ldots, b_m$, for $t \in \mathbf{A}$ not necessarily in $[r, s]$. The only difference is that in the more general case, certain properties holding for the curve segment $F([r, s])$ may not hold for larger curve segments of F, such as the fact that the curve segment $F([r, s])$ is contained in the convex hull of the control polygon (or control polyline) determined by the control points $b_0, b_1, \ldots, b_m$.

What's good about the algorithm is that it does not assume any prior knowledge of the curve. All that is given is the sequence $b_0, b_1, \ldots, b_m$ of $m + 1$ control points, and the idea is to approximate the shape of the polygonal line consisting of the m line segments $(b_0, b_1), (b_1, b_2), \ldots, (b_{m-1}, b_m)$.[1] The curve goes through the two end points b_0 and b_m, but not through the other control points. The essence of the de Casteljau algorithm is to compute $f(t, \ldots, t)$ by repeated linear interpolations, using the fact that f is symmetric and m-affine. The computation consists of m phases, where in phase j, $m + 1 - j$ interpolations are performed. In phase m (the last phase), only one interpolation is performed, and the result is the point $F(t)$ on the curve, corresponding to the parameter value $t \in \mathbf{A}$.

Since f is symmetric, we can think of its m arguments as a *multiset* rather than a sequence, and thus, we can write the arguments in any order we please.

We already discussed the de Casteljau algorithm in some detail in Section 3.8. We strongly advise our readers to look at de Casteljau's original presentation in de Casteljau [23]. Let us review this case (polynomial cubic curves). As we observed, the computation of the point $F(t)$ on a polynomial cubic curve F can be arranged in a triangular array, as shown below:

$$
\begin{array}{ccccc}
 & 1 & 2 & 3 & \\
f(r,r,r) & & & & \\
 & f(r,r,t) & & & \\
f(r,r,s) & & f(t,t,r) & & \\
 & f(r,t,s) & & f(t,t,t) & \\
f(r,s,s) & & f(t,t,s) & & \\
 & f(t,s,s) & & & \\
f(s,s,s) & & & & \\
\end{array}
$$

The above computation is usually performed for $t \in [r, s]$, but it works just as well for any $t \in \mathbf{A}$, even outside $[r, s]$. When t is outside $[r, s]$, we usually say that $F(t) = f(t, t, t)$ is computed by *extrapolation.*

Figure 5.1 shows an example of the de Casteljau algorithm for computing the point $F(t)$ on a cubic, where r, s, and t are arbitrary.

---

1. Actually, some of the points b_k and b_{k+1} may coincide, but the algorithm still works fine.

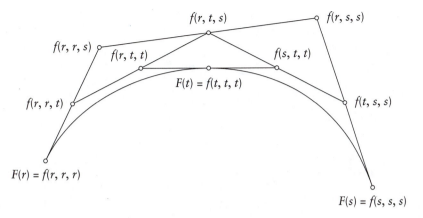

FIG. 5.1 The de Casteljau algorithm

The de Casteljau algorithm can also be used to compute any polar value $f(t_1, t_2, t_3)$ (which is not generally on the curve). All we have to do is to use t_j during phase j, as shown below in the case where $m = 3$:

$$
\begin{array}{ccccc}
 & 1 & 2 & 3 \\
f(r,r,r) \\
 & f(r,r,t_1) \\
f(r,r,s) & & f(t_1,t_2,r) \\
 & f(r,t_1,s) & & f(t_1,t_2,t_3) \\
f(r,s,s) & & f(t_1,t_2,s) \\
 & f(t_1,s,s) \\
f(s,s,s)
\end{array}
$$

Since control points are polar values, the de Casteljau algorithm can also be used for computing other control points. This turns out to be very useful.

Figure 5.2 shows an example of the de Casteljau algorithm for computing the polar value $f(t_1, t_2, t_3)$ on a cubic, where $r = 0$, $s = 6$, $t_1 = 2$, $t_2 = 3$, and $t_3 = 4$. There are several possible computations. The figure shows the computation of the polar values $f(0, 0, t_1)$, $f(0, t_1, 6)$, $f(t_1, 6, 6)$, $f(0, t_1, t_2)$, and $f(6, t_1, t_2)$.

The polar value $f(t_1, t_2, t_3)$ is also obtained by computing the polar values $f(0, 0, t_3)$, $f(0, t_3, 6)$, $f(t_3, 6, 6)$, $f(0, t_2, t_3)$, and $f(6, t_2, t_3)$, as shown in Figure 5.3.

The general case for computing the point $F(t)$ on the curve F determined by the sequence of control points $b_0, \ldots, b_m$, where $b_k = f(r^{m-k} s^k)$, is shown below. We will abbreviate

$$
f(\underbrace{t, \ldots, t}_{i},\ \underbrace{r, \ldots, r}_{j},\ \underbrace{s, \ldots, s}_{k}),
$$

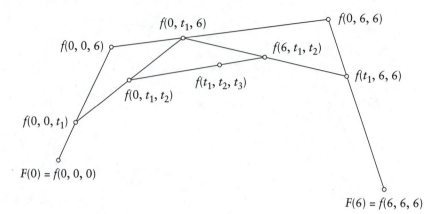

FIG. 5.2 The de Casteljau algorithm, for $t_1 = 2, t_2 = 3, t_3 = 4$

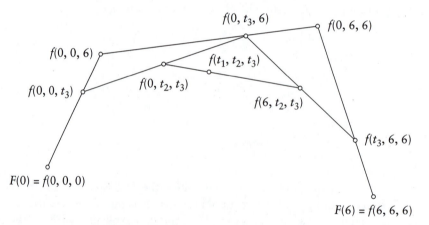

FIG. 5.3 A de Casteljau algorithm, for $t_1 = 2, t_2 = 3, t_3 = 4$, different geometry

as $f(t^i r^j s^k)$, where $i + j + k = m$. The point $f(t^j r^{m-i-j} s^i)$ is obtained at step i of phase j, for $1 \leq j \leq m$, $0 \leq i \leq m - j$, by the interpolation step

$$f(t^j r^{m-i-j} s^i) = \left(\frac{s-t}{s-r} \right) f(t^{j-1} r^{m-i-j+1} s^i) + \left(\frac{t-r}{s-r} \right) f(t^{j-1} r^{m-i-j} s^{i+1}).$$

$$0 \qquad 1 \qquad 2 \; \ldots \qquad j-1 \qquad\qquad j \qquad \ldots \quad m-1 \qquad m$$

$f(r^m)$

$\qquad f(tr^{m-1})$

$f(r^{m-1}s)$

$\vdots$

$\qquad\qquad\qquad\qquad f(t^{j-1}r^{m-j+1})$

$\qquad\qquad\qquad\qquad\qquad\qquad f(t^j r^{m-j})$

$\qquad\qquad\qquad\qquad\; f(t^{j-1}r^{m-j}s)$

$\vdots \qquad\qquad\qquad\qquad\qquad\qquad\vdots \qquad\qquad\vdots$

$\qquad\qquad\qquad\qquad f(t^{j-1}r^{m-i-j+1}s^i)$

$\qquad\qquad\qquad\qquad\qquad\qquad\qquad f(t^j r^{m-i-j}s^i)$

$\qquad\qquad\qquad\qquad f(t^{j-1}r^{m-i-j}s^{i+1})$

$\qquad\qquad\qquad\qquad\qquad\qquad\qquad\qquad\qquad\qquad f(t^{m-1}r)$

$\qquad\qquad\qquad\qquad\qquad\qquad\qquad\qquad\qquad\qquad\qquad\qquad\qquad f(t^m)$

$\vdots \qquad\qquad\qquad\qquad\qquad\qquad\vdots \qquad\qquad\vdots \qquad\qquad f(t^{m-1}s)$

$\qquad\qquad\qquad\qquad f(t^{j-1}rs^{m-j})$

$\qquad\qquad\qquad\qquad\qquad\qquad f(t^j s^{m-j})$

$\qquad\qquad\qquad\qquad f(t^{j-1}s^{m-j+1})$

$\vdots$

$f(rs^{m-1})$

$\qquad f(ts^{m-1})$

$f(s^m)$

In order to make the above triangular array a bit more readable, let us define the following points $b_{i,j}$, used during the computation:

$$b_{i,j} = \begin{cases} b_i & \text{if } j = 0,\ 0 \le i \le m, \\ f(t^j r^{m-i-j}s^i) & \text{if } 1 \le j \le m,\ 0 \le i \le m - j. \end{cases}$$

Then, we have the following equations:

$$b_{i,j} = \left(\frac{s-t}{s-r}\right) b_{i,j-1} + \left(\frac{t-r}{s-r}\right) b_{i+1,j-1}.$$

Such a computation can be conveniently represented in the triangular form shown at the top of the next page.

When $r \le t \le s$, each interpolation step computes a convex combination, and $b_{i,j}$ lies between $b_{i,j-1}$ and $b_{i+1,j-1}$. In this case, geometrically, the algorithm consists of a diagram consisting of the m polylines

0	1	$\ldots$	$j-1$	j	$\ldots$	$m-k$	$\ldots$	m
$b_{0,0}$								
	$b_{0,1}$							
$b_{1,0}$		$\ddots$						
			$b_{0,j-1}$					
			$\vdots$	$b_{0,j}$				
			$b_{i,j-1}$	$\vdots$	$\ddots$			
				$b_{i,j}$		$b_{0,m-k}$		
			$b_{i+1,j-1}$	$\vdots$				
			$\vdots$	$b_{m-k-j,j}$		$\vdots$		$b_{0,m}$
			$b_{m-k-j+1,j-1}$					
				$\vdots$		$b_{k,m-k}$		
			$\vdots$					
	$b_{m-k-1,1}$		$\vdots$					
$b_{m-k,0}$				$b_{m-j,j}$				
	$\vdots$		$b_{m-j+1,j-1}$					
$\vdots$								
$b_{m-1,0}$								
	$b_{m-1,1}$							
$b_{m,0}$								

$$(b_{0,0},\ b_{1,0}),\ (b_{1,0},\ b_{2,0}),\ (b_{2,0},\ b_{3,0}),\ (b_{3,0},\ b_{4,0}),\ \ldots,(b_{m-1,0},\ b_{m,0})$$
$$(b_{0,1},\ b_{1,1}),\ (b_{1,1},\ b_{2,1}),\ (b_{2,1},\ b_{3,1}),\ \ldots,(b_{m-2,1},\ b_{m-1,1})$$
$$(b_{0,2},\ b_{1,2}),\ (b_{1,2},\ b_{2,2}),\ \ldots,(b_{m-3,2},\ b_{m-2,2})$$
$$\vdots$$
$$(b_{0,m-2},\ b_{1,m-2}),\ (b_{1,m-2},\ b_{2,m-2})$$
$$(b_{0,m-1},\ b_{1,m-1})$$

called *shells*, and with the point $b_{0,m}$, they form the *de Casteljau diagram*. Note that the shells are nested nicely. The polyline

$$(b_0,\ b_1),\ (b_1,\ b_2),\ (b_2,\ b_3),\ (b_3,\ b_4),\ \ldots,(b_{m-1},\ b_m)$$

is also called a *control polygon* of the curve. When t is outside $[r, s]$, we still obtain m shells and a de Casteljau diagram, but the shells are not nicely nested.

By Lemma 4.3.1, we have an explicit formula giving any point $F(t)$ associated with a parameter $t \in \mathbf{A}$, on the unique polynomial curve $F \colon \mathbf{A} \to \mathcal{E}$ of degree m

determined by the sequence of control points $b_0, \ldots, b_m$. The point $F(t)$ is given by the formula

$$F(t) = \sum_{k=0}^{m} B_k^m[r, s](t)\, b_k,$$

where the polynomials

$$B_k^m[r, s](t) = \binom{m}{k} \left(\frac{s - t}{s - r}\right)^{m-k} \left(\frac{t - r}{s - r}\right)^k$$

are the *Bernstein polynomials of degree m over* $[r, s]$. Thus, the de Casteljau algorithm provides an iterative method for computing $F(t)$, without actually using the Bernstein polynomials. This can be advantageous for numerical stability. We will sometimes denote the Bézier curve determined by the sequence of control points $b_0, \ldots, b_m$, and defined with respect to the interval $[r, s]$, in the sense that

$$f(\underbrace{r, \ldots, r}_{m-i}, \underbrace{s, \ldots, s}_{i}) = b_i,$$

where f is the polar form of the Bézier curve, as $\mathcal{B}[b_0, \ldots, b_m; [r, s]]$, or $\mathcal{B}[r, s]$, and the point corresponding to the parameter value t as $\mathcal{B}[b_0, \ldots, b_m; [r, s]](t)$. Note that the parameter t can take any value in $\mathbf{A}$, and not necessarily only in $[r, s]$, but when we refer to the Bézier curve segment over $[r, s]$, we are assuming that $t \in [r, s]$.

The de Casteljau algorithm is very easy to implement, and we give below several versions in Mathematica. These functions all use a simple function lerp performing affine interpolation between two points $p1$ and $p2$, with respect to the affine frame $[r, s]$, for a value t of the parameter. The function badecas simply computes the point $F(t)$ on a polynomial curve F specified by a control polygon cpoly (over $[r, s]$). The result is the point $F(t)$. The function decas computes the point $F(t)$ on a polynomial curve F specified by a control polygon cpoly (over $[r, s]$), but also the shells of the de Casteljau diagram. The output is a list consisting of two sublists, the first one being the shells of the de Casteljau diagram and the second one being $F(t)$ itself.

```
(* Performs general affine interpolation between two points p, q *)
(* w.r.t. affine basis [r, s], and interpolating value t *)

lerp[p_List,q_List,r_,s_,t_] :=
(s - t)/(s - r)  p + (t - r)/(s - r)  q;

(* computes a point F(t) on a curve using the de Casteljau algorithm *)
(* this is the simplest version of de Casteljau *)
(* the auxiliary points involved in the algorithm are not computed *)
```

```
badecas[{cpoly__}, r_, s_, t_] :=
Block[
{bb = {cpoly}, b = {}, m, i, j},
(m = Length[bb] - 1;
Do[
   Do[
     b = Append[b, lerp[bb[[i]], bb[[i+1]], r, s, t]], {i, 1, m - j + 1}
     ]; bb = b; b = {}, {j, 1, m}
  ];
bb[[1]]
)
];
```

```
(* computes the point F(t) and the line segments involved in
   computing F(t) using the de Casteljau algorithm *)
```

```
decas[{cpoly__}, r_, s_, t_] :=
Block[
{bb = {cpoly}, b = {},
m, i, j, lseg = {}, res},
(m = Length[bb] - 1;
Do[
   Do[
     b = Append[b, lerp[bb[[i]], bb[[i+1]], r, s, t]];
     If[i > 1, lseg = Append[lseg, {b[[i - 1]], b[[i]]}]]
     , {i, 1, m - j + 1}
     ]; bb = b; b = {}, {j, 1, m}
  ];
res := Append[lseg, bb[[1]]];
res
)
];
```

The following function pdecas creates a list consisting of Mathematica line segments and of the point of the curve, ready for display.

```
(* this function calls decas, and computes the line segments
   in Mathematica, with colors *)
```

```
pdecas[{cpoly__}, r_, s_, t_] :=
Block[
{bb = {cpoly}, pt, ll, res, i, ll, edge},
res = decas[bb, r, s, t];
pt = Last[res]; res = Drop[res, -1];
ll = Length[res];
ll = {};
```

```
Do[
   edge = res[[i]];
   ll = Append[ll, Line[edge]], {i, 1, ll}
   ];
res = Append[ll, {RGBColor[1,0,0], PointSize[0.01], Point[pt]}];
res
];
```

The general computation of the polar value $f(t_1, \dots, t_m)$ is shown below:

$$
\begin{array}{cccccc}
0 & 1 & j-1 & & j & m \\
f(r^m) & & & & & \\
& f(t_1 r^{m-1}) & & & & \\
f(r^{m-1}s) & & & & & \\
\vdots & & & & & \\
& & f(t_1 \dots t_{j-1} r^{m-j+1}) & & & \\
& & & & f(t_1 \dots t_j r^{m-j}) & \\
& & f(t_1 \dots t_{j-1} r^{m-j} s) & & & \\
\vdots & & \vdots & & \vdots & \\
& & f(t_1 \dots t_{j-1} r^{m-i-j+1} s^i) & & & \\
& & & & f(t_1 \dots t_j r^{m-i-j} s^i) & \\
& & f(t_1 \dots t_{j-1} r^{m-i-j} s^{i+1}) & & & \\
& & \vdots & & \vdots & f(t_1 \dots t_m) \\
& & f(t_1 \dots t_{j-1} r s^{m-j}) & & & \\
& & & & f(t_1 \dots t_j s^{m-j}) & \\
& & f(t_1 \dots t_{j-1} s^{m-j+1}) & & & \\
\vdots & & & & & \\
f(r s^{m-1}) & & & & & \\
& f(t_1 s^{m-1}) & & & & \\
f(s^m) & & & & &
\end{array}
$$

We abbreviate

$$
f(\underbrace{t_1, \dots, t_j}_{j}, \underbrace{r, \dots, r}_{m-i-j}, \underbrace{s, \dots, s}_{i})
$$

as $f(t_1 \dots t_j r^{m-i-j} s^i)$, where $1 \le j \le m$, and $0 \le i \le m - j$, and in the case where $j = 0$, we abbreviate

$$
f(\underbrace{r, \dots, r}_{m-i}, \underbrace{s, \dots, s}_{i})
$$

as $f(r^{m-i}s^i)$, where $0 \le i \le m$. The point $f(t_1 \ldots t_j r^{m-i-j} s^i)$ is obtained at step i of phase j, for $1 \le j \le m$, $0 \le i \le m - j$, by the interpolation step

$$f(t_1 \ldots t_j r^{m-i-j} s^i)$$

$$= \left(\frac{s - t_j}{s - r}\right) f(t_1 \ldots t_{j-1} r^{m-i-j+1} s^i) + \left(\frac{t_j - r}{s - r}\right) f(t_1 \ldots t_{j-1} r^{m-i-j} s^{i+1}).$$

Again, defining the points $b_{i,j}$ used during the computation as

$$b_{i,j} = \begin{cases} b_i & \text{if } j = 0, \ 0 \le i \le m, \\ f(t_1 \ldots t_j r^{m-i-j} s^i) & \text{if } 1 \le j \le m, \ 0 \le i \le m - j, \end{cases}$$

we have the following more readable equations:

$$b_{i,j} = \left(\frac{s - t_j}{s - r}\right) b_{i,j-1} + \left(\frac{t_j - r}{s - r}\right) b_{i+1,j-1}.$$

The computation of polar values is implemented in Mathematica as follows:

```
(* computes a polar value using the de Casteljau algorithm *)
(* and the line segments involved in computing f(t1, ..., tm) *)
(* the input is a list tt of m numbers *)

gdecas[{cpoly__}, {tt__}, r_, s_] :=
Block[
{bb = {cpoly}, b = {}, t = {tt},
m, i, j, lseg = {}, res},
(m = Length[bb] - 1;
Do[
   Do[
       b = Append[b, lerp[bb[[i]], bb[[i+1]], r, s, t[[j]]]];
       If[i > 1, lseg = Append[lseg, {b[[i - 1]], b[[i]]}]],
       {i, 1, m - j + 1}
    ]; bb = b; b = {}, {j, 1, m}
  ];
res := Append[lseg, bb[[1]]];
res
)
];
```

Remark: The version of the de Casteljau algorithm for computing polar values provides a geometric argument for proving that the function $f(t_1, \ldots, t_m)$ that it computes is a symmetric multiaffine map. Since the algorithm proceeds by affine interpolation steps, it is clear that it yields a multiaffine map. What is not entirely obvious is symmetry. Since every permutation is a product of transpositions, we only need to show that $f(t_1, \ldots, t_m)$ remains invariant if we exchange any two arguments.

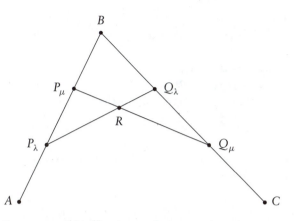

Symmetry of biaffine interpolation

We can establish this fact as follows. Let A, B, C be three points, and let

$$P_\lambda = (1 - \lambda)A + \lambda B, \qquad P_\mu = (1 - \mu)A + \mu B,$$

and also

$$Q_\lambda = (1 - \lambda)B + \lambda C, \qquad Q_\mu = (1 - \mu)B + \mu C.$$

Then, we claim that

$$(1 - \mu)P_\lambda + \mu Q_\lambda = (1 - \lambda)P_\mu + \lambda Q_\mu,$$

which is obvious, since both of these points coincide with the point

$$R = (1 - \lambda)(1 - \mu)A + (\lambda + \mu - 2\lambda\mu)B + \lambda\mu C.$$

Thus, interpolating first with respect to λ, and then with respect to μ, yields the same result as interpolating first with respect to μ, and then with respect to λ, as illustrated in Figure 5.4.

The above result is closely related to a standard result known as Menelaus's theorem.

We now consider a number of remarkable properties of Bézier curves.

- *Affine invariance.* This means that if an affine map h is applied to a Bézier curve F specified by the sequence of control points $b_0, \ldots, b_m$, obtaining a curve $h(F)$, then the Bézier curve F' determined by the sequence of control points $h(b_0), \ldots, h(b_m)$, images of the original control points $b_0, \ldots, b_m$, is identical to the curve $h(F)$. This can be expressed as

$$h(\mathcal{B}[b_0, \ldots, b_m; \ [r, s]]) = \mathcal{B}\ [h(b_0), \ldots, h(b_m), \ [r, \ s]] \,.$$

This is because points on a Bézier curve specified by a sequence of control points $b_0, \ldots, b_m$ are obtained by computing affine combinations, and because affine maps preserve affine combinations.

This property can be used to save a lot of computation time. If we want to move a curve using an affine map, rather than applying the affine map to all the points computed on the original curve, we simply apply the affine map to the control points, and then construct the new Bézier curve. This is usually a lot cheaper than moving every point around.

- *Invariance under affine parameter change.* The Bézier curve $F(t)$ specified by the sequence of control points $b_0, \ldots, b_m$, over the interval $[r, s]$, is the same as the Bézier curve

$$
F\left(\frac{t - r}{r - s}\right),
$$

over $[0, 1]$, with the same sequence of control points $b_0, \ldots, b_m$. This can be expressed as

$$
B[b_0, \ldots, b_m; \; [r, s]](t) = B[b_0, \ldots, b_m; \; [0, 1]]\left(\frac{t - r}{r - s}\right).
$$

This fact is basically obvious and left to verify, along with the following two properties:

$$
B[b_0, \ldots, b_m; \; [r, r + h]](t) = B[b_0, \ldots, b_m; \; [0, h]](t - r),
$$

and

$$
B[b_0, \ldots, b_m; \; [r, s]](t) = B[b_m, \ldots, b_0; \; [s, r]](t).
$$

- *Convex hull property.* The segment of Bézier curve $F(t)$ specified by the sequence of control points $b_0, \ldots, b_m$ and defined over the interval $[r, s]$ $(r < s)$ is contained within the convex hull of the control points $b_0, \ldots, b_m$. This is because, when $r \leq t \leq s$, all affine combinations involved in computing a point $F(t)$ on the curve segment are convex barycentric combinations.

  This property can be used to determine whether two Bézier curve segments intersect each other.

- *End point interpolation.* The Bézier curve $F(t)$ specified by the sequence of control points $b_0, \ldots, b_m$, over the interval $[r, s]$, passes through the points b_0 and b_m.

- *Symmetry.* The Bézier curve $F(r + s - t)$ specified by the sequence of control points $b_0, \ldots, b_m$, over the interval $[r, s]$, is equal to the Bézier curve $F'(t)$ specified by the sequence of control points $b_m, \ldots, b_0$, over the interval $[r, s]$. This can be expressed as

$$
B[b_0, \ldots, b_m; \; [r, s]](r + s - t) = B[b_m, \ldots, b_0; \; [r, s]](t).
$$

This can be seen easily using the symmetry of the Bernstein polynomials. Another way to see it is to observe that the curve $F(r + s - t)$, whose polar form is

$$g(t_1, \ldots, t_m) = f(r + s - t_1, \ldots, r + s - t_m),$$

where f is the polar form of the original curve $F(t)$ specified by the sequence of control points $b_0, \ldots, b_m$, satisfies the conditions

$$g(\underbrace{r, \ldots, r}_{m-i}, \underbrace{s, \ldots, s}_{i}) = f(\underbrace{s, \ldots, s}_{m-i}, \underbrace{r, \ldots, r}_{i}) = b_{m-i},$$

and since this curve is unique, it is indeed $F'(t)$.

- *Linear precision.* If the points $b_0, \ldots, b_m$ are collinear (belong to the same line), then the Bézier curve determined by the sequence of control points $b_0, \ldots, b_m$ is that same line. This is obvious since the points on the curve are obtained by affine combinations.

- *Pseudolocal control.* Given a Bézier curve F specified by a sequence of control points $b_0, \ldots, b_m$, if some control point b_i is moved a little bit, the curve is most affected around the points whose parameter value is close to i/n. This is because it can be shown that the Bernstein polynomial B_i^n reaches its maximum at $t = i/n$.

- *Determination of tangents.* It will be shown in Section 5.4 that, when b_0 and b_1 are distinct, the tangent to the Bézier curve at the point b_0 is the line determined by b_0 and b_1. Similarly, the tangent at the point b_m is the line determined by b_{m-1} and b_m (provided that these points are distinct). Furthermore, the tangent at the current point $F(t)$, determined by the parameter t, is determined by the two points

$$b_{0, m-1} = f(\underbrace{t, \ldots, t}_{m-1}, r)$$

and

$$b_{1, m-1} = f(\underbrace{t, \ldots, t}_{m-1}, s),$$

given by the de Casteljau algorithm.

- *Variation diminishing property.* Given a Bézier curve F specified by a sequence of control points $b_0, \ldots, b_m$, over $[r, s]$, for every hyperplane H, the number of intersections between the Bézier curve segment $F[r, s]$ and the hyperplane H is less than or equal to the number of intersections between the control polygon determined by $b_0, \ldots, b_m$ and the hyperplane H. As a consequence, a convex control polygon corresponds to a convex curve. We will prove the variation diminishing property as a consequence of another property, the subdivision property.

5.2   Subdivision Algorithms for Polynomial Curves

We now consider the subdivision method. As we will see, subdivision can be used to approximate a curve using a polygon, and the convergence is very fast. Given a sequence of control points $b_0, \ldots, b_m$, and an interval $[r, s]$, for every $t \in \mathbf{A}$, we saw how the de Casteljau algorithm gives a way of computing the point $\mathcal{B}[b_0, \ldots, b_m;\ [r, s]](t) = b_{0,m}$ on the Bézier curve, and the computation can be conveniently represented in the following triangular form:

$$
\begin{array}{ccccccc}
0 & 1 & \ldots & j-1 & j & \ldots\ m-k\ \ldots & m
\end{array}
$$

$b_{0,0}$

$\qquad b_{0,1}$

$b_{1,0} \qquad\qquad \ddots$

$\qquad\qquad\qquad\qquad b_{0,j-1}$

$\qquad\qquad\qquad\qquad \vdots \qquad\qquad b_{0,j}$

$\qquad\qquad\qquad b_{i,j-1} \qquad \vdots \qquad \ddots$

$\qquad\qquad\qquad\qquad\qquad b_{i,j} \qquad\qquad b_{0,m-k}$

$\qquad\qquad\qquad b_{i+1,j-1} \qquad \vdots$

$\qquad\qquad\qquad\qquad \vdots \qquad b_{m-k-j,j} \qquad\qquad \vdots \qquad\qquad b_{0,m}$

$\qquad\qquad b_{m-k-j+1,j-1}$

$\qquad\qquad\qquad\qquad\qquad \vdots \qquad\qquad b_{k,m-k}$

$\qquad b_{m-k-1,1} \qquad\qquad\qquad \vdots$

$b_{m-k,0} \qquad\qquad\qquad\qquad\qquad b_{m-j,j}$

$\qquad \vdots \qquad\qquad b_{m-j+1,j-1}$

$\vdots$

$b_{m-1,0}$

$\qquad b_{m-1,1}$

$b_{m,0}$

Let us now assume that $r < t < s$. Observe that the two diagonals

$$b_{0,0},\ b_{0,1}, \ldots, b_{0,j}, \ldots, b_{0,m}$$

and

$$b_{0,m},\ b_{1,m-1}, \ldots, b_{m-j,j}, \ldots, b_{m,0}$$

each consist of $m + 1$ points. We claim that we have

$$\mathcal{B}[b_0, \ldots, b_m;\ [r, s]](u) = \mathcal{B}[b_{0,0}, \ldots, b_{0,j}, \ldots, b_{0,m};\ [r, t]](u)$$

$$= \mathcal{B}[b_{0,m}, \ldots, b_{m-j,j}, \ldots, b_{m,0};\ [t, s]](u),$$

for all $u \in \mathbf{A}$.

This can be seen easily using the symmetry of the Bernstein polynomials. Another way to see it is to observe that the curve $F(r + s - t)$, whose polar form is

$$g(t_1, \ldots, t_m) = f(r + s - t_1, \ldots, r + s - t_m),$$

where f is the polar form of the original curve $F(t)$ specified by the sequence of control points $b_0, \ldots, b_m$, satisfies the conditions

$$g(\underbrace{r, \ldots, r}_{m-i}, \underbrace{s, \ldots, s}_{i}) = f(\underbrace{s, \ldots, s}_{m-i}, \underbrace{r, \ldots, r}_{i}) = b_{m-i},$$

and since this curve is unique, it is indeed $F'(t)$.

- *Linear precision.* If the points $b_0, \ldots, b_m$ are collinear (belong to the same line), then the Bézier curve determined by the sequence of control points $b_0, \ldots, b_m$ is that same line. This is obvious since the points on the curve are obtained by affine combinations.

- *Pseudolocal control.* Given a Bézier curve F specified by a sequence of control points $b_0, \ldots, b_m$, if some control point b_i is moved a little bit, the curve is most affected around the points whose parameter value is close to i/n. This is because it can be shown that the Bernstein polynomial B_i^n reaches its maximum at $t = i/n$.

- *Determination of tangents.* It will be shown in Section 5.4 that, when b_0 and b_1 are distinct, the tangent to the Bézier curve at the point b_0 is the line determined by b_0 and b_1. Similarly, the tangent at the point b_m is the line determined by b_{m-1} and b_m (provided that these points are distinct). Furthermore, the tangent at the current point $F(t)$, determined by the parameter t, is determined by the two points

$$b_{0, m-1} = f(\underbrace{t, \ldots, t}_{m-1}, r)$$

and

$$b_{1, m-1} = f(\underbrace{t, \ldots, t}_{m-1}, s),$$

given by the de Casteljau algorithm.

- *Variation diminishing property.* Given a Bézier curve F specified by a sequence of control points $b_0, \ldots, b_m$, over $[r, s]$, for every hyperplane H, the number of intersections between the Bézier curve segment $F[r, s]$ and the hyperplane H is less than or equal to the number of intersections between the control polygon determined by $b_0, \ldots, b_m$ and the hyperplane H. As a consequence, a convex control polygon corresponds to a convex curve. We will prove the variation diminishing property as a consequence of another property, the subdivision property.

5.2   Subdivision Algorithms for Polynomial Curves

We now consider the subdivision method. As we will see, subdivision can be used to approximate a curve using a polygon, and the convergence is very fast. Given a sequence of control points $b_0, \ldots, b_m$, and an interval $[r, s]$, for every $t \in \mathbf{A}$, we saw how the de Casteljau algorithm gives a way of computing the point $\mathcal{B}[b_0, \ldots, b_m; [r, s]](t) = b_{0,m}$ on the Bézier curve, and the computation can be conveniently represented in the following triangular form:

$$
\begin{array}{ccccccccc}
0 & 1 & \cdots & j-1 & j & \cdots & m-k & \cdots & m \\
b_{0,0} & & & & & & & & \\
& b_{0,1} & & & & & & & \\
b_{1,0} & & \ddots & & & & & & \\
& & & b_{0,j-1} & & & & & \\
& & & \vdots & b_{0,j} & & & & \\
& & b_{i,j-1} & & \vdots & \ddots & & & \\
& & & & b_{i,j} & & b_{0,m-k} & & \\
& & b_{i+1,j-1} & & \vdots & & & & \\
& & \vdots & & b_{m-k-j,j} & & \vdots & & b_{0,m} \\
& & b_{m-k-j+1,j-1} & & & & & & \\
& & & & & & \vdots & & b_{k,m-k} \\
& b_{m-k-1,1} & & \vdots & & & & & \\
b_{m-k,0} & & & & & b_{m-j,j} & & & \\
& & \vdots & & b_{m-j+1,j-1} & & & & \\
\vdots & & & & & & & & \\
b_{m-1,0} & & & & & & & & \\
& b_{m-1,1} & & & & & & & \\
b_{m,0} & & & & & & & &
\end{array}
$$

Let us now assume that $r < t < s$. Observe that the two diagonals

$$b_{0,0}, \; b_{0,1}, \ldots, b_{0,j}, \ldots, b_{0,m}$$

and

$$b_{0,m}, \; b_{1,m-1}, \ldots, b_{m-j,j}, \ldots, b_{m,0}$$

each consist of $m + 1$ points. We claim that we have

$$\mathcal{B}[b_0, \ldots, b_m; [r, s]](u) = \mathcal{B}[b_{0,0}, \ldots, b_{0,j}, \ldots, b_{0,m}; [r, t]](u)$$

$$= \mathcal{B}[b_{0,m}, \ldots, b_{m-j,j}, \ldots, b_{m,0}; [t, s]](u),$$

for all $u \in \mathbf{A}$.

Indeed, if f is the polar form associated with the Bézier curve specified by the sequence of control points $b_0, \ldots, b_m$ over $[r, s]$, g is the polar form associated with the Bézier curve specified by the sequence of control points $b_{0,0}, \ldots, b_{0,j}, \ldots, b_{0,m}$ over $[r, t]$, and h is the polar form associated with the Bézier curve specified by the sequence of control points $b_{0,m}, \ldots, b_{m-j,j}, \ldots, b_{m,0}$ over $[t, s]$, since f and g agree on the sequence of $m + 1$ points

$$b_{0,0}, \ldots, b_{0,j}, \ldots, b_{0,m},$$

and f and h agree on the sequence of $m + 1$ points

$$b_{0,m}, \ldots, b_{m-j,j}, \ldots, b_{m,0},$$

by Lemma 4.3.1, we have $f = g = h$.

For $t \in [r, \ s]$ as above, we say that the two curve segments

$$\mathcal{B}[b_{0,0}, \ldots, b_{0,j}, \ldots, b_{0,m}; \ [r, t]]$$

and

$$\mathcal{B}[b_{0,m}, \ldots, b_{m-j,j}, \ldots, b_{m,0}; \ [t, s]]$$

form a *subdivision* of the curve segment $\mathcal{B}[b_0, \ldots, b_m; \ [r, s]]$. Clearly, we can in turn subdivide each of the two segments, and continue recursively in this manner. It seems intuitively clear that the polygon obtained by repeated subdivision converges to the original curve segment. This is indeed the case, and the convergence is in fact very fast. Assuming for simplicity that $r = 0$ and $s = 1$, if we first choose $t = \frac{1}{2}$, and then $t = \frac{1}{4}$ and $t = \frac{3}{4}$, and so on, at the nth step, we have 2^n Bézier segments, and 2^n control subpolygons, whose union forms a polygon Π_n with $m2^n + 1$ nodes. Among these points, there are $2^n + 1$ points on the original curve, the points corresponding to parameter values $t = k/2^n$, $0 \leq k \leq 2^n$. For the following lemma, we assume that $\mathcal{E}$ is a normed affine space. Also, given a control polygon Π with m sides, we assume that Π is viewed as the piecewise linear curve defined such that over $[i/m, \ (i + 1)/m]$, with $0 \leq i \leq m - 1$,

$$\Pi(u) = (i + 1 - m \, u)a_i + (m \, u - i)a_{i+1}.$$

Lemma 5.2.1

Given a Bézier curve specified by a sequence of $m + 1$ control points $b_0, \ldots, b_m$, over the interval $[0, 1]$, if we subdivide in a binary fashion, the polygon Π_n, obtained after n steps of subdivision, converges uniformly to the curve segment $F = \mathcal{B}[b_0, \ldots, b_m; \ [0, 1]]$, in the sense that

$$\max_{0 \leq u \leq 1} \left\| \overrightarrow{\Pi_n(u) F(u)} \right\| \leq \frac{C}{2^n},$$

for some constant $C > 0$ independent of n.

Proof: If Π is any control polygon with $m + 1$ nodes, for a Bézier curve segment F, since F is contained in the convex hull of the control polygon, the distance between the Bézier curve segment F and the control polygon satisfies the inequality

$$\max_{0 \leq u \leq 1} \left\| \overrightarrow{\Pi(u)F(u)} \right\| \leq \max_{0 \leq i,j \leq m} \left\| \overrightarrow{b_i b_j} \right\| \leq m \max_{0 \leq i \leq m-1} \left\| \overrightarrow{b_i b_{i+1}} \right\|,$$

by the triangle inequality. Let $M = \max \left\| \overrightarrow{b_i b_{i+1}} \right\|$, for the original control polygon with control points $b_0, \ldots, b_m$. Since we are subdividing in a binary fashion, and since only convex combinations are involved, by the triangle inequality, the maximum length of the sides of the polygon Π_n is $M/2^n$. Then, from above, we have

$$\max_{0 \leq u \leq 1} \left\| \overrightarrow{\Pi_n(u)F(u)} \right\| \leq \max_{\Pi \subseteq \Pi_n, |\Pi| = m} \max_{0 \leq u \leq 1} \left\| \overrightarrow{\Pi(u)F(u)} \right\| \leq \frac{mM}{2^n},$$

where Π is any subpolygon of Π_n consisting of m sides, whose end points are on the curve F, which proves the lemma. ∎

The above lemma is the key to efficient methods for rendering polynomial (and rational) curves. After a certain number of steps, due to the screen resolution, the polygon obtained by subdivision becomes indistinguishable from the curve, and thus, this yields a fast method for plotting the curve segment! The subdivision method can easily be implemented. Given a polynomial curve F defined by a control polygon $\mathcal{B} = (b_0, \ldots, b_m)$ over an affine frame $[r, s]$, for every $t \in \mathbf{A}$, we denote as $\mathcal{B}_{[r,t]}$ the control polygon

$$b_{0,0}, \ b_{0,1}, \ldots, b_{0,j}, \ldots, b_{0,m},$$

and as $\mathcal{B}_{[t,s]}$ the control polygon

$$b_{0,m}, \ b_{1,m-1}, \ldots, b_{m-j,j}, \ldots, b_{m,0}.$$

The following Mathematica function returns a pair consisting of $\mathcal{B}_{[r,t]}$ and $\mathcal{B}_{[t,s]}$, from an input control polygon cpoly.

```
(* Performs a single subdivision step using the de Casteljau algorithm *)
(* Returns the control poly (f(r,...,r, t, ..., t)) and *)
(* (f(t, ..., t, s, ..., s)) *)

subdecas[{cpoly__}, r_, s_, t_] :=
Block[
{bb = {cpoly}, b = {}, ud = {}, ld = {},
m, i, j, res},
(m = Length[bb] - 1; ud = {bb[[1]]}; ld = {bb[[m + 1]]};
Do[
```

```
Do[
   b = Append[b, lerp[bb[[i]], bb[[i+1]], r, s, t]], {i, 1, m - j + 1}
   ];
   ud = Append[ud, b[[1]]];
   ld = Prepend[ld, b[[m - j + 1]]];
   bb = b; b = {}, {j, 1, m}
  ];
res := Join[{ud},{ld}];
res
)
];
```

In order to approximate the curve segment over $[r, s]$, we recursively apply subdivision to a list consisting originally of a single control polygon. The function subdivstep subdivides each control polygon in a list of control polygons. The function subdiv performs n calls to subdivstep. Finally, in order to display the resulting curve, the function makedgelis makes a list of Mathematica line segments from a list of control polygons.

```
(* subdivides each control polygon in a list of control polygons *)
(* using  subdecas. Uses t = (r + s)/2 *)

subdivstep[{poly__}, r_, s_] :=
Block[
{cpoly = {poly}, lpoly = {},  t, l, i},
(l = Length[cpoly]; t = (r + s)/2;
Do[
    lpoly = Join[lpoly, subdecas[cpoly[[i]], r, s, t]] , {i, 1, l}
   ];
lpoly
)
];


(* calls subdivstep n times *)

subdiv[{poly__}, r_, s_, n_] :=
Block[
{pol1 = {poly}, newp = {}, i},
(
 newp = {pol1};
 Do[
   newp = subdivstep[newp, r, s], {i, 1, n}
  ];
 newp
)
];
```

```
(* To create a list of line segments from a list of control polygons *)

makedgelis[{poly__}] :=
Block[
{res, sl,  newsl = {poly},
 i, j, l1, l2},
 (l1 = Length[newsl];  res = {};
 Do[
    sl = newsl[[i]]; l2 = Length[sl];
    Do[
       If[j > 1, res = Append[res, Line[{sl[[j-1]], sl[[j]]}]]],
                {j, 1, l2}
       ], {i, 1, l1}
    ];
  res
  )
  ];
```

The subdivision method is illustrated by the following example of a curve of degree 4 given by the control polygon

$$cpoly = ((0, -4), (10, 30), (5, -20), (0, 30), (10, -4)).$$

Figures 5.5–5.10 show polygonal approximations of the curve segment over $[0, 1]$ using subdiv, for $n = 1, 2, 3, 4, 5, 6$.

The convergence is indeed very fast. Another nice application of the subdivision method is that we can compute very cheaply the control polygon $\mathcal{B}_{[a,b]}$ over a new affine frame $[a, b]$ of a polynomial curve given by a control polygon $\mathcal{B}$ over $[r, s]$. Indeed, assuming $a \neq r$, by subdividing once with respect to $[r, s]$ using the

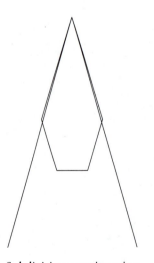

FIG. 5.5 Subdivision, one iteration

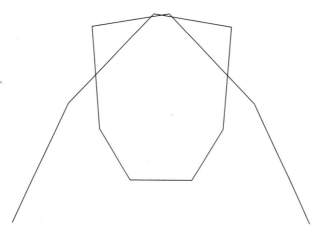

**FIG. 5.6** Subdivision, two iterations

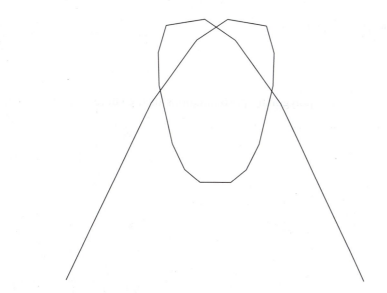

FIG. 5.7 Subdivision, three iterations

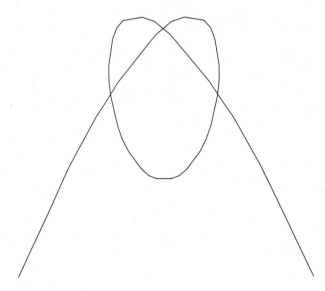

FIG. 5.8 Subdivision, four iterations

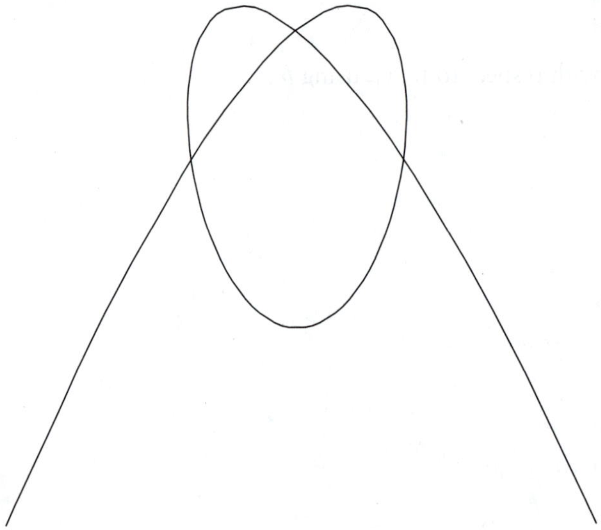

FIG. 5.9 Subdivision, five iterations

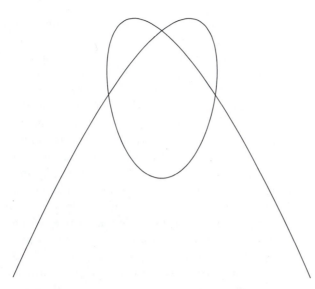

FIG. 5.10 Subdivision, six iterations

parameter a, we get the control polygon $\mathcal{B}_{[r,a]}$, and then we reverse this control polygon and subdivide again with respect to $[a, r]$ using b, to get $\mathcal{B}_{[a,b]}$. When $r = a$, we subdivide with respect to $[r, s]$, using b.

```
(* Computes the control polygon w.r.t. new affine frame (a, b) *)
(* Assumes that a = (1 - lambda) r + lambda t and *)
(* that b = (1 - mu) r + mu t, w.r.t. original frame (s, t) *)
(* Returns control poly  (f(a, ..., a, b, ..., b)) *)

newcpoly[{cpoly__}, r_, s_, a_, b_] :=
Block[
{poly = {cpoly}, m, i, pol1, pola, pol2, npoly, pt},
(
  If[a =!= r, pol1 = subdecas[poly, r, s, a];
              pola = pol1[[1]]; pol2 = {};
              m = Length[pola];
              Do[
                  pt = pola[[i]];
                  pol2 = Prepend[pol2, pt], {i, 1, m}
                ];
              npoly = subdecas[pol2, a, r, b],
        (* Print[" npoly: ", npoly] *)
              npoly = subdecas[poly, r, s, b]
    ];
 npoly[[1]]
 )
];
```

The above function can be used to render curve segments over intervals $[a, b]$ different from the interval $[r, s]$ over which the original control polygon is defined.

We can now prove the variation diminishing property. Observe that the subdivision process only involves convex affine combinations. Given any two adjacent edges (a, b) and (b, c) of the control polygon, if we construct the points $b' = (1 - \lambda)a + \lambda b$ and $b'' = (1 - \lambda)b + \lambda c$, where $0 \leq \lambda \leq 1$, and modify the control polygon so that instead of having the two edges (a, b) and (b, c), we now have the three edges (a, b'), (b', b''), and (b'', c), we observe that a hyperplane intersects the new polygon in a number of points that is at most the number of times that it intersects the original polygon. This immediately follows by convexity. Then, by induction, we can show that a hyperplane intersects any polygon obtained by subdivision in a number of points that is at most the number of times that it intersects the original control polygon. Since these polygons obtained via subdivision converge to the Bézier curve, a hyperplane intersects the Bézier curve in a number of points that is at most the number of times that it intersects its control polygon.

We consider one more property of Bézier curves, *degree raising*. Given a Bézier curve F of polar degree m, and specified by a sequence of $m + 1$ control points $b_0, \ldots, b_m$, it is sometimes necessary to view F as a curve of polar degree $m + 1$. For example, certain algorithms can only be applied to curve segments of the same degree. Or a system may only accept curves of a specified degree, say, 3, and thus, in order to use such a system on a curve of lower degree, for example, a curve of degree 2, it may be necessary to raise the (polar) degree of the curve. This can be done very easily in terms of polar forms. Indeed, if F is defined by the polar form $f \colon \mathbf{A}^m \to \mathcal{E}$, the polar form $g \colon \mathbf{A}^{m+1} \to \mathcal{E}$ that will yield the same curve F, in the sense that

$$g(\underbrace{t, \ldots, t}_{m+1}) = f(\underbrace{t, \ldots, t}_{m}) = F(t),$$

is necessarily

$$g(t_1, \ldots, t_{m+1}) = \frac{1}{m+1} \left(\sum_{1 \leq i_1 < \ldots < i_m \leq m+1} f(t_{i_1}, \ldots, t_{i_m}) \right).$$

Indeed, g as defined above is clearly $m + 1$-affine and symmetric, it is equal to F on the diagonal, and since it is unique, it is the desired polar form. Instead of the above notation, the following notation is often used:

$$g(t_1, \ldots, t_{m+1}) = \frac{1}{m+1} \sum_{i=1}^{m+1} f(t_1, \ldots, \widehat{t_i}, \ldots, t_{m+1}),$$

where the hat over the argument $\widehat{t_i}$ indicates that this argument is omitted. For example, if f is biaffine, we have

$$g(t_1, t_2, t_3) = \frac{f(t_1, t_2) + f(t_1, t_3) + f(t_2, t_3)}{3}.$$

If F (and thus f) is specified by the $m + 1$ control points $b_0, \ldots, b_m$, then F, considered of degree $m + 1$ (and thus g), is specified by $m + 2$ control points $b_0^1, \ldots, b_{m+1}^1$, and it is an easy exercise to show that the points b_j^1 are given in terms of the original points b_i, by the equations

$$b_i^1 = \frac{i}{m+1} b_{i-1} + \frac{m+1-i}{m+1} b_i,$$

where $1 \leq i \leq m$, with $b_0^1 = b_0$, and $b_{m+1}^1 = b_m$.

We can also raise the degree again, and so on. It can be shown that the control polygons obtained by successive degree raising, converge to the original curve segment. However, this convergence is much slower than the convergence obtained by subdivision, and it is not useful in practice.

5.3   The Progressive Version of the de Casteljau Algorithm (the de Boor Algorithm)

We now consider one more generalization of the de Casteljau algorithm that will be useful when we deal with splines. Such a version will be called the *progressive version*, for reasons that will become clear shortly. When dealing with splines, it is convenient to consider control points not just of the form $f(r^{m-i} s^i)$, but of the form $f(u_{k+1}, \ldots, u_{k+m})$, where the u_i are real numbers taken from a sequence $\langle u_1, \ldots, u_{2m} \rangle$ of length $2m$, satisfying certain inequality conditions. Let us begin with the case $m = 3$.

Given a sequence $\langle u_1, u_2, u_3, u_4, u_5, u_6 \rangle$, we say that this sequence is *progressive* iff the inequalities indicated in the following array hold:

$$
\begin{array}{cccc}
u_1 & \neq & & \\
u_2 & \neq & \neq & \\
u_3 & \neq & \neq & \neq \\
& u_4 & u_5 & u_6
\end{array}
$$

Then, we consider the following four control points:

$$f(u_1, u_2, u_3), \ f(u_2, u_3, u_4), \ f(u_3, u_4, u_5), \ f(u_4, u_5, u_6).$$

Observe that these points are obtained from the sequence $\langle u_1, u_2, u_3, u_4, u_5, u_6 \rangle$, by sliding a window of length 3 over the sequence, from left to right. This explains the name "progressive case". Now, we can compute any polar value $f(t_1, t_2, t_3)$ from the above control points, using the following triangular array obtained using the de Casteljau algorithm:

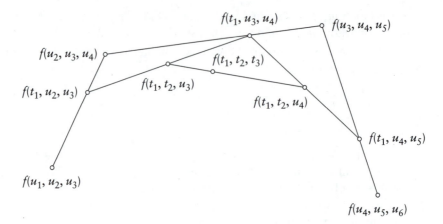

FIG. 5.11 The de Casteljau algorithm, progressive case

0	1	2	3
$f(u_1, u_2, u_3)$			
	$f(t_1, u_2, u_3)$		
$f(u_2, u_3, u_4)$		$f(t_1, t_2, u_3)$	
	$f(t_1, u_3, u_4)$		$f(t_1, t_2, t_3)$
$f(u_3, u_4, u_5)$		$f(t_1, t_2, u_4)$	
	$f(t_1, u_4, u_5)$		
$f(u_4, u_5, u_6)$			

At stage 1, we can successfully interpolate because $u_1 \neq u_4$, $u_2 \neq u_5$, and $u_3 \neq u_6$. This corresponds to the inequalities on the main descending diagonal of the array of inequality conditions. At stage 2, we can successfully interpolate because $u_2 \neq u_4$, and $u_3 \neq u_5$. This corresponds to the inequalities on the second descending diagonal of the array of inequality conditions. At stage 3 we can successfully interpolate because $u_3 \neq u_4$. This corresponds to the third-lowest descending diagonal. Thus, we used exactly all of the "progressive" inequality conditions.

Figure 5.11 shows an example of the de Casteljau algorithm for computing the polar value $f(t_1, t_2, t_3)$ on a cubic, given the progressive sequence $\langle u_1, u_2, u_3, u_4, u_5, u_6 \rangle$.

In the general case, we have a sequence $\langle u_1, \ldots, u_{2m} \rangle$ of numbers $u_i \in \mathbf{R}$.

Definition 5.3.1

A sequence $\langle u_1, \ldots, u_{2m} \rangle$ of numbers $u_i \in \mathbf{R}$ is progressive iff $u_j \neq u_{m+i}$, for all j, and all i, $1 \leq i \leq j \leq m$. These $m(m+1)/2$ conditions correspond to the lower triangular part of the following array:

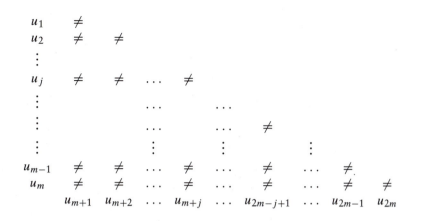

Note that the jth descending diagonal of the array of progressive inequalities begins with u_j (on the vertical axis) and ends with u_{2m-j+1} (on the horizontal axis). The entry u_{2m-j+1} will be before or after u_{m+j}, depending on the inequality $2j \leq m + 1$. We will abbreviate

$$f(\underbrace{t_1, \ldots, t_j}_{j}, \underbrace{u_{i+j+1}, \ldots, u_{m+i}}_{m-j})$$

as $f(t_1 \ldots t_j u_{i+j+1} \ldots u_{m+i})$, and when $j = 0$, we abbreviate

$$f(\underbrace{u_{i+1}, \ldots, u_{m+i}}_{m})$$

as $f(u_{i+1} \ldots u_{m+i})$.

The point $f(t_1 \ldots t_j u_{i+j+1} \ldots u_{m+i})$ is obtained at step i of phase j, for $1 \leq j \leq m$, $0 \leq i \leq m - j$, by the interpolation step

$$f(t_1 \ldots t_j u_{i+j+1} \ldots u_{m+i}) = \left(\frac{u_{m+i+1} - t_j}{u_{m+i+1} - u_{i+j}} \right) f(t_1 \ldots t_{j-1} u_{i+j} \ldots u_{m+i})$$

$$+ \left(\frac{t_j - u_{i+j}}{u_{m+i+1} - u_{i+j}} \right) f(t_1 \ldots t_{j-1} u_{i+j+1} \ldots u_{m+i+1}).$$

Phase j of the general computation of the polar value $f(t_1, \ldots, t_m)$, in the progressive case, is shown below:

$$j - 1$$
$$f(t_1 \ldots t_{j-1} u_j \ldots u_m)$$

$$j$$
$$f(t_1 \ldots t_j u_{j+1} \ldots u_m)$$

$$f(t_1 \ldots t_{j-1} u_{j+1} \ldots u_{m+1})$$

$$\vdots$$

$$\vdots$$

$$f(t_1 \ldots t_{j-1} u_{i+j} \ldots u_{m+i})$$

$$f(t_1 \ldots t_j u_{i+j+1} \ldots u_{m+i})$$

$$f(t_1 \ldots t_{j-1} u_{i+j+1} \ldots u_{m+i+1})$$

$$\vdots$$

$$\vdots$$

$$f(t_1 \ldots t_{j-1} u_m \ldots u_{2m-j})$$

$$f(t_1 \ldots t_j u_{m+1} \ldots u_{2m-j})$$

$$f(t_1 \ldots t_{j-1} u_{m+1} \ldots u_{2m-j+1})$$

Note that the reason why the interpolation steps can be performed is that we have the inequalities

$$u_j \neq u_{m+1}, \; u_{j+1} \neq u_{m+2}, \ldots, u_{i+j} \neq u_{m+i+1}, \ldots, u_m \neq u_{2m-j+1},$$

which correspond to the jth descending diagonal of the array of progressive inequalities, counting from the main descending diagonal.

In order to make the above triangular array a bit more readable, let us define the following points $b_{i,j}$, used during the computation:

$$b_{i,j} = f(t_1 \ldots t_j u_{i+j+1} \ldots u_{m+i}),$$

for $1 \leq j \leq m$, $0 \leq i \leq m - j$, with

$$b_{i,0} = f(u_{i+1}, \ldots, u_{m+i}),$$

for $0 \leq i \leq m$. Then, we have the following equations:

$$b_{i,j} = \left(\frac{u_{m+i+1} - t_j}{u_{m+i+1} - u_{i+j}} \right) b_{i,j-1} + \left(\frac{t_j - u_{i+j}}{u_{m+i+1} - u_{i+j}} \right) b_{i+1,j-1}.$$

The progressive version of the de Casteljau algorithm is also called the *de Boor algorithm*. It is the major algorithm used in dealing with splines.

You may wonder whether it is possible to give a closed form for $f(t_1, \ldots, t_m)$, as computed by the progressive case of the de Casteljau algorithm, and come up with a version of Lemma 4.3.1. This turns out to be difficult, as the case $m = 2$ already reveals!

Consider a progressive sequence $\langle u_1, u_2, u_3, u_4 \rangle$, where the following inequalities hold:

$$u_1 \quad \neq$$
$$u_2 \quad \neq \quad \neq$$
$$\qquad u_3 \quad u_4$$

We would like to compute $f(t_1, t_2)$ in terms of $f(u_1, u_2)$, $f(u_2, u_3)$, and $f(u_3, u_4)$. We could apply the algorithm, but we can also proceed directly as follows. Since $u_1 \neq u_3$ and $u_2 \neq u_4$, we can express t_1 in two ways using two parameters λ_1 and λ_2, as

$$t_1 = (1 - \lambda_1)u_1 + \lambda_1 u_3 = (1 - \lambda_2)u_2 + \lambda_2 u_4,$$

and since $u_2 \neq u_3$, we can express t_2 in terms of λ_3, as

$$t_2 = (1 - \lambda_3)u_2 + \lambda_3 u_3.$$

Now, we compute $f(t_1, t_2)$, by first expanding t_2:

$$
\begin{aligned}
f(t_1, t_2) &= f(t_1, (1 - \lambda_3)u_2 + \lambda_3 u_3) \\
&= (1 - \lambda_3)\, f(t_1, u_2) + \lambda_3\, f(t_1, u_3) \\
&= (1 - \lambda_3)\, f((1 - \lambda_1)u_1 + \lambda_1 u_3, u_2) + \lambda_3\, f((1 - \lambda_2)u_2 + \lambda_2 u_4, u_3) \\
&= (1 - \lambda_1)(1 - \lambda_3)\, f(u_1, u_2) + [\lambda_1(1 - \lambda_3) + \lambda_3(1 - \lambda_2)]\, f(u_2, u_3) \\
&\quad + \lambda_2 \lambda_3\, f(u_3, u_4),
\end{aligned}
$$

and by expressing $\lambda_1, \lambda_2, \lambda_3$ in terms of t_1 and t_2, we get

$$
\begin{aligned}
f(t_1, t_2) ={}& \left(\frac{u_3 - t_1}{u_3 - u_1}\right)\left(\frac{u_3 - t_2}{u_3 - u_2}\right) f(u_1, u_2) \\
&+ \left[\left(\frac{t_1 - u_1}{u_3 - u_1}\right)\left(\frac{u_3 - t_2}{u_3 - u_2}\right) + \left(\frac{t_2 - u_2}{u_3 - u_2}\right)\left(\frac{u_4 - t_1}{u_4 - u_2}\right)\right] f(u_2, u_3) \\
&+ \left(\frac{t_1 - u_2}{u_4 - u_2}\right)\left(\frac{t_2 - u_2}{u_3 - u_2}\right) f(u_3, u_4).
\end{aligned}
$$

The coefficients of $f(u_1, u_2)$ and $f(u_3, u_4)$ are symmetric in t_1 and t_2, but it is certainly not obvious that the coefficient of $f(u_2, u_3)$ is symmetric in t_1 and t_2. Actually, by doing more calculations, it can be verified that

$$\left[\left(\frac{t_1 - u_1}{u_3 - u_1}\right)\left(\frac{u_3 - t_2}{u_3 - u_2}\right) + \left(\frac{t_2 - u_2}{u_3 - u_2}\right)\left(\frac{u_4 - t_1}{u_4 - u_2}\right)\right]$$

is symmetric.

These calculations are already rather involved for $m = 2$. What are we going to do for the general case $m \geq 3$?

We can still prove the following theorem, generalizing Lemma 4.3.1 to the progressive case. The easy half follows from the progressive version of the de Casteljau algorithm, and the converse will be proved later.

Theorem 5.3.2

Let $\langle u_1, \ldots, u_{2m} \rangle$ be a progressive sequence of numbers $u_i \in \mathbf{R}$. Given any sequence of $m + 1$ points $b_0, \ldots, b_m$ in some affine space $\mathcal{E}$, there is a unique polynomial curve $F: \mathbf{A} \to \mathcal{E}$ of degree m, whose polar form $f: \mathbf{A}^m \to \mathcal{E}$ satisfies the conditions

$$f(u_{k+1}, \ldots, u_{m+k}) = b_k,$$

for every k, $0 \le k \le m$.

Proof: If such a curve exists, and $f: \mathbf{A}^m \to \mathcal{E}$ is its polar form, the progressive version of the de Casteljau algorithm shows that $f(t_1, \ldots, t_m) = b_{0,m}$, where $b_{0,m}$ is uniquely determined by the inductive computation

$$b_{i,j} = \left(\frac{u_{m+i+1} - t_j}{u_{m+i+1} - u_{i+j}} \right) b_{i,j-1} + \left(\frac{t_j - u_{i+j}}{u_{m+i+1} - u_{i+j}} \right) b_{i+1,j-1},$$

where

$$b_{i,j} = f(t_1 \ldots t_j u_{i+j+1} \ldots u_{m+i}),$$

for $1 \le j \le m$, $0 \le i \le m - j$, and with

$$b_{i,0} = f(u_{i+1}, \ldots, u_{m+i}) = b_i,$$

for $0 \le i \le m$. The above computation is well defined because the sequence $\langle u_1, \ldots, u_{2m} \rangle$ is progressive.

The existence of a curve is much more difficult to prove, and we postpone giving such an argument until Section 11.1. ∎

There are at least two ways of proving the existence of a curve satisfying the conditions of Theorem 5.3.2. One proof is fairly computational and requires computing a certain determinant, which turns out to be nonzero precisely because the sequence is progressive. The other proof is more elegant and conceptual, but it uses the more sophisticated concept of symmetric tensor product (see Section 11.1).

5.4 Derivatives of Polynomial Curves

In this section, it is assumed that $\mathcal{E}$ is some affine space $\mathbf{A}^n$, with $n \ge 2$. Our intention is to give the formulae for the derivatives of polynomial curves $F: \mathbf{A} \to \mathcal{E}$ in terms of control points. This way, we will be able to describe the tangents to polynomial curves, as well as the higher-order derivatives, in terms of control points. This characterization will be used in the next section dealing with the conditions for joining polynomial curves with C^k-continuity.

A more general treatment of (directional) derivatives of affine polynomial functions $F: \mathbf{A}^m \to \mathcal{E}$ will be given in Section 10.5, as an application of the homogenization of an affine space presented in Chapter 10. In this section, we decided to go easy on our readers, and proofs are omitted. Such proofs are easily supplied (by direct computation). Our experience shows that most readers are happy to skip proofs, since they can find them later in Chapter 10.

In this section, following Ramshaw, it will be convenient to denote a point in $\mathbf{A}$ as $\bar{a}$, to distinguish it from the vector $a \in \mathbf{R}$. The unit vector $1 \in \mathbf{R}$ is denoted as δ. When dealing with derivatives, it is also more convenient to denote the vector $\overrightarrow{ab}$ as $b - a$.

Given a polynomial curve $F \colon \mathbf{A} \to \mathcal{E}$, for any $\bar{a} \in \mathbf{A}$, recall that the derivative $DF(\bar{a})$ is the limit

$$\lim_{t \to 0, \, t \neq 0} \frac{F(\bar{a} + t\delta) - F(\bar{a})}{t},$$

if it exists.

Recall that since $F \colon \mathbf{A} \to \mathcal{E}$, where $\mathcal{E}$ is an affine space, the derivative $DF(\bar{a})$ of F at $\bar{a}$ is a *vector* in $\overrightarrow{\mathcal{E}}$, and not a point in $\mathcal{E}$.

Since coefficients of the form $m(m - 1) \cdots (m - k + 1)$ occur a lot when taking derivatives, following Knuth, it is useful to introduce the *falling power* notation. We define the falling power $m^{\underline{k}}$ as

$$m^{\underline{k}} = m(m - 1) \cdots (m - k + 1),$$

for $0 \leq k \leq m$, with $m^{\underline{0}} = 1$, and with the convention that $m^{\underline{k}} = 0$ when $k > m$. The falling powers $m^{\underline{k}}$ have some interesting combinatorial properties of their own.

The following lemma giving the kth derivative $D^k F(\bar{r})$ of F at $\bar{r}$ in terms of polar values can be shown.

Lemma 5.4.1

Given an affine polynomial function $F \colon \mathbf{A} \to \mathcal{E}$ of polar degree m, for any $\bar{r}, \bar{s} \in \mathbf{A}$, with $r \neq s$, the kth derivative $D^k F(\bar{r})$ can be computed from the polar form f of F as follows, where $1 \leq k \leq m$:

$$D^k F(\bar{r}) = \frac{m^{\underline{k}}}{(s - r)^k} \sum_{i=0}^{i=k} \binom{k}{i} (-1)^{k-i} f(\underbrace{\bar{r}, \ldots, \bar{r}}_{m-i}, \underbrace{\bar{s}, \ldots, \bar{s}}_{i}).$$

A proof is given in Section 10.5. It is also possible to obtain this formula by expressing $F(\bar{r})$ in terms of the Bernstein polynomials and computing their derivatives.

If F is specified by the sequence of $m + 1$ control points $b_i = f(\bar{r}^{m-i}\bar{s}^i)$, $0 \leq i \leq m$, the above lemma shows that the kth derivative $D^k F(\bar{r})$ of F at $\bar{r}$ depends only on the $k + 1$ control points $b_0, \ldots, b_k$. In terms of the control points $b_0, \ldots, b_k$, the formula of Lemma 5.4.1 reads as follows:

$$D^k F(\bar{r}) = \frac{m^{\underline{k}}}{(s-r)^k} \sum_{i=0}^{i=k} \binom{k}{i} (-1)^{k-i} b_i.$$

In particular, if $b_0 \neq b_1$, then $DF(\bar{r})$ is the velocity vector of F at b_0, and it is given by

$$DF(\bar{r}) = \frac{m}{s-r} \overrightarrow{b_0 b_1} = \frac{m}{s-r}(b_1 - b_0).$$

This shows that when b_0 and b_1 are distinct, the tangent to the Bézier curve at the point b_0 is the line determined by b_0 and b_1. Similarly, the tangent at the point b_m is the line determined by b_{m-1} and b_m (provided that these points are distinct).

More generally, the tangent at the current point $F(\bar{t})$, defined by the parameter $\bar{t}$, is determined by the two points

$$b_{0,m-1} = f(\underbrace{\bar{t},\ldots,\bar{t}}_{m-1},\bar{r}) \quad \text{and} \quad b_{1,m-1} = f(\underbrace{\bar{t},\ldots,\bar{t}}_{m-1},\bar{s}),$$

given by the de Casteljau algorithm. It can be shown that

$$DF(\bar{t}) = \frac{m}{s-r}(b_{1,m-1} - b_{0,m-1}).$$

The acceleration vector $D^2 F(\bar{r})$ is given by

$$D^2 F(\bar{r}) = \frac{m(m-1)}{(s-r)^2} (\overrightarrow{b_0 b_2} - 2\overrightarrow{b_0 b_1}) = \frac{m(m-1)}{(s-r)^2}(b_2 - 2b_1 + b_0).$$

More generally, if $b_0 = b_1 = \ldots = b_k$, and $b_k \neq b_{k+1}$, it can be shown that the tangent at the point b_0 is determined by the points b_0 and b_{k+1}.

In the next section, we use Lemma 5.4.1 to give a very nice condition for joining two polynomial curves with certain specified smoothness conditions. This material will be useful when we deal with splines. Also, if you have not yet looked at the treatment of derivatives given in Section 10.5, we urge you to read Chapter 10.

5.5   Joining Affine Polynomial Functions

When dealing with splines, we have several curve segments that need to be joined with certain required continuity conditions ensuring smoothness. The typical situation is that we have two intervals $[\bar{p}, \bar{q}]$ and $[\bar{q}, \bar{r}]$, where $\bar{p}, \bar{q}, \bar{r} \in \mathbf{A}$, with $p < q < r$, and two affine curve segments $F: [\bar{p}, \bar{q}] \to \mathcal{E}$ and $G: [\bar{q}, \bar{r}] \to \mathcal{E}$, of polar degree m, that we wish to join at $\bar{q}$.

The weakest condition is no condition at all, called C^{-1}-continuity. This means that we don't even care whether $F(\bar{q}) = G(\bar{q})$, that is, there could be a discontinuity at $\bar{q}$. In this case, we say that $\bar{q}$ is a *discontinuity knot*. The next weakest condition, called C^0-continuity, is that $F(\bar{q}) = G(\bar{q})$. In other words, we impose continuity at $\bar{q}$, but no conditions on the derivatives. Generally, we have the following definition.

Definition 5.5.1

Two curve segments $F([\overline{p},\overline{q}])$ *and* $G[\overline{q},\overline{r}])$ *of polar degree m are said to* join with C^k*-continuity at* $\overline{q}$*, where* $0 \le k \le m$*, iff*

$$D^i F(\overline{q}) = D^i G(\overline{q}),$$

for all i, $0 \le i \le k$, where by convention, $D^0 F(\overline{q}) = F(\overline{q})$, and $D^0 G(\overline{q}) = G(\overline{q})$.

As we will see, for curve segments F and G of polar degree m, C^m-continuity imposes that $F = G$, which is too strong, and thus, we usually consider C^k-continuity, where $0 \le k \le m - 1$ (or even $k = -1$, as mentioned above). The continuity conditions of Definition 5.5.1 are usually referred to as *parametric continuity*. There are other useful kinds of continuity, for example *geometric continuity*.

We can characterize C^k-continuity of joins of curve segments very conveniently in terms of polar forms. A more conceptual proof of a slightly more general lemma will be given in Section 11.1, using symmetric tensor products (see Lemma B.4.5). The proof below uses Lemma 10.5.1, which is given in Section 10.5. As a consequence, if you have only read Section 5.4, you may skip the proof.

Lemma 5.5.2

Given two intervals $[\overline{p},\overline{q}]$ and $[\overline{q},\overline{r}]$, where $\overline{p},\overline{q},\overline{r} \in A$, with $p < q < r$, and two affine curve segments $F\colon [\overline{p},\overline{q}] \to \mathcal{E}$ and $G\colon [\overline{q},\overline{r}] \to \mathcal{E}$, of polar degree m, the curve segments $F([\overline{p},\overline{q}])$ and $G[\overline{q},\overline{r}])$ join with continuity C^k at $\overline{q}$, where $0 \le k \le m$, iff their polar forms $f\colon A^m \to \mathcal{E}$ and $g\colon A^m \to \mathcal{E}$ agree on all multisets of points that contain at most k points distinct from $\overline{q}$, that is,

$$f(\overline{u_1},\ldots,\overline{u_k},\underbrace{\overline{q},\ldots,\overline{q}}_{m-k}) = g(\overline{u_1},\ldots,\overline{u_k},\underbrace{\overline{q},\ldots,\overline{q}}_{m-k}),$$

for all $\overline{u_1},\ldots,\overline{u_k} \in A$.

Proof: First, assume that the polar forms f and g satisfy the condition

$$f(\overline{u_1},\ldots,\overline{u_k},\underbrace{\overline{q},\ldots,\overline{q}}_{m-k}) = g(\overline{u_1},\ldots,\overline{u_k},\underbrace{\overline{q},\ldots,\overline{q}}_{m-k}),$$

for all $\overline{u_1},\ldots,\overline{u_k} \in A$. If $\overline{u_i} = \overline{q}$, $1 \le i \le k$, we are requiring that

$$f(\underbrace{\overline{q},\ldots,\overline{q}}_{m}) = g(\underbrace{\overline{q},\ldots,\overline{q}}_{m}),$$

that is, $F(\overline{q}) = G(\overline{q})$, which is C^0-continuity. Let $\widehat{f}\colon (\widehat{A})^m \to \widehat{\mathcal{E}}$ and $\widehat{g}\colon (\widehat{A})^m \to \widehat{\mathcal{E}}$ be the homogenized versions of f and g. For every j, $1 \le j \le k$, by Lemma 5.4.1, the jth derivative $D^j F(\overline{q})$ can be computed from the polar form f of F as follows:

$$D^j F(\overline{q}) = \frac{m^{\underline{j}}}{(r-q)^j} \sum_{i=0}^{i=j} \binom{j}{i} (-1)^{j-i} f(\underbrace{\overline{q},\ldots,\overline{q}}_{m-i},\underbrace{\overline{r},\ldots,\overline{r}}_{i}).$$

Similarly, we have

$$D^j G(\overline{q}) = \frac{m^{\underline{j}}}{(r-q)^j} \sum_{i=0}^{i=j} \binom{j}{i} (-1)^{j-i} g(\underbrace{\overline{q},\ldots,\overline{q}}_{m-i},\underbrace{\overline{r},\ldots,\overline{r}}_{i}).$$

Since $i \le j \le k$, by the assumption, we have

$$f(\underbrace{\overline{q},\ldots,\overline{q}}_{m-i},\underbrace{\overline{r},\ldots,\overline{r}}_{i}) = g(\underbrace{\overline{q},\ldots,\overline{q}}_{m-i},\underbrace{\overline{r},\ldots,\overline{r}}_{i}),$$

and thus, $D^j F(\overline{q}) = D^j G(\overline{q})$. Thus, we have C^k-continuity of the join at $\overline{q}$.

Conversely, assume that we have C^k-continuity at $\overline{q}$. Thus, we have

$$D^i F(\overline{q}) = D^i G(\overline{q}),$$

for all i, $0 \le i \le k$, where by convention, $D^0 F(\overline{q}) = F(\overline{q})$, and $D^0 G(\overline{q}) = G(\overline{q})$. Thus, for $i = 0$, we get

$$f(\underbrace{\overline{q},\ldots,\overline{q}}_{m}) = g(\underbrace{\overline{q},\ldots,\overline{q}}_{m}).$$

By Lemma 10.5.1, we have

$$D^i F(\overline{q}) = m^{\underline{i}} \widehat{f}(\underbrace{\overline{q},\ldots,\overline{q}}_{m-i},\underbrace{\delta,\ldots,\delta}_{i}),$$

and similarly,

$$D^i G(\overline{q}) = m^{\underline{i}} \widehat{g}(\underbrace{\overline{q},\ldots,\overline{q}}_{m-i},\underbrace{\delta,\ldots,\delta}_{i}),$$

for $1 \le i \le m$. Then, the assumption of C^k-continuity implies that

$$\widehat{f}(\underbrace{\overline{q},\ldots,\overline{q}}_{m-i},\underbrace{\delta,\ldots,\delta}_{i}) = \widehat{g}(\underbrace{\overline{q},\ldots,\overline{q}}_{m-i},\underbrace{\delta,\ldots,\delta}_{i}),$$

for $1 \le i \le k$. However, for any $\overline{u_i} \in \mathbf{A}$, we have (in $\widehat{\mathbf{A}}$)

$$\overline{u_i} = \overline{q} + (u_i - q)\delta,$$

and thus, for any j, $1 \le j \le k$, we have

$$\widehat{f}(\overline{u_1},\ldots,\overline{u_j},\underbrace{\overline{q},\ldots,\overline{q}}_{m-j}) = \widehat{f}(\overline{q}+(u_1-q)\delta,\ldots,\overline{q}+(u_j-q)\delta,\underbrace{\overline{q},\ldots,\overline{q}}_{m-j}),$$

which can be expanded using multilinearity and symmetry, and yields

$$\widehat{f}(\overline{u_1},\ldots,\overline{u_j},\underbrace{\overline{q},\ldots,\overline{q}}_{m-j}) = \sum_{i=0}^{i=j} \sum_{\substack{L\subseteq\{1,\ldots,j\}\\|L|=i}} \prod_{l\in L}(u_l-q)\widehat{f}(\underbrace{\delta,\ldots,\delta}_{i},\underbrace{\overline{q},\ldots,\overline{q}}_{m-i}).$$

Similarly, we have

$$\widehat{g}(\overline{u_1},\ldots,\overline{u_j},\underbrace{\overline{q},\ldots,\overline{q}}_{m-j}) = \sum_{i=0}^{i=j} \sum_{\substack{L\subseteq\{1,\ldots,j\}\\|L|=i}} \prod_{l\in L}(u_l-q)\widehat{g}(\underbrace{\delta,\ldots,\delta}_{i},\underbrace{\overline{q},\ldots,\overline{q}}_{m-i}).$$

However, we know that

$$\widehat{f}(\underbrace{\delta,\ldots,\delta}_{i},\underbrace{\overline{q},\ldots,\overline{q}}_{m-i}) = \widehat{g}(\underbrace{\delta,\ldots,\delta}_{i},\underbrace{\overline{q},\ldots,\overline{q}}_{m-i}),$$

for all i, $1 \le i \le k$, and thus, we have

$$\widehat{f}(\overline{u_1},\ldots,\overline{u_j},\underbrace{\overline{q},\ldots,\overline{q}}_{m-j}) = \widehat{g}(\overline{u_1},\ldots,\overline{u_j},\underbrace{\overline{q},\ldots,\overline{q}}_{m-j}),$$

for all j, $1 \le j \le k$. Since $\widehat{f}$ extends f and $\widehat{g}$ extends g, together with

$$f(\underbrace{\overline{q},\ldots,\overline{q}}_{m}) = g(\underbrace{\overline{q},\ldots,\overline{q}}_{m}),$$

which we already proved, we have established the conditions of the lemma. ■

Another way to state Lemma 5.5.2 is to say that the curve segments $F([\overline{p},\overline{q}])$ and $G[\overline{q},\overline{r}])$ join with continuity C^k at $\overline{q}$, where $0 \le k \le m$, iff their polar forms $f\colon \mathbf{A}^m \to \mathcal{E}$ and $g\colon \mathbf{A}^m \to \mathcal{E}$ agree on all multisets of points that contain at least $m - k$ copies of the argument $\overline{q}$. Thus, the number k is the number of arguments that can be varied away from $\overline{q}$ without disturbing the values of the polar forms f and g. When $k = 0$, we can't change any of the arguments, and this means that f and g agree on the multiset

$$\underbrace{\overline{q},\ldots,\overline{q}}_{m},$$

that is, the curve segments F and G simply join at $\overline{q}$, without any further conditions. On the other hand, for $k = m - 1$, we can vary $m - 1$ arguments away from $\overline{q}$ without changing the value of the polar forms, which means that the curve segments F and G join with a high degree of smoothness (C^{m-1}-continuity). In the extreme case where $k = m$ (C^m-continuity), the polar forms f and g must agree when all arguments vary, and thus $f = g$, that is, F and G coincide. We will see that Lemma 5.5.2 yields a very pleasant treatment of parametric continuity for splines.

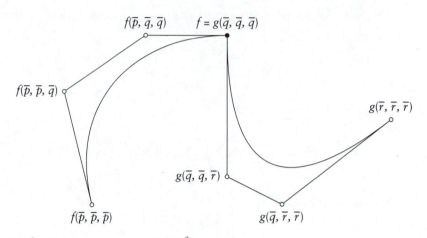

FIG. 5.12 Cubic curves joining at $\bar{q}$ with C^0-continuity

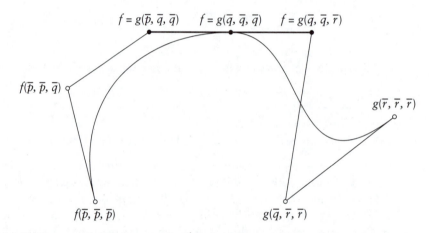

FIG. 5.13 Cubic curves joining at $\bar{q}$ with C^1-continuity

Figures 5.12–5.15 illustrate the geometric conditions that must hold so that two segments of cubic curves $F: \mathbf{A} \to \mathcal{E}$ and $G: \mathbf{A} \to \mathcal{E}$, defined on the intervals $[\bar{p}, \bar{q}]$ and $[\bar{q}, \bar{r}]$, join at $\bar{q}$ with C^k-continuity, for $k = 0, 1, 2, 3$. Let f and g denote the polar forms of F and G.

The curve segments F and G join at $\bar{q}$ with C^0-continuity iff the polar forms f and g agree on the (multiset) triplet $\bar{q}, \bar{q}, \bar{q}$ (see Figure 5.12).

The curve segments F and G join at $\bar{q}$ with C^1-continuity iff the polar forms f and g agree on all (multiset) triplets including two copies of the argument $\bar{q}$ (see Figure 5.13).

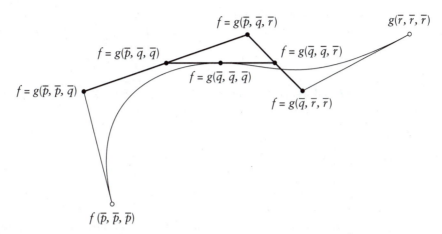

FIG. 5.14 Cubic curves joining at $\overline{q}$ with C^2-continuity

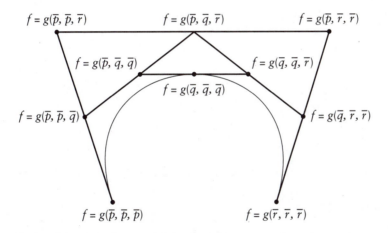

FIG. 5.15 Cubic curves joining at $\overline{q}$ with C^3-continuity

The curve segments F and G join at $\overline{q}$ with C^2-continuity iff the polar forms f and g agree on all (multiset) triplets including the argument $\overline{q}$ (see Figure 5.14).

The curve segments F and G join at $\overline{q}$ with C^3-continuity iff the polar forms f and g agree on all (multiset) triplets, that is, iff $f = g$ (see Figure 5.15).

The above examples show that the points corresponding to the common values

$$f(\overline{p}^i, \overline{r}^j, \overline{q}^{3-i-j}) = g(\overline{p}^i, \overline{r}^j, \overline{q}^{3-i-j})$$

of the polar forms f and g, where $i + j \leq k \leq 3$, constitute a de Casteljau diagram with k shells, where k is the degree of continuity required. These de Casteljau diagrams are represented in bold. This is a general fact. When two polynomial curves F and G of degree m join at $\overline{q}$ with C^k-continuity (where $0 \leq k \leq m$), then

$$f(\overline{p}^i, \overline{r}^j, \overline{q}^{m-i-j}) = g(\overline{p}^i, \overline{r}^j, \overline{q}^{m-i-j})$$

for all i, j with $i + j \leq k \leq m$, and these points form a de Casteljau diagram with k shells. We are now ready to consider B-spline curves.

Problems

[60 pts]   **1.** Write a computer program implementing the subdivision version of the de Casteljau algorithm, over some interval $[r, s]$.

        You may use Mathematica or any other available software in which graphics primitives are available. Test your program extensively.

        In the next three problems, it is assumed that $r = 0$ and $s = 1$.

[10 pts]   **2.** Consider (in the plane) the curve F defined by the following five control points:

$$b_0 = (6, 0),$$
$$b_1 = (0, 0),$$
$$b_2 = (6, 6),$$
$$b_3 = (0, 6),$$
$$b_4 = (6, -1).$$

        Use the de Casteljau algorithm to find the coordinates of the points $F(\frac{1}{2})$ and $F(\frac{3}{4})$. Does the curve self-intersect? Plot the curve segment (in the convex hull of the control polygon) as well as you can.

[10 pts]   **3.** Consider (in the plane) the curve F defined by the following five control points:

$$b_0 = (6, 0),$$
$$b_1 = (3, -1),$$
$$b_2 = (6, 6),$$
$$b_3 = (0, 6),$$
$$b_4 = (6.5, -1).$$

        Use the de Casteljau algorithm to find the coordinates of the points $F(\frac{1}{4})$ and $F(\frac{1}{2})$. Does the curve self-intersect? Plot the curve segment (in the convex hull of the control polygon) as well as you can.

[20 pts]   **4.** Consider (in the plane) the curve F defined by the following five control points:

$$b_0 = (0, -4),$$
$$b_1 = (10, 30),$$
$$b_2 = (5, -20),$$
$$b_3 = (0, 30),$$
$$b_4 = (10, -4).$$

Use the de Casteljau algorithm to find the coordinates of the point $F(\frac{1}{2})$. Does the curve self-intersect? Plot the curve segment (in the convex hull of the control polygon) as well as you can.

[10 pts]   **5.** (baby Lagrange interpolation via control points)   Given any affine space $\mathcal{E}$, given any four distinct values $t_0 < t_1 < t_2 < t_3$, and given any sequence of four points (x_0, x_1, x_2, x_3), we would like to find a cubic $F: A \to \mathcal{E}$ such that $F(t_i) = x_i$ (i.e., an interpolating cubic curve). To simplify the calculations, assume that $t_0 = 0$ and $t_3 = 1$.

Prove that there exists a unique cubic satisfying the above conditions, and compute its control points b_0, b_1, b_2, b_3, in terms of x_0, x_1, x_2, x_3, and $t_1 < t_2$.

[20 pts]   **6.** Let F be a cubic curve given by its control points b_0, b_1, b_2, b_3. Consider the arc of cubic $F[0, 1]$. If any of the control points b_i changes (one only) to a new point b_i', we get a different cubic F'. Show that for any $t \in [0, 1]$, we have

$$\left\| F'(t) - F(t) \right\| = B_i^3(t) \left\| b_i' - b_i \right\|,$$

where $B_i^3(t)$ is the ith Bernstein polynomial of degree 3. What is $\left\| F'(t) - F(t) \right\|$ for $i = 2, t = \frac{1}{2}$, and $t = \frac{1}{4}$?

[30 pts]   **7.** (cubic Hermite interpolation)   Let a_0, a_1 be any two points in A^3, and let $\overrightarrow{u_0}$ and $\overrightarrow{u_1}$ be any two vectors in $\mathbf{R}^3$. Show that there is a unique cubic curve $F: A \to A^3$ such that

$$F(0) = a_0,$$
$$F(1) = a_1,$$
$$F'(0) = \overrightarrow{u_0},$$
$$F'(1) = \overrightarrow{u_1},$$

and show that its control points are given by

$$b_0 = a_0, \quad b_1 = a_0 + \frac{1}{3}\overrightarrow{u_0}, \quad b_2 = a_1 - \frac{1}{3}\overrightarrow{u_1}, \quad b_3 = a_1.$$

Show that

$$F(t) = a_0 H_0^3(t) + \vec{u_0} H_1^3(t) + \vec{u_1} H_2^3(t) + a_1 H_3^3(t),$$

where

$$H_0^3(t) = B_0^3(t) + B_1^3(t),$$

$$H_1^3(t) = \frac{1}{3} B_1^3(t),$$

$$H_2^3(t) = -\frac{1}{3} B_2^3(t),$$

$$H_3^3(t) = B_2^3(t) + B_3^3(t).$$

Compute explicitly the polynomials $H_i^3(t)$, $0 \leq i \leq 3$. The polynomials $H_i^3(t)$ are called the *cubic Hermite polynomials*. Show that they are linearly independent.

[40 pts]   8. (quintic Hermite interpolation)   Let a_0, a_1 be any two points in $\mathbf{A}^3$, and let $\vec{u_0}, \vec{u_1}$, $\vec{v_0}, \vec{v_1}$, be any four vectors in $\mathbf{R}^3$. Show that there is a unique quintic curve $F \colon \mathbf{A} \to \mathbf{A}^3$ such that

$$F(0) = a_0,$$

$$F(1) = a_1,$$

$$F'(0) = \vec{u_0},$$

$$F'(1) = \vec{u_1},$$

$$F''(0) = \vec{v_0},$$

$$F''(1) = \vec{v_1},$$

and compute its control points. Show that

$$F(t) = a_0 H_0^5(t) + \vec{u_0} H_1^5(t) + \vec{v_0} H_2^5(t) + \vec{v_1} H_3^5(t) + \vec{u_1} H_4^5(t) + a_1 H_5^5(t),$$

where

$$H_0^5(t) = B_0^5(t) + B_1^5(t) + B_2^5(t),$$

$$H_1^5(t) = \frac{1}{5}(B_1^5(t) + 2B_2^5(t)),$$

$$H_2^5(t) = \frac{1}{20} B_2^5(t),$$

$$H_3^5(t) = \frac{1}{20} B_3^5(t),$$

$$H_4^5(t) = -\frac{1}{5}(2B_3^5(t) + B_4^5(t)),$$

$$H_5^5(t) = B_3^5(t) + B_4^5(t) + B_5^5(t).$$

Compute explicitly the polynomials $H_i^5(t)$, $0 \le i \le 5$. The polynomials $H_i^5(t)$ are called the *quintic Hermite polynomials*. Show that they are linearly independent.

[30 pts]   9. Use your implementation of the subdivision version of the de Casteljau algorithm to experiment with cubic and quintic Hermite interpolants. Try many different cases.

[20 pts]   10. Hermite interpolants were defined with respect to the interval $[0, 1]$. What happens if the affine map $t \mapsto (1 - t)a + tb$ is applied to the domain of the Hermite interpolants? How can you modify the Hermite polynomials to obtain the same kind of expression as in Problems 7 and 8?

[20 pts]   11. Plot the Hermite polynomials $H_i^3(t)$, $0 \le i \le 3$, over $[0, 1]$. Plot the Hermite polynomials $H_i^5(t)$, $0 \le i \le 5$, over $[0, 1]$.

[20 pts]   12. Use the de Casteljau algorithm to design a curve of degree 4 whose third control point b_2 belongs to the curve (in fact, for $t = \frac{1}{2}$).

[30 pts]   13. Assume that two Bézier curve segments F and G are defined over $[0, 1]$ in terms of their control points. Give a method for finding all the intersection points between the curve segments F and G. What if F and G have a common component? What if F and G have different degrees?

[30 pts]   14. Write a computer program implementing the progressive version of the de Casteljau algorithm, over some interval $[r, s]$.

You may use Mathematica or any other available software in which graphics primitives are available.

[30 pts]   15. Draw diagrams showing C^3-continuity for curves of degree 4. Draw diagrams showing C^4-continuity for curves of degree 5. Draw diagrams showing C^5-continuity for curves of degree 6. You may want to write computer programs to draw such diagrams.

[30 pts]   16. Write a computer program implementing a version of the de Casteljau algorithm applied to curves of degree 4 modified as explained below. During a subdivision step, allow the middle control point (b_2) to be perturbed in each of the two subpolygons. Experiment with various ways of perturbing the middle control point, by a random displacement or a controlled displacement. After a number of subdivision steps, you should get "fractal-style" curves with C^1-continuity.

[20 pts]   17. Let F be a polynomial curve defined by its control polygon $\mathcal{B} = (b_0, \ldots, b_m)$. Let $\mathcal{B}^{(r)} = (b_0^{(r)}, \ldots, b_{m+r}^{(r)})$ be the control polygon for the curve F obtained after r steps of degree elevation. Prove that

$$b_i^{(r)} = \sum_{j=0}^{m} \binom{m}{j} \frac{\binom{r}{i-j}}{\binom{m+r}{i}} b_j.$$

Remark: For any $t \in [0, 1]$, for each $r \geq 1$, there is some i such that $i/(m + r)$ is closest to t. Then, as $r \to \infty$, it can be shown (using Stirling's formula) that

$$\lim_{i/(m+r) \to t} \frac{\dbinom{r}{i-j}}{\dbinom{m+r}{i}} = t^j (1 - t)^{m-j}.$$

As a consequence,

$$\lim_{i/(m+r) \to t} b_i^{(r)} = \sum_{j=0}^{m} b_j B_j^m(t) = F(t).$$

This means that the control polygons $\mathcal{B}^{(r)}$ converge towards the curve segment $F[0, 1]$. However, this convergence is very slow and is not useful in practice.

CHAPTER 6

B-Spline Curves

6.1 Introduction: Knot Sequences, de Boor Control Points

Polynomial curves have many virtues for CAGD, but they are also unsatisfactory in a number of ways:

1. Given a control polygon containing m sides ($m + 1$ vertices), the degree of the polynomial curve determined by these control points is m. We know that it takes $m(m + 1)/2$ steps to compute a point on the curve. When m is large, this may be too costly, and thus impractical.

2. Moving any control point will affect the entire curve. It would be desirable to have better local control, in the sense that moving a control point only affects a small region of the curve.

3. If we are interested in interpolation rather than just approximating a shape, we will have to compute control points from points on the curve. This leads to systems of linear equations, and solving such systems can be impractical when the degree of the curve is large.

For the above reasons, people thought about segmenting a curve specified by a complex control polygon into smaller and more manageable segments. This is the idea behind splines. In this chapter, we present a class of spline curves known as *B*-splines and explain how to use knots to control the degree of continuity between the curve segments forming a spline curve. We show how knot sequences and sequences of de Boor control points can be used to specify *B*-splines, and we present the de Boor algorithm for *B*-splines, as well as the useful knot insertion algorithm. We also discuss interpolation using *B*-splines and briefly present the more traditional approach to *B*-splines in terms of basis functions.

Each segment of the curve will be controlled by some small subpolygon of the global polygon, and the segments will be joined together in some smooth fashion. In order to achieve this, it becomes necessary to consider several contiguous parameter intervals, rather than a single interval $[r, s]$ as in the case of polynomial curves. For example, we could have the intervals

$$[1, 2], \ [2, 3], \ [3, 5], \ [5, 6], \ [6, 9],$$

and if we want to use cubic segments, we would need four control points for each of these intervals. Let us denote the corresponding cubic curve segments as $F[1, 2]$, $F[2, 3]$, $F[3, 5]$, $F[5, 6]$, $F[6, 9]$. Since we want to join these cubic curve segments, we will assume that the fourth control point of the curve segment $F[1, 2]$ is equal to the first control point of the curve segment $F[2, 3]$, that the fourth control point of the curve segment $F[2, 3]$ is equal to the first control point of the curve segment $F[3, 5]$, and so on, and finally, that the fourth control point of the curve segment $F[5, 6]$ is equal to the first control point of the curve segment $F[6, 9]$.

Usually, we will want better continuity at the junction points (2, 3, 5, 6) than just contact. This can be achieved, as we will explain shortly.

Why did we choose a nonuniform spacing of the intervals? Because it would not really simplify anything, and because such flexibility is in fact useful, as we shall see later. Clearly, we may also want to be more careful about end points (in this case, 1 and 9). For the time being, we can assume that we are dealing with infinite sequences of contiguous intervals, where the sequences extend to infinity in both directions. When looking at a finite sequence such as

$$\ldots, [1, 2], \ [2, 3], \ [3, 5], \ [5, 6], \ [6, 9], \ldots,$$

we are just focusing on a particular subsequence of some bi-infinite sequence. It is also possible to handle cyclic sequences.

Note that it is slightly more economical to specify the sequence of intervals by just listing the junction points of these intervals, as in the following sequence:

$$\ldots, 1, 2, 3, 5, 6, 9, \ldots.$$

Such a sequence is called a *knot sequence*.

We will see that it is useful to collapse intervals, since this is a way to lower the degree of continuity of a join. This can be captured by a knot sequence by letting a knot appear more than once. For example, if we want to collapse the interval $[3, 5]$ to $[3, 3]$, the above knot sequence becomes

$$\ldots, 1, 2, 3, 3, 6, 9, \ldots.$$

We also allow collapsing several consecutive intervals. For example, we can also collapse $[2, 3]$ to $[3, 3]$, obtaining the sequence

$$\ldots, 1, 3, 3, 3, 6, 9, \ldots.$$

The number of consecutive occurrences of a knot is called its *multiplicity*. Thus, in the above sequence, 3 has multiplicity 3. Extending our sequence a bit, say, to

$$\ldots, 1, \ 3, \ 3, \ 3, \ 6, \ 9, \ 10, \ 12, \ 15, \ldots,$$

we can collapse several intervals and get several multiple knots, as shown by collapsing [10, 12] to [10, 10]:

$$\ldots, 1, \ 3, \ 3, \ 3, \ 6, \ 9, \ 10, \ 10, \ 15, \ldots.$$

The above sequence has a triple knot 3 and a double knot 10. Knots of multiplicity 1 are called *simple knots*, and knots of multiplicity greater than 1 are called *multiple knots*. As we will see, it does not make sense for the knot multiplicity to exceed $m + 1$, where m is the degree of each curve segment (in fact, multiplicity $m + 1$ corresponds to a discontinuity at the control point associated with that multiple knot).

The problem now is to find a convenient way of specifying the degree of continuity that we want at each join, and to find more convenient control points than the Bézier control points of the curve segments (in our example, $F[1, 2]$, $F[2, 3]$, $F[3, 5]$, $F[5, 6]$, $F[6, 9]$). Fortunately, there is a nice answer to both questions. Lemma 5.5.2 will yield a very pleasant answer to the problem of continuity of joins, and this answer will also show that there are natural control points called *de Boor points*, which turn out to be more convenient (and more economical) than the Bézier control points of the curve segments. We will also see how to extend the de Casteljau algorithm in order to compute points on any curve segment directly from the de Boor control points, without having to first compute the Bézier control points for the given curve segment. However, we could compute the Bézier control points using this algorithm, which is called the *de Boor algorithm*.

Since we are now using knot sequences to represent contiguous intervals, we can simplify our notation of curve segments by using the index (position) of the knot corresponding to the beginning of an interval as the index of the curve segment on that interval. For example, given the knot sequence

$$\ldots, 1, \ 2, \ 3, \ 5, \ 6, \ 9, \ldots,$$

we will denote $F[1, 2]$, $F[2, 3]$, $F[3, 5]$, $F[5, 6]$, $F[6, 9]$ simply as F_1, F_2, F_3, F_4, and F_5. Note that we need to take care of multiple knots, as in the sequence

$$\ldots, 1, \ 3, \ 3, \ 3, \ 6, \ 9, \ 10, \ 10, \ 15, \ 16 \ldots.$$

We simply consider the subsequence of strictly increasing knots, and we index each curve segment by the index (position) of the *last* occurrence of the knot corresponding to the left of its interval domain, and thus, we have curve segments: F_1, F_4, F_5, F_6, F_8, F_9.

We now have to explain how the de Boor control points arise. There are several possible presentations. The more mathematical presentation is to consider the polar form f_i of each curve segment F_i associated with an interval $[u_i, u_{i+1}]$, and to figure out the conditions that C^n-continuity at u_{i+1} impose on the polar forms f_i and f_{i+1}. If the degree of all curve segments is $\leq m$, and for simplicity, we allow knot multiplicity at most m (although it is easy to accommodate knots of multiplicity $m + 1$), it turns out that we are led to consider sequences of consecutive knots of length m of the form

$$\langle u_{k+1}, \ldots, u_{k+m} \rangle,$$

and that for all $i \in [k, k + m]$, the value

$$f_i(u_{k+1}, \ldots, u_{k+m})$$

of the polar form f_i associated with the interval beginning with knot u_i is constant and denoted as d_k. These points d_k are the *de Boor points*. Then, for any simple knot u_k, that is, a knot such that $u_k < u_{k+1}$, the sequence of $2m$ consecutive knots

$$\langle u_{k-m+1}, \ldots, u_k, u_{k+1}, \ldots, u_{k+m} \rangle$$

yields $m + 1$ sequences of consecutive knots

$$\langle u_{k-m+i+1}, \ldots, u_{k+i} \rangle,$$

each of length m, where $0 \leq i \leq m$, and these sequences turn out to define $m + 1$ de Boor control points for the curve segment F_k associated with the middle interval $[u_k, u_{k+1}]$. In fact, if f_k is the polar form of F_k, these de Boor points are the polar values

$$d_{k+i} = f_k(u_{k-m+i+1}, \ldots, u_{k+i}),$$

where $0 \leq i \leq m$.

For example, given the following (portion of a) knot sequence

$$\ldots, 1, 2, 3, 5, 6, 8, 9, 11, 14, 15, \ldots,$$

if $m = 3$, $k = 5$, and $u_k = u_5 = 6$, we have the sequence

$$\langle 3, 5, 6, 8, 9, 11 \rangle$$

consisting of $6 = 2 \cdot 3$ knots, and so $u_{k+1} = u_6 = 8$, the middle interval is $[6, 8]$, $u_{k-m+1} = u_3 = 3$, and $u_{k+m} = u_8 = 11$.

Since $u_k < u_{k+1}$, the sequence

$$\langle u_{k-m+1}, \ldots, u_k, u_{k+1}, \ldots, u_{k+m} \rangle$$

is progressive, and thus, it is possible to use the progressive version of the de Casteljau algorithm presented in Section 5.3, also called the de Boor algorithm, to compute points on the curve F_k, and more generally, any polar value of f_k

for parameter values in $[u_k, u_{k+1}]$. This is illustrated by the following progressive sequence of six knots:

$$\langle 3,\ 5,\ 6,\ 8,\ 9,\ 11 \rangle.$$

Observe that if u_k is a simple knot as above, then the $m+1$ sequences of consecutive knots

$$\langle u_{k-m+i+1}, \ldots, u_{k+i} \rangle,$$

each of length m (where $0 \leq i \leq m$), overlap precisely on the middle interval $[u_k, u_{k+1}]$ of the sequence

$$\langle u_{k-m+1}, \ldots, u_k, u_{k+1}, \ldots, u_{k+m} \rangle.$$

This property is the point of departure of another rather intuitive explanation of the de Boor algorithm, due to Ken Shoemake. Let us now forget that we have curve segments. Instead, we fix the maximum degree m of the curve segments that will arise, and we assume that we are given a bi-infinite knot sequence $\langle u_j \rangle$,

$$\ldots, u_j, \ldots, u_{j+k}, \ldots,$$

which for simplicity, consists only of simple knots (i.e., where $u_j < u_{j+1}$ for all j), and a bi-infinite sequence $\langle d_i \rangle$,

$$\ldots, d_i, \ldots, d_{i+l}, \ldots,$$

of (distinct) control points, with an additional constraint: we assume that there is a bijective function from the sequence $\langle d_i \rangle$ of control points to the knot sequence $\langle u_j \rangle$, with the property that for every control point d_i, if d_i is mapped to the knot u_{k+1}, then d_{i+1} is mapped to u_{k+2}.

Since consecutive control points map to consecutive knots, there is obviously an affine bijection mapping the interval $[u_{k+1}, u_{k+m+1}]$ onto the line segment (d_i, d_{i+1}), defined as

$$u \mapsto \frac{u_{k+m+1} - u}{u_{k+m+1} - u_{k+1}}\, d_i + \frac{u - u_{k+1}}{u_{k+m+1} - u_{k+1}}\, d_{i+1},$$

where $u \in [u_{k+1}, u_{k+m+1}]$. Thus, we can view each side (d_i, d_{i+1}) of the control polygon as being divided into m subsegments. If we color the m intervals

$$[u_{k+1},\ u_{k+2}], \ldots, [u_{k+m},\ u_{k+m+1}]$$

with different colors, the line segment (d_i, d_{i+1}) is also colored in a similar fashion. Assuming that we color all intervals $[u_{k+1}, u_{k+2}]$ (assuming infinitely many colors), we can see that m consecutive line segments $(d_i, d_{i+1}), \ldots, (d_{i+m-1}, d_{i+m})$ of the control polygon share exactly one color: that of the interval $[u_{k+m}, u_{k+m+1}]$.

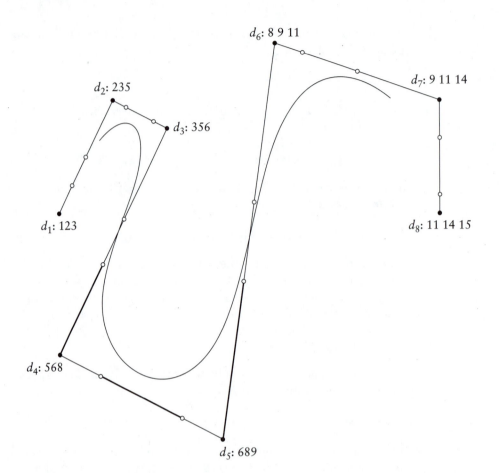

d_6: 8 9 11

d_7: 9 11 14

d_2: 235

d_3: 356

d_1: 123

d_8: 11 14 15

d_4: 568

d_5: 689

FIG. 6.1 Part of a cubic spline with knot sequence ..., 1, 2, 3, 5, 6, 8, 9, 11, 14, 15, ... Thick segments are images of [6, 8].

For example, assuming $m = 3$, given the following (portion of a) knot sequence,

$$\ldots, 1, 2, 3, 5, 6, 8, 9, 11, 14, 15, \ldots,$$

and given the following (portion of a) sequence of control points,

$$\ldots, d_1, d_2, d_3, d_4, d_5, d_6, d_7, d_8, \ldots,$$

Figure 6.1 shows part of a cubic spline, and the interval [1, 5] maps onto (d_1, d_2), the interval [2, 6] maps onto (d_2, d_3), ..., and the interval [9, 15] maps onto (d_7, d_8).

For $k = 5$, and $u_k = u_5 = 6$, the sequence

$$\langle 3, 5, 6, 8, 9, 11 \rangle,$$

whose middle interval is [6, 8], corresponds to the three line segments (d_3, d_4), (d_4, d_5), and (d_5, d_6). The line segment (d_4, d_5) is the affine image of the interval [5, 9], which itself consists of the three subintervals [5, 6], [6, 8], and [8, 9].

Therefore, m consecutive line segments $(d_i, d_{i+1}), \ldots, (d_{i+m-1}, d_{i+m})$ on the control polygon, or equivalently, $m + 1$ consecutive control points $d_i, \ldots, d_{i+m}$, correspond to a sequence of $2m$ knots

$$\langle u_{k+1}, u_{k+2}, \ldots, u_{k+2m} \rangle.$$

Note that any two consecutive line segments (d_i, d_{i+1}) and (d_{i+1}, d_{i+2}) are the affine images of intervals that overlap on exactly $m - 1$ consecutive subintervals of the knot sequence.

For example, the line segments (d_3, d_4) and (d_4, d_5) both contain images of the interval [5, 8], which consists of [5, 6] and [6, 8], and the line segments (d_4, d_5) and (d_5, d_6) both contain images of the interval [6, 9], which consists of [6, 8] and [8, 9].

The connection with the previous explanation becomes clearer. Since any two consecutive line segments (d_i, d_{i+1}) and (d_{i+1}, d_{i+2}) correspond to intervals that overlap on $m - 1$ consecutive subintervals of the knot sequence, we can index each control point d_i by the knot sequence

$$\langle u_{k+1}, \ldots, u_{k+m} \rangle$$

of m knots, where d_i is mapped to u_{k+1}. Note that the control point d_i corresponds to the knot sequence $\langle u_{k+1}, \ldots, u_{k+m} \rangle$, and that the control point d_{i+1} corresponds to the knot sequence $\langle u_{k+2}, \ldots, u_{k+m+1} \rangle$. Thus, the interval $[u_{k+1}, u_{k+m+1}]$, which is mapped affinely onto the line segment (d_i, d_{i+1}), corresponds to the leftmost knot in the sequence associated with d_i and to the rightmost knot in the sequence associated with d_{i+1}. This is an easy way to remember which interval maps onto the line segment (d_i, d_{i+1}).

For example, d_1 corresponds to $\langle 1, 2, 3 \rangle$, d_2 corresponds to $\langle 2, 3, 5 \rangle, \ldots$, and d_8 corresponds to $\langle 11, 14, 15 \rangle$.

Given a sequence of $2m$ knots

$$\langle u_{k+1}, u_{k+2}, \ldots, u_{k+2m} \rangle,$$

for any parameter value in the middle interval $t \in [u_{k+m}, u_{k+m+1}]$, a point on the curve segment specified by the $m + 1$ control points $d_i, d_{i+1}, \ldots, d_{i+m}$ (where d_i is mapped onto u_{k+1}) is computed by repeated affine interpolation, as follows:

Using the mapping

$$t \mapsto \frac{u_{k+m+j+1} - t}{u_{k+m+j+1} - u_{k+j+1}} d_{i+j} + \frac{t - u_{k+j+1}}{u_{k+m+j+1} - u_{k+j+1}} d_{i+j+1},$$

mapping the interval $[u_{k+j+1}, u_{k+m+j+1}]$ onto the line segment (d_{i+j}, d_{i+j+1}), where $0 \leq j \leq m - 1$, we map $t \in [u_{k+m}, u_{k+m+1}]$ onto the line segment (d_{i+j}, d_{i+j+1}), which gives us a point $d_{j,1}$. Then, we consider the new control polygon determined by the m points

$$d_{0,1}, \ d_{1,1}, \ \ldots, \ d_{m-1,1},$$

and we map affinely each of the $m - 1$ intervals $[u_{k+j+2}, \ u_{k+m+j+1}]$ onto the line segment $(d_{j,1}, \ d_{j+1,1})$, where $0 \leq j \leq m - 2$, and for $t \in [u_{k+m}, \ u_{k+m+1}]$, we get a point $d_{j,2}$ on $(d_{j,1}, \ d_{j+1,1})$. Note that each interval $[u_{k+j+2}, \ u_{k+m+j+1}]$ now consists of $m - 1$ consecutive subintervals, and that the leftmost interval $[u_{k+2}, \ u_{k+m+1}]$ starts at knot u_{k+2}, the immediate successor of the starting knot u_{k+1} of the leftmost interval used at the previous stage. The above round gives us a new control polygon determined by the $m - 1$ points

$$d_{0,2}, \ d_{1,2}, \ \ldots, \ d_{m-2,2},$$

and we repeat the procedure.

At every round, the number of consecutive intervals affinely mapped onto a line segment of the current control polygon decreases by one, and the starting knot of the leftmost interval used during this round is the (right) successor of the starting knot of the leftmost interval used at the previous round, so that at the mth round, we only have one interval, the middle interval $[u_{k+m}, \ u_{k+m+1}]$, the intersection of the m original intervals $[u_{k+j+1}, \ u_{k+m+j+1}]$, where $0 \leq j \leq m - 1$. The point $d_{0,m}$ obtained during the mth round is a point on the curve segment.

Figure 6.2 illustrates the computation of the point corresponding to $t = 7$ on the spline of the previous figure. These points are also shown as labels of polar values. For example, we have $d_{0,1}: 567$, $d_{1,1}: 678$, $d_{2,1}: 789$, $d_{0,2}: 677$, $d_{1,2}: 778$, and $d_{0,3}: 777$. The interpolation ratio associated with the point $d_{0,1}$ is

$$\frac{7-3}{8-3} = \frac{4}{5}.$$

The interpolation ratio associated with the point $d_{1,1}$ is

$$\frac{7-5}{9-5} = \frac{2}{4} = \frac{1}{2}.$$

The interpolation ratio associated with the point $d_{2,1}$ is

$$\frac{7-6}{11-6} = \frac{1}{5}.$$

The interpolation ratio associated with the point $d_{0,2}$ is

$$\frac{7-5}{8-5} = \frac{2}{3}.$$

The interpolation ratio associated with the point $d_{1,2}$ is

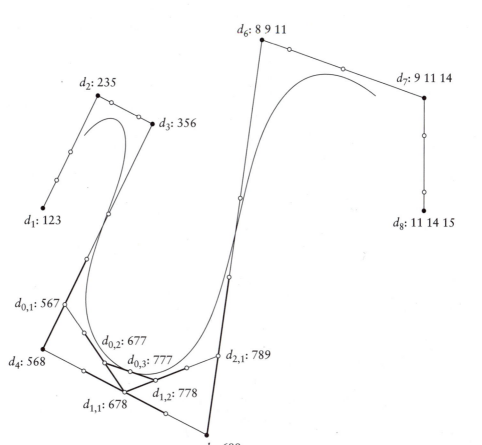

FIG. 6.2 Part of a cubic spline with knot sequence $\ldots, 1, 2, 3, 5, 6, 8, 9, 11, 14, 15, \ldots$, and construction of the point corresponding to $t = 7$. Thick segments are images of $[6, 8]$.

$$\frac{7 - 6}{9 - 6} = \frac{1}{3}.$$

And the interpolation ratio associated with the point $d_{0,3}$ is

$$\frac{7 - 6}{8 - 6} = \frac{1}{2}.$$

We recognize the progressive version of the de Casteljau algorithm presented in Section 5.3. The bookkeeping that consists in labeling control points using sequences of m consecutive knots becomes clearer: it is used to keep track of the consecutive intervals (on the knot line) and how they are mapped onto line segments of the current control polygon. Figure 6.3 shows the construction of the Bézier control points of the five Bézier segments forming this part of the spline.

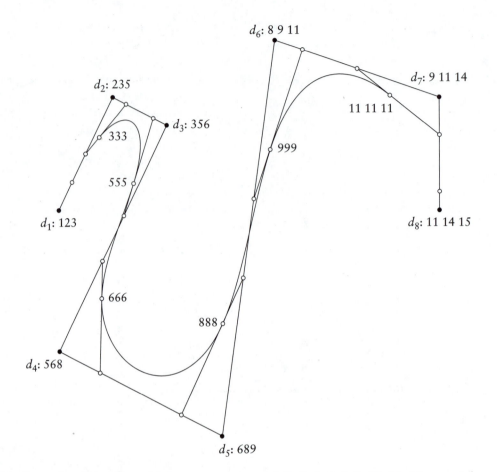

FIG. 6.3 Part of a cubic spline with knot sequence ..., 1, 2, 3, 5, 6, 8, 9, 11, 14, 15, ..., and some of its Bézier control points

We can now provide a better intuition for the use of multiple knots. Going back to the previous example of the (portion of a) knot sequence

$$..., 1, 2, 3, 5, 6, 8, 9, 11, 14, 15, ...,$$

and the (portion of a) sequence of control points

$$..., d_1, d_2, d_3, d_4, d_5, d_6, d_7, d_8, ...,$$

we can see that these control points determine five curve segments, corresponding to the intervals [3, 5], [5, 6], [6, 8], [8, 9], and [9, 11]. If we "squeeze" any of these intervals, say, [5, 6], to the empty interval [5, 5], this will have the effect that the corresponding curve segment shrinks to a single point, and the result will be that the degree of continuity of the junction between the curve segments associated with [3, 5] and [5, 8] (which used to be [6, 8]) will be lower. If we also squeeze the interval [5, 8] to the empty interval, we are also shrinking the corresponding curve segment to a single point. This time, the curve segments corresponding to the intervals [3, 5] and [5, 9] (previously [8, 9]) will join with even less continuity, and in fact, now that 5 is a triple knot, we may not even have C^1-continuity, meaning that the tangents may not agree. The extreme is to squeeze one more interval, say, [5, 9] (previously [8, 9]), and now, we may even have a discontinuity at the parameter value 5, in the sense that the curve segments associated with [3, 5] and [5, 11] (previously [9, 11]) may not even join at the point associated with the knot 5.

Thus, we see how the knot multiplicity can be used to control the degree of continuity of joins between curve segments.

We can now be more precise and prove some results showing that splines are uniquely determined by de Boor control points (given a knot sequence).

6.2   Infinite Knot Sequences, Open *B*-Spline Curves

We begin with knot sequences. As usual, to distinguish between real numbers in **R** and points in **A**, we will denote knots as points of the real affine line **A**, as $\overline{u} \in \mathbf{A}$ (as explained in Section 5.4).

Definition 6.2.1

A knot sequence *is a bi-infinite nondecreasing sequence* $\langle \overline{u}_k \rangle_{k \in \mathbf{Z}}$ *of points* $\overline{u}_k \in \mathbf{A}$ *(i.e.,* $\overline{u}_k \leq \overline{u}_{k+1}$ *for all* $k \in \mathbf{Z}$*), such that every knot in the sequence has finitely many occurrences. A knot* $\overline{u}_k$ *in a knot sequence* $\langle \overline{u}_k \rangle_{k \in \mathbf{Z}}$ *has* multiplicity *n (n* $\geq$ *1) iff it occurs exactly n (consecutive) times in the knot sequence. Given any natural number* $m \geq 1$*, a knot sequence has* degree of multiplicity at most $m + 1$ *iff every knot has multiplicity at most* $m + 1$*, that is, there are at most* $m + 1$ *occurrences of identical knots in the sequence. Thus, for a knot sequence of degree of multiplicity at most* $m + 1$*, we must have* $\overline{u}_k \leq \overline{u}_{k+1}$ *for all* $k \in \mathbf{Z}$*, and for every* $k \in \mathbf{Z}$*, if*

$$\overline{u}_{k+1} = \overline{u}_{k+2} = \ldots = \overline{u}_{k+n},$$

then $1 \leq n \leq m + 1$*. A knot* $\overline{u}_k$ *of multiplicity* $m + 1$ *is called a* discontinuity *(knot). A knot of multiplicity 1 is called a* simple *knot. A knot sequence* $\langle \overline{u}_k \rangle_{k \in \mathbf{Z}}$ *is* uniform *iff* $\overline{u}_{k+1} = \overline{u}_k + h$*, for some fixed* $h \in \mathbf{R}_+$*.*

We can now define spline (*B*-spline) curves.

Definition 6.2.2

Given any natural number $m \geq 1$*, and any knot sequence* $\langle \overline{u}_k \rangle_{k \in \mathbf{Z}}$ *of degree of multiplicity at most* $m + 1$*, a* piecewise polynomial curve of degree m based on the knot sequence $\langle \overline{u}_k \rangle_{k \in \mathbf{Z}}$ *is a function* $F: \mathbf{A} \to \mathcal{E}$*, where* $\mathcal{E}$ *is some affine space (of dimension at least 2), such that, for any two consecutive distinct knots* $\overline{u}_i < \overline{u}_{i+1}$*, if* $\overline{u}_{i+1}$ *is a knot of multiplicity n, the next distinct knot being* $\overline{u}_{i+n+1}$ *(since we must have* $\overline{u}_{i+1} = \ldots = \overline{u}_{i+n} < \overline{u}_{i+n+1}$*), then the following condition holds:*

1. *The restriction of F to $[\bar{u}_i, \bar{u}_{i+1}[$ agrees with a polynomial curve F_i of polar degree m, with associated polar form f_i.*

    A spline curve F of degree m based on the knot sequence $\langle \bar{u}_k \rangle_{k \in \mathbb{Z}}$ is a piecewise polynomial curve $F : \mathbf{A} \to \mathcal{E}$, such that, for every two consecutive distinct knots $\bar{u}_i < \bar{u}_{i+1}$, the following condition holds:

2. *The curve segments F_i and F_{i+n} join with continuity (at least) C^{m-n} at $\bar{u}_{i+1}$, in the sense of Definition 5.5.1, where n is the multiplicity of the knot $\bar{u}_{i+1}$ $(1 \le n \le m+1)$.*

    Thus, in particular, if $\bar{u}_{i+1}$ is a discontinuity knot, that is, a knot of multiplicity $m+1$, then we have C^{-1}-continuity, and $F_i(\bar{u}_{i+1})$ and $F_{i+n}(\bar{u}_{i+1})$ may differ. The set $F(\mathbf{A})$ is called the trace *of the spline F.*

Remarks:

1. Note that by definition, F agrees with a polynomial curve F_i on the interval $[\bar{u}_i, \bar{u}_{i+1}[$, and with a polynomial curve F_{i+n} on the interval $[\bar{u}_{i+1}, \bar{u}_{i+n+1}[$, so that the junction knot is indeed $\bar{u}_{i+1}$. Thus, it is more convenient to index the curve segment on the interval $[\bar{u}_i, \bar{u}_{i+1}[$ by the *last* occurrence of the knot $\bar{p} = \bar{u}_i$ in the knot sequence, rather than its first occurrence.

2. If we assume that there are no discontinuities, that is, every knot has multiplicity $\le m$, then clause (1) can be simplified a little bit: we simply require that the restriction of F to the closed interval $[\bar{u}_i, \bar{u}_{i+1}]$ agrees with a polynomial curve F_i of polar degree m. However, when $\bar{u}_{i+1}$ is a knot of multiplicity $m+1$, we want the spline function F to be defined at $\bar{u}_{i+1}$, although possibly discontinuous. This is achieved by requiring that the restriction of F to the interval $[\bar{u}_{i+1}, \bar{u}_{i+m+2}[$, *open on the right*, agrees with a polynomial curve F_{i+m+1}. This ensures that $F(\bar{u}_{i+1}) = F_{i+m+1}(\bar{u}_{i+1})$. Since F agrees with F_i on $[\bar{u}_i, \bar{u}_{i+1}[$, the limit $F(\bar{u}_{i+1}-)$ of $F(\bar{t})$ when $\bar{t}$ approaches $\bar{u}_{i+1}$ from below is equal to the limit of $F_i(\bar{t})$ when $\bar{t}$ approaches $\bar{u}_{i+1}$ (from below), and thus,

$$F(\bar{u}_{i+1}-) = \lim_{\bar{t} \to \bar{u}_{i+1}, \bar{t} < \bar{u}_{i+1}} F(\bar{t}) = F_i(\bar{u}_{i+1}).$$

   Thus, when $\bar{u}_{i+1}$ has multiplicity $n \le m$, we have

$$F(\bar{u}_{i+1}) = F_i(\bar{u}_{i+1}) = F_{i+n}(\bar{u}_{i+1}),$$

   since we have at least C^0-continuity.

3. The number $m+1$ is often called the *order* of the B-spline curve.

   We could have instead used intervals $]\bar{u}_{i+1}, \bar{u}_{i+m+2}]$, open on the left. The first option seems the one used in most books. We could also have used a more symmetric approach, where we require that the restriction of F to the open interval $]\bar{u}_{i+1}, \bar{u}_{i+m+2}[$, agrees with a polynomial curve F_{i+m+1}, and by giving an arbitrary value to $F(\bar{u}_{i+1})$. In this case, when $\bar{u}_{i+1}$ has multiplicity $m+1$, we would have

$$F(\bar{u}_{i+1}-) = \lim_{\bar{t} \to \bar{u}_{i+1}, \bar{t} < \bar{u}_{i+1}} F(\bar{t}) = F_i(\bar{u}_{i+1}),$$

and

$$F(\overline{u}_{i+1}+) = \lim_{\overline{t} \to \overline{u}_{i+1}, \overline{t} > \overline{u}_{i+1}} F(\overline{t}) = F_{i+m+1}(\overline{u}_{i+1}).$$

However, this would complicate the treatment of control points (we would need special control points corresponding to the "discontinuity values" $F(\overline{u}_{i+1})$). In case you are curious, the kind of discontinuity arising at a discontinuity knot $\overline{u}_{i+1}$ is called a discontinuity of the first kind (see Schwartz [71]). Practically, discontinuities are rare anyway, and we can safely ignore these subtleties.

4. Note that no requirements at all are placed on the joins of a piecewise polynomial curve, which amounts to saying that each join has continuity C^{-1} (but may be better).

5. It is possible for a piecewise polynomial curve, or for a spline curve, to have C^m-continuity at all joins: this is the case when F is a polynomial curve! In this case, there is no advantage in viewing F as a spline.

Figure 6.4 represents a part of a cubic spline based on the uniform knot sequence

$$\ldots, 0, 1, 2, 3, 4, 5, 6, 7, \ldots.$$

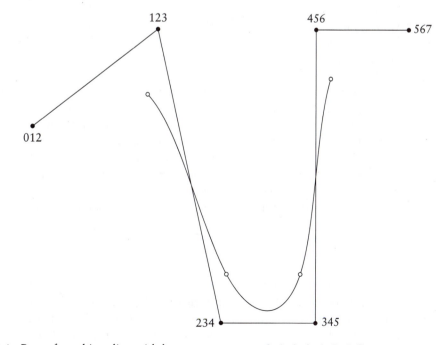

FIG. 6.4 Part of a cubic spline with knot sequence $\ldots, 0, 1, 2, 3, 4, 5, 6, 7, \ldots$

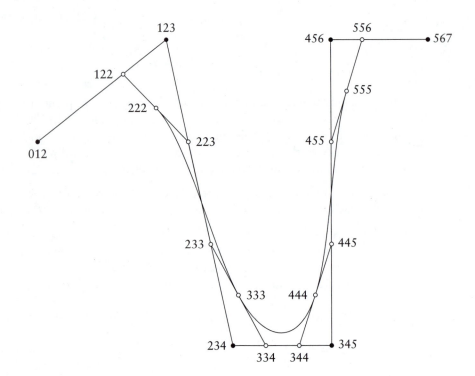

123   556

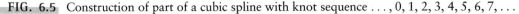

FIG. 6.5 Construction of part of a cubic spline with knot sequence ..., 0, 1, 2, 3, 4, 5, 6, 7, ...

For simplicity of notation, the polar values are denoted as triplets of consecutive knots $\bar{u}_i \bar{u}_{i+1} \bar{u}_{i+2}$, when in fact, they should be denoted as $f_k(\bar{u}_i, \bar{u}_{i+1}, \bar{u}_{i+2})$, for some appropriate k.

When considering part of a spline curve obtained by restricting our attention to a finite subsequence of an infinite knot sequence, we often say that the spline has *floating ends*. Figure 6.5 shows the construction of the control points for the three Bézier curve segments constituting this part of the spline (with floating ends).

By Lemma 5.5.2, the curve segments F_i and F_{i+n} join with continuity C^{m-n} at $\bar{q} = \bar{u}_{i+1}$ (where $1 \leq n \leq m+1$), iff their polar forms $f_i: \mathbf{A}^m \to \mathcal{E}$ and $f_{i+n}: \mathbf{A}^m \to \mathcal{E}$ agree on all multisets of points that contain at most $m - n$ points distinct from $\bar{q} = \bar{u}_{i+1}$, or equivalently, iff the polar forms $f_i: \mathbf{A}^m \to \mathcal{E}$ and $f_{i+n}: \mathbf{A}^m \to \mathcal{E}$ agree on all multisets (supermultisets) of m points from $\mathbf{A}$ containing the multiset

$$\{\bar{u}_{i+1}, \bar{u}_{i+2}, \ldots, \bar{u}_{i+n}\} = \{\underbrace{\bar{q}, \ldots, \bar{q}}_{n}\}.$$

Thus, the continuity conditions for joining curve segments forming a spline impose constraints on the polar forms of adjacent curve segments. In fact, two nonadjacent curve segments F_i and F_j are still related to each other as long as the number $j - i$ of intervening knots is at most m. As we will prove, the polar forms f_i and f_j must agree on all supermultisets (of m elements) of the multiset $\{\overline{u}_{i+1}, \overline{u}_{i+2}, \ldots, \overline{u}_j\}$.

Lemma 6.2.3

Given any $m \geq 1$, and any knot sequence $\langle \overline{u}_k \rangle_{k \in \mathbf{Z}}$ of degree of multiplicity at most $m + 1$, for any piecewise polynomial curve F of (polar) degree m based on the knot sequence $\langle \overline{u}_k \rangle_{k \in \mathbf{Z}}$, the curve F is a spline iff the following condition holds:
    For all i, j, with $i < j \leq i + m$, $\overline{u}_i < \overline{u}_{i+1}$ and $\overline{u}_j < \overline{u}_{j+1}$, the polar forms f_i and f_j agree on all multisets of m elements from $\mathbf{A}$ (supermultisets) containing the multiset of intervening knots

$$\{\overline{u}_{i+1}, \overline{u}_{i+2}, \ldots, \overline{u}_j\}.$$

Proof: If the polar forms f_i and f_j agree on all multisets of m elements from $\mathbf{A}$ containing the multiset of intervening knots

$$\{\overline{u}_{i+1}, \overline{u}_{i+2}, \ldots, \overline{u}_j\},$$

where $i < j \leq i + m$, $\overline{u}_i < \overline{u}_{i+1}$ and $\overline{u}_j < \overline{u}_{j+1}$, then for any two adjacent line segments F_i and F_{i+n} ($1 \leq n \leq m$), f_i and f_{i+n} agree on all multisets containing the multiset

$$\{\overline{u}_{i+1}, \overline{u}_{i+2}, \ldots, \overline{u}_{i+n}\},$$

which by Lemma 5.5.2, implies that the join at $\overline{u}_{i+1} = \overline{u}_{i+n}$ has continuity at least C^{m-n}. When $n = m + 1$, the condition is vacuous, but that's fine, since C^{-1}-continuity does not impose any continuity at all!

In the other direction, suppose that the curve segments F_i fit together to form a spline. Consider any two curve segments F_i and F_j, where $i < j \leq i + m$, $\overline{u}_i < \overline{u}_{i+1}$, and $\overline{u}_j < \overline{u}_{j+1}$. Let $n_1, n_2, \ldots, n_h$ be the multiplicities of the knots of the intervening sequence of knots

$$\{\overline{u}_{i+1}, \ldots, \overline{u}_j\},$$

so that $n_1 + n_2 + \cdots + n_h = j - i$. We proceed by induction on h. Since F_i and F_{i+n_1} join with C^{m-n_1}-continuity at $\overline{u}_{i+1} = \overline{u}_{i+n_1}$, by Lemma 5.5.2, f_i and f_{i+n_1} agree on all multisets containing the multiset

$$\{\overline{u}_{i+1}, \ldots, \overline{u}_{i+n_1}\}.$$

By the induction hypothesis, f_{i+n_1} and f_j agree on all multisets containing the multiset

$$\{\overline{u}_{i+n_1+1}, \ldots, \overline{u}_j\},$$

and by transitivity, f_i and f_j agree on all multisets containing the multiset

$$\{\overline{u}_{i+1}, \ldots, \overline{u}_j\}. \quad \blacksquare$$

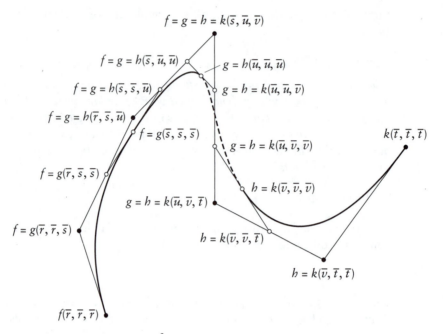

$$f = g = b = k(\bar{s}, \bar{u}, \bar{v})$$

$$f = g = b(\bar{s}, \bar{u}, \bar{u})$$

$$g = b(\bar{u}, \bar{u}, \bar{u})$$

$$f = g = b(\bar{s}, \bar{s}, \bar{u})$$

$$g = b = k(\bar{u}, \bar{u}, \bar{v})$$

$$f = g = b(\bar{r}, \bar{s}, \bar{u})$$

$$f = g(\bar{s}, \bar{s}, \bar{s})$$

$$k(\bar{t}, \bar{t}, \bar{t})$$

$$f = g(\bar{r}, \bar{s}, \bar{s})$$

$$g = b = k(\bar{u}, \bar{v}, \bar{v})$$

$$b = k(\bar{v}, \bar{v}, \bar{v})$$

$$g = b = k(\bar{u}, \bar{v}, \bar{t})$$

$$f = g(\bar{r}, \bar{r}, \bar{s})$$

$$b = k(\bar{v}, \bar{v}, \bar{t})$$

$$b = k(\bar{v}, \bar{t}, \bar{t})$$

$$f(\bar{r}, \bar{r}, \bar{r})$$

FIG. 6.6 Part of a cubic spline with C^2-continuity at the knots $\bar{s}, \bar{u}, \bar{v}$

Figure 6.6 shows part of a cubic spline corresponding to the knot sequence

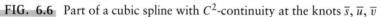

$$\ldots, \bar{r}, \bar{s}, \bar{u}, \bar{v}, \bar{t}, \ldots$$

with C^2-continuity at the knots $\bar{s}, \bar{u}, \bar{v}$. Recall that C^2-continuity at the knots $\bar{s}, \bar{u}, \bar{v}$ means that if we let f, g, h, k denote the polar forms corresponding to the intervals $[\bar{r}, \bar{s}]$, $[\bar{s}, \bar{u}]$, $[\bar{u}, \bar{v}]$, and $[\bar{v}, \bar{t}]$, then f and g agree on all (multiset) triplets including the argument $\bar{s}$, g and h agree on all triplets including the argument $\bar{u}$, and h and k agree on all triplets including the argument $\bar{v}$.

The fact that a knot $\bar{u}$ of multiplicity 2 generally corresponds to a join with only C^1-continuity can be derived by the following reasoning. If we assume that the points labeled $f(\bar{r}, \bar{r}, \bar{r})$, $f(\bar{r}, \bar{r}, \bar{s})$, $f(\bar{r}, \bar{s}, \bar{u})$, $f(\bar{s}, \bar{u}, \bar{v})$, $g(\bar{u}, \bar{v}, \bar{t})$, $k(\bar{v}, \bar{t}, \bar{t})$, and $k(\bar{t}, \bar{t}, \bar{t})$ do not change, and if we let $\bar{u}$ and $\bar{v}$ converge to a common value, in the limit, the curve segment between $g(\bar{u}, \bar{u}, \bar{u})$ and $h(\bar{v}, \bar{v}, \bar{v})$ (displayed as a dashed curve) is contracted to the single point $g(\bar{u}, \bar{u}, \bar{u})$ on the line segment between $f(\bar{s}, \bar{u}, \bar{v}) = f(\bar{s}, \bar{u}, \bar{u})$ and $g(\bar{u}, \bar{v}, \bar{t}) = g(\bar{u}, \bar{u}, \bar{t})$ (since the polar form h vanishes), and the two curve segments between $f(\bar{s}, \bar{s}, \bar{s})$ and $g(\bar{u}, \bar{u}, \bar{u})$, and between $k(\bar{v}, \bar{v}, \bar{v})$ and $k(\bar{t}, \bar{t}, \bar{t})$, end up joining at the new point $g(\bar{u}, \bar{u}, \bar{u})$ with different acceleration vectors, that is, only with C^1-continuity. Figure 6.7 illustrates this situation.

Note that C^1-continuity at the double knot $\bar{u}$ corresponds to the fact that the polar forms g and k agree on all (multiset) triplets that include two copies of the

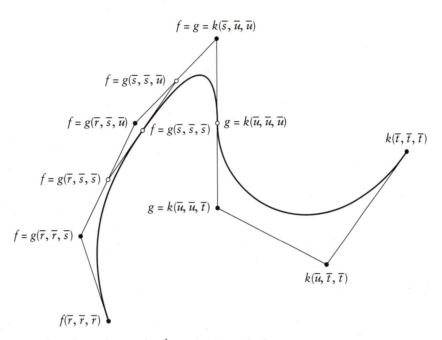

FIG. 6.7 Part of a cubic spline with C^1-continuity at the knot $\bar{u}$

argument $\bar{u}$. Let us now go back to our original figure showing part of a cubic spline corresponding to the knot sequence

$$\ldots, \bar{r}, \bar{s}, \bar{u}, \bar{v}, \bar{t}, \ldots$$

with C^2-continuity at the knots $\bar{s}, \bar{u}, \bar{v}$, and let us see what happens when the knot $\bar{s}$ becomes a knot of multiplicity 3 (see Figure 6.8).

The fact that a knot $\bar{s}$ of multiplicity 3 generally corresponds to a join with only C^0-continuity can be derived by the following reasoning. As in the previous case, if we assume that the points labeled $f(\bar{r}, \bar{r}, \bar{r})$, $f(\bar{r}, \bar{r}, \bar{s})$, $f(\bar{r}, \bar{s}, \bar{u})$, $f(\bar{s}, \bar{u}, \bar{v})$, $g(\bar{u}, \bar{v}, \bar{t})$, $k(\bar{v}, \bar{t}, \bar{t})$, and $k(\bar{t}, \bar{t}, \bar{t})$ do not change, and if we let $\bar{s}, \bar{u}$, and $\bar{v}$ converge to a common value, in the limit, the two curve segments between $f(\bar{s}, \bar{s}, \bar{s})$ and $g(\bar{u}, \bar{u}, \bar{u})$ and between $g(\bar{u}, \bar{u}, \bar{u})$ and $h(\bar{v}, \bar{v}, \bar{v})$ (displayed as dashed curves) are contracted to the single point $f(\bar{s}, \bar{u}, \bar{v}) = f(\bar{s}, \bar{s}, \bar{s})$ (since the polar forms g and h vanish), and the two curve segments between $f(\bar{r}, \bar{r}, \bar{r})$ and $f(\bar{s}, \bar{s}, \bar{s})$ and between $k(\bar{v}, \bar{v}, \bar{v})$ and $k(\bar{t}, \bar{t}, \bar{t})$ end up joining at $f(\bar{s}, \bar{u}, \bar{v}) = f(\bar{s}, \bar{s}, \bar{s})$ with different tangents, that is, only with C^0-continuity. Figure 6.9 illustrates this situation.

Note that C^0-continuity at the triple knot $\bar{s}$ corresponds to the fact that the polar forms f and k agree on the (multiset) triplet $\bar{s}, \bar{s}, \bar{s}$.

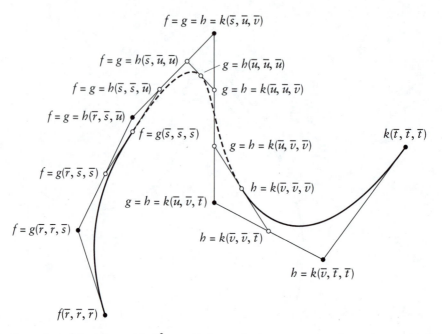

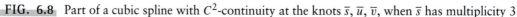

FIG. 6.8 Part of a cubic spline with C^2-continuity at the knots $\bar{s}, \bar{u}, \bar{v}$, when $\bar{s}$ has multiplicity 3

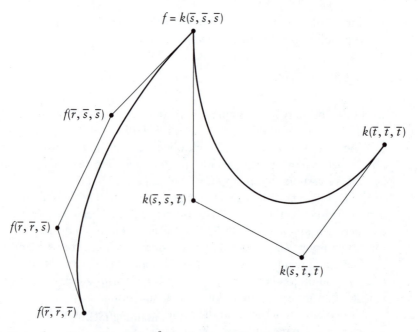

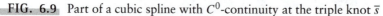

FIG. 6.9 Part of a cubic spline with C^0-continuity at the triple knot $\bar{s}$

If F is a spline curve of degree m, let us see what Lemma 6.2.3 tells us about the values of polar forms on multisets of arguments of the form

$$\{\overline{u}_{k+1}, \ldots, \overline{u}_{k+m}\}.$$

Consider $i < j$ such that $k \leq i < j \leq k + m$. Then, the multiset $\{\overline{u}_{i+1}, \ldots, \overline{u}_j\}$ is a submultiset of the multiset $\{\overline{u}_{k+1}, \ldots, \overline{u}_{k+m}\}$, and by Lemma 6.2.3, f_i and f_j agree on $\{\overline{u}_{k+1}, \ldots, \overline{u}_{k+m}\}$.

The polar values $f_i(\overline{u}_{k+1}, \ldots, \overline{u}_{k+m})$ (where $k \leq i \leq k + m$), are called *de Boor points*, and they play an important role for splines. Basically, they play for splines the role that Bézier control points play for polynomial curves. This is confirmed formally by the following theorem, which can be viewed as a generalization of Lemma 4.3.1. The proof is due to Ramshaw.

Theorem 6.2.4

Given any $m \geq 1$, and any knot sequence $\langle \overline{u}_k \rangle_{k \in \mathbb{Z}}$ of degree of multiplicity at most $m + 1$, for any bi-infinite sequence $\langle d_k \rangle_{k \in \mathbb{Z}}$ of points in some affine space $\mathcal{E}$, there exists a unique spline curve $F \colon \mathbf{A} \to \mathcal{E}$, such that the following condition holds:

$$d_k = f_i(\overline{u}_{k+1}, \ldots, \overline{u}_{k+m}),$$

for all k, i, where $\overline{u}_i < \overline{u}_{i+1}$ and $k \leq i \leq k + m$.

Proof: Assume that such a spline curve F exists. Let $\overline{u}_i < \overline{u}_{i+1}$ be two consecutive distinct knots, and consider the sequence of $2m$ knots

$$\langle \overline{u}_{i-m+1}, \ldots, \overline{u}_{i+m} \rangle,$$

centered at the interval $[\overline{u}_i, \overline{u}_{i+1}]$. Since we have

$$\overline{u}_{i-m+1} \leq \ldots \leq \overline{u}_i < \overline{u}_{i+1} \leq \ldots \leq \overline{u}_{i+m},$$

the sequence is progressive. Then, by Theorem 5.3.2, there is a unique polynomial curve F_i of polar degree m, such that

$$d_k = f_i(\overline{u}_{k+1}, \ldots, \overline{u}_{k+m}),$$

for all k, where $i - m \leq k \leq i$.

Since the requirements of Theorem 6.2.4 uniquely determine every curve segment F_i, we have shown that the spline curve F is unique, if it exists. Thus, we need to show the existence of such a spline curve. For this, we have to show that the curve segments F_i fit together in the right way to form a spline with the required continuity conditions. We will use Lemma 6.2.3. Let i, j be such that $i < j \leq i + m$, $\overline{u}_i < \overline{u}_{i+1}$, and $\overline{u}_j < \overline{u}_{j+1}$. We must show that the polar forms f_i and f_j agree on all multisets of m elements from $\mathbf{A}$ (supermultisets) containing the multiset of intervening knots

$$\{\overline{u}_{i+1}, \ldots, \overline{u}_j\}.$$

From the requirements of Theorem 6.2.4, we know that

$$f_i(\overline{u}_{k+1}, \ldots, \overline{u}_{k+m}) = f_j(\overline{u}_{k+1}, \ldots, \overline{u}_{k+m}) = d_k,$$

for k, with $j - m \leq k \leq i$. This means that f_i and f_j agree on the rows of the following parallelogram:

$$
\begin{matrix}
\overline{u}_{j-m+1} & \overline{u}_{j-m+2} & \cdots & \overline{u}_i & \overline{u}_{i+1} & \cdots & \overline{u}_j & & & \\
& \overline{u}_{j-m+2} & \cdots & \overline{u}_i & \overline{u}_{i+1} & \cdots & \overline{u}_j & \overline{u}_{j+1} & & \\
& & \ddots & \vdots & \vdots & & \vdots & \vdots & \ddots & \\
& & & \overline{u}_i & \overline{u}_{i+1} & \cdots & \overline{u}_j & \overline{u}_{j+1} & \cdots & \overline{u}_{i+m-1} \\
& & & & \overline{u}_{i+1} & \cdots & \overline{u}_j & \overline{u}_{j+1} & \cdots & \overline{u}_{i+m-1} & \overline{u}_{i+m}
\end{matrix}
$$

Now, cut the middle $j - i$ columns out of this parallelogram, and collapse the remaining two triangles to form a smaller parallelogram.

Let $l = m - j + i$, and let $g_i: \mathbf{A}^l \to \mathcal{E}$ and $g_j: \mathbf{A}^l \to \mathcal{E}$ denote the symmetric multiaffine functions of l arguments defined as follows:

$$g_i(\overline{v}_1, \ldots, \overline{v}_l) = f_i(\overline{v}_1, \ldots, \overline{v}_l, \overline{u}_{i+1}, \ldots, \overline{u}_j)$$

and

$$g_j(\overline{v}_1, \ldots, \overline{v}_l) = f_j(\overline{v}_1, \ldots, \overline{v}_l, \overline{u}_{i+1}, \ldots, \overline{u}_j),$$

for all $\overline{v}_1, \ldots, \overline{v}_l \in \mathbf{A}$. Proving that f_i and f_j agree on all supermultisets of $\{\overline{u}_{i+1}, \ldots, \overline{u}_j\}$ is equivalent to proving that $g_i = g_j$. Note that the sequence of $2l$ knots

$$\langle \overline{u}_{j-m+1}, \ldots, \overline{u}_i, \overline{u}_{j+1}, \ldots, \overline{u}_{i+m} \rangle$$

is progressive, since each element of the left half is strictly less than each element of the right half (since $\overline{u}_i < \overline{u}_{i+1} \leq \overline{u}_j$), and since f_i and f_j agree on the previous parallelogram, then g_i and g_j agree on the $l + 1$ sequences associated with the progressive sequence

$$\langle \overline{u}_{j-m+1}, \ldots, \overline{u}_i, \overline{u}_{j+1}, \ldots, \overline{u}_{i+m} \rangle,$$

which by Theorem 5.3.2 implies that $g_i = g_j$, and thus, that $f_i = f_j$. ∎

Given a knot $\overline{u}_i$ in the knot sequence, such that $\overline{u}_i < \overline{u}_{i+1}$, the inequality $k \leq i \leq k + m$ can be interpreted in two ways. If we think of k as fixed the theorem tells us which curve segments F_i of the spline F are influenced by the specific de Boor point d_k: the de Boor point d_k influences at most $m + 1$ curve segments. This is achieved when all the knots are simple. On the other hand, we can consider i as fixed and think of the inequalities as $i - m \leq k \leq i$. In this case, the theorem tells us which de Boor points influence the specific curve segment F_i: there are $m + 1$ de Boor points that influence the curve segment F_i. This does not depend on the knot multiplicity.

Given a spline curve $F: \mathbf{A} \to \mathcal{E}$, it is important to realize that F itself is generally *not* the polar form of some (unique) symmetric multiaffine map, although for every knot $\overline{u}_i$ such that $\overline{u}_i < \overline{u}_{i+1}$, the curve segment F_i that is the restriction of F to $[\overline{u}_i, \overline{u}_{i+1}[$ is defined by a unique symmetric multiaffine map. We can only say that F is a piecewise polar form. Nevertheless, it is convenient to denote polar values $f_i(\overline{u}_{k+1}, \ldots, \overline{u}_{k+m})$, corresponding to control points, simply as $f(\overline{u}_{k+1}, \ldots, \overline{u}_{k+m})$, omitting the subscript i, and we will often do so. We may even denote polar values $f_i(\overline{t}_1, \ldots, \overline{t}_m)$ as $f(\overline{t}_1, \ldots, \overline{t}_m)$, when the index i is clear from the context.

A clean way to handle this overloading problem is to define the notion of a validity interval. Given a knot sequence $\langle \overline{u}_k \rangle_{k \in \mathbb{Z}}$ of degree of multiplicity at most $m + 1$, for any multiset of arguments $\{\overline{u}_1, \ldots, \overline{u}_m\}$, if we know that for some nonempty set S of knots, the polar forms f_i, where $i \in S$, agree on the multiset $\{\overline{u}_1, \ldots, \overline{u}_m\}$, we denote this common value $f_i(\overline{u}_1, \ldots, \overline{u}_m)$ as $f_S(\overline{u}_1, \ldots, \overline{u}_m)$. According to this convention, when $i < j \leq i + m$, $\overline{u}_i < \overline{u}_{i+1}$, and $\overline{u}_j < \overline{u}_{j+1}$, the common value of f_i and f_j is denoted as

$$f_{\{i,j\}}(\overline{u}_{i+1}, \ldots, \overline{u}_j, \overline{t}_{j-i+1}, \ldots, \overline{t}_m),$$

where $\overline{t}_{j-i+1}, \ldots, \overline{t}_m$ are arbitrary.

Although the notation f_S is helpful, it is quite complex. We prefer using the notation f_I, where I is an open interval $]\overline{p}, \overline{q}[$. We have to be a little careful to deal with knots of multiplicity ≥ 2. Given a nonempty open interval I, for any multiset of arguments $\{\overline{u}_1, \ldots, \overline{u}_m\}$, we define $f_I(\overline{u}_1, \ldots, \overline{u}_m)$ as the common value $f_S(\overline{u}_1, \ldots, \overline{u}_m)$, where

$$S = \{i \mid \overline{u}_i, \overline{u}_{i+1}[\cap I \neq \emptyset\},$$

provided that this common value makes sense. The interval I is called a *validity interval*. Then,

$$f_{]\overline{u}_i, \overline{u}_{j+1}[}(\overline{u}_{i+1}, \ldots, \overline{u}_j, \overline{t}_{j-i+1}, \ldots, \overline{t}_m)$$

is well defined iff $\overline{u}_i < \overline{u}_{j+1}$. In particular, the terms $f_{]\overline{u}_i, \overline{u}_{i+m+1}[}(\overline{u}_{i+1}, \ldots, \overline{u}_{i+m})$ (the de Boor points) are always well defined. It is possible to introduce conventions for overloading the notation, that is, omitting validity intervals in polar forms. Under some reasonable conventions, validity intervals can be inferred automatically. Ramshaw introduced two such conventions, *tame overloading* and *wild overloading*. For details, see Ramshaw [65].

Having considered the case of bi-infinite knot sequences, we will next consider what kinds of adjustments are needed to handle finite knot sequences and infinite cyclic knot sequences. These adjustments are minor.

6.3   Finite Knot Sequences, Finite *B*-Spline Curves

In the case of a finite knot sequence, we have to deal with the two end knots. A reasonable method is to assume that the end knots have multiplicity $m + 1$. This way the first curve segment is unconstrained at its left end, and the last curve segment is unconstrained at its right end. Actually, multiplicity m will give the same results, but multiplicity $m + 1$ allows us to view a finite spline curve as a fragment of an infinite spline curve delimited by two discontinuity knots. Another reason for letting the end knots have multiplicity $m + 1$ is that it is needed for the inductive definition of *B*-spline basis functions (see Section 6.7).

Definition 6.3.1

Given any natural numbers $m \geq 1$ and $N \geq 0$, a finite knot sequence of degree of multiplicity at most $m + 1$ with N intervening knots is any finite nondecreasing sequence $\langle \bar{u}_k \rangle_{-m \leq k \leq N+m+1}$, such that $\bar{u}_{-m} < \bar{u}_{N+m+1}$, and every knot $\bar{u}_k$ has multiplicty at most $m + 1$. A knot $\bar{u}_k$ of multiplicity $m + 1$ is called a discontinuity (knot). A knot of multiplicity 1 is called a simple knot.

Given a finite knot sequence $\langle \bar{u}_k \rangle_{-m \leq k \leq N+m+1}$, of degree of multiplicity at most $m + 1$ and with N intervening knots, we now define the number L of subintervals in the knot sequence. If $N = 0$, the knot sequence $\langle \bar{u}_k \rangle_{-m \leq k \leq m+1}$ consists of $2(m + 1)$ knots, where $\bar{u}_{-m}$ and $\bar{u}_{m+1}$ are distinct and of multiplicity $m + 1$, and we let $L = 1$. If $N \geq 1$, then we let $L - 1 \geq 1$ be the number of distinct knots in the sequence $\langle \bar{u}_1, \ldots, \bar{u}_N \rangle$. If the multiplicities of the $L - 1$ distinct knots in the sequence $\langle \bar{u}_1, \ldots, \bar{u}_N \rangle$ are $n_1, \ldots, n_{L-1}$ (where $1 \leq n_i \leq m + 1$, and $1 \leq i \leq L - 1$), then

$$N = n_1 + \cdots + n_{L-1},$$

and the knot sequence $\langle \bar{u}_k \rangle_{-m \leq k \leq N+m+1}$ consists of $2(m + 1) + N = 2(m + 1) + n_1 + \cdots + n_{L-1}$ knots, with $L + 1$ of them distinct.

Given a finite sequence, when $N \geq 1$ and $L \geq 2$, if $\langle \bar{v}_1, \ldots, \bar{v}_{L-1} \rangle$ is the subsequence of leftmost occurrences of distinct knots in the sequence $\langle \bar{u}_1, \ldots, \bar{u}_N \rangle$, in general, $\bar{v}_i \neq \bar{u}_i$. Instead, if the multiplicity of each knot $\bar{v}_i$ is n_i (where $1 \leq i \leq L - 1$, and $1 \leq n_i \leq m + 1$), then $\bar{v}_i = \bar{u}_{n_1 + \cdots + n_{i-1} + 1}$, with the convention that $n_1 + \cdots + n_0 = 0$ when $i - 1 = 0$.

A finite knot sequence of length $2(m + 1) + N$ containing $L + 1$ distinct knots looks as follows:

$$\underbrace{\bar{u}_{-m}, \ldots, \bar{u}_0}_{m+1}, \underbrace{\bar{u}_1, \ldots, \bar{u}_{n_1}}_{n_1}, \underbrace{\bar{u}_{n_1+1}, \ldots, \bar{u}_{n_1+n_2}}_{n_2}, \ldots,$$

$$\underbrace{\bar{u}_{N-n_{L-1}+1}, \ldots, \bar{u}_N}_{n_{L-1}}, \underbrace{\bar{u}_{N+1}, \ldots, \bar{u}_{N+m+1}}_{m+1},$$

where

$$N = n_1 + \cdots + n_{L-1}.$$

The picture below gives a clearer idea of the knot multiplicities:

$$\bar{u}_{-m}, \quad \bar{u}_1, \quad \bar{u}_{n_1+1}, \quad \ldots, \quad \bar{u}_{N-n_{L-1}+1}, \quad \bar{u}_{N+1},$$

$$\vdots \qquad \vdots \qquad \vdots \qquad \ldots \qquad \vdots \qquad \vdots$$

$$\bar{u}_0 \qquad \bar{u}_{n_1} \quad \bar{u}_{n_1+n_2} \quad \ldots \qquad \bar{u}_N \qquad \bar{u}_{N+m+1}$$

$$m+1 \quad n_1 \qquad n_2 \qquad \ldots \qquad n_{L-1} \qquad m+1$$

We can now define finite B-spline curves based on finite knot sequences. Note that some authors use the terminology *closed B-splines* for such B-splines. We do not favor this terminology, since it is inconsistent with the traditional meaning of a closed curve. Instead, we propose to use the terminology *finite B-splines*.

Definition 6.3.2

Given any natural numbers $m \geq 1$ and $N \geq 0$, given any finite knot sequence $\langle \bar{u}_k \rangle_{-m \leq k \leq N+m+1}$ of degree of multiplicity at most $m+1$ and with N intervening knots, a piecewise polynomial curve of degree m based on the finite knot sequence $\langle \bar{u}_k \rangle_{-m \leq k \leq N+m+1}$ is a function $F: [\bar{u}_0, \bar{u}_{N+1}] \to \mathcal{E}$, where $\mathcal{E}$ is some affine space (of dimension at least 2), such that the following condition holds:

1. *If $N = 0$, then $F: [\bar{u}_0, \bar{u}_{m+1}] \to \mathcal{E}$ agrees with a polynomial curve F_0 of polar degree m, with associated polar form f_0. When $N \geq 1$, then for any two consecutive distinct knots $\bar{u}_i < \bar{u}_{i+1}$, if $0 \leq i \leq N - n_{L-1}$, then the restriction of F to $[\bar{u}_i, \bar{u}_{i+1}[$ agrees with a polynomial curve F_i of polar degree m with associated polar form f_i, and if $i = N$, then the restriction of F to $[\bar{u}_N, \bar{u}_{N+1}]$ agrees with a polynomial curve F_N of polar degree m, with associated polar form f_N.*

   A spline curve F of degree m based on the finite knot sequence $\langle \bar{u}_k \rangle_{-m \leq k \leq N+m+1}$ or for short, a finite B-spline, is a piecewise polynomial curve $F: [\bar{u}_0, \bar{u}_{N+1}] \to \mathcal{E}$, such that, when $N \geq 1$ and $L \geq 2$, for every two consecutive distinct knots $\bar{u}_i < \bar{u}_{i+1}$ (where $0 \leq i \leq N - n_{L-1}$), if $\bar{u}_{i+1}$ has multiplicity $n \leq m+1$, the following condition holds:

2. *The curve segments F_i and F_{i+n} join with continuity (at least) C^{m-n} at $\bar{u}_{i+1}$, in the sense of Definition 5.5.1.*

   The set $F([\bar{u}_0, \bar{u}_{N+1}])$ is called the trace *of the finite spline F.*

Remark: The remarks about discontinuities made after Definition 6.2.2 also apply. However, we also want the last curve segment F_N to be defined at $\bar{u}_{N+1}$. Note that if we assume that $\bar{u}_0$ and $\bar{u}_{N+1}$ have multiplicity m, then we get the same curve. However, using multiplicity $m+1$ allows us to view a finite spline as a fragment of an infinite spline. Another reason for letting the end knots have multiplicity $m+1$ is that it is needed for the inductive definition of B-spline basis functions (see Section 6.7).

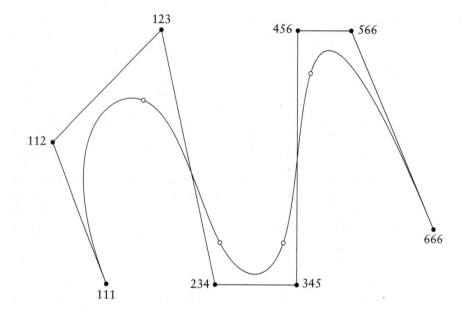

A cubic spline with knot sequence 1, 1, 1, 1, 2, 3, 4, 5, 6, 6, 6, 6

Note that a spline curve defined on the finite knot sequence

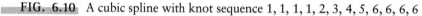

$$\begin{array}{ccccc} \bar{u}_{-m}, & \bar{u}_1, & \bar{u}_{n_1+1}, & \ldots, & \bar{u}_{N-n_{L-1}+1}, & \bar{u}_{N+1}, \\ \vdots & \vdots & \vdots & \ldots & \vdots & \vdots \\ \bar{u}_0 & \bar{u}_{n_1} & \bar{u}_{n_1+n_2} & \ldots & \bar{u}_N & \bar{u}_{N+m+1} \\ m+1 & n_1 & n_2 & \ldots & n_{L-1} & m+1 \end{array}$$

where

$$N = n_1 + \cdots + n_{L-1},$$

consists of L curve segments, $F_0, F_{n_1}, \ldots, F_{n_1+\cdots+n_{L-1}} = F_N$.

Let us look at some examples of splines.

To simplify notation, in the following figures representing cubic splines, polar values are denoted as triplets of consecutive knots $\bar{u}_i \bar{u}_{i+1} \bar{u}_{i+2}$, when in fact they should be denoted as $f_k(\bar{u}_i, \bar{u}_{i+1}, \bar{u}_{i+2})$, for some appropriate k.

Several Bézier curve segments of a cubic spline are shown in Figure 6.10, and the construction of the corresponding control points is shown in Figure 6.11.

Figure 6.12 shows another cubic spline with knot sequence

$$0, 0, 0, 0, 1, 2, 3, 4, 5, 6, 7, 7, 7, 7.$$

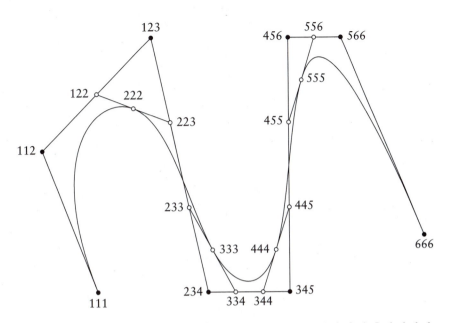

FIG. 6.11 Construction of a cubic spline with knot sequence 1, 1, 1, 1, 2, 3, 4, 5, 6, 6, 6, 6

Figure 6.13 shows the construction of the control points for the Bézier curve segments constituting the previous spline.

Figures 6.14 and 6.15 show a cubic spline with knot sequence

$$0, 0, 0, 0, 1, 2, 3, 4, 5, 6, 7, 7, 8, 9, 10, 11, 11, 11, 12, 13, 13, 13, 13,$$

and the construction of the control points of the Bézier curves that constitute the spline.

Figure 6.16 shows a cubic spline based on the nonuniform knot sequence

$$0, 0, 0, 0, 1, 2, 3, 5, 6, 7, 8, 8, 9, 10, 10, 10, 10$$

with intervening double knot 8, and Figure 6.17 shows the details of the construction of this spline.

Since the knot sequence is nonuniform, the interpolation ratios vary. For example, the nodes labeled 112, 122, 223, 233, 335, 355, 556, 566, 667, 677, 222, 333, 555, and 666 correspond to the ratios $\frac{1}{3}, \frac{2}{3}, \frac{1}{4}, \frac{1}{2}, \frac{1}{4}, \frac{3}{4}, \frac{1}{2}, \frac{3}{4}, \frac{1}{3}, \frac{2}{3}, \frac{1}{2}, \frac{1}{3}, \frac{2}{3}, \frac{1}{2}$.

The nonuniformity of the knot sequence causes the Bézier control points 333 and 555 to be pulled towards the edges of the control polygon, and thus, the corresponding part of the spline is also pulled towards the control polygon. We now consider closed *B*-spline curves over cyclic knot sequences.

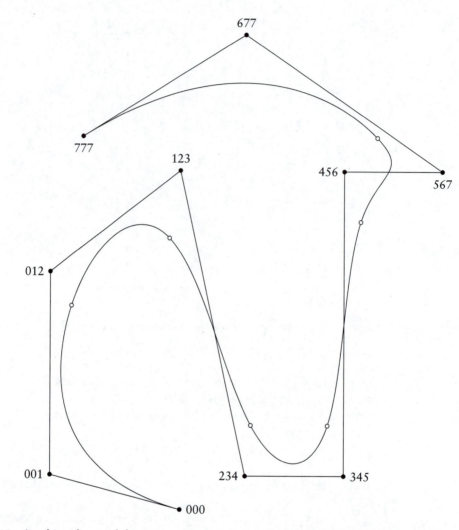

FIG. 6.12 A cubic spline with knot sequence 0, 0, 0, 0, 1, 2, 3, 4, 5, 6, 7, 7, 7, 7

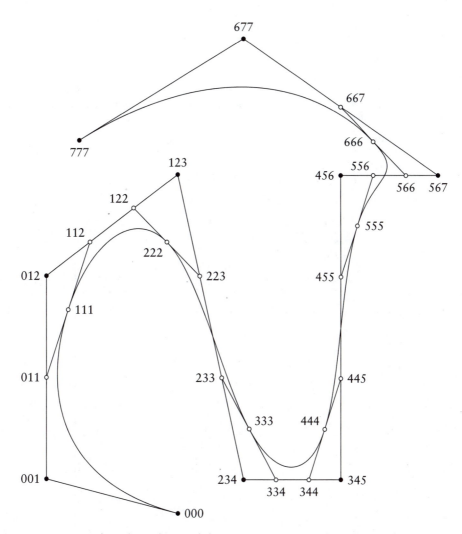

FIG. 6.13 Construction of a cubic spline with knot sequence 0, 0, 0, 0, 1, 2, 3, 4, 5, 6, 7, 7, 7, 7

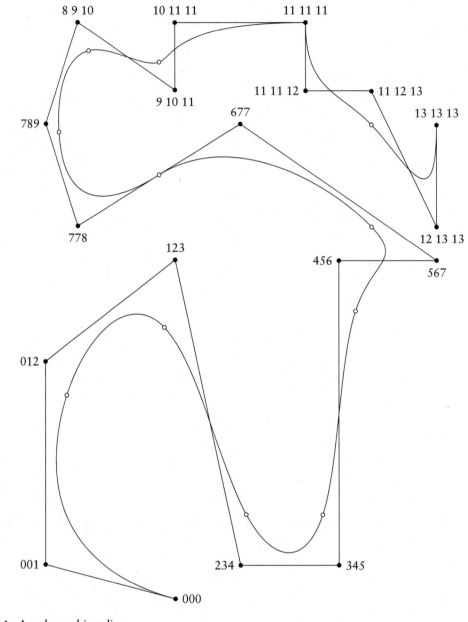

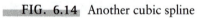
FIG. 6.14 Another cubic spline

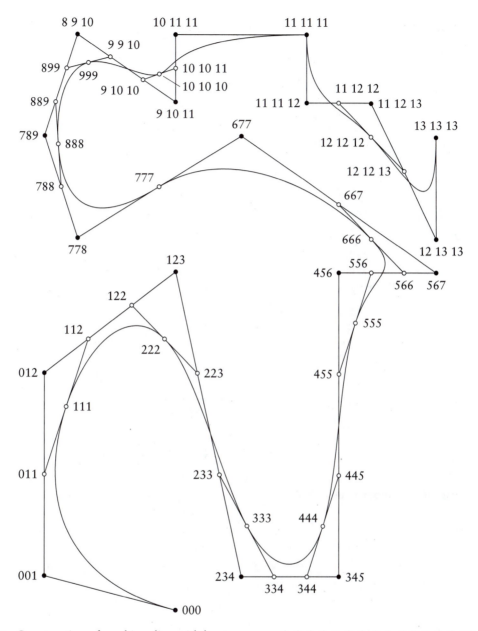

FIG. 6.15 Construction of a cubic spline with knot sequence 0, 0, 0, 0, 1, 2, 3, 4, 5, 6, 7, 7, 8, 9, 10, 11, 11, 11, 12, 13, 13, 13, 13

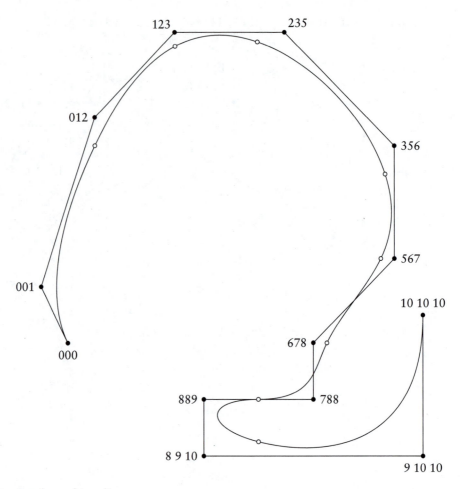

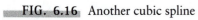

FIG. 6.16 Another cubic spline

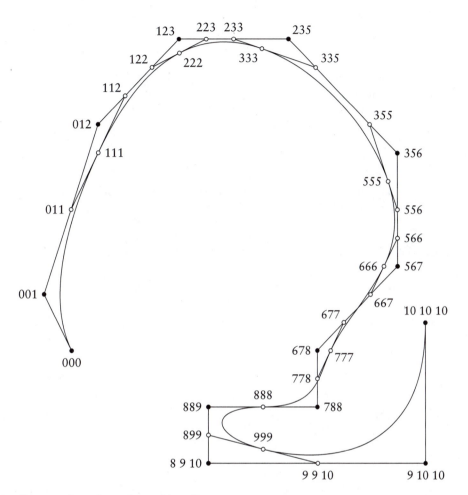

Construction of another cubic spline

6.4   Cyclic Knot Sequences, Closed (Cyclic) B-Spline Curves

First, we define cyclic knot sequences.

Definition 6.4.1

A cyclic knot sequence of period L, cycle length N, and period size T is any bi-infinite nondecreasing sequence $\langle \overline{u}_k \rangle_{k \in \mathbf{Z}}$ of points $\overline{u}_k \in \mathbf{A}$ (i.e., $\overline{u}_k \leq \overline{u}_{k+1}$ for all $k \in \mathbf{Z}$), where $L, N, T \in \mathbf{N}$, $L \geq 2$, and $N \geq L$, such that there is some subsequence

$$\langle \overline{u}_{j+1}, \ldots, \overline{u}_{j+N} \rangle$$

of N consecutive knots containing exactly L distinct knots, with multiplicities $n_1, \ldots, n_L,$ $\overline{u}_{j+N} < \overline{u}_{j+N+1},$ *and* $\overline{u}_{k+N} = \overline{u}_k + T,$ *for every* $k \in \mathbf{Z}.$ *Note that we must have* $N = n_1 + \cdots + n_L$ *(and* $n_i \geq 1$*). Given any natural number* $m \geq 1,$ *a cyclic knot sequence of period L, cycle length N, and period size T has degree of multiplicity at most m, iff every knot has multiplicity at most m.*

As before, a knot sequence (finite, or cyclic) is uniform iff $\overline{u}_{k+1} = \overline{u}_k + h,$ for some fixed $h \in \mathbf{R}_+.$

A cyclic knot sequence of period L, cycle length N, and period size T is completely determined by a sequence of $N + 1$ consecutive knots, which looks as follows (assuming for simplicity that the index of the starting knot of the cycle that we are looking at is $k = 1$):

$$\ldots, \underbrace{\overline{u}_1, \ldots, \overline{u}_{n_1}}_{n_1}, \underbrace{\overline{u}_{n_1+1}, \ldots, \overline{u}_{n_1+n_2}}_{n_2}, \ldots, \underbrace{\overline{u}_{n_1+\cdots+n_{L-1}+1}, \ldots, \overline{u}_N}_{n_L}, \overline{u}_{N+1}, \ldots,$$

or showing the knot multiplicities more clearly, as

$$
\begin{array}{ccccc}
\ldots, & \overline{u}_1, & \overline{u}_{n_1+1}, & \ldots, & \overline{u}_{N-n_L+1}, & \overline{u}_{N+1}, & \ldots \\
 & \vdots & \vdots & \ldots & \vdots & \vdots & \\
 & \overline{u}_{n_1} & \overline{u}_{n_1+n_2} & \ldots & \overline{u}_N & \overline{u}_{N+n_1} & \\
 & & & & & & \\
 & n_1 & n_2 & \ldots & n_L & n_1 &
\end{array}
$$

where

$$N = n_1 + \cdots + n_L, \quad \overline{u}_N < \overline{u}_{N+1},$$

and $\overline{u}_{k+N} = \overline{u}_k + T,$ for every $k \in \mathbf{Z}.$ Observe that we can think of the knots as labeling N points distributed on a circle, where any two knots $\overline{u}_{k+N}$ and $\overline{u}_k + T$ label the same point (see Figure 6.18).

We will see when we define closed spline curves that it does not make sense to allow knots of multiplicity $m + 1$ in a cyclic knot sequence. This is why the multiplicity of knots is at most m.

The following is an example of a cyclic knot sequence of period 3, cycle length $N = 3$, and period size 5:

$\ldots,$ **1, 3, 4, 6, 8, 9, 11, 13,** $\ldots$.

Another example of a cyclic knot sequence of period 4, cycle length $N = 5$, and period size 6 is

$\ldots,$ **1, 2, 2, 5, 6, 7, 8, 8, 11, 12, 13,** $\ldots$.

We now define *B*-spline curves based on cyclic knot sequences. Some authors use the terminology *cyclic B-splines*, and we will also call them *closed B-splines*.

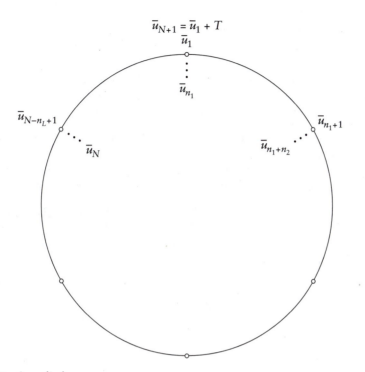

FIG. 6.18 A cyclic knot sequence

Definition 6.4.2

Given any natural number $m \geq 1$, given any cyclic knot sequence $\langle \overline{u}_k \rangle_{k \in \mathbb{Z}}$ of period L, cycle length N, period size T, and of degree of multiplicity at most m, a piecewise polynomial curve of degree m based on the cyclic knot sequence $\langle \overline{u}_k \rangle_{k \in \mathbb{Z}}$ is a function $F: \mathbf{A} \rightarrow \mathcal{E}$, where $\mathcal{E}$ is some affine space (of dimension at least 2), such that, for any two consecutive distinct knots $\overline{u}_i < \overline{u}_{i+1}$, if $\overline{u}_{i+1}$ is a knot of multiplicity n, the next distinct knot being $\overline{u}_{i+n+1}$, then the following condition holds:

1. *The restriction of F to $[\overline{u}_i, \overline{u}_{i+1}]$ agrees with a polynomial curve F_i of polar degree m, with associated polar form f_i, and $F_{i+N}(\overline{t} + T) = F_i(\overline{t})$, for all $\overline{t} \in [\overline{u}_i, \overline{u}_{i+1}]$.*

    A spline curve F of degree m based on the cyclic knot sequence $\langle \overline{u}_k \rangle_{k \in \mathbb{Z}}$, or for short, a closed (or cyclic) B-spline, is a closed piecewise polynomial curve $F: \mathbf{A} \rightarrow \mathcal{E}$, such that, for every two consecutive distinct knots $\overline{u}_i < \overline{u}_{i+1}$, the following condition holds:

2. *The curve segments F_i and F_{i+n} join with continuity (at least) C^{m-n} at $\overline{u}_{i+1}$, in the sense of Definition 5.5.1, where n is the multiplicity of the knot $\overline{u}_{i+1}$ $(1 \leq n \leq m)$.*

    The set $F(\mathbf{A})$ is called the trace *of the closed spline F.*

Remarks:

1. Recall that a cyclic knot sequence of period L, cycle length N, and period size T satisfies the property that $\bar{u}_{k+N} = \bar{u}_k + T$, for every $k \in \mathbb{Z}$. We must have $\bar{u}_{i+N} = \bar{u}_i + T$, $\bar{u}_{i+1+N} = \bar{u}_{i+1} + T$, and thus, the curve segment F_{i+N} is defined on the interval $[\bar{u}_i + T, \bar{u}_{i+1} + T]$, and it makes sense to require the periodicity condition $F_{i+N}(\bar{t} + T) = F_i(\bar{t})$, for all $\bar{t} \in [\bar{u}_i, \bar{u}_{i+1}]$.

2. In the case of a closed spline curve, it does not make sense to allow discontinuities, because if we do, we obtain a spline curve with discontinuities, which is not a closed curve in the usual mathematical sense. Thus, we allow knots of multiplicity at most m (rather than $m + 1$). When every knot is simple, we have $L = N$.

   Note that a closed spline curve based on the following cyclic knot sequence of period L, cycle length N, and period size T,

$$
\begin{array}{ccccc}
\ldots, & \bar{u}_1, & \bar{u}_{n_1+1}, & \ldots, & \bar{u}_{N-n_L+1}, & \bar{u}_{N+1}, & \ldots \\
& \vdots & \vdots & \ldots & \vdots & \vdots \\
& \bar{u}_{n_1} & \bar{u}_{n_1+n_2} & \ldots & \bar{u}_N & \bar{u}_{N+n_1} \\
\\
& n_1 & n_2 & \ldots & n_L & n_1
\end{array}
$$

   where

$$
N = n_1 + \cdots + n_L, \quad \bar{u}_N < \bar{u}_{N+1},
$$

   and $\bar{u}_{k+N} = \bar{u}_k + T$ for every $k \in \mathbb{Z}$, consists of L curve segments (the period of the knot sequence).

   Some examples of closed splines are given next.

   Figure 6.19 shows a closed cubic spline based on the uniform cyclic knot sequence

$$
\ldots, 0, 1, 2, 3, 4, 5, 6, 7, 8, 9, 10, 11, 12, 13, 14, 15, 16, 17, \ldots
$$

   of period $L = 16$, cycle length $N = 16$, and period size $T = 16$. As usual, for simplicity of notation, the control points are denoted as triplets of consecutive knots $\bar{u}_i \bar{u}_{i+1} \bar{u}_{i+2}$. The cyclicity condition is

$$
f_k(\bar{u}_i, \bar{u}_{i+1}, \bar{u}_{i+2}) = f_{k+16}(\bar{u}_i + 16, \bar{u}_{i+1} + 16, \bar{u}_{i+2} + 16),
$$

   which we write more simply as

$$
\bar{u}_i \bar{u}_{i+1} \bar{u}_{i+2} = (\bar{u}_i + 16)(\bar{u}_{i+1} + 16)(\bar{u}_{i+2} + 16).
$$

   Since the knot sequence is uniform, all the interpolation ratios are equal to $\frac{1}{3}$, $\frac{2}{3}$, or $\frac{1}{2}$. Figure 6.20 shows the details of the construction of the spline.

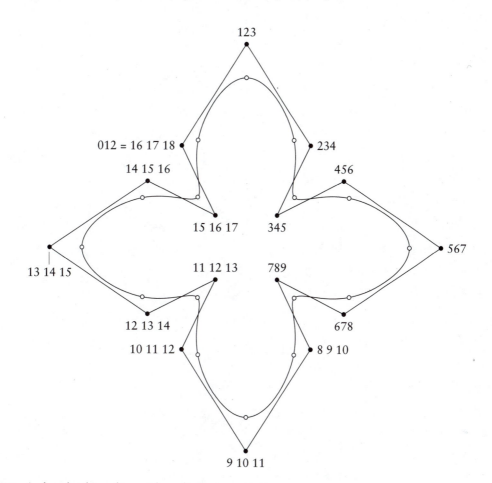

123

012 = 16 17 18

234

14 15 16

456

15 16 17   345

13 14 15

567

11 12 13   789

12 13 14

678

10 11 12

8 9 10

9 10 11

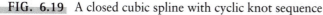**FIG. 6.19** A closed cubic spline with cyclic knot sequence

Figure 6.21 shows a closed cubic spline based on the nonuniform cyclic knot sequence

$$\ldots, -3, -2, 1, 3, 4, 5, 6, 9, 11, 12, \ldots$$

of period $L = 5$, cycle length $N = 5$, and period size $T = 8$. As usual, for simplicity of notation, the control points are denoted as triplets of consecutive knots $\bar{u}_i \bar{u}_{i+1} \bar{u}_{i+2}$. The cyclicity condition is

$$f_k(\bar{u}_i, \bar{u}_{i+1}, \bar{u}_{i+2}) = f_{k+5}(\bar{u}_i + 8, \bar{u}_{i+1} + 8, \bar{u}_{i+2} + 8),$$

which we write more simply as

$$\bar{u}_i \bar{u}_{i+1} \bar{u}_{i+2} = (\bar{u}_i + 8)(\bar{u}_{i+1} + 8)(\bar{u}_{i+2} + 8).$$

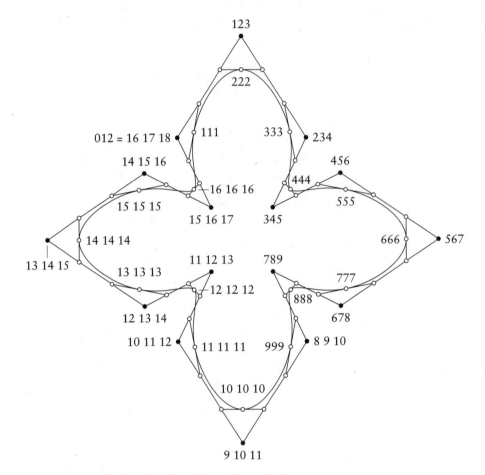

FIG. 6.20 Construction of a closed cubic spline with cyclic knot sequence

Because the knot sequence is nonuniform, the interpolation ratios vary. The interpolation ratios for the nodes labeled 113, 133, 334, 344, 445, 455, 556, 566, 669, −2 11 = 699, 111, 333, 444, 555, 666 are $\frac{1}{3}, \frac{5}{6}, \frac{1}{2}, \frac{3}{4}, \frac{1}{3}, \frac{2}{3}, \frac{1}{5}, \frac{2}{5}, \frac{1}{6}, \frac{2}{3}, \frac{3}{5}, \frac{2}{3}, \frac{1}{2}, \frac{1}{2}, \frac{1}{4}$.

Figure 6.22 shows the details of the construction of the spline.

It is easy to show that Lemma 6.2.3 can be simply modified to hold for finite spline curves and for closed spline curves. We can also modify Theorem 6.2.4 as follows.

Theorem 6.4.3

1. *Given any $m \geq 1$, and any finite knot sequence $\langle \bar{u}_k \rangle_{-m \leq k \leq N+m+1}$ of degree of multiplicity at most $m + 1$, for any sequence $\langle d_{-m}, \ldots, d_N \rangle$ of $N + m + 1$ points in some affine space $\mathcal{E}$, there exists a unique spline curve $F: [\bar{u}_0, \bar{u}_{N+1}] \to \mathcal{E}$, such that*

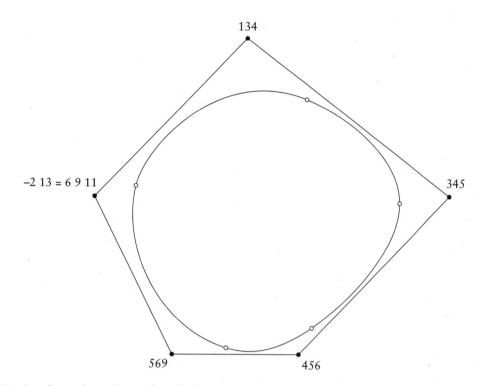

134

−2 13 = 6 9 11

345

569

456

FIG. 6.21 Another cubic spline with cyclic knot sequence

$$d_k = f_i(\bar{u}_{k+1}, \ldots, \bar{u}_{k+m}),$$

for all k, i, where $-m \leq k \leq N$, $\bar{u}_i < \bar{u}_{i+1}$, and $k \leq i \leq k + m$.

2. *Given any $m \geq 1$, and any finite cyclic knot sequence $\langle \bar{u}_k \rangle_{k \in \mathbb{Z}}$ of period L, cycle length N, period size T, and of degree of multiplicity at most m, for any bi-infinite periodic sequence $\langle d_k \rangle_{k \in \mathbb{Z}}$ of period N of points in some affine space $\mathcal{E}$, that is, a sequence such that $d_{k+N} = d_k$ for all $k \in \mathbb{Z}$, there exists a unique closed spline curve $F : \mathbf{A} \to \mathcal{E}$, such that*

$$d_k = f_i(\bar{u}_{k+1}, \ldots, \bar{u}_{k+m}),$$

for all k, i, where $\bar{u}_i < \bar{u}_{i+1}$ and $k \leq i \leq k + m$.

Proof: (1) The finite knot sequence is of the form

$$\underbrace{\bar{u}_{-m}, \ldots, \bar{u}_0}_{m+1}, \underbrace{\bar{u}_1, \ldots, \bar{u}_{n_1}}_{n_1}, \underbrace{\bar{u}_{n_1+1}, \ldots, \bar{u}_{n_1+n_2}}_{n_2}, \ldots,$$

$$\underbrace{\bar{u}_{n_1+\cdots+n_{L-2}+1}, \ldots, \bar{u}_N}_{n_{L-1}}, \underbrace{\bar{u}_{N+1}, \ldots, \bar{u}_{N+m+1}}_{m+1},$$

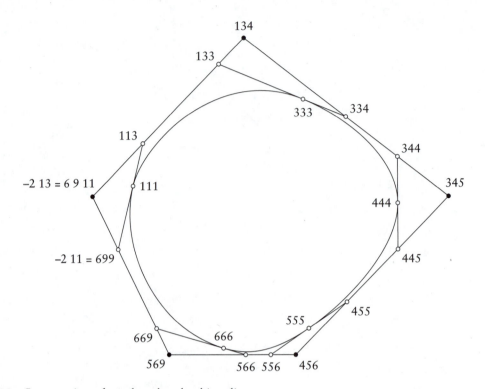

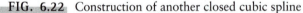

FIG. 6.22   Construction of another closed cubic spline

where $N = n_1 + \cdots + n_{L-1}$, and it consists of $2(m+1) + N$ knots. Note that there are $(2(m+1) + N) - m + 1 = m + N + 3$ subsequences of m consecutive knots in the entire knot sequence. Assume that a spline satisfying condition (1) exists. Observe that

$$d_{-m} = f_0(\overline{u}_{-m+1}, \ldots, \overline{u}_0),$$

and

$$d_N = f_N(\overline{u}_{N+1}, \ldots, \overline{u}_{N+m}),$$

and since the first and the last knot have multiplicity $m + 1$, this means that the sequences $\langle \overline{u}_{-m}, \ldots, \overline{u}_{-1} \rangle$ and $\langle \overline{u}_{N+2}, \ldots, \overline{u}_{N+m+1} \rangle$ do not correspond to any control points (but this is fine!). Also observe that there are $m + N + 1$ subsequences of m consecutive knots in the knot sequence $\langle \overline{u}_{-m+1}, \ldots, \overline{u}_{N+m} \rangle$. Let $\overline{u}_i < \overline{u}_{i+1}$ be two consecutive distinct knots in the sequence $\langle \overline{u}_{-m+1}, \ldots, \overline{u}_{N+m} \rangle$, and consider the sequence of $2m$ knots

$$\langle \overline{u}_{i-m+1}, \ldots, \overline{u}_{i+m} \rangle,$$

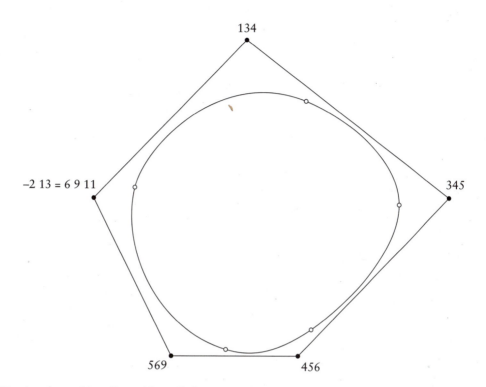

Another cubic spline with cyclic knot sequence

$$d_k = f_i(\overline{u}_{k+1}, \ldots, \overline{u}_{k+m}),$$

for all k, i, where $-m \leq k \leq N$, $\overline{u}_i < \overline{u}_{i+1}$, and $k \leq i \leq k + m$.

2. *Given any $m \geq 1$, and any finite cyclic knot sequence $\langle \overline{u}_k \rangle_{k \in \mathbf{Z}}$ of period L, cycle length N, period size T, and of degree of multiplicity at most m, for any bi-infinite periodic sequence $\langle d_k \rangle_{k \in \mathbf{Z}}$ of period N of points in some affine space $\mathcal{E}$, that is, a sequence such that $d_{k+N} = d_k$ for all $k \in \mathbf{Z}$, there exists a unique closed spline curve $F : \mathrm{A} \to \mathcal{E}$, such that*

$$d_k = f_i(\overline{u}_{k+1}, \ldots, \overline{u}_{k+m}),$$

for all k, i, where $\overline{u}_i < \overline{u}_{i+1}$ and $k \leq i \leq k + m$.

Proof: (1) The finite knot sequence is of the form

$$\underbrace{\overline{u}_{-m}, \ldots, \overline{u}_0}_{m+1}, \underbrace{\overline{u}_1, \ldots, \overline{u}_{n_1}}_{n_1}, \underbrace{\overline{u}_{n_1+1}, \ldots, \overline{u}_{n_1+n_2}}_{n_2}, \ldots,$$

$$\underbrace{\overline{u}_{n_1+\cdots+n_{L-2}+1}, \ldots, \overline{u}_N}_{n_{L-1}}, \underbrace{\overline{u}_{N+1}, \ldots, \overline{u}_{N+m+1}}_{m+1},$$

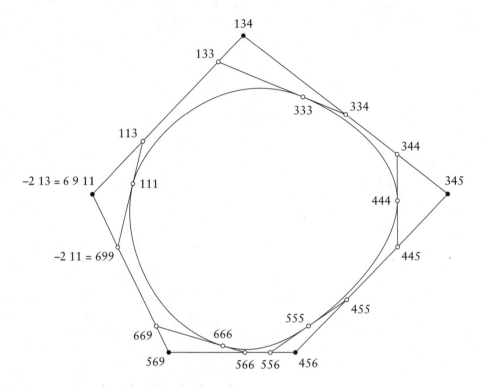

Construction of another closed cubic spline

where $N = n_1 + \cdots + n_{L-1}$, and it consists of $2(m + 1) + N$ knots. Note that there are $(2(m + 1) + N) - m + 1 = m + N + 3$ subsequences of m consecutive knots in the entire knot sequence. Assume that a spline satisfying condition (1) exists. Observe that

$$d_{-m} = f_0(\bar{u}_{-m+1}, \ldots, \bar{u}_0),$$

and

$$d_N = f_N(\bar{u}_{N+1}, \ldots, \bar{u}_{N+m}),$$

and since the first and the last knot have multiplicity $m + 1$, this means that the sequences $\langle \bar{u}_{-m}, \ldots, \bar{u}_{-1} \rangle$ and $\langle \bar{u}_{N+2}, \ldots, \bar{u}_{N+m+1} \rangle$ do not correspond to any control points (but this is fine!). Also observe that there are $m + N + 1$ subsequences of m consecutive knots in the knot sequence $\langle \bar{u}_{-m+1}, \ldots, \bar{u}_{N+m} \rangle$. Let $\bar{u}_i < \bar{u}_{i+1}$ be two consecutive distinct knots in the sequence $\langle \bar{u}_{-m+1}, \ldots, \bar{u}_{N+m} \rangle$, and consider the sequence of $2m$ knots

$$\langle \bar{u}_{i-m+1}, \ldots, \bar{u}_{i+m} \rangle,$$

centered at the interval $[\bar{u}_i, \bar{u}_{i+1}]$. The rest of the proof is similar to the proof of Theorem 6.2.4. Since there are $m + N + 1$ subsequences of m consecutive knots in the knot sequence $\langle \bar{u}_{-m+1}, \ldots, \bar{u}_{N+m} \rangle$, there are indeed $m + N + 1$ control points associated with the original knot sequence.

(2) It will be enough to consider a cycle of the knot sequence, say,

$$\ldots, \underbrace{\bar{u}_1, \ldots, \bar{u}_{n_1}}_{n_1}, \underbrace{\bar{u}_{n_1+1}, \ldots, \bar{u}_{n_1+n_2}}_{n_2}, \ldots, \underbrace{\bar{u}_{n_1+\cdots+n_{L-1}+1}, \ldots, \bar{u}_N}_{n_L}, \bar{u}_{N+1}, \ldots,$$

where $N = n_1 + \cdots + n_L$, $\bar{u}_N < \bar{u}_{N+1}$, and $\bar{u}_{k+N} = \bar{u}_k + T$, for every $k \in \mathbf{Z}$. If a closed spline curve exists, the proof of Theorem 6.2.4 applied to the distinct knots in the above cycle shows that the curve segments F_i are uniquely determined, and that the periodicity condition on curve segments, namely, the condition $F_{i+N}(\bar{t} + T) = F_i(\bar{t})$, for all $\bar{t} \in [\bar{u}_i, \bar{u}_{i+1}]$, implies that the sequence of control points $d_k = f_i(\bar{u}_{k+1}, \ldots, \bar{u}_{k+m})$ is periodic of period N. Conversely, given a periodic sequence $\langle d_k \rangle_{k \in \mathbf{Z}}$ of control points with period N, the proof of Theorem 6.2.4 applied to the distinct knots in the knot sequence shows that the curve segments F_i are uniquely defined and fit well together for joining knots, and since the cycle length N of the knot sequence agrees with the periodicity N of the sequence of control points, and $\bar{u}_{i+N} = \bar{u}_i + T$, we have $F_{i+N}(\bar{t} + T) = F_i(\bar{t})$, for all $\bar{t} \in [\bar{u}_i, \bar{u}_{i+1}]$. ∎

Remark: Theorem 6.4.3 (1) shows that the first and the last knots $\bar{u}_{-m}$ and $\bar{u}_{N+m+1}$ can be safely ignored. Indeed, they do not contribute to any control points. Thus, from a practical point of view, we can assume that $\bar{u}_0$ and $\bar{u}_{N+1}$ have multiplicity m.

We now reconsider the de Boor algorithm, present the very useful "knot insertion" method, and look at some properties of spline curves.

6.5   The de Boor Algorithm

In Section 5.3, we presented the progressive version of the de Casteljau algorithm. Its relationship to spline curves is that, given a knot sequence $\langle \bar{u}_k \rangle$ (infinite, finite, or cyclic), and a sequence $\langle d_k \rangle$ of control points (corresponding to the nature of the knot sequence), given any parameter $\bar{t} \in \mathbf{A}$ (where $\bar{t} \in [\bar{u}_0, \bar{u}_{N+1}]$, in the case of a finite spline), in order to compute the point $F(\bar{t})$ on the spline curve F determined by $\langle \bar{u}_k \rangle$ and $\langle d_k \rangle$, we just have to find the interval $[\bar{u}_I, \bar{u}_{I+1}]$ for which $\bar{u}_I \le \bar{t} < \bar{u}_{I+1}$, and then to apply the progressive version of the de Casteljau algorithm, starting from the $m + 1$ control points indexed by the sequences $\langle \bar{u}_{I-m+k}, \ldots, \bar{u}_{I+k-1} \rangle$, where $1 \le k \le m + 1$.

As in Section 5.3, let us assume for simplicity that $I = m$, since the indexing will be a bit more convenient. Indeed, in this case $[\bar{u}_m, \bar{u}_{m+1}]$ is the middle of the sequence $\langle \bar{u}_1, \ldots, \bar{u}_{2m} \rangle$ of length $2m$. For the general case, we translate all knots by $I - m$.

Recall that $F(\bar{t}) = f(\bar{t}, \ldots, \bar{t})$ is computed by iteration as the point $b_{0,m}$ determined by the inductive computation

$$b_{k,j} = \left(\frac{u_{m+k+1} - t}{u_{m+k+1} - u_{k+j}} \right) b_{k,j-1} + \left(\frac{t - u_{k+j}}{u_{m+k+1} - u_{k+j}} \right) b_{k+1,j-1},$$

where

$$b_{k,j} = f(\bar{t}^{\,j} \overline{u}_{k+j+1} \ldots \overline{u}_{m+k}),$$

for $1 \le j \le m$, $0 \le k \le m - j$, and with $b_{k,0} = f(\overline{u}_{k+1}, \ldots, \overline{u}_{m+k}) = d_k$, for $0 \le k \le m$.

The computation proceeds by rounds, and during round j, the points $b_{0,j}, b_{1,j}, \ldots, b_{m-j,j}$ are computed. Such a computation can be conveniently represented in the following triangular form:

	1	$\ldots$	$j-1$	j	$\ldots$	$m-r$	$\ldots$	m
$b_{0,0}$								
	$b_{0,1}$							
$b_{1,0}$		$\ddots$						
			$b_{0,j-1}$					
			$\vdots$	$b_{0,j}$				
			$b_{k,j-1}$	$\vdots$	$\ddots$			
				$b_{k,j}$		$b_{0,m-r}$		
			$b_{k+1,j-1}$	$\vdots$				
			$\vdots$	$b_{m-r-j,j}$		$\vdots$		$b_{0,m}$
			$b_{m-r-j+1,j-1}$					
						$\vdots$		$b_{r,m-r}$
	$b_{m-r-1,1}$		$\vdots$					
$b_{m-r,0}$				$b_{m-j,j}$				
	$\vdots$		$b_{m-j+1,j-1}$					
$\vdots$								
$b_{m-1,0}$								
	$b_{m-1,1}$							
$b_{m,0}$								

If $\bar{t} = \overline{u}_m$ and the knot $\overline{u}_m$ has multiplicity r $(1 \le r \le m)$, we notice that

$$b_{0,m-r} = b_{0,m-r+1} = \ldots = b_{0,m},$$

because $b_{0,m-r} = f(\bar{t}^{\,m-r} \overline{u}_{m-r+1} \ldots \overline{u}_m) = F(\bar{t})$, since $\overline{u}_m$ is of multiplicity r, and $\bar{t} = \overline{u}_{m-r+1} = \ldots = \overline{u}_m$. Thus, in this case, we only need to start with the $m - r + 1$ control points $b_{0,0}, \ldots, b_{m-r,0}$, and we only need to construct the part of the triangle above the ascending diagonal

$$b_{m-r,0}, \ b_{m-r-1,1}, \ \ldots, \ b_{0,m-r}.$$

In order to present the de Boor algorithm, it is convenient to index the points $b_{k,j}$ differently. First, we will label the starting control points as $d_{1,0}, \ldots, d_{m+1,0}$, and second, for every round j, rather than indexing the points on the jth column with an index k always starting from 0, and running up to $m - j$, it will be convenient to index the points in the jth column with an index i starting at $j + 1$, and always ending at $m + 1$. Thus, at round j, the points $b_{0,j}, b_{1,j}, \ldots, b_{k,j}, \ldots, b_{m-j,j}$, indexed using our original indexing, will correspond to the points $d_{j+1,j}, d_{j+2,j}, \ldots,$ $b_{k+j+1,j}, \ldots, d_{m+1,j}$, under our new indexing. Rewriting the triangular array representing the computation with our new indexing, we get the following:

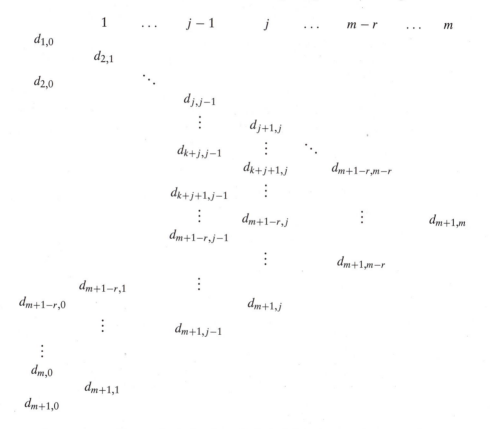

As we can easily see, the inductive relation giving $d_{k+j+1,j}$ in terms of $d_{k+j+1,j-1}$ and $d_{k+j,j-1}$ is given by the equation

$$d_{k+j+1,j} = \left(\frac{u_{m+k+1} - t}{u_{m+k+1} - u_{k+j}} \right) d_{k+j,j-1} + \left(\frac{t - u_{k+j}}{u_{m+k+1} - u_{k+j}} \right) d_{k+j+1,j-1},$$

where $1 \leq j \leq m - r$, $0 \leq k \leq m - r - j$, and with $d_{k+1,0} = d_k$, when $0 \leq k \leq m - r$, where r is the multiplicity of $\bar{u}_m$ when $\bar{t} = \bar{u}_m$, and $r = 0$ otherwise. Letting $i = k + j + 1$, the above equation becomes

$$d_{i,j} = \left(\frac{u_{m+i-j} - t}{u_{m+i-j} - u_{i-1}} \right) d_{i-1,j-1} + \left(\frac{t - u_{i-1}}{u_{m+i-j} - u_{i-1}} \right) d_{i,j-1},$$

where $1 \le j \le m - r$, $j + 1 \le i \le m + 1 - r$, and with $d_{i,0} = d_{i-1}$, when $1 \le i \le m + 1 - r$. The point $F(\bar{t})$ on the spline curve is $d_{m+1-r,m-r}$.

Finally, in order to deal with the general case where $\bar{t} \in [\bar{u}_I, \bar{u}_{I+1}[$, we translate all the knot indices by $I - m$, which does not change differences of indices, and we get the equation

$$d_{i,j} = \left(\frac{u_{m+i-j} - t}{u_{m+i-j} - u_{i-1}} \right) d_{i-1,j-1} + \left(\frac{t - u_{i-1}}{u_{m+i-j} - u_{i-1}} \right) d_{i,j-1},$$

where $1 \le j \le m - r$, $I - m + j + 1 \le i \le I + 1 - r$, and with $d_{i,0} = d_{i-1}$, when $I - m + 1 \le i \le I + 1 - r$, where r is the multiplicity of the knot $\bar{u}_I$ when $\bar{t} = \bar{u}_I$, and $r = 0$ when $\bar{u}_I < \bar{t} < \bar{u}_{I+1}$ $(1 \le r \le m)$.

The point $F(\bar{t})$ on the spline curve is $d_{I+1-r,m-r}$. This is the de Boor algorithm. Note that other books often use a superscript for the "round index" j, and write our $d_{i,j}$ as d_i^j. The de Boor algorithm can be described as follows in pseudocode:

begin
$\quad I = \max\{k \mid \bar{u}_k \le \bar{t} < \bar{u}_{k+1}\};$
$\quad\quad$ **if** $\bar{t} = \bar{u}_I$ **then** $r := multiplicity(\bar{u}_I)$ **else** $r := 0$ **endif**;
$\quad\quad$ **for** $i := I - m + 1$ **to** $I + 1 - r$ **do**
$\quad\quad\quad d_{i,0} := d_{i-1}$
$\quad\quad$ **endfor**;
$\quad\quad$ **for** $j := 1$ **to** $m - r$ **do**
$\quad\quad\quad$ **for** $i := I - m + j + 1$ **to** $I + 1 - r$ **do**
$\quad\quad\quad\quad d_{i,j} := \left(\frac{u_{m+i-j} - t}{u_{m+i-j} - u_{i-1}} \right) d_{i-1,j-1} + \left(\frac{t - u_{i-1}}{u_{m+i-j} - u_{i-1}} \right) d_{i,j-1}$
$\quad\quad\quad$ **endfor**
$\quad\quad$ **endfor**;
$\quad\quad F(\bar{t}) := d_{I+1-r,m-r}$
end

6.6   The de Boor Algorithm and Knot Insertion

The process of knot insertion consists of inserting a knot $\bar{w}$ into a given knot sequence without altering the spline curve. The knot $\bar{w}$ may be new or may coincide with some existing knot of multiplicity $r < m$, and in the latter case, the effect will be to increase the degree of multiplicity of $\bar{w}$ by 1. Knot insertion can be used either to construct new control points, Bézier control points associated with the curve segments forming a spline curve, and even for computing a point on a spline curve.

If I is the largest knot index such that $\bar{u}_I \le \bar{w} < \bar{u}_{I+1}$, inserting the knot $\bar{w}$ will affect the $m - 1 - r$ control points $f(\bar{u}_{I-m+k+1}, \ldots, \bar{u}_{I+k})$ associated with the sequences $\langle \overline{u}_{I-m+k+1}, \ldots, \overline{u}_{I+k} \rangle$ containing the subinterval $[\overline{u}_I, \overline{u}_{I+1}]$, where $1 \leq k \leq m-1-r$, and where r is the multiplicity of $\overline{u}_I$ if $\overline{w} = \overline{u}_I$ (with $1 \leq r < m$), and $r = 0$ if $\overline{u}_I < \overline{w}$:

$$\ldots, \overline{u}_{I-m+2}, \ldots, \overline{u}_{I-r}, \overline{u}_{I-r+1}, \ldots, \overline{u}_I, \overline{u}_{I+1}, \ldots, \overline{u}_{I+m-1-r}, \ldots, \overline{u}_{I+m-1}, \ldots.$$

For example, given the knot sequence

$$\ldots, 1, 2, 3, 5, 6, 8, 9, 11, 14, 15, \ldots,$$

insertion of the knot 7 yields the knot sequence

$$\ldots, 1, 2, 3, 5, 6, 7, 8, 9, 11, 14, 15, \ldots,$$

for which the two polar values $f(568)$ and $f(689)$ no longer exist.

After insertion of $\overline{w}$, we get the new sequence $(\overline{v}_k)$, where $\overline{v}_k = \overline{u}_k$, for all $k \leq I$, $\overline{v}_{I+1} = \overline{w}$, and $\overline{v}_{k+1} = \overline{u}_k$, for all $k \geq I+1$:

$$\ldots, \overline{v}_{I-m+2}, \ldots, \overline{v}_{I-r}, \overline{v}_{I-r+1}, \ldots, \overline{v}_I, \overline{v}_{I+1}, \overline{v}_{I+2}, \ldots, \overline{v}_{I+m-r}, \ldots, \overline{v}_{I+m}, \ldots.$$

Thus, we need to compute the $m - r$ new control points

$$f(\overline{v}_{I-m+k+1}, \ldots, \overline{v}_{I+1}, \ldots, \overline{v}_{I+k}),$$

which are just the polar values corresponding to the $m - r$ subsequences of $m-1$ consecutive subintervals $\langle \overline{v}_{I-m+k+1}, \ldots, \overline{v}_{I+1}, \ldots, \overline{v}_{I+k} \rangle$, where $1 \leq k \leq m - r$ ($\overline{w} = \overline{v}_{I+1}$ belongs to one of these subintervals). For example, after insertion of the knot 7 in the knot sequence

$$\ldots, 1, 2, 3, 5, 6, 8, 9, 11, 14, 15, \ldots,$$

we have the knot sequence

$$\ldots, 1, 2, 3, 5, 6, 7, 8, 9, 11, 14, 15, \ldots,$$

and the three polar values $f(567)$, $f(678)$, and $f(789)$ need to be computed.

We can use the de Boor algorithm to compute the new $m - r$ control points. In fact, note that these points constitute the first column obtained during the first round of the de Boor algorithm. Thus, we can describe knot insertion in pseudocode as follows:

begin

    $I = \max\{k \mid \overline{u}_k \leq \overline{w} < \overline{u}_{k+1}\}$;

    if $\overline{w} = \overline{u}_I$ **then** $r := multiplicity(\overline{u}_I)$ **else** $r := 0$ **endif**;

    for $i := I - m + 1$ **to** $I + 1 - r$ **do**

        $d_{i,0} := d_{i-1}$

    endfor;

for $i := I - m + 2$ **to** $I + 1 - r$ **do**

$$d_{i,1} := \left(\frac{u_{m+i-1}-w}{u_{m+i-1}-u_{i-1}}\right)d_{i-1,0} + \left(\frac{w-u_{i-1}}{u_{m+i-1}-u_{i-1}}\right)d_{i,0}$$

endfor

return $\langle d_{I-m+2,1}, \ldots, d_{I+1-r,1}\rangle$

end

Note that evaluation of a point $F(\bar{t})$ on the spline curve amounts to repeated knot insertions: we perform $m - r$ rounds of knot insertion, to raise the original multiplicity r of the knot $\bar{t}$ to m (again, $r = 0$ if $\bar{t}$ is distinct from all existing knots).

Figure 6.23 illustrates the process of inserting the knot $\bar{t} = 7$, in the knot sequence

$$\ldots, 1, 2, 3, 5, 6, 8, 9, 11, 14, 15, \ldots.$$

The interpolation ratios associated with the points $d_{1,1}$, $d_{2,1}$, and $d_{3,1}$ are

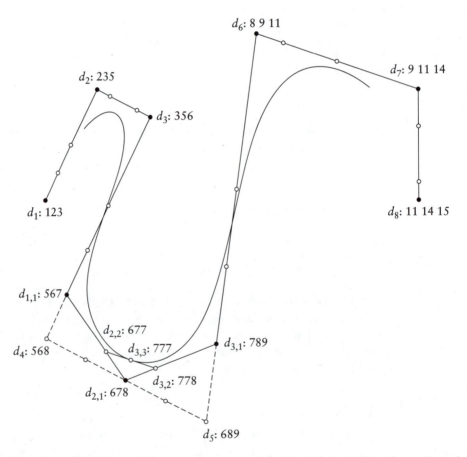

FIG. 6.23 Part of a cubic spline with knot sequence $\ldots, 1, 2, 3, 5, 6, 8, 9, 11, 14, 15, \ldots$, insertion of the knot $\bar{t} = 7$

$$\frac{7-3}{8-3} = \frac{4}{5}, \quad \frac{7-5}{9-5} = \frac{2}{4} = \frac{1}{2}, \quad \frac{7-6}{11-6} = \frac{1}{5}.$$

Evaluation of the point $F(7)$ on the spline curve above consists in inserting the knot $\bar{t} = 7$ three times.

It is also possible to formulate a version of knot insertion where a whole sequence of knots, as opposed to a single knot, is inserted. Such an algorithm, often coined "Olso algorithm," is described in Cohen, Lyche, and Riesenfeld [20]. It is rather straightforward to give an equivalent (and in fact, more illuminating) presentation of this algorithm in terms of polar forms, in the spirit of our treatment of single knot insertion. We leave the formulation of such an algorithm as an exercise (for help, see Risler [68] or Bartels, Beatty, and Barsky [4]).

An amusing application of this algorithm is that it yields simple rules for inserting knots at every interval midpoint of a uniform cyclic knot sequence. For instance, in the case of a quadratic B-spline curve specified by a closed polygon of de Boor control points, for every edge (b_i, b_{i+1}), create two new control points according to the formulae

$$b'_{2i+1} = \frac{3}{4} b_i + \frac{1}{4} b_{i+1}$$

and

$$b'_{2i+2} = \frac{1}{4} b_i + \frac{3}{4} b_{i+1}.$$

This is Chaikin's subdivision method [18]. For a cubic B-spline curve specified by a closed polygon of de Boor control points, for any three consecutive control points b_i, b_{i+1}, and b_{i+2}, two new control points b'_{2i+1} and b'_{2i+2} are created according to the formulae

$$b'_{2i+1} = \frac{1}{2} b_i + \frac{1}{2} b_{i+1}$$

and

$$b'_{2i+2} = \frac{1}{8} b_i + \frac{6}{8} b_{i+1}, + \frac{1}{8} b_{i+2}.$$

Spline curves inherit a number of the properties of Bézier curves, which we now briefly review.

- *Linear precision.* Given a finite knot sequence

$$\bar{u}_0, \bar{u}_1, \bar{u}_2, \ldots, \bar{u}_{N-1}, \bar{u}_N, \bar{u}_{N+1},$$

where $\bar{u}_0$ and $\bar{u}_{N+1}$ are of multiplicity $m + 1$, given the $N + m + 1$ knots (known as *Greville abscissas*)

$$\xi_i = \frac{1}{m}(u_i + u_{i+1} + \cdots + u_{i+m-1}),$$

where $0 \leq i \leq N + m$, given a straight line of the form $l(u) = au + b$, if we read off control points on this line at the Greville abscissas, the resulting spline curve reproduces the straight line.

- *Strong convex hull property.* Every point on the spline curve lies in the convex hull of no more than $m + 1$ nearby de Boor control points.

- *Variation diminishing property.* The spline curve is not intersected by any straight line more often than is the control polygon. An easy way to prove this property is to use knot insertion. Insert every knot until it has multiplicity m. This is a variation diminishing property, since it consists in affine interpolation steps. At that stage, the control polygon consists of Bézier subpolygons, for which the variation diminishing property has been established.

- *Local control.* If one of the de Boor control points is changed, this affects $m + 1$ curve segments.

- *Affine invariance.* This property is inherited from the corresponding property of the Bézier segments.

- *End point interpolation.* In case of a finite knot sequence

$$\overline{u}_0, \overline{u}_1, \overline{u}_2, \ldots, \overline{u}_{N-1}, \overline{u}_N, \overline{u}_{N+1},$$

where $\overline{u}_0$ and $\overline{u}_{N+1}$ are of multiplicity $m + 1$, a spline curve passes through the first and the last de Boor control points.

6.7   Polar Forms of *B*-Splines

Our multiaffine approach to spline curves led us to the de Boor algorithm, and we learned that the current point $F(\overline{t})$ on a spline curve F can be expressed as an affine combination of its de Boor control points. The coefficients of the de Boor points can be viewed as real functions of the real parameter $\overline{t}$. In the traditional theory of Bézier curves, a Bézier curve is viewed as the result of blending together its Bézier control points using the Bernstein basis polynomials as the weights. Similarly, a spline curve can be viewed as the result of blending together its de Boor control points using certain piecewise polynomial functions called *B-splines* as the weights. In the traditional theory, *B*-splines are usually not defined in terms of the de Boor algorithm, but instead in terms of a recurrence relation, or by a formula involving so-called divided differences. We will now show briefly how the multiaffine approach to spline curves leads to the recurrence relation defining *B*-splines, thus showing the equivalence with the traditional approach.

For simplicity, we will only consider an infinite knot sequence $\langle \overline{u}_k \rangle_{k \in \mathbf{Z}}$ where every knot has multiplicity at most $m + 1$, since the adaptations needed to handle a finite or a cyclic knot sequence are quite trivial. *B*-splines are piecewise polynomial functions that can be viewed as spline curves whose range is the affine line $\mathbf{A}$. We define *B*-splines as follows.

Definition 6.7.1

Given an infinite knot sequence $\langle \overline{u}_k \rangle_{k \in Z}$, *where every knot has multiplicity at most* $m + 1$, *the jth normalized (univariate) B-spline* $B_{j,m+1} : \mathbf{A} \to \mathbf{A}$ *(or* $N_{j,m+1} : \mathbf{A} \to \mathbf{A}$*) of order* $m + 1$ *is the unique spline curve whose de Boor control points are the reals* $x_i = \delta_{i,j}$, *where* $\delta_{i,j}$ *is the Kronecker delta symbol, such that* $\delta_{i,j} = 1$ *iff* $i = j$, *and* $\delta_{i,j} = 0$ *otherwise.*

Remark: The normalized *B*-spline $B_{j,m+1}$ is actually of degree $\leq m$, and it would perhaps make more sense to denote it as $B_{j,m}$, but the notation $B_{j,m+1}$ is well established. Some authors use the notation N_j^m.

Given any spline curve (really, any *B*-spline curve) $F : \mathbf{A} \to \mathcal{E}$ over the knot sequence $\langle \overline{u}_k \rangle_{k \in Z}$ (where $\mathcal{E}$ is an arbitrary affine space), and defined by the de Boor control points $\langle d_k \rangle_{k \in Z}$, where $d_k = f_{]\overline{u}_k, \overline{u}_{k+m+1}[}(\overline{u}_{k+1}, \ldots, \overline{u}_{k+m})$, for every k such that $\overline{u}_k < \overline{u}_{k+1}$, for every $\overline{t} \in [\overline{u}_k, \overline{u}_{k+1}[$, we know that

$$F_k(\overline{t}) = \sum_j B_{j,m+1,k}(\overline{t})\, d_j = \sum_j B_{j,m+1,k}(\overline{t})\, f_{]\overline{u}_j, \overline{u}_{j+m+1}[}(\overline{u}_{j+1}, \ldots, \overline{u}_{j+m}),$$

where $B_{j,m+1,k}$ is the segment forming the spline curve $B_{j,m+1}$ over $[\overline{u}_k, \overline{u}_{k+1}[$. Thus, the normalized *B*-splines $B_{j,m+1,k}$ are indeed the weights used for blending the de Boor control points of a spline curve.

Remark: The word "curve" is sometimes omitted when referring to *B*-spline curves, which may cause a slight confusion with the (normalized) *B*-splines $B_{j,m+1}$, which are piecewise polynomial functions and not curves in the traditional sense. Thus, we tried to be careful in keeping the word "curve" whenever necessary, to avoid ambiguities.

If we polarize both sides of the equation

$$F_k(\overline{t}) = \sum_j B_{j,m+1,k}(\overline{t})\, f_{]\overline{u}_j, \overline{u}_{j+m+1}[}(\overline{u}_{j+1}, \ldots, \overline{u}_{j+m}),$$

we get

$$f_k(\overline{t}_1, \ldots, \overline{t}_m) = \sum_j b_{j,m+1,k}(\overline{t}_1, \ldots, \overline{t}_m)\, f_{]\overline{u}_j, \overline{u}_{j+m+1}[}(\overline{u}_{j+1}, \ldots, \overline{u}_{j+m}),$$

where $b_{j,m+1,k}$ is the polar form of $B_{j,m+1,k}$. Recall that the above sum only contains at most $m + 1$ nonzero factors, since F_k is influenced by the $m + 1$ de Boor control points d_j only when $j \in [k - m, k]$. Thus, for j outside $[k - m, k]$, the polynomial $B_{j,m+1,k}$ is null. Our goal is to find a recurrence formula for $b_{j,m+1,k}$.

The de Boor algorithm provides a method for computing the polar value $f_k(\overline{t}_1, \ldots, \overline{t}_m)$ from the de Boor control points $f_{]\overline{u}_j, \overline{u}_{j+m+1}[}(\overline{u}_{j+1}, \ldots, \overline{u}_{j+m})$. Recall that the computation can be arranged into a triangle. An interesting phenomenon occurs if we fix the multiset $\{\overline{t}_1, \ldots, \overline{t}_m\}$ and we compute $f_k(\overline{t}_1, \ldots, \overline{t}_m)$, where we

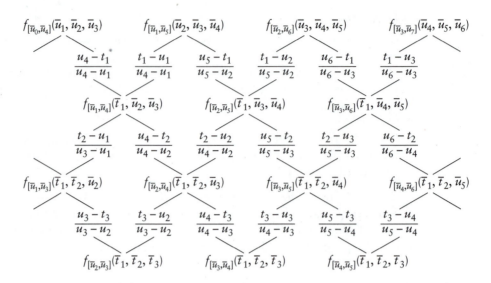

FIG. 6.24 Computation scheme of the de Boor algorithm when $m = 3$

let k vary. We discover that the triangles used in the computation of the polar values $f_k(\bar{t}_1, \ldots, \bar{t}_m)$ overlap in large parts, forming a kind of lattice with $m + 1$ rows, where each subsequent row is computed from the row above by taking affine combinations controlled by one of the arguments $\bar{t}_i$, as specified in the de Boor algorithm. The top row consists of the de Boor control points $d_j = f_{]\bar{u}_j, \bar{u}_{j+m+1}[}(\bar{u}_{j+1}, \ldots, \bar{u}_{j+m})$, and the bottom row consists of the values $y_k = f_k(\bar{t}_1, \ldots, \bar{t}_m)$. If there are multiple knots, this lattice will have triangular notches cut out of the bottom of it, whose heights correspond to knot multiplicity. More specifically, if $\bar{t}_{k+1} = \ldots = \bar{t}_{k+n}$, then we have a computation triangle for f_k and for f_{k+n}, but there are no triangles for f_{k+1} through f_{k+n-1}, and this is what generates a triangular hole of height n at the bottom of the lattice.

Figure 6.24 shows a portion of this lattice in the case of a cubic spline. The nodes of the lattice are labeled to reflect the computation of the polar value $f_k(\bar{t}_1, \ldots, \bar{t}_m)$. It is interesting to draw the same lattice in the case where the object space is the affine line **A**, but this time, omitting the node labels, except that we label the top row with the de Boor points x_i (which are real numbers) and the bottom row with the polar values y_k (see Figure 6.25).

We now show how this second lattice can be used to compute the polar value

$$b_{j,m+1,k}(\bar{t}_1, \ldots, \bar{t}_m)$$

associated with the normalized B-spline $B_{j,m+1}$.

The first method proceeds from the top down, and it is just the de Boor algorithm. Fixing an index j, if we let $x_i = \delta_{i,j}$ for the top nodes, then the bottom row node y_k gives the value $b_{j,m+1,k}(\bar{t}_1, \ldots, \bar{t}_m)$ (where $\bar{u}_k < \bar{u}_{k+1}$). Intuitively, we have

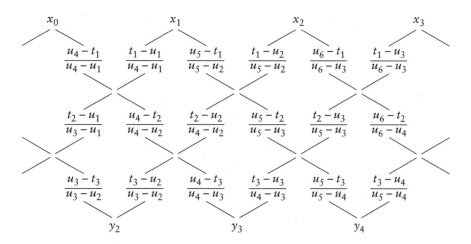

FIG. 6.25 The computation lattice underlying the de Boor algorithm when $m = 3$

computed the influence of the chosen jth de Boor control point on all segments f_k of the spline, at the fixed multiset $\{\bar{t}_1, \ldots, \bar{t}_m\}$.

If we label the intermediate nodes as we do this top-down computation, we obtain another interpretation for $b_{j,m+1,k}(\bar{t}_1, \ldots, \bar{t}_m)$. It is easily seen that the label assigned to every node is the sum of the products of the edge weights along all descending paths from x_j to that node, and $b_{j,m+1,k}(\bar{t}_1, \ldots, \bar{t}_m)$ is the sum of the products of the edge weights along all descending paths from x_j to y_k (there are $\binom{m}{m-j}$ such paths).

The symmetry of this second approach suggests a bottom-up computation. This time, we choose a fixed k with $\bar{u}_k < \bar{u}_{k+1}$, and we let $y_i = \delta_{i,k}$ for the bottom nodes. We then assign labels to the nodes in a bottom-up fashion, taking linear combinations as specified by the edge weights. Note that the combinations involved are no longer affine (as in the top-down approach), but under the symmetric path interpretation, it is easy to see that the label of the top row node x_j is the polar value $b_{j,m+1,k}(\bar{t}_1, \ldots, \bar{t}_m)$. Intuitively, the bottom-up approach chooses a spline segment f_k and computes how this segment is influenced by all de Boor control points.

The bottom-up approach yields a recurrence relation for computing $b_{j,m+1,k}(\bar{t}_1, \ldots, \bar{t}_m)$. We have

$$b_{j,1,k}() = \delta_{j,k},$$

$$b_{j,m+1,k}(\bar{t}_1, \ldots, \bar{t}_m) = \frac{t_m - u_j}{u_{j+m} - u_j} b_{j,m,k}(\bar{t}_1, \ldots, \bar{t}_{m-1})$$

$$+ \frac{u_{j+m+1} - t_m}{u_{j+m+1} - u_{j+1}} b_{j+1,m,k}(\bar{t}_1, \ldots, \bar{t}_{m-1}).$$

If we set all $\bar{t}_i$ to $\bar{t}$, and drop the subscript k, we get the standard recurrence relation defining B-splines, due to Mansfield, de Boor, and Cox (see de Boor [22] and Farin [32]):

$$B_{j,1}(\bar{t}) = \begin{cases} 1 & \text{if } \bar{t} \in [\bar{u}_j, \bar{u}_{j+1}[\\ 0 & \text{otherwise,} \end{cases}$$

$$B_{j,m+1}(\bar{t}) = \frac{t - u_j}{u_{j+m} - u_j} B_{j,m}(\bar{t}) + \frac{u_{j+m+1} - t}{u_{j+m+1} - u_{j+1}} B_{j+1,m}(\bar{t}).$$

It is easily shown that $B_{j,m+1}$ is null outside $[\bar{u}_j, \bar{u}_{j+m+1}[$. A nice property about this recurrence relation is that it is not necessary to know the degree m ahead of time if we want to compute the B-spline $B_{j,m+1}$.

Remarks: In the case of a finite spline based on a finite knot sequence $\langle \bar{u}_k \rangle_{-m \le k \le N+m+1}$, the above recurrence equations show the necessity for the knots $\bar{u}_{-m}$ and $\bar{u}_{N+m+1}$. This justifies the introduction of end knots $\bar{u}_0$ and $\bar{u}_{N+1}$ of multiplicity $m + 1$.

Observe that

$$b_{j,m+1,k}(\bar{t}_{i+1}, \dots, \bar{t}_{i+m}) = \delta_{i,j}.$$

If we consider the tensored version $\widehat{b}_{\odot\, j,m+1,k}$ of the homogenized version $\widehat{b}_{j,m+1,k}$ of $b_{j,m+1,k}$, the above equations show that the sequence of symmetric tensors $(\widehat{b}_{\odot\, j,m+1,k})_{k-m \le j \le k}$ is the dual basis of the basis of symmetric tensors $(\bar{u}_{j+1} \cdots \bar{u}_{j+m})_{k-m \le j \le k}$. Thus, the sequence of tensors $(\widehat{b}_{\odot\, j,m+1,k})_{k-m \le j \le k}$ forms a basis of the vector space $(\bigodot^m \widehat{A})^*$, the dual space of $\bigodot^m \widehat{A}$. As a consequence, the polynomials $(B_{j,m+1,k})_{k-m \le j \le k}$ are linearly independent.

It is also possible to define B-splines using divided differences or in various other ways. For more on B-splines, see de Boor [22], Risler [68], Farin [32], Hoschek and Lasser [45], or Piegl and Tiller [62].

We conclude this section by showing how the multiaffine approach to B-spline curves yields a quick solution to the "degree-raising" problem. First, we consider an example. Figure 6.26 shows a cubic spline curve F based on the knot sequence

$$\bar{0}, \bar{0}, \bar{0}, \bar{0}, \bar{1}, \bar{2}, \bar{2}, \bar{2}, \bar{2}.$$

We would like to view this spline curve F as a spline curve G of degree 4. For this, we need to find the polar form g of this spline curve G of degree 4, in terms of the polar form f of the original cubic spline curve F. First, in order for the spline curve to retain the same order of continuity, we must increase the degree of multiplicity of each knot by 1, so that the quartic spline curve G is based on the knot sequence

$$\bar{0}, \bar{0}, \bar{0}, \bar{0}, \bar{0}, \bar{1}, \bar{1}, \bar{2}, \bar{2}, \bar{2}, \bar{2}, \bar{2}.$$

Then, it is immediate that the answer is

$$g(\bar{t}_1, \bar{t}_2, \bar{t}_3, \bar{t}_4) = \frac{f(\bar{t}_1, \bar{t}_2, \bar{t}_3) + f(\bar{t}_1, \bar{t}_2, \bar{t}_4) + f(\bar{t}_1, \bar{t}_3, \bar{t}_4) + f(\bar{t}_2, \bar{t}_3, \bar{t}_4)}{4}.$$

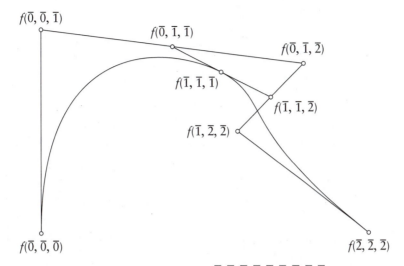

$f(\bar{0}, \bar{0}, \bar{1})$
$f(\bar{0}, \bar{1}, \bar{1})$
$f(\bar{0}, \bar{1}, \bar{2})$
$f(\bar{1}, \bar{1}, \bar{1})$
$f(\bar{1}, \bar{1}, \bar{2})$
$f(\bar{1}, \bar{2}, \bar{2})$
$f(\bar{0}, \bar{0}, \bar{0})$
$f(\bar{2}, \bar{2}, \bar{2})$

FIG. 6.26 A cubic spline F with knot sequence $\bar{0}, \bar{0}, \bar{0}, \bar{0}, \bar{1}, \bar{2}, \bar{2}, \bar{2}, \bar{2}$

It is then an easy matter to compute the de Boor control points of the quartic spline curve G. For example, we have

$$g(\bar{0}, \bar{0}, \bar{1}, \bar{1}) = \frac{2f(\bar{0}, \bar{0}, \bar{1}) + 2f(\bar{0}, \bar{1}, \bar{1})}{4} = f(\bar{0}, \overline{0.5}, \bar{1}),$$

and

$$g(\bar{0}, \bar{1}, \bar{1}, \bar{2}) = \frac{2f(\bar{0}, \bar{1}, \bar{1}) + 2f(\bar{0}, \bar{1}, \bar{2}) + f(\bar{1}, \bar{1}, \bar{2})}{4}.$$

The point $g(\bar{0}, \bar{1}, \bar{1}, \bar{2})$ is easily seen to be the middle of the line segment between $f(\bar{0}, \bar{1}, \bar{2})$ and $f(\bar{1}, \bar{1}, \bar{1})$. Figure 6.27 shows the de Boor control points of the quartic spline curve G and its associated control polygon, in bold lines.

We note that the control polygon of G is "closer" to the curve. This is a general phenomenon. It can be shown that as the degree is raised, the control polygon converges to the spline curve.

In the general case, given a knot sequence $\langle \bar{u}_k \rangle_{k \in Z}$, where each knot is of multiplicity at most $m + 1$, given a spline curve F of degree m based on this knot sequence, it is first necessary to form a new knot sequence $\langle \bar{v}_k \rangle_{k \in Z}$, which consists of the knots in the sequence $\langle \bar{u}_k \rangle_{k \in Z}$, with the multiplicity of each knot incremented by 1. Then, as in Section 5.1, the polar form g_k of the spline curve segment G of degree $m + 1$ over the interval $[\bar{u}_v, \bar{v}_{k+1}]$, where $\bar{v}_k < \bar{v}_{k+1}$, is related to the polar form f_k of the original spline curve F of degree m by the identity

$$g_k(\bar{t}_1, \ldots, \bar{t}_{m+1}) = \frac{1}{m+1} \sum_{i=1}^{i=m+1} f_k(\bar{t}_1, \ldots, \widehat{\bar{t}_i}, \ldots, \bar{t}_{m+1}),$$

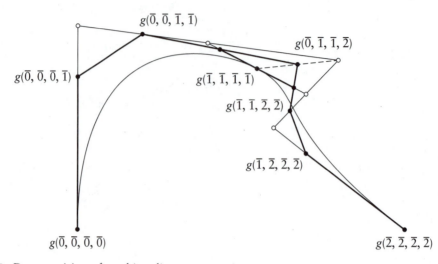

$g(\overline{0}, \overline{0}, \overline{1}, \overline{1})$

$g(\overline{0}, \overline{1}, \overline{1}, \overline{2})$

$g(\overline{0}, \overline{0}, \overline{0}, \overline{1})$

$g(\overline{1}, \overline{1}, \overline{1}, \overline{1})$

$g(\overline{1}, \overline{1}, \overline{2}, \overline{2})$

$g(\overline{1}, \overline{2}, \overline{2}, \overline{2})$

$g(\overline{0}, \overline{0}, \overline{0}, \overline{0})$

$g(\overline{2}, \overline{2}, \overline{2}, \overline{2})$

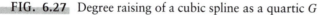

FIG. 6.27 Degree raising of a cubic spline as a quartic G

where the hat over the argument $\overline{i}_i$ indicates that this argument is omitted. We observe that the above expression is indeed well defined because if the left-hand side is well defined, then the right-hand side is also well defined, since the multiplicity of every knot goes down by 1 as we move from F to G. Thus, the de Boor control points of the spline curve G of degree $m + 1$ are given by the formula

$$g_{]\overline{v}_l, \overline{v}_{l+m+2}[}(\overline{v}_{l+1}, \ldots, \overline{v}_{l+m+1})$$

$$= \frac{1}{m+1} \sum_{i=1}^{i=m+1} f_{]\overline{u}_k, \overline{v}_{k+m+1}[}(\overline{v}_{l+1}, \ldots, \widehat{\overline{v}_{l+i}}, \ldots, \overline{v}_{l+m+1}),$$

where $[\overline{v}_l, \overline{v}_{l+m+2}] = [\overline{u}_k, \overline{u}_{k+m+1}]$, and where the hat over the argument $\overline{v}_{l+i}$ indicates that this argument is omitted. In general, it is not possible to obtain a more explicit formula, as in the case of Bézier curves.

6.8   Cubic Spline Interpolation

We now consider the problem of interpolation by smooth curves. Unlike the problem of approximating a shape by a smooth curve, interpolation problems require finding curves passing through some given data points and possibly satisfying some extra constraints. There are a number of interpolation problems. We consider one of the most common problems, which can be stated as follows:

Interpolation Problem 1: Given $N + 1$ data points $x_0, \ldots, x_N$, and a sequence of $N + 1$ knots $\overline{u}_0, \ldots, \overline{u}_N$, with $\overline{u}_i < \overline{u}_{i+1}$ for all i, $0 \leq i \leq N - 1$, find a C^2 cubic spline curve F, such that $F(\overline{u}_i) = x_i$, for all i, $0 \leq i \leq N$.

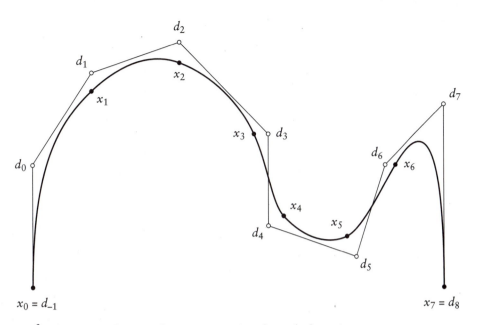

FIG. 6.28 A C^2 cubic interpolation spline curve passing through the points $x_0, x_1, x_2, x_3, x_4, x_5,$ x_6, x_7

It is well known that Lagrange interpolation is not very satisfactory when N is greater than 5, since Lagrange interpolants tend to oscillate in an undesirable manner. Thus, we turn to spline curves. Cubic spline curves happen to do very well for a large class of interpolation problems. In order to solve the above problem, we can try to find the de Boor control points of a C^2 cubic spline curve F based on the finite knot sequence

$$\overline{u}_0, \overline{u}_0, \overline{u}_0, \overline{u}_1, \overline{u}_2, \ldots, \overline{u}_{N-2}, \overline{u}_{N-1}, \overline{u}_N, \overline{u}_N, \overline{u}_N.$$

We note that we are looking for a total of $N+3$ de Boor control points $d_{-1}, \ldots,$ d_{N+1}. Actually, since the first control point d_{-1} coincides with x_0, and the last control point d_{N+1} coincides with x_N, we are looking for $N+1$ de Boor control points $d_0, \ldots, d_N$. However, using the de Boor evaluation algorithm, we only come up with $N-1$ equations expressing $x_1, \ldots, x_{N-1}$ in terms of the $N+1$ unknown variables $d_0, \ldots, d_N$.

Figure 6.28 shows $N+1 = 7+1 = 8$ data points, and a C^2 cubic spline curve F passing through these points, for a uniform knot sequence. The control points d_0 and $d_7 = d_N$ were chosen arbitrarily.

Thus, the above problem has two degrees of freedom, and it is underdetermined. To remove these degrees of freedom, we can add various "end conditions," which amount to the assumption that the de Boor control points d_0 and d_N are known. For example, we can specify that the tangent vectors at x_0 and x_N be equal to some

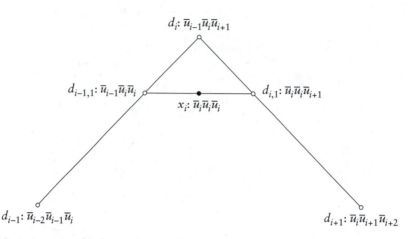

d_i: $\bar{u}_{i-1}\bar{u}_i\bar{u}_{i+1}$

$d_{i-1,1}$: $\bar{u}_{i-1}\bar{u}_i\bar{u}_i$ $d_{i,1}$: $\bar{u}_i\bar{u}_i\bar{u}_{i+1}$

x_i: $\bar{u}_i\bar{u}_i\bar{u}_i$

d_{i-1}: $\bar{u}_{i-2}\bar{u}_{i-1}\bar{u}_i$ d_{i+1}: $\bar{u}_i\bar{u}_{i+1}\bar{u}_{i+2}$

FIG. 6.29 Computation of x_i from d_{i-1}, d_i, d_{i+1}

desired value. We now have a system of $N-1$ linear equations in the $N-1$ variables $d_1, \ldots, d_{N-1}$.

In order to derive this system of linear equations, we use the de Boor evaluation algorithm. Note that for all i, with $1 \le i \le N-1$, the de Boor control point d_i corresponds to the polar label $\bar{u}_{i-1}\,\bar{u}_i\,\bar{u}_{i+1}$; x_i corresponds to the polar label $\bar{u}_i\,\bar{u}_i\,\bar{u}_i$; and d_{-1}, d_0, d_N, and d_{N+1} correspond, respectively, to $\bar{u}_0\,\bar{u}_0\,\bar{u}_0$, $\bar{u}_0\,\bar{u}_0\,\bar{u}_1$, $\bar{u}_{N-1}\,\bar{u}_N\,\bar{u}_N$, and $\bar{u}_N\,\bar{u}_N\,\bar{u}_N$. For every i, with $1 \le i \le N-1$, x_i can be computed from d_{i-1}, d_i, d_{i+1}, using the de Boor algorithm represented in Figure 6.29.

Thus, for all i, $1 \le i \le N-1$, we have

$$d_{i-1,1} = \frac{u_{i+1} - u_i}{u_{i+1} - u_{i-2}}\, d_{i-1} + \frac{u_i - u_{i-2}}{u_{i+1} - u_{i-2}}\, d_i,$$

$$d_{i,1} = \frac{u_{i+2} - u_i}{u_{i+2} - u_{i-1}}\, d_i + \frac{u_i - u_{i-1}}{u_{i+2} - u_{i-1}}\, d_{i+1},$$

$$x_i = \frac{u_{i+1} - u_i}{u_{i+1} - u_{i-1}}\, d_{i-1,1} + \frac{u_i - u_{i-1}}{u_{i+1} - u_{i-1}}\, d_{i,1}.$$

From the above formulae, we get

$$x_i = \frac{\alpha_i}{u_{i+1} - u_{i-1}}\, d_{i-1} + \frac{\beta_i}{u_{i+1} - u_{i-1}}\, d_i + \frac{\gamma_i}{u_{i+1} - u_{i-1}}\, d_{i+1},$$

with

$$\alpha_i = \frac{(u_{i+1} - u_i)^2}{u_{i+1} - u_{i-2}},$$

$$\beta_i = \frac{(u_{i+1} - u_i)(u_i - u_{i-2})}{u_{i+1} - u_{i-2}} + \frac{(u_i - u_{i-1})(u_{i+2} - u_i)}{u_{i+2} - u_{i-1}},$$

$$\gamma_i = \frac{(u_i - u_{i-1})^2}{u_{i+2} - u_{i-1}}.$$

At the end points, it is easily verified that we get

$$x_1 = \frac{\alpha_1}{u_2 - u_0} d_0 + \frac{\beta_1}{u_2 - u_0} d_1 + \frac{\gamma_1}{u_2 - u_0} d_2,$$

$$x_{N-1} = \frac{\alpha_{N-1}}{u_N - u_{N-2}} d_{N-2} + \frac{\beta_{N-1}}{u_N - u_{N-2}} d_{N-1} + \frac{\gamma_{N-1}}{u_N - u_{N-2}} d_N,$$

where

$$\alpha_1 = \frac{(u_2 - u_1)^2}{u_2 - u_0},$$

$$\beta_1 = \frac{(u_2 - u_1)(u_1 - u_0)}{u_2 - u_0} + \frac{(u_1 - u_0)(u_3 - u_1)}{u_3 - u_0},$$

$$\gamma_1 = \frac{(u_1 - u_0)^2}{u_3 - u_0},$$

$$\alpha_{N-1} = \frac{(u_N - u_{N-1})^2}{u_N - u_{N-3}},$$

$$\beta_{N-1} = \frac{(u_N - u_{N-1})(u_{N-1} - u_{N-3})}{u_N - u_{N-3}} + \frac{(u_{N-1} - u_{N-2})(u_N - u_{N-1})}{u_N - u_{N-2}},$$

$$\gamma_{N-1} = \frac{(u_{N-1} - u_{N-2})^2}{u_N - u_{N-2}}.$$

Letting

$$r_i = (u_{i+1} - u_{i-1}) x_i,$$

for all i, $1 \le i \le N - 1$, and r_0 and r_N be arbitrary points, we obtain the following $(N + 1) \times (N + 1)$ system of linear equations in the unknowns $d_0, \ldots, d_N$:

$$\begin{pmatrix} 1 & & & & & & \\ \alpha_1 & \beta_1 & \gamma_1 & & & & \\ & \alpha_2 & \beta_2 & \gamma_2 & & 0 & \\ & & & \ddots & & & \\ & 0 & & \alpha_{N-2} & \beta_{N-2} & \gamma_{N-2} & \\ & & & & \alpha_{N-1} & \beta_{N-1} & \gamma_{N-1} \\ & & & & & & 1 \end{pmatrix} \begin{pmatrix} d_0 \\ d_1 \\ d_2 \\ \vdots \\ d_{N-2} \\ d_{N-1} \\ d_N \end{pmatrix} = \begin{pmatrix} r_0 \\ r_1 \\ r_2 \\ \vdots \\ r_{N-2} \\ r_{N-1} \\ r_N \end{pmatrix}$$

The matrix of the system of linear equations is tridiagonal, and it is clear that $\alpha_i, \beta_i, \gamma_i \geq 0$. It is also easy to show that

$$\alpha_i + \gamma_i + \beta_i = u_{i+1} - u_{i-1}$$

for all i, $1 \leq i \leq N - 1$. Such conditions should not come as a surprise, since the d_i and the x_i are points. If

$$\alpha_i + \gamma_i < \beta_i,$$

for all i, $1 \leq i \leq N - 1$, which means that the matrix is diagonally dominant, then it can be shown that the matrix is invertible. In particular, this is the case for a uniform knot sequence. There are methods for solving diagonally dominant systems of linear equations very efficiently, for example, using an LU-decomposition.

In the case of a uniform knot sequence, it is an easy exercise to show that the linear system can be written as

$$\begin{pmatrix} 1 & & & & & & \\ \frac{3}{2} & \frac{7}{2} & 1 & & & & \\ 1 & 4 & 1 & & 0 & & \\ & & \ddots & & & & \\ & 0 & & 1 & 4 & 1 & \\ & & & & 1 & \frac{7}{2} & \frac{3}{2} \\ & & & & & & 1 \end{pmatrix} \begin{pmatrix} d_0 \\ d_1 \\ d_2 \\ \vdots \\ d_{N-2} \\ d_{N-1} \\ d_N \end{pmatrix} = \begin{pmatrix} r_0 \\ 6x_1 \\ 6x_2 \\ \vdots \\ 6x_{N-2} \\ 6x_{N-1} \\ r_N \end{pmatrix}$$

It can also be shown that the general system of linear equations has a unique solution when the knot sequence is strictly increasing, that is, when $u_i < u_{i+1}$ for all i, $0 \leq i \leq N - 1$. For example, this can be shown by expressing each spline segment in terms of the Hermite polynomials. Writing the C^2 conditions leads to a tridiagonal system that is diagonally dominant when the knot sequence is strictly increasing. For details, see Farin [32].

We can also solve the problem of finding a closed interpolating spline curve, formulated as follows.

Interpolation Problem 2: Given N data points $x_0, \ldots, x_{N-1}$, and a sequence of $N + 1$ knots $\bar{u}_0, \ldots, \bar{u}_N$, with $\bar{u}_i < \bar{u}_{i+1}$ for all i, $0 \leq i \leq N - 1$, find a C^2 closed cubic spline curve F, such that $F(\bar{u}_i) = x_i$, for all i, $0 \leq i \leq N$, where we let $x_N = x_0$.

This time, we consider the cyclic knot sequence determined by the $N + 1$ knots $\bar{u}_0, \ldots, \bar{u}_N$, which means that we consider the infinite cyclic knot sequence $\langle \bar{u}_k \rangle_{k \in \mathbf{Z}}$ that agrees with $\bar{u}_0, \ldots, \bar{u}_N$ for $i = 0, \ldots, N$, and such that

$$\bar{u}_{k+N} = \bar{u}_k + u_N - u_0,$$

for all $k \in \mathbf{Z}$. We observe that we are now looking for N de Boor control points $d_0, \ldots, d_{N-1}$, since the condition $x_0 = x_N$ implies that $d_0 = d_N$, so that we can write a system of N linear equations in the N unknowns $d_0, \ldots, d_{N-1}$. The following system of linear equations is easily obtained:

$$\begin{pmatrix} \beta_0 & \gamma_0 & & & & & & \alpha_0 \\ \alpha_1 & \beta_1 & \gamma_1 & & & & & \\ & \alpha_2 & \beta_2 & \gamma_2 & & & 0 & \\ & & & \ddots & & & & \\ & 0 & & & \alpha_{N-3} & \beta_{N-3} & \gamma_{N-3} & \\ & & & & & \alpha_{N-2} & \beta_{N-2} & \gamma_{N-2} \\ \gamma_{N-1} & & & & & & \alpha_{N-1} & \beta_{N-1} \end{pmatrix} \begin{pmatrix} d_0 \\ d_1 \\ d_2 \\ \vdots \\ d_{N-3} \\ d_{N-2} \\ d_{N-1} \end{pmatrix} = \begin{pmatrix} r_0 \\ r_1 \\ r_2 \\ \vdots \\ r_{N-3} \\ r_{N-2} \\ r_{N-1} \end{pmatrix}$$

where

$$r_i = (u_{i+1} - u_{i-1}) \, x_i,$$

for all i, $1 \leq i \leq N - 1$, since the knot sequence is cyclic,

$$r_0 = (u_N - u_{N-1} + u_1 - u_0) \, x_0,$$

and for all i, $2 \leq i \leq N - 2$, we have

$$\alpha_i = \frac{(u_{i+1} - u_i)^2}{u_{i+1} - u_{i-2}},$$

$$\beta_i = \frac{(u_{i+1} - u_i)(u_i - u_{i-2})}{u_{i+1} - u_{i-2}} + \frac{(u_i - u_{i-1})(u_{i+2} - u_i)}{u_{i+2} - u_{i-1}},$$

$$\gamma_i = \frac{(u_i - u_{i-1})^2}{u_{i+2} - u_{i-1}}.$$

Since the knot sequence is cyclic, we also get

$$\alpha_0 = \frac{(u_1 - u_0)^2}{u_N - u_{N-2} + u_1 - u_0},$$

$$\beta_0 = \frac{(u_1 - u_0)(u_N - u_{N-2})}{u_N - u_{N-2} + u_1 - u_0} + \frac{(u_N - u_{N-1})(u_2 - u_0)}{u_N - u_{N-1} + u_2 - u_0},$$

$$\gamma_0 = \frac{(u_N - u_{N-1})^2}{u_N - u_{N-1} + u_2 - u_0},$$

$$\alpha_1 = \frac{(u_2 - u_1)^2}{u_N - u_{N-1} + u_2 - u_0},$$

$$\beta_1 = \frac{(u_2 - u_1)(u_N - u_{N-1} + u_1 - u_0)}{u_N - u_{N-1} + u_2 - u_0} + \frac{(u_1 - u_0)(u_3 - u_1)}{u_3 - u_0},$$

$$\gamma_1 = \frac{(u_1 - u_0)^2}{u_3 - u_0},$$

$$\alpha_{N-1} = \frac{(u_N - u_{N-1})^2}{u_N - u_{N-3}},$$

$$\beta_{N-1} = \frac{(u_N - u_{N-1})(u_{N-1} - u_{N-3})}{u_N - u_{N-3}} + \frac{(u_{N-1} - u_{N-2})(u_N - u_{N-1} + u_1 - u_0)}{u_N - u_{N-2} + u_1 - u_0},$$

$$\gamma_{N-1} = \frac{(u_{N-1} - u_{N-2})^2}{u_N - u_{N-2} + u_1 - u_0}.$$

The system is no longer tridiagonal, but it can still be solved efficiently.

The coefficients $\alpha_i, \beta_i, \gamma_i$ can be written in a uniform fashion for both the open and the closed interpolating C^2 cubic spline curves, if we let $\Delta_i = u_{i+1} - u_i$. It is immediately verified that we have

$$\alpha_i = \frac{\Delta_i^2}{\Delta_{i-2} + \Delta_{i-1} + \Delta_i},$$

$$\beta_i = \frac{\Delta_i(\Delta_{i-2} + \Delta_{i-1})}{\Delta_{i-2} + \Delta_{i-1} + \Delta_i} + \frac{\Delta_{i-1}(\Delta_i + \Delta_{i+1})}{\Delta_{i-1} + \Delta_i + \Delta_{i+1}},$$

$$\gamma_i = \frac{\Delta_{i-1}^2}{\Delta_{i-1} + \Delta_i + \Delta_{i+1}},$$

where in the case of an open spline curve, $\Delta_{-1} = \Delta_N = 0$, and in the case of a closed spline curve, $\Delta_{-1} = \Delta_{N-1}$, $\Delta_{-2} = \Delta_{N-2}$.

In the case of an open C^2 cubic spline interpolant, several end conditions have been proposed to determine $r_0 = d_0$ and $r_N = d_N$, and we quickly review these conditions:

1. The first method consists in specifying the tangent vectors m_0 and m_N at x_0 and x_N, usually called the *clamped condition* method. Since the tangent vector at x_0 is given by

$$\mathrm{D}F(\overline{u}_0) = \frac{3}{u_1 - u_0}(d_0 - x_0),$$

we get

$$r_0 = d_0 = x_0 + \frac{u_1 - u_0}{3} m_0,$$

and similarly

$$r_N = d_N = x_N - \frac{u_N - u_{N-1}}{3} m_N.$$

One specific method is the *Bessel end condition*. If we consider the parabola interpolating the first three data points x_0, x_1, x_2, the method consists in picking the tangent vector to this parabola at x_0. A similar selection is made using the parabola interpolating the last three points x_{N-2}, x_{N-1}, x_N.

2. Another method is the *quadratic end condition*. In this method, we require that

$$\mathrm{D}^2 F(\overline{u}_0) = \mathrm{D}^2 F(\overline{u}_1)$$

and

$$\mathrm{D}^2 F(\overline{u}_{N-1}) = \mathrm{D}^2 F(\overline{u}_N).$$

3. Another method is the *natural end condition*. In this method, we require that

$$\mathrm{D}^2 F(\overline{u}_0) = \mathrm{D}^2 F(\overline{u}_N) = \vec{0}.$$

4. Finally, we have the *not-a-knot condition*, which forces the first two cubic segments to merge into a single cubic segment and similarly for the last two cubic segments. This amounts to requiring that $\mathrm{D}^3 F$ is continuous at $\overline{u}_1$ and at $\overline{u}_{N-1}$.

We leave the precise formulation of these conditions as an exercise (see Farin [32] or Hoschek and Lasser [45]).

In practice, when attempting to solve an interpolation problem, the knot sequence $\overline{u}_0, \ldots, \overline{u}_N$ is not given. Thus, it is necessary to find knot sequences that produce reasonable results. We now briefly survey methods for producing knot sequences.

The simplest method consists in choosing a *uniform* knot sequence. Although simple, this method may produce bad results when the data points are heavily clustered in some areas.

Another popular method is to use a *chord length* knot sequence. In this method, after choosing $\overline{u}_0$ and $\overline{u}_N$, we determine the other knots in such a way that

$$\frac{u_{i+1} - u_i}{u_{i+2} - u_{i+1}} = \frac{\|x_{i+1} - x_i\|}{\|x_{i+2} - x_{i+1}\|},$$

where $\|x_{i+1} - x_i\|$ is the length of the chord between x_i and x_{i+1}. This method usually works quite well.

Another method is the so-called *centripedal* method, derived from physical heuristics, where we set

$$\frac{u_{i+1} - u_i}{u_{i+2} - u_{i+1}} = \left(\frac{\|x_{i+1} - x_i\|}{\|x_{i+2} - x_{i+1}\|} \right)^{1/2}.$$

There are other methods, in particular due to Foley. For details, see Farin [32].

Problems

[30 pts]   **1.** Consider the following cubic spline F with finite knot sequence

$$1, 1, 1, 1, 2, 3, 4, 5, 6, 6, 6, 6,$$

and with the de Boor control points:

$$d_{-3} = (2, 0), \text{ labeled } 111,$$
$$d_{-2} = (0, 5), \text{ labeled } 112,$$
$$d_{-1} = (4, 9), \text{ labeled } 123,$$
$$d_0 = (6, 0), \text{ labeled } 234,$$
$$d_1 = (9, 0), \text{ labeled } 345,$$
$$d_2 = (9, 9), \text{ labeled } 456,$$
$$d_3 = (11, 9), \text{ labeled } 566,$$
$$d_4 = (14, 2), \text{ labeled } 666.$$

(a) Compute the Bézier points corresponding to 222, 333, 444, and 555, and plot the Bézier segments forming the spline as well as possible (you may use programs you have written for previous assignments).

(b) Insert the knot 3.5 three times. Give a geometric construction of the point $F(3.5)$ on the spline curve. Construct (geometrically) the tangent at $t = 3.5$.

[10 pts]   **2.** Show that if a *B*-spline curve consisting of quadratic curve segments ($m = 2$) has an inflection point, then this point is associated with a knot.

[30 pts]   **3.** Consider the following quadratic spline F with finite knot sequence

$$0, 0, 0, 1, 2, 3, 4, 4, 5, 5, 5,$$

and with the de Boor control points:

$$d_{-2} = (-6, -1), \text{ labeled } 00,$$

$$d_{-1} = (-5, 2), \text{ labeled } 01,$$

$$d_0 = (-3, 3), \text{ labeled } 12,$$

$$d_1 = (-1, 2), \text{ labeled } 23,$$

$$d_2 = (0, 0), \text{ labeled } 34,$$

$$d_3 = (3, 1), \text{ labeled } 44,$$

$$d_4 = (3, 3), \text{ labeled } 45,$$

$$d_5 = (1, 5), \text{ labeled } 55.$$

(a) Compute the Bézier points corresponding to 11, 22, and 33, and plot the Bézier segments forming the spline as well as possible (you may use programs you have written for previous assignments).

(b) Compute $F(\frac{5}{4})$ by repeated knot insertion. Determine the tangent at $F(\frac{5}{4})$.

(c) Which knot should be inserted so that $(-\frac{3}{4}, \frac{3}{2})$ becomes a control point?

[30 pts] **4.** Find the Bézier control points of a closed spline of degree 4 whose control polygon consists of the edges of a square, and whose knot sequence is uniform and consists of simple knots. Repeat the problem for a uniform knot sequence in which all knots have multiplicity 2.

[50 pts] **5.** Implement the de Boor algorithm for finite and closed splines. Design a subdivision version of the de Boor algorithm.

[30 pts] **6.** Implement the knot insertion algorithm.

[40 pts] **7.** It is shown in Section 6.7 how a B-spline of degree m can be defined in terms of the normalized B-splines $B_{j,m+1}$.

(a) Given a finite knot sequence

$$\bar{u}_{-m}, \quad \bar{u}_1, \quad \bar{u}_{n_1+1}, \quad \cdots, \quad \bar{u}_{N-n_{L-1}+1}, \quad \bar{u}_{N+1},$$

$$\vdots \qquad \vdots \qquad \vdots \qquad \cdots \qquad \vdots \qquad \vdots$$

$$\bar{u}_0 \qquad \bar{u}_{n_1} \quad \bar{u}_{n_1+n_2} \quad \cdots \qquad \bar{u}_N \qquad \bar{u}_{N+m+1}$$

$$m+1 \quad n_1 \qquad n_2 \qquad \cdots \qquad n_{L-1} \qquad m+1$$

and a sequence of de Boor control points $\langle d_j \rangle_{-m \le j \le N}$, show that the finite B-spline F defined by the above knot sequence and de Boor control points can be expressed as

$$F(\bar{t}) = \sum_{j=-m}^{N} d_j B_{j,m+1}(\bar{t}),$$

where the *B*-splines $B_{j,m+1}$ are defined inductively as follows:

$$B_{j,1}(\bar{t}) = \begin{cases} 1 & \text{if } \bar{t} \in [\bar{u}_j, \bar{u}_{j+1}[\\ 0 & \text{otherwise,} \end{cases}$$

$$B_{j,m+1}(\bar{t}) = \frac{t - u_j}{u_{j+m} - u_j} B_{j,m}(\bar{t}) + \frac{u_{j+m+1} - t}{u_{j+m+1} - u_{j+1}} B_{j+1,m}(\bar{t}).$$

(b) Show that $B_{j,m+1}$ is null outside $[\bar{u}_j, \bar{u}_{j+m+1}[$.

(c) Show that

$$\sum_{j=-m}^{N} B_{j,m+1}(\bar{t}) = 1$$

for all $\bar{t}$.

(d) Compute the functions $B_{j,4}$ associated with Problem 1.

[20 pts]   **8.** Under the assumptions of Problem 7, prove *Marsden's formula*:

$$(x - t)^m = \sum_{i=-m}^{N} (x - \bar{t}_{i+1}) \cdots (x - \bar{t}_{i+m}) B_{i,m+1}(t).$$

[10 pts]   **9.** The *B*-spline basis functions $B_{j,m+1}(\bar{t})$ being defined as in Problem 7, prove that

$$B'_{j,m+1}(\bar{t}) = \frac{m}{u_{j+m} - u_j} B_{j,m}(\bar{t}) - \frac{m}{u_{j+m+1} - u_{j+1}} B_{j+1,m}(\bar{t}).$$

[20 pts]   **10.** Given the knot sequence

$$0, 0, 0, 0, 1, 2, 3, 4, 4, 4, 4,$$

show that the spline basis function $B_{0,4}$ is given by

$$B_{0,4}(t) = \begin{cases} \frac{1}{6}t^3 & \text{for } 0 \le t < 1 \\ \frac{1}{6}(-3t^3 + 12t^2 - 12t + 4) & \text{for } 1 \le t < 2 \\ \frac{1}{6}(3t^3 - 24t^2 + 60t - 44) & \text{for } 2 \le t < 3 \\ \frac{1}{6}(-t^3 + 12t^2 - 48t + 64) & \text{for } 3 \le t < 4. \end{cases}$$

[40 pts]   **11.** Given any uniform sequence $t_0, \ldots, t_m$ of real numbers, where $t_{i+1} = t_i + h$ for some $h > 0$ $(0 \le i \le m - 1)$, given any sequence $y_0, \ldots, y_m$ of real numbers, given any two real numbers α, β, prove that there exists a unique cubic *B*-spline function *F* based on the knot sequence

$$\underbrace{t_0, \ldots, t_0}_{m}, t_1, \ldots, t_{m-1}, \underbrace{t_m, \ldots, t_m}_{m},$$

such that

$$F(t_i) = y_i,$$

$$F'(t_0) = \alpha,$$

$$F'(t_m) = \beta.$$

Prove that the above B-spline function F is the only C^2 function among all C^2 functions φ over $[t_0, t_m]$ such that

$$F(t_i) = y_i,$$

$$F'(t_0) = \alpha,$$

$$F'(t_m) = \beta,$$

that minimizes the integral

$$\int_{t_0}^{t_m} [\varphi''(t)]^2 dt.$$

Hint: Given any two spline functions F, G as above, and any piecewise linear function h, show that

$$\int_{t_0}^{t_m} [F''(t) - G''(t)]h(t)dt = 0.$$

[20 pts]   **12.** (a) Prove that

$$\alpha_i + \gamma_i + \beta_i = u_{i+1} - u_{i-1}$$

for all i, $1 \leq i \leq N - 1$, where $\alpha_i, \gamma_i, \beta_i$ are defined in Section 6.8 (Interpolation Problem 1 and Interpolation Problem 2).

(b) Let $(x_1, \ldots, x_n)$ and $(y_1, \ldots, y_n)$ be two sequences of n points (say, in $\mathbf{A}^3$), and assume that each point y_i is an affine combination of the points x_j, say,

$$y_i = \sum_{j=1}^{n} a_{i\,j} x_j.$$

Let $A = (a_{i\,j})$ be the $n \times n$ matrix expressing the y_i in terms of the x_j. Show that

$$\sum_{j=1}^{n} a_{i\,j} = 1$$

for every i, $1 \le i \le n$, that is, the sum of the elements of every row is 1. Prove that if A is invertible, then the sum of the elements of every row of A^{-1} is also 1.

[20 pts]   **13.** Prove that the matrix below is invertible.

$$
\begin{pmatrix}
1 & & & & & & \\
\frac{3}{2} & \frac{7}{2} & 1 & & & & \\
& 1 & 4 & 1 & & 0 & \\
& & & \ddots & & & \\
& 0 & & 1 & 4 & 1 & \\
& & & & 1 & \frac{7}{2} & \frac{3}{2} \\
& & & & & & 1
\end{pmatrix}
$$

[40 pts]   **14.** Compute the de Boor points d_0 and d_N arising in Interpolation Problem 1 in the following cases:

(a) Bessel end condition.

(b) Quadratic end condition.

(c) Natural end condition.

(d) Not-a-knot condition.

[20 pts]   **15.** (a) Show that interpolating cubic B-splines reproduce straight lines, provided that the end conditions are clamped, and that the tangents are read off the straight line.

(b) Prove a similar result for quadratic and cubic polynomial curves.

[30 pts]   **16.** Study the interpolation problem when the end conditions are to prescribe the first and the second derivatives at x_0.

[40 pts]   **17.** Implement the interpolation method proposed for solving Interpolation Problem 1. In solving this problem, find (or look up) a linear-time method for solving a tridiagonal linear system.

[40 pts]   **18.** Implement the interpolation method proposed for solving Problem 2. In solving this problem, find (or look up) a linear-time method for solving a tridiagonal linear system.

[20 pts]   **19.** (a) For a quadratic B-spline curve specified by a closed polygon of de Boor control points, prove that knot insertion at midpoints of intervals yields new control points defined such that for every edge (b_i, b_{i+1}),

$$
b'_{2i+1} = \frac{3}{4} b_i + \frac{1}{4} b_{i+1},
$$

and

$$
b'_{2i+2} = \frac{1}{4} b_i + \frac{3}{4} b_{i+1}.
$$

(b) For a cubic B-spline curve specified by a closed polygon of de Boor control points, prove that knot insertion at midpoints of intervals yields new control points defined such that, for any three consecutive control points b_i, b_{i+1}, and b_{i+2},

$$b'_{2i+1} = \frac{1}{2} b_i + \frac{1}{2} b_{i+1},$$

and

$$b'_{2i+2} = \frac{1}{8} b_i + \frac{6}{8} b_{i+1}, + \frac{1}{8} b_{i+2}.$$

PART III

POLYNOMIAL SURFACES
AND SPLINE SURFACES

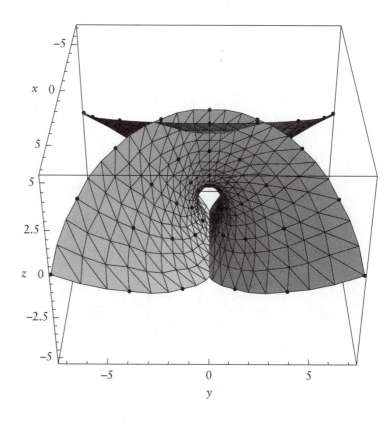

CHAPTER 7

Polynomial Surfaces

7.1   Polarizing Polynomial Surfaces

In this chapter, we take up the study of polynomial surfaces. After a quick review of the traditional parametric definition in terms of polynomials, we investigate the possibility of defining polynomial surfaces in terms of polar forms. Because the polynomials involved contain two variables, there are two natural ways to polarize a polynomial surface. The first approach yields bipolynomial surfaces (also called tensor product surfaces), and the second approach yields total degree surfaces. Bipolynomial surfaces are completely determined by rectangular nets of control points, and total degree surfaces are completely determined by triangular nets of control points. The de Casteljau algorithm splits into two versions, one for rectangular nets and the other one for triangular nets. We show how these versions of the de Casteljau algorithm can be turned into subdivision methods. In the case of rectangular nets, it is easy to use the algorithms developed for polynomial curves. However, in the case of triangular nets, things are more tricky, and we give an efficient method for performing subdivision. We also show how to compute a new control net with respect to a new rectangle (or new triangle) from a given net.

We begin with the traditional definition of polynomial surfaces. As we shall see, there are two natural ways to polarize a polynomial surface. Intuitively, this depends on whether we decide to tile the parameter plane with rectangles or with triangles. This is one of the many indications that dealing with surfaces is far more complex than dealing with curves.

Recall that the affine line is denoted as $\mathbf{A}$, and that the affine plane is denoted as $\mathbf{A}^2$. To reduce the amount of superscripts, we will also denote the affine plane as $\mathcal{P}$. We assume that some fixed affine frame $(O, (\vec{i_1}, \vec{i_2}))$ for $\mathcal{P}$ is chosen, typically, the canonical affine frame where $O = (0, 0)$, $\vec{i_1} = \binom{1}{0}$, and $\vec{i_2} = \binom{0}{1}$. Let $\mathcal{E}$ be some affine space of finite dimension $n \geq 3$, and let $(\Omega_1, (\vec{e_1}, \ldots, \vec{e_n}))$ be an affine frame for $\mathcal{E}$.

Definition 7.1.1

A polynomial surface *is a function* $F: \mathcal{P} \to \mathcal{E}$, *such that, for all* $u, v \in \mathbf{R}$, *we have*

$$F(O + u\vec{i_1} + v\vec{i_2}) = \Omega_1 + F_1(u, v)\vec{e_1} + \cdots + F_n(u, v)\vec{e_n},$$

where $F_1(U, V), \ldots, F_n(U, V)$ *are polynomials in* $\mathbf{R}[U, V]$. *Given natural numbers* p, q, *and* m, *if each polynomial* $F_i(U, V)$ *has total degree* $\leq m$, *we say that* F *is a polynomial surface of total degree* m. *If the maximum degree of* U *in all the* $F_i(U, V)$ *is* $\leq p$, *and the maximum degree of* V *in all the* $F_i(U, V)$ *is* $\leq q$, *we say that* F *is a bipolynomial surface of degree* $\langle p, q \rangle$. *The trace of the surface* F *is the set* $F(\mathcal{P})$.

The affine frame $(O, (\vec{i_1}, \vec{i_2}))$ for $\mathcal{P}$ being fixed, for simplicity of notation, we denote $F(O + u\vec{i_1} + v\vec{i_2})$ as $F(u, v)$. Intuitively, a polynomial surface is obtained by bending and twisting the real affine plane $\mathbf{A}^2$ using a polynomial map. For example, the following polynomials define a polynomial surface of total degree 2 in $\mathbf{A}^3$:

$$F_1(U, V) = U^2 + V^2 + UV + 2U + V - 1,$$

$$F_2(U, V) = U - V + 1,$$

$$F_3(U, V) = UV + U + V + 1.$$

The above is also a bipolynomial surface of degree $\langle 2, 2 \rangle$. Another example, known as *Enneper's surface*, is as follows:

$$F_1(U, V) = U - \frac{U^3}{3} + UV^2,$$

$$F_2(U, V) = V - \frac{V^3}{3} + U^2V,$$

$$F_3(U, V) = U^2 - V^2.$$

As defined above, Enneper's surface is a surface of total degree 3, and a bipolynomial surface of degree $\langle 3, 3 \rangle$.

Given a polynomial surface $F: \mathcal{P} \to \mathcal{E}$, there are two natural ways to polarize.

The first way is to treat the variables u and v separately, and polarize separately in u and v. This way, if p and q are such that F is a bipolynomial surface of degree $\langle p, q \rangle$, we get a $(p + q)$-multiaffine map

$$f: (\mathbf{A})^p \times (\mathbf{A})^q \to \mathcal{E},$$

which is symmetric separately in its first p arguments and in its last q arguments, but not symmetric in all its arguments.

Note that we are intentionally denoting

$$\underbrace{\mathbf{A} \times \cdots \times \mathbf{A}}_{p} \times \underbrace{\mathbf{A} \times \cdots \times \mathbf{A}}_{q}$$

as $(\mathbf{A})^p \times (\mathbf{A})^q$, with parentheses around each factor $\mathbf{A}$, instead of $\mathbf{A}^p \times \mathbf{A}^q$, to avoid the confusion between the affine space $\mathbf{A}^p$ and the cartesian product $\underbrace{\mathbf{A} \times \cdots \times \mathbf{A}}_{p}$.

We get what are traditionally called *tensor product surfaces*. The advantage of this method is that it allows the use of many algorithms applying in the case of curves. Note that in this case, since

$$F(u, v) = f(\underbrace{u, \ldots, u}_{p}, \underbrace{v, \ldots, v}_{q}),$$

the surface F is really a map $F \colon \mathbf{A} \times \mathbf{A} \to \mathcal{E}$. However, since $\mathbf{A} \times \mathbf{A}$ is isomorphic to $\mathcal{P} = \mathbf{A}^2$, we can view F as a polynomial surface $F \colon \mathcal{P} \to \mathcal{E}$.

The second way to polarize is to treat the variables u and v as a whole, namely, as the coordinates of a point (u, v) in $\mathcal{P}$, and to polarize the polynomials in both variables simultaneously. This way, if m is such that F is a polynomial surface of total degree m, we get an m-multiaffine map

$$f \colon \mathcal{P}^m \to \mathcal{E},$$

which is symmetric in all of its m arguments. In some sense, this method is the immediate generalization of Bézier curves. Indeed, since

$$F(u, v) = f(\underbrace{(u, v), \ldots, (u, v)}_{m}),$$

the surface F is indeed a map $F \colon \mathcal{P} \to \mathcal{E}$.

We will present both methods and investigate appropriate generalizations of the de Casteljau algorithm. First, we consider several examples to illustrate the two ways of polarizing. We begin with the first method for polarizing, in which we polarize separately in u and v. Using linearity, it is enough to explain how to polarize a monomial $F(u, v)$ of the form $u^h v^k$ with respect to the bidegree $\langle p, q \rangle$, where $h \le p$ and $k \le q$. It is easily seen that

$$f(u_1, \ldots, u_p, v_1, \ldots, v_q) = \frac{1}{\binom{p}{h}\binom{q}{k}} \sum_{\substack{I \subseteq \{1,\ldots,p\},\, |I|=h \\ J \subseteq \{1,\ldots,q\},\, |J|=k}} \left(\prod_{i \in I} u_i \right) \left(\prod_{j \in J} v_j \right).$$

Example 1: Consider the following surface viewed as a bipolynomial surface of degree $\langle 2, 2 \rangle$:

$$F_1(U, V) = U^2 + V^2 + UV + 2U + V - 1,$$

$$F_2(U, V) = U - V + 1,$$

$$F_3(U, V) = UV + U + V + 1.$$

In order to find the polar form $f(U_1, U_2, V_1, V_2)$ of F, viewed as a bipolynomial surface of degree $\langle 2, 2 \rangle$, we polarize each of the $F_i(U, V)$ separately in U and V. It is quite obvious that the same result is obtained if we first polarize with respect to U, and then with respect to V, or conversely. After polarizing with respect to U, we have

$$f_1^U(U_1, U_2, V) = U_1 U_2 + V^2 + \frac{U_1 + U_2}{2} V + U_1 + U_2 + V - 1,$$

$$f_2^U(U_1, U_2, V) = \frac{U_1 + U_2}{2} - V + 1,$$

$$f_3^U(U_1, U_2, V) = \frac{U_1 + U_2}{2} V + \frac{U_1 + U_2}{2} + V + 1,$$

and after polarizing with respect to V, we have

$$f_1(U_1, U_2, V_1, V_2) = U_1 U_2 + V_1 V_2 + \frac{(U_1 + U_2)(V_1 + V_2)}{4} + U_1 + U_2$$
$$+ \frac{V_1 + V_2}{2} - 1,$$

$$f_2(U_1, U_2, V_1, V_2) = \frac{U_1 + U_2}{2} - \frac{V_1 + V_2}{2} + 1,$$

$$f_3(U_1, U_2, V_1, V_2) = \frac{(U_1 + U_2)(V_1 + V_2)}{4} + \frac{U_1 + U_2}{2} + \frac{V_1 + V_2}{2} + 1.$$

Now, we can express every point $\bar{u} \in \mathbf{A}$ over the affine basis $(\bar{0}, \bar{1})$ as a barycentric combination $\bar{u} = u = (1 - u)0 + u1 = (1 - u)\bar{0} + u\bar{1}$, and expanding

$$f_i(\bar{u}_1, \bar{u}_2, \bar{v}_1, \bar{v}_2) = f_i\big((1 - u_1)\bar{0} + u_1\bar{1}, (1 - u_2)\bar{0} + u_2\bar{1}, (1 - v_1)\bar{0} + v_1\bar{1},$$
$$(1 - v_2)\bar{0} + v_2\bar{1}\big),$$

using multiaffineness and symmetry in $\bar{u}_1, \bar{u}_2$, and $\bar{v}_1, \bar{v}_2$, we see, similarly to the case of curves, that $f_i(\bar{u}_1, \bar{u}_2, \bar{v}_1, \bar{v}_2)$ can be expressed as a barycentric combination involving nine control points $b_{i,j}$, $0 \le i, j \le 2$, corresponding to the 27 polar values $f_i(\bar{u}_1, \bar{u}_2, \bar{v}_1, \bar{v}_2)$, where the multiset of polar arguments $\{\bar{u}_1, \bar{u}_2\}$ can take as values any of the three multisets $\{\bar{0}, \bar{0}\}$, $\{\bar{0}, \bar{1}\}$, $\{\bar{1}, \bar{1}\}$, and similarly for the multiset of polar arguments $\{\bar{v}_1, \bar{v}_2\}$.

Denoting $f_i(\bar{u}_1, \bar{u}_2, \bar{v}_1, \bar{v}_2)$ as $b_{u_1+u_2, v_1+v_2}^i$, the coordinates of the control point $b_{u_1+u_2, v_1+v_2}$ are

$$(b_{u_1+u_2, v_1+v_2}^1, b_{u_1+u_2, v_1+v_2}^2, b_{u_1+u_2, v_1+v_2}^3).$$

Letting $i = u_1 + u_2$, and $j = v_1 + v_2$, we get

$b^1_{i,j}$ $\overline{u}_1, \overline{u}_2$	$\overline{v}_1, \overline{v}_2$	$\overline{0}, \overline{0}$	$\overline{0}, \overline{1}$	$\overline{1}, \overline{1}$
$\overline{0}, \overline{0}$		-1	$-\frac{1}{2}$	1
$\overline{0}, \overline{1}$		0	$\frac{3}{4}$	$\frac{5}{2}$
$\overline{1}, \overline{1}$		2	3	5

$b^2_{i,j}$ $\overline{u}_1, \overline{u}_2$	$\overline{v}_1, \overline{v}_2$	$\overline{0}, \overline{0}$	$\overline{0}, \overline{1}$	$\overline{1}, \overline{1}$
$\overline{0}, \overline{0}$		1	$\frac{1}{2}$	0
$\overline{0}, \overline{1}$		$\frac{3}{2}$	1	$\frac{1}{2}$
$\overline{1}, \overline{1}$		2	$\frac{3}{2}$	1

$b^3_{i,j}$ $\overline{u}_1, \overline{u}_2$	$\overline{v}_1, \overline{v}_2$	$\overline{0}, \overline{0}$	$\overline{0}, \overline{1}$	$\overline{1}, \overline{1}$
$\overline{0}, \overline{0}$		1	$\frac{3}{2}$	2
$\overline{0}, \overline{1}$		$\frac{3}{2}$	$\frac{9}{4}$	3
$\overline{1}, \overline{1}$		2	3	4

and the nine control points $b_{i,j}$ have coordinates

$b_{i,j}$ j i	0	1	2
0	$(-1, 1, 1)$	$(-\frac{1}{2}, \frac{1}{2}, \frac{3}{2})$	$(1, 0, 2)$
1	$(0, \frac{3}{2}, \frac{3}{2})$	$(\frac{3}{4}, 1, \frac{9}{4})$	$(\frac{5}{2}, \frac{1}{2}, 3)$
2	$(2, 2, 2)$	$(3, \frac{3}{2}, 3)$	$(5, 1, 4)$

Note that the surface contains the four control points $b_{0,0}$, $b_{2,0}$, $b_{0,2}$, and $b_{2,2}$, corresponding to the polar values $f(\overline{0}, \overline{0}, \overline{0}, \overline{0})$, $f(\overline{1}, \overline{1}, \overline{0}, \overline{0})$, $f(\overline{0}, \overline{0}, \overline{1}, \overline{1})$, and $f(\overline{1}, \overline{1}, \overline{1}, \overline{1})$, but the other five control points are not on the surface. There are also some pleasant properties regarding tangent planes. Note that a bipolynomial surface can be viewed as a polynomial curve of polynomial curves. Indeed, if we fix the parameter u, we get a polynomial curve in v, and the surface is obtained by letting this curve vary as a function of u. A similar interpretation applies if we exchange the roles of u and v.

Let us now review how to polarize a polynomial in two variables as a polynomial of total degree m, in preparation for Example 2. Using linearity, it is enough to deal with a single monomial. According to Lemma 4.5.1, given the monomial $U^h V^k$, with $h + k = d \leq m$, we get the following polar form of degree m:

$$f((u_1, v_1), \ldots, (u_m, v_m)) = \frac{h!k!(m - (h + k))!}{m!} \sum_{\substack{I \cup J \subseteq \{1, \ldots, m\} \\ I \cap J = \emptyset \\ |I| = h, |J| = k}} \left(\prod_{i \in I} u_i \right) \left(\prod_{j \in J} v_j \right).$$

Example 2: Let us now polarize the surface of Example 1 as a surface of total degree 2. Starting from

$$F_1(U, V) = U^2 + V^2 + UV + 2U + V - 1,$$

$$F_2(U, V) = U - V + 1,$$

$$F_3(U, V) = UV + U + V + 1,$$

we get

$$f_1((U_1, V_1), (U_2, V_2)) = U_1 U_2 + V_1 V_2 + \frac{U_1 V_2 + U_2 V_1}{2} + U_1 + U_2 + \frac{V_1 + V_2}{2} - 1,$$

$$f_2((U_1, V_1), (U_2, V_2)) = \frac{U_1 + U_2}{2} - \frac{V_1 + V_2}{2} + 1,$$

$$f_3((U_1, V_1), (U_2, V_2)) = \frac{U_1 V_2 + U_2 V_1}{2} + \frac{U_1 + U_2}{2} + \frac{V_1 + V_2}{2} + 1.$$

Digression: This time, if we want to find control points, it appears that we have a problem. Indeed, the symmetric multiaffine map $f: \mathcal{P}^2 \to \mathcal{E}$ is defined in terms of the coordinates (u, v) of points in the plane $\mathcal{P}$, with respect to the affine frame $(O, (\vec{i_1}, \vec{i_2}))$, and not the barycentric affine frame $(O + \vec{i_1}, O + \vec{i_2}, O)$. In order to expand $f(u_1, v_1, u_2, v_2)$ by multiaffineness, the polar form f needs to be expressed in terms of barycentric coordinates. It is possible to convert polar forms expressed in terms of coordinates with respect to the affine frame $(O, (\vec{i_1}, \vec{i_2}))$ to barycentric coordinates, but there is a simple way around this apparent problem, and we leave such a conversion as an exercise. The way around the problem is to observe that every point in $\mathcal{P}$ of coordinates (u, v) with respect to the affine frame $(O, (\vec{i_1}, \vec{i_2}))$ is also represented by its barycentric coordinates $(u, v, 1 - u - v)$ with respect to the barycentric affine frame $(r, s, t) = (O + \vec{i_1}, O + \vec{i_2}, O)$. Now, with respect to the barycentric affine frame $(r, s, t) = (O + \vec{i_1}, O + \vec{i_2}, O)$, every point $b_i \in \mathcal{P}$, where $i = 1, 2$, can be expressed as $\lambda_i r + \mu_i s + \nu_i t$, where $\lambda_i + \mu_i + \nu_i = 1$. We can expand

$$f(b_1, b_2) = f(\lambda_1 r + \mu_1 s + \nu_1 t, \lambda_2 r + \mu_2 s + \nu_2 t)$$

by multiaffineness and symmetry, and we see that $f(b_1, b_2)$ can be expressed as a barycentric combination of the six control points $f(r, r)$, $f(r, s)$, $f(r, t)$, $f(s, s)$, $f(s, t)$, $f(t, t)$. Thus, if we only want the coordinates of the six control points, we just have to evaluate the original polar forms f_1, f_2, f_3, expressed in terms of the (u, v) coordinates, on the (u, v) coordinates of (r, s, t), namely, $(1, 0)$, $(0, 1)$, and $(0, 0)$.

So, in fact, there is no problem in computing the coordinates of control points using the original (nonbarycentric) polar forms, and we now go back to Example 2.

Example 2 (continued): Evaluating the polar forms

$$f_1((U_1, V_1), (U_2, V_2)) = U_1 U_2 + V_1 V_2 + \frac{U_1 V_2 + U_2 V_1}{2} + U_1 + U_2 + \frac{V_1 + V_2}{2} - 1,$$

$$f_2((U_1, V_1), (U_2, V_2)) = \frac{U_1 + U_2}{2} - \frac{V_1 + V_2}{2} + 1,$$

$$f_3((U_1, V_1), (U_2, V_2)) = \frac{U_1 V_2 + U_2 V_1}{2} + \frac{U_1 + U_2}{2} + \frac{V_1 + V_2}{2} + 1,$$

for argument pairs (U_1, V_1) and (U_2, V_2) ranging over $(1, 0)$, $(0, 1)$, and $(0, 0)$, we get the following coordinates:

$$\begin{array}{ccc}
 & \begin{array}{c} f(r,r) \\ (2,2,2) \end{array} & \\[4pt]
\begin{array}{c} f(r,t) \\ \left(0, \dfrac{3}{2}, \dfrac{3}{2}\right) \end{array} & & \begin{array}{c} f(r,s) \\ \left(1, 1, \dfrac{5}{2}\right) \end{array} \\[12pt]
\begin{array}{c} f(t,t) \\ (-1,1,1) \end{array} & \begin{array}{c} f(s,t) \\ \left(-\dfrac{1}{2}, \dfrac{1}{2}, \dfrac{3}{2}\right) \end{array} & \begin{array}{c} f(s,s) \\ (1,0,2) \end{array}
\end{array}$$

Example 3: Let us also find the polar forms of the Enneper's surface, considered as a total degree surface (of degree 3):

$$F_1(U, V) = U - \frac{U^3}{3} + UV^2,$$

$$F_2(U, V) = V - \frac{V^3}{3} + U^2 V,$$

$$F_3(U, V) = U^2 - V^2.$$

We get

$$f_1((U_1, V_1), (U_2, V_2), (U_3, V_3)) = \frac{U_1 + U_2 + U_3}{3} - \frac{U_1 U_2 U_3}{3}$$

$$+ \frac{U_1 V_2 V_3 + U_2 V_1 V_3 + U_3 V_1 V_2}{3}$$

$$f_2((U_1, V_1), (U_2, V_2), (U_3, V_3)) = \frac{V_1 + V_2 + V_3}{3} - \frac{V_1 V_2 V_3}{3}$$

$$+ \frac{U_1 U_2 V_3 + U_1 U_3 V_2 + U_2 U_3 V_1}{3}$$

$$f_3((U_1, V_1), (U_2, V_2), (U_3, V_3)) = \frac{U_1 U_2 + U_1 U_3 + U_2 U_3}{3} - \frac{V_1 V_2 + V_1 V_3 + V_2 V_3}{3},$$

and evaluating these polar forms for argument pairs (U_1, V_1), (U_2, V_2), and (U_3, V_3), ranging over $(1, 0)$, $(0, 1)$, and $(0, 0)$, we find the following 10 control points:

$$f(r, r, r)$$
$$\left(\frac{2}{3}, 0, 1\right)$$

$$f(r, r, t) \qquad\qquad f(r, r, s)$$
$$\left(\frac{2}{3}, 0, \frac{1}{3}\right) \qquad\qquad \left(\frac{2}{3}, \frac{2}{3}, \frac{1}{3}\right)$$

$$f(r, t, t) \qquad\qquad f(r, s, t) \qquad\qquad f(r, s, s)$$
$$\left(\frac{1}{3}, 0, 0\right) \qquad \left(\frac{1}{3}, \frac{1}{3}, 0\right) \qquad \left(\frac{2}{3}, \frac{2}{3}, -\frac{1}{3}\right)$$

$$f(t, t, t) \qquad\quad f(s, t, t) \qquad\quad f(s, s, t) \qquad\quad f(s, s, s)$$
$$(0, 0, 0) \qquad \left(0, \frac{1}{3}, 0\right) \qquad \left(0, \frac{2}{3}, -\frac{1}{3}\right) \qquad \left(0, \frac{2}{3}, -1\right)$$

Let us consider two more examples.

Example 4: Let F be the surface considered as a total degree surface, and defined such that

$$F_1(U, V) = U,$$

$$F_2(U, V) = V,$$

$$F_3(U, V) = U^2 - V^2.$$

The polar forms are

$$f_1((U_1, V_1), (U_2, V_2)) = \frac{U_1 + U_2}{2},$$

$$f_2((U_1, V_1), (U_2, V_2)) = \frac{V_1 + V_2}{2},$$

$$f_3((U_1, V_1), (U_2, V_2)) = U_1 U_2 - V_1 V_2.$$

With respect to the barycentric affine frame $(r, s, t) = (O + \vec{i_1}, O + \vec{i_2}, O)$, the control net consists of the following six points, obtained by evaluating the polar forms f_1, f_2, f_3 on the (u, v) coordinates of (r, s, t), namely, $(1, 0)$, $(0, 1)$, and $(0, 0)$:

$$f(r, r)$$
$$(1, 0, 1)$$

$$f(r, t) \qquad\qquad f(r, s)$$
$$\left(\frac{1}{2}, 0, 0\right) \qquad\qquad \left(\frac{1}{2}, \frac{1}{2}, 0\right)$$

$$f(t, t) \qquad\qquad f(s, t) \qquad\qquad f(s, s)$$
$$(0, 0, 0) \qquad \left(0, \frac{1}{2}, 0\right) \qquad (0, 1, -1)$$

The resulting surface is a *hyperbolic paraboloid*, of implicit equation

$$z = x^2 - y^2.$$

Its general shape is that of a saddle. Its intersection with planes parallel to the plane yOz is a parabola, and similarly with its intersection with planes parallel to the plane xOz. Its intersection with planes parallel to the plane xOy is a hyperbola. If we rotate the x, y-axes to the X, Y-axes such that

$$X = \frac{x - y}{2},$$

$$Y = \frac{x + y}{2},$$

we get the parametric representation

$$F_1'(U, V) = \frac{U - V}{2},$$

$$F_2'(U, V) = \frac{U + V}{2},$$

$$F_3'(U, V) = U^2 - V^2.$$

After the change of parameters

$$u = \frac{U - V}{2},$$

$$v = \frac{U + V}{2},$$

since $U^2 - V^2 = (U + V)(U - V) = 4uv$, we see that the same hyperbolic paraboloid is also defined by

$$F_1''(u, v) = u,$$

$$F_2''(u, v) = v,$$

$$F_3''(u, v) = 4uv.$$

Thus, when u is constant, the curve traced on the surface is a straight line, and similarly when v is constant. We say that the hyperbolic paraboloid is a *ruled surface*.

Example 5: Let F be the surface considered as a total degree surface, and defined such that

$$F_1(U, V) = U,$$

$$F_2(U, V) = V,$$

$$F_3(U, V) = 2U^2 + V^2.$$

The polar forms are

$$f_1((U_1, V_1), (U_2, V_2)) = \frac{U_1 + U_2}{2},$$

$$f_2((U_1, V_1), (U_2, V_2)) = \frac{V_1 + V_2}{2},$$

$$f_3((U_1, V_1), (U_2, V_2)) = 2U_1U_2 + V_1V_2.$$

With respect to the barycentric affine frame $(r, s, t) = (O + \vec{i_1}, O + \vec{i_2}, O)$, the control net consists of the following six points, obtained by evaluating the polar forms f_1, f_2, f_3 on the (u, v) coordinates of (r, s, t), namely, $(1, 0)$, $(0, 1)$, and $(0, 0)$:

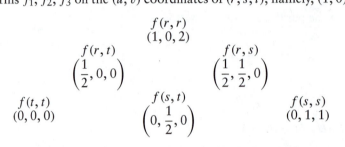

The resulting surface is an *elliptic paraboloid* of implicit equation

$$z = 2x^2 + y^2.$$

Its general shape is that of a "boulder hat." Its intersection with planes parallel to the plane yOz is a parabola, and similarly with its intersection with planes parallel to the plane xOz. Its intersection with planes parallel to the plane xOy is an ellipse.

Generally, we leave as an exercise to show that, except for some degenerate cases, the algebraic surfaces defined by implicit equations of degree 2 that are also defined as polynomial surfaces of degree 2 are either a *hyperbolic paraboloid*, defined by an implicit equation of the form

$$z = \frac{x^2}{a^2} - \frac{y^2}{b^2},$$

or an *elliptic paraboloid*, defined by an implicit equation of the form

$$z = \frac{x^2}{a^2} + \frac{y^2}{b^2},$$

or a *parabolic cylinder*, defined by an implicit equation of the form

$$y^2 = 4ax.$$

It should be noted that parametric polynomial surfaces of degree 2 may correspond to implicit algebraic surfaces of degree > 2, as shown by the following example:

$$x = u,$$

$$y = u^2 + v,$$

$$z = v^2.$$

An implicit equation for this surface is

$$z = (y - x^2)^2,$$

which is of degree 4, and it is easy to see that this is the smallest degree.

We will now consider bipolynomial surfaces and total degree surfaces in more detail. First, we go back to bipolynomial surfaces.

7.2   Bipolynomial Surfaces in Polar Form

Given a bipolynomial surface $F: \mathcal{P} \to \mathcal{E}$ of degree $\langle p, q \rangle$, where $\mathcal{E}$ is of dimension n, applying Lemma 4.5.1 to each polynomial $F_i(U, V)$ defining F, first with respect to U, and then with respect to V, we get polar forms

$$f_i: (\mathbf{A})^p \times (\mathbf{A})^q \to \mathbf{A},$$

which together, define a $(p + q)$-multiaffine map

$$f: (\mathbf{A})^p \times (\mathbf{A})^q \to \mathcal{E},$$

such that $f(U_1, \ldots, U_p; V_1, \ldots, V_q)$ is symmetric in its first p arguments, and symmetric in its last q arguments, and with

$$F(u, v) = f(\underbrace{u, \ldots, u}_{p}; \underbrace{v, \ldots, v}_{q}),$$

for all $u, v \in \mathbf{R}$.

Remark: It is immediately verified that the same polar form is obtained if we first polarize with respect to V and then with respect to U.

By analogy with polynomial curves, it is natural to propose the following definition.

Definition 7.2.1

Given any affine space $\mathcal{E}$ of dimension ≥ 3, a bipolynomial surface of degree $\langle p, q \rangle$ in polar form is a map $F: \mathbf{A} \times \mathbf{A} \to \mathcal{E}$, such that there is some multiaffine map

$$f: (\mathbf{A})^p \times (\mathbf{A})^q \to \mathcal{E},$$

which is symmetric in its first p arguments, and symmetric in its last q arguments, and with

$$F(\overline{u}, \overline{v}) = f(\underbrace{\overline{u}, \ldots, \overline{u}}_{p}; \underbrace{\overline{v}, \ldots, \overline{v}}_{q}),$$

for all $\overline{u}, \overline{v} \in A$. We also say that f is $\langle p, q \rangle$-symmetric. *The* trace of the surface F is the set $F(A, A)$.

The advantage of Definition 7.2.1 is that it does not depend on the dimension of $\mathcal{E}$.

Remark: This note is intended for those who are fond of tensors and can be safely omitted by other readers. Let $F: A \times A \to \mathcal{E}$ be a bipolynomial surface of degree $\langle p, q \rangle$, and let

$$f: (A)^p \times (A)^q \to \mathcal{E}$$

be its polar form. Let

$$\widehat{f}: (\widehat{A})^p \times (\widehat{A})^q \to \widehat{\mathcal{E}}$$

be its homogenized $\langle p, q \rangle$-symmetric multilinear map. It is easily verified that the set of all symmetric q-linear maps $h: (\widehat{A})^q \to \widehat{\mathcal{E}}$ forms a vector space $\mathrm{SML}((\widehat{A})^q, \widehat{\mathcal{E}})$, and thus, the $\langle p, q \rangle$-symmetric multilinear map

$$\widehat{f}: (\widehat{A})^p \times (\widehat{A})^q \to \widehat{\mathcal{E}}$$

is in bijection with the symmetric p-linear map

$$g: (\widehat{A})^p \to \mathrm{SML}((\widehat{A})^q, \widehat{\mathcal{E}}).$$

From the universal property of the symmetric tensor power $\bigodot^p \widehat{A}$, the symmetric p-linear map g is in bijection with a linear map

$$g_\odot: \overset{p}{\bigodot} \widehat{A} \to \mathrm{SML}((\widehat{A})^q, \widehat{\mathcal{E}}).$$

We can now view the linear map $g_\odot$ as a symmetric q-linear map

$$h: (\widehat{A})^q \to \mathrm{SML}\left(\overset{p}{\bigodot} \widehat{A}^p, \widehat{\mathcal{E}}\right),$$

which, in turn, is in bijection with a linear map

$$h_\odot: \overset{q}{\bigodot} \widehat{A} \to \mathrm{SML}\left(\overset{p}{\bigodot} \widehat{A}, \widehat{\mathcal{E}}\right).$$

But then, the linear map $h_\odot$ is in bijection with a bilinear map

$$f_{\odot;\odot}: \left(\overset{p}{\bigodot} \widehat{A}\right) \times \left(\overset{q}{\bigodot} \widehat{A}\right) \to \widehat{\mathcal{E}}.$$

Note that $f_{\odot;\odot}$ is bilinear, but not necessarily symmetric. However, using the universal property of the tensor product $(\bigodot^p \widehat{\mathbf{A}}) \otimes (\bigodot^q \widehat{\mathbf{A}})$, we note that the bilinear map

$$f_{\odot;\odot} \colon \left(\overset{p}{\bigodot} \widehat{\mathbf{A}} \right) \times \left(\overset{q}{\bigodot} \widehat{\mathbf{A}} \right) \to \widehat{\mathcal{E}}$$

is in bijection with a linear map

$$f_{\otimes} \colon \left(\overset{p}{\bigodot} \widehat{\mathbf{A}} \right) \otimes \left(\overset{q}{\bigodot} \widehat{\mathbf{A}} \right) \to \widehat{\mathcal{E}},$$

and it is immediately verified that

$$f(\overline{u}_1, \ldots, \overline{u}_p; \overline{v}_1, \ldots, \overline{v}_q) = f_{\otimes}((\overline{u}_1 \odot \cdots \odot \overline{u}_p) \otimes (\overline{v}_1 \odot \cdots \odot \overline{v}_q)).$$

This explains the terminology "tensor product surface," but it also explains why this terminology is slightly unfortunate. Indeed, the tensor product involved,

$$\left(\overset{p}{\bigodot} \widehat{\mathbf{A}} \right) \otimes \left(\overset{q}{\bigodot} \widehat{\mathbf{A}} \right),$$

is "mixed," in the sense that it uses both the symmetric tensor product $\odot$, and the ordinary tensor product $\otimes$.

Now, let $(\overline{r}_1, \overline{s}_1)$ and $(\overline{r}_2, \overline{s}_2)$ be two affine frames for the affine line $\mathbf{A}$. Every point $\overline{u} \in \mathbf{A}$ can be written as

$$\overline{u} = \left(\frac{s_1 - u}{s_1 - r_1} \right) \overline{r}_1 + \left(\frac{u - r_1}{s_1 - r_1} \right) \overline{s}_1,$$

and similarly any point $\overline{v} \in \mathbf{A}$ can be written as

$$\overline{v} = \left(\frac{s_2 - v}{s_2 - r_2} \right) \overline{r}_2 + \left(\frac{v - r_2}{s_2 - r_2} \right) \overline{s}_2.$$

We can expand

$$f(\overline{u}_1, \ldots, \overline{u}_p; \overline{v}_1, \ldots, \overline{v}_q),$$

using multiaffineness. For example, the first two steps yield

$$f(\bar{u}_1, \ldots, \bar{u}_p; \bar{v}_1, \ldots, \bar{v}_q) = \left(\frac{s_1 - u_1}{s_1 - r_1}\right)\left(\frac{s_2 - v_1}{s_2 - r_2}\right) f(\bar{r}_1, \bar{u}_2, \ldots, \bar{u}_p; \bar{r}_2, \bar{v}_2, \ldots, \bar{v}_q)$$

$$+ \left(\frac{s_1 - u_1}{s_1 - r_1}\right)\left(\frac{v_1 - r_2}{s_2 - r_2}\right) f(\bar{r}_1, \bar{u}_2, \ldots, \bar{u}_p; \bar{s}_2, \bar{v}_2, \ldots, \bar{v}_q)$$

$$+ \left(\frac{u_1 - r_1}{s_1 - r_1}\right)\left(\frac{s_2 - v_1}{s_2 - r_2}\right) f(\bar{s}_1, \bar{u}_2, \ldots, \bar{u}_p; \bar{r}_2, \bar{v}_2, \ldots, \bar{v}_q)$$

$$+ \left(\frac{u_1 - r_1}{s_1 - r_1}\right)\left(\frac{v_1 - r_2}{s_2 - r_2}\right) f(\bar{s}_1, \bar{u}_2, \ldots, \bar{u}_p; \bar{s}_2, \bar{v}_2, \ldots, \bar{v}_q).$$

By induction, the following can easily be shown:

$$f(\bar{u}_1, \ldots, \bar{u}_p; \bar{v}_1, \ldots, \bar{v}_q)$$

$$= \sum_{\substack{I \cap J = \emptyset \\ I \cup J = \{1,\ldots,p\} \\ K \cap L = \emptyset \\ K \cup L = \{1,\ldots,q\}}} \prod_{i \in I} \left(\frac{s_1 - u_i}{s_1 - r_1}\right) \prod_{j \in J} \left(\frac{u_j - r_1}{s_1 - r_1}\right) \prod_{k \in K} \left(\frac{s_2 - v_k}{s_2 - r_2}\right) \prod_{l \in L} \left(\frac{v_l - r_2}{s_2 - r_2}\right) b_{|J|, |L|},$$

where

$$b_{|J|, |L|} = f(\underbrace{\bar{r}_1, \ldots, \bar{r}_1}_{|I|}, \underbrace{\bar{s}_1, \ldots, \bar{s}_1}_{|J|}; \underbrace{\bar{r}_2, \ldots, \bar{r}_2}_{|K|}, \underbrace{\bar{s}_2, \ldots, \bar{s}_2}_{|L|}).$$

The polar values

$$b_{|J|, |L|} = f(\underbrace{\bar{r}_1, \ldots, \bar{r}_1}_{|I|}, \underbrace{\bar{s}_1, \ldots, \bar{s}_1}_{|J|}; \underbrace{\bar{r}_2, \ldots, \bar{r}_2}_{|K|}, \underbrace{\bar{s}_2, \ldots, \bar{s}_2}_{|L|})$$

can obviously be treated as control points.

Indeed, conversely, given any family $(b_{i,j})_{0 \le i \le p, 0 \le j \le q}$ of $(p+1)(q+1)$ points in $\mathcal{E}$, it is easily seen that the map defined such that

$$f(\bar{u}_1, \ldots, \bar{u}_p; \bar{v}_1, \ldots, \bar{v}_q)$$

$$= \sum_{\substack{I \cap J = \emptyset \\ I \cup J = \{1,\ldots,p\} \\ K \cap L = \emptyset \\ K \cup L = \{1,\ldots,q\}}} \prod_{i \in I} \left(\frac{s_1 - u_i}{s_1 - r_1}\right) \prod_{j \in J} \left(\frac{u_j - r_1}{s_1 - r_1}\right) \prod_{k \in K} \left(\frac{s_2 - v_k}{s_2 - r_2}\right) \prod_{l \in L} \left(\frac{v_l - r_2}{s_2 - r_2}\right) b_{|J|, |L|}$$

defines a multiaffine map that is $\langle p, q \rangle$-symmetric, and such that

$$f(\underbrace{\bar{r}_1, \ldots, \bar{r}_1}_{p-|J|}, \underbrace{\bar{s}_1, \ldots, \bar{s}_1}_{|J|}; \underbrace{\bar{r}_2, \ldots, \bar{r}_2}_{q-|L|}, \underbrace{\bar{s}_2, \ldots, \bar{s}_2}_{|L|}) = b_{|J|, |L|}.$$

We summarize the above in the following lemma.

Lemma 7.2.2

Let $(\overline{r}_1, \overline{s}_1)$ and $(\overline{r}_2, \overline{s}_2)$ be any two affine frames for the affine line $\mathbf{A}$, and let $\mathcal{E}$ be an affine space (of finite dimension $n \geq 3$). For any natural numbers p, q, for any family $(b_{i,j})_{0 \leq i \leq p, 0 \leq j \leq q}$ of $(p+1)(q+1)$ points in $\mathcal{E}$, there is a unique bipolynomial surface $F: \mathbf{A} \times \mathbf{A} \to \mathcal{E}$ of degree $\langle p, q \rangle$, whose polar form is the $(p+q)$-multiaffine $\langle p, q \rangle$-symmetric map

$$f: (\mathbf{A})^p \times (\mathbf{A})^q \to \mathcal{E},$$

such that

$$f(\underbrace{\overline{r}_1, \ldots, \overline{r}_1}_{p-i}, \underbrace{\overline{s}_1, \ldots, \overline{s}_1}_{i}; \underbrace{\overline{r}_2, \ldots, \overline{r}_2}_{q-j}, \underbrace{\overline{s}_2, \ldots, \overline{s}_2}_{j}) = b_{i,j},$$

for all $i, 1 \leq i \leq p$ and all $j, 1 \leq j \leq q$. Furthermore, f is given by the expression

$$f(\overline{u}_1, \ldots, \overline{u}_p; \overline{v}_1, \ldots, \overline{v}_q)$$

$$= \sum_{\substack{I \cap J = \emptyset \\ I \cup J = \{1, \ldots, p\} \\ K \cap L = \emptyset \\ K \cup L = \{1, \ldots, q\}}} \prod_{i \in I} \left(\frac{s_1 - u_i}{s_1 - r_1} \right) \prod_{j \in J} \left(\frac{u_j - r_1}{s_1 - r_1} \right) \prod_{k \in K} \left(\frac{s_2 - v_k}{s_2 - r_2} \right) \prod_{l \in L} \left(\frac{v_l - r_2}{s_2 - r_2} \right) b_{|J|, |L|}.$$

A point $F(\overline{u}, \overline{v})$ on the surface F can be expressed in terms of the Bernstein polynomials $B_i^p[r_1, s_1](u)$ and $B_j^q[r_2, s_2](v)$, as

$$F(\overline{u}, \overline{v}) = \sum_{\substack{0 \leq i \leq p \\ 0 \leq j \leq q}} B_i^p[r_1, s_1](u)\, B_j^q[r_2, s_2](v)$$

$$\cdot f(\underbrace{\overline{r}_1, \ldots, \overline{r}_1}_{p-i}, \underbrace{\overline{s}_1, \ldots, \overline{s}_1}_{i}; \underbrace{\overline{r}_2, \ldots, \overline{r}_2}_{q-j}, \underbrace{\overline{s}_2, \ldots, \overline{s}_2}_{j}).$$

Thus, we see that the Bernstein polynomials show up again, and indeed, in traditional presentations of bipolynomial surfaces, they are used in the definition itself. We can also show that when $\mathcal{E}$ is of finite dimension, the class of bipolynomial surfaces in polar form as in Definition 7.2.1 is identical to the class of polynomial surfaces as in Definition 7.1.1. Indeed, we have already shown using polarization that a polynomial surface according to Definition 7.1.1 is a bipolynomial surface in polar form, as in Definition 7.2.1. For the converse, simply apply Lemma 4.2.3. Note that in both cases we use the isomorphism between $\mathbf{A} \times \mathbf{A}$ and $\mathcal{P}$.

A family $\mathcal{N} = (b_{i,j})_{0 \leq i \leq p, 0 \leq j \leq q}$ of $(p+1)(q+1)$ points in $\mathcal{E}$ is often called a (rectangular) control net, or Bézier net. Note that we can view the set of pairs

$$\square_{p,q} = \{(i, j) \in \mathbf{N}^2 \mid 0 \leq i \leq p,\ 0 \leq j \leq q\}$$

as a rectangular grid of $(p+1)(q+1)$ points in $\mathbf{A} \times \mathbf{A}$. The control net $\mathcal{N} = (b_{i,j})_{(i,j) \in \square_{p,q}}$ can be viewed as an image of the rectangular grid $\square_{p,q}$ in the affine space $\mathcal{E}$. By Lemma 7.2.2, such a control net $\mathcal{N}$ determines a unique bipolynomial surface F of degree $\langle p, q \rangle$. The portion of the surface F corresponding to the points $F(\overline{u}, \overline{v})$ for which the parameters $\overline{u}, \overline{v}$ satisfy the inequalities $r_1 \le u \le s_1$ and $r_2 \le v \le s_2$ is called a *rectangular (surface) patch*, or *rectangular Bézier patch*, and $F([\overline{r}_1, \overline{s}_1], [\overline{r}_2, \overline{s}_2])$ is the *trace of the rectangular patch*. The surface F (or rectangular patch) determined by a control net $\mathcal{N}$ contains the four control points $b_{0,0}, b_{0,q}, b_{p,0}$, and $b_{p,q}$, the *corners* of the surface patch. Note that there is a natural way of connecting the points in a control net $\mathcal{N}$: every point $b_{i,j}$, where $0 \le i \le p - 1$, and $0 \le j \le q - 1$, is connected to the three points $b_{i+1,j}, b_{i,j+1}$, and $b_{i+1,j+1}$. Generally, pq quadrangles are obtained in this manner, and together, they form a polyhedron that gives a rough approximation of the surface patch.

When we fix the parameter $\overline{u}$, the map $F_{\overline{u}}: \mathbf{A} \to \mathcal{E}$, defined such that $F_{\overline{u}}(\overline{v}) = F(\overline{u}, \overline{v})$ for all $\overline{u} \in \mathbf{A}$, is a curve on the bipolynomial surface F. Similarly, when we fix the parameter $\overline{v}$, the map $F_{\overline{v}}: \mathbf{A} \to \mathcal{E}$, defined such that $F_{\overline{v}}(\overline{u}) = F(\overline{u}, \overline{v})$ for all $\overline{v} \in \mathbf{A}$, is a curve on the bipolynomial surface F. Such curves are called *isoparametric curves*. When we fix $\overline{u}$, we obtain a Bézier curve of degree q, and when we fix $\overline{v}$, we obtain a Bézier curve of degree p. In particular, the images of the line segments $[\overline{r}_1, \overline{r}_2], [\overline{r}_1, \overline{s}_1], [\overline{s}_1, \overline{s}_2]$, and $[\overline{r}_2, \overline{s}_2]$ are Bézier curve segments, called the *boundary curves* of the rectangular surface patch.

Remark: We can also consider curves on a bipoynomial surface, defined by the constraint $u + v = \lambda$, for some $\lambda \in \mathbf{R}$. They are Bézier curves, but of degree $p + q$.

The de Casteljau algorithm can be generalized very easily to bipolynomial surfaces.

7.3   The de Casteljau Algorithm for Rectangular Surface Patches

Given a rectangular control net $\mathcal{N} = (b_{i,j})_{(i,j) \in \square_{p,q}}$, we can first compute the points

$$b_{0*}, \ldots, b_{p*},$$

where b_{i*} is obtained by applying the de Casteljau algorithm to the Bézier control points

$$b_{i,0}, \ldots, b_{i,q},$$

with $0 \le i \le p$, and then compute b_{0*}^p, by applying the de Casteljau algorithm to the control points

$$b_{0*}, \ldots, b_{p*}.$$

For every i, with $0 \le i \le p$, we first compute the points $b_{i*,k}^j$, where $b_{i*,j}^0 = b_{i,j}$, and

$$b^j_{i*,\,k} = \left(\frac{s_2 - v}{s_2 - r_2}\right) b^{j-1}_{i*,\,k} + \left(\frac{v - r_2}{s_2 - r_2}\right) b^{j-1}_{i*,\,k+1},$$

with $1 \leq j \leq q$ and $0 \leq k \leq q - j$, and we let $b_{i*} = b^q_{i*,\,0}$.

It is easily shown by induction that

$$b^j_{i*,\,k} = f(\underbrace{\overline{r}_1, \ldots, \overline{r}_1}_{p-i}, \underbrace{\overline{s}_1, \ldots, \overline{s}_1}_{i}; \underbrace{\overline{v}, \ldots, \overline{v}}_{j}, \underbrace{\overline{r}_2, \ldots, \overline{r}_2}_{q-j-k}, \underbrace{\overline{s}_2, \ldots, \overline{s}_2}_{k}),$$

and since $b_{i*} = b^q_{i*,\,0}$, we have

$$b_{i*} = f(\underbrace{\overline{r}_1, \ldots, \overline{r}_1}_{p-i}, \underbrace{\overline{s}_1, \ldots, \overline{s}_1}_{i}; \underbrace{\overline{v}, \ldots, \overline{v}}_{q}).$$

Next, we compute the points b^j_{i*}, where $b^0_{i*} = b_{i*}$, and

$$b^j_{i*} = \left(\frac{s_1 - u}{s_1 - r_1}\right) b^{j-1}_{i*} + \left(\frac{u - r_1}{s_1 - r_1}\right) b^{j-1}_{i+1*},$$

with $1 \leq j \leq p$ and $0 \leq i \leq p - j$, and we let $F(\overline{u}, \overline{v}) = b^p_{0*}$.

It is easily shown by induction that

$$b^j_{i*} = f(\underbrace{\overline{u}, \ldots, \overline{u}}_{j}, \underbrace{\overline{r}_1, \ldots, \overline{r}_1}_{p-i-j}, \underbrace{\overline{s}_1, \ldots, \overline{s}_1}_{i}; \underbrace{\overline{v}, \ldots, \overline{v}}_{q}),$$

and thus,

$$F(\overline{u}, \overline{v}) = b^p_{0*} = f(\underbrace{\overline{u}, \ldots, \overline{u}}_{p}; \underbrace{\overline{v}, \ldots, \overline{v}}_{q}).$$

Alternatively, we can first compute the points

$$b_{*0}, \ldots, b_{*q},$$

where b_{*j} is obtained by applying the de Casteljau algorithm to the Bézier control points

$$b_{0,\,j}, \ldots, b_{p,\,j},$$

with $0 \leq j \leq q$, and then compute b^q_{*0}, by applying the de Casteljau algorithm to the control points

$$b_{*0}, \ldots, b_{*q}.$$

The same result, $b^p_{0*} = b^q_{*0}$, is obtained.

We give in pseudocode the version of the algorithm in which we compute first the control points

$$b_{0*}, \ldots, b_{p*},$$

and then b_{0*}^p. You should easily be able to write the other version where the control points

$$b_{*0}, \ldots, b_{*q}$$

are computed first, and then b_{*0}^q. Although logically equivalent, one of these two programs may be more efficient than the other, depending on p and q. We assume that the input is a control net $\mathcal{N} = (b_{i,j})_{(i,j)\in\square_{p,q}}$.

begin
   for $i := 0$ **to** p **do**
      for $j := 0$ **to** q **do**
         $b_{i*,j}^0 := b_{i,j}$
      endfor;
      for $j := 1$ **to** q **do**
         for $k := 0$ **to** $q - j$ **do**
            $b_{i*,k}^j := \left(\frac{s_2-v}{s_2-r_2}\right) b_{i*,k}^{j-1} + \left(\frac{v-r_2}{s_2-r_2}\right) b_{i*,k+1}^{j-1}$
         endfor
      endfor;
      $b_{i*} = b_{i*,0}^q;$
   endfor;
   for $i := 0$ **to** p **do**
      $b_{i*}^0 = b_{i*}$
   endfor;
   for $j := 1$ **to** p **do**
      for $i := 0$ **to** $p - j$ **do**
         $b_{i*}^j := \left(\frac{s_1-u}{s_1-r_1}\right) b_{i*}^{j-1} + \left(\frac{u-r_1}{s_1-r_1}\right) b_{i+1*}^{j-1},$
      endfor
   endfor;
   $F(\overline{u}, \overline{v}) := b_{0*}^p$
end

From the above algorithm, it is clear that the rectangular surface patch defined by a control net $\mathcal{N}$ is contained inside the convex hull of the control net. It is also clear that bipolynomial surfaces are closed under affine maps, and that the image by an affine map h of a bipolynomial surface defined by a control net $\mathcal{N}$ is the bipolynomial surface defined by the image of the control net $\mathcal{N}$ under the affine map h.

Figure 7.1 illustrates the de Casteljau algorithm in the case of a bipolynomial surface of degree $\langle 3, 3 \rangle$. It is assumed that $(\overline{r}, \overline{s})$ and $(\overline{x}, \overline{y})$ have been chosen as affine bases of $\mathbf{A}$, and for simplicity of notation, the polar value $f(\overline{u}_1, \overline{u}_2, \overline{u}_3; \overline{v}_1, \overline{v}_2, \overline{v}_3)$ is denoted as $u_1u_2u_3; v_1v_2v_3$; for instance, $f(\overline{r}, \overline{r}, \overline{s}; \overline{x}, \overline{x}, \overline{x})$ is denoted as $rrs; xxx$. The

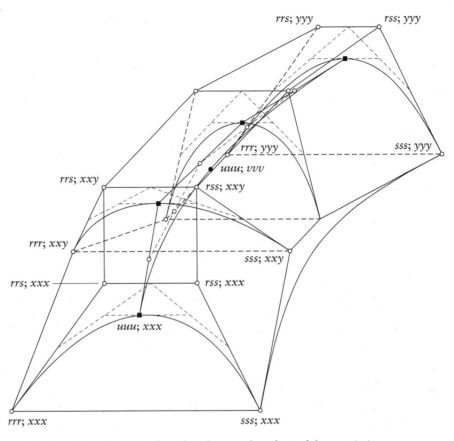

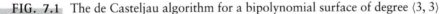

FIG. 7.1 The de Casteljau algorithm for a bipolynomial surface of degree $\langle 3, 3 \rangle$

figure shows the computation of the point $F(\overline{u}; \overline{v})$. The computation shows that the points $f(\overline{u}, \overline{u}, \overline{u}; \overline{x}, \overline{x}, \overline{x})$, $f(\overline{u}, \overline{u}, \overline{u}; \overline{x}, \overline{x}, \overline{y})$, $f(\overline{u}, \overline{u}, \overline{u}; \overline{x}, \overline{y}, \overline{y})$, and $f(\overline{u}, \overline{u}, \overline{u}; \overline{y}, \overline{y}, \overline{y})$ are computed first, and then, using these points (shown as square dark dots) as control points, the point $f(\overline{u}, \overline{u}, \overline{u}; \overline{v}, \overline{v}, \overline{v})$ (shown as a round dark dot) is computed. Since the figure is quite crowded, not all points have been labeled.

There are other interesting properties of tangent planes, which will be proved at the end of this chapter. For example, if the control points $b_{0,0}$, $b_{1,0}$, and $b_{0,1}$ are not collinear, then the plane that they define is the tangent plane to the surface at the corner point $b_{0,0}$. A similar property holds for the other corner control points $b_{0,q}$, $b_{p,0}$, and $b_{p,q}$. Thus, in general, the four tangent planes at the corner points are known. Also, the tangent plane to the surface at $F(\overline{u}, \overline{v})$ is determined by the points b_{0*}^{p-1}, b_{1*}^{p-1}, which determine one tangent line, and the points b_{*0}^{q-1}, b_{*1}^{q-1}, which determine another tangent line (unless these points are all collinear).

We now go back to total degree surfaces.

7.4   Total Degree Surfaces in Polar Form

Given a surface $F: \mathcal{P} \to \mathcal{E}$ of total degree m, where $\mathcal{E}$ is of dimension n, applying Lemma 4.5.1 to each polynomial $F_i(U, V)$ defining F, with respect to both U and V, we get polar forms

$$f_i: \mathcal{P}^m \to \mathbf{A},$$

which together, define an m-multiaffine and symmetric map

$$f: \mathcal{P}^m \to \mathcal{E},$$

such that

$$F(u, v) = f(\underbrace{(u, v), \ldots, (u, v)}_{m}).$$

Note that each $f((U_1, V_1), \ldots, (U_m, V_m))$ is multiaffine and symmetric in the pairs (U_i, V_i).

By analogy with polynomial curves, it is also natural to propose the following definition.

Definition 7.4.1

Given any affine space $\mathcal{E}$ of dimension ≥ 3, a surface of total degree m in polar form, is a map $F: \mathcal{P} \to \mathcal{E}$, such that there is some symmetric multiaffine map

$$f: \mathcal{P}^m \to \mathcal{E},$$

and with

$$F(a) = f(\underbrace{a, \ldots, a}_{m}),$$

for all $a \in \mathcal{P}$. The trace of the surface F is the set $F(\mathcal{P})$.

The advantage of Definition 7.4.1 is that it does not depend on the dimension of $\mathcal{E}$.

Given any barycentric affine frame $(r, s, t) \in \mathcal{P}$, for any $a_i = \lambda_i r + \mu_i s + \nu_i t$, where $\lambda_i + \mu_i + \nu_i = 1$, and $1 \leq i \leq m$, we can expand

$$f(a_1, \ldots, a_m) = f(\lambda_1 r + \mu_1 s + \nu_1 t, \ldots, \lambda_m r + \mu_m s + \nu_m t)$$

by multiaffineness and symmetry. As a first step, we have

$$f(\lambda_1 r + \mu_1 s + \nu_1 t, \ldots, \lambda_m r + \mu_m s + \nu_m t)$$
$$= \lambda_1 f(r, \lambda_2 r + \mu_2 s + \nu_2 t, \ldots, \lambda_m r + \mu_m s + \nu_m t)$$
$$+ \mu_1 f(s, \lambda_2 r + \mu_2 s + \nu_2 t, \ldots, \lambda_m r + \mu_m s + \nu_m t)$$
$$+ \nu_1 f(t, \lambda_2 r + \mu_2 s + \nu_2 t, \ldots, \lambda_m r + \mu_m s + \nu_m t).$$

By induction, it is easily shown that

$$f(a_1, \ldots, a_m) = \sum_{\substack{I \cup J \cup K = \{1,\ldots,m\} \\ I,J,K \text{ pairwise disjoint}}} \left(\prod_{i \in I} \lambda_i \right) \left(\prod_{j \in J} \mu_j \right) \left(\prod_{k \in K} \nu_k \right)$$
$$\cdot f(\underbrace{r, \ldots, r}_{|I|}, \underbrace{s, \ldots, s}_{|J|}, \underbrace{t, \ldots, t}_{|K|}).$$

There are 3^m terms in this sum, but it can be verified that there are only $\binom{m+2}{2} = (m+1)(m+2)/2$ terms corresponding to the points

$$f(\underbrace{r, \ldots, r}_{i}, \underbrace{s, \ldots, s}_{j}, \underbrace{t, \ldots, t}_{k}),$$

where $i + j + k = m$. Also, when $a_1 = a_2 = \ldots = a_m = a$, we get

$$F(a) = f(\underbrace{a, \ldots, a}_{m}) = \sum_{i+j+k=m} \frac{m!}{i!j!k!} \lambda^i \mu^j \nu^k \, f(\underbrace{r, \ldots, r}_{i}, \underbrace{s, \ldots, s}_{j}, \underbrace{t, \ldots, t}_{k}).$$

where $a = \lambda r + \mu s + \nu t$, with $\lambda + \mu + \nu = 1$.

The polynomials in three variables U, V, T, defined such that

$$B_{i,j,k}^m(U, V, T) = \frac{m!}{i!j!k!} U^i V^j T^k,$$

where $i + j + k = m$, are also called *Bernstein polynomials*.
Clearly, the points

$$f(\underbrace{r, \ldots, r}_{i}, \underbrace{s, \ldots, s}_{j}, \underbrace{t, \ldots, t}_{k}),$$

where $i + j + k = m$, can be viewed as control points. Let

$$\Delta_m = \{(i, \, j, \, k) \in \mathbf{N}^3 \mid i + j + k = m\}.$$

Then, given any family $(b_{i, \, j, k})_{(i,j,k) \in \Delta_m}$ of $(m + 1)(m + 2)/2$ points in $\mathcal{E}$, the map defined such that

$$f(a_1, \ldots, a_m) = \sum_{\substack{I \cup J \cup K = \{1, \ldots, m\} \\ I, J, K \text{ disjoint}}} \left(\prod_{i \in I} \lambda_i \right) \left(\prod_{j \in J} \mu_j \right) \left(\prod_{k \in K} \nu_k \right) b_{|I|, |J|, |K|},$$

is symmetric and multiaffine.

We summarize all this in the following lemma. From now on, we will usually denote a barycentric affine frame (r, s, t) in the affine plane $\mathcal{P}$ as Δrst and call it a *reference triangle*.

Lemma 7.4.2

Given a reference triangle Δrst in the affine plane $\mathcal{P}$, given any family $(b_{i,\,j,\,k})_{(i,j,k) \in \Delta_m}$ of $(m+1)(m+2)/2$ points in $\mathcal{E}$, there is a unique surface $F \colon \mathcal{P} \to \mathcal{E}$ of total degree m, defined by a symmetric m-affine polar form $f \colon \mathcal{P}^m \to \mathcal{E}$, such that

$$f(\underbrace{r, \ldots, r}_{i}, \underbrace{s, \ldots, s}_{j}, \underbrace{t, \ldots, t}_{k}) = b_{i,\,j,\,k},$$

for all $(i, j, k) \in \Delta_m$. Furthermore, f is given by the expression

$$f(a_1, \ldots, a_m) = \sum_{\substack{I \cup J \cup K = \{1, \ldots, m\} \\ I, J, K \text{ pairwise disjoint}}} \left(\prod_{i \in I} \lambda_i \right) \left(\prod_{j \in J} \mu_j \right) \left(\prod_{k \in K} \nu_k \right)$$

$$\cdot f(\underbrace{r, \ldots, r}_{|I|}, \underbrace{s, \ldots, s}_{|J|}, \underbrace{t, \ldots, t}_{|K|}),$$

where $a_i = \lambda_i r + \mu_i s + \nu_i t$, with $\lambda_i + \mu_i + \nu_i = 1$, and $1 \leq i \leq m$. A point $F(a)$ on the surface F can be expressed in terms of the Bernstein polynomials

$$B_{i,j,k}^m(U, V, T) = \frac{m!}{i! \, j! \, k!} U^i V^j T^k$$

as

$$F(a) = f(\underbrace{a, \ldots, a}_{m}) = \sum_{(i,\,j,\,k) \in \Delta_m} B_{i,j,k}^m(\lambda, \mu, \nu) \, f(\underbrace{r, \ldots, r}_{i}, \underbrace{s, \ldots, s}_{j}, \underbrace{t, \ldots, t}_{k}),$$

where $a = \lambda r + \mu s + \nu t$, with $\lambda + \mu + \nu = 1$.

We can show that when $\mathcal{E}$ is of finite dimension, the class of polynomial surfaces of total degree m in polar form as in Definition 7.4.1 is identical to the class of polynomial surfaces as in Definition 7.1.1. Indeed, we have already shown using polarization that a polynomial surface according to Definition 7.1.1 is a polynomial surface of total degree m in polar form as in Definition 7.4.1. For the converse, simply apply Lemma 4.2.3.

A family $\mathcal{N} = (b_{i,\,j,\,k})_{(i,j,k)\in\Delta_m}$ of $(m+1)(m+2)/2$ points in $\mathcal{E}$ is called a *(triangular) control net*, or *Bézier net*. Note that the points in

$$\Delta_m = \{(i,\ j,\ k) \in \mathbf{N}^3 \mid i + j + k = m\}$$

can be thought of as a triangular grid of points in $\mathcal{P}$. For example, when $m = 5$, we have the following grid of 21 points:

$$
\begin{array}{ccccccccccc}
 & & & & & 500 & & & & & \\
 & & & & 401 & & 410 & & & & \\
 & & & 302 & & 311 & & 320 & & & \\
 & & 203 & & 212 & & 221 & & 230 & & \\
 & 104 & & 113 & & 122 & & 131 & & 140 & \\
005 & & 014 & & 023 & & 032 & & 041 & & 050
\end{array}
$$

We intentionally let i be the row index, starting from the left lower corner, and j be the column index, also starting from the left lower corner. The control net $\mathcal{N} = (b_{i,\,j,\,k})_{(i,j,k)\in\Delta_m}$ can be viewed as an image of the triangular grid Δ_m in the affine space $\mathcal{E}$. By Lemma 7.4.2, such a control net $\mathcal{N}$ determines a unique polynomial surface F of total degree m. The portion of the surface F corresponding to the points $F(a)$ for which the barycentric coordinates (λ, μ, ν) of a (with respect to the reference triangle Δrst) satisfy the inequalities $0 \le \lambda$, $0 \le \mu$, $0 \le \nu$, with $\lambda + \mu + \nu = 1$, is called a *triangular (surface) patch*, or *triangular Bézier patch*, and $F(\Delta rst)$ is called the *trace of the triangular surface patch*. The surface F (or triangular patch) determined by a control net $\mathcal{N}$ contains the three control points $b_{m,0,0}, b_{0,m,0}$, and $b_{0,0,m}$, the *corners* of the surface patch.

Unlike rectangular patches, given a triangular control net $\mathcal{N} = (b_{i,\,j,\,k})_{(i,j,k)\in\Delta_m}$, there isn't a unique natural way to connect the nodes in $\mathcal{N}$ to form triangular faces that form a polyhedron. In order to understand the difficulty, we can associate with each triple $(i, j, k) \in \Delta_m$ the points

$$\frac{i}{m}r + \frac{j}{m}s + \frac{k}{m}t,$$

where Δrst is the reference triangle. Then, various triangulations of the triangle Δrst, using the points just defined, yield various ways of forming triangular faces using the control net. To be definite, we can assume that we pick a Delaunay triangulation (see O'Rourke [58], Preparata and Shamos [64], Boissonnat and Yvinec [13], or Risler [68]).

The de Casteljau algorithm generalizes quite easily.

7.5   The de Casteljau Algorithm for Triangular Surface Patches

Given a reference triangle Δrst, given a triangular control net $\mathcal{N} = (b_{i,j,k})_{(i,j,k) \in \Delta_m}$, recall that in terms of the polar form $f : \mathcal{P}^m \to \mathcal{E}$ of the polynomial surface $F : \mathcal{P} \to \mathcal{E}$ defined by $\mathcal{N}$, for every $(i, j, k) \in \Delta_m$, we have

$$b_{i,j,k} = f(\underbrace{r, \ldots, r}_{i}, \underbrace{s, \ldots, s}_{j}, \underbrace{t, \ldots, t}_{k}).$$

Given $a = \lambda r + \mu s + \nu t$ in $\mathcal{P}$, where $\lambda + \mu + \nu = 1$, in order to compute $F(a) = f(a, \ldots, a)$, the computation builds a sort of tetrahedron consisting of $m + 1$ layers. The base layer consists of the original control points in $\mathcal{N}$, which are also denoted as $(b^0_{i,j,k})_{(i,j,k) \in \Delta_m}$. The other layers are computed in m stages, where at stage l, $1 \leq l \leq m$, the points $(b^l_{i,j,k})_{(i,j,k) \in \Delta_{m-l}}$ are computed such that

$$b^l_{i,j,k} = \lambda b^{l-1}_{i+1,j,k} + \mu b^{l-1}_{i,j+1,k} + \nu b^{l-1}_{i,j,k+1}.$$

During the last stage, the single point $b^m_{0,0,0}$ is computed. An easy induction shows that

$$b^l_{i,j,k} = f(\underbrace{a, \ldots, a}_{l}, \underbrace{r, \ldots, r}_{i}, \underbrace{s, \ldots, s}_{j}, \underbrace{t, \ldots, t}_{k}),$$

where $(i, j, k) \in \Delta_{m-l}$, and thus, $F(a) = b^m_{0,0,0}$.

Similarly, given m points $a_1, \ldots, a_m$ in $\mathcal{P}$, where $a_l = \lambda_l r + \mu_l s + \nu_l t$, with $\lambda_l + \mu_l + \nu_l = 1$, we can compute the polar value $f(a_1, \ldots, a_m)$ as follows. Again, the base layer of the tetrahedron consists of the original control points in $\mathcal{N}$, which are also denoted as $(b^0_{i,j,k})_{(i,j,k) \in \Delta_m}$. At stage l, where $1 \leq l \leq m$, the points $(b^l_{i,j,k})_{(i,j,k) \in \Delta_{m-l}}$ are computed such that

$$b^l_{i,j,k} = \lambda_l b^{l-1}_{i+1,j,k} + \mu_l b^{l-1}_{i,j+1,k} + \nu_l b^{l-1}_{i,j,k+1}.$$

An easy induction shows that

$$b^l_{i,j,k} = f(a_1, \ldots, a_l, \underbrace{r, \ldots, r}_{i}, \underbrace{s, \ldots, s}_{j}, \underbrace{t, \ldots, t}_{k}),$$

where $(i, j, k) \in \Delta_{m-l}$, and thus, $f(a_1, \ldots, a_m) = b^m_{0,0,0}$.

In order to present the algorithm, it may be helpful to introduce some abbreviations. For example, a triple $(i, j, k) \in \Delta_m$ is denoted as $\mathbf{i}$, and we let $\mathbf{e}_1 = (1, 0, 0)$, $\mathbf{e}_2 = (0, 1, 0)$, $\mathbf{e}_3 = (0, 0, 1)$, and $\mathbf{0} = (0, 0, 0)$. Let $a = \lambda r + \mu s + \nu t$, where $\lambda + \mu + \nu = 1$. We are assuming that we have initialized the family $(b^0_{\mathbf{i}})_{\mathbf{i} \in \Delta_m}$, such that $b^0_{\mathbf{i}} = b_{\mathbf{i}}$, for all $\mathbf{i} \in \Delta_m$. Then, we can describe the de Casteljau algorithm as follows:

begin

   for $l := 1$ **to** m **do**

      for $i := 0$ **to** $m - l$ **do**

         for $j := 0$ **to** $m - i - l$ **do**

$$k := m - i - j - l;$$

$$i := (i, j, k);$$

$$b_i^l := \lambda b_{i+e_1}^{l-1} + \mu b_{i+e_2}^{l-1} + \nu b_{i+e_3}^{l-1}$$

         endfor

      endfor

   endfor;

$$F(a) := b_0^m$$

end

In order to compute the polar value $f(a_1, \ldots, a_m)$, for m points $a_1, \ldots, a_m$ in $\mathcal{P}$, where $a_l = \lambda_l r + \mu_l s + \nu_l t$, with $\lambda_l + \mu_l + \nu_l = 1$, we simply replace λ, μ, ν by λ_l, μ_l, ν_l.

It is clear from the above algorithm that the triangular patch defined by the control net $\mathcal{N}$ is contained in the convex hull of the control net $\mathcal{N}$.

Figure 7.2 illustrates the de Casteljau algorithm in the case of a polynomial surface of total degree 3. It is assumed that the triangle Δrst has been chosen as an affine base of $\mathcal{P}$, and for simplicity of notation, the polar value $f(u_1, u_2, u_3)$ is denoted as $u_1 u_2 u_3$; for example, $f(r, r, s)$ is denoted as rrs. The diagram shows the computation of the point $F(u)$, and it consists of three shells, each one obtained via two-dimensional interpolation steps.

There are other interesting properties of tangent planes, which will be proved at the end of this chapter. For example, if the control points $b_{m,0,0}, b_{m-1,1,0}$, and $b_{m-1,0,1}$, are not collinear, then the plane that they define is the tangent plane to the surface at the corner point $b_{m,0,0}$. A similar property holds for the other corner control points $b_{0,m,0}$ and $b_{0,0,m}$. Thus, in general, the three tangent planes at the corner points are known. Also, the tangent plane to the surface at $F(a)$ is determined by the points $b_{1,0,0}^{m-1}, b_{0,1,0}^{m-1}$, and $b_{0,0,1}^{m-1}$ (unless these points are all collinear).

Given a polynomial surface $F: \mathcal{P} \to \mathcal{E}$, by considering points $a \in \mathcal{P}$ of barycentric coordinates $(0, \mu, 1 - \mu)$, we get a curve on the surface F passing through $F(s)$ and $F(t)$, and similarly, considering points of barycentric coordinates $(\lambda, 0, 1 - \lambda)$, we get a curve on the surface F passing through $F(r)$ and $F(t)$. Finally, considering points of barycentric coordinates $(\lambda, 1 - \lambda, 0)$, we get a curve on the surface F passing through $F(r)$ and $F(s)$. These curves are Bézier curves of degree m, and they are called the *boundary curves* of the triangular patch. If we consider the points $F(\lambda r + \mu s + \nu t)$ on the surface F, obtained by holding λ constant, they form a polynomial curve called an *isoparametric curve*. Other isoparametric curves are

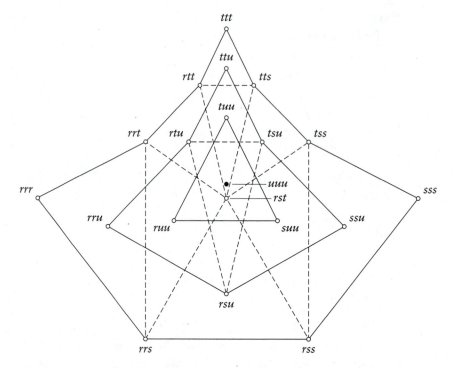

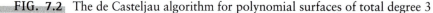

FIG. 7.2   The de Casteljau algorithm for polynomial surfaces of total degree 3

obtained by holding μ constant or ν constant. More generally, we can consider curves on a surface F of total degree m, determined by the constraint that the parameter point $a = \lambda r + \mu s + \nu t \in \mathcal{P}$ lies on a line. This way, we also get a Bézier curve of degree m.

It is interesting to note that the same polynomial surface F, when represented as a bipolynomial surface of degree $\langle p, q \rangle$, requires a control net of $(p + 1)(q + 1)$ control points, and when represented as a surface of total degree m, requires a control net of $(m + 1)(m + 2)/2$ points.

We conclude this chapter by considering directional derivatives of polynomial surfaces.

7.6   Directional Derivatives of Polynomial Surfaces

In Section 10.5, it is shown that if $F: E \to \mathcal{E}$ is an affine polynomial function of polar degree m, where E and $\mathcal{E}$ are normed affine spaces, and if $\vec{u}$ is any nonnull vector in $\vec{E}$, for any $a \in E$, the directional derivative $D_{\vec{u}}F(a)$ is given by

$$D_{\vec{u}} F(a) = m \widehat{f}(\underbrace{a, \ldots, a}_{m-1}, \vec{u}).$$

Now, let $F: \mathbf{A} \times \mathbf{A} \to \mathcal{E}$ be a bipolynomial surface of degree $\langle p, q \rangle$, and let

$$f: (\mathbf{A})^p \times (\mathbf{A})^q \to \mathcal{E}$$

be its polar form. Let

$$\widehat{f}: (\widehat{\mathbf{A}})^p \times (\widehat{\mathbf{A}})^q \to \widehat{\mathcal{E}}$$

be its homogenized $\langle p, q \rangle$-symmetric multilinear map. Using some very similar calculations, it is easily shown that for any two nonnull vectors $\vec{u}, \vec{v} \in \mathbf{R}$, for any two points $\overline{a}, \overline{b} \in \mathbf{A}$, the directional derivative $D_{\vec{u}} D_{\vec{v}} F(\overline{a}, \overline{b})$ is given by

$$D_{\vec{u}} D_{\vec{v}} F(\overline{a}, \overline{b}) = p \, q \, \widehat{f}(\underbrace{\overline{a}, \ldots, \overline{a}}_{p-1}, \vec{u}, \underbrace{\overline{b}, \ldots, \overline{b}}_{q-1}, \vec{v}).$$

This directional derivative is also denoted as

$$\frac{\partial^2 F}{\partial \vec{u} \, \partial \vec{v}}(\overline{a}, \overline{b}).$$

When $\vec{u} = 1$ and $\vec{v} = 1$, by definition, the directional derivative $\frac{\partial^2 F}{\partial \vec{u} \, \partial \vec{v}}(\overline{a}, \overline{b})$ is the partial derivative $\frac{\partial^2 F}{\partial u \, \partial v}(\overline{a}, \overline{b})$, and the vector $\frac{\partial^2 F}{\partial u \, \partial v}(\overline{a}, \overline{b})$ is often called the *twist* at $(\overline{a}, \overline{b})$.

The following lemma, analogous to Lemma 10.5.3, can be shown easily.

Lemma 7.6.1

Given a bipolynomial surface $F: \mathbf{A} \times \mathbf{A} \to \mathcal{E}$ of degree $\langle p, q \rangle$, with polar form $f: (\mathbf{A})^p \times (\mathbf{A})^q \to \mathcal{E}$, where $\mathcal{E}$ is any normed affine space, for any nonzero vectors $\vec{u}, \vec{v} \in \mathbf{R}$, for any two points $\overline{a}, \overline{b} \in \mathbf{A}$, for any i, j, where $0 \leq i, j \leq m$, the directional derivative

$$\underbrace{D_{\vec{u}} \ldots D_{\vec{u}}}_{i} \underbrace{D_{\vec{v}} \ldots D_{\vec{v}}}_{j} F(\overline{a}, \overline{b})$$

can be computed from the homogenized polar form $\widehat{f}$ of F as follows:

$$\underbrace{D_{\vec{u}} \ldots D_{\vec{u}}}_{i} \underbrace{D_{\vec{v}} \ldots D_{\vec{v}}}_{j} F(\overline{a}, \overline{b}) = p^{\underline{i}} \, q^{\underline{j}} \, \widehat{f}(\underbrace{\overline{a}, \ldots, \overline{a}}_{p-i}, \underbrace{\vec{u}, \ldots, \vec{u}}_{i}, \underbrace{\overline{b}, \ldots, \overline{b}}_{q-j}, \underbrace{\vec{v}, \ldots, \vec{v}}_{j}).$$

The directional derivative

$$\underbrace{D_{\vec{u}} \ldots D_{\vec{u}}}_{i} \underbrace{D_{\vec{v}} \ldots D_{\vec{v}}}_{j} F(\overline{a}, \overline{b})$$

is also denoted as

$$\frac{\partial^{i+j} F}{\partial \vec{u}^i \partial \vec{v}^j} (\overline{a}, \overline{b}),$$

and when $i = 0$ or $j = 0$, it is denoted as $\frac{\partial^i F}{\partial \vec{u}^i}(\overline{a}, \overline{b})$ or $\frac{\partial^j F}{\partial \vec{v}^j}(\overline{a}, \overline{b})$, respectively.

If $(\overline{r}_1, \overline{s}_1)$ and $(\overline{r}_2, \overline{s}_2)$ are any two affine frames for the affine line $\mathbf{A}$, every vector $\vec{u} \in \mathbf{R}$ can be expressed as

$$\vec{u} = \lambda_1 \overline{s}_1 - \lambda_1 \overline{r}_1,$$

and similarly, every vector $\vec{v} \in \mathbf{R}$ can be expressed as

$$\vec{v} = \lambda_2 \overline{s}_2 - \lambda_2 \overline{r}_2,$$

and thus, for any $\overline{a}, \overline{b} \in \mathbf{A}$, since

$$\frac{\partial F}{\partial \vec{u}} (\overline{a}, \overline{b}) = p \, \widehat{f} (\underbrace{\overline{a}, \ldots, \overline{a}}_{p-1}, \vec{u}, \underbrace{\overline{b}, \ldots, \overline{b}}_{q}),$$

and

$$\frac{\partial F}{\partial \vec{v}} (\overline{a}, \overline{b}) = q \, \widehat{f} (\underbrace{\overline{a}, \ldots, \overline{a}}_{p}, \underbrace{\overline{b}, \ldots, \overline{b}}_{q-1}, \vec{v}),$$

we get

$$\frac{\partial F}{\partial \vec{u}} (\overline{a}, \overline{b}) = p \, \lambda_1 \, (f (\underbrace{\overline{a}, \ldots, \overline{a}}_{p-1}, \overline{s}_1, \underbrace{\overline{b}, \ldots, \overline{b}}_{q}) - f (\underbrace{\overline{a}, \ldots, \overline{a}}_{p-1}, \overline{r}_1, \underbrace{\overline{b}, \ldots, \overline{b}}_{q})),$$

and

$$\frac{\partial F}{\partial \vec{v}} (\overline{a}, \overline{b}) = q \, \lambda_2 \, (f (\underbrace{\overline{a}, \ldots, \overline{a}}_{p}, \underbrace{\overline{b}, \ldots, \overline{b}}_{q-1}, \overline{s}_2) - f (\underbrace{\overline{a}, \ldots, \overline{a}}_{p}, \underbrace{\overline{b}, \ldots, \overline{b}}_{q-1}, \overline{r}_2)).$$

Since these vectors, provided that they are not linearly dependent, span the tangent plane at $(\overline{a}, \overline{b})$ to F, the four points

$$f (\underbrace{\overline{a}, \ldots, \overline{a}}_{p-1}, \overline{r}_1, \underbrace{\overline{b}, \ldots, \overline{b}}_{q}), \quad f (\underbrace{\overline{a}, \ldots, \overline{a}}_{p-1}, \overline{s}_1, \underbrace{\overline{b}, \ldots, \overline{b}}_{q}),$$

$$f (\underbrace{\overline{a}, \ldots, \overline{a}}_{p}, \underbrace{\overline{b}, \ldots, \overline{b}}_{q-1}, \overline{r}_2), \quad f (\underbrace{\overline{a}, \ldots, \overline{a}}_{p}, \underbrace{\overline{b}, \ldots, \overline{b}}_{q-1}, \overline{s}_2),$$

are coplanar, and provided that they are not collinear, they determine the tangent plane at $(\overline{a}, \overline{b})$ to the bipolynomial surface F. However, these points are just the points $b_{0*}^{p-1}, b_{1*}^{p-1}$, and $b_{*0}^{q-1}, b_{*1}^{q-1}$, computed by the two versions of the de Casteljau algorithm. Thus, we have proved the claim that the tangent plane at $(\bar{a}, \bar{b})$ to the bipolynomial surface F is determined by the points $b_{0*}^{p-1}, b_{1*}^{p-1}$ and $b_{*0}^{q-1}, b_{*1}^{q-1}$, computed by the two versions of the de Casteljau algorithm (provided that they are not collinear). In particular, letting $\bar{a} = \bar{r}_1$ and $\bar{b} = \bar{r}_2$, we find that the control points $b_{0,0}$, $b_{1,0}$, and $b_{0,1}$ define the tangent plane to the surface at the corner point $b_{0,0}$.

Assuming $\vec{u} = 1$ and $\vec{v} = 1$, by a similar reasoning, since

$$\frac{\partial^2 F}{\partial u \partial v}(\bar{a}, \bar{b}) = p\, q\, \widehat{f}(\underbrace{\bar{a}, \ldots, \bar{a}}_{p-1}, \vec{u}, \underbrace{\bar{b}, \ldots, \bar{b}}_{q-1}, \vec{v}),$$

we get

$$\frac{\partial^2 F}{\partial u \partial v}(\bar{a}, \bar{b}) = p\, q\, \Bigg(f(\underbrace{\bar{a}, \ldots, \bar{a}}_{p-1}, \bar{s}_1, \underbrace{\bar{b}, \ldots, \bar{b}}_{q-1}, \bar{s}_2) - f(\underbrace{\bar{a}, \ldots, \bar{a}}_{p-1}, \bar{s}_1, \underbrace{\bar{b}, \ldots, \bar{b}}_{q-1}, \bar{r}_2)$$

$$- (f(\underbrace{\bar{a}, \ldots, \bar{a}}_{p-1}, \bar{r}_1, \underbrace{\bar{b}, \ldots, \bar{b}}_{q-1}, \bar{s}_2) - f(\underbrace{\bar{a}, \ldots, \bar{a}}_{p-1}, \bar{r}_1, \underbrace{\bar{b}, \ldots, \bar{b}}_{q-1}, \bar{r}_2)) \Bigg).$$

Letting $d_{1,1}, d_{1,2}, d_{2,1}, d_{2,2}$ be the points

$$d_{1,1} = f(\underbrace{\bar{a}, \ldots, \bar{a}}_{p-1}, \bar{r}_1, \underbrace{\bar{b}, \ldots, \bar{b}}_{q-1}, \bar{r}_2), \quad d_{1,2} = f(\underbrace{\bar{a}, \ldots, \bar{a}}_{p-1}, \bar{r}_1, \underbrace{\bar{b}, \ldots, \bar{b}}_{q-1}, \bar{s}_2),$$

$$d_{2,1} = f(\underbrace{\bar{a}, \ldots, \bar{a}}_{p-1}, \bar{s}_1, \underbrace{\bar{b}, \ldots, \bar{b}}_{q-1}, \bar{r}_2), \quad d_{2,2} = f(\underbrace{\bar{a}, \ldots, \bar{a}}_{p-1}, \bar{s}_1, \underbrace{\bar{b}, \ldots, \bar{b}}_{q-1}, \bar{s}_2),$$

we can express $\frac{\partial^2 F}{\partial u \partial v}(\bar{a}, \bar{b})$ as

$$\frac{\partial^2 F}{\partial u \partial v}(\bar{a}, \bar{b}) = p\, q\, (d_{2,2} - d_{2,1} - d_{1,2} + d_{1,1}),$$

which, in terms of vectors, can be written either as

$$\frac{\partial^2 F}{\partial u \partial v}(\bar{a}, \bar{b}) = p\, q\, \left((d_{2,2} - d_{2,1}) - (d_{1,2} - d_{1,1}) \right)$$

or as

$$\frac{\partial^2 F}{\partial u \partial v}(\bar{a}, \bar{b}) = p\, q\, \left((d_{2,2} - d_{1,2}) - (d_{2,1} - d_{1,1}) \right).$$

The twist vector $\frac{\partial^2 F}{\partial u \partial v}(\bar{a}, \bar{b})$ can be given an interesting interpretation in terms of the points $d_{1,1}, d_{1,2}, d_{2,1}, d_{2,2}$. Let c be the point determined such that $d_{1,1}, d_{1,2}, d_{2,1}$, and c form a parallelogram; that is, let

$$c = d_{2,1} + (d_{1,2} - d_{1,1}).$$

Then, it is immediately verified that

$$(d_{2,2} - d_{2,1}) - (d_{1,2} - d_{1,1}) = d_{2,2} - c,$$

and thus (since $\vec{u} = 1$ and $\vec{v} = 1$), we get

$$\frac{\partial^2 F}{\partial u \partial v}(\overline{a}, \overline{b}) = p \, q \, (d_{2,2} - c).$$

Thus, up to the factor $p \, q$, the twist vector is a measure for how much the quadrangle $d_{1,1}, d_{1,2}, d_{2,1}, d_{2,2}$ deviates from the parallelogram $d_{1,1}, d_{1,2}, d_{2,1}, c$, and roughly, it is a measure of the deviation of $d_{2,2}$ from the plane determined by $d_{1,1}, d_{1,2}$, and $d_{2,1}$ (when these points are not collinear). In particular, when $\overline{a} = \overline{r}_1$ and $\overline{b} = \overline{r}_2$, this plane is just the tangent plane at $d_{1,1} = b_{0,0}$.

Remark: If we assume that $\vec{u} = 1$ and $\vec{v} = 1$, then by definition, the directional derivative $\frac{\partial^2 F}{\partial \vec{u} \partial \vec{v}}(\overline{a}, \overline{b})$ is the partial derivative $\frac{\partial^2 F}{\partial u \partial v}(\overline{a}, \overline{b})$, and since

$$\frac{\partial^2 F}{\partial \vec{u} \partial \vec{v}}(\overline{a}, \overline{b}) = p \, q \, (d_{2,2} - d_{2,1} - d_{1,2} + d_{1,1}),$$

and

$$d_{1,1} = f(\underbrace{\overline{a}, \dots, \overline{a}}_{p-1}, \overline{r}_1, \underbrace{\overline{b}, \dots, \overline{b}}_{q-1}, \overline{r}_2), \quad d_{1,2} = f(\underbrace{\overline{a}, \dots, \overline{a}}_{p-1}, \overline{r}_1, \underbrace{\overline{b}, \dots, \overline{b}}_{q-1}, \overline{s}_2),$$

$$d_{2,1} = f(\underbrace{\overline{a}, \dots, \overline{a}}_{p-1}, \overline{s}_1, \underbrace{\overline{b}, \dots, \overline{b}}_{q-1}, \overline{r}_2), \quad d_{2,2} = f(\underbrace{\overline{a}, \dots, \overline{a}}_{p-1}, \overline{s}_1, \underbrace{\overline{b}, \dots, \overline{b}}_{q-1}, \overline{s}_2),$$

letting

$$\overline{a} = (1 - \lambda_1)\overline{r}_1 + \lambda_1 \overline{s}_1,$$

and

$$\overline{b} = (1 - \lambda_2)\overline{r}_2 + \lambda_2 \overline{s}_2,$$

after expansion using multiaffineness, we get

$$\frac{\partial^2 F}{\partial u \partial v}(\overline{a}, \overline{b}) = p \, q \sum_{i=0}^{i=p-1} \sum_{j=0}^{j=q-1} (b_{i+1,j+1} - b_{i+1,j} - b_{i,j+1} + b_{i,j}) B_i^{p-1}(\lambda_1) B_j^{q-1}(\lambda_2),$$

where B_i^{p-1} and B_j^{q-1} are the Bernstein polynomials, and the $b_{i,j}$ are the Bézier control points of F.

If we now consider a polynomial Bézier surface $F \colon \mathcal{P} \to \mathcal{E}$ of total degree m, defined by a symmetric m-affine polar form $f \colon \mathcal{P}^m \to \mathcal{E}$, the results of Section 10.5 apply immediately. Thus, by Lemma 10.5.3, for any k nonzero vectors $\vec{u}_1, \dots, \vec{u}_k \in$

$\mathbf{R}^2$, where $1 \le k \le m$, for any $a \in \mathcal{P}$, the kth directional derivative $D_{\overrightarrow{u_1}} \ldots D_{\overrightarrow{u_k}} F(a)$ can be computed as follows:

$$D_{\overrightarrow{u_1}} \ldots D_{\overrightarrow{u_k}} F(a) = m^{\underline{k}} \, \widehat{f}(\underbrace{a, \ldots, a}_{m-k}, \overrightarrow{u_1}, \ldots, \overrightarrow{u_k}).$$

When $u_1 = \ldots = u_k$, we also denote $D_{\overrightarrow{u_1}} \ldots D_{\overrightarrow{u_k}} F(a)$ as $\frac{\partial^k F}{\partial \overrightarrow{u}^k}(a)$.

Given any reference triangle Δrst, since every vector $\overrightarrow{u} \in \mathbf{R}^2$ can be written as

$$\overrightarrow{u} = \lambda r + \mu s + vt,$$

where $\lambda + \mu + v = 0$, for $k = 1$, we get

$$\frac{\partial F}{\partial \overrightarrow{u}}(a) = m(\lambda f(\underbrace{a, \ldots, a}_{m-1}, r) + \mu f(\underbrace{a, \ldots, a}_{m-1}, s) + vf(\underbrace{a, \ldots, a}_{m-1}, t)).$$

When λ, μ, v vary, subject to $\lambda + \mu + v = 0$, provided that the points

$$f(\underbrace{a, \ldots, a}_{m-1}, r), \; f(\underbrace{a, \ldots, a}_{m-1}, s), \; f(\underbrace{a, \ldots, a}_{m-1}, t)$$

are not collinear, the vectors $\frac{\partial F}{\partial \overrightarrow{u}}(a)$ span the tangent plane to F at a. However, we recognize that the above points are just the points $b_{(1,0,0)}^{m-1}$, $b_{(0,1,0)}^{m-1}$, and $b_{(0,0,1)}^{m-1}$, computed by the de Casteljau algorithm. Thus, we have proved the claim that the tangent plane to the surface at $F(a)$ is determined by the points $b_{(1,0,0)}^{m-1}$, $b_{(0,1,0)}^{m-1}$, and $b_{(0,0,1)}^{m-1}$ (unless these points are all collinear). In particular, letting $a = r$, if the control points $b_{m,0,0}$, $b_{m-1,1,0}$, and $b_{m-1,0,1}$ are not collinear, then the plane that they define is the tangent plane to the surface at the corner point $b_{m,0,0}$.

Remark: From

$$D_{\overrightarrow{u_1}} \ldots D_{\overrightarrow{u_k}} F(a) = m^{\underline{k}} \, \widehat{f}(\underbrace{a, \ldots, a}_{m-k}, \overrightarrow{u_1}, \ldots, \overrightarrow{u_k}),$$

we deduce that

$$\frac{\partial^{i+j} F}{\partial \overrightarrow{u}^i \partial \overrightarrow{v}^j}(a) = m^{\underline{i+j}} \, \widehat{f}(\underbrace{a, \ldots, a}_{m-i-j}, \underbrace{\overrightarrow{u}, \ldots, \overrightarrow{u}}_{i}, \underbrace{\overrightarrow{v}, \ldots, \overrightarrow{v}}_{j}).$$

Problems

[10 pts]   **1.** Compute the rectangular control net for the surface defined by the equation $z = xy$, with respect to the affine frames $(0, 1)$ and $(0, 1)$. Plot the surface patch over $[0, 1] \times [0, 1]$.

[20 pts]   **2.** Recall that the polar form of the monomial $u^h v^k$ with respect to the bidegree $\langle p, q \rangle$ (where $h \leq p$ and $k \leq q$) is

$$f_{h,k}^{p,q} = \frac{1}{\binom{p}{h}\binom{q}{k}} \sum_{\substack{I \subseteq \{1,\ldots,p\},|I|=h \\ J \subseteq \{1,\ldots,q\},|J|=k}} \left(\prod_{i \in I} u_i \right) \left(\prod_{j \in J} v_j \right).$$

Letting $\sigma_{h,k}^{p,q} = \binom{p}{h}\binom{q}{k} f_{h,k}^{p,q}$, prove that we have the following recurrence equations:

$$\sigma_{h,k}^{p,q} = \begin{cases} \sigma_{h,k}^{p-1,q-1} + u_p \sigma_{h-1,k}^{p-1,q-1} + v_q \sigma_{h,k-1}^{p-1,q-1} + u_p v_q \sigma_{h-1,k-1}^{p-1,q-1} & \text{if } 1 \leq h \leq p \text{ and } 1 \leq k \leq q, \\ \sigma_{0,k}^{p,q-1} + v_q \sigma_{0,k-1}^{p,q-1} & \text{if } h = 0 \leq p \text{ and } 1 \leq k \leq q, \\ \sigma_{h,0}^{p-1,q} + u_p \sigma_{h-1,0}^{p-1,q} & \text{if } 1 \leq h \leq p \text{ and } k = 0 \leq q, \\ 1 & \text{if } h = k = 0, \ p \geq 0, \text{ and } q \geq 0, \\ 0 & \text{otherwise.} \end{cases}$$

Alternatively, prove that $f_{h,k}^{p,q}$ can be computed directly using the recurrence formula

$$f_{h,k}^{p,q} = \frac{(p-h)(q-k)}{pq} f_{h,k}^{p-1,q-1} + \frac{h(q-k)}{pq} u_p f_{h-1,k}^{p-1,q-1} + \frac{(p-h)k}{pq} v_q f_{h,k-1}^{p-1,q-1}$$

$$+ \frac{hk}{pq} u_p v_q f_{h-1,k-1}^{p-1,q-1},$$

where $1 \leq h \leq p$ and $1 \leq k \leq q$,

$$f_{0,k}^{p,q} = \frac{(q-k)}{q} f_{0,k}^{p,q-1} + \frac{k}{q} v_q f_{0,k-1}^{p,q-1},$$

where $h = 0 \leq p$ and $1 \leq k \leq q$, and

$$f_{h,0}^{p,q} = \frac{(p-h)}{p} f_{h,0}^{p-1,q} + \frac{h}{p} u_p f_{h-1,0}^{p-1,q},$$

where $1 \leq h \leq p$ and $k = 0 \leq q$.

Show that for any $(u_1, \ldots, u_p, v_1, \ldots, v_q)$, computing all the polar values

$$f_{h,k}^{i,j}(u_1, \ldots, u_p, v_1, \ldots, v_q),$$

where $1 \leq h \leq i$, $1 \leq k \leq j$, $1 \leq i \leq p$, and $1 \leq j \leq q$, can be done in time $O(p^2 q^2)$.

[30 pts]   **3.** Using the result of Problem 2, write a computer program for computing the control points of a rectangular surface patch defined parametrically.

[20 pts]   **4.** Prove that the polar form of the monomial $u^h v^k$ with respect to the total degree m (where $h + k \leq m$) can be expressed as

$$f_{h,k}^m = \frac{1}{\binom{m}{h}\binom{m-h}{k}} \sum_{\substack{I \cup J \subseteq \{1,\dots,m\} \\ |I|=h, |J|=k, I \cap J=\emptyset}} \left(\prod_{i \in I} u_i\right)\left(\prod_{j \in J} v_j\right).$$

Letting $\sigma_{h,k}^m = \binom{m}{h}\binom{m-h}{k} f_{h,k}^m$, prove that we have the following recurrence equations:

$$\sigma_{h,k}^m = \begin{cases} \sigma_{h,k}^{m-1} + u_m \sigma_{h-1,k}^{m-1} + v_m \sigma_{h,k-1}^{m-1} & \text{if } h, k \geq 0 \text{ and } 1 \leq h+k \leq m, \\ 1 & \text{if } h = k = 0 \text{ and } m \geq 0, \\ 0 & \text{otherwise.} \end{cases}$$

Alternatively, prove that $f_{h,k}^m$ can be computed directly using the recurrence formula

$$f_{h,k}^m = \frac{(m-h-k)}{m} f_{h,k}^{m-1} + \frac{h}{m} u_m f_{h-1,k}^{m-1} + \frac{k}{m} v_m f_{h,k-1}^{m-1},$$

where $h, k \geq 0$ and $1 \leq h+k \leq m$.

Show that for any $((u_1, v_1), \dots, (u_m, v_m))$, computing all the polar values

$$f_{h,k}^i((u_1, v_1), \dots, (u_m, v_m)),$$

where $h, k \geq 0$, $1 \leq h+k \leq i$, and $1 \leq i \leq m$, can be done in time $O(m^3)$.

[30 pts] 5. Using the result of Problem 4, write a computer program for computing the control points of a triangular surface patch defined parametrically.

[20 pts] 6. Compute a rectangular net for the surface defined by the equation

$$z = x^3 - 3xy^2$$

with respect to the affine frames $(-1, 1)$ and $(-1, 1)$. Compute a triangular net for the same surface with respect to the affine frame $((1, 0), (0, 1), (0, 0))$.

Note that z is the real part of the complex number $(u + iv)^3$. This surface is called a *monkey saddle*.

[20 pts] 7. Compute a rectangular net for the surface defined by the equation

$$z = x^4 - 6x^2y^2 + y^4$$

with respect to the affine frames $(-1, 1)$ and $(-1, 1)$. Compute a triangular net for the same surface with respect to the affine frame $((1, 0), (0, 1), (0, 0))$.

Note that z is the real part of the complex number $(u + iv)^4$. This surface is a more complex kind of monkey saddle.

[20 pts] 8. Compute a rectangular net for the surface defined by the equation

$$z = 1/6(x^3 + y^3)$$

with respect to the affine frames $(-1, 1)$ and $(-1, 1)$. Compute a triangular net for the same surface with respect to the affine frame $((1, 0), (0, 1), (0, 0))$.

[20 pts]   **9.** Compute a rectangular net for the surface defined by

$$x = u(u^2 + v^2),$$

$$y = v(u^2 + v^2),$$

$$z = u^2 v - v^3/3,$$

with respect to the affine frames $(0, 1)$ and $(0, 1)$. Compute a triangular net for the same surface with respect to the affine frame $((1, 0), (0, 1), (0, 0))$.

Explain what happens for $(u, v) = (0, 0)$.

[20 pts]   **10.** Give the details of the proof of Lemma 7.2.2 and Lemma 7.4.2; that is, give the details of the induction steps.

[10 pts]   **11.** Prove that when $\mathcal{E}$ is of finite dimension, the class of bipolynomial surfaces in polar form as in Definition 7.2.1 is identical to the class of polynomial surfaces as in Definition 7.1.1.

[10 pts]   **12.** Prove that when $\mathcal{E}$ is of finite dimension, the class of polynomial surfaces of total degree m in polar form as in Definition 7.4.1 is identical to the class of polynomial surfaces as in Definition 7.1.1.

[20 pts]   **13.** Let F be a bipolynomial surface of bidegree $\langle n, n \rangle$ given by some control net $\mathcal{N} = (b_{i, j})_{(i,j) \in \square_{n,n}}$ with respect to the affine frames $(\overline{r}_1, \overline{s}_1)$ and $(\overline{r}_2, \overline{s}_2)$. Define a sequence of nets $(b^r_{i, j})_{(i,j) \in \square_{n-r,n-r}}$ inductively as follows: For $r = 0$, we have $b^r_{i, j} = b_{i, j}$ for all i, j with $0 \leq i, j \leq n$, and for $r = 1, \ldots, n$,

$$b^r_{i, j} = (1 - u)(1 - v)\, b^{r-1}_{i, j} + u(1 - v)\, b^{r-1}_{i+1, j} + (1 - u)v\, b^{r-1}_{i, j+1} + uv\, b^{r-1}_{i+1, j+1},$$

where $0 \leq i, j \leq n - r$. This method is known as the *direct de Casteljau algorithm*.

(a) Prove that $F(u, v) = b^n_{0, 0}$.

(b) Let F be a bipolynomial surface of bidegree $\langle p, q \rangle$ given by some control net $\mathcal{N} = (b_{i, j})_{(i,j) \in \square_{p,q}}$ with respect to the affine frames $(\overline{r}_1, \overline{s}_1)$ and $(\overline{r}_2, \overline{s}_2)$. What happens to the direct de Casteljau algorithm when $p \neq q$? Modify the direct de Casteljau algorithm to compute $F(u, v)$ when $p \neq q$.

[20 pts]   **14.** Given a bipolynomial surface F of bidegree $\langle p, q \rangle$ given by some control net $\mathcal{N} = (b_{i, j})_{(i,j) \in \square_{p,q}}$ with respect to the affine frames $(\overline{r}_1, \overline{s}_1)$ and $(\overline{r}_2, \overline{s}_2)$, there are three versions of the de Casteljau algorithm to compute a point $F(u, v)$ on the surface F. The first version is the direct de Casteljau algorithm described in Problem 13. In the second version, we first compute the points

$$b_{0*}, \ldots, b_{p*},$$

where b_{i*} is obtained by applying the de Casteljau algorithm to the Bézier control points

$$b_{i,0}, \ldots, b_{i,q},$$

with $0 \leq i \leq p$, and then compute b_{0*}^p, by applying the de Casteljau algorithm to the control points

$$b_{0*}, \ldots, b_{p*}.$$

In the third version, we first compute the points

$$b_{*0}, \ldots, b_{*q},$$

where b_{*j} is obtained by applying the de Casteljau algorithm to the Bézier control points

$$b_{0,j}, \ldots, b_{p,j},$$

with $0 \leq j \leq q$, and then compute b_{*0}^q, by applying the de Casteljau algorithm to the control points

$$b_{*0}, \ldots, b_{*q}.$$

Compare the complexity of the three algorithms depending on relative values of p and q.

[40 pts] **15.** Write a computer program implementing the de Casteljau algorithm(s) for rectangular surface patches.

[30 pts] **16.** Write a computer program implementing the de Casteljau algorithm for triangular surface patches.

CHAPTER 8

Subdivision Algorithms for Polynomial Surfaces

8.1 Subdivision Algorithms for Triangular Patches

In this section, we explain in detail how the de Casteljau algorithm can be used to subdivide a triangular patch into subpatches, in order to obtain a triangulation of a surface patch using recursive subdivision. A similar method is described in Farin [30]. Given a reference triangle Δrst, given a triangular control net $\mathcal{N} = (b_{i,j,k})_{(i,j,k)\in\Delta_m}$, recall that in terms of the polar form $f\colon \mathcal{P}^m \to \mathcal{E}$ of the polynomial surface $F\colon \mathcal{P} \to \mathcal{E}$ defined by $\mathcal{N}$, for every $(i,j,k) \in \Delta_m$, we have

$$b_{i,j,k} = f(\underbrace{r,\ldots,r}_{i},\underbrace{s,\ldots,s}_{j},\underbrace{t,\ldots,t}_{k}).$$

Given $a = \lambda r + \mu s + \nu t$ in $\mathcal{P}$, where $\lambda + \mu + \nu = 1$, in order to compute $F(a) = f(a,\ldots,a)$, the computation builds a sort of tetrahedron consisting of $m+1$ layers. The base layer consists of the original control points in $\mathcal{N}$, which are also denoted as $(b^0_{i,j,k})_{(i,j,k)\in\Delta_m}$. The other layers are computed in m stages, where at stage l, $1 \leq l \leq m$, the points $(b^l_{i,j,k})_{(i,j,k)\in\Delta_{m-l}}$ are computed such that

$$b^l_{i,j,k} = \lambda b^{l-1}_{i+1,j,k} + \mu b^{l-1}_{i,j+1,k} + \nu b^{l-1}_{i,j,k+1}.$$

During the last stage, the single point $b^m_{0,0,0}$ is computed. An easy induction shows that

$$b^l_{i,j,k} = f(\underbrace{a,\ldots,a}_{l},\underbrace{r,\ldots,r}_{i},\underbrace{s,\ldots,s}_{j},\underbrace{t,\ldots,t}_{k}),$$

where $(i,j,k) \in \Delta_{m-l}$, and thus, $F(a) = b^m_{0,0,0}$.

Assuming that a is not on one of the edges of $\triangle rst$, the crux of the subdivision method is that the three other faces of the tetrahedron of polar values $b^l_{i,j,k}$, besides the face corresponding to the original control net, yield three control nets:

$$\mathcal{N}ast = (b^l_{0,j,k})_{(l,j,k)\in\triangle_m},$$

corresponding to the base triangle $\triangle ast$,

$$\mathcal{N}rat = (b^l_{i,0,k})_{(i,l,k)\in\triangle_m},$$

corresponding to the base triangle $\triangle rat$, and

$$\mathcal{N}rsa = (b^l_{i,j,0})_{(i,j,l)\in\triangle_m},$$

corresponding to the base triangle $\triangle rsa$.

From an implementation point of view, we found it convenient to assume that a triangular net $\mathcal{N} = (b_{i,j,k})_{(i,j,k)\in\triangle_m}$ is represented as the list consisting of the concatenation of the $m+1$ rows

$$b_{i,0,m-i}, \ b_{i,1,m-i-1}, \ \ldots, \ b_{i,m-i,0},$$

that is,

$$f(\underbrace{r,\ldots,r}_{i}, \underbrace{t,\ldots,t}_{m-i}), \ f(\underbrace{r,\ldots,r}_{i}, s, \underbrace{t,\ldots,t}_{m-i-1}), \ \ldots,$$

$$f(\underbrace{r,\ldots,r}_{i}, \underbrace{s,\ldots,s}_{m-i-1}, t), \ f(\underbrace{r,\ldots,r}_{i}, \underbrace{s,\ldots,s}_{m-i}),$$

where $0 \le i \le m$. As a triangle, the net $\mathcal{N}$ is listed (from top down) as

$$f(\underbrace{t,\ldots,t}_{m}) \quad f(\underbrace{t,\ldots,t}_{m-1}, s) \quad \cdots \quad f(t, \underbrace{s,\ldots,s}_{m-1}) \quad f(\underbrace{s,\ldots,s}_{m})$$

$$\vdots \qquad\qquad\qquad \vdots$$

$$\vdots$$

$$f(\underbrace{r,\ldots,r}_{m-1}, t) \quad f(\underbrace{r,\ldots,r}_{m-1}, s)$$

$$f(\underbrace{r,\ldots,r}_{m})$$

The main advantage of this representation is that we can view the net $\mathcal{N}$ as a two-dimensional array net, such that $net[i,j] = b_{i,j,k}$ (with $i+j+k=m$). In fact, only a triangular portion of this array is filled. This way of representing control nets fits well with the convention that the reference triangle $\triangle rst$ is represented as in Figure 8.1.

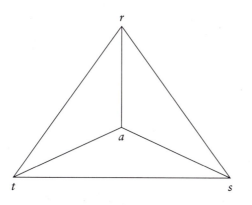

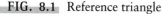

FIG. 8.1 Reference triangle

Instead of simply computing $F(a) = b_{0,0,0}^m$, the de Casteljau algorithm can be easily adapted to output the three nets $Nast$, $Nrat$, and $Nrsa$. We call this version of the de Casteljau algorithm the *subdivision algorithm*. In implementing such a program, we found that it was convenient to compute the nets $Nast$, $Nart$, and $Nars$. In order to compute $Nrat$ from $Nart$, we wrote a very simple function transnetj, and in order to compute $Nrsa$ from $Nars$, we wrote a very simple function transnetk. We also have a function, convtomat, that converts a control net, given as a list of rows, into a two-dimensional array. The corresponding Mathematica functions are given below:

```
(* Converts a triangular net into a triangular matrix *)

convtomat[{cnet__},m_] :=
Block[
{cc = {cnet},  i, j, n, mat = {}, row},
(
 Do[n = m + 2 - i;
    row = {};
    Do[
       pt = cc[[j]];
       row = Append[row, pt], {j, 1, n}
      ];
    cc = Drop[cc, n]; mat = Append[mat, row], {i, 1, m + 1}
   ];
 mat
 )
];

(* To transpose a triangular net w.r.t. left edge *)
(* Converts (r, s, t) to (s, r, t) *)
```

```
transnetj[{cnet__},m_] :=
Block[
{cc = {cnet},  i, j, n, aux1, aux2, row, pt, res},
(
 aux1 = {}; res = {};
 Do[
    pt = cc[[j]];
    aux1 = Append[aux1, {pt}], {j, 1, m + 1}
    ];
 cc = Drop[cc, m + 1];
 Do[n = m + 1 - i;
    Do[
       pt = cc[[j]];
       aux2 = Append[aux1[[j]], pt];
       aux1 = ReplacePart[aux1, aux2, j], {j, 1, n}
       ];
       cc = Drop[cc, n], {i, 1, m}
    ];
 Do[
    row = aux1[[j]];
    res = Join[res, row], {j, 1, m + 1}
    ];
 res
)
];


(* To rotate a triangular net *)
(* Converts (r, s, t) to (s, t, r) *)

transnetk[{cnet__},m_] :=
Block[
{cc = {cnet},  i, j, n, aux1, aux2, row, pt, res},
(
 aux1 = {}; res = {};
 Do[
    pt = cc[[j]];
    aux1 = Append[aux1, {pt}], {j, 1, m + 1}
    ];
 cc = Drop[cc, m + 1];
 Do[n = m + 1 - i;
    Do[
       pt = cc[[j]];
       aux2 = Prepend[aux1[[j]], pt];
       aux1 = ReplacePart[aux1, aux2, j], {j, 1, n}
       ];
```

```
            cc = Drop[cc, n], {i, 1, m}
        ];
    Do[
        row = aux1[[j]];
        res = Join[res, row], {j, 1, m + 1}
        ];
      res
    )
    ];
```

We found it convenient to write three distinct functions subdecas3ra, sub-decas3sa, and subdecas3ta, computing the control nets with respect to the reference triangles Δast, Δart, and Δars. The variables net, mm, and a correspond to the input control net represented as a list of points, as explained above, the degree of the net, and the barycentric coordinates of a point in the parameter plane. The output is a control net.

```
(* de Casteljau for triangular patches, with subdivision *)
(* this version returns the control net for the ref triangle (a, s, t) *)

subdecas3ra[{net__}, mm_, {a__}] :=
Block[
{cc = {net}, dd, row, row0, row1, row2, barcor = {a},   net0,
 cctr = {}, ccts = {}, ccsr = {},
 m, i, j, k, l, pt},
(m = mm;
 net0 = convtomat[cc,m];
 row0 = {}; row1 = {}; row2 = {};
 Do[
     row1 = Append[row1, net0[[1, j + 1]]], {j, 0, m}
     ];
 ccts = row1;
 Do[
     dd = {};
     Do[
         row = {};
         Do[
             pt = barcor[[1]] * net0[[i + 2, j + 1]] +
                  barcor[[2]] * net0[[i + 1, j + 2]] +
                  barcor[[3]] * net0[[i + 1, j + 1]];
             row = Append[row, pt], {j, 0, m - i - 1}
             ];
         dd = Join[dd, row], {i, 0, m - 1}
         ];
     If[m - 1 =!= 0, net0 = convtomat[dd,m - 1];
         row0 = {}; row1 = {}; row2 = {};
```

```
          Do[
             row1 = Append[row1, net0[[1, j + 1]]], {j, 0, m - 1}
             ];
          ccts = Join[ccts, row1],
          ccts = Join[ccts, dd]
          ], {1, 1, m}
    ];
  ccts
  )
  ];


(* de Casteljau for triangular patches, with subdivision *)
(* this version returns the control net for the ref triangle (a, r, t) *)

subdecas3sa[{net__}, mm_, {a__}] :=
Block[
{cc = {net}, dd, row, row0, row1, row2, barcor = {a},  net0,
 cctr = {}, ccts = {}, ccsr = {},
 m, i, j, k, l, pt},
(m = mm;
 net0 = convtomat[cc,m];
 row0 = {}; row1 = {}; row2 = {};
 Do[
    row0 = Append[row0, net0[[i + 1, 1]]], {i, 0, m}
   ];
 cctr = row0;
 Do[
    dd = {};
    Do[
       row = {};
       Do[
          pt = barcor[[1]] * net0[[i + 2, j + 1]] +
               barcor[[2]] * net0[[i + 1, j + 2]] +
               barcor[[3]] * net0[[i + 1, j + 1]];
          row = Append[row, pt], {j, 0, m - i - 1}
      ];
      dd = Join[dd, row], {i, 0, m - 1}
      ];
    If[m - 1 =!= 0, net0 = convtomat[dd,m - 1];
       row0 = {}; row1 = {}; row2 = {};
       Do[
          row0 = Append[row0, net0[[i + 1, 1]]], {i, 0, m - 1}
          ];
       cctr = Join[cctr, row0],
       cctr = Join[cctr, dd]
       ], {1, 1, m}
```

```
    ];
cctr
)
];



(* de Casteljau for triangular patches, with subdivision *)
(* this version returns the control net for the ref triangle (a, r, s) *)

subdecas3ta[{net__}, mm_, {a__}] :=
Block[
{cc = {net}, dd, row, row0, row1, row2, barcor = {a},  net0,
 cctr = {}, ccts = {}, ccsr = {},
 m, i, j, k, l, pt},
(m = mm;
 net0 = convtomat[cc,m];
 row0 = {}; row1 = {}; row2 = {};
 Do[
    row2 = Append[row2, net0[[i + 1, m - i + 1]]], {i, 0, m}
   ];
 ccsr = row2;
 Do[
     dd = {};
     Do[
       row = {};
       Do[
          pt = barcor[[1]] * net0[[i + 2, j + 1]] +
                barcor[[2]] * net0[[i + 1, j + 2]] +
                barcor[[3]] * net0[[i + 1, j + 1]];
          row = Append[row, pt], {j, 0, m - i - 1}
        ];
       dd = Join[dd, row], {i, 0, m - 1}
      ];
      If[m - 1 =!= 0, net0 = convtomat[dd,m - 1];
         row0 = {}; row1 = {}; row2 = {};
         Do[
           row2 = Append[row2, net0[[i + 1, m - 1 - i + 1]]],
                     {i, 0, m - 1}
           ];
         ccsr = Join[ccsr, row2],
         ccsr = Join[ccsr, dd]
        ], {l, 1, m}
   ];
ccsr
)
];
```

The following function computes a polar value, given a control net net, and a list a of mm points given by their barycentric coordinates.

```
(* polar value by de Casteljau for triangular patches *)

poldecas3[{net__}, mm_, {a__}] :=
Block[
{cc = {net}, dd,  barcor = {a},  net0,
 row,  m, i, j, k, l, pt, res},
(m = mm;
 net0 = convtomat[cc,m];
 Do[
     dd = {};
     Do[
        row = {};
        Do[
           pt = barcor[[l,1]] * net0[[i + 2, j + 1]] +
                barcor[[l,2]] * net0[[i + 1, j + 2]] +
                barcor[[l,3]] * net0[[i + 1, j + 1]];
           row = Append[row, pt], {j, 0, m - i - 1}
          ];
        dd = Join[dd, row], {i, 0, m - 1}
       ];
     If[m - 1 =!= 0, net0 = convtomat[dd,m - 1],
                     res = dd
       ],  {l, 1, m}
   ];
 res
 )
];
```

If we want to render a triangular surface patch *F* defined over the reference triangle Δrst, it seems natural to subdivide Δrst into the three subtriangles Δars, Δast, and Δart, where $a = (\frac{1}{3}, \frac{1}{3}, \frac{1}{3})$ is the center of gravity of the triangle Δrst, getting new control nets $\mathcal{N}ars$, $\mathcal{N}ast$, and $\mathcal{N}art$ using the functions described earlier, and repeat this process recursively. However, this process does not yield a good triangulation of the surface patch because no progress is made on the edges *rs*, *st*, and *tr*, and thus such a triangulation does not converge to the surface patch. Therefore, in order to compute triangulations that converge to the surface patch, we need to subdivide the triangle Δrst in such a way that the edges of the reference triangle are subdivided. There are many ways of performing such subdivisions, and we will propose a rather efficient method that yields a very regular triangulation. In fact, we give a method for subdividing a reference triangle using 4 calls to the de Casteljau algorithm in its subdivision version. A naive method would require 12 calls.

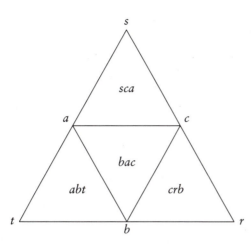

FIG. 8.2 Subdividing a reference triangle $\triangle rst$

Subdivision methods based on a version of the de Casteljau algorithm that splits a control net into three control subnets were investigated by Goldman [38], Böhm and Farin [9], Böhm [12], and Seidel [75] (see also Böhm, Farin, and Kahman [10], and Filip [34]). However, some of these authors were not particularly concerned with minimizing the number of calls to the de Casteljau algorithm, and they use a version of the de Casteljau algorithm computing a five-dimensional simplex of polar values, which is more expensive than the standard three-dimensional version. It was brought to our attention by Gerald Farin (and it is mentioned at the end of Seidel's paper [75]) that Helmut Prautzsch showed in his dissertation (in German) [63] that regular subdivision into four subtriangles can be achieved in four calls to the de Casteljau algorithm. This algorithm is also sketched in Böhm [12] (see pages 348–349). We rediscovered this algorithm and present a variant of it below.

The subdivision strategy that we will follow is to divide the reference triangle $\triangle rst$ into four subtriangles $\triangle abt$, $\triangle bac$, $\triangle crb$, and $\triangle sca$, where $a = (0, \frac{1}{2}, \frac{1}{2})$, $b = (\frac{1}{2}, 0, \frac{1}{2})$, and $c = (\frac{1}{2}, \frac{1}{2}, 0)$ are the middle points of the sides st, rt, and rs, respectively, as shown in Figure 8.2.

The first step is to compute the control net for the reference triangle $\triangle bat$. This can be done using two steps. In the first step, split the triangle $\triangle rst$ into the two triangles $\triangle art$ and $\triangle ars$, where $a = (0, \frac{1}{2}, \frac{1}{2})$ is the middle of st. Using the function sdecas3 (with $a = (0, \frac{1}{2}, \frac{1}{2})$), the nets $\mathcal{N}art$, $\mathcal{N}ast$, and $\mathcal{N}ars$ are obtained, and we throw away $\mathcal{N}ast$ (which is degenerate anyway). Then, we split $\triangle art$ into the two triangles $\triangle bat$ and $\triangle bar$. For this, we need the barycentric coordinates of b with respect to the triangle $\triangle art$, which turns out to be $(0, \frac{1}{2}, \frac{1}{2})$. Using the function sdecas3, the nets $\mathcal{N}bat$, $\mathcal{N}brt$, and $\mathcal{N}bar$ are obtained, and we throw away $\mathcal{N}brt$, obtaining the triangles shown in Figure 8.3.

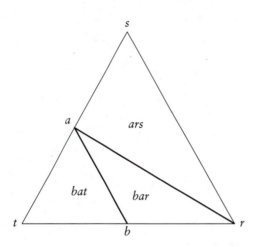

FIG. 8.3 Computing the nets $\mathcal{N}bat$, $\mathcal{N}bar$, and $\mathcal{N}ars$ from $\mathcal{N}rst$

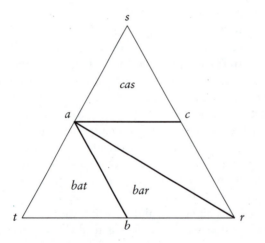

FIG. 8.4 Computing the net $\mathcal{N}cas$ from $\mathcal{N}ars$

We will now compute the net $\mathcal{N}cas$ from the net $\mathcal{N}ars$ (see Figure 8.4). For this, we need the barycentric coordinates of c with respect to the triangle $\triangle ars$, which turns out to be $(0, \frac{1}{2}, \frac{1}{2})$. Using the function subdecas3sa, the net $\mathcal{N}cas$ is obtained.

We can now compute the nets $\mathcal{N}cbr$ and $\mathcal{N}cba$ from the net $\mathcal{N}bar$ (see Figure 8.5). For this, we need the barycentric coordinates of c with respect to the reference triangle $\triangle bar$, which turns out to be $(-1, 1, 1)$. Using the function sdecas3, the nets $\mathcal{N}cbr$, $\mathcal{N}car$, and $\mathcal{N}cba$ are obtained, and we throw away $\mathcal{N}car$.

Finally, we apply transposej to the net $\mathcal{N}bat$ to get the net $\mathcal{N}abt$, transposek to $\mathcal{N}cba$ to get the net $\mathcal{N}bac$, transposej followed by transposek to the net

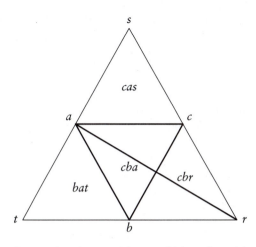

FIG. 8.5 Computing the nets $\mathcal{N}cbr$ and $\mathcal{N}cba$ from $\mathcal{N}bar$

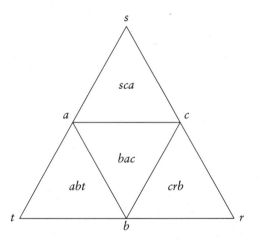

FIG. 8.6 Subdividing $\triangle rst$ into $\triangle abt$, $\triangle bac$, $\triangle crb$, and $\triangle sca$

$\mathcal{N}cbr$ to get the net $\mathcal{N}crb$, and `transposek` twice to $\mathcal{N}cas$ to get the net $\mathcal{N}sca$ (see Figure 8.6).

Thus, using four calls to the de Casteljau algorithm, we obtained the nets $\mathcal{N}abt$, $\mathcal{N}bac$, $\mathcal{N}crb$, and $\mathcal{N}sca$.

Remark: For debugging purposes, we assigned different colors to the patches corresponding to $\mathcal{N}abt$, $\mathcal{N}bac$, $\mathcal{N}crb$, and $\mathcal{N}sca$, and we found that they formed a particularly nice pattern under this ordering of the vertices of the triangles. In fact, $\mathcal{N}abt$ is blue, $\mathcal{N}bac$ is red, $\mathcal{N}crb$ is green, and $\mathcal{N}sca$ is yellow.

The subdivision algorithm just presented is implemented in Mathematica as follows:

```
(* Computes the polar degree m associated with a
   net cnet of size (m + 1)*(m + 2)/2 *)

netsize[cnet__] := Block[
{cc = cnet, ll, s, i,  stop, res},
(ll = Length[cc]; s = N[Sqrt[2 * ll]]; i = 1; stop = 1; res = 1;
 While[i <= s  && stop === 1,
      If[(res === ll), stop = 0, i = i + 1; res = res + i]
      ];
  res = i - 1;
  res
)
];


(* Subdivides into four subpatches, by dividing the base triangle *)
(* into four subtriangles using the middles of the original sides *)
(* uses a tricky scheme involving 4 de Casteljau steps *)
(* basic version that does not try to resolve singularities *)
(* The triangles are  abt, sca, bac, and crb *)

mainsubdecas4[{net__}, oldm_, debug_] :=
Block[
{cc = {net}, newnet, m, art, ars, barcor2},
(m = netsize[cc];
 (* Print[" calling mainsubdecas4 with netsize = ", m]; *)
 barcor1 = {-1, 1, 1};
 barcor2 = {0, 1/2, 1/2};
 newnet = sdecas3[cc, m, barcor2];
 art = newnet[[1]]; ars = newnet[[3]];
 newnet = nsubdecas4[art, ars, m, debug];
 newnet
)
];


(* Subdivides into four subpatches, by dividing the base triangle *)
(* into four subtriangles using the middles of the original sides *)
(* uses a tricky scheme involving 4 de Casteljau steps *)
(* basic version that does not try to resolve singularities *)
(* The triangles are  abt, sca, bac, and crb *)

nsubdecas4[{net1__}, {net2__}, oldm_, debug_] :=
Block[
{newnet, m, art = {net1}, ars = {net2},
  bat, bar, cas, sca, cbr, cba, bac, crb,
```

```
      barcor1, barcor2},
   (m = netsize[art];
   (* Print[" calling mainsubdecas4 with netsize = ", m]; *)
   barcor1 = {-1, 1, 1};
   barcor2 = {0, 1/2, 1/2};
      If[debug === -20, Print["*** art: ",art]];
      If[debug === -20, Print["*** ars: ",ars]];
   newnet = sdecas3[art, m, barcor2];
   bat = newnet[[1]]; bar = newnet[[3]];
   abt =  transnetj[bat, m];
      If[debug === -20, Print["*** abt: ",abt]];
      If[debug === -20, Print["*** bar: ",bar]];
   cas = subdecas3sa[ars, m, barcor2];
   sca = transnetk[cas, m];
   sca = transnetk[sca, m];
   newnet = sdecas3[bar, m, barcor1];
   cbr = newnet[[1]]; cba = newnet[[3]];
   bac =  transnetk[cba, m];
   crb =  transnetj[cbr, m];
   crb =  transnetk[crb, m];
   newnet = Join[{abt}, {sca}];
   newnet = Join[newnet, {bac}];
   newnet = Join[newnet, {crb}];
   newnet
   )
   ];
```

Using `mainsubdecas4`, starting from a list consisting of a single control net net, we can repeatedly subdivide the nets in a list of nets, in order to obtain a triangulation of the surface patch specified by the control net net. The function `rsubdiv4` shown below performs n recursive steps of subdivision, starting with an input control net net. The function `itersub4` takes a list of nets and subdivides each net in this list into four subnets.

```
(* performs a subdivision step on each net in a list *)
(* using subdecas4, i.e., splitting into four patches *)

itersub4[{net__}, m_, debug_] :=
Block[
{cnet = {net},  lnet = {}, l, i},
(l = Length[cnet];
Do[
   lnet = Join[lnet, mainsubdecas4[cnet[[i]], m, debug]] , {i, 1, l}
  ];
lnet
)
];
```

```
(* performs n subdivision steps using itersub4,
   i.e., recursively splits into 4 patches *)

rsubdiv4[{net__}, m_, n_, debug_] :=
Block[
{newnet = {net}, i},
(
newnet = {newnet};
Do[
   newnet = itersub4[newnet, m, debug], {i, 1, n}
 ];
 newnet
)
];
```

The function `rsubdiv4` creates a list of nets, where each net is a list of points. In order to render the surface patch, it is necessary to triangulate each net, that is, to join the control points in a net by line segments. This can be done in a number of ways and is left as an exercise. The best thing to do is to use the `Polygon` construct of Mathematica. Indeed, polygons are considered nontransparent, and the rendering algorithm automatically removes hidden parts. It is also very easy to use the shading options of Mathematica or color the polygons as desired. This is very crucial to understand complicated surfaces.

The subdivision method is illustrated Figures 8.7–8.9, showing a cubic patch specified by the control net

```
net = {{0, 0, 0}, {2, 0, 2}, {4, 0, 2}, {6, 0, 0},
       {1, 2, 2}, {3, 2, 5}, {5, 2, 2},
       {2, 4, 2}, {4, 4, 2},  {3, 6, 0}};
```

We show the output of the subdivision algorithm for $n = 1, 2, 3$. After only three subdivision steps, the triangulation approximates the surface patch very well.

Figure 8.10 shows a cubic patch specified by the control net `sink`:

```
sink = {{0, 0, 0}, {2, 0, 2}, {4, 0, 2}, {6, 0, 0},
        {1, 2, 2}, {3, 2, -8}, {5, 2, 2},
        {2, 4, 2}, {4, 4, 2},  {3, 6, 0}};
```

This surface patch looks like a sink!

Another pleasant application of the subdivision method is that it yields an efficient method for computing a control net $\mathcal{N}abc$ over a new reference triangle Δabc, from a control net $\mathcal{N}$ over an original reference triangle Δrst. Such an algorithm is useful if we wish to render a surface patch over a bigger or different reference triangle than the originally given one. Before discussing such an algorithm, we need to review how a change of reference triangle is performed. Let Δrst and Δabc be two reference triangles, and let $(\lambda_1, \mu_1, \nu_1)$, $(\lambda_2, \mu_2, \nu_2)$, and $(\lambda_3, \mu_3, \nu_3)$ be the barycentric coordinates of a, b, c with respect to Δrts. Given any arbitrary point d, if d has

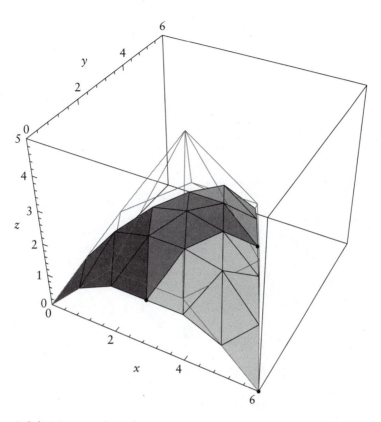

 **FIG. 8.7** Subdivision, one iteration

coordinates (λ, μ, ν) with respect to $\triangle rst$, and coordinates (λ', μ', ν') with respect to $\triangle abc$, since

$$d = \lambda r + \mu s + \nu t = \lambda' a + \mu' b + \nu' c$$

and

$$a = \lambda_1 r + \mu_1 s + \nu_1 t,$$
$$b = \lambda_2 r + \mu_2 s + \nu_2 t,$$
$$c = \lambda_3 r + \mu_3 s + \nu_3 t,$$

we easily get

$$\begin{pmatrix} \lambda \\ \mu \\ \nu \end{pmatrix} = \begin{pmatrix} \lambda_1 & \lambda_2 & \lambda_3 \\ \mu_1 & \mu_2 & \mu_3 \\ \nu_1 & \nu_2 & \nu_3 \end{pmatrix} \begin{pmatrix} \lambda' \\ \mu' \\ \nu' \end{pmatrix},$$

and thus,

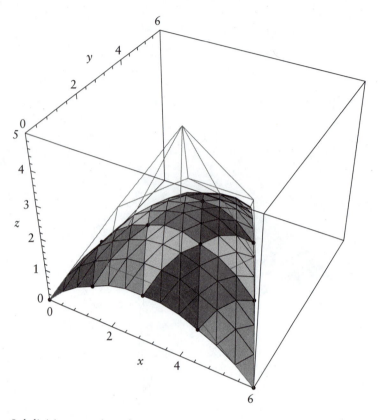

FIG. 8.8 Subdivision, two iterations

$$
\begin{pmatrix} \lambda' \\ \mu' \\ \nu' \end{pmatrix} = \begin{pmatrix} \lambda_1 & \lambda_2 & \lambda_3 \\ \mu_1 & \mu_2 & \mu_3 \\ \nu_1 & \nu_2 & \nu_3 \end{pmatrix}^{-1} \begin{pmatrix} \lambda \\ \mu \\ \nu \end{pmatrix},
$$

Thus, the coordinates (λ', μ', ν') of d with respect to $\triangle abc$ can be computed from the coordinates (λ, μ, ν) of d with respect to $\triangle rst$, by inverting a matrix. In this case, this is easily done using determinants by Cramer's formulae (see Lang [47] or Strang [81]).

Now, given a reference triangle $\triangle rst$ and a control net $\mathcal{N}$ over $\triangle rst$, we can compute the new control net $\mathcal{N}abc$ over the new reference triangle $\triangle abc$ using three subdivision steps as explained below. In the first step, we compute the control net $\mathcal{N}ast$ over the reference triangle $\triangle ast$ using subdecas3ra. In the second step, we compute the control net $\mathcal{N}bat$ using subdecas3sa, and then the control net $\mathcal{N}abt$ over the reference triangle $\triangle abt$ using transnetj. In the third step, we compute the control net $\mathcal{N}cab$ using subdecas3ta, and then the control net $\mathcal{N}abc$ over the reference triangle $\triangle abc$ using transnetk.

Note that in the second step, we need the coordinates of b with respect to the reference triangle $\triangle ast$, and in the third step, we need the coordinates of c with

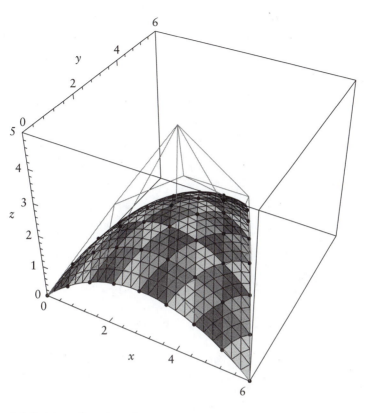

Subdivision, three iterations

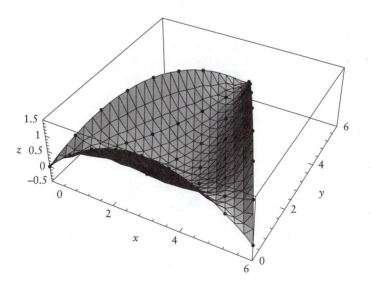

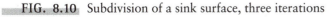 FIG. 8.10 Subdivision of a sink surface, three iterations

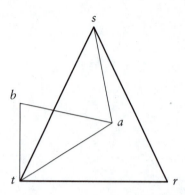

FIG. 8.11   Case 1a: $a \notin st$, $b \notin at$

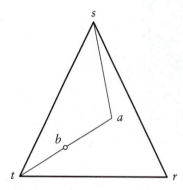

FIG. 8.12   Case 1b: $a \notin st$, $b \in at$

respect to the reference triangle $\triangle abt$. This can be easily done by inverting a matrix of order 3, as explained earlier. Observe also that the above method is only correct if a does not belong to st and b does not belong to at. In general, some adaptations are needed. We used the strategy explained below, implemented in Mathematica.

Case 1: $a \notin st$.

Compute $\mathcal{N}ast$ using `subdecas3ra`.

Case 1a: $b \notin at$ (Figure 8.11).

First, compute $\mathcal{N}bat$ using `subdecas3sa`, and then $\mathcal{N}abt$ using `transnetj`. Next, compute $\mathcal{N}cab$ using `subdecas3ta`, and then $\mathcal{N}abc$ using `transnetk`.

Case 1b: $b \in at$ (Figure 8.12).

First, compute $\mathcal{N}tas$ from $\mathcal{N}ast$ using `transnetk` twice, then compute $\mathcal{N}bas$ using `subdecas3ra`, and then $\mathcal{N}abs$ using `transnetj`. Finally, compute $\mathcal{N}abc$ using `subdecas3ta`.

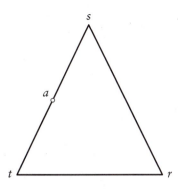

FIG. 8.13 Case 2b: $a \in st$, $s \neq a$

Case 2a: $s = a$ (and thus, $a \in st$).

In this case, $\Delta rst = \Delta rat$. First compute $\mathcal{N}art$ using `transnetj`, and then go back to Case 1.

Case 2b: $a \in st$ and $s \neq a$ (Figure 8.13).

Compute $\mathcal{N}ars$ using `subdecas3ta`, and then go back to Case 1.

The implementation in Mathematica requires some auxiliary functions. The function `collin` checks whether three points in the plane are collinear.

```
(* checks for collinearity of three points in the plane *)

collin[a__, b__, c__] :=    Block[
{a1, a2, b1, b2, c1, c2, d1, d2, res},
a1 = a[[1]]; a2 = a[[2]]; b1 = b[[1]]; b2 = b[[2]];
c1 = c[[1]]; c2 = c[[2]];
d1 =  (c1 - a1)*(b2 - a2); d2 = (c2 - a2)*(b1 - a1);
If[d1 === d2, res = 1, res = 0];
res
];
```

The function `solve3` solves a linear system of three equations in three variables. It uses the function `det3` computing a 3×3 determinant.

```
(* Computes a 3 X 3 determinant *)

det3[a_, b_, c_] :=
Block[
{a1, a2, a3, b1, b2, b3, c1, c2, c3, d1, d2, d3, res},
(
a1 = a[[1]]; a2 = a[[2]]; a3 = a[[3]];
b1 = b[[1]]; b2 = b[[2]]; b3 = b[[3]];
c1 = c[[1]]; c2 = c[[2]]; c3 = c[[3]];
d1 = b1*c2 - b2*c1; d2 = a1*c2 - a2*c1;
```

```
d3 = a1*b2 - a2*b1;
res = a3*d1 - b3*d2 + c3*d3;
res
)
];


(* Solves  a 3 X 3 linear system *)
(* Assuming a, b, c, d are column vectors *)

solve3[a_, b_, c_, d_] :=
Block[
{a1, a2, a3, b1, b2, b3, c1, c2, c3, d1, d2, d3,
 x1, x2, x3, dd, res},
 (dd = det3[a, b, c];
  If[dd === 0. || dd === 0, Print["*** Null Determinant ***"];
  dd = 10^(-10)];
  x1 = det3[d, b, c]/dd;
  x2 = det3[a, d, c]/dd;
  x3 = det3[a, b, d]/dd;
  res = {x1, x2, x3};
  res
 )
];
```

Finally, the function newcnet3 computes a new net $\mathcal{N}abc$ over the triangle Δrts, from a net $\mathcal{N}$ over the triangle Δrts. The function newcnet3 uses the auxiliary function fnewaux.

```
(* computes new control net, given barycentric coords for *)
(* new reference triangle (a, b, c) w.r.t  (r, s, t) *)
(* In the simplest case where a, s, t are not collinear and *)
(* b is not on (a, t), *)
(* the algorithm first computes the control net w.r.t *)
(* (a, s, t) using subdecas3ra, then the control net w.r.t *)
(* (a, b, t) using subdecas3sa and transnetj, and *)
(* the control net w.r.t  (a, b, c) using subdecas3ta and *)
(* transnetk *)
(* The other cases are also treated *)
(* The function returns the net (a, b, c) *)

newcnet3[{net__}, m_, {reftrig__}] :=
Block[
{cc = {net}, newtrig = {reftrig}, neta, netb, newnet, a, b, c,
 nb, nc, rr, ss, tt},
 (newnet = {}; a = newtrig[[1]]; b = newtrig[[2]]; c = newtrig[[3]];
  rr = {1, 0, 0}; ss = {0, 1, 0}; tt = {0, 0, 1};
```

```
      If[collin[a, ss, tt] === 0,
                          (* In this case, a is not on (s, t).
                             Want (a, s, t) *)
                          (* Print[" a NOT on (s, t) "]; *)
                                  neta = subdecas3ra[cc, m, a];
                          (* Now, the net is (a, s, t) *)
                          newnet = fnewaux[neta, m, a, b, c, ss, tt],
                          (* In this case, a is on (s, t) *)
                          (* Print[" a IS on (s, t) "]; *)
          If[a === ss,
                          (* In this case, a is on (s, t) and a = s.
                             Want (a, r, t) *)
                          (* Print[" a on (s, t) and a = ss"]; *)
                                  neta = transnetj[cc, m];
                          (* Now, the net is (a, r, t) *)
                          newnet = fnewaux[neta, m, a, b, c, rr, tt],
                          (* In this case,  a is on (s, t) and a <> s.
                             Want (a, r, s) *)
                          (* Print[" a on (s, t) and a <> ss"]; *)
                                  neta = subdecas3ta[cc, m, a];
                          (* Now, the net is (a, r, s) *)
                          newnet = fnewaux[neta, m, a, b, c, rr, ss],
          ]
      ];
    newnet
  )
];


(* This routine is used by newcnet3 *)
(* Initially, neta = (a,s,t) *)

fnewaux[{net__}, m_, a_, b_, c_, ss_, tt_] :=
Block[
{neta = {net}, netb, newnet, nb, nc},
( If[collin[b, a, tt] === 0,
                          (* In this case, b is not on (a, t). Want (a, b, t) *)
                          (* Print[" b NOT on (a, t) "]; *)
                                  nb = solve3[a, ss, tt, b];
                                  netb = subdecas3sa[neta, m, nb];
                                  netb = transnetj[netb, m];
                          (* Now, the net is (a, b, t) *)
                                  nc = solve3[a, b, tt, c];
                                  newnet = subdecas3ta[netb, m, nc];
                                  newnet = transnetk[newnet, m],
                          (* In this case, b is on (a, t). Want (a, b, s) *)
```

```
                          (* Print[" b IS on (a, t) "]; *)
                                 neta = transnetk[neta, m];
                                 neta = transnetk[neta, m];
                  (* Now, the net (a, s, t) is (t, a, s) *)
                                 nb = solve3[tt, a, ss, b];
                                 netb = subdecas3ra[neta, m, nb];
                                 netb = transnetj[netb, m];
                  (* Now, the net is (a, b, s) *)
                                 nc = solve3[a, b, ss, c];
                                 newnet = subdecas3ta[netb, m, nc];
                                 newnet = transnetk[newnet, m]
          ];
       newnet
       )
       ];
```

As an example of the use of the above functions, we can display a portion of a well-known surface known as the "monkey saddle," defined by the equations

$$x = u,$$

$$y = v,$$

$$z = u^3 - 3uv^2.$$

Note that z is the real part of the complex number $(u + iv)^3$. It is easily shown that the monkey saddle is specified by the following triangular control net monknet over the standard reference triangle Δrst, where $r = (1, 0, 0)$, $s = (0, 1, 0)$, and $t = (0, 0, 1)$.

```
monknet = {{0, 0, 0}, {0, 1/3, 0}, {0, 2/3, 0}, {0, 1, 0},
           {1/3, 0, 0}, {1/3, 1/3, 0}, {1/3, 2/3, -1},
           {2/3, 0, 0}, {2/3, 1/3, 0}, {1, 0, 1}};
```

Using newcnet3 twice to get some new nets net1 and net2, and then subdividing both nets three times, we get Figure 8.14.

We used the triangles

$$reftrig1 = ((-1, 1, 1), (-1, -1, 3), (1, 1, -1))$$

and

$$reftrig2 = ((1, -1, 1), (1, 1, -1), (-1, -1, 3))$$

with newcnet3.

Another nice application of the subdivision algorithms is an efficient method for computing the control points of a curve on a triangular surface patch, where the curve is the image of a line in the parameter plane, specified by two points a and b.

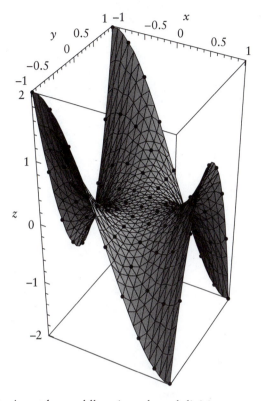

FIG. 8.14 A monkey saddle, triangular subdivision

What we need is to compute the control points

$$d_i = f(\underbrace{a, \ldots, a}_{m-i}, \underbrace{b, \ldots, b}_{i}),$$

where m is the degree of the surface. We could compute these polar values directly, but there is a much faster method. Indeed, assuming that the surface is defined by some net $\mathcal{N}$ over the reference triangle Δrts, if r does not belong to the line (a, b), we simply have to compute $\mathcal{N}rba$ using `newcnet3`, and the control points $(d_0, \ldots, d_m)$ are simply the bottom row of the net $\mathcal{N}rba$, assuming the usual representation of a triangular net as the list of rows

$$b_{i, 0, m-i}, \ b_{i, 1, m-i-1}, \ \ldots, \ b_{i, m-i, 0}.$$

More precisely, we have the following cases.

Case 1: $r \notin ab$ (Figure 8.15).

We compute $\mathcal{N}rba$ using `newcnet3`.

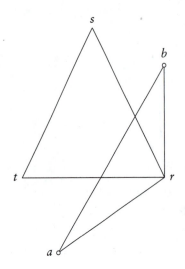

 **FIG. 8.15** Case 1: $r \notin ab$

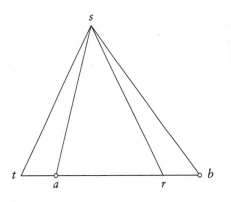

FIG. 8.16 Case 2a: $r \in ab$ and $a \in rt$

Case 2a: $r \in ab$ and $a \in rt$ (Figure 8.16).
  We compute $\mathcal{N}sba$ using newcnet3.

Case 2b: $r \in ab$ and $a \notin rt$ (Figure 8.17).
  In this case, we must have $t \notin ab$, since $r \in ab$, and we compute $\mathcal{N}tba$ using newcnet3.

  The corresponding Mathematica program is given below.

```
(* computes a control net for a curve on the surface, *)
(* given two points a = (a1, a2, a3) and b = (b1, b2, b3) *)
(* in  the parameter plane, w.r.t. the reference triangle (r, s, t) *)
```

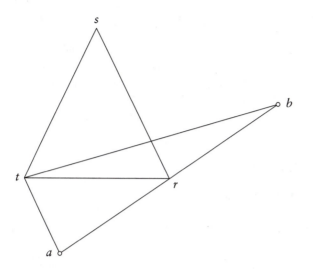

FIG. 8.17 Case 2b: $r \in ab$ and $a \notin rt$

```
(* We use newcnet3 to get the control points of the *)
(* curve segment defined over [0, 1], with end points a, b. *)

curvcpoly[{net__}, m_, a_, b_] :=
Block[
{cc = {net}, res, net1, trigr, trigs, trigt, i, r, s, t, aa, bb},
(r = {1, 0, 0};  s = {0, 1, 0}; t = {0, 0, 1};
 aa = a; bb = b;
 trigr = {r, bb, aa}; trigs = {s, bb, aa}; trigt = {t, bb, aa};
 If[collin[aa,bb,r] === 0, net1 = newcnet3[cc, m, trigr],
     If[collin[aa,t,r] === 1, net1 = newcnet3[cc, m, trigs],
                              net1 = newcnet3[cc, m, trigt]
       ]
   ];
  res = {};
  Do[
     res = Append[res, net1[[i]]], {i, 1, m + 1}
    ];
  res
)
];
```

Using the function curvcpoly, it is easy to render a triangular patch by rendering a number of u-curves and v-curves.

8.2   Subdivision Algorithms for Rectangular Patches

We now consider algorithms for approximating rectangular patches using recursive subdivision. Given two affine frames $(\overline{r}_1, \overline{s}_1)$ and $(\overline{r}_2, \overline{s}_2)$ for the affine line $\mathbf{A}$, given a rectangular control net $\mathcal{N} = (b_{i,j})_{(i,j)\in\square_{p,q}}$, recall that in terms of the polar form $f\colon (\mathbf{A})^p \times (\mathbf{A})^q \to \mathcal{E}$ of the bipolynomial surface $F\colon \mathbf{A} \times \mathbf{A} \to \mathcal{E}$ of degree $\langle p, q \rangle$ defined by $\mathcal{N}$, for every $(i, j) \in \square_{p,q}$, we have

$$b_{i,j} = f(\underbrace{\overline{r}_1, \ldots, \overline{r}_1}_{p-i}, \underbrace{\overline{s}_1, \ldots, \overline{s}_1}_{i}; \underbrace{\overline{r}_2, \ldots, \overline{r}_2}_{q-j}, \underbrace{\overline{s}_2, \ldots, \overline{s}_2}_{j}).$$

Unlike subdividing triangular patches, subdividing rectangular patches is quite simple. Indeed, it is possible to subdivide a rectangular control net $\mathcal{N}$ in two ways. The first way is to compute the two nets $\mathcal{N}[r_1, u; *]$ and $\mathcal{N}[u, s_1; *]$, where

$$\mathcal{N}[r_1, u; *]_{i,j} = f(\underbrace{\overline{r}_1, \ldots, \overline{r}_1}_{p-i}, \underbrace{\overline{u}, \ldots, \overline{u}}_{i}; \underbrace{\overline{r}_2, \ldots, \overline{r}_2}_{q-j}, \underbrace{\overline{s}_2, \ldots, \overline{s}_2}_{j}),$$

with $0 \leq i \leq p$, and $0 \leq j \leq q$, and

$$\mathcal{N}[u, s_1; *]_{i,j} = f(\underbrace{\overline{u}, \ldots, \overline{u}}_{p-i}, \underbrace{\overline{s}_1, \ldots, \overline{s}_1}_{i}; \underbrace{\overline{r}_2, \ldots, \overline{r}_2}_{q-j}, \underbrace{\overline{s}_2, \ldots, \overline{s}_2}_{j}),$$

with $0 \leq i \leq p$, and $0 \leq j \leq q$. This can be achieved in $q + 1$ calls to the version of the de Casteljau algorithm performing subdivision (in the case of curves). This algorithm has been implemented in Mathematica as the function urecdecas. The second way is to compute the two nets $\mathcal{N}[*; r_2, v]$ and $\mathcal{N}[*; v, s_2]$, where

$$\mathcal{N}[*; r_2, v]_{i,j} = f(\underbrace{\overline{r}_1, \ldots, \overline{r}_1}_{p-i}, \underbrace{\overline{s}_1, \ldots, \overline{s}_1}_{i}; \underbrace{\overline{r}_2, \ldots, \overline{r}_2}_{q-j}, \underbrace{\overline{v}, \ldots, \overline{v}}_{j}),$$

with $0 \leq i \leq p$, and $0 \leq j \leq q$, and

$$\mathcal{N}[*; v, s_2]_{i,j} = f(\underbrace{\overline{r}_1, \ldots, \overline{r}_1}_{p-i}, \underbrace{\overline{s}_1, \ldots, \overline{s}_1}_{i}; \underbrace{\overline{v}, \ldots, \overline{v}}_{q-j}, \underbrace{\overline{s}_2, \ldots, \overline{s}_2}_{j}),$$

with $0 \leq i \leq p$, and $0 \leq j \leq q$. This can be achieved in $p + 1$ calls to the version of the de Casteljau algorithm performing subdivision (in the case of curves). This algorithm has been implemented in Mathematica as the function vrecdecas.

Then, given an input net $\mathcal{N}$ over $[r_1, s_1] \times [r_2, s_2]$, for any $\overline{u}, \overline{v} \in \mathbf{A}$, we can subdivide the net $\mathcal{N}$ into four subnets $\mathcal{N}[r_1, u; r_2, v]$, $\mathcal{N}[u, s_1; r_2, v]$, $\mathcal{N}[r_1, u; v, s_2]$, $\mathcal{N}[u, s_1; v, s_2]$, by first subdviding $\mathcal{N}$ into $\mathcal{N}[*; r_2, v]$ and $\mathcal{N}[*; v, s_2]$ using the function vrecdecas, and then by splitting each of these two nets using urecdecas. The four nets have the common corner $F(\overline{u}, \overline{v})$ (Figure 8.18).

In order to implement these algorithms, we represent a rectangular control net $\mathcal{N} = (b_{i,j})_{(i,j)\in\square_{p,q}}$ as the list of $p + 1$ rows

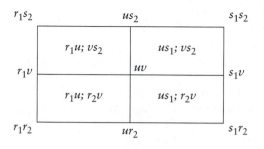

FIG. 8.18 Subdividing a rectangular patch

$$b_{i,0},\ b_{i,1},\ \ldots,\ b_{i,q},$$

where $0 \leq i \leq p$. This has the advantage that we can view $\mathcal{N}$ as a rectangular array *net*, with $net[i, j] = b_{i,j}$. The function `makerecnet` converts an input net into such a two-dimensional array.

```
(* To make a rectangular net of degree (p, q) from a list
   of length (p + 1)x(q + 1) *)

makerecnet[{net__}, p_, q_] :=
Block[
{oldnet = {net}, newnet = {}, row, pt, i, j, n},
 n = Length[oldnet];
    Do[row = {};
       Do[
           pt = oldnet[[i*(q + 1) + j + 1]];
           row = Append[row,pt],   {j, 0, q}
          ];
         newnet = Append[newnet, row], {i, 0, p}
       ];
newnet
];
```

The subdivision algorithm is implemented in Mathematica by the function `recdecas`, which uses the functions `vrecdecas` and `urecdecas`. In turn, these functions use the function `subdecas`, which performs the subdivision of a control polygon. It turns out that an auxiliary function `rectrans`, converting a matrix given as a list of columns into a linear list of rows, is needed.

```
(* de Casteljau algorithm with subdivision into four rectangular nets *)
(* for a rectangular net of degree (p, q) *)

recdecas[{oldnet__}, p_, q_, r1_, s1_, r2_, s2_, u_, v_, debug_] :=
Block[
{net = {oldnet}, temp, newneta, newnetb,
```

```
   newnet1, newnet2, newnet},
   newneta = {}; newnetb = {};
   Print[" p = ", p, ", q = ", q, ", in recdecas"];
   temp = vrecdecas[net, p, q, r2, s2, v, debug];
   newneta = temp[[1]]; newnetb = temp[[2]];
   newnet1 = urecdecas[newneta, p, q, r1, s1, u, debug];
   newnet2 = urecdecas[newnetb, p, q, r1, s1, u, debug];
   newnet = Join[newnet1, newnet2];
   If[debug === 2, Print[" Subdivided nets: ", newnet]];
   newnet
   ];


(* de Casteljau algorithm with subdivision into two rectangular nets *)
(* for a rectangular net of degree (p,  q).
   Subdivision along the u-curves *)

urecdecas[{oldnet__}, p_, q_, r1_, s1_, u_, debug_] :=
Block[
{net = {oldnet}, i, j, temp, bistar, row1, row2, pt,
 newnet1, newnet2, newnet},
 bistar = {}; row1 = {}; row2 = {};
 newnet1 = {}; newnet2 = {};
 Do[
    bistar = {}; row1 = {}; row2 = {};
    Do[
       pt = net[[(q + 1)*i + j + 1]];
       bistar = Append[bistar, pt], {i, 0, p}
      ];
    If[debug === 2, Print[" bistar: ", bistar]];
    temp = subdecas[bistar, r1, s1, u];
    row1 = temp[[1]]; row2 = temp[[2]];
    newnet1 = Join[newnet1, {row1}];
    newnet2 = Join[newnet2, {row2}], {j, 0, q}
   ];
 newnet1 = rectrans[newnet1];  newnet2 = rectrans[newnet2];
 newnet = Join[{newnet1}, {newnet2}];
 If[debug === 2, Print[" Subdivided nets: ", newnet]];
 newnet
 ];


(* Converts a matrix given as a list of columns
   into a linear list of rows *)

rectrans[{oldnet__}] :=
Block[
{net = {oldnet}, i, j, pp, qq, row, pt, newnet},
```

```
row = {};    newnet = {}; qq = Length[net]; pp = Length[net[[1]]];
Do[
    Do[
        row = net[[j]];    pt = row[[i]];
        newnet = Append[newnet, pt], {j, 1, qq}
      ], {i, 1, pp}
  ];
  newnet
];


(* de Casteljau algorithm with subdivision into two rectangular nets *)
(* for a rectangular net of degree (p, q).
   Subdivision along the v-curves *)

vrecdecas[{oldnet__}, p_, q_, r2_, s2_, v_, debug_] :=
Block[
{net = {oldnet}, i, j, temp, bstarj, row1, row2, pt,
 newneta, newnetb, newnet},
 bistar = {}; row1 = {}; row2 = {}; newneta = {}; newnetb = {};
 Do[
    bstarj = {}; row1 = {}; row2 = {};
    Do[
        pt = net[[(q + 1)*i + j + 1]];
        bstarj = Append[bstarj, pt], {j, 0, q}
      ];
    If[debug === 2, Print[" bstarj: ", bstarj]];
    temp = subdecas[bstarj, r2, s2, v];
    row1 = temp[[1]]; row2 = temp[[2]];
    newneta = Join[newneta, row1];
    newnetb = Join[newnetb, row2], {i, 0, p}
   ];
 newnet = Join[{newneta}, {newnetb}];
 If[debug === 2, Print[" Subdivided nets: ", newnet]];
 newnet
];
```

Given a rectangular net oldnet of degree (p, q), the function recpoldecas computes the polar value for argument lists u and v. This function calls the function bdecas, which computes a point on a curve from a control polygon.

```
(* Computation of a polar value for a rectangular net of
   degree (p, q) *)

recpoldecas[{oldnet__}, p_, q_, r1_, s1_, r2_, s2_, u_, v_, debug_] :=
Block[
{net = {oldnet}, i, j, bistar, bstarj, pt, res},
 bistar = {};
```

```
Do[
   bstarj = {};
   Do[
       pt = net[[(q + 1)*i + j + 1]];
       bstarj = Append[bstarj, pt], {j, 0, q}
       ];
     If[debug === 2, Print[" bstarj: ", bstarj]];
     pt = bdecas[bstarj, v, r2, s2];
     bistar = Append[bistar, pt], {i, 0, p}
   ];
  If[debug === 2, Print[" bistar: ", bistar]];
  res = bdecas[bistar, u, r1, s1];
  If[debug === 2, Print[" polar value: ", res]];
  res
];
```

As in the case of triangular patches, using the function recdecas, starting from a list consisting of a single control net net, we can repeatedly subdivide the nets in a list of nets, in order to obtain an approximation of the surface patch specified by the control net net. The function recsubdiv4 shown below performs n recursive steps of subdivision, starting with an input control net net. The function recitersub4 takes a list of nets and subdivides each net in this list into four subnets.

```
(* performs a subdivision step on each rectangular net in a list *)
(* using recdecas4, i.e., splitting into four subpatches *)

recitersub4[{net__}, p_, q_, r1_, s1_, r2_, s2_, debug_] :=
Block[
{cnet = {net},  lnet = {}, l, i, u, v},
(l = Length[cnet]; u = 1/2; v = 1/2;
Do[
   lnet = Join[lnet, recdecas[cnet[[i]], p, q, r1, s1,
                             r2, s2, u, v, debug]] , {i, 1, l}
   ];
lnet
)
];

(* performs n subdivision steps using recitersub4, i.e., splits *)
(* a rectangular patch into 4 subpatches *)

recsubdiv4[{net__}, p_, q_, n_, debug_] :=
Block[
{newnet = {net},  i, r1, s1, r2, s2},
(r1 = 0; s1 = 1; r2 = 0; s2 = 1;
newnet = {newnet};
```

```
Do[
    newnet = recitersub4[newnet, p, q, r1, s1, r2, s2, debug], {i, 1, n}
    ];
  newnet
  )
];
```

The function `recsubdiv4` returns a list of rectangular nets. In order to render the surface patch, it is necessary to link the nodes in each net. This is easily done and is left as an exercise.

The functions `urecdecas` and `vrecdecas` can also be used to compute the control net $N[a, b; c, d]$ over new affine bases $[a, b]$ and $[c, d]$, from a control net N over some affine bases $[r_1, s_1]$ and $[r_2, s_2]$. If $d \neq r_2$ and $b \neq r_1$, we first compute $N[r_1, s_1; r_2, d]$ using `vrecdecas`, then $N[r_1, b; r_2, d]$ using `urecdecas`, and then $N[r_1, b; c, d]$ using `vrecdecas`, and finally $N[a, b; c, d]$ using `urecdecas`. It is easy to take care of the cases where $d = r_2$ or $b = r_1$, and such a program is implemented as follows:

```
(* Computes a new rectangular net of degree (p, q) *)
(* w.r.t. frames (a, b) and (c, d) on the affine line *)
(* In the hat space *)

recnewnet[{oldnet__}, p_, q_, a_, b_, c_, d_, debug_] :=
Block[
{net = {oldnet}, temp, newnet1, newnet2, newnet3, newnet4, rnet,
r1, s1, r2, s2, ll, i},
r1 = 0; s1 = 1; r2 = 0; s2 = 1;
newnet1 = {};   newnet2 = {};   newnet3 = {};   newnet4 = {};
If[d =!= r2,   temp = vrecdecas[net, p, q, r2, s2, d, debug];
               newnet1 = temp[[1]],
               newnet1 = net
    ];
If[debug === 2, Print[" newnet1: ", newnet1]];
If[b =!= r1, temp = urecdecas[newnet1, p, q, r1, s1, b, debug];
             newnet2 = temp[[1]],
             newnet2 = newnet1
    ];
If[debug === 2, Print[" newnet2: ", newnet2]];
If[d =!= r2,   temp = vrecdecas[newnet2, p, q, r2, d, c, debug];
               newnet3 = temp[[2]],
               temp = vrecdecas[newnet2, p, q, r2, s2, c, debug];
               newnet3 = temp[[1]]
    ];
If[debug === 2, Print[" newnet3: ", newnet3]];
If[b =!= r1, temp = urecdecas[newnet3, p, q, r1, b, a, debug];
             newnet4 = temp[[2]],
```

```
temp = urecdecas[newnet3, p, q, r1, s1, a, debug];
(* needs to reverse the net in this case *)
rnet = temp[[1]]; newnet4 = {}; ll = Length[rnet];
Do[
    newnet4 = Prepend[newnet4, rnet[[i]]], {i, 1, ll}
    ]
];
If[debug === 2, Print[" newnet4: ", newnet4]];
newnet4
];
```

Let us go back to the example of the monkey saddle, to illustrate the use of the functions `recsubdiv4` and `recnewnet`. It is easily shown that the monkey saddle is specified by the following rectangular control net of degree $(3, 2)$, `sqmonknet1`, over $[0, 1] \times [0, 1]$:

```
sqmonknet1 =  {{0, 0, 0}, {0, 1/2, 0}, {0, 1, 0}, {1/3, 0, 0},
    {1/3, 1/2, 0}, {1/3, 1, -1}, {2/3, 0, 0}, {2/3, 1/2, 0},
    {2/3, 1, -2}, {1, 0, 1}, {1, 1/2, 1}, {1, 1, -2}}
```

Using `recnewnet`, we can compute a rectangular net `sqmonknet` over $[-1, 1] \times [-1, 1]$:

```
sqmonknet =   {{-1, -1, 2}, {-1, 0, -4}, {-1, 1, 2}, {-1/3, -1, 2},
    {-1/3, 0, 0}, {-1/3, 1, 2}, {1/3, -1, -2}, {1/3, 0, 0},
    {1/3, 1, -2}, {1, -1, -2}, {1, 0, 4}, {1, 1, -2}}
```

Finally, Figures 8.19–8.21 show the output of the subdivision algorithm `recsubdiv4`, for $n = 1, 2, 3$. The advantage of rectangular nets is that we get the patch over $[-1, 1] \times [-1, 1]$ directly, as opposed to the union of two triangular patches.

The final picture (corresponding to three iterations), Figure 8.21, is basically as good as the triangulation shown earlier and is obtained faster.

Actually, it is possible to convert a triangular net of degree m into a rectangular net of degree (m, m), and conversely to convert a rectangular net of degree (p, q) into a triangular net of degree $p + q$, but we will postpone this until we deal with rational surfaces.

Problems

[10 pts] **1.** Let $F: \mathbf{A}^2 \to \mathbf{A}^3$ be a bilinear map. Consider the rectangular net $\mathcal{N} = (b_{i, j})$ of bidegree $\langle p, q \rangle$ defined such that

$$b_{i, j} = F\left(\frac{i}{p}, \frac{j}{q}\right)$$

for all i, j, where $0 \leq i \leq p$ and $0 \leq j \leq q$. Prove that the rectangular surface defined by $\mathcal{N}$ is equal to F (we say that rectangular patches have *bilinear precision*).

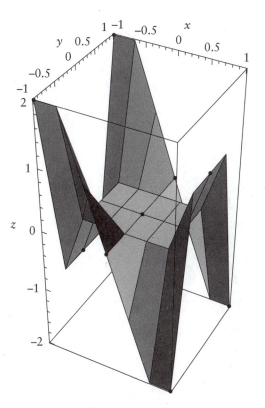

FIG. 8.19 A monkey saddle, rectangular subdivision, one iteration

[20 pts]   **2.** Give a method for recursively subdividing a triangular patch into four subpatches, using only three calls to the de Casteljau algorithm. Show the result of performing three levels of subdivision on the original reference triangle (r, s, t).

[20 pts]   **3.** Investigate the method for recursively subdividing a triangular patch into six subpatches, using four calls to the de Casteljau algorithm as follows: first apply the subdivision version of the de Casteljau algorithm to the center of gravity of the reference triangle, and then to the middle of every side of the triangle. Show the result of performing three levels of subdivision on the original reference triangle (r, s, t).

[40 pts]   **4.** Implement your own version of the de Casteljau algorithm splitting a triangular patch into four triangles, as in Section 8.1. Use your algorithm to draw the surface patch over $[-1, 1] \times [-1, 1]$ defined by the following control net:

```
domenet3 = {{0, 0, 0}, {3/4, 3/2, 3/10}, {-1/4, -1/2, 3/10}, {1/2, 1, 0},
       {3/2, 0, 3/10}, {1/2, 1/2, 1/2}, {5/4, -1/2, 3/10},
       {-1/2, 0, 3/10}, {1/4, 3/2, 3/10},  {1, 0, 0}};
```

[40 pts]   **5.** Implement your own version of the de Casteljau algorithm splitting a rectangular patch into four rectangles, as in Section 8.2.

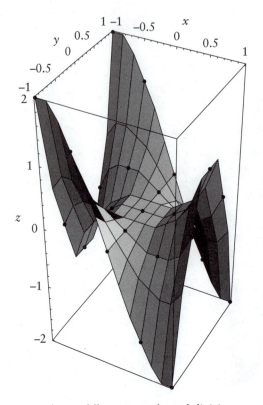

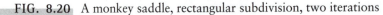

FIG. 8.20 A monkey saddle, rectangular subdivision, two iterations

[40 pts] **6.** Given a surface specified by a triangular net, implement a program drawing the u-curves and the v-curves of the patch over $[a, b] \times [c, d]$, using the function `curvcpoly`.

[20 pts] **7.** Prove that any method for obtaining a regular subdivision into four subpatches using the standard de Casteljau algorithm requires at least four calls.

[20 pts] **8.** Let F be a surface of total degree m defined by a triangular control net $\mathcal{N} = (b_{i,j,k})_{(i,j,k) \in \Delta_m}$, with respect to the affine frame Δrst. For any n points $p_i = u_i r + v_i s + w_i t$ (where $u_i + v_i + w_i = 1$), define the following $(n + 2)$-simplex of points $b_{i,j,k}^{l_1,\dots,l_n}$, where $i + j + k + l_1 + \dots + l_n = m$, inductively as follows:

$$b_{i,j,k}^{0,\dots,0} = b_{i,j,k},$$

$$b_{i,j,k}^{l_1,\dots,l_h+1,\dots,l_n} = u_h\, b_{i+1,j,k}^{l_1,\dots,l_h,\dots,l_n} + v_h\, b_{i,j+1,k}^{l_1,\dots,l_h,\dots,l_n} + w_h\, b_{i,j,k+1}^{l_1,\dots,l_h,\dots,l_n},$$

where $1 \leq h \leq n$.

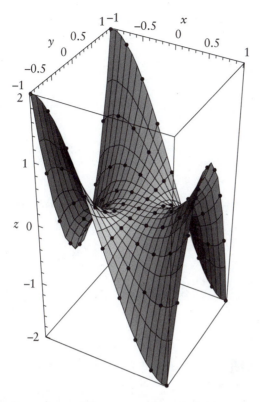

FIG. 8.21 A monkey saddle, rectangular subdivision, three iterations

(a) If f is the polar form of F, prove that

$$b_{i,j,k}^{l_1,\ldots,l_n} = f(\underbrace{r,\ldots,r}_{i}, \underbrace{s,\ldots,s}_{j}, \underbrace{t,\ldots,t}_{k}, \underbrace{p_1,\ldots,p_1}_{l_1}, \ldots, \underbrace{p_n,\ldots,p_n}_{l_n}).$$

(b) For $n=0$, show that $F(p) = b_{0,0,0}^n$, as in the standard de Casteljau algorithm.

For $n=1$, prove that $(b_{i,j,0}^{l_1})_{(i,j,l_1)\in\Delta_m}$ is a control net of F with respect to Δrsp_1, $(b_{0,j,k}^{l_1})_{(j,k,l_1)\in\Delta_m}$ is a control net of F with respect to Δstp_1, and $(b_{i,0,k}^{l_1})_{(i,k,l_1)\in\Delta_m}$ is a control net of F with respect to Δtrp_1.

For $n=2$, prove that $(b_{i,0,0}^{l_1,l_2})_{(i,l_1,l_2)\in\Delta_m}$ is a control net of F with respect to Δrp_1p_2, $(b_{0,j,0}^{l_1,l_2})_{(j,l_1,l_2)\in\Delta_m}$ is a control net of F with respect to Δsp_1p_2, and $(b_{0,0,k}^{l_1,l_2})_{(k,l_1,l_2)\in\Delta_m}$ is a control net of F with respect to Δtp_1p_2.

For $n=3$, prove that $(b_{0,0,0}^{l_1,l_2,l_3})_{(l_1,l_2,l_2)\in\Delta_m}$ is a control net of F with respect to $\Delta p_1p_2p_3$.

[20 pts]   9. Given any two integers $p, q \geq 1$, we define the rectangular grid $\square_{p,q}$ as the grid consisting of all points of coordinates

$$g_{i,j} = \left(\frac{i}{p}, \frac{j}{q} \right),$$

where $0 \leq i \leq p$ and $0 \leq j \leq q$. Prove that the rectangular patch G defined by $\square_{p,q}$ satisfies the property that

$$(x, y) = \sum_{i=0}^{p} \sum_{j=0}^{q} B_i^p(x) B_j^q(y) \, g_{i,j}$$

for all $(x, y) \in \mathbf{A}^2$, where B_i^p and B_j^q are Bernstein polynomials. Given any rectangular net

$$\mathcal{N} = (b_{i,j})_{0 \leq i \leq p, \, 0 \leq j \leq q}$$

in $\mathbf{A}^2$, we define the map from $\mathbf{A}^2$ to $\mathbf{A}^2$ as

$$(x, y) \mapsto \sum_{i=0}^{p} \sum_{j=0}^{q} B_i^p(x) B_k^q(j) \, b_{i,j}.$$

Show that this map behaves like a global deformation of the original rectangular grid $\square_{p,q}$. Show how to use such maps to globally deform a Bézier curve specified by its control points $(c_0, \ldots, c_m)$ (where each c_i is inside the grid defined by $\square_{p,q}$).

CHAPTER 9

Polynomial Spline Surfaces and Subdivision Surfaces

9.1   Joining Polynomial Surfaces

We now attempt to generalize the idea of splines to polynomial surfaces. As we shall see, this is far more subtle than it is for curves. In the case of a curve, the parameter space is the affine line $\mathbf{A}$, and the only reasonable choice is to divide the affine line into intervals, and to view the curve as the result of joining curve segments defined over these intervals. However, in the case of a surface, the parameter space is the affine *plane* $\mathcal{P}$, and even if we just want to subdivide the plane into convex regions, there is a tremendous variety of ways of doing so. Thus, we will restrict our attention to subdivisions of the plane into convex polygons, where the edges are line segments. In fact, we will basically only consider subdivisions made of rectangles or of (equilateral) triangles. We also need to decide what kind of continuity we want to enforce. As in the case of curves, we will first consider parametric continuity.

First, we will find necessary and sufficient conditions on polar forms for two surface patches to meet with C^n-continuity. Next, we will take a closer look at spline surfaces of degree m based on a triangular subdivision of the plane. We will discover that C^n-continuity is only possible if $2m \geq 3n + 2$. We will find necessary conditions on spline surfaces of degree $m = 3n + 1$ to meet with C^{2n}-continuity, but unfortunately, we will not be able to propose a nice scheme involving control points, in the line of de Boor control points. To the best of our knowledge, finding such a scheme is still an open problem. We will then consider spline surfaces of degree m based on a rectangular subdivision of the plane. This time, we will find that C^n-continuity is only possible if $m \geq 2n + 2$. This is not quite as good as in the triangular case, but on the positive side, we will see that there is a nice scheme, involving de Boor control points, for bipolynomial splines of bidegree $\langle n, n \rangle$ meeting with C^{n-1}-continuity.

We conclude this chapter with a section on subdivision surfaces (Section 9.4). Subdivision surfaces provide an attractive alternative to spline surfaces in modeling applications where the topology of surfaces is rather complex, and where the initial control polyhedron consists of various kinds of faces, not just triangles or rectangles. The idea is to start with a rough polyhedron specified by a mesh (a collection of points and edges connected so that it defines the boundary of a polyhedron) and to apply recursively a subdivision scheme, which, in the limit, yields a smooth surface (or solid). Subdivision schemes typically produce surfaces with at least C^1-continuity, except for a finite number of so-called extraordinary points, where it is tangent-plane continuous. A number of spectacular applications of subdivision surfaces can be found in the 1998 SIGGRAPH conference proceedings, notably, Geri, a computer model of a character from the short movie *Geri's Game*. We present three subdivision schemes due to Doo and Sabin [27, 29, 28], Catmull and Clark [17], and Charles Loop [50]. We discuss Loop's convergence proof in some detail, and for this, we give a crash course on discrete Fourier transforms and (circular) discrete convolutions.

In this section, we restrict our attention to total degree polynomial surfaces. This is not a real restriction, since it is always possible to convert a rectangular net to a triangular net. It is also easier to deal with bipolynomial surfaces than total degree surfaces, and we concentrate on the more difficult case.

Given two polynomial surfaces F and G of degree m, for any point $a \in \mathcal{P}$, as we will see in Section 11.1, we say that *F and G agree to kth order at a*, iff

$$D_{\vec{u_1}} \ldots D_{\vec{u_i}} F(a) = D_{\vec{u_1}} \ldots D_{\vec{u_i}} G(a),$$

for all $\vec{u_1}, \ldots, \vec{u_i} \in \mathbf{R}^2$, where $0 \leq i \leq k$.

Definition 9.1.1

Let A and B be two adjacent convex polygons in the plane, and let (r, s) be the line segment along which they are adjacent (where $r, s \in \mathcal{P}$ are distinct vertices of A and B). Given two polynomial surfaces F_A and F_B of degree m, F_A and F_B join with C^k-continuity along (r, s) iff F_A and F_B agree to kth order for all $a \in (r, s)$.

Lemma B.4.5 (in Appendix B) tells us that for any $a \in (r, s)$, F_A and F_B agree to kth order at a iff their polar forms $f_A \colon \mathcal{P}^m \to \mathcal{E}$ and $f_B \colon \mathcal{P}^m \to \mathcal{E}$ agree on all multisets of points that contain at least $m - k$ copies of a, that is, iff

$$f_A(u_1, \ldots, u_k, \underbrace{a, \ldots, a}_{m-k}) = f_B(u_1, \ldots, u_k, \underbrace{a, \ldots, a}_{m-k}),$$

for all $u_1, \ldots, u_k \in \mathcal{P}$. Using this fact, we can prove the following crucial lemma.

Lemma 9.1.2

Let A and B be two adjacent convex polygons in the plane, and let (r, s) be the line segment along which they are adjacent (where $r, s \in \mathcal{P}$ are distinct vertices of A

and B). Given two polynomial surfaces F_A and F_B of degree m, F_A and F_B join with
C^k-*continuity along (r, s) iff their polar forms $f_A: \mathcal{P}^m \to \mathcal{E}$ and $f_B: \mathcal{P}^m \to \mathcal{E}$ agree on*
all multisets of points that contain at least $m - k$ points on the line (r, s), that is, iff

$$f_A(u_1, \ldots, u_k, a_{k+1}, \ldots, a_m) = f_B(u_1, \ldots, u_k, a_{k+1}, \ldots, a_m),$$

for all $u_1, \ldots, u_k \in \mathcal{P}$, and all $a_{k+1}, \ldots, a_m \in (r, s)$.

Proof: As we just said, for every $a \in (r, s)$, F_A and F_B agree to kth order at a iff

$$f_A(u_1, \ldots, u_k, \underbrace{a, \ldots, a}_{m-k}) = f_B(u_1, \ldots, u_k, \underbrace{a, \ldots, a}_{m-k}),$$

for all $u_1, \ldots, u_k \in \mathcal{P}$. However, if we consider

$$a \mapsto f_A(u_1, \ldots, u_k, \underbrace{a, \ldots, a}_{m-k})$$

and

$$a \mapsto f_B(u_1, \ldots, u_k, \underbrace{a, \ldots, a}_{m-k})$$

as affine polynomial functions $F_A(u_1, \ldots, u_k)$ and $F_B(u_1, \ldots, u_k)$, Lemma 4.4.1
shows that if these functions agree on all points in (r, s), then the corresponding
polar forms $f_A(u_1, \ldots, u_k)$ and $f_B(u_1, \ldots, u_k)$ agree for all points $a_{k+1}, \ldots, a_m \in$
(r, s). Since every point on the line (r, s) can be expressed as an affine combination
of r and s, the polar forms $f_A(u_1, \ldots, u_k)$ and $f_B(u_1, \ldots, u_k)$ agree for all points
$a_{k+1}, \ldots, a_m$ on the line (r, s). Since this holds for all $u_1, \ldots, u_k \in \mathcal{P}$, we have shown
that

$$f_A(u_1, \ldots, u_k, a_{k+1}, \ldots, a_m) = f_B(u_1, \ldots, u_k, a_{k+1}, \ldots, a_m),$$

for all $u_1, \ldots, u_k \in \mathcal{P}$, and all $a_{k+1}, \ldots, a_m \in (r, s)$, as desired.   ■

As a consequence of Lemma 9.1.2, we obtain the necessary and sufficient conditions on control nets for F_A and F_B for having C^n-continuity along (r, s). Let
$A = \Delta prs$ and $B = \Delta qrs$ be two reference triangles in the plane, sharing the edge
(r, s), as shown in Figure 9.1.

Then, Lemma 9.1.2 tells us that F_A and F_B join with C^n-continuity along (r, s)
iff

$$f_A(p^i q^j r^k s^l) = f_B(p^i q^j r^k s^l),$$

for all i, j, k, l such that $i + j + k + l = m$, and $k + l \geq m - n$ $(0 \leq n \leq m)$.
For $n = 0$, we just have

$$f_A(r^k s^{m-k}) = f_B(r^k s^{m-k}),$$

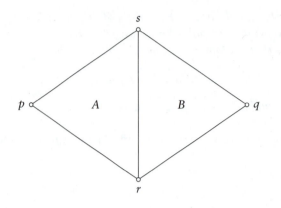

Two adjacent reference triangles

with $0 \leq k \leq m$, which means that the control points of the boundary curves along (r, s) must agree. This is natural; the two surfaces join along this curve! Let us now see what the continuity conditions mean for $m = 3$ and $n = 1, 2, 3$.

For C^1-continuity, the following 10 polar values must agree:

$$f_A(r, r, r) = f_B(r, r, r),$$
$$f_A(r, r, s) = f_B(r, r, s),$$
$$f_A(r, s, s) = f_B(r, s, s),$$
$$f_A(s, s, s) = f_B(s, s, s),$$
$$f_A(p, r, r) = f_B(p, r, r),$$
$$f_A(p, r, s) = f_B(p, r, s),$$
$$f_A(p, s, s) = f_B(p, s, s),$$
$$f_A(q, s, s) = f_B(q, s, s),$$
$$f_A(q, r, s) = f_B(q, r, s),$$
$$f_A(q, r, r) = f_B(q, r, r).$$

Denoting these common polar values as $f_{A,B}(\cdot, \cdot, \cdot)$, note that these polar values naturally form the vertices of three diamonds,

$$(f_{A,B}(p, r, r), \ f_{A,B}(r, r, r), \ f_{A,B}(q, r, r), \ f_{A,B}(s, r, r)),$$
$$(f_{A,B}(p, r, s), \ f_{A,B}(r, r, s), \ f_{A,B}(q, r, s), \ f_{A,B}(s, r, s)),$$
$$(f_{A,B}(p, s, s), \ f_{A,B}(r, s, s), \ f_{A,B}(q, s, s), \ f_{A,B}(s, s, s)),$$

images of the diamond (p, r, q, s). In particular, the vertices of each of these diamonds must be coplanar, but this is not enough to ensure C^1-continuity. The above conditions are depicted in Figure 9.2.

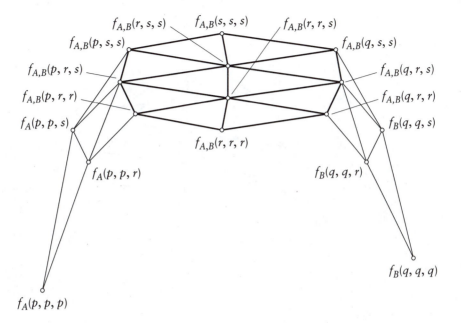

$f_{A,B}(r, s, s)$ $f_{A,B}(s, s, s)$ $f_{A,B}(r, r, s)$
$f_{A,B}(p, s, s)$ $f_{A,B}(q, s, s)$
$f_{A,B}(p, r, s)$ $f_{A,B}(q, r, s)$
$f_{A,B}(p, r, r)$ $f_{A,B}(q, r, r)$
$f_A(p, p, s)$ $f_B(q, q, s)$
$f_{A,B}(r, r, r)$

$f_A(p, p, r)$ $f_B(q, q, r)$

$f_B(q, q, q)$

$f_A(p, p, p)$

FIG. 9.2 Control nets of cubic surfaces joining with C^1-continuity

We can view this figure as three pairs of overlapping de Casteljau diagrams each with one shell.

Let us now consider C^2-continuity, that is, $n = 2$. In addition to the 10 constraints necessary for C^1-continuity, we have 6 additional equations among polar values:

$$f_A(p, p, r) = f_B(p, p, r),$$
$$f_A(p, p, s) = f_B(p, p, s),$$
$$f_A(p, q, r) = f_B(p, q, r),$$
$$f_A(p, q, s) = f_B(p, q, s),$$
$$f_A(q, q, r) = f_B(q, q, r),$$
$$f_A(q, q, s) = f_B(q, q, s).$$

Again, denoting these common polar values as $f_{A,B}(\cdot, \cdot, \cdot)$, note that these polar values naturally form the vertices of four diamonds, images of the diamond (p, r, q, s). For example, the left two diamonds are

$$(f_{A,B}(p, p, r),\ f_{A,B}(r, p, r),\ f_{A,B}(q, p, r),\ f_{A,B}(s, p, r)),$$
$$(f_{A,B}(p, p, s),\ f_{A,B}(r, p, s),\ f_{A,B}(q, p, s),\ f_{A,B}(s, p, s)).$$

In particular, the vertices of each of these diamonds must be coplanar, but this is not enough to ensure C^2-continuity. Note that the polar values $f_A(p, q, r) = f_B(p, q, r)$

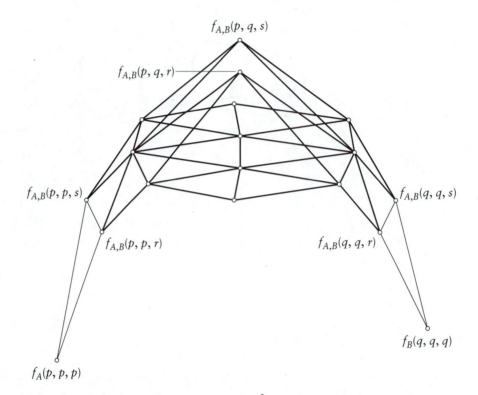

FIG. 9.3   Control nets of cubic surfaces joining with C^2-continuity

and $f_A(p, q, s) = f_B(p, q, s)$ are not control points of the original nets. The above conditions are depicted in Figure 9.3.

We can view this figure as two pairs of overlapping de Casteljau diagrams each with two shells.

Finally, in the case of C^3-continuity, that is, $n = 3$, all the control points agree, which means that $f_A = f_B$. In general, C^n-continuity is ensured by the overlapping of $m - n + 1$ pairs of de Casteljau diagrams, each with n shells. We now investigate the realizability of the continuity conditions in the two cases where the parameter plane is subdivided into rectangles or triangles. We assume that the parameter plane has its natural Euclidean structure.

9.2   Spline Surfaces with Triangular Patches

In this section, we study what happens with the continuity conditions between surface patches, if the parameter plane is divided into equilateral triangles. In the case of spline curves, recall that it was possible to achieve C^{m-1}-continuity with curve segments of degree m. Also, spline curves have *local flexibility*, which means that changing some control points in a small area does not affect the entire spline

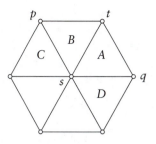

FIG. 9.4 Constraints on triangular patches

curve. In the case of surfaces, the situation is not as pleasant. For simplicity, we will consider surface patches of degree m joining with the *same* degree of continuity n for all common edges. First, we will prove that if $2m \leq 3n + 1$, then it is generally impossible to construct a spline surface. More precisely, given any four adjacent patches as shown in Figure 9.4, if f_C and f_D are known, then f_A and f_B are completely determined.

The proof is more complicated than it might appear. The difficulty is that even though A and D join with C^n-continuity along (s, q), A and B join with C^n-continuity along (s, t), and B and C join with C^n-continuity along (s, p), there is no reference triangle containing all of these three edges!

Lemma 9.2.1

Surface splines consisting of triangular patches of degree $m \geq 1$ joining with C^n-continuity cannot be locally flexible if $2m \leq 3n + 1$. This means that given any four adjacent patches D, A, B, C as in Figure 9.4, if f_D and f_C are known, then f_A and f_B are completely determined. Furthermore, when $2m = 3n + 2$, there is at most one free control point for every two internal adjacent patches.

Proof: The idea is to show that the two control nets of polar values $f_A(s^i t^j q^l)$ and $f_B(s^i t^j p^k)$ are completely determined, where $i + j + l = m$ in the first case, and $i + j + k = m$ in the second case. Since D and A meet with C^n-continuity along (s, q), by Lemma 9.1.2,

$$f_A(s^i t^j p^k q^l) = f_D(s^i t^j p^k q^l),$$

for all $j + k \leq n$ (where $i + j + k + l = m$). Similarly, since A and B join with C^n-continuity along (s, t), and B and C join with C^n-continuity along (s, p), we get

$$f_A(s^i t^j p^k q^l) = f_B(s^i t^j p^k q^l),$$

for all $k + l \leq n$, and

$$f_B(s^i t^j p^k q^l) = f_C(s^i t^j p^k q^l),$$

for all $j + l \leq n$ (where $i + j + k + l = m$).

In summary, $f_A(s^i t^j p^k q^l)$ is determined for all $j + k \leq n$, $f_B(s^i t^j p^k q^l)$ is determined for all $j + l \leq n$, and $f_A(s^i t^j p^k q^l) = f_B(s^i t^j p^k q^l)$ for all $k + l \leq n$. These conditions do not seem to be sufficient to show that f_A and f_B are completely determined, but we haven't yet taken advantage of the symmetries of the situation. Indeed, note that (p, q) and (s, t) have the same middle point, that is,

$$p + q = s + t.$$

If $n = 2h$, the condition $2m \leq 3n + 1$ becomes $2m \leq 6h + 1$, which implies that $m \leq 3h$. If $n = 2h + 1$, the condition $2m \leq 3n + 1$ becomes $2m \leq 6h + 4$, which implies $m \leq 3h + 2$. If we can show that the polar values for F_A and F_B are completely determined when $n = 2h$ and $m = 3h$, or when $n = 2h + 1$ and $m = 3h + 2$, which are the worst cases, we will be done. We will first reformulate the C^n-continuity conditions between A and B, using the identity $p + q = s + t$. Recall that these conditions are

$$f_A(s^i t^j p^k q^l) = f_B(s^i t^j p^k q^l)$$

for all $k + l \leq n$. Replacing p by $s + t - q$ on the left-hand side and q by $s + t - p$ on the right-hand side, we get

$$\sum_{i_1 + i_2 + i_3 = k} (-1)^{i_3} \frac{k!}{i_1! i_2! i_3!} \, f_A(s^{i + i_1} t^{j + i_2} q^{l + i_3})$$

$$= \sum_{j_1 + j_2 + j_3 = l} (-1)^{j_3} \frac{l!}{j_1! j_2! j_3!} \, f_B(s^{i + j_1} t^{j + j_2} p^{k + j_3}),$$

where $k + l \leq n$, and $i + j + k + l = m$. This is an equation relating some affine combination of polar values from a triangular net of $(k + 1)(k + 2)/2$ polar values associated with A and some affine combination of polar values from a triangular net of $(l + 1)(l + 2)/2$ polar values associated with B. A similar rewriting of the C^n-continuity equations between A and D and between C and B shows that the polar values $f_A(s^{m - j - l} t^j q^l)$ are known for $0 \leq l \leq m - j$ and $0 \leq j \leq n$, and that the polar values $f_B(s^{m - j - k} t^j p^k)$ are known for $0 \leq k \leq m - j$ and $0 \leq j \leq n$. In Figure 9.5, the polar values of the form $f_A(s^{m - j - l} t^j q^l)$ are located in the trapezoid (s, q_1, q_2, t), and the polar values of the form $f_B(s^{m - j - k} t^j p^k)$ are located in the trapezoid (s, p_1, p_2, t).

If $n = 2h$ and $m = 3h$, the polar values associated with A and B that are not already determined are contained in the diamond (t, u, v, w), and there are $(m - n)^2 = h^2$ such polar values, since $f_A(s^i t^j) = f_B(s^i t^j)$ along (s, t) (where $i + j = m$). If $n = 2h + 1$ and $m = 3h + 2$, the polar values associated with A and B that are not already determined are also contained in the diamond (t, u, v, w), and there are $(m - n)^2 = (h + 1)^2$ such polar values.

In either case, the polar values in the diamond (t, u, v, w) can be determined inductively from right to left and from bottom up (referring to Figure 9.5). First, we consider the case where $n = 2h + 1$ and $m = 3h + 2$, so that the diamond (t, u, v, w)

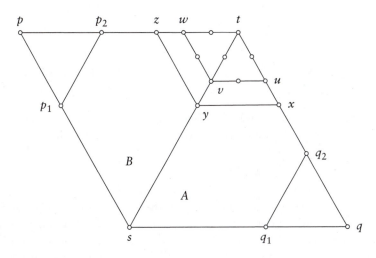

FIG. 9.5 Determining polar values in A and B

contains $(h+1)^2$ polar values. The proof proceeds by induction on h. Assume inductively that the h^2 polar values inside the diamond (t, u, v, w) and not on (u, v) and (v, w) can be computed from the other polar values inside (s, p_1, p_2, w, v, s) and (s, q_1, q_2, u, v, s). We explain how the $h+1$ polar values on the edge (u, v) can be computed, the computation of the h polar values on the edge (v, w) being analogous. When $k = h+1, l = h, i = 0$, and $j = h+1$, observe that in the equation

$$\sum_{i_1+i_2+i_3=h+1} (-1)^{i_3} \frac{(h+1)!}{i_1!i_2!i_3!} \, f_A(s^{i_1}t^{h+1+i_2}q^{h+i_3})$$

$$= \sum_{j_1+j_2+j_3=h} (-1)^{j_3} \frac{h!}{j_1!j_2!j_3!} \, f_B(s^{j_1}t^{h+1+j_2}p^{h+1+j_3}),$$

the only undetermined polar value is the one associated with u, namely,

$$f_A(t^{2h+2}q^h),$$

since all the other polar values involved in this equation are inside (s, p_1, p_2, z, y, s) and (s, q_1, q_2, x, y, s). Thus, $f_A(t^{2h+2}q^h)$ can be computed. Generally, if $0 \le l_1 \le h$, the polar value

$$f_A(s^{h-l_1}t^{2h+2}q^{l_1})$$

along (u, v) can be computed from the equation obtained by letting $k = l_1 + 1, l = l_1$, $i = h - l_1$, and $j = 2h + 1 - l_1$,

$$\sum_{i_1+i_2+i_3=l_1+1} (-1)^{i_3} \frac{(l_1+1)!}{i_1!i_2!i_3!} f_A(s^{h-l_1+i_1}t^{2h+1-l_1+i_2}q^{l_1+i_3})$$

$$= \sum_{j_1+j_2+j_3=l_1} (-1)^{j_3} \frac{l_1!}{j_1!j_2!j_3!} f_B(s^{h-l_1+j_1}t^{2h+1-l_1+j_2}p^{l_1+1+j_3}),$$

since all the other polar values involved are inside (s, p_1, p_2, z, y, s) and (s, q_1, q_2, x, y, s). After a similar computation to determine the polar values

$$f_B(s^{h-l_1}t^{2h+2}p^{l_1}),$$

where $1 \le l_1 \le h$, we get a strictly smaller diamond of h^2 polar values contained in (t, u, v, w), and we use the induction hypothesis to compute these polar values.

We now consider the case $n = 2h$ and $m = 3h$, so that the diamond (t, u, v, w) contains h^2 polar values. Again, the proof proceeds by induction on h. This time, the polar value associated with u is $f_A(t^{2h+1}q^{h-1})$, and the polar value associated with w is $f_B(t^{2h+1}p^{h-1})$. Thus, the argument for the previous case can be used, and in fact, this argument uses C^{2h}-continuity between A and D and between B and C, but only C^{2h-1}-continuity between A and B.

In both cases, note that C^n-continuity was only needed to compute the polar values associated with u and w, and that once they are determined, all the other polar values in the diamond (t, u, v, w) can be computed using only C^{n-1}-continuity constraints. When $2m = 3n + 2$, which implies that $n = 2h$ and $m = 3h + 1$, both polar values $f_A(t^{2h+1}q^h)$ and $f_B(t^{2h+1}p^h)$ are undetermined, but there is an equation relating them, and thus there is at most one degree of freedom for both patches F_A and F_B. ∎

Knowing that we must have $2m \ge 3n + 2$ to have local flexibility, and thus, to find any reasonable scheme to constuct triangular spline surfaces, the problem remains to actually find a method for constructing spline surfaces when $2m = 3n + 2$. Such a method using convolutions is described by Ramshaw [65], but it is not practical. Instead of presenting this method, we attempt to understand better what are the constraints on triangular patches when $n = 2N$ and $m = 3N + 1$. The key is to look at "derived surfaces."

Given a polynomial surface $F: \mathcal{P} \to \mathcal{E}$ of degree m, for any vector $\vec{u} \in \mathbf{R}^2$, the map $D_{\vec{u}}F: \mathcal{P} \to \vec{\mathcal{E}}$, defined by the directional derivative of F in the fixed direction $\vec{u}$, is a polynomial surface of degree $m - 1$, called a *derived surface* of F. Given two triangular surfaces $F: \mathcal{P} \to \mathcal{E}$ and $G: \mathcal{P} \to \mathcal{E}$, the following lemmas show that if F and G join with C^n-continuity along a line L and if $\vec{u}$ is parallel to L, then $D_{\vec{u}}F$ and $D_{\vec{u}}G$ also join with C^n-continuity along L.

Lemma 9.2.2

Given two triangular surfaces $F: \mathcal{P} \to \mathcal{E}$ and $G: \mathcal{P} \to \mathcal{E}$, if F and G meet with C^0-continuity along a line L, and if $\vec{u} \in \mathbf{R}^2$ is parallel to L, then $D_{\vec{u}}F$ and $D_{\vec{u}}G$ also meet with C^0-continuity along L.

Proof: If $a \in L$, we can compute $D_{\vec{u}} F(a)$ by evaluating F at a and at points near a on L, and since F and G agree on L, we will get the same value for $D_{\vec{u}} F(a)$ and $D_{\vec{u}} G(a)$. ∎

Lemma 9.2.3

Given two triangular surfaces $F: \mathcal{P} \to \mathcal{E}$ and $G: \mathcal{P} \to \mathcal{E}$, if F and G meet with C^n-continuity along a line L, and if $\vec{u}$ is parallel to L, then $D_{\vec{u}} F$ and $D_{\vec{u}} G$ also meet with C^n-continuity along L.

Proof: Let $\vec{u_1}, \ldots, \vec{u_n}$ be any vectors in $\mathbf{R}^2$. If F and G meet with C^n-continuity along L, then it is clear that the derived surfaces $D_{\vec{u_1}} \ldots D_{\vec{u_n}} F$ and $D_{\vec{u_1}} \ldots D_{\vec{u_n}} G$ meet with C^0-continuity along L. Taking the derivative in the direction $\vec{u}$, by Lemma 9.2.3, the derived surfaces $D_{\vec{u}} D_{\vec{u_1}} \ldots D_{\vec{u_n}} F$ and $D_{\vec{u}} D_{\vec{u_1}} \ldots D_{\vec{u_n}} G$ also meet with C^0-continuity. Since the various directional derivatives commute, $D_{\vec{u_1}} \ldots D_{\vec{u_n}} D_{\vec{u}} F$ and $D_{\vec{u_1}} \ldots D_{\vec{u_n}} D_{\vec{u}} G$ meet with C^0-continuity, which means that $D_{\vec{u}} F$ and $D_{\vec{u}} G$ also meet with C^n-continuity along L. ∎

We can now derive necessary conditions on surfaces F and G of degree $3n + 1$ to join with C^{2n}-continuity. Consider three vectors $\vec{\alpha}$, $\vec{\beta}$, $\vec{\gamma}$, parallel to the three directions of the edges of triangles in the triangular grid, and such that

$$\vec{\alpha} + \vec{\beta} + \vec{\gamma} = \vec{0},$$

as shown in Figure 9.6.

We have the following lemma.

Lemma 9.2.4

Given a spline surface $F: \mathcal{P} \to \mathcal{E}$ of degree $3n + 1$ having C^{2n}-continuity, for any three vectors $\vec{\alpha}$, $\vec{\beta}$, $\vec{\gamma}$, parallel to the three directions of the edges of triangles in the triangular grid, and such that $\vec{\alpha} + \vec{\beta} + \vec{\gamma} = \vec{0}$, for every triangle A, the derived surface $D_{\vec{\alpha}}^{n+1} D_{\vec{\beta}}^{n+1} F_A$ is the same in any stripe in the direction $\vec{\gamma}$, the derived surface $D_{\vec{\beta}}^{n+1} D_{\vec{\gamma}}^{n+1} F_A$ is the same in any stripe in the direction $\vec{\alpha}$, and the derived surface $D_{\vec{\alpha}}^{n+1} D_{\vec{\gamma}}^{n+1} F_A$ is the same in any stripe in the direction $\vec{\beta}$.

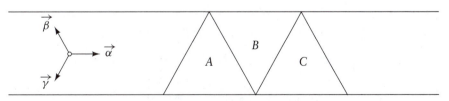

FIG. 9.6 A stripe in the parameter plane for triangular patches

Proof: If $F_A \colon \mathcal{P} \to \mathcal{E}$ and $F_B \colon \mathcal{P} \to \mathcal{E}$ are any two adjacent triangular patches, since F_A and F_B meet with C^{2n}-continuity and have degree $3n + 1$, the derived surfaces $D_{\vec{\gamma}}^{n+1} F_A$ and $D_{\vec{\gamma}}^{n+1} F_B$ have degree $2n$ and meet with continuity C^{n-1}. The derived surfaces $D_{\vec{\beta}}^{n+1} D_{\vec{\gamma}}^{n+1} F_A$ and $D_{\vec{\beta}}^{n+1} D_{\vec{\gamma}}^{n+1} F_B$ have degree $n - 1$, and by applying Lemma 9.2.3 $n + 1$ times, they join with C^{n-1}-continuity along their common boundary in the direction $\vec{\beta}$. But then, they must be identical. The same argument applies to F_B and F_C, with the roles of $\vec{\gamma}$ and $\vec{\beta}$ reversed, and thus, $D_{\vec{\beta}}^{n+1} D_{\vec{\gamma}}^{n+1} F_B$ and $D_{\vec{\beta}}^{n+1} D_{\vec{\gamma}}^{n+1} F_C$ are identical. Thus, the derived surface $D_{\vec{\beta}}^{n+1} D_{\vec{\gamma}}^{n+1} F_A$ has a constant value in any horizontal stripe. A similar argument applies to the stripes in the other two directions, which proves the lemma. ∎

From Lemma 9.2.4, in order to find spline surfaces of degree $3n + 1$ with C^{2n}-continuity, it is natural to attempt to satisfy the conditions

$$D_{\vec{\alpha}}^{n+1} D_{\vec{\beta}}^{n+1} F_A = D_{\vec{\beta}}^{n+1} D_{\vec{\gamma}}^{n+1} F_A = D_{\vec{\alpha}}^{n+1} D_{\vec{\gamma}}^{n+1} F_A = \vec{0},$$

for all triangles A. Each derived surface patch has degree $n - 1$, and thus, setting it to zero corresponds to $(n + 1)n/2$ conditions. If we can show that for $\vec{\alpha}, \vec{\beta}, \vec{\gamma}$, these conditions are independent, we have a total of $3(n + 1)n/2$ conditions. A surface of degree $3n + 1$ is determined by $(3n + 3)(3n + 2)/2$ control points. Subtracting the $3(n + 1)n/2$ conditions, we see that each patch F_A is specified by $3(n + 1)^2$ control points.

We can show that these conditions are indeed independent using tensors. Indeed, if $f_A \colon \mathcal{P}^m \to \mathcal{E}$ is the polar form of $F_A \colon \mathcal{P} \to \mathcal{E}$, and $\widehat{f_A} \colon (\widehat{\mathcal{P}})^m \to \widehat{\mathcal{E}}$ is the homogenized version of f_A, then as we will see from Lemma 10.5.3,

$$D_{\vec{u_1}} \ldots D_{\vec{u_k}} F_A(a) = m^{\underline{k}} \, \widehat{f_A}(\underbrace{a, \ldots, a}_{m-k}, \vec{u_1}, \ldots, \vec{u_k}).$$

If $\widehat{f_A}_{\odot} \colon (\widehat{\mathcal{P}})^{\odot m} \to \widehat{\mathcal{E}}$ is the linear map from the tensor power $(\widehat{\mathcal{P}})^{\odot m}$ to $\widehat{\mathcal{E}}$ associated with the symmetric multilinear map $\widehat{f_A}$, since $(\widehat{\mathcal{P}})^{\odot(n-1)}$ is spanned by the simple $(n-1)$-tensors of the form a^{n-1}, where $a \in \mathcal{P}$ (see Section 11.1), saying that $D_{\vec{\alpha}}^{n+1} D_{\vec{\beta}}^{n+1} F_A = \vec{0}$ is equivalent to saying that

$$\widehat{f_A}_{\odot}(\vec{\alpha}^{n+1} \odot \vec{\beta}^{n+1} \odot \eta) = \vec{0},$$

where $\eta \in (\widehat{\mathcal{P}})^{\odot(n-1)}$. Thus, the conditions

$$D_{\vec{\alpha}}^{n+1} D_{\vec{\beta}}^{n+1} F_A = D_{\vec{\beta}}^{n+1} D_{\vec{\gamma}}^{n+1} F_A = D_{\vec{\alpha}}^{n+1} D_{\vec{\gamma}}^{n+1} F_A = \vec{0}$$

correspond to three subspaces of $(\widehat{\mathcal{P}})^{\odot(3n+1)}$,

$$\{\vec{\alpha}^{n+1} \odot \vec{\beta}^{n+1} \odot \eta \mid \eta \in (\widehat{\mathcal{P}})^{\odot(n-1)}\},$$

$$\{\vec{\alpha}^{n+1} \odot \vec{\gamma}^{n+1} \odot \eta \mid \eta \in (\widehat{\mathcal{P}})^{\odot(n-1)}\},$$

$$\{\vec{\beta}^{n+1} \odot \vec{\gamma}^{n+1} \odot \eta \mid \eta \in (\widehat{\mathcal{P}})^{\odot(n-1)}\}.$$

However, reasoning on dimensions, it is easy to see that these subspaces are pairwise disjoint, and the conditions are indeed independent. For example, if the three subspaces above had a nontrivial intersection, they would contain a tensor of the form $\vec{\alpha}^{n+1} \odot \vec{\beta}^{n+1} \odot \vec{\gamma}^{n+1} \odot \delta$, which is impossible since such a tensor has order at least $3n + 3$.

It can be shown that if we consider surface splines of degree $3n + 3$ with C^{2n+1}-continuity, then for every triangle A, the derived surface $D_{\vec{\alpha}}^{n+2} D_{\vec{\beta}}^n F_A$ is the same in any stripe in the direction $\vec{\gamma}$, the derived surface $D_{\vec{\beta}}^{n+2} D_{\vec{\gamma}}^n F_A$ is the same in any stripe in the direction $\vec{\alpha}$, and the derived surface $D_{\vec{\alpha}}^{n+2} D_{\vec{\gamma}}^n F_A$ is the same in any stripe in the direction $\vec{\beta}$. As a consequence, it is easy to show that each patch is defined by $3(n + 1)^2 - 2$ control points.

In summary, we were led to consider surface splines of degree $3n + 1$ with C^{2n}-continuity, satisfying the independent conditions

$$D_{\vec{\alpha}}^{n+1} D_{\vec{\beta}}^{n+1} F_A = D_{\vec{\beta}}^{n+1} D_{\vec{\gamma}}^{n+1} F_A = D_{\vec{\alpha}}^{n+1} D_{\vec{\gamma}}^{n+1} F_A = \vec{0}.$$

Each patch is then defined by $3(n + 1)^2$ control points. We can also consider surface splines of degree $3n + 3$ with C^{2n+1}-continuity, satisfying the independent conditions

$$D_{\vec{\alpha}}^{n+2} D_{\vec{\beta}}^n F_A = D_{\vec{\beta}}^{n+2} D_{\vec{\gamma}}^n F_A = D_{\vec{\alpha}}^{n+2} D_{\vec{\gamma}}^n F_A = \vec{0}.$$

Each patch is then defined by $3(n + 1)^2 - 2$ control points.

Such spline surfaces do exist, and their existence can be shown using convolutions. Unfortunately, to the best of our knowledge, no nice scheme involving de Boor control points is known for such triangular spline surfaces. This is one of the outstanding open problems for spline surfaces, as discussed very lucidly by Ramshaw [65]. Some interesting related work on joining triangular patches with geometric continuity (G^1-continuity) can be found in Loop [51].

Next we will see that we have better luck with rectangular spline surfaces.

9.3   Spline Surfaces with Rectangular Patches

We now study what happens with the continuity conditions between surface patches if the parameter plane is divided into rectangles. For simplicity, we will consider surface patches of degree m joining with the *same* degree of continuity n for all common edges. First, we will prove that if $m \leq 2n + 1$, then it is generally impossible

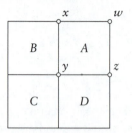

Constraints on rectangular patches

to construct a spline surface. More precisely, given any four adjacent patches as shown in Figure 9.7, if f_B and f_D are known, then f_A is completely determined.

As opposed to the triangular case, the proof is fairly simple.

Lemma 9.3.1

Surface splines consisting of rectangular patches of degree $m \geq 1$ joining with C^n-continuity cannot be locally flexible if $m \leq 2n + 1$. This means that given any three adjacent patches A, B, D as in Figure 9.7, if f_B and f_D are known, then f_A is completely determined. Furthermore, when $m = 2n + 2$, there is at most one free control point for every two internal adjacent patches.

Proof: Take Δxyz as the reference triangle. Since A and B meet with C^n-continuity along (x, y), by Lemma 9.1.2,

$$f_A(x^i y^{m-i-j} z^j) = f_B(x^i y^{m-i-j} z^j),$$

for all $j \leq n$. Similarly, since A and D join with C^n-continuity along (y, z), we have

$$f_A(x^i y^{m-i-j} z^j) = f_D(x^i y^{m-i-j} z^j),$$

for all $i \leq n$. However, $i + j \leq m \leq 2n + 1$, and so either $i \leq n$ or $j \leq n$, which shows that $f_A(x^i y^{m-i-j} z^j)$ is completely determined. When $m = 2n + 2$, the only control point that is not determined is $f_A(x^{n+1} z^{n+1})$. ∎

Thus, in order to have rectangular spline surfaces with C^n-continuity, we must have $m \geq 2n + 2$. We shall consider the case of rectangular spline surfaces of degree $2n$ meeting with C^{n-1}-continuity. We can prove using convolutions (see Ramshaw [65]) that such spline surfaces exist, but the construction is not practical. Instead, as in the case of triangular spline surfaces, we will look for necessary conditions in terms of derived surfaces. This time, we will be successful in finding a nice class of spline surfaces specifiable in terms of de Boor control points. The following lemma is the key result.

Lemma 9.3.2

Given two triangular surfaces $F: \mathcal{P} \to \mathcal{E}$ and $G: \mathcal{P} \to \mathcal{E}$ of degree $2n$, if F and G meet with C^{n-1}-continuity along a line L, and if $\vec{u}$ is parallel to L, then $D_{\vec{u}}^{n+1} F = D_{\vec{u}}^{n+1} G$.

Proof: Applying Lemma 9.2.3 $n + 1$ times, we deduce that $D_{\vec{u}}^{n+1} F$ and $D_{\vec{u}}^{n+1} G$ meet with C^{n-1}-continuity along L. But these surfaces have degree at most $n - 1$, so they must be identical. ∎

We can now derive necessary conditions on surfaces F and G of degree $2n$ to join with C^{n-1} continuity.

Lemma 9.3.3

Given a spline surface $F: \mathcal{P} \to \mathcal{E}$ of degree $2n$ having C^{n-1}-continuity, for any horizontal vector $\vec{\alpha}$, and any vertical vector $\vec{\beta}$, for every triangle A, the derived surface $D_{\vec{\alpha}}^{n+1} F_A$ is the same in any stripe in the direction $\vec{\alpha}$, and the derived surface $D_{\vec{\beta}}^{n+1} F_A$ is the same in any stripe in the direction $\vec{\beta}$.

Proof: An immediate consequence of Lemma 9.3.2. ∎

In view of Lemma 9.3.3, it makes sense to look for rectangular spline surfaces of degree $2n$ with continuity C^{n-1} satisfying the constraints

$$D_{\vec{\alpha}}^{n+1} F_A = D_{\vec{\beta}}^{n+1} F_A = \vec{0}$$

for all rectangles A. Since $D_{\vec{\alpha}}^{n+1} F_A$ has degree $n - 1$, setting it to zero corresponds to $(n + 1)n/2$ constraints, and thus, we have a total of $(n + 1)n$ constraints. A surface of degree $2n$ is specified by $(2n + 2)(2n + 1)/2$ control points, and subtracting the $(n + 1)n$ constraints, we find that each rectangular patch is determined by $(n + 1)^2$ control points. However, note that a surface of degree $2n$ such that

$$D_{\vec{\alpha}}^{n+1} F_A = D_{\vec{\beta}}^{n+1} F_A = \vec{0}$$

is equivalent to a bipolynomial surface of bidegree $\langle n, n \rangle$.

Thus, in the present case of rectangular spline surfaces, we discover that bipolynomial spline surfaces of bidegree $\langle n, n \rangle$ are an answer to our quest. Furthermore, since each rectangle is the product of two intervals, we can easily adapt what we have done for spline curves to bipolynomial spline surfaces. In fact, we can do this for bipolynomial spline surfaces of bidegree $\langle p, q \rangle$. Given a knot sequence $(\bar{s}_i)$ along the u-direction, and a knot sequence $(\bar{t}_j)$ along the v-direction, we have de Boor control points of the form

$$x_{i,j} = f(\bar{s}_{i+1}, \ldots, \bar{s}_{i+p}; \bar{t}_{j+1}, \ldots, \bar{t}_{j+q}).$$

The patches of the spline surface have domain rectangles of the form

$$R_{k,l} = [\bar{s}_k, \bar{s}_{k+1}] \times [\bar{t}_l, \bar{t}_{l+1}],$$

where $\bar{s}_k < \bar{s}_{k+1}$ and $\bar{t}_l < \bar{t}_{l+1}$. The patch defined on the rectangle $R_{k,l}$ has the $(p+1)(q+1)$ de Boor control points $x_{i,j}$, where $k - p \le i \le k$ and $l - q \le i \le l$. Two patches adjacent in the u-direction meet with C^{p-r}-continuity, where r is the multiplicity of the knot $\bar{s}_i$ that divides them, and two patches adjacent in the v-direction meet with C^{q-r}-continuity, where r is the multiplicity of the knot $\bar{t}_j$ that divides them. The progressive version of the de Casteljau algorithm can be generalized quite easily. Since the study of bipolynomial spline surfaces of bidegree $\langle p, q \rangle$ basically reduces to the study of spline curves, we will not elaborate any further and leave this topic as an interesting project.

In summary, contrary to the case of triangular spline surfaces, in the case of rectangular spline surfaces, we were able to generalize the treatment of spline curves in terms of knot sequences and de Boor control points to bipolynomial spline surfaces. You should have no trouble filling in the details. The challenge of finding such a scheme for triangular spline surfaces remains open.

9.4   Subdivision Surfaces

An alternative to spline surfaces is provided by subdivision surfaces. The idea is to start with a rough polyhedron specified by a mesh (a collection of points and edges connected so that it defines the boundary of a polyhedron), and to apply recursively a subdivision scheme, which, in the limit, yields a smooth surface (or solid). One of the major advantages of such a scheme is that it applies to surfaces of arbitrary topology, and that it is not restricted to a rectangular mesh (i.e., a mesh based on a rectangular grid). Furthermore, except for a finite number of so-called extraordinary points, a "good" subdivision scheme produces large portions of spline surfaces.

The idea of defining a curve or a surface via a limit process involving subdivision goes back to Chaikin, who (in 1974) defined a simple subdivision scheme applying to curves defined by a closed control polygon [18]. Soon after that, Riesenfeld [67] realized that Chaikin's scheme was simply the de Boor subdivision method for quadratic uniform B-splines, that is, the process of recursively inserting a knot at the midpoint of every interval in a cyclic knot sequence. In 1978, two subdivision schemes for surfaces were proposed by Doo and Sabin [27, 29, 28] and by Catmull and Clark [17]. The main difference between the two schemes is the following. After one round of subdivision, the Doo-Sabin scheme produces a mesh whose vertices all have the same degree 4, and most faces are rectangular, except for faces arising from original vertices of degree not equal to 4 and from nonrectangular faces. After one round of subdivision, the number of nonrectangular faces remains constant, and it turns out that these faces shrink and tend to a limit that is their common centroid. The centroid of each nonrectangular face is referred to as an *extraordinary point*. Furthermore, large regions of the mesh define biquadratic B-splines. The limit surface is C^1-continuous except at extraordinary points. On the other hand, after one round of subdivision, the Catmull-Clark scheme produces rectangular faces, and most vertices have degree 4, except for vertices arising from original nonrectangular faces and from vertices of degree not equal to 4, also referred to as extraordinary points. The limit surface is C^2-continuous except at extraordinary points. Large regions of the mesh define bicubic B-splines. Although both schemes can be viewed as cutting off corners, not unlike a sculptor at work, the Catmull-Clark scheme is closer to a process of face shrinking.

Several years later, Charles Loop in his master's thesis (1987) introduced a subdivision scheme based on a mesh consisting strictly of triangular faces [50]. In Loop's scheme, every triangular face is refined into four subtriangles. Most vertices have degree 6, except for original vertices whose degree is not equal to 6, referred to as extraordinary points. Large regions of the mesh define triangular splines based on hexagons consisting of 24 small triangles each of degree 4 (each edge of such a hexagon consists of two edges of a small triangle). The limit surface is C^2-continuous except at extraordinary points.

Although such subdivision schemes had been around for some time, it was not until roughly 1994 that subdivision surfaces became widely used in computer graphics and geometric modeling applications. However, in 1998, subdivision hit the big screen with Pixar's *Geri's Game*.

Since 1994, refinements of previous subdivision schemes and new subdivision schemes have been proposed. Due to the lack of space, we will restrict ourselves to a brief description of the Doo-Sabin method, Catmull-Clark method, and Loop method (for more details, see the *Proceedings of SIGGRAPH '98 and Course Notes on Subdivision for Modeling and Animation*).

The Doo-Sabin scheme is described very clearly in Nasri [56], who also proposed a method for improving the design of boundary curves, a nontrivial problem. During every round of the subdivision process, new vertices and new faces are created as follows. Every vertex v of the current mesh yields a new vertex v_F called *image of v in F*, for every face F having v as a vertex. Then, image vertices are connected to form three kinds of new faces: F-faces, E-faces, and V-faces.

An F-face is a smaller version of a face F, and it is obtained by connecting the image vertices of the boundary vertices of F in F. Note that if F is an n-sided face, so is the new F-face. This process is illustrated in Figure 9.8.

A new E-face is created as follows. For every edge E common to two faces F_1 and F_2, the four image vertices v_{F_1}, v_{F_2} of the end vertex v of E, and w_{F_1}, w_{F_2} of the other end vertex w of E, are connected to form a rectangular face, as illustrated in Figure 9.9.

A new V-face is obtained by connecting the image vertices v_F of a given vertex v in all the faces adjacent to v, provided that v has degree $n \geq 3$. If v has degree n, the new V-face is also n-sided. This process is illustrated in Figure 9.10.

The scheme just described applies to surfaces without boundaries. Special rules are needed to handle boundary edges, that is, vertices of degree $n \leq 2$. One way to handle boundaries is to treat them as quadratic B-splines. For every boundary vertex v, if v_F is the image of v in the face F containing v, create the new vertex

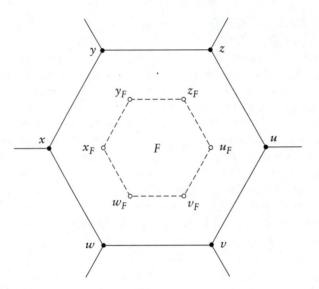

FIG. 9.8 Vertices of a new F-face

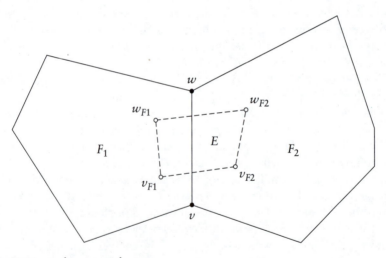

FIG. 9.9 Vertices of a new E-face

$$v' = \frac{1}{4} v_F + \frac{3}{4} v.$$

Another method was proposed by Nasri [56].

Various rules are used to determine the image vertex v_F of a vertex v in some face F. A simple scheme used by Doo is to compute the centroid c of the face F, and the image v_F of v in F as the midpoint of c and v (if F has n sides, the centroid of F is the barycenter of the weighted points $(v, 1/n)$, where the vs are the vertices of F).

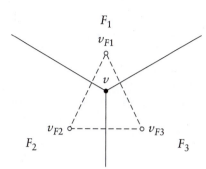

FIG. 9.10 Vertices of a new V-face

Another rule is

$$v_i = \sum_{j=1}^{n} \alpha_{ij} w_j,$$

where the w_j are the vertices of the face F, and v_i is the image of w_i in F, with

$$\alpha_{ij} = \begin{cases} \frac{n+5}{4n} & \text{if } i = j, \\ \frac{3+2\cos(2\pi(i-j)/n)}{4n} & \text{if } i \neq j, \end{cases}$$

where $1 \leq i, j \leq n$, and $n \geq 3$ is the number of boundary edges of F.

Note that the above weights add up to 1, since

$$\sum_{k=1}^{n} \cos(2\pi k/n) = 0,$$

because it is the real part of the sum of the nth roots of unity, and thus, for every i, $1 \leq i \leq n$,

$$\sum_{j \neq i} \cos(2\pi(i - j)/n) = -1.$$

Observe that after one round of subdivision, all vertices have degree 4, and the number of nonrectangular faces remains constant. It is also easy to check that these faces shrink and tend to a limit that is their common centroid. However, it is not obvious that such subdivision schemes converge, and what kind of smoothness is obtained at extraordinary points. These matters were investigated by Doo and Sabin [28] and by Peters and Reif [60]. Roughly, the idea is to analyze the iteration of subdivision around extraordinary points. This can be achieved by eigenvalue analysis, or better, using discrete Fourier transforms. The Doo-Sabin method has been generalized to accommodate features such as creases, darts, or cusps by Sederberg et al. [74].

Such features are desirable in human modeling, for example, to model clothes or human skin. The subdivision rules are modified to allow for nonuniform knot spacing, called "NURSS" by the authors.

We now turn to a description of the Catmull-Clark scheme. Unlike the previous one, this method consists in subdividing every face into smaller rectangular faces obtained by connecting new face points, edge points, and vertex points.

Given a face F with vertices $v_1, \ldots, v_n$, the new face point v_F is computed as the centroid of the v_i, that is,

$$v_F = \sum_{i=1}^{n} \frac{1}{n} v_i.$$

Given an edge E with end points v and w, if F_1 and F_2 are the two faces sharing E as a common edge, the new edge point v_E is the average of the four points v, w, v_{F_1}, v_{F_2}, where v_{F_1} and v_{F_2} are the centroids of F_1 and F_2, that is,

$$v_E = \frac{v + w + v_{F_1} + v_{F_2}}{4}.$$

The computation of new vertex points is slightly more involved. In fact, there are several different versions. The version presented in Catmull and Clark [17] is as follows. Given a vertex v (an old one), if $\mathcal{F}$ denotes the average of the new face points of all (old) faces adjacent to v and $\mathcal{E}$ denotes the average of the midpoints of all (old) n edges incident with v, the new vertex point v' associated with v is

$$v' = \frac{1}{n} \mathcal{F} + \frac{2}{n} \mathcal{E} + \frac{n-3}{n} v.$$

New faces are then determined by connecting the new points as follows: each new face point v_F is connected by an edge to the new edge points v_E associated with the boundary edges E of the face F; each new vertex point v' is connected by an edge to the new edge points v_E associated with all the edges E incident with v.

Note that only rectangular faces are created. Figure 9.11 shows this process. New face points are denoted as solid square points, new edge points are denoted as hollow round points, and new vertex points are denoted as hollow square points.

An older version of the rule for vertex points is

$$v' = \frac{1}{4} \mathcal{F} + \frac{1}{2} \mathcal{E} + \frac{1}{4} v,$$

but it was observed that the resulting surfaces could be too "pointy" (for example, starting from a tetrahedron). Another version studied by Doo and Sabin is

$$v' = \frac{1}{n} \mathcal{F} + \frac{1}{n} \mathcal{E} + \frac{n-2}{n} v.$$

Doo and Sabin analyzed the tangent-plane continuity of this scheme using discrete Fourier transforms [28]. Observe that after one round of subdivision, all faces

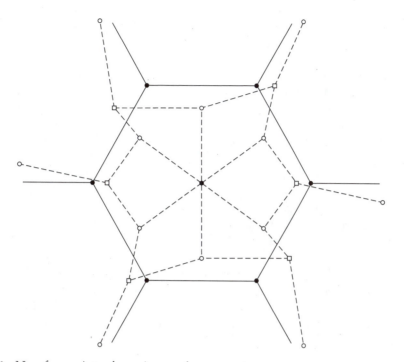

FIG. 9.11 New face point, edge points, and vertex points

are rectangular, and the number of extraordinary points (vertices of degree different from 4) remains constant. The tangent-plane continuity of various versions of
Catmull-Clark schemes are also investigated in Ball and Storry [3] (using discrete
Fourier transforms), and C^1-continuity is investigated by Peters and Reif [60]. A
more general study of the convergence of subdivision methods can be found in Zorin
[89] (see also Zorin, Schroder, and Swelders [88]).

We have only presented the Catmull-Clark scheme for surfaces without boundaries. It is also possible to accommodate boundary vertices and edges. Boundaries
can be easily handled by treating the boundary curves as cubic B-splines, and using
rules for knot insertion at midpoints of intervals in a closed knot sequence. Then
for any three consecutive control points p_i^l, p_{i+1}^l, and p_{i+2}^l of a boundary curve, two
new control points p_{2i+1}^{l+1} and p_{2i+2}^{l+1} are created according to the formulae

$$p_{2i+1}^{l+1} = \frac{1}{2}\, p_i^l + \frac{1}{2}\, p_{i+1}^l,$$

and

$$p_{2i+2}^{l+1} = \frac{1}{8}\, p_i^l + \frac{6}{8}\, p_{i+1}^l, + \frac{1}{8}\, p_{i+2}^l.$$

DeRose, Kass, and Truong [24] have generalized the Catmull-Clark subdivision rules to accommodate sharp edges and creases. Their work is inspired by the previous work of Hoppe et al. [44], in which the Loop scheme was extended to allow (infinitely) sharp creases, except that DeRose, Kass, and Truong's method applies to Catmull-Clark surfaces. The method of DeRose, Kass, and Truong [24] also allows semisharp creases in addition to (infinitely) sharp creases. This new scheme was used in modeling the character Geri in the short film *Geri's Game*. A common criticism of subdivision surfaces is that they do not provide immediate access to the points on the limit surface, as opposed to parametric models that obviously do. However, it was shown by Stam [78] that it is in fact possible to evaluate points on Catmull-Clark subdivision surfaces. One of the techniques involved is called *eigenbasis functions*, which were also studied by Zorin [89].

Before presenting Loop's scheme, let us mention that a particularly simple subdivision method termed "midedge subdivison" was discovered by Peters and Reif [61].

Unlike the previous methods, Loop's method only applies to meshes whose faces are all triangles. Loop's method consists in splitting each (triangular) face into four triangular faces, using rules to determine new edge points and new vertex points. For every edge (rs), since exactly two triangles Δprs and Δqrs share the edge (rs), we compute the new edge point η_{rs} as the following convex combination:

$$\eta_{rs} = \frac{1}{8}\, p + \frac{3}{8}\, r + \frac{3}{8}\, s + \frac{1}{8}\, q,$$

as illustrated in Figure 9.12. This corresponds to computing the affine combination of three points assigned, respectively, the weights $\frac{3}{8}, \frac{3}{8}$, and $\frac{2}{8}$: the centroids of the two triangles Δprs and Δqrs, and the midpoint of the edge (rs).

For any vertex v of degree n, if $p_0, \ldots, p_{n-1}$ are the other end points of all (old) edges incident with v, the new vertex point v' associated with v is

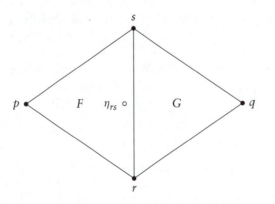

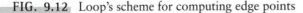

FIG. 9.12 Loop's scheme for computing edge points

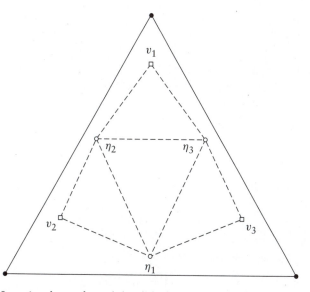

Loop's scheme for subdividing faces

$$v' = (1 - \alpha_n) \left(\sum_{i=0}^{n-1} \frac{1}{n} \, p_i \right) + \alpha_n v,$$

where α_n is a coefficient dependent on n. Loop's method is illustrated in Figure 9.13, where hollow round points denote new edge points, and hollow square points denote new vertex points.

Observe that after one round of subdivision, all vertices have degree 6, except for vertices coming from original vertices of degree different from 6, but such vertices are surrounded by ordinary vertices of degree 6. Vertices of degree different from 6 are called extraordinary points. Loop determined that the value $\alpha_n = \frac{5}{8}$ produces good results [50], but in some cases, tangent-plane continuity is lost at extraordinary points. Large regions of the mesh define triangular splines based on hexagons consisting of small triangles each of degree 4 (each edge of such a hexagon consists of two edges of a small triangle). Thus, ordinary points have a well-defined limit that can be computed by subdividing the quartic triangular patches. The limit surface is C^2-continuous except at extraordinary points.

Loop's method was first formulated for surfaces without boundaries. Boundaries can be easily handled by treating the boundary curves as cubic B-splines, as in the Catmull-Clark scheme.

In his master's thesis [50], Loop rigorously investigates the convergence and smoothness properties of his scheme. He proves convergence of extraordinary points to a limit. He also figures out in which interval α_n should belong, in order to ensure convergence and better smoothness at extraordinary points. Since the principles of Loop's analysis are seminal and yet quite simple, we will present its main lines.

As we already remarked, after one round of subdivision, extraordinary points are surrounded by ordinary points, which makes the analysis of convergence possible. Since points are created during every iteration of the subdivision process, it is convenient to label points with the index of the subdivision round during which they are created. Then, the rule for creating a new vertex point v^l associated with a vertex v^{l-1} can be written as

$$v^l = (1 - \alpha_n)q^{l-1} + \alpha_n v^{l-1},$$

where

$$q^{l-1} = \sum_{i=0}^{n-1} \frac{1}{n} p_i^{l-1}$$

is the centroid of the points $p_0^{l-1}, \ldots, p_{n-1}^{l-1}$, the other end points of all edges incident with v^{l-1}. Loop proves that as l tends to ∞,

1. every extraordinary vertex v^l tends to the same limit as q^l;

2. the ordinary vertices $p_0^l, \ldots, p_{n-1}^l$ surrounding v^l also tend to the same limit as q^l.

Since q^l is the centroid of ordinary points, this proves the convergence for extraordinary points. Keep in mind that the lower indices of the p_i^l are taken modulo n.

Proving that $\lim_{l \to \infty} v^l = \lim_{l \to \infty} q^l$ is fairly easy. Using the fact that

$$p_i^l = \frac{1}{8} p_{i-1}^{l-1} + \frac{3}{8} p_i^{l-1} + \frac{3}{8} v^{l-1} + \frac{1}{8} p_{i+1}^{l-1}$$

and some calculations, it is easy to show that

$$q^l = \sum_{i=0}^{n-1} \frac{1}{n} p_i^l = \frac{3}{8} v^{l-1} + \frac{5}{8} q^{l-1}.$$

From this, we have

$$v^l - q^l = (1 - \alpha_n)q^{l-1} + \alpha_n v^{l-1} - \frac{3}{8} v^{l-1} - \frac{5}{8} q^{l-1} = \left(\alpha_n - \frac{3}{8}\right)(v^{l-1} - q^{l-1}).$$

By a trivial induction, we get

$$v^l - q^l = \left(\alpha_n - \frac{3}{8}\right)^l (v^0 - q^0).$$

Thus, if $-1 < \alpha_n - \frac{3}{8} < 1$, that is,

$$-\frac{5}{8} < \alpha_n < \frac{11}{5},$$

we get convergence of v^l to q^l. The value $\alpha_n = \frac{5}{8}$ is certainly acceptable.

Proving (2) is a little more involved. Loop makes a clever use of discrete Fourier transforms. Let us quickly review some basic facts about discrete Fourier series (see Strang [80, 82] for a more comprehensive treatment).

Discrete Fourier series deal with finite sequences $c \in \mathbf{C}^n$ of complex numbers. It is convenient to view a finite sequence $c \in \mathbf{C}^n$ as a periodic sequence over $\mathbf{Z}$, by letting $c_k = c_h$ iff $k - h = 0 \bmod n$. It is also more convenient to index n-tuples starting from 0 instead of 1, thus writing $c = (c_0, \dots, c_{n-1})$. Every sequence $c = (c_0, \dots, c_{n-1}) \in \mathbf{C}^n$ of "Fourier coefficients" $c = (c_0, \dots, c_{n-1})$ determines a periodic function $f_c \colon \mathbf{R} \to \mathbf{C}$ (of period 2π) known as *discrete Fourier series,* or *phase polynomial,* defined such that

$$f_c(\theta) = c_0 + c_1 e^{i\theta} + \cdots + c_{n-1} e^{i(n-1)\theta} = \sum_{k=0}^{n-1} c_k e^{ik\theta}.$$

Then, given any sequence $f = (f_0, \dots, f_{n-1})$ of data points, it is desirable to find the "Fourier coefficients" $c = (c_0, \dots, c_{n-1})$ of the discrete Fourier series f_c such that

$$f_c(2\pi k/n) = f_k,$$

for every k, $0 \le k \le n - 1$.

The problem amounts to solving the linear system

$$F_n c = f,$$

where F_n is the symmetric $n \times n$ matrix (with complex coefficients)

$$F_n = \left(e^{i2\pi kl/n} \right)_{\substack{0 \le k \le n-1 \\ 0 \le l \le n-1}},$$

assuming that we index the entries in F_n over $[0, 1, \dots, n - 1] \times [0, 1, \dots, n - 1]$, the standard kth row now being indexed by $k - 1$ and the standard lth column now being indexed by $l - 1$. The matrix F_n is called a *Fourier matrix.* Letting

$$\overline{F_n} = \left(e^{-i2\pi kl/n} \right)_{\substack{0 \le k \le n-1 \\ 0 \le l \le n-1}}$$

be the conjugate of F_n, it is easily checked that

$$F_n \overline{F_n} = \overline{F_n} F_n = n\, I_n.$$

Thus, the Fourier matrix is invertible, and its inverse $F_n^{-1} = (1/n)\overline{F_n}$ is computed very cheaply.

The purpose of the *discrete Fourier transform* is to find the Fourier coefficients $c = (c_0, \dots, c_{n-1})$ from the data points $f = (f_0, \dots, f_{n-1})$. The discrete Fourier transform is a linear map $\widehat{} \colon \mathbf{C}^n \to \mathbf{C}^n$. Now, the other major player in Fourier analysis is the convolution. In the discrete case, it is natural to define the discrete convolution as a circular type of convolution rule. The *discrete convolution* is a map $\star \colon \mathbf{C}^n \times \mathbf{C}^n \to \mathbf{C}^n$, taking two sequences $c, d \in \mathbf{C}^n$, and forming the new sequence

$c \star d$. The Fourier transform and the convolution rule (discrete or not!) must be defined in such a way that they form a harmonious pair, which means that the transform of a convolution should be the product of the transforms, that is,

$$\widehat{c \star d} = \widehat{c}\,\widehat{d},$$

where the multiplication on the right-hand side is just the inner product of $\widehat{c}$ and $\widehat{d}$ (vectors of length n).

Inspired by the continuous case, and following Strang [82], it is natural to define the *discrete Fourier transform* $\widehat{f}$ of a sequence $f = (f_0, \ldots, f_{n-1}) \in \mathbf{C}^n$ as

$$\widehat{f} = \overline{F_n} f,$$

or equivalently, as

$$\widehat{f}(k) = \sum_{j=0}^{n-1} f_j e^{-i2\pi jk/n}$$

for every k, $0 \le k \le n-1$. We also define the *inverse discrete Fourier transform* (taking c back to f) as

$$\overline{\widehat{c}} = F_n\, c.$$

In view of the formula $F_n \overline{F_n} = \overline{F_n} F_n = n\, I_n$, the Fourier coefficients $c = (c_0, \ldots, c_{n-1})$ are then given by the formulae

$$c_k = \frac{1}{n}\, \widehat{f}(k) = \frac{1}{n} \sum_{j=0}^{n-1} f_j e^{-i2\pi jk/n}.$$

Note the analogy with the continuous case, where the Fourier transform $\widehat{f}$ of the function f is given by

$$\widehat{f}(x) = \int_{-\infty}^{\infty} f(t) e^{-ixt}\, dt,$$

and the Fourier coefficients of the Fourier series

$$f(x) = \sum_{k=-\infty}^{\infty} c_k e^{ikx}$$

are given by the formulae

$$c_k = \frac{1}{2\pi} \int_{-\pi}^{\pi} f(x) e^{-ikx}\, dx.$$

Remark: Others authors (including Strang in his older book [80]) define the discrete Fourier transform as

$$\widehat{f} = \frac{1}{n}\overline{F_n}f.$$

The drawback of this choice is that the convolution rule has an extra factor of n. Loop defines the discrete Fourier transform as $F_n f$, which causes problems with the convolution rule. We will come back to this point shortly.

The simplest definition of discrete convolution is, in our opinion, the definition in terms of *circulant matrices*. Again, for details, see Strang [80] and Strang and Truong [82]. The fascinating book on circulants, Fourier matrices, and more, by Davis [21], is highly recommended. We define the *circular shift matrix* S_n *(of order n)* as the matrix

$$S_n = \begin{pmatrix} 0 & 0 & 0 & 0 & \cdots & 0 & 1 \\ 1 & 0 & 0 & 0 & \cdots & 0 & 0 \\ 0 & 1 & 0 & 0 & \cdots & 0 & 0 \\ 0 & 0 & 1 & 0 & \cdots & 0 & 0 \\ \vdots & \vdots & \vdots & \vdots & \ddots & \vdots & \vdots \\ 0 & 0 & 0 & 0 & \cdots & 1 & 0 \end{pmatrix}$$

consisting of cyclic permutations of its first column. For any sequence $f = (f_0, \ldots, f_{n-1}) \in \mathbf{C}^n$, we define the *circulant matrix* $H(f)$ as

$$H(f) = \sum_{j=0}^{n-1} f_j S_n^j,$$

where $S_n^0 = I_n$, as usual. For example, the circulant matrix associated with the sequence $f = (a, b, c, d)$ is

$$\begin{pmatrix} a & d & c & b \\ b & a & d & c \\ c & b & a & d \\ d & c & b & a \end{pmatrix}$$

We can now define the *convolution* $f \star g$ of two sequences $f = (f_0, \ldots, f_{n-1})$ and $g = (g_0, \ldots, g_{n-1})$ as

$$f \star g = H(f)\, g,$$

viewing f and g as column vectors. Then, the miracle (which is not too hard to prove!) is that we have

$$H(f)F_n = F_n\widehat{f},$$

which means that the columns of the Fourier matrix F_n are the eigenvectors of the circulant matrix $H(f)$, and that the eigenvalue associated with the lth eigenvector is $(\widehat{f})_l$, the lth component of the Fourier transform $\widehat{f}$ of f (counting from 0). If we recall that $F_n \overline{F_n} = \overline{F_n} F_n = n\, I_n$, multiplying the equation $H(f)F_n = F_n \widehat{f}$ both on the left and on the right by $\overline{F_n}$, we get

$$\overline{F_n} H(f)(n\, I_n) = (n\, I_n) \widehat{f}\, \overline{F_n},$$

that is,

$$\overline{F_n} H(f) = \widehat{f}\, \overline{F_n}.$$

If we apply both sides to any sequence $g \in \mathbf{C}^n$, we get

$$\overline{F_n} H(f) g = \widehat{f}\, \overline{F_n} g,$$

which, since $\widehat{g} = \overline{F_n} g$, $f \star g = H(f)g$, and $\widehat{f \star g} = \overline{F_n}(f \star g)$, can be rewritten as the *(circular) convolution rule*

$$\widehat{f \star g} = \widehat{f}\, \widehat{g},$$

where the multiplication on the right-hand side is just the inner product of the vectors $\widehat{f}$ and $\widehat{g}$.

If the sequence $f = (f_0, \dots, f_{n-1})$ is even, which means that $f_{-j} = f_j$ for all $j \in \mathbf{Z}$ (viewed as a periodic sequence), or equivalently, that $f_{n-j} = f_j$ for all j, $0 \le j \le n-1$, it is easily seen that the Fourier transform $\widehat{f}$ can be expressed as

$$\widehat{f}(k) = \sum_{j=0}^{n-1} f_j \cos\left(2\pi jk/n\right),$$

for every k, $0 \le k \le n-1$. Similarly, the inverse Fourier transform (taking c back to f) is expressed as

$$\overline{\overline{c}}(k) = \sum_{j=0}^{n-1} c_j \cos\left(2\pi jk/n\right),$$

for every k, $0 \le k \le n-1$. Observe that it is the same as the (forward) discrete Fourier transform. This is what saves Loop's proof (see below)!

After this digression, we get back to Loop's master's thesis [50]. However, we should warn you that Loop defines the discrete Fourier transform as

$$\mathcal{F}(f) = F_n f,$$

(which is our inverse Fourier transform $\overline{\overline{f}}$) and not as $\overline{F_n} f$, which is our Fourier transform $\widehat{f}$ (following Strang and Truong [82]). Loop defines convolution using the formula

$$(f \star g)_k = \sum_{j=0}^{n-1} f_j g_{k-j},$$

for every j, $0 \leq j \leq n - 1$, which requires interpreting indexes modulo n, but is equivalent to the circulant definition. However, Loop states the convolution rule as

$$\mathcal{F}(f \star g) = \mathcal{F}(f)\mathcal{F}(g),$$

which is incorrect, since $\mathcal{F}$ uses the Fourier matrix F_n, when it should be using its conjugate $\overline{F_n}$.

Nevertheless, even though Loop appears to be using an incorrect definition of the Fourier transform, what saves his argument is that for even sequences, his $\mathcal{F}(f)$ and our $\widehat{f}$ are identical, as observed earlier. With these remarks in mind, we go back to Loop's proof that the ordinary vertices $p_0^l, \ldots, p_{n-1}^l$ surrounding v^l also tend to the same limit as q^l.

The trick is to rewrite the equations

$$q^l = \sum_{i=0}^{n-1} \frac{1}{n} \, p_i^l$$

and

$$p_i^l = \frac{1}{8} \, p_{i-1}^{l-1} + \frac{3}{8} \, p_i^{l-1} + \frac{3}{8} \, v^{l-1} + \frac{1}{8} \, p_{i+1}^{l-1}$$

in terms of discrete convolutions. To do so, define the sequences

$$M = \left(\frac{3}{8}, \frac{1}{8}, \underbrace{0, \ldots, 0}_{n-3}, \frac{1}{8} \right)$$

and

$$A = \left(\frac{1}{n}, \ldots, \frac{1}{n} \right),$$

both of length n. Note that these sequences are even! We also define the sequence P^l as

$$P^l = (p_0^l, \ldots, p_{n-1}^l),$$

and treat q^l and v^l as constant sequences Q^l and V^l of length n. Then, equation

$$p_i^l = \frac{1}{8} \, p_{i-1}^{l-1} + \frac{3}{8} \, p_i^{l-1} + \frac{3}{8} \, v^{l-1} + \frac{1}{8} \, p_{i+1}^{l-1}$$

is rewritten as

$$P^l = M \star P^{l-1} + \frac{3}{8} \, V^{l-1},$$

and equation

$$q^l = \sum_{i=0}^{n-1} \frac{1}{n}\, p_i^l$$

is rewritten as

$$Q^l = A \star P^l.$$

From these equations, we get

$$P^l = \left(M - \frac{5}{8} A\right) \star P^{l-1} + Q^l.$$

Taking advantage of certain special properties of M and A, namely,

$$\sum_{j=0}^{n-1} \left(M - \frac{5}{8} A\right)_j = 0,$$

we get

$$P^l = \left(M - \frac{5}{8} A\right)^{l\star} \star P^0 + Q^l,$$

where $c^{n\star}$ stands for the n-fold convolution $\underbrace{c \star \cdots \star c}_{n}$.

At this stage, letting

$$R = \left(M - \frac{5}{8} A\right),$$

all we have to prove is that $R^{l\star}$ tends to the null sequence as l goes to infinity. Since both M and A are even sequences, applying the Fourier transform in its cosine form and the convolution rule, we have

$$\widehat{R^{l\star}} = (\widehat{R})^l,$$

and so, we just have to compute the discrete Fourier transform of R. However, this is easy to do, and we get

$$(\widehat{R})_j = \begin{cases} 0 & \text{if } j = 0, \\ \frac{3}{8} + \frac{1}{4} \cos\left(2\pi j/n\right) & \text{if } j \neq 0. \end{cases}$$

Since the absolute value of the cosine is bounded by 1,

$$\frac{1}{8} \leq (\widehat{R})_j \leq \frac{5}{8}$$

for all j, $0 \leq j \leq n - 1$, and thus

$$\lim_{l \to \infty} (\widehat{R})^l = 0_n,$$

which proves that

$$\lim_{l \to \infty} \widehat{R^{l\star}} = \lim_{l \to \infty} R^{l\star} = 0_n,$$

and consequently that

$$\lim_{l \to \infty} p_i^l = \lim_{l \to \infty} q^l.$$

Therefore, the faces surrounding extraordinary points converge to the same limit as the centroid of these faces. Loop gives explicit formulae for the limit of extraordinary points. He proves that q^l (and thus v^l) has the limit

$$(1 - \beta_n)q^0 + \beta_n v^0,$$

where

$$\beta_n = \frac{3}{11 - 8\alpha_n}.$$

The bounds to ensure convergence are the same as the bounds to ensure convergence of v^l to q^l, namely,

$$-\frac{5}{8} < \alpha_n < \frac{11}{5}.$$

In particular, $\alpha_n = \frac{5}{8}$ yields $\beta_n = \frac{1}{2}$. Loop also investigates the tangent-plane continuity at these limit points. He proves that tangent-plane continuity is ensured if α_n is chosen so that

$$-\frac{1}{4} \cos (2\pi/n) < \alpha_n < \frac{3}{4} + \frac{1}{4} \cos (2\pi/n).$$

For instance, for a vertex of degree 3 ($n = 3$), the value $\alpha_3 = \frac{5}{8}$ is outside the correct range, as Loop first observed experimentally. If α_n is chosen in the correct range, it is possible to find a formula for the tangent vector function at each extraordinary point. Loop also discusses curvature continuity at extraordinary points, but his study is more tentative. He proposes the following "optimal" value for α_n:

$$\alpha_n = \frac{3}{8} + \left(\frac{3}{8} + \frac{1}{4} \cos (2\pi/n) \right)^2.$$

Note that $\alpha_6 = \frac{5}{8}$ is indeed this value for regular vertices (of degree $n = 6$).

In summary, Loop proves that his subdivision scheme is C^2-continuous, except at a finite number of extraordinary points. At extraordinary points, there is convergence, and there is a range of values from which α_n can be chosen to ensure tangent-plane continuity. The implementation of the method is discussed, and it is nontrivial. Stam [78] also implemented a method for computing points on Loop surfaces. Loop's scheme was extended to accommodate sharp edges and creases on boundaries (see Hoppe et al. [44]).

We conclude this section on subdivision surfaces with a few comments. First, general approaches to study the properties (convergence, smoothness) of subdivision surfaces have been investigated in Reif [66] and by Zorin [89]. The related issue of adaptive parameterization of surfaces is investigated in Lee et al. [49]. Their method makes use of Loop's scheme. There are many other papers on the subject of subdivision surfaces, and we apologize for not being more thorough, but we hope that we have at least given pointers to the most important research directions. Again, we advise our readers to consult the SIGGRAPH proceedings and course notes, especially after 1996.

Although subdivision surfaces have many attractive features, such as arbitrary topology of the mesh, uniformity of representation, numerical stability, and code simplicity, they have their problems too. For example, there are problems with curvature continuity at extraordinary points (the curvature can be zero). Extraordinary points of large degree may exhibit poor smoothness. The phenomenon of "eigenvalue clustering" can also cause ripples on the surface. Another phenomenon related to the eigenvalue distribution of the local subdivision matrix is the possible unevenness of the mesh, with certain triangles being significantly larger than others near extraordinary points.

Problems

[30 pts]   **1.** Show that the number of conditions required for two triangular patches of degree m to meet with C^1-continuity is $3m + 1$. Show that the number of independent conditions is generally $2m + 1$. Show that the number of conditions required for two triangular patches of degree m to meet with C^2-continuity is $6m - 2$. Show that the number of independent conditions is generally $3m$.

[20 pts]   **2.** Formulate a de Boor algorithm for rectangular B-spline surfaces.

[30 pts]   **3.** Formulate a knot insertion algorithm for rectangular B-spline surfaces. Use it to convert a B-spline surface into rectangular Bézier patches.

[30 pts]   **4.** Let $u_0, \ldots, u_M$ and $v_0, \ldots, u_N$ be two knot sequences consisting of simple knots, and let $(x_{i,j})_{0 \leq i \leq M, 0 \leq j \leq N}$ be a net of data points. We would like to find a rectangular bicubic C^1-continuous B-spline surface F interpolating the points $x_{i,j}$, that is, such that

$$F(u_i, v_j) = x_{i,j}.$$

(a) Using the method of Section 6.8, show that the control points on the boundary curves of each rectangular patch can be computed, accounting for 12 control points per patch.

(b) However, each patch requires 16 control points. Show that the other 4 interior control points can be found by computing the corner twists of each patch (twist vectors are defined in Section 7.6).

(c) Various methods exist to determine twist vectors. One method (*Bessel twist*) consists in estimating the twist at (u_i, v_j) to be the bilinear interpolant of the four bilinear patches determined by the nine points $x_{i+r, j+s}$, where $r = -1, 0, 1$ and $s = -1, 0, 1$. Compute the Bessel twists.

[40 pts]   5. Implement the interpolation method proposed in Problem 4. Experiment with various methods for determining corner twists.

[20 pts]   6. (a) If we consider surface splines of degree $3n + 3$ with C^{2n+1}-continuity, prove that for every triangle A, the derived surface $D_{\vec{\alpha}}^{n+2} D_{\vec{\beta}}^{n} F_A$ is the same in any stripe in the direction $\vec{\gamma}$, the derived surface $D_{\vec{\beta}}^{n+2} D_{\vec{\gamma}}^{n} F_A$ is the same in any stripe in the direction $\vec{\alpha}$, and the derived surface $D_{\vec{\alpha}}^{n+2} D_{\vec{\gamma}}^{n} F_A$ is the same in any stripe in the direction $\vec{\beta}$.

(b) Prove that the conditions

$$D_{\vec{\alpha}}^{n+2} D_{\vec{\beta}}^{n} F_A = D_{\vec{\beta}}^{n+2} D_{\vec{\gamma}}^{n} F_A = D_{\vec{\alpha}}^{n+2} D_{\vec{\gamma}}^{n} F_A = \vec{0}$$

are independent, and that in this case, each patch is defined by $3(n + 1)^2 - 2$ control points.

[30 pts]   7. Let F_n be the symmetric $n \times n$ matrix (with complex coefficients)

$$F_n = \left(e^{i2\pi kl/n} \right)_{\substack{0 \le k \le n-1 \\ 0 \le l \le n-1}},$$

assuming that we index the entries in F_n over $[0, 1, \ldots, n-1] \times [0, 1, \ldots, n-1]$, the standard kth row now being indexed by $k - 1$ and the standard lth column now being indexed by $l - 1$. The matrix F_n is called a *Fourier matrix*.

(a) Letting

$$\overline{F_n} = \left(e^{-i2\pi kl/n} \right)_{\substack{0 \le k \le n-1 \\ 0 \le l \le n-1}}$$

be the conjugate of F_n, prove that

$$F_n \overline{F_n} = \overline{F_n} F_n = n \, I_n.$$

(b) Prove that

$$H(f) F_n = F_n \widehat{f}.$$

Hint: Prove that

$$S_n F_n = F_n \, diag(v^1),$$

where $diag(v^1)$ is the diagonal matrix with the following entries on the diagonal:

$$v^1 = \left(1, e^{-i2\pi/n}, \ldots, e^{-ik2\pi/n}, \ldots, e^{-i(n-1)2\pi/n}\right).$$

(c) If the sequence $f = (f_0, \ldots, f_{n-1})$ is even, which means that $f_{-j} = f_j$ for all $j \in \mathbf{Z}$ (viewed as a periodic sequence), or equivalently, that $f_{n-j} = f_j$ for all j, $0 \le j \le n - 1$, prove that the Fourier transform $\widehat{f}$ is expressed as

$$\widehat{f}(k) = \sum_{j=0}^{n-1} f_j \cos\left(2\pi jk/n\right),$$

and that the inverse Fourier transform (taking c back to f) is expressed as

$$\overline{\widehat{c}}(k) = \sum_{j=0}^{n-1} c_j \cos\left(2\pi jk/n\right),$$

for every k, $0 \le k \le n - 1$.

[10 pts] 8. Prove that the Fourier transform of Loop's matrix

$$R = \left(M - \frac{5}{8}A\right)$$

is given by

$$(\widehat{R})_j = \begin{cases} 0 & \text{if } j = 0, \\ \frac{3}{8} + \frac{1}{4}\cos\left(2\pi j/n\right) & \text{if } j \ne 0. \end{cases}$$

[50 pts] 9. Implement the Doo-Sabin subdivision method for closed meshes. Generalize your program to handle boundaries.

[50 pts] 10. Implement the Catmull-Clark subdivision method for closed meshes. Generalize your program to handle boundaries.

[60 pts] 11. Implement the Loop subdivision method for closed meshes. Generalize your program to handle boundaries. Experiment with various values of α_n.

Embedding an Affine Space in a Vector Space

10.1   The "Hat Construction," or Homogenizing

For all practical purposes, curves and surfaces live in affine spaces. A disadvantage of the affine world is that points and vectors live in disjoint universes. It is often more convenient, at least mathematically, to deal with linear objects (vector spaces, linear combinations, linear maps) rather than affine objects (affine spaces, affine combinations, affine maps). Actually, it would also be advantageous if we could manipulate points and vectors as if they lived in a common universe, using perhaps an extra bit of information to distinguish between them if necessary.

Such a "homogenization" (or "hat construction") can be achieved. Such a homogenization of an affine space and its associated vector space is very useful to define and manipulate rational curves and surfaces. However, such a treatment will be given elsewhere. It also leads to a very elegant method for obtaining the various formulae giving the derivatives of a polynomial curve, or the directional derivatives of polynomial surfaces.

This chapter proceeds as follows. First, the construction of a vector space $\widehat{E}$ in which both E and $\vec{E}$ are embedded as (affine) hyperplanes is described. It is shown how affine frames in E become bases in $\widehat{E}$. It turns out that $\widehat{E}$ is characterized by a universality property: affine maps to vector spaces extend uniquely to linear maps. As a consequence, affine maps between affine spaces E and F extend to linear maps between $\widehat{E}$ and $\widehat{F}$. Similarly, multiaffine maps extend to multilinear maps. Next, the linearization of multiaffine maps is used to obtain formulae for the directional derivatives of polynomial maps. In turn, these formulae lead to a very convenient way of formulating the continuity conditions for joining polynomial curves or surfaces.

Let us first explain how to distinguish between points and vectors practically, using what amounts to a "hacking trick." Then, we will show that such a procedure can be put on firm mathematical grounds.

Assume that we consider the real affine space E of dimension 3, and that we have some affine frame $(a_0, (\overrightarrow{v_1}, \overrightarrow{v_2}, \overrightarrow{v_2}))$. With respect to this affine frame, every point $x \in E$ is represented by its coordinates (x_1, x_2, x_3), where

$$a = a_0 + x_1\overrightarrow{v_1} + x_2\overrightarrow{v_2} + x_3\overrightarrow{v_3}.$$

A vector $\vec{u} \in \vec{E}$ is also represented by its coordinates (u_1, u_2, u_3) over the basis $(\overrightarrow{v_1}, \overrightarrow{v_2}, \overrightarrow{v_2})$. One way to distinguish between points and vectors is to add a fourth coordinate, and to agree that points are represented by (row) vectors $(x_1, x_2, x_3, 1)$ whose fourth coordinate is 1, and that vectors are represented by (row) vectors $(v_1, v_2, v_3, 0)$ whose fourth coordinate is 0. This "programming trick" works actually very well. Of course, we are opening the door for strange elements such as $(x_1, x_2, x_3, 5)$, where the fourth coordinate is neither 1 nor 0.

The question is, can we make sense of such elements, and of such a construction? The answer is yes. We will present a construction in which an affine space $(E, \vec{E})$ is embedded in a vector space $\widehat{E}$, in which $\vec{E}$ is embedded as a hyperplane passing through the origin, and E itself is embedded as an affine hyperplane, defined as $\omega^{-1}(1)$, for some linear form $\omega: \widehat{E} \to \mathbf{R}$. In the case of an affine space E of dimension 2, we can think of $\widehat{E}$ as the vector space $\mathbf{R}^3$ of dimension 3, in which $\vec{E}$ corresponds to the (x, y)-plane, and E corresponds to the plane of equation $z = 1$, parallel to the (x, y)-plane, and passing through the point on the z-axis of coordinates $(0, 0, 1)$. The construction of the vector space $\widehat{E}$ is presented in some detail in Berger [5]. Berger explains the construction in terms of vector fields. Ramshaw explains the construction using the symmetric tensor power of an affine space [65]. We prefer a more geometric and simpler description in terms of simple geometric transformations, translations and dilatations.

Remark: Readers with a good knowledge of geometry will recognize the first step in embedding an affine space into a projective space. We will also show that the homogenization $\widehat{E}$ of an affine space $(E, \vec{E})$ satisfies a universal property with respect to the extension of affine maps to linear maps. As a consequence, the vector space $\widehat{E}$ is unique up to isomorphism, and its actual construction is not so important. However, it is quite useful to visualize the space $\widehat{E}$.

As usual, for simplicity, it is assumed that all vector spaces are defined over the field $\mathbf{R}$ of real numbers, and that all families of scalars (points and vectors) are finite. The extension to arbitrary fields and to families of finite support is immediate. We begin by defining two very simple kinds of geometric (affine) transformations. Given an affine space $(E, \vec{E})$, every $\vec{u} \in \vec{E}$ induces a mapping $t_{\vec{u}}: E \to E$, called a *translation*, and defined such that $t_{\vec{u}}(a) = a + \vec{u}$, for every $a \in E$. Clearly, the set of translations is a vector space isomorphic to $\vec{E}$. Thus, we will use the same notation $\vec{u}$ for both the vector $\vec{u}$ and the translation $t_{\vec{u}}$. Given any point a and any scalar $\lambda \in \mathbf{R}$, we define the mapping $H_{a,\lambda}: E \to E$, called *dilatation* (or *central dilatation*, or *homothety*) of *center a and ratio λ*, and defined such that

$$H_{a,\lambda}(x) = a + \lambda \overrightarrow{ax},$$

for every $x \in E$. We have $H_{a,\lambda}(a) = a$, and when $\lambda \neq 0$ and $x \neq a$, $H_{a,\lambda}(x)$ is on the line defined by a and x, and is obtained by "scaling" $\overrightarrow{ax}$ by λ. The effect is a uniform dilatation (or contraction, if $\lambda < 1$). When $\lambda = 0$, $H_{a,0}(x) = a$ for all $x \in E$, and $H_{a,0}$ is the constant affine map sending every point to a. If we assume $\lambda \neq 1$, note that $H_{a,\lambda}$ is never the identity, and since a is a fixed point, $H_{a,\lambda}$ is never a translation.

We now consider the set $\widehat{E}$ of geometric transformations from E to E, consisting of the union of the (disjoint) sets of translations and dilatations of ratio $\lambda \neq 1$. We would like to give this set the structure of a vector space, in such a way that both E and $\vec{E}$ can be naturally embedded into $\widehat{E}$. In fact, it will turn out that barycenters show up quite naturally too!

In order to "add" two dilatations H_{a_1,λ_1} and H_{a_2,λ_2}, it turns out that it is more convenient to consider dilatations of the form $H_{a,1-\lambda}$, where $\lambda \neq 0$. To see this, let us see the effect of such a dilatation on a point $x \in E$: we have

$$H_{a,1-\lambda}(x) = a + (1-\lambda)\overrightarrow{ax} = a + \overrightarrow{ax} - \lambda\overrightarrow{ax} = x + \lambda\overrightarrow{xa}.$$

For simplicity of notation, let us denote $H_{a,1-\lambda}$ as $\langle a, \lambda \rangle$. Then, we have

$$\langle a, \lambda \rangle(x) = x + \lambda\overrightarrow{xa}.$$

Remarks:

1. Note that $H_{a,1-\lambda}(x) = H_{x,\lambda}(a)$.

2. Berger defines a map $h: E \to \vec{E}$ as a *vector field*. Thus, each $\langle a, \lambda \rangle$ can be viewed as the vector field $x \mapsto \lambda\overrightarrow{xa}$. Similarly, a translation $\vec{u}$ can be viewed as the constant vector field $x \mapsto \vec{u}$. Thus, we could define $\widehat{E}$ as the (disjoint) union of these two vector fields. We prefer our view in terms of geometric transformations.

Then, since

$$\langle a_1, \lambda_1 \rangle(x) = x + \lambda_1\overrightarrow{xa_1}$$

and

$$\langle a_2, \lambda_2 \rangle(x) = x + \lambda_2\overrightarrow{xa_2},$$

if we want to define $\langle a_1, \lambda_1 \rangle \,\widehat{+}\, \langle a_2, \lambda_2 \rangle$, we see that we have to distinguish between two cases:

Case 1: $\lambda_1 + \lambda_2 = 0$. In this case, since

$$\lambda_1\overrightarrow{xa_1} + \lambda_2\overrightarrow{xa_2} = \lambda_1\overrightarrow{xa_1} - \lambda_1\overrightarrow{xa_2} = \lambda_1\overrightarrow{a_2a_1},$$

we let

$$\langle a_1, \lambda_1 \rangle \,\widehat{+}\, \langle a_2, \lambda_2 \rangle = \lambda_1 \overrightarrow{a_2 a_1},$$

where $\lambda_1 \overrightarrow{a_2 a_1}$ denotes the translation associated with the vector $\lambda_1 \overrightarrow{a_2 a_1}$.

Case 2: $\lambda_1 + \lambda_2 \neq 0$. In this case, the points a_1 and a_2 assigned the weights

$$\frac{\lambda_1}{\lambda_1 + \lambda_2}$$

and

$$\frac{\lambda_2}{\lambda_1 + \lambda_2}$$

have a barycenter

$$b = \frac{\lambda_1}{\lambda_1 + \lambda_2} a_1 + \frac{\lambda_2}{\lambda_1 + \lambda_2} a_2,$$

such that

$$\overrightarrow{xb} = \frac{\lambda_1}{\lambda_1 + \lambda_2} \overrightarrow{xa_1} + \frac{\lambda_2}{\lambda_1 + \lambda_2} \overrightarrow{xa_2}.$$

Since

$$\lambda_1 \overrightarrow{xa_1} + \lambda_2 \overrightarrow{xa_2} = (\lambda_1 + \lambda_2) \overrightarrow{xb},$$

we let

$$\langle a_1, \lambda_1 \rangle \,\widehat{+}\, \langle a_2, \lambda_2 \rangle = \left\langle \frac{\lambda_1}{\lambda_1 + \lambda_2} a_1 + \frac{\lambda_2}{\lambda_1 + \lambda_2} a_2, \lambda_1 + \lambda_2 \right\rangle,$$

the dilatation associated with the point b and the scalar $\lambda_1 + \lambda_2$.

Given a translation defined by $\vec{u}$ and a dilatation $\langle a, \lambda \rangle$, since $\lambda \neq 0$, we have

$$\lambda \overrightarrow{xa} + \vec{u} = \lambda(\overrightarrow{xa} + \lambda^{-1}\vec{u}),$$

and so, letting $b = a + \lambda^{-1}\vec{u}$, since $\overrightarrow{ab} = \lambda^{-1}\vec{u}$, we have

$$\lambda \overrightarrow{xa} + \vec{u} = \lambda(\overrightarrow{xa} + \lambda^{-1}\vec{u}) = \lambda(\overrightarrow{xa} + \overrightarrow{ab}) = \lambda \overrightarrow{xb},$$

and we let

$$\langle a, \lambda \rangle \,\widehat{+}\, \vec{u} = \langle a + \lambda^{-1}\vec{u}, \lambda \rangle,$$

the dilatation of center $a + \lambda^{-1}\vec{u}$ and ratio λ.

The sum of two translations $\vec{u}$ and $\vec{v}$ is of course defined as the translation $\vec{u} + \vec{v}$.

It is also natural to define multiplication by a scalar as follows:

$$\mu \cdot \langle a, \lambda \rangle = \langle a, \lambda\mu \rangle,$$

and

$$\lambda \cdot \vec{u} = \lambda\vec{u},$$

where $\lambda\vec{u}$ is the product by a scalar in $\vec{E}$.

We can now use the definition of the above operations to state the following lemma, showing that the "hat construction" described above has allowed us to achieve our goal of embedding both E and $\vec{E}$ in the vector space $\widehat{E}$.

Lemma 10.1.1

The set $\widehat{E}$, consisting of the disjoint union of the translations and the dilatations $H_{a,1-\lambda} = \langle a, \lambda \rangle$, $\lambda \in \mathbf{R}$, $\lambda \neq 0$, is a vector space under the following operations of addition and multiplication by a scalar:
If $\lambda_1 + \lambda_2 = 0$, then

$$\langle a_1, \lambda_1 \rangle \mathbin{\widehat{+}} \langle a_2, \lambda_2 \rangle = \lambda_1\overrightarrow{a_2a_1}.$$

If $\lambda_1 + \lambda_2 \neq 0$, then

$$\langle a_1, \lambda_1 \rangle \mathbin{\widehat{+}} \langle a_2, \lambda_2 \rangle = \left\langle \frac{\lambda_1}{\lambda_1 + \lambda_2}a_1 + \frac{\lambda_2}{\lambda_1 + \lambda_2}a_2, \lambda_1 + \lambda_2 \right\rangle,$$

$$\langle a, \lambda \rangle \mathbin{\widehat{+}} \vec{u} = \langle a + \lambda^{-1}\vec{u}, \lambda \rangle,$$

$$\vec{u} \mathbin{\widehat{+}} \vec{v} = \vec{u} + \vec{v}.$$

If $\mu \neq 0$, then

$$\mu \cdot \langle a, \lambda \rangle = \langle a, \lambda\mu \rangle,$$

$$0 \cdot \langle a, \lambda \rangle = \vec{0},$$

and

$$\lambda \cdot \vec{u} = \lambda\vec{u}.$$

Furthermore, the map $\omega \colon \widehat{E} \to \mathbf{R}$ defined such that

$$\omega(\langle a, \lambda \rangle) = \lambda,$$

$$\omega(\vec{u}) = 0,$$

is a linear form, $\omega^{-1}(0)$ is a hyperplane isomorphic to $\vec{E}$ under the injective linear map $i \colon \vec{E} \to \widehat{E}$ such that $i(\vec{u}) = t_{\vec{u}}$ (the translation associated with $\vec{u}$), and $\omega^{-1}(1)$ is an affine hyperplane isomorphic to E with direction $i(\vec{E})$, under the injective affine *map* $j: E \to \widehat{E}$, *where* $j(a) = \langle a, 1 \rangle$, *for every* $a \in E$. *Finally, for every* $a \in E$, *we have*

$$\widehat{E} = i(\vec{E}) \oplus \mathbf{R} j(a).$$

Proof: The verification that $\widehat{E}$ is a vector space is straightforward. The linear map mapping a vector $\vec{u}$ to the translation defined by $\vec{u}$ is clearly an injection $i: \vec{E} \to \widehat{E}$ embedding $\vec{E}$ as a hyperplane in $\widehat{E}$. It is also clear that ω is a linear form. Note that

$$j(a + \vec{u}) = \langle a + \vec{u}, 1 \rangle = \langle a, 1 \rangle \,\widehat{+}\, \vec{u},$$

where $\vec{u}$ stands for the translation associated with the vector $\vec{u}$, and thus, j is an affine injection with associated linear map i. Thus, $\omega^{-1}(1)$ is indeed an affine hyperplane isomorphic to E with direction $i(\vec{E})$, under the map $j: E \to \widehat{E}$. Finally, from the definition of $\widehat{+}$, for every $a \in E$, for every $\vec{u} \in \vec{E}$, since

$$i(\vec{u}) \,\widehat{+}\, \lambda \cdot j(a) = \vec{u} \,\widehat{+}\, \langle a, \lambda \rangle = \langle a + \lambda^{-1} \vec{u}, \lambda \rangle,$$

when $\lambda \neq 0$, we get any arbitrary $\vec{v} \in \widehat{E}$ by picking $\lambda = 0$ and $\vec{u} = \vec{v}$, and we get any arbitrary element $\langle b, \mu \rangle$, $\mu \neq 0$, by picking $\lambda = \mu$ and $\vec{u} = \mu \vec{ab}$. Thus,

$$\widehat{E} = i(\vec{E}) + \mathbf{R} j(a),$$

and since $i(\vec{E}) \cap \mathbf{R} j(a) = \{\vec{0}\}$, we have

$$\widehat{E} = i(\vec{E}) \oplus \mathbf{R} j(a),$$

for every $a \in E$.   ∎

Figure 10.1 illustrates the embedding of the affine space E into the vector space $\widehat{E}$, when E is an affine plane.

Note that $\widehat{E}$ is isomorphic to $\vec{E} \cup (E \times \mathbf{R}^*)$ (where $\mathbf{R}^* = \mathbf{R} - \{0\}$). Other authors use the notation E_* for $\widehat{E}$. Ramshaw calls the linear form $\omega: \widehat{E} \to \mathbf{R}$ a *weight* (or *flavor*), and he says that an element $z \in \widehat{E}$ such that $\omega(z) = \lambda$ is *λ-heavy* (or *has flavor* λ) [65]. The elements of $j(E)$ are 1-heavy and are called *points*, and the elements of $i(\vec{E})$ are 0-heavy and are called *vectors*. In general, the λ-heavy elements all belong to the hyperplane $\omega^{-1}(\lambda)$ parallel to $i(\vec{E})$. Thus, intuitively, we can think of $\widehat{E}$ as a stack of parallel hyperplanes, one for each λ, a little bit like an infinite stack of very thin pancakes! There are two privileged pancakes: one corresponding to E, for $\lambda = 1$, and one corresponding to $\vec{E}$, for $\lambda = 0$.

From now on, we will identify $j(E)$ and E, and $i(\vec{E})$ and $\vec{E}$. We will also write λa instead of $\langle a, \lambda \rangle$, which we will call a *weighted point*, and write $1a$ just as a. When we want to be more precise, we may also write $\langle a, 1 \rangle$ as $\bar{a}$. In particular, when we consider the homogenized version $\widehat{\mathbf{A}}$ of the affine space $\mathbf{A}$ associated with the field $\mathbf{R}$ considered as an affine space, we write $\bar{\lambda}$ for $\langle \lambda, 1 \rangle$ when viewing λ as a point in both $\mathbf{A}$ and $\widehat{\mathbf{A}}$, and simply λ when viewing λ as a vector in $\mathbf{R}$ and in $\widehat{\mathbf{A}}$. The elements of $\widehat{\mathbf{A}}$ are called *Bézier sites* by Ramshaw. As an example, the expression $2 + 3$ denotes the real number 5 in $\mathbf{A}$, $\frac{\bar{2} + \bar{3}}{2}$ denotes the middle point of the segment $[\bar{2}, \bar{3}]$, which can

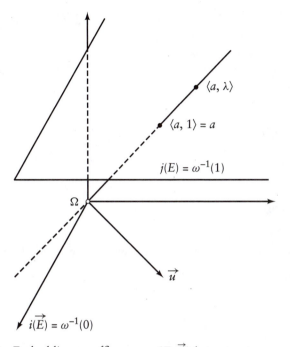

$\langle a, \lambda \rangle$

$\langle a, 1 \rangle = a$

$j(E) = \omega^{-1}(1)$

Ω

$\vec{u}$

$i(\vec{E}) = \omega^{-1}(0)$

FIG. 10.1 Embedding an affine space $(E, \vec{E})$ into a vector space $\widehat{E}$

be denoted as $\overline{2.5}$, and $\overline{2} + \overline{3}$ does not make sense in **A**, since it is not a barycentric combination. However, in $\widehat{\textbf{A}}$, the expression $\overline{2} + \overline{3}$ makes sense: it is the weighted point $\langle \overline{2.5}, 2 \rangle$.

Then, in view of the fact that

$$\langle a + \vec{u}, 1 \rangle = \langle a, 1 \rangle \mathbin{\widehat{+}} \vec{u},$$

and since we are identifying $a + \vec{u}$ with $\langle a + \vec{u}, 1 \rangle$ (under the injection j), in the simplified notation, the above reads as $a + \vec{u} = a \mathbin{\widehat{+}} \vec{u}$. Thus, we go one step further and denote $a \mathbin{\widehat{+}} \vec{u}$ as $a + \vec{u}$. However, since

$$\langle a, \lambda \rangle \mathbin{\widehat{+}} \vec{u} = \langle a + \lambda^{-1}\vec{u}, \lambda \rangle,$$

we will refrain from writing $\lambda a \mathbin{\widehat{+}} \vec{u}$ as $\lambda a + \vec{u}$, because we find it too confusing. From Lemma 10.1.1, for every $a \in E$, every element of $\widehat{E}$ can be written uniquely as $\vec{u} \mathbin{\widehat{+}} \lambda a$. We also denote

$$\lambda a \mathbin{\widehat{+}} (-\mu)b$$

as

$$\lambda a \mathbin{\widehat{-}} \mu b.$$

We can now justify rigorously the programming trick of the introduction of an extra coordinate to distinguish between points and vectors. First, we make a few observations. Given any family $(a_i)_{i \in I}$ of points in E, and any family $(\lambda_i)_{i \in I}$ of scalars in $\mathbf{R}$, it is easily shown by induction on the size of I that the following holds:

1. If $\sum_{i \in I} \lambda_i = 0$, then

$$\sum_{i \in I} \langle a_i, \lambda_i \rangle = \overrightarrow{\sum_{i \in I} \lambda_i a_i},$$

where

$$\overrightarrow{\sum_{i \in I} \lambda_i a_i} = \sum_{i \in I} \lambda_i \overrightarrow{b a_i}$$

for any $b \in E$, which, by Lemma 2.4.1, is a vector independent of b, or

2. If $\sum_{i \in I} \lambda_i \neq 0$, then

$$\sum_{i \in I} \langle a_i, \lambda_i \rangle = \left\langle \sum_{i \in I} \frac{\lambda_i}{\sum_{i \in I} \lambda_i} a_i, \sum_{i \in I} \lambda_i \right\rangle.$$

Thus, we see how barycenters reenter the scene quite naturally, and that in $\widehat{E}$, we can make sense of $\sum_{i \in I} \langle a_i, \lambda_i \rangle$, regardless of the value of $\sum_{i \in I} \lambda_i$. When $\sum_{i \in I} \lambda_i = 1$, the element $\sum_{i \in I} \langle a_i, \lambda_i \rangle$ belongs to the hyperplane $\omega^{-1}(1)$, and thus, it is a point. When $\sum_{i \in I} \lambda_i = 0$, the linear combination of points $\sum_{i \in I} \lambda_i a_i$ is a vector, and when $I = \{1, \ldots, n\}$, we allow ourselves to write

$$\lambda_1 a_1 \widehat{+} \cdots \widehat{+} \lambda_n a_n,$$

where some of the occurrences of $\widehat{+}$ can be replaced by $\widehat{-}$, as

$$\lambda_1 a_1 + \cdots + \lambda_n a_n,$$

where the occurrences of $\widehat{-}$ (if any) are replaced by $-$. This will be convenient when dealing with derivatives in Section 10.5.

In fact, we have the following slightly more general property, which is left as an exercise.

Lemma 10.1.2

Given any affine space $(E, \overrightarrow{E})$, for any family $(a_i)_{i \in I}$ of points in E, for any family $(\lambda_i)_{i \in I}$ of scalars in $\mathbf{R}$, and any family $(\overrightarrow{v_j})_{j \in J}$ of vectors in $\overrightarrow{E}$, with $I \cap J = \emptyset$, the following properties hold:

1. *If $\sum_{i \in I} \lambda_i = 0$, then*

$$\sum_{i \in I} \langle a_i, \lambda_i \rangle \,\widehat{+}\, \sum_{j \in J} \vec{v}_j = \overline{\sum_{i \in I} \lambda_i a_i} + \sum_{j \in J} \vec{v}_j,$$

where

$$\overline{\sum_{i \in I} \lambda_i a_i} = \sum_{i \in I} \lambda_i \overrightarrow{ba_i}$$

for any $b \in E$, which, by Lemma 2.4.1, is a vector independent of b, or

2. *if $\sum_{i \in I} \lambda_i \neq 0$, then*

$$\sum_{i \in I} \langle a_i, \lambda_i \rangle \,\widehat{+}\, \sum_{j \in J} \vec{v}_j = \left\langle \sum_{i \in I} \frac{\lambda_i}{\sum_{i \in I} \lambda_i} a_i + \sum_{j \in J} \frac{\vec{v}_j}{\sum_{i \in I} \lambda_i}, \sum_{i \in I} \lambda_i \right\rangle.$$

Proof: By induction on the size of I and the size of J. ∎

The above formulae show that we have some kind of extended barycentric calculus. Operations on weighted points and vectors were introduced by H. Grassmann, in his book published in 1844!

10.2   Affine Frames of E and Bases of $\widehat{E}$

There is also a nice relationship between affine frames in $(E, \vec{E})$ and bases of $\widehat{E}$, stated in the following lemma.

Lemma 10.2.1

Given any affine space $(E, \vec{E})$, for any affine frame $(a_0, (\overrightarrow{a_0 a_1}, \ldots, \overrightarrow{a_0 a_m}))$ for E, the family $(\overrightarrow{a_0 a_1}, \ldots, \overrightarrow{a_0 a_m}, a_0)$ is a basis for $\widehat{E}$, and for any affine frame $(a_0, \ldots, a_m)$ for E, the family $(a_0, \ldots, a_m)$ is a basis for $\widehat{E}$. Furthermore, given any element $\langle x, \lambda \rangle \in \widehat{E}$, if

$$x = a_0 + x_1 \overrightarrow{a_0 a_1} + \cdots + x_m \overrightarrow{a_0 a_m}$$

over the affine frame $(a_0, (\overrightarrow{a_0 a_1}, \ldots, \overrightarrow{a_0 a_m}))$ in E, then the coordinates of $\langle x, \lambda \rangle$, over the basis $(\overrightarrow{a_0 a_1}, \ldots, \overrightarrow{a_0 a_m}, a_0)$ in $\widehat{E}$, are

$$(\lambda x_1, \ldots, \lambda x_m, \lambda).$$

For any vector $\vec{v} \in \vec{E}$, if

$$\vec{v} = v_1 \overrightarrow{a_0 a_1} + \cdots + v_m \overrightarrow{a_0 a_m}$$

over the basis $(\overrightarrow{a_0 a_1}, \ldots, \overrightarrow{a_0 a_m})$ in $\vec{E}$, then over the basis $(\overrightarrow{a_0 a_1}, \ldots, \overrightarrow{a_0 a_m}, a_0)$ in $\widehat{E}$, the coordinates of $\vec{v}$ are

$$(v_1, \ldots, v_m, 0).$$

For any element $\langle a, \lambda \rangle$, where $\lambda \neq 0$, if the barycentric coordinates of a with respect to the affine basis $(a_0, \ldots, a_m)$ in E are $(\lambda_0, \ldots, \lambda_m)$ with $\lambda_0 + \cdots + \lambda_m = 1$, then the coordinates of $\langle a, \lambda \rangle$ with respect to the basis $(a_0, \ldots, a_m)$ in $\widehat{E}$ are

$$(\lambda\lambda_0, \ldots, \lambda\lambda_m).$$

If a vector $\vec{v} \in \vec{E}$ is expressed as

$$\vec{v} = v_1\overrightarrow{a_0a_1} + \cdots + v_m\overrightarrow{a_0a_m} = -(v_1 + \cdots + v_m)a_0 + v_1a_1 + \cdots + v_ma_m,$$

with respect to the affine basis $(a_0, \ldots, a_m)$ in E, then its coordinates with respect to the basis $(a_0, \ldots, a_m)$ in $\widehat{E}$ are

$$(-(v_1 + \cdots + v_m), v_1, \ldots, v_m).$$

Proof: We sketch parts of the proof, leaving the details as an exercise. If we assume that we have a nontrivial linear combination

$$\lambda_1\overrightarrow{a_0a_1} \,\widehat{+}\, \cdots \,\widehat{+}\, \lambda_m\overrightarrow{a_0a_m} \,\widehat{+}\, \mu a_0 = \vec{0},$$

if $\mu \neq 0$, then we have

$$\lambda_1\overrightarrow{a_0a_1} \,\widehat{+}\, \cdots \,\widehat{+}\, \lambda_m\overrightarrow{a_0a_m} \,\widehat{+}\, \mu a_0 = \langle a_0 + \mu^{-1}\lambda_1\overrightarrow{a_0a_1} + \cdots + \mu^{-1}\lambda_m\overrightarrow{a_0a_m}, \mu \rangle,$$

which is never null, and thus, we must have $\mu = 0$, but since $(\overrightarrow{a_0a_1}, \ldots, \overrightarrow{a_0a_m})$ is a basis of $\vec{E}$, we must also have $\lambda_i = 0$ for all i, $1 \leq i \leq m$.

Given any element $\langle x, \lambda \rangle \in \widehat{E}$, if

$$x = a_0 + x_1\overrightarrow{a_0a_1} + \cdots + x_m\overrightarrow{a_0a_m}$$

over the affine frame $(a_0, (\overrightarrow{a_0a_1}, \ldots, \overrightarrow{a_0a_m}))$ in E, in view of the definition of $\widehat{+}$, we have

$$\langle x, \lambda \rangle = \langle a_0 + x_1\overrightarrow{a_0a_1} + \cdots + x_m\overrightarrow{a_0a_m}, \lambda \rangle = \langle a_0, \lambda \rangle \,\widehat{+}\, \lambda x_1\overrightarrow{a_0a_1} \,\widehat{+}\, \cdots \,\widehat{+}\, \lambda x_m\overrightarrow{a_0a_m},$$

which shows that the coordinates of $\langle x, \lambda \rangle$ over the basis $(\overrightarrow{a_0a_1}, \ldots, \overrightarrow{a_0a_m}, a_0)$ in $\widehat{E}$ are

$$(\lambda x_1, \ldots, \lambda x_m, \lambda). \quad \blacksquare$$

Figure 10.2 shows the basis $(\overrightarrow{a_0a_1}, \overrightarrow{a_0a_2}, a_0)$ corresponding to the affine frame (a_0, a_1, a_2) in E.

If $(x_1, \ldots, x_m)$ are the coordinates of x with respect to the affine frame $(a_0, (\overrightarrow{a_0a_1}, \ldots, \overrightarrow{a_0a_m}))$ in E, then $(x_1, \ldots, x_m, 1)$ are the coordinates of x in $\widehat{E}$ (i.e., the last coordinate is 1), and if $\vec{u}$ has coordinates $(u_1, \ldots, u_m)$ with respect to the basis $(\overrightarrow{a_0a_1}, \ldots, \overrightarrow{a_0a_m})$ in $\vec{E}$, then $\vec{u}$ has coordinates $(u_1, \ldots, u_m, 0)$ in $\widehat{E}$ (i.e., the last coordinate is 0).

Figure 10.3 shows the affine frame (a_0, a_1, a_2) in E viewed as a basis in $\widehat{E}$.

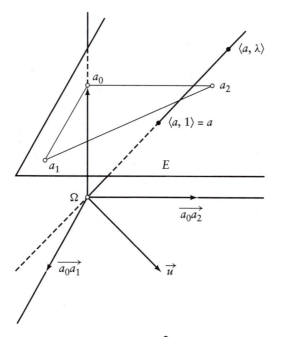

FIG. 10.2 The basis $(\overrightarrow{a_0a_1}, \overrightarrow{a_0a_2}, a_0)$ in $\widehat{E}$

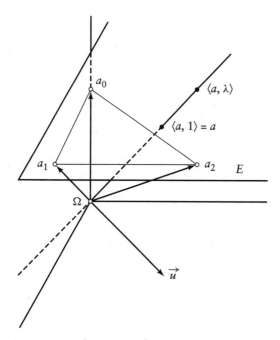

FIG. 10.3 The basis (a_0, a_1, a_2) in $\widehat{E}$

We now consider the universal property of $\widehat{E}$ mentioned at the beginning of this section.

10.3   Extending Affine Maps to Linear Maps

Roughly, the vector space $\widehat{E}$ has the property that for any vector space $\vec{F}$ and any affine map $f\colon E \to \vec{F}$, there is a unique linear map $\widehat{f}\colon \widehat{E} \to \vec{F}$ extending $f\colon E \to \vec{F}$. As a consequence, given two affine spaces E and F, every affine map $f\colon E \to F$ extends uniquely to a linear map $\widehat{f}\colon \widehat{E} \to \widehat{F}$. Other authors use the notation f_* for $\widehat{f}$. First, we define rigorously the notion of homogenization of an affine space.

Definition 10.3.1

Given any affine space $(E, \vec{E})$, a homogenization *(or* linearization*) of $(E, \vec{E})$ is a triple $\langle \mathcal{E}, j, \omega \rangle$, where $\mathcal{E}$ is a vector space, $j\colon E \to \mathcal{E}$ is an injective affine map with associated injective linear map $i\colon \vec{E} \to \mathcal{E}$, $\omega\colon \mathcal{E} \to \mathbf{R}$ is a linear form such that $\omega^{-1}(0) = i(\vec{E})$, $\omega^{-1}(1) = j(E)$, and for every vector space $\vec{F}$ and every affine map $f\colon E \to \vec{F}$, there is a unique linear map $\widehat{f}\colon \mathcal{E} \to \vec{F}$ extending f, that is, $f = \widehat{f} \circ j$, as in the following diagram:*

$$
\begin{array}{ccc}
E & \xrightarrow{\ j\ } & \mathcal{E} \\
& {\scriptstyle f}\searrow & \downarrow{\scriptstyle \widehat{f}} \\
& & \vec{F}
\end{array}
$$

Thus, $j(E) = \omega^{-1}(1)$ is an affine hyperplane with direction $i(\vec{E}) = \omega^{-1}(0)$. Note that we could have defined a homogenization of an affine space $(E, \vec{E})$ as a triple $\langle \mathcal{E}, j, H \rangle$, where $\mathcal{E}$ is a vector space, H is an affine hyperplane in $\mathcal{E}$, and $j\colon E \to \mathcal{E}$ is an injective affine map such that $j(E) = H$, and such that the universal property stated above holds. However, Definition 10.3.1 is more convenient for our purposes, since it makes the notion of weight more evident.

The obvious candidate for $\mathcal{E}$ is the vector space $\widehat{E}$ that we just constructed. The next lemma will indeed show that $\widehat{E}$ has the required extension property. As usual, objects defined by a universal property are unique up to isomorphism. This property is left as an exercise.

Lemma 10.3.2

Given any affine space $(E, \vec{E})$ and any vector space $\vec{F}$, for any affine map $f\colon E \to \vec{F}$, there is a unique linear map $\widehat{f}\colon \widehat{E} \to \vec{F}$ extending f such that

$$\widehat{f}(\vec{u} \mathbin{\widehat{+}} \lambda a) = \lambda f(a) + \vec{f}(\vec{u})$$

for all $a \in E$, all $\vec{u} \in \vec{E}$, and all $\lambda \in \mathbf{R}$, where $\vec{f}$ is the linear map associated with f. In particular, when $\lambda \neq 0$, we have

$$\widehat{f}(\vec{u} \mathbin{\widehat{+}} \lambda a) = \lambda f(a + \lambda^{-1} \vec{u}).$$

Proof: Assuming that $\widehat{f}$ exists, recall that from Lemma 10.1.1, for every $a \in E$, every element of $\widehat{E}$ can be written uniquely as $\vec{u} \,\widehat{+}\, \lambda a$. By linearity of $\widehat{f}$ and since $\widehat{f}$ extends f, we have

$$\widehat{f}(\vec{u} \,\widehat{+}\, \lambda a) = \widehat{f}(\vec{u}) + \lambda \widehat{f}(a) = \widehat{f}(\vec{u}) + \lambda f(a) = \lambda f(a) + \widehat{f}(\vec{u}).$$

If $\lambda = 1$, since $a \,\widehat{+}\, \vec{u}$ and $a + \vec{u}$ are identified, and since $\widehat{f}$ extends f, we must have

$$f(a) + \widehat{f}(\vec{u}) = \widehat{f}(a) + \widehat{f}(\vec{u}) = \widehat{f}(a \,\widehat{+}\, \vec{u}) = f(a + \vec{u}) = f(a) + \vec{f}(\vec{u}),$$

and thus, $\widehat{f}(\vec{u}) = \vec{f}(\vec{u})$ for all $\vec{u} \in \vec{E}$. Then, we have

$$\widehat{f}(\vec{u} \,\widehat{+}\, \lambda a) = \lambda f(a) + \vec{f}(\vec{u}),$$

which proves the uniqueness of $\widehat{f}$. On the other hand, the map $\widehat{f}$ defined as above is clearly a linear map extending f.

When $\lambda \neq 0$, we have

$$\widehat{f}(\vec{u} \,\widehat{+}\, \lambda a) = \widehat{f}(\lambda(a + \lambda^{-1}\vec{u})) = \lambda \widehat{f}(a + \lambda^{-1}\vec{u}) = \lambda f(a + \lambda^{-1}\vec{u}). \quad \blacksquare$$

Lemma 10.3.2 shows that $\langle \widehat{E}, j, \omega \rangle$ is a homogenization of $(E, \vec{E})$. As a corollary, we obtain the following lemma.

Lemma 10.3.3

Given two affine spaces E and F and an affine map $f: E \to F$, there is a unique linear map $\widehat{f}: \widehat{E} \to \widehat{F}$ extending f, as in the following diagram,

$$
\begin{array}{ccc}
E & \xrightarrow{f} & F \\
j\downarrow & & \downarrow j \\
\widehat{E} & \xrightarrow[\widehat{f}]{} & \widehat{F}
\end{array}
$$

such that

$$\widehat{f}(\vec{u} \,\widehat{+}\, \lambda a) = \vec{f}(\vec{u}) \,\widehat{+}\, \lambda f(a),$$

for all $a \in E$, all $\vec{u} \in \vec{E}$, and all $\lambda \in \mathbf{R}$, where $\vec{f}$ is the linear map associated with f. In particular, when $\lambda \neq 0$, we have

$$\widehat{f}(\vec{u} \,\widehat{+}\, \lambda a) = \lambda f(a + \lambda^{-1}\vec{u}).$$

Proof: Consider the vector space $\widehat{F}$, and the affine map $j \circ f: E \to \widehat{F}$. By Lemma 10.3.2, there is a unique linear map $\widehat{f}: \widehat{E} \to \widehat{F}$, extending $j \circ f$, and thus extending f. $\quad \blacksquare$

Note that $\widehat{f}: \widehat{E} \to \widehat{F}$ has the property that $\widehat{f}(\vec{E}) \subseteq \vec{F}$. More generally, since

$$\widehat{f}(\vec{u} \,\widehat{+}\, \lambda a) = \vec{f}(\vec{u}) \,\widehat{+}\, \lambda f(a),$$

the linear map $\widehat{f}$ is weight-preserving. Also observe that we recover f from $\widehat{f}$, by letting $\lambda = 1$ in

$$\widehat{f}(\vec{u} \mathbin{\widehat{+}} \lambda a) = \lambda f(a + \lambda^{-1}\vec{u}),$$

that is, we have

$$f(a + \vec{u}) = \widehat{f}(\vec{u} \mathbin{\widehat{+}} a).$$

From a practical point of view, Lemma 10.3.3 shows us how to homogenize an affine map to turn it into a linear map between the two homogenized spaces. Assume that E and F are of finite dimension, and that $(a_0, (\vec{u_1}, \ldots, \vec{u_n}))$ is an affine frame of E, with origin a_0, and $(b_0, (\vec{v_1}, \ldots, \vec{v_m}))$ is an affine frame of F, with origin b_0. Then, with respect to the two bases $(\vec{u_1}, \ldots, \vec{u_n}, a_0)$ in $\widehat{E}$ and $(\vec{v_1}, \ldots, \vec{v_m}, b_0)$ in $\widehat{F}$, a linear map $h \colon \widehat{E} \to \widehat{F}$ is given by an $(m+1) \times (n+1)$ matrix A. If this linear map h is equal to the homogenized version $\widehat{f}$ of an affine map f, since

$$\widehat{f}(\vec{u} \mathbin{\widehat{+}} \lambda a) = \vec{f}(\vec{u}) \mathbin{\widehat{+}} \lambda f(a),$$

since over the basis $(\vec{u_1}, \ldots, \vec{u_n}, a_0)$ in $\widehat{E}$, points are represented by vectors whose last coordinate is 1, and vectors are represented by vectors whose last coordinate is 0, the last row of the matrix $A = M(\widehat{f})$ with respect to the given bases is

$$(0, 0, \ldots, 0, 1),$$

with m occurrences of 0, the last column contains the coordinates

$$(\mu_1, \ldots, \mu_m, 1)$$

of $f(a_0)$ with respect to the basis $(\vec{v_1}, \ldots, \vec{v_m}, b_0)$. The submatrix of A obtained by deleting the last row and the last column is the matrix of the linear map $\vec{f}$ with respect to the bases $(\vec{u_1}, \ldots, \vec{u_n})$ and $(\vec{v_1}, \ldots, \vec{v_m})$, and since

$$f(a_0 + \vec{u}) = \widehat{f}(\vec{u} \mathbin{\widehat{+}} a_0),$$

given any $x \in E$ and $y \in F$, with coordinates $(x_1, \ldots, x_n, 1)$ and $(y_1, \ldots, y_m, 1)$, for $X = (x_1, \ldots, x_n, 1)^\top$ and $Y = (y_1, \ldots, y_m, 1)^\top$, we have $y = f(x)$ iff

$$Y = AX.$$

For example, consider the affine map $f \colon \mathbf{A}^2 \to \mathbf{A}^2$ defined as follows:

$$y_1 = ax_1 + bx_2 + \mu_1,$$
$$y_2 = cx_1 + dx_2 + \mu_2.$$

The matrix of $\widehat{f}$ is

$$\begin{pmatrix} a & b & \mu_1 \\ c & d & \mu_2 \\ 0 & 0 & 1 \end{pmatrix}$$

and we have

$$\begin{pmatrix} y_1 \\ y_2 \\ 1 \end{pmatrix} = \begin{pmatrix} a & b & \mu_1 \\ c & d & \mu_2 \\ 0 & 0 & 1 \end{pmatrix} \begin{pmatrix} x_1 \\ x_2 \\ 1 \end{pmatrix}$$

In $\widehat{E}$, we have

$$\begin{pmatrix} y_1 \\ y_2 \\ y_3 \end{pmatrix} = \begin{pmatrix} a & b & \mu_1 \\ c & d & \mu_2 \\ 0 & 0 & 1 \end{pmatrix} \begin{pmatrix} x_1 \\ x_2 \\ x_3 \end{pmatrix}$$

which means that the homogeneous map $\widehat{f}$ is obtained from f by "adding the variable of homogeneity x_3":

$$y_1 = ax_1 + bx_2 + \mu_1 x_3,$$

$$y_2 = cx_1 + dx_2 + \mu_2 x_3,$$

$$y_3 = x_3.$$

10.4   From Multiaffine Maps to Multilinear Maps

We now show how to homogenize multiaffine maps.

Lemma 10.4.1

Given any affine space E and any vector space $\vec{F}$, for any m-affine map $f \colon E^m \to \vec{F}$, there is a unique m-linear map $\widehat{f} \colon (\widehat{E})^m \to \vec{F}$ extending f, such that, if

$$f(a_1 + \vec{v}_1, \ldots, a_m + \vec{v}_m) = f(a_1, \ldots, a_m) + \sum_{\substack{S \subseteq \{1,\ldots,m\},\, k=|S| \\ S=\{i_1,\ldots,i_k\},\, k \geq 1}} f_S(\vec{v_{i_1}}, \ldots, \vec{v_{i_k}}),$$

for all $a_1 \ldots, a_m \in E$, and all $\vec{v}_1, \ldots, \vec{v}_m \in \vec{E}$, where the f_S are uniquely determined multilinear maps (by Lemma 4.1.3), then

$$\widehat{f}(\vec{v_1} \,\widehat{+}\, \lambda_1 a_1, \ldots, \vec{v_m} \,\widehat{+}\, \lambda_m a_m)$$

$$= \lambda_1 \cdots \lambda_m f(a_1, \ldots, a_m) + \sum_{\substack{S \subseteq \{1,\ldots,m\},\, k=|S| \\ S=\{i_1,\ldots,i_k\},\, k \geq 1}} \left(\prod_{\substack{j \in \{1,\ldots,m\} \\ j \notin S}} \lambda_j \right) f_S(\vec{v_{i_1}}, \ldots, \vec{v_{i_k}}),$$

for all $a_1 \ldots, a_m \in E$, all $\vec{v}_1, \ldots, \vec{v}_m \in \vec{E}$, and all $\lambda_1, \ldots, \lambda_m \in \mathbf{R}$. Furthermore, for $\lambda_i \neq 0$, $1 \leq i \leq m$, we have

$$\widehat{f}(\overrightarrow{v_1} \,\widehat{+}\, \lambda_1 a_1, \ldots, \overrightarrow{v_m} \,\widehat{+}\, \lambda_m a_m) = \lambda_1 \cdots \lambda_m f(a_1 + \lambda_1^{-1}\overrightarrow{v_1}, \ldots, a_m + \lambda_m^{-1}\overrightarrow{v_m}).$$

Proof: The proof is very technical and can be found in Appendix B (Section B.2). ■

As a corollary, we obtain the following useful lemma.

Lemma 10.4.2

Given any two affine spaces E and F and an m-affine map $f\colon E^m \to F$, there is a unique m-linear map $\widehat{f}\colon (\widehat{E})^m \to \widehat{F}$ extending f as in the following diagram,

$$
\begin{array}{ccc}
E^m & \xrightarrow{\ f\ } & F \\
{\scriptstyle j \times \cdots \times j}\downarrow & & \downarrow{\scriptstyle j} \\
(\widehat{E})^m & \xrightarrow[\widehat{f}]{} & \widehat{F}
\end{array}
$$

such that, if

$$f(a_1 + \overrightarrow{v_1}, \ldots, a_m + \overrightarrow{v_m}) = f(a_1, \ldots, a_m) + \sum_{\substack{S \subseteq \{1,\ldots,m\},\, k=|S| \\ S=\{i_1,\ldots,i_k\},\, k \geq 1}} f_S(\overrightarrow{v_{i_1}}, \ldots, \overrightarrow{v_{i_k}}),$$

for all $a_1 \ldots, a_m \in E$, and all $\overrightarrow{v_1}, \ldots, \overrightarrow{v_m} \in \vec{E}$, where the f_S are uniquely determined multilinear maps (by Lemma 4.1.3), then

$$\widehat{f}(\overrightarrow{v_1} \,\widehat{+}\, \lambda_1 a_1, \ldots, \overrightarrow{v_m} \,\widehat{+}\, \lambda_m a_m)$$

$$= \lambda_1 \cdots \lambda_m f(a_1, \ldots, a_m) \,\widehat{+}\, \sum_{\substack{S \subseteq \{1,\ldots,m\},\, k=|S| \\ S=\{i_1,\ldots,i_k\},\, k \geq 1}} \left(\prod_{\substack{j \in \{1,\ldots,m\} \\ j \notin S}} \lambda_j \right) f_S(\overrightarrow{v_{i_1}}, \ldots, \overrightarrow{v_{i_k}}),$$

for all $a_1 \ldots, a_m \in E$, all $\overrightarrow{v_1}, \ldots, \overrightarrow{v_m} \in \vec{E}$, and all $\lambda_1, \ldots, \lambda_m \in \mathbf{R}$. Furthermore, for $\lambda_i \neq 0$, $1 \leq i \leq m$, we have

$$\widehat{f}(\overrightarrow{v_1} \,\widehat{+}\, \lambda_1 a_1, \ldots, \overrightarrow{v_m} \,\widehat{+}\, \lambda_m a_m) = \lambda_1 \cdots \lambda_m f(a_1 + \lambda_1^{-1}\overrightarrow{v_1}, \ldots, a_m + \lambda_m^{-1}\overrightarrow{v_m}).$$

Proof: Immediate from Lemma 10.4.1 (see the proof of Lemma 10.3.3 from Lemma 10.3.2). ■

The homogenized version $\widehat{f}$ of an m-affine map f is weight-multiplicative, in the sense that

$$\omega(\widehat{f}(z_1, \ldots, z_m)) = \omega(z_1) \cdots \omega(z_m),$$

for all $z_1, \ldots, z_m \in \widehat{E}$.

From a practical point of view,

$$\widehat{f}(\overrightarrow{v_1} \,\widehat{+}\, \lambda_1 a_1, \ldots, \overrightarrow{v_m} \,\widehat{+}\, \lambda_m a_m) = \lambda_1 \cdots \lambda_m f(a_1 + \lambda_1^{-1}\overrightarrow{v_1}, \ldots, a_m + \lambda_m^{-1}\overrightarrow{v_m})$$

shows us that f is recovered from $\widehat{f}$ by setting $\lambda_i = 1$, for $1 \leq i \leq m$. We can use this formula to find the homogenized version $\widehat{f}$ of the map f. For example, if we consider the affine space $\mathbf{A}$ with its canonical affine frame (the origin is $\overline{0}$, and the basis consists of the single vector 1), if $f: \mathbf{A} \times \mathbf{A} \to \mathbf{A}$ is the biaffine map defined such that

$$f(x_1, x_2) = ax_1x_2 + bx_1 + cx_2 + d,$$

the bilinear map $\widehat{f}: \widehat{\mathbf{A}} \times \widehat{\mathbf{A}} \to \widehat{\mathbf{A}}$ is given by

$$\widehat{f}((x_1, \lambda_1), (x_2, \lambda_2)) = (\lambda_1\lambda_2[a(x_1\lambda_1^{-1})(x_2\lambda_2^{-1}) + bx_1\lambda_1^{-1} + cx_2\lambda_2^{-1} + d], \ \lambda_1\lambda_2)$$

$$= (ax_1x_2 + bx_1\lambda_2 + cx_2\lambda_1 + d\lambda_1\lambda_2, \ \lambda_1\lambda_2),$$

where we choose the basis $(1, \overline{0})$, in $\widehat{\mathbf{A}}$.

Note that $f(x_1, x_2)$ is indeed recovered from $\widehat{f}$ by setting $\lambda_1 = \lambda_2 = 1$. Since multiaffine maps can be homogenized, polynomial maps can also be homogenized. This is very useful in practice. In fact, using the characterization of multiaffine maps $f: E^m \to F$ given by Lemma 4.2.3, when E is of finite dimension, we can get an explicit formula for the homogenized version $\widehat{f}$ of f, generalizing our previous example. If $(a, (\vec{e_1}, \ldots, \vec{e_n}))$ is an affine frame for E, we know that for any m vectors

$$\vec{v_j} = v_{1,j}\vec{e_1} + \cdots + v_{n,j}\vec{e_n} \in \vec{E},$$

we have

$$f(a + \vec{v_1}, \ldots, a + \vec{v_m})$$

$$= b + \sum_{1 \leq p \leq m} \sum_{\substack{I_1 \cup \ldots \cup I_n = \{1, \ldots, p\} \\ I_i \cap I_j = \emptyset, \, i \neq j \\ 1 \leq i, j \leq n}} \left(\prod_{i_1 \in I_1} v_{1, i_1} \right) \cdots \left(\prod_{i_n \in I_n} v_{n, i_n} \right) \vec{w}_{|I_1|, \ldots, |I_n|} \, ,$$

for some $b \in F$, and some $\vec{w}_{|I_1|, \ldots, |I_n|} \in \vec{F}$, and since $\widehat{E} = \vec{E} \oplus Ra$, with respect to the basis $(\vec{e_1}, \ldots, \vec{e_n}, \langle a, 1 \rangle)$ of $\widehat{E}$, we have

$$\widehat{f}(\vec{v_1} \mathbin{\widehat{+}} \lambda_1 a, \ldots, \vec{v_m} \mathbin{\widehat{+}} \lambda_m a)$$

$$= \lambda_1 \cdots \lambda_m b \mathbin{\widehat{+}} \sum_{1 \leq p \leq m} \sum_{\substack{I_1 \cup \ldots \cup I_n = \{1, \ldots, p\} \\ I_i \cap I_j = \emptyset, \, i \neq j \\ 1 \leq i, j \leq n}} \left(\prod_{i_1 \in I_1} v_{1, i_1} \right) \cdots \left(\prod_{i_n \in I_n} v_{n, i_n} \right)$$

$$\cdot \left(\prod_{\substack{j \in \{1, \ldots, m\} \\ j \notin (I_1 \cup \ldots \cup I_n)}} \lambda_j \right) \vec{w}_{|I_1|, \ldots, |I_n|}.$$

In other words, we obtain the expression for $\widehat{f}$ by homogenizing the polynomials that are the coefficients of $\vec{w}_{|I_1|,\ldots,|I_n|}$. For the homogenized version $\widehat{h}$ of the affine polynomial h associated with f, we get

$$\widehat{h}(\vec{v} \mathbin{\widehat{+}} \lambda a) = \lambda^m b \mathbin{\widehat{+}} \sum_{1 \leq p \leq m} \sum_{\substack{k_1 + \cdots + k_n = p \\ 0 \leq k_i,\, 1 \leq i \leq n}} v_1^{k_1} \cdots v_n^{k_n} \lambda^{m-p}\, \vec{w}_{k_1,\ldots,k_n}.$$

Remark: Recall that homogenizing a polynomial $P(X_1, \ldots, X_n) \in \mathbf{R}[X_1, \ldots, X_n]$ is done as follows. If $P(X_1, \ldots, X_n)$ is of total degree p, and we want to find a homogeneous polynomial $Q(X_1, \ldots, X_n, Z)$ of total degree $m \geq p$, such that

$$P(X_1, \ldots, X_n) = Q(X_1, \ldots, X_n, 1),$$

we let

$$Q(X_1, \ldots, X_n, Z) = Z^m P\left(\frac{X_1}{Z}, \ldots, \frac{X_n}{Z}\right).$$

10.5 Differentiating Affine Polynomial Functions Using Their Homogenized Polar Forms, Osculating Flats

In this section, we assume that $\mathcal{E}$ is a normed affine space. One of the major benefits of homogenization is that the derivatives of an affine polynomial function $F \colon A \to \mathcal{E}$ can be obtained in a very simple way from the homogenized version $\widehat{f} \colon (\widehat{A})^m \to \widehat{\mathcal{E}}$, of its m-polar form $f \colon A^m \to \mathcal{E}$. In this section, following Ramshaw, it will be convenient to denote a point in A (and in $\widehat{A}$, since we view A as embedded as a line in $\widehat{A}$) as $\overline{a}$, to distinguish it from the vector $a \in \mathbf{R}$ (and $a \in \widehat{A}$, since we view $\mathbf{R}$ as embedded in $\widehat{A}$). When dealing with derivatives, it is also more convenient to denote the vector $\overrightarrow{ab}$ as $b - a$.

The vector 1 of $\widehat{A}$ will be denoted as $\vec{1}$, or as δ. Note that

$$\delta = \vec{1} = \overline{a+1} - \overline{a},$$

for any $a \in \mathbf{R}$.

Remark: When we write $\overline{a+1} - \overline{a}$, we mean $\overline{a+1} \mathbin{\widehat{-}} \overline{a}$ in $\widehat{A}$, but we prefer to be less pedantic, and we write simply $\overline{a+1} - \overline{a}$. In this section, given $a_1, \ldots, a_n \in \mathcal{E}$, and $\lambda_1, \ldots, \lambda_n \in \mathbf{R}$, such that $\lambda_1 + \cdots + \lambda_n = 0$, as suggested in Section 10.1, we will write

$$\lambda_1 a_1 \mathbin{\widehat{+}} \cdots \mathbin{\widehat{+}} \lambda_n a_n,$$

as

$$\lambda_1 a_1 + \cdots + \lambda_n a_n.$$

However, remember that such combinations are vectors in $\vec{\mathcal{E}}$ (and in $\widehat{\mathcal{E}}$).

For any $\overline{a} \in \mathbf{A}$, the derivative $DF(\overline{a})$ is the limit

$$\lim_{t \to 0,\, t \neq 0} \frac{F(\overline{a} + t\delta) - F(\overline{a})}{t},$$

if it exists. However, since $\widehat{F}$ agrees with F on $\mathbf{A}$, we have

$$F(\overline{a} + t\delta) - F(\overline{a}) = \widehat{F}(\overline{a} + t\delta) - \widehat{F}(\overline{a}),$$

and thus, we need to see what is the limit of

$$\frac{\widehat{F}(\overline{a} + t\delta) - \widehat{F}(\overline{a})}{t},$$

when $t \to 0$, $t \neq 0$, with $t \in \mathbf{R}$.

Recall that since $F: \mathbf{A} \to \mathcal{E}$, where $\mathcal{E}$ is an affine space, the derivative $DF(\overline{a})$ of F at $\overline{a}$ is a *vector* in $\vec{\mathcal{E}}$, and not a point in $\mathcal{E}$. However, the structure of $\widehat{\mathcal{E}}$ takes care of this, since $\widehat{F}(\overline{a} + t\delta) - \widehat{F}(\overline{a})$ is indeed a vector (remember our convention that $-$ is an abbreviation for $\widehat{-}$).

Since

$$\widehat{F}(\overline{a} + t\delta) = \widehat{f}(\underbrace{\overline{a} + t\delta, \ldots, \overline{a} + t\delta}_{m}),$$

where $\widehat{f}$ is the homogenized version of the polar form f of F, and $\widehat{F}$ is the homogenized version of F, since

$$\widehat{F}(\overline{a} + t\delta) - \widehat{F}(\overline{a}) = \widehat{f}(\underbrace{\overline{a} + t\delta, \ldots, \overline{a} + t\delta}_{m}) - \widehat{f}(\underbrace{\overline{a}, \ldots, \overline{a}}_{m}),$$

by multilinearity and symmetry, we have

$$\widehat{F}(\overline{a} + t\delta) - \widehat{F}(\overline{a}) = m\, t\, \widehat{f}(\underbrace{\overline{a}, \ldots, \overline{a}}_{m-1}, \delta) + \sum_{k=2}^{k=m} \binom{m}{k} t^{k}\, \widehat{f}(\underbrace{\overline{a}, \ldots, \overline{a}}_{m-k}, \underbrace{\delta, \ldots, \delta}_{k}),$$

and thus,

$$\lim_{t \to 0,\, t \neq 0} \frac{\widehat{F}(\overline{a} + t\delta) - \widehat{F}(\overline{a})}{t} = m\widehat{f}(\underbrace{\overline{a}, \ldots, \overline{a}}_{m-1}, \delta).$$

However, since $\widehat{F}$ extends F on $\mathbf{A}$, we have $DF(\overline{a}) = D\widehat{F}(\overline{a})$, and thus, we showed that

$$DF(\overline{a}) = m\widehat{f}(\underbrace{\overline{a}, \ldots, \overline{a}}_{m-1}, \delta).$$

This shows that the derivative of F at $\overline{a} \in \mathbf{A}$ can be computed by evaluating the homogenized version $\widehat{f}$ of the polar form f of F, by replacing just one occurrence of $\overline{a}$ in $\widehat{f}(\overline{a}, \ldots, \overline{a})$ by δ.

More generally, we have the following useful lemma.

Lemma 10.5.1

Given an affine polynomial function $F \colon \mathbf{A} \to \mathcal{E}$ of polar degree m, where $\mathcal{E}$ is a normed affine space, the kth derivative $D^k F(\overline{a})$ can be computed from the homogenized polar form $\widehat{f}$ of F as follows, where $1 \le k \le m$:

$$D^k F(\overline{a}) = m(m-1) \cdots (m-k+1)\,\widehat{f}(\underbrace{\overline{a}, \ldots, \overline{a}}_{m-k}, \underbrace{\delta, \ldots, \delta}_{k}).$$

Proof: A simple induction on k. ∎

When $k > m$, we have $D^k F(\overline{a}) = \vec{0}$.

Recall from Section 5.4 that the *falling power* $m^{\underline{k}}$ is defined as

$$m^{\underline{k}} = m(m-1) \cdots (m-k+1),$$

We define the *falling power* $m^{\underline{k}}$, for $0 \le k \le m$, with $m^{\underline{0}} = 1$, and with the convention that $m^{\underline{k}} = 0$ when $k > m$. The falling powers $m^{\underline{k}}$ have some interesting combinatorial properties of their own. Using the falling power notation, the previous lemma reads as

$$D^k F(\overline{a}) = m^{\underline{k}}\,\widehat{f}(\underbrace{\overline{a}, \ldots, \overline{a}}_{m-k}, \underbrace{\delta, \ldots, \delta}_{k}).$$

We also get the following explicit formula in terms of control points.

Lemma 10.5.2

Given an affine polynomial function $F \colon \mathbf{A} \to \mathcal{E}$ of polar degree m, where $\mathcal{E}$ is a normed affine space, for any $\overline{r}, \overline{s} \in \mathbf{A}$, with $r \ne s$, the kth derivative $D^k F(\overline{r})$ can be computed from the polar form f of F as follows, where $1 \le k \le m$:

$$D^k F(\overline{r}) = \frac{m^{\underline{k}}}{(s-r)^k} \sum_{i=0}^{i=k} \binom{k}{i} (-1)^{k-i} f(\underbrace{\overline{r}, \ldots, \overline{r}}_{m-i}, \underbrace{\overline{s}, \ldots, \overline{s}}_{i}).$$

Proof: Since

$$\delta = \frac{\overline{s} - \overline{r}}{s - r},$$

we can expand

$$D^k F(\bar{r}) = m^{\underline{k}} \,\widehat{f}\left(\underbrace{\bar{r}, \ldots, \bar{r}}_{m-k}, \underbrace{\frac{\bar{s} - \bar{r}}{s - r}, \ldots, \frac{\bar{s} - \bar{r}}{s - r}}_{k}\right)$$

by multilinearity and symmetry, and by induction on k, we get

$$D^k F(\bar{r}) = \frac{m^{\underline{k}}}{(s - r)^k} \sum_{i=0}^{i=k} \binom{k}{i} (-1)^{k-i} \,\widehat{f}(\underbrace{\bar{r}, \ldots, \bar{r}}_{m-i}, \underbrace{\bar{s}, \ldots, \bar{s}}_{i}),$$

and we conclude using the fact that $\widehat{f}$ agrees with f on $\mathcal{E}$. ∎

Lemma 10.5.2 is usually derived via more traditional methods involving finite differences. We believe that the approach via polar forms is more conceptual and gives more insight into what's really going on. It also extends fairly easily to the case when the domain **A** is replaced by a more general normed affine space (to define surfaces).

If F is specified by the sequence of $m + 1$ control points $b_i = f(\bar{r}^{\,m-i}\,\bar{s}^{\,i})$, $0 \le i \le m$, the above lemma shows that the kth derivative $D^k F(\bar{r})$ of F at $\bar{r}$ depends only on the $k + 1$ control points $b_0, \ldots, b_k$. In terms of the control points $b_0, \ldots, b_k$, the formula of Lemma 10.5.2 reads as follows:

$$D^k F(\bar{r}) = \frac{m^{\underline{k}}}{(s - r)^k} \sum_{i=0}^{i=k} \binom{k}{i} (-1)^{k-i} \, b_i.$$

In particular, if $b_0 \neq b_1$, then $DF(\bar{r})$ is the velocity vector of F at b_0, and it is given by

$$DF(\bar{r}) = \frac{m}{s - r}\,\overrightarrow{b_0 b_1} = \frac{m}{s - r}\,(b_1 - b_0),$$

the last expression making sense in $\widehat{\mathcal{E}}$. This shows that when b_0 and b_1 are distinct, the tangent to the Bézier curve at the point b_0 is the line determined by b_0 and b_1. Similarly, the tangent at the point b_m is the line determined by b_{m-1} and b_m (provided that these points are distinct). In order to see that the tangent at the current point $F(\bar{t})$ defined by the parameter $\bar{t}$, is determined by the two points

$$b_{0, m-1} = f(\underbrace{\bar{t}, \ldots, \bar{t}}_{m-1}, \bar{r})$$

and

$$b_{1, m-1} = f(\underbrace{\bar{t}, \ldots, \bar{t}}_{m-1}, \bar{s}),$$

given by the de Casteljau algorithm, note that since

$$\delta = \frac{\bar{s} - \bar{r}}{s - r}$$

and

$$\mathrm{D}F(\bar{t}) = m\widehat{f}(\underbrace{\bar{t}, \ldots, \bar{t}}_{m-1}, \delta) = \frac{m}{s - r}(\widehat{f}(\underbrace{\bar{t}, \ldots, \bar{t}}_{m-1}, \bar{r}) - \widehat{f}(\underbrace{\bar{t}, \ldots, \bar{t}}_{m-1}, \bar{s})),$$

and since $\widehat{f}$ agrees with f on $\mathbf{A}^m$, we have

$$\mathrm{D}F(\bar{t}) = \frac{m}{s - r}(b_{1,m-1} - b_{0,m-1}).$$

Thus, we have justified the claims about tangents to Bézier curves made in Section 5.1.

Similarly, the acceleration vector $\mathrm{D}^2 F(\bar{r})$ is given by

$$\mathrm{D}^2 F(\bar{r}) = \frac{m(m-1)}{(s-r)^2}(\overrightarrow{b_0 b_2} - 2\overrightarrow{b_0 b_1}) = \frac{m(m-1)}{(s-r)^2}(b_2 - 2b_1 + b_0),$$

the last expression making sense in $\widehat{\mathcal{E}}$. More generally, if $b_0 = b_1 = \ldots = b_k$, and $b_k \neq b_{k+1}$, the above reasoning can be used to show that the tangent at the point b_0 is determined by the points b_0 and b_{k+1}.

Later on when we deal with surfaces, it will be necessary to generalize the above results to directional derivatives. However, we have basically done all the work already. Let us assume that E and $\mathcal{E}$ are normed affine spaces, and consider a map $F \colon E \to \mathcal{E}$. From Definition D.1.2 in Appendix D, if A is any open subset of E, for any $a \in A$, for any $\vec{u} \neq \vec{0}$ in $\vec{E}$, the *directional derivative of F at a with respect to the vector $\vec{u}$*, denoted as $\mathrm{D}_{\vec{u}} F(a)$, is the limit, if it exists,

$$\lim_{t \to 0, t \in U, t \neq 0} \frac{F(a + t\vec{u}) - F(a)}{t},$$

where $U = \{t \in \mathbf{R} \mid a + t\vec{u} \in A\}$.

If $F \colon E \to \mathcal{E}$ is a polynomial function of degree m, and if the symmetric multiaffine map $f \colon E^m \to \mathcal{E}$ is its polar form, then

$$F(a + t\vec{u}) - F(a) = \widehat{F}(a + t\vec{u}) - \widehat{F}(a),$$

where $\widehat{F}$ is the homogenized version of F, that is, the polynomial map $\widehat{F} \colon \widehat{E} \to \widehat{\mathcal{E}}$ associated with the homogenized version $f \colon (\widehat{E})^m \to \widehat{\mathcal{E}}$ of the polar form $f \colon E^m \to \mathcal{E}$ of $F \colon E \to \mathcal{E}$. Thus, $\mathrm{D}_{\vec{u}} F(a)$ exists iff the limit

$$\lim_{t \to 0, t \neq 0} \frac{\widehat{F}(a + t\vec{u}) - \widehat{F}(a)}{t}$$

exists, and in this case, this limit is $\mathrm{D}_{\vec{u}} F(a) = \mathrm{D}_{\vec{u}} \widehat{F}(a)$.

Furthermore,

$$\widehat{F}(a + t\vec{u}) = \widehat{f}(\underbrace{a + t\vec{u}, \ldots, a + t\vec{u}}_{m}),$$

and since

$$\widehat{F}(a + t\vec{u}) - \widehat{F}(a) = \widehat{f}(\underbrace{a + t\vec{u}, \ldots, a + t\vec{u}}_{m}) - \widehat{f}(\underbrace{a, \ldots, a}_{m}),$$

by multilinearity and symmetry, we have

$$\widehat{F}(a + t\vec{u}) - \widehat{F}(a) = m\, t\, \widehat{f}(\underbrace{a, \ldots, a}_{m-1}, \vec{u}) + \sum_{k=2}^{k=m} \binom{m}{k} t^k \widehat{f}(\underbrace{a, \ldots, a}_{m-k}, \underbrace{\vec{u}, \ldots, \vec{u}}_{k}),$$

and thus,

$$D_{\vec{u}}\widehat{F}(a) = \lim_{t \to 0,\, t \neq 0} \frac{\widehat{F}(a + t\vec{u}) - \widehat{F}(a)}{t} = m\widehat{f}(\underbrace{a, \ldots, a}_{m-1}, \vec{u}).$$

However, we showed previously that $D_{\vec{u}}F(a) = D_{\vec{u}}\widehat{F}(a)$, and thus, we showed that

$$D_{\vec{u}}F(a) = m\widehat{f}(\underbrace{a, \ldots, a}_{m-1}, \vec{u}).$$

By a simple induction, we can prove the following lemma.

Lemma 10.5.3

Given an affine polynomial function $F: E \to \mathcal{E}$ of polar degree m, where E and $\mathcal{E}$ are normed affine spaces, for any k nonzero vectors $\vec{u}_1, \ldots, \vec{u}_k \in \vec{E}$, where $1 \le k \le m$, the kth directional derivative $D_{\vec{u}_1} \ldots D_{\vec{u}_k}F(a)$ can be computed from the homogenized polar form $\widehat{f}$ of F as follows:

$$D_{\vec{u}_1} \ldots D_{\vec{u}_k}F(a) = m^{\underline{k}}\, \widehat{f}(\underbrace{a, \ldots, a}_{m-k}, \vec{u}_1, \ldots, \vec{u}_k).$$

Lemma 10.5.3 is a generalization of Lemma 10.5.1 to any domain E that is a normed affine space. We are going to make use of this lemma to study local approximations of a polynomial map $F: E \to \mathcal{E}$, in the neighborhood of a point $F(a)$, where a is any point in E. In order to be sure that the polar form $f: E^m \to \mathcal{E}$ is continuous, let us now assume that E is of finite dimension.

Since by Lemma 10.5.3, the directional derivatives $D_{\vec{u}_1} \ldots D_{\vec{u}_k}F(a)$ exist for all $\vec{u}_1, \ldots, \vec{u}_k$ and all $k \ge 1$, and since E is of finite dimension, all multiaffine maps are continuous and the derivatives $D^k F$ exist for all $k \ge 1$ and are of class C^∞ (recall that

$D^k F(a)$ is a symmetric k-linear map, see Lang [48]). Furthermore, we know that

$$D^k F(a)(\overrightarrow{u_1}, \ldots, \overrightarrow{u_k}) = D_{\overrightarrow{u_1}} \ldots D_{\overrightarrow{u_k}} F(a).$$

Thus, Lemma 10.5.3 actually shows that

$$D^k F(a)(\overrightarrow{u_1}, \ldots, \overrightarrow{u_k}) = m^{\underline{k}} \widehat{f}(\underbrace{a, \ldots, a}_{m-k}, \overrightarrow{u_1}, \ldots, \overrightarrow{u_k}).$$

This shows that $D^k F(a)$ is the symmetric k-linear map

$$(\overrightarrow{u_1}, \ldots, \overrightarrow{u_k}) \mapsto m^{\underline{k}} \widehat{f}(\underbrace{a, \ldots, a}_{m-k}, \overrightarrow{u_1}, \ldots, \overrightarrow{u_k}).$$

Of course, for $k > m$, the derivative $D^k F(a)$ is the null k-linear map.

Remark: As usual, for $k = 0$, we agree that $D^0 F(a) = F(a)$. We could also relax the condition that E is of finite dimension, and assume that the polar form f is a continuous map.

Now, let a be any point in E. For any k, with $0 \le k \le m$, we can truncate the Taylor expansion of $F \colon E \to \mathcal{E}$ at a at the $(k+1)$-th order, getting the polynomial map $G_a^k \colon E \to \mathcal{E}$ defined such that, for all $b \in E$,

$$G_a^k(b) = F(a) + \frac{1}{1!} D^1 F(a)(\overrightarrow{ab}) + \cdots + \frac{1}{k!} D^k F(a)(\overrightarrow{ab}^k).$$

The polynomial function G_a^k agrees with F to kth order at a, which means that

$$D^i G_a^k(a) = D^i F(a),$$

for all i, $0 \le i \le k$. We say that G_a^k *osculates F to kth order at a*. For example, in the case of a curve $F \colon \mathbf{A} \to \mathcal{E}$, for $k = 1$, the map G_a^1 is simply the affine map determined by the tangent line at a, and for $k = 2$, G_a^2 is a parabola tangent to the curve F at a.

As pointed out by Ramshaw, it is tempting to believe that the polar form g_a^k of G_a^k is simply obtained from the polar form f of F, by fixing $m - k$ arguments of f at the point a, more precisely, if

$$g_a^k(b_1, \ldots, b_k) = f(b_1, \ldots, b_k, \underbrace{a, \ldots, a}_{m-k}),$$

for all $b_1, \ldots, b_k \in E$.

Unfortunately, this is false, even for curves. The problem is a silly one and has to do with the falling power $m^{\underline{k}}$. For example, if we consider a parabola $F \colon \mathbf{A} \to \mathbf{A}^2$, it is easy to see from Taylor's formula that

$$G_{\overline{b}}^1(\overline{a}) = 2 f(\overline{a}, \overline{b}) - f(\overline{b}, \overline{b}),$$

and

$$G_{\overline{a}}^1(\overline{b}) = 2f(\overline{a}, \overline{b}) - f(\overline{a}, \overline{a}),$$

which means that $f(\overline{a}, \overline{b})$ is both the middle of the two line segments $(f(\overline{a}, \overline{a}), G_{\overline{a}}^1(\overline{b}))$ and $(f(\overline{b}, \overline{b}), G_{\overline{b}}^1(\overline{a}))$, which happen to be tangent to F at $F(\overline{a})$ and $F(\overline{b})$. Unfortunately, it is not true that $G_{\overline{a}}^1(\overline{b}) = G_{\overline{b}}^1(\overline{a}) = f(\overline{a}, \overline{b})$.

It is possible to fix this problem and to find the relationship between the polar forms f and g_a^k, but this is done most conveniently using symmetric tensors and will be postponed until Section 11.1 (see Lemma B.4.3).

The annoying coefficients $m^{\underline{k}}$ can also be washed out, if we consider the affine subspaces spanned by the range of G_a^k, instead of osculating curves or surfaces.

Definition 10.5.4

Given any two normed affine spaces E and $\mathcal{E}$, where E is of finite dimension, for any polynomial map $F: E \to \mathcal{E}$ of degree m, for any $a \in E$, for any k, with $0 \le k \le m$, the polynomial map $G_a^k: E \to \mathcal{E}$ is defined such that, for all $b \in E$,

$$G_a^k(b) = F(a) + \frac{1}{1!}D^1 F(a)(\overrightarrow{ab}) + \cdots + \frac{1}{k!}D^k F(a)(\overrightarrow{ab}^k).$$

We say that G_a^k osculates F to kth order at a. The osculating flat $\mathrm{Osc}_k F(a)$ is the affine subspace of $\mathcal{E}$ generated by the range of G_a^k.

If $F: \mathbf{A} \to \mathcal{E}$ is a curve, then we say that F is *nondegenerate* iff $\mathrm{Osc}_k F(\overline{a})$ has dimension k for all $\overline{a} \in \mathbf{A}$. In such a case, the flat $\mathrm{Osc}_1 F(\overline{a})$ is the tangent line to F at $\overline{a}$, and $\mathrm{Osc}_2 F(\overline{a})$ is the *osculating plane to F at a*, that is, the plane determined by the point $F(\overline{a})$, the velocity vector $D^1 F(\overline{a})$, and the acceleration vector $D^2 F(\overline{a})$. The osculating plane is the usual notion used in differential geometry. The osculating plane to the curve F at the point $F(\overline{a})$ is the limit of any plane containing the tangent line at $F(\overline{a})$ and any other point $F(\overline{b})$ on the curve F, when $\overline{b}$ approaches $\overline{a}$.

If $F: \mathcal{P} \to \mathcal{E}$ is a surface, assuming that $(\Omega, (\overrightarrow{e_1}, \overrightarrow{e_2}))$ is an affine frame of $\mathcal{P}$, recall that we denote $D_{\overrightarrow{e_{j_k}}} \dots D_{\overrightarrow{e_{j_1}}} F(a)$ as

$$\frac{\partial^k F}{\partial x_{j_1} \dots \partial x_{j_k}}(a).$$

These are the partial derivatives at a. Also, letting $b = a + h_1 \overrightarrow{e_1} + h_2 \overrightarrow{e_2}$, in terms of partial derivatives, the truncated Taylor expansion is written as

$$G_a^k(b) = F(a) + \sum_{1 \le i_1 + i_2 \le k} \frac{h_1^{i_1} h_2^{i_2}}{i_1! i_2!} \left(\frac{\partial}{\partial x_1}\right)^{i_1} \left(\frac{\partial}{\partial x_2}\right)^{i_2} F(a).$$

It is not too difficult to show that there are

$$\frac{(k+1)(k+2)}{2} - 1 = \frac{k(k+3)}{2}$$

partial derivatives in the above expression, and we say that the surface *F is nondegenerate* iff $\mathrm{Osc}_k F(a)$ has dimension $k(k+3)/2$ for all $a \in \mathcal{P}$. For a nondegenerate surface, $\mathrm{Osc}_1 F(a)$ is the tangent plane to F at a, and $\mathrm{Osc}_2 F(a)$ is a flat of dimension 5, spanned by the vectors $\frac{\partial F}{\partial x_1}(a)$, $\frac{\partial F}{\partial x_2}(a)$, $\frac{\partial^2 F}{\partial x_1^2}(a)$, $\frac{\partial^2 F}{\partial x_2^2}(a)$, and $\frac{\partial^2 F}{\partial x_1 \partial x_2}(a)$. The flat $\mathrm{Osc}_3 F(a)$ is a flat of dimension 9, and we leave as an exercise to list the vectors spanning it. Thus, plane curves are degenerate in the above sense, except lines, and surfaces in $\mathbf{A}^3$ are degenerate in the above sense, except planes.

There is a simple relationship between osculating flats and polar forms, but it is much more convenient to use tensors to prove it, and we postpone the proof until Section 11.1 (see Lemma B.4.4). Let us simply mention a useful corollary. Given a polynomial map $F \colon E \to \mathcal{E}$ of degree m with polar form $f \colon E^m \to \mathcal{E}$, the affine subspace spanned by the range of the multiaffine map

$$(b_1, \ldots, b_{m-k}) \mapsto f(\underbrace{a, \ldots, a}_{k}, b_1, \ldots, b_{m-k})$$

is the osculating flat $\mathrm{Osc}_{m-k} F(a)$. This leads to a geometric interpretation of polar values. We note in passing that the geometric interpretation of polar forms, in terms of osculating flats, was investigated by S. Jolles, as early as 1886.

Let $F \colon \mathbf{A} \to \mathcal{E}$ be a nondegenerate curve of degree 3 (and thus, a space curve). By the previous corollary, the polar value $f(\bar{r}, \bar{s}, \bar{t})$ is the unique intersection of the three osculating planes $\mathrm{Osc}_2 F(\bar{r})$, $\mathrm{Osc}_2 F(\bar{s})$, and $\mathrm{Osc}_2 F(\bar{t})$. The polar value $f(\bar{s}, \bar{s}, \bar{t})$ is the intersection of the tangent line $\mathrm{Osc}_1 F(\bar{s})$ with the osculating plane $\mathrm{Osc}_2 F(\bar{t})$. More generally, given a nondegenerate curve or surface $F \colon E \to \mathcal{E}$, the polar value $f(b_1, \ldots, b_m)$ is the unique intersection of the osculating flats corresponding to all of the distinct points a that occur in the multiset $\{b_1, \ldots, b_m\}$.

This interpretation is so nice that you may wonder why it was not chosen as a definition of polar forms. Unfortunately, this idea does not work as soon as $F \colon \mathbf{A} \to \mathcal{E}$ is degenerate, which happens a lot. Indeed, Bézier points are usually not affinely independent. Thus, we had to use a more algebraic definition.

In the case of surfaces, osculating flats intersect more often than we would expect. For example, given a nondegenerate cubic surface, we know that it lies in an affine space of dimension 9. But for each $a \in \mathcal{P}$, the osculating flat $\mathrm{Osc}_2 F(a)$ has dimension 5. In general, three 5-flats in a 9-space do not intersect, but any three 5-flats $\mathrm{Osc}_2 F(a)$, $\mathrm{Osc}_2 F(b)$, and $\mathrm{Osc}_2 F(c)$ intersect at the polar value $f(a, b, c)$.

If you would like to have an in-depth understanding of the foundations of geometric design and a more conceptual view of the material on curves and surfaces, we urge you to read the next chapter on tensors. However, skipping this chapter will only have very minor consequences (basically, ignoring the proofs of a few results).

Problems

[10 pts] 1. Prove that $\widehat{E}$ as defined in Lemma 10.1.1 is indeed a vector space.

[10 pts] 2. Prove Lemma 10.1.2.

[10 pts] 3. Fill in the missing details in the proof of Lemma 10.2.1.

[10 pts] 4. Fill in the missing details in the proof of Lemma 10.5.2.

[10 pts] 5. Give some vectors spanning the flat $\mathrm{Osc}_3 F(a)$ of dimension 9.

CHAPTER 11

Tensor Products and Symmetric Tensor Products

11.1   Tensor Products

This chapter is not absolutely essential and can be omitted if you are willing to accept some of the deeper results without proofs (or are willing to go through rather nasty computations!). On the other hand, if you would like to have an in-depth understanding of the foundations of computer-aided geometric design and a more conceptual view of the material on curves and surfaces, you should make an effort to read this chapter. We hope that you will find it rewarding!

First, tensor products are defined, and some of their basic properties are shown. Next, symmetric tensor products are defined, and some of their basic properties are shown. Symmetric tensor products of affine spaces are also briefly discussed. The machinery of symmetric tensor products is then used to prove some important results of CAGD. For example, an elegant proof of Theorem 5.3.2 is given.

We have seen that multilinear maps play an important role. Given a linear map $f: E \to F$, we know that if we have a basis $(\vec{u_i})_{i \in I}$ for E, then f is completely determined by its values $f(\vec{u_i})$ on the basis vectors. For a multilinear map $f: E^n \to F$, we don't know if there is such a nice property, but it would certainly be very useful.

In many respects, tensor products allow us to define multilinear maps in terms of their action on a suitable basis. Once again, as in Section 10.1, we *linearize*, that is, we create a new vector space $E \otimes \cdots \otimes E$, such that the multilinear map $f: E^n \to F$ is turned into a *linear map* $f_\otimes: E \otimes \cdots \otimes E \to F$, which is equivalent to f in a strong sense. If, in addition, f is symmetric, then we can define a symmetric tensor product $E \odot \cdots \odot E$, and every symmetric multilinear map $f: E^n \to F$ is turned into a *linear map* $f_\odot: E \odot \cdots \odot E \to F$, which is equivalent to f in a strong sense.

Tensor products can be defined in various ways, some more abstract than others. We tried to stay down to earth, without excess!

373

Let K be a given field, and let $E_1, \ldots, E_n$ be $n \geq 2$ given vector spaces. First, we define tensor products, and then we prove their existence and uniqueness up to isomorphism.

Definition 11.1.1

A tensor product of $n \geq 2$ vector spaces $E_1, \ldots, E_n$ is a vector space T, together with a multilinear map $\varphi \colon E_1 \times \cdots \times E_n \to T$, such that, for every vector space F and for every multilinear map $f \colon E_1 \times \cdots \times E_n \to F$, there is a unique linear map $f_\otimes \colon T \to F$, with

$$f(\overrightarrow{u_1}, \ldots, \overrightarrow{u_n}) = f_\otimes(\varphi(\overrightarrow{u_1}, \ldots, \overrightarrow{u_n})),$$

for all $\overrightarrow{u_1} \in E_1, \ldots, \overrightarrow{u_n} \in E_n$, or for short

$$f = f_\otimes \circ \varphi.$$

Equivalently, there is a unique linear map $f_\otimes$ such that the following diagram commutes:

$$
\begin{array}{ccc}
E_1 \times \cdots \times E_n & \xrightarrow{\ \varphi\ } & T \\
& {}^{f}\searrow & \downarrow {}^{f_\otimes} \\
& & F
\end{array}
$$

First, we show that any two tensor products (T_1, φ_1) and (T_2, φ_2), for $E_1, \ldots, E_n$, are isomorphic.

Lemma 11.1.2

Given any two tensor products (T_1, φ_1) and (T_2, φ_2), for $E_1, \ldots, E_n$, there is an isomorphism $h \colon T_1 \to T_2$ such that

$$\varphi_2 = h \circ \varphi_1.$$

Proof: Focusing on (T_1, φ_1), we have a multilinear map $\varphi_2 \colon E_1 \times \cdots \times E_n \to T_2$, and thus, there is a unique linear map $(\varphi_2)_\otimes \colon T_1 \to T_2$, with

$$\varphi_2 = (\varphi_2)_\otimes \circ \varphi_1.$$

Similarly, focusing now on (T_2, φ_2), we have a multilinear map $\varphi_1 \colon E_1 \times \cdots \times E_n \to T_1$, and thus, there is a unique linear map $(\varphi_1)_\otimes \colon T_2 \to T_1$, with

$$\varphi_1 = (\varphi_1)_\otimes \circ \varphi_2.$$

But then, we get

$$\varphi_1 = (\varphi_1)_\otimes \circ (\varphi_2)_\otimes \circ \varphi_1,$$

and

$$\varphi_2 = (\varphi_2)_\otimes \circ (\varphi_1)_\otimes \circ \varphi_2.$$

On the other hand, focusing on (T_1, φ_1), we have a multilinear map $\varphi_1 \colon E_1 \times \cdots \times E_n \to T_1$, but the unique linear map $h \colon T_1 \to T_1$, with

$$\varphi_1 = h \circ \varphi_1$$

is $h = \mathrm{id}$, and since $(\varphi_1)_\otimes \circ (\varphi_2)_\otimes$ is linear, as a composition of linear maps, we must have

$$(\varphi_1)_\otimes \circ (\varphi_2)_\otimes = \mathrm{id} \,.$$

Similarly, we must have

$$(\varphi_2)_\otimes \circ (\varphi_1)_\otimes = \mathrm{id} \,.$$

This shows that $(\varphi_1)_\otimes$ and $(\varphi_2)_\otimes$ are inverse linear maps, and thus, $(\varphi_2)_\otimes \colon T_1 \to T_2$ is an isomorphism between T_1 and T_2. $\blacksquare$

Now that we have shown that tensor products are unique up to isomorphism, we give a construction that produces one.

Lemma 11.1.3

Given $n \geq 2$ vector spaces $E_1, \ldots, E_n$, a tensor product $(E_1 \otimes \cdots \otimes E_n, \varphi)$ for $E_1, \ldots, E_n$ can be constructed. Furthermore, denoting $\varphi(\vec{u_1}, \ldots, \vec{u_n})$ as $\vec{u_1} \otimes \cdots \otimes \vec{u_n}$, the tensor product $E_1 \otimes \cdots \otimes E_n$ is generated by the vectors $\vec{u_1} \otimes \cdots \otimes \vec{u_n}$, where $\vec{u_1} \in E_1, \ldots, \vec{u_n} \in E_n$, and for every multilinear map $f \colon E_1 \times \cdots \times E_n \to F$, the unique linear map $f_\otimes \colon E_1 \otimes \cdots \otimes E_n \to F$, such that $f = f_\otimes \circ \varphi$, is defined by

$$f_\otimes(\vec{u_1} \otimes \cdots \otimes \vec{u_n}) = f(\vec{u_1}, \ldots, \vec{u_n}),$$

on the generators $\vec{u_1} \otimes \cdots \otimes \vec{u_n}$ of $E_1 \otimes \cdots \otimes E_n$.

Proof: First, we apply the construction of Definition A.1.11 to the cartesian product $I = E_1 \times \cdots \times E_n$, and we get the free vector space $M = K^{(I)}$ on $I = E_1 \times \cdots \times E_n$. Recall that the family $(\vec{e_i})_{i \in I}$ is defined such that $\overrightarrow{(e_i)}_j = 0$ if $j \neq i$ and $\overrightarrow{(e_i)}_i = 1$. It is a basis of the vector space $K^{(I)}$, so that every $\vec{w} \in K^{(I)}$ can be uniquely written as a finite linear combination of the $\vec{e_i}$. There is also an injection $\iota \colon I \to K^{(I)}$ such that $\iota(i) = \vec{e_i}$ for every $i \in I$. Since every $\vec{e_i}$ is uniquely associated with some n-tuple $i = (\vec{u_1}, \ldots, \vec{u_n}) \in E_1 \times \cdots \times E_n$, we will denote $\vec{e_i}$ as $(\vec{u_1}, \ldots, \vec{u_n})$. Also, by Lemma A.2.4, for any vector space F, and for any function $f \colon I \to F$, there is a unique linear map $\overline{f} \colon K^{(I)} \to F$, such that

$$f = \overline{f} \circ \iota,$$

as in the following diagram:

$$E_1 \times \cdots \times E_n \;\xrightarrow{\;\iota\;}\; K^{(E_1 \times \cdots \times E_n)}$$
$$f \searrow \qquad \downarrow \overline{f}$$
$$F$$

Next, let N be the subspace of M generated by the vectors of the following type:

$$(\vec{u_1}, \ldots, \vec{u_i} + \vec{v_i}, \ldots, \vec{u_n}) - (\vec{u_1}, \ldots, \vec{u_i}, \ldots, \vec{u_n}) - (\vec{u_1}, \ldots, \vec{v_i}, \ldots, \vec{u_n}),$$

$$(\vec{u_1}, \ldots, \lambda\vec{u_i}, \ldots, \vec{u_n}) - \lambda(\vec{u_1}, \ldots, \vec{u_i}, \ldots, \vec{u_n}).$$

We let $E_1 \otimes \cdots \otimes E_n$ be the quotient M/N of the free vector space M by N, which is well defined, by Lemma A.3.1. Let $\pi \colon M \to M/N$ be the quotient map, and let

$$\varphi = \pi \circ \iota.$$

By construction, φ is multilinear, and since π is surjective and the $\iota(i) = \vec{e_i}$ generate M, since i is of the form $i = (\vec{u_1}, \ldots, \vec{u_n}) \in E_1 \times \cdots \times E_n$, the $\varphi(\vec{u_1}, \ldots, \vec{u_n})$ generate M/N. Thus, if we denote $\varphi(\vec{u_1}, \ldots, \vec{u_n})$ as $\vec{u_1} \otimes \cdots \otimes \vec{u_n}$, the tensor product $E_1 \otimes \cdots \otimes E_n$ is generated by the vectors $\vec{u_1} \otimes \cdots \otimes \vec{u_n}$, where $\vec{u_1} \in E_1, \ldots, \vec{u_n} \in E_n$.

For every multilinear map $f \colon E_1 \times \cdots \times E_n \to F$, if a linear map $f_\otimes \colon E_1 \otimes \cdots \otimes E_n \to F$ exists such that $f = f_\otimes \circ \varphi$, since the vectors $\vec{u_1} \otimes \cdots \otimes \vec{u_n}$ generate $E_1 \otimes \cdots \otimes E_n$, the map $f_\otimes$ is uniquely defined by

$$f_\otimes(\vec{u_1} \otimes \cdots \otimes \vec{u_n}) = f(\vec{u_1}, \ldots, \vec{u_n}).$$

On the other hand, because $M = K^{(E_1 \times \cdots \times E_n)}$ is free on $I = E_1 \times \cdots \times E_n$, there is a unique linear map $\overline{f} \colon K^{(E_1 \times \cdots \times E_n)} \to F$, such that

$$f = \overline{f} \circ \iota,$$

as in the diagram below:

$$
\begin{array}{ccc}
E_1 \times \cdots \times E_n & \overset{\iota}{\longrightarrow} & K^{(E_1 \times \cdots \times E_n)} \\
 & {\scriptstyle f}\searrow & \downarrow {\scriptstyle \overline{f}} \\
 & & F
\end{array}
$$

Because f is multilinear, note that we must have $\overline{f}(\vec{w}) = \vec{0}$, for every $\vec{w} \in N$. But then, $\overline{f} \colon M \to F$ induces a linear map $h \colon M/N \to F$, such that

$$f = h \circ \pi \circ \iota,$$

by defining $h([\vec{z}]) = \overline{f}(\vec{z})$, for every $\vec{z} \in M$, where $[\vec{z}]$ denotes the equivalence class in M/N of $\vec{z} \in M$:

$$
\begin{array}{ccc}
E_1 \times \cdots \times E_n & \overset{\pi \circ \iota}{\longrightarrow} & K^{(E_1 \times \cdots \times E_n)/N} \\
 & {\scriptstyle f}\searrow & \downarrow {\scriptstyle h} \\
 & & F
\end{array}
$$

Indeed, the fact that $\overline{f}$ vanishes on N ensures that h is well defined on M/N, and it is clearly linear by definition. However, we showed that such a linear map h is unique, and thus it agrees with the linear map $f_\otimes$ defined by

$$f_\otimes(\vec{u_1} \otimes \cdots \otimes \vec{u_n}) = f(\vec{u_1}, \ldots, \vec{u_n})$$

on the generators of $E_1 \otimes \cdots \otimes E_n$. ∎

What is important about Lemma 11.1.3 is not so much the construction itself, but the fact that a tensor product with the universal property with respect to multilinear maps stated in that lemma holds. Indeed, Lemma 11.1.3 yields an isomorphism between the vector space of linear maps $L(E_1 \otimes \cdots \otimes E_n; F)$ and the vector space of multilinear maps $L(E_1, \ldots, E_n; F)$, via the linear map $- \circ \varphi$ defined by

$$h \mapsto h \circ \varphi,$$

where $h \in L(E_1 \otimes \cdots \otimes E_n; F)$. Indeed, $h \circ \varphi$ is clearly multilinear, and since by Lemma 11.1.3, for every multilinear map $f \in L(E_1, \ldots, E_n; F)$, there is a unique linear map $f_\otimes \in L(E_1 \otimes \cdots \otimes E_n; F)$ such that $f = f_\otimes \circ \varphi$, the map $- \circ \varphi$ is bijective. As a matter of fact, its inverse is the map

$$f \mapsto f_\otimes.$$

Remark: For $F = K$, the base field, we obtain a natural isomorphism between the vector space $L(E_1 \otimes \cdots \otimes E_n; K)$ and the vector space of multilinear forms $L(E_1, \ldots, E_n; K)$. However, $L(E_1 \otimes \cdots \otimes E_n; K)$ is the dual space $(E_1 \otimes \cdots \otimes E_n)^*$, and thus, the vector space of multilinear forms $L(E_1, \ldots, E_n; K)$ is naturally isomorphic to $(E_1 \otimes \cdots \otimes E_n)^*$. When all the spaces have finite dimension, this yields a (noncanonical) isomorphism between the vector space of multilinear forms $L(E_1^*, \ldots, E_n^*; K)$ and $E_1 \otimes \cdots \otimes E_n$.

The fact that the map $\varphi \colon E_1 \times \cdots \times E_n \to E_1 \otimes \cdots \otimes E_n$ is multilinear can also be expressed as follows:

$$\vec{u_1} \otimes \cdots \otimes (\vec{u_i} + \vec{v_i}) \otimes \cdots \otimes \vec{u_n}$$
$$= (\vec{u_1} \otimes \cdots \otimes \vec{u_i} \otimes \cdots \otimes \vec{u_n}) + (\vec{u_1} \otimes \cdots \otimes \vec{v_i} \otimes \cdots \otimes \vec{u_n}),$$
$$\vec{u_1} \otimes \cdots \otimes (\lambda \vec{u_i}) \otimes \cdots \otimes \vec{u_n}$$
$$= \lambda(\vec{u_1} \otimes \cdots \otimes \vec{u_i} \otimes \cdots \otimes \vec{u_n}).$$

Of course, this is just what we wanted! Tensors in $E_1 \otimes \cdots \otimes E_n$ are also called *n-tensors*, and tensors of the form $\vec{u_1} \otimes \cdots \otimes \vec{u_n}$, where $\vec{u_i} \in E_i$, are called *simple* (or *decomposable*) *n-tensors*. Those *n*-tensors that are not simple are often called *compound n-tensors*.

We showed that $E_1 \otimes \cdots \otimes E_n$ is generated by the vectors of the form $\vec{u_1} \otimes \cdots \otimes \vec{u_n}$. However, these vectors are not linearly independent. This situation can be fixed when considering bases, which is the object of the next lemma.

Lemma 11.1.4

Given $n \geq 2$ vector spaces $E_1, \ldots, E_n$, if $(\vec{u_i^k})_{i \in I_k}$ is a basis for E_k, $1 \leq k \leq n$, then the family of vectors

$$(\vec{u_{i_1}^1} \otimes \cdots \otimes \vec{u_{i_n}^n})_{(i_1, \ldots, i_n) \in I_1 \times \ldots \times I_n}$$

is a basis of the tensor product $E_1 \otimes \cdots \otimes E_n$.

Proof: For each k, $1 \le k \le n$, every $\vec{v^k} \in E_k$ can be written uniquely as

$$\vec{v^k} = \sum_{j \in I_k} v_j^k \vec{u_j^k},$$

for some family of scalars $(v_j^k)_{j \in I_k}$. Let F be any nontrivial vector space. We will show that for every family

$$(\overrightarrow{w_{i_1,\ldots,i_n}})_{(i_1,\ldots,i_n) \in I_1 \times \ldots \times I_n}$$

of vectors in F, there is some linear map $h \colon E_1 \otimes \cdots \otimes E_n \to F$, such that

$$h(\overrightarrow{u_{i_1}^1} \otimes \cdots \otimes \overrightarrow{u_{i_n}^n}) = \overrightarrow{w_{i_1,\ldots,i_n}}.$$

Then, by Lemma A.2.5 (2), it will follow that

$$(\overrightarrow{u_{i_1}^1} \otimes \cdots \otimes \overrightarrow{u_{i_n}^n})_{(i_1,\ldots,i_n) \in I_1 \times \ldots \times I_n}$$

is linearly independent. However, since $(\overrightarrow{u_i^k})_{i \in I_k}$ is a basis for E_k, the $\overrightarrow{u_{i_1}^1} \otimes \cdots \otimes \overrightarrow{u_{i_n}^n}$ also generate $E_1 \otimes \cdots \otimes E_n$, and thus, they form a basis of $E_1 \otimes \cdots \otimes E_n$.

We define the function $f \colon E_1 \times \cdots \times E_n \to F$ as follows:

$$f\left(\sum_{j_1 \in I_1} v_{j_1}^1 \overrightarrow{u_{j_1}^1}, \ldots, \sum_{j_n \in I_n} v_{j_n}^n \overrightarrow{u_{j_n}^n}\right) = \sum_{j_1 \in I_1, \ldots, j_n \in I_n} v_{j_1}^1 \cdots v_{j_n}^n \overrightarrow{w_{j_1,\ldots,j_n}}.$$

It is immediately verified that f is multilinear. By the universal property of the tensor product, the linear map $f_\otimes \colon E_1 \otimes \cdots \otimes E_n \to F$, such that $f = f_\otimes \circ \varphi$, is the desired map h. ∎

In particular, when each I_k is finite and of size m_k, we see that the dimension of the tensor product $E_1 \otimes \cdots \otimes E_n$ is $m_1 \cdots m_n$. As a corollary of Lemma 11.1.4, if $(\overrightarrow{u_i^k})_{i \in I_k}$ is a basis for E_k, $1 \le k \le n$, then every tensor $\vec{z} \in E_1 \otimes \cdots \otimes E_n$ can be written in a unique way as

$$\vec{z} = \sum_{(i_1,\ldots,i_n) \in I_1 \times \ldots \times I_n} \lambda_{i_1,\ldots,i_n} \overrightarrow{u_{i_1}^1} \otimes \cdots \otimes \overrightarrow{u_{i_n}^n},$$

for some unique family of scalars $\lambda_{i_1,\ldots,i_n} \in K$, all zero except for a finite number.

We also mention the following useful isomorphisms.

Lemma 11.1.5

Given three vector spaces E, F, G, there exist unique isomorphisms

1. $E \otimes F \simeq F \otimes E$

2. $(E \otimes F) \otimes G \simeq E \otimes (F \otimes G) \simeq E \otimes F \otimes G$

3. $(E \oplus F) \otimes G \simeq (E \otimes G) \oplus (F \otimes G)$

4. $K \otimes E \simeq E$

such that, respectively,

$$\vec{u} \otimes \vec{v} \mapsto \vec{v} \otimes \vec{u}$$

$$(\vec{u} \otimes \vec{v}) \otimes \vec{w} \mapsto \vec{u} \otimes (\vec{v} \otimes \vec{w}) \mapsto \vec{u} \otimes \vec{v} \otimes \vec{w}$$

$$(\vec{u}, \ \vec{v}) \otimes \vec{w} \mapsto (\vec{u} \otimes \vec{w}, \ \vec{v} \otimes \vec{w})$$

$$\lambda \otimes \vec{u} \mapsto \lambda \vec{u}.$$

Proof: These isomorphisms are proved using the universal property of tensor products. We illustrate the proof method on (2). Fix some $\vec{w} \in G$. The map

$$(\vec{u}, \ \vec{v}) \mapsto \vec{u} \otimes \vec{v} \otimes \vec{w}$$

from $E \times F$ to $E \otimes F \otimes G$ is bilinear, and thus, there is a linear map $f_{\vec{w}} \colon E \otimes F \to E \otimes F \otimes G$, such that $f_{\vec{w}}(\vec{u} \otimes \vec{v}) = \vec{u} \otimes \vec{v} \otimes \vec{w}$.

Next, consider the map

$$(\vec{z}, \ \vec{w}) \mapsto f_{\vec{w}}(\vec{z}),$$

from $(E \otimes F) \times G$ into $E \otimes F \otimes G$. It is easily seen to be bilinear, and thus, it induces a linear map

$$f \colon (E \otimes F) \otimes G \to E \otimes F \otimes G,$$

such that $f((\vec{u} \otimes \vec{v}) \otimes \vec{w}) = \vec{u} \otimes \vec{v} \otimes \vec{w}$.

Also consider the map

$$(\vec{u}, \ \vec{v}, \vec{w}) \mapsto (\vec{u} \otimes \vec{v}) \otimes \vec{w}$$

from $E \times F \times G$ to $(E \otimes F) \otimes G$. It is trilinear, and thus, there is a linear map

$$g \colon E \otimes F \otimes G \to (E \otimes F) \otimes G,$$

such that $g(\vec{u} \otimes \vec{v} \otimes \vec{w}) = (\vec{u} \otimes \vec{v}) \otimes \vec{w}$. Clearly, $f \circ g$ and $g \circ f$ are identity maps, and thus, f and g are isomorphisms. The other cases are similar. ∎

Not only do tensor products act on spaces, but they also act on linear maps (they are functors). Given two linear maps $f \colon E \to E'$ and $g \colon F \to F'$, we can define $h \colon E \times F \to E' \otimes F'$ by

$$h(\vec{u}, \ \vec{v}) = f(\vec{u}) \otimes g(\vec{v}).$$

It is immediately verified that h is bilinear, and thus, it induces a unique linear map

$$f \otimes g \colon E \otimes F \to E' \otimes F',$$

such that

$$(f \otimes g)(\vec{u} \otimes \vec{v}) = f(\vec{u}) \otimes g(\vec{u}).$$

If we also have linear maps $f' \colon E' \to E''$ and $g' \colon F' \to F''$, we can easily verify that the linear maps $(f' \circ f) \otimes (g' \circ g)$ and $(f' \otimes g') \circ (f \otimes g)$ agree on all vectors of the form $\vec{u} \otimes \vec{v} \in E \otimes F$. Since these vectors generate $E \otimes F$, we conclude that

$$(f' \circ f) \otimes (g' \circ g) = (f' \otimes g') \circ (f \otimes g).$$

The generalization to the tensor product $f_1 \otimes \cdots \otimes f_n$ of $n \geq 3$ linear maps $f_i \colon E_i \to F_i$ is immediate and left to the reader.

Remark: The tensor product

$$\underbrace{E \otimes \cdots \otimes E}_{m}$$

is also denoted as

$$\overset{m}{\bigotimes} E,$$

and is called the *mth tensor power of E* (with $\bigotimes^1 E = E$ and $\bigotimes^0 E = K$). The vector space

$$T(E) = \bigoplus_{m \geq 0} \overset{m}{\bigotimes} E,$$

called the *tensor algebra of E*, is an interesting object. When E is of finite dimension n, it corresponds to the algebra of polynomials with coefficients in K in n noncommuting variables. However, we would have to define a multiplication operation on $T(E)$, which is easily done.

We now turn to symmetric tensors.

11.2   Symmetric Tensor Products

Our goal is to come up with a notion of tensor product that will allow us to treat symmetric multilinear maps as linear maps. First, note that we have to restrict ourselves to a single vector space E, rather than n vector spaces $E_1, \ldots, E_n$, so that symmetry makes sense.

We could proceed directly as in Lemma 11.1.3 and construct symmetric tensor products from scratch. However, since we already have the notion of a tensor product, there is a more economical method. First, we define symmetric tensor products (powers).

Definition 11.2.1

A symmetric nth tensor power (or tensor product) of a vector space E, where $n \geq 2$, is a vector space S, together with a symmetric multilinear map $\varphi \colon E^n \to S$, such that, *for every vector space F and for every symmetric multilinear map $f\colon E^n \to F$, there is a unique linear map $f_\odot\colon S \to F$, with*

$$f(\overrightarrow{u_1}, \ldots, \overrightarrow{u_n}) = f_\odot(\varphi(\overrightarrow{u_1}, \ldots, \overrightarrow{u_n})),$$

for all $\overrightarrow{u_1}, \ldots, \overrightarrow{u_n} \in E$, or for short,

$$f = f_\odot \circ \varphi.$$

Equivalently, there is a unique linear map $f_\odot$ such that the following diagram commutes:

$$
\begin{array}{ccc}
E^n & \xrightarrow{\ \varphi\ } & S \\
& {\scriptstyle f}\searrow & \downarrow{\scriptstyle f_\odot} \\
& & F
\end{array}
$$

First, we show that any two symmetric nth tensor powers (S_1, φ_1) and (S_2, φ_2) for E are isomorphic.

Lemma 11.2.2

Given any two symmetric nth tensor powers (S_1, φ_1) and (S_2, φ_2) for E, there is an isomorphism $h\colon S_1 \to S_2$ such that

$$\varphi_2 = h \circ \varphi_1.$$

Proof: Replace tensor product by symmetric nth tensor power in the proof of Lemma 11.1.2.   ■

We now give a construction that produces a symmetric nth tensor power of a vector space E.

Lemma 11.2.3

Given a vector space E, a symmetric nth tensor power $(\bigodot^n E, \varphi)$ for E can be constructed ($n \geq 2$). Furthermore, denoting $\varphi(\overrightarrow{u_1}, \ldots, \overrightarrow{u_n})$ as $\overrightarrow{u_1} \odot \cdots \odot \overrightarrow{u_n}$, the symmetric tensor power $\bigodot^n E$ is generated by the vectors $\overrightarrow{u_1} \odot \cdots \odot \overrightarrow{u_n}$, where $\overrightarrow{u_1}, \ldots, \overrightarrow{u_n} \in E$, and for every symmetric multilinear map $f\colon E^n \to F$, the unique linear map $f_\odot\colon \bigodot^n E \to F$ such that $f = f_\odot \circ \varphi$, is defined by

$$f_\odot(\overrightarrow{u_1} \odot \cdots \odot \overrightarrow{u_n}) = f(\overrightarrow{u_1}, \ldots, \overrightarrow{u_n}),$$

on the generators $\overrightarrow{u_1} \odot \cdots \odot \overrightarrow{u_n}$ of $\bigodot^n E$.

Proof: The tensor power $\bigotimes^n E$ is too big, and thus, we define an appropriate quotient. Let C be the subspace of $\bigotimes^n E$ generated by the vectors of the form

$$\overrightarrow{u_1} \otimes \cdots \otimes \overrightarrow{u_n} - \overrightarrow{u_{\pi(1)}} \otimes \cdots \otimes \overrightarrow{u_{\pi(n)}},$$

for all $\overrightarrow{u_i} \in E$, and all permutations $\pi\colon \{1, \ldots, n\} \to \{1, \ldots, n\}$. We claim that the quotient space $(\bigotimes^n E)/C$ does the job.

Let $p\colon \bigotimes^n E \to (\bigotimes^n E)/C$ be the quotient map. Let $\varphi\colon E^n \to (\bigotimes^n E)/C$ be the map

$$(\overrightarrow{u_1}, \ldots, \overrightarrow{u_n}) \mapsto p(\overrightarrow{u_1} \otimes \cdots \otimes \overrightarrow{u_n}),$$

or equivalently, $\varphi = p \circ \varphi_0$, where $\varphi_0(\overrightarrow{u_1}, \ldots, \overrightarrow{u_n}) = \overrightarrow{u_1} \otimes \cdots \otimes \overrightarrow{u_n}$.

Let us denote $\varphi(\overrightarrow{u_1}, \ldots, \overrightarrow{u_n})$ as $\overrightarrow{u_1} \odot \cdots \odot \overrightarrow{u_n}$. It is clear that φ is symmetric. Since the vectors $\overrightarrow{u_1} \otimes \cdots \otimes \overrightarrow{u_n}$ generate $\bigotimes^n E$, and p is surjective, the vectors $\overrightarrow{u_1} \odot \cdots \odot \overrightarrow{u_n}$ generate $(\bigotimes^n E)/C$.

Given any symmetric multilinear map $f\colon E^n \to F$, there is a linear map $f_\otimes\colon \bigotimes^n E \to F$ such that $f = f_\otimes \circ \varphi_0$, as in the diagram below:

$$
\begin{array}{ccc}
E^n & \xrightarrow{\ \varphi_0\ } & \bigotimes^n E \\
& f \searrow & \downarrow f_\otimes \\
& & F
\end{array}
$$

However, since f is symmetric, we have $f_\otimes(\overrightarrow{z}) = \overrightarrow{0}$ for every $\overrightarrow{z} \in \bigotimes^n E$. Thus, we get an induced linear map $h\colon (\bigotimes^n E)/C \to F$, such that $h([\overrightarrow{z}]) = f_\otimes(\overrightarrow{z})$, where $[\overrightarrow{z}]$ is the equivalence class in $(\bigotimes^n E)/C$ of $\overrightarrow{z} \in \bigotimes^n E$:

$$
\begin{array}{ccc}
E^n & \xrightarrow{\ p\circ\varphi_0\ } & (\bigotimes^n E)/C \\
& f \searrow & \downarrow h \\
& & F
\end{array}
$$

However, if a linear map $f_\odot\colon (\bigotimes^n E)/C \to F$ exists, since the vectors $\overrightarrow{u_1} \odot \cdots \odot \overrightarrow{u_n}$ generate $(\bigotimes^n E)/C$, we must have

$$f_\odot(\overrightarrow{u_1} \odot \cdots \odot \overrightarrow{u_n}) = f(\overrightarrow{u_1}, \ldots, \overrightarrow{u_n}),$$

which shows that h and $f_\odot$ agree. Thus, $\odot^n E = (\bigotimes^n E)/C$ and φ constitute a symmetric nth tensor power of E. ∎

Again, the actual construction is not important. What is important is that the symmetric nth power has the universal property with respect to symmetric multilinear maps.

Remark: The notation $\odot^n E$ for the symmetric nth tensor power of E is borrowed from Ramshaw. It may not be standard. Other authors use the notation $\mathrm{Sym}^n(E)$, or $S^n(E)$. We will adopt Ramshaw's notation.

The fact that the map $\varphi\colon E^n \to \odot^n E$ is symmetric and multilinear can also be expressed as follows:

$$\vec{u_1} \odot \cdots \odot (\vec{u_i} + \vec{v_i}) \odot \cdots \odot \vec{u_n}$$
$$= (\vec{u_1} \odot \cdots \odot \vec{u_i} \odot \cdots \odot \vec{u_n}) + (\vec{u_1} \odot \cdots \odot \vec{v_i} \odot \cdots \odot \vec{u_n}),$$
$$\vec{u_1} \odot \cdots \odot (\lambda \vec{u_i}) \odot \cdots \odot \vec{u_n}$$
$$= \lambda(\vec{u_1} \odot \cdots \odot \vec{u_i} \odot \cdots \odot \vec{u_n}), \vec{u_1} \odot \cdots \odot \vec{u_n} = \vec{u_{\pi(1)}} \odot \cdots \odot \vec{u_{\pi(n)}},$$

for all permutations π on n elements.

The last identity shows that the "operation" $\odot$ is commutative. Thus, we can view the symmetric tensor $\vec{u_1} \odot \cdots \odot \vec{u_n}$ as a multiset.

Lemma 11.2.3 yields an isomorphism between the vector space of linear maps $L(\bigodot^n E; F)$ and the vector space of symmetric multilinear maps $S(E^n; F)$, via the linear map $- \circ \varphi$ defined by

$$h \mapsto h \circ \varphi,$$

where $h \in L(\bigodot^n E; F)$. Indeed, $h \circ \varphi$ is clearly symmetric multilinear, and since by Lemma 11.2.3, for every symmetric multilinear map $f \in S(E^n; F)$, there is a unique linear map $f_\odot \in L(\bigodot^n E; F)$ such that $f = f_\odot \circ \varphi$, the map $- \circ \varphi$ is bijective. As a matter of fact, its inverse is the map

$$f \mapsto f_\odot.$$

Remark: As in the case of general tensors, the vector space of symmetric multilinear forms $S(E^n; K)$ is naturally isomorphic to $(\bigodot^n E)^*$. When the space E has finite dimension, this yields a (noncanonical) isomorphism between the vector space of symmetric multilinear forms $S((E^*)^n; K)$ and $\bigodot^n E$.

Symmetric tensors in $\bigodot^n E$ are also called *symmetric n-tensors*, and tensors of the form $\vec{u_1} \odot \cdots \odot \vec{u_n}$, where $\vec{u_i} \in E$, are called *simple* (or *decomposable*) *symmetric n-tensors*. Those symmetric n-tensors that are not simple are often called *compound symmetric n-tensors*.

It is also possible to define tensor products of affine spaces and symmetric tensor powers of affine spaces.

11.3   Affine Symmetric Tensor Products

Ramshaw gives a construction for the symmetric tensor powers of an affine space, using polynomials. The motivation is to be able to deal with symmetric multiaffine maps $f: E^m \to F$, as affine maps $f_\odot: \bigodot^m E \to F$. Actually, it turns out that we can easily construct symmetric tensor powers of affine spaces from what we have done so far. Thus, we now briefly discuss symmetric tensor powers of affine spaces, since this might also be helpful to those readers who wish to study Ramshaw's paper [65] carefully.

Definition 11.3.1

A symmetric nth tensor power (or tensor product) of an affine space E, where $n \geq 2$, is an affine space S, together with a symmetric multiaffine map $\varphi: E^n \to S$, such that, for every affine space F and for every symmetric multiaffine map $f: E^n \to F$, there is a unique affine map $f_{\odot}: S \to F$, with

$$f(a_1, \ldots, a_n) = f_{\odot}(\varphi(a_1, \ldots, a_n)),$$

for all $a_1, \ldots, a_n \in E$, or for short,

$$f = f_{\odot} \circ \varphi.$$

Equivalently, there is a unique affine map $f_{\odot}$ such that the following diagram commutes:

$$
\begin{array}{ccc}
E^n & \xrightarrow{\varphi} & S \\
& f \searrow & \downarrow f_{\odot} \\
& & F
\end{array}
$$

As usual, it is easy to show that symmetric tensor powers are unique up to isomorphism. In order to prove the existence of such tensor products, we can proceed in at least two ways.

The first method is to mimic the constructions of this section, but with affine spaces and affine and multiaffine maps. Indeed, tensor products of affine spaces can be constructed, for the following reasons:

1. The notion of affine space freely generated by a set I makes sense. In fact, it is identical to the construction of the free vector space $K^{(I)}$.

2. Quotients of affine spaces can be defined and behave well. Given an affine space E and a subspace $\overrightarrow{F}$ of $\overrightarrow{E}$, an *affine congruence on E* is defined as a relation $\equiv_{\overrightarrow{F}}$ on E, determined such that

$$a \equiv_{\overrightarrow{F}} b \quad \text{iff} \quad \overrightarrow{ab} \in \overrightarrow{F}.$$

Then, it can be shown that $E / \equiv_{\overrightarrow{F}}$ is an affine space with associated vector space $\overrightarrow{E}/\overrightarrow{F}$.

However, there is a more direct approach. It turns out that if we first homogenize the affine space E, getting the vector space $\widehat{E}$, and then construct the symmetric tensor power $\bigodot^n \widehat{E}$, then the symmetric tensor power $\bigodot^n E$ of the affine space E already sits inside $\bigodot^n \widehat{E}$ as an affine space! As a matter of fact, the affine space $\bigodot^n E$ consists of all affine combinations of simple n-tensors of the form $a_1 \odot \cdots \odot a_n$, where $a_1, \ldots, a_n$ are *points* in E. The following lemma, whose proof is left as an exercise, makes what we just claimed more precise.

Lemma 11.3.2

Given an affine space E, the subset $\bigodot^n E$ of the vector space $\bigodot^n \widehat{E}$ consisting of all affine combinations of simple n-tensors of the form $a_1 \odot \cdots \odot a_n$, where $a_1, \ldots, a_n$ are points in E, is an affine space, and together with the multiaffine map $\varphi \colon E^n \to \bigodot^n E$, defined as the restriction to E^n of the multilinear map

$$\overrightarrow{u_1}, \ldots, \overrightarrow{u_n} \mapsto \overrightarrow{u_1} \odot \cdots \odot \overrightarrow{u_n}$$

from $(\widehat{E})^n$ to $\bigodot^n \widehat{E}$, is a symmetric nth tensor power for E. If $\varphi(a_1, \ldots, a_n)$ is denoted as $a_1 \odot \cdots \odot a_n$, the symmetric tensor power $\bigodot^n E$ is spanned by the tensors $a_1 \odot \cdots \odot a_n$, where $a_1, \ldots, a_n \in E$, and for every symmetric multiaffine map $f \colon E^n \to F$, the unique affine map $f_\odot \colon \bigodot^n E \to F$, such that $f = f_\odot \circ \varphi$, is defined by

$$f_\odot(a_1 \odot \cdots \odot a_n) = f(a_1, \ldots, a_n),$$

on the generators $a_1 \odot \cdots \odot a_n$ of $\bigodot^n E$.

Proof: Left as an exercise. ■

Let E and $\mathcal{E}$ be two affine spaces. From Lemma 11.3.2, given any polynomial affine map $F \colon E \to \mathcal{E}$ of degree m with polar form $f \colon E^m \to \mathcal{E}$, we can associate a unique affine map $f_\odot \colon \bigodot E^m \to \mathcal{E}$, such that

$$f(a_1, \ldots, a_m) = f_\odot(a_1 \odot \cdots \odot a_m),$$

for all $a_1, \ldots, a_m \in E$. Following Ramshaw, we call the affine map $f_\odot$, the *affine blossom of F*. The existence of the symmetric tensor power $\bigodot E^m$ justifies the multiplicative notation $f(a_1 \cdots a_m)$ for the polar value $f(a_1, \ldots, a_m)$: view the notation $f(a_1 \cdots a_m)$ as an abbreviation for $f_\odot(a_1 \odot \cdots \odot a_m)$, that is, drop the subscript $\odot$ from $f_\odot$, and write tensors $a_1 \odot \cdots \odot a_m$ simply as $a_1 \cdots a_m$, omitting the symbol $\odot$.

It is worth noting that the affine tensor power $\bigodot^n E$ is spanned not only by the simple n-tensors $a_1 \cdots a_n$, where $a_1, \ldots, a_n \in E$, but also by the simple n-tensors of the form a^n, where $a \in E$. Indeed, by Lemma A.2.5, it is sufficient to show that every linear map $h \colon \bigodot^n E \to F$ is uniquely determined by the tensors of the form a^n. By Lemma 11.3.2, if we let $f = h \circ \varphi$, since f is symmetric multiaffine and $h = f_\odot$ is the unique affine map such that $f(a_1, \ldots, a_n) = h(a_1 \cdots a_n)$, for all $a_1, \ldots, a_n \in E$, we just have to show that a symmetric multiaffine map is uniquely determined by its behavior on the diagonal. However, this is a consequence of Lemma 4.4.1.

Given an affine space E, you may wonder what is the relationship between $\widehat{\bigodot^n E}$ and $\bigodot^n \widehat{E}$. The answer is that they are isomorphic, and this is quite easy to show. We personally favor the reading $\bigodot^n \widehat{E}$, but Ramshaw favors the reading $\widehat{\bigodot^n E}$. This is because Ramshaw defines the hat construction as a special case of his construction of the affine symmetric tensor power. In the end, the two approaches are equivalent, and we simply followed an approach closer to traditional linear algebra, whereas Ramshaw followed an approach in which affine spaces played a more predominant role.

11.4   Properties of Symmetric Tensor Products

Going back to vector spaces, again, the vectors $\vec{u_1} \odot \cdots \odot \vec{u_n}$, where $\vec{u_1}, \ldots, \vec{u_n} \in E$, generate $\odot^n E$, but they are not linearly independent. We will prove a version of Lemma 11.1.4 for symmetric tensor powers. For this, recall that a (finite) multiset over a set I is a function $M: I \to \mathbf{N}$, such that $M(i) \neq 0$ for finitely many $i \in I$, and that the set of all multisets over I is denoted as $\mathbf{N}^{(I)}$. We let $\mathrm{dom}(M) = \{i \in I \mid M(i) \neq 0\}$, which is a finite set. Then, for any multiset $M \in \mathbf{N}^{(I)}$, note that the sum $\sum_{i \in I} M(i)$ makes sense, since $\sum_{i \in I} M(i) = \sum_{i \in \mathrm{dom}(M)} M(i)$, and $\mathrm{dom}(M)$ is finite. For every multiset $M \in \mathbf{N}^{(I)}$, for any $n \geq 2$, we define the set J_M of functions $\eta: \{1, \ldots, n\} \to \mathrm{dom}(M)$ as follows:

$$J_M = \{\eta \mid \eta: \{1, \ldots, n\} \to \mathrm{dom}(M),\ |\eta^{-1}(i)| = M(i),\ i \in \mathrm{dom}(M),\ \sum_{i \in I} M(i) = n\}.$$

In other words, if $\sum_{i \in I} M(i) = n$ and $\mathrm{dom}(M) = \{i_1, \ldots, i_k\}$,[1] any function $\eta \in J_M$ specifies a sequence of length n, consisting of $M(i_1)$ occurrences of i_1, $M(i_2)$ occurrences of $i_2, \ldots, M(i_k)$ occurrences of i_k. Intuitively, any η defines a "permutation" of the sequence (of length n)

$$\langle \underbrace{i_1, \ldots, i_1}_{M(i_1)},\ \underbrace{i_2, \ldots, i_2}_{M(i_2)},\ \ldots,\ \underbrace{i_k, \ldots, i_k}_{M(i_k)} \rangle.$$

Given any $k \geq 1$, and any $\vec{u} \in E$, we denote

$$\underbrace{\vec{u} \odot \cdots \odot \vec{u}}_{k}$$

as $\vec{u}^{\odot k}$.

We can now prove the following lemma.

Lemma 11.4.1

Given a vector space E, if $(\vec{u_i})_{i \in I}$ is a basis for E, then the family of vectors

$$\left(\vec{u_{i_1}}^{\odot M(i_1)} \odot \cdots \odot \vec{u_{i_k}}^{\odot M(i_k)} \right)_{M \in \mathbf{N}^{(I)}, \sum_{i \in I} M(i) = n, \{i_1, \ldots, i_k\} = \mathrm{dom}(M)}$$

is a basis of the symmetric nth tensor power $\odot^n E$.

---

1. Note that we must have $k \leq n$.

Proof: The proof is very similar to that of Lemma 11.1.4. For any nontrivial vector space F, for any family of vectors

$$(\vec{w}_M)_{M \in \mathbf{N}^{(I)}, \sum_{i \in I} M(i)=n},$$

we show the existence of a symmetric multilinear map $h \colon \bigodot^n E \to F$, such that for every $M \in \mathbf{N}^{(I)}$ with $\sum_{i \in I} M(i) = n$, we have

$$h(\vec{u_{i_1}}^{\odot M(i_1)} \odot \cdots \odot \vec{u_{i_k}}^{\odot M(i_k)}) = \vec{w}_M,$$

where $\{i_1, \ldots, i_k\} = \operatorname{dom}(M)$. We define the map $f \colon E^n \to F$ as follows:

$$f\left(\sum_{j_1 \in I} v_{j_1}^1 \vec{u_{j_1}^1}, \ldots, \sum_{j_n \in I} v_{j_n}^n \vec{u_{j_n}^n}\right) = \sum_{\substack{M \in \mathbf{N}^{(I)} \\ \sum_{i \in I} M(i)=n}} \left(\sum_{\eta \in J_M} v_{\eta(1)}^1 \cdots v_{\eta(n)}^n\right) \vec{w_M}.$$

It is not difficult to verify that f is symmetric and multilinear. By the universal property of the symmetric tensor product, the linear map $f_\odot \colon \bigodot^n E \to F$ such that $f = f_\odot \circ \varphi$, is the desired map h. Then, by Lemma A.2.5 (2), it follows that the family

$$\left(\vec{u_{i_1}}^{\odot M(i_1)} \odot \cdots \odot \vec{u_{i_k}}^{\odot M(i_k)}\right)_{M \in \mathbf{N}^{(I)}, \sum_{i \in I} M(i)=n, \{i_1, \ldots, i_k\}=\operatorname{dom}(M)}$$

is linearly independent. Using the commutativity of $\odot$, we can also show that these vectors generate $\bigodot^n E$, and thus, they form a basis for $\bigodot^n E$. The details are left as an exercise. ∎

As a consequence, when I is finite, say, of size p, the dimension of $\bigodot^n E$ is the number of finite sequences $(j_1, \ldots, j_p)$, such that $j_1 + \cdots + j_p = n$, $j_k \geq 0$. We leave as an exercise to show that this number is $\binom{p+n-1}{n}$. Thus the dimension of $\bigodot^n E$ is $\binom{p+n-1}{n}$. Compare with the dimension of $\bigotimes^n E$, which is p^n. In particular, when $p = 2$, the dimension of $\bigodot^n E$ is $n + 1$. This can also be seen directly.

Remark: The number $\binom{p+n-1}{n}$ is also the number of homogeneous monomials

$$X_1^{j_1} \cdots X_p^{j_p}$$

of total degree n in p variables (we have $j_1 + \cdots + j_p = n$). This is not a coincidence! Symmetric tensor products are closely related to polynomials (for more on this, see the next remark).

Given a vector space E and a basis $(\vec{u_i})_{i \in I}$ for E, Lemma 11.4.1 shows that every symmetric tensor $\vec{z} \in \bigodot^n E$ can be written in a unique way as

$$\vec{z} = \sum_{\substack{M \in \mathbf{N}^{(I)} \\ \sum_{i \in I} M(i)=n \\ \{i_1, \ldots, i_k\}=\operatorname{dom}(M)}} \lambda_M \, \vec{u_{i_1}}^{\odot M(i_1)} \odot \cdots \odot \vec{u_{i_k}}^{\odot M(i_k)},$$

for some unique family of scalars $\lambda_M \in K$, all zero except for a finite number.

This looks like a homogeneous polynomial of total degree n, where the monomials of total degree n are the symmetric tensors

$$\overrightarrow{u_{i_1}}^{\odot M(i_1)} \odot \cdots \odot \overrightarrow{u_{i_k}}^{\odot M(i_k)},$$

in the "indeterminates" $\overrightarrow{u_i}$, where $i \in I$ (recall that $M(i_1) + \cdots + M(i_k) = n$). Again, this is not a coincidence. Polynomials can be defined in terms of symmetric tensors.

We can also show the following properties of the symmetric tensor product, using the proof technique of Lemma 11.1.5: there exist unique isomorphisms

1. $(E \odot E) \odot E \simeq E \odot (E \odot E) \simeq E \odot E \odot E$

2. $K \odot E \simeq E$

such that, respectively,

$$(\vec{u} \odot \vec{v}) \odot \vec{w} \mapsto \vec{u} \odot (\vec{v} \odot \vec{w}) \mapsto \vec{u} \odot \vec{v} \odot \vec{w}$$

$$\lambda \odot \vec{u} \mapsto \lambda \vec{u}.$$

Given two linear maps $f: E \to E'$ and $g: E \to E'$, we can define $h: E \times E \to E' \odot E'$ by

$$h(\vec{u}, \vec{v}) = f(\vec{u}) \odot g(\vec{v}).$$

It is immediately verified that h is bilinear, and thus, it induces a unique linear map

$$f \odot g: E \odot E \to E' \odot E',$$

such that

$$(f \odot g)(\vec{u} \odot \vec{v}) = f(\vec{u}) \odot g(\vec{u}).$$

If we also have linear maps $f': E' \to E''$ and $g': E' \to E''$, we can easily verify that

$$(f' \circ f) \odot (g' \circ g) = (f' \odot g') \circ (f \odot g).$$

The generalization to the symmetric tensor product $f_1 \odot \cdots \odot f_n$ of $n \geq 3$ linear maps $f_i: E_i \to F_i$ is immediate and left to the reader.

Remark: The vector space

$$S(E) = \bigoplus_{m \geq 0} \overset{m}{\bigodot} E$$

(with $\bigodot^1 E = E$ and $\bigodot^0 E = K$), called the *symmetric tensor algebra of* E, is an interesting object. When E is of finite dimension n, it can be shown to correspond to the ring of polynomials with coefficients in K in n variables (this can be seen from Lemma 11.4.1). When E is of infinite dimension and $(\vec{u}_i)_{i \in I}$ is a basis of E, the vector space $S(E)$ (also denoted as $\text{Sym}(E)$) corresponds to the ring of polynomials in infinitely many variables in I. However, we would have to define a multiplication operation on $T(E)$, which is easily done. Actually, we have avoided talking about algebras (even though polynomial rings are a prime example of algebra), and we will continue to do so.[2] What's nice about the symmetric tensor algebra is that $S(E)$ provides an intrinsic definition of a polynomial ring (algebra!) in any set I of variables. We could also have defined $S(E)$ from $T(E)$, but this would also require defining a multiplication operation $(\otimes)$ on $T(E)$. If this is done, then $S(E)$ is obtained as the quotient of $T(E)$, by the subspace of $T(E)$ generated by all vectors in $T(E)$, of the form $\vec{u} \otimes \vec{v} - \vec{v} \otimes \vec{u}$. Very elegant, isn't it?

We can finally apply this powerful machinery to CAGD.

11.5   Polar Forms Revisited

When $E = \widehat{\mathbf{A}}$, multisets of size $n + 1$ consisting of points $\overline{u}_1, \ldots, \overline{u}_{n+1}$ in $\widehat{\mathbf{A}}$ can be viewed as symmetric tensors $\overline{u}_1 \odot \cdots \odot \overline{u}_{n+1}$. Then, given any progressive sequence $\langle \overline{u}_1, \ldots, \overline{u}_{2n} \rangle$, we have $n + 1$ tensors $\overline{u}_{k+1} \odot \cdots \odot \overline{u}_{n+k}$, where $0 \le k \le n$, and if these tensors are linearly independent in $\odot^n \widehat{\mathbf{A}}$, then they form a basis of $\odot^n \widehat{\mathbf{A}}$.

As your reward for bravely reading through this chapter, we give a short proof of the hard part of Theorem 5.3.2. This elegant proof is due to Ramshaw. First, we recall Theorem 5.3.2.

Theorem 5.3.2

Let $\langle u_1, \ldots, u_{2m} \rangle$ be a progressive sequence of numbers $u_i \in \mathbf{R}$. Given any sequence of $m + 1$ points $b_0, \ldots, b_m$ in some affine space $\mathcal{E}$, there is a unique polynomial curve $F: \mathbf{A} \to \mathcal{E}$ of degree m, whose polar form $f: \mathbf{A}^m \to \mathcal{E}$ satisfies the conditions

$$f(u_{k+1}, \ldots, u_{m+k}) = b_k,$$

for every k, $0 \le k \le m$.

Proof: Uniqueness has already been shown, and so, we want to prove that there exists a polynomial curve $F: \mathbf{A} \to \mathcal{E}$ of degree m, whose polar form $f: \mathbf{A}^m \to \mathcal{E}$ satisfies the conditions

$$f(u_{k+1}, \ldots, u_{m+k}) = b_k,$$

for every k, $0 \le k \le m$.

---

2. Let me tease the reader anyway, by saying that an algebra over a field K (or a ring A) consists basically of a vector space (or module) structure, together with a multiplication operation that is bilinear. When this operation is associative and has an identity, an algebra essentially has both a vector space (or module) structure and a ring structure.

If we can show that there exists a symmetric multilinear map $g\colon (\widehat{\mathbf{A}})^m \to \widehat{\mathcal{E}}$ satisfying the conditions

$$g(\overline{u}_{k+1}, \ldots, \overline{u}_{m+k}) = b_k,$$

for every k, $0 \le k \le m$, we will have succeeded, since we can define f as the restriction of g to $\mathbf{A}^m$. Now, using symmetric tensors, we just have to prove the existence of a *linear map*

$$h\colon \overset{m}{\bigodot} \widehat{\mathbf{A}} \to \widehat{\mathcal{E}},$$

satisfying the conditions

$$h(\overline{u}_{k+1} \odot \cdots \odot \overline{u}_{m+k}) = b_k,$$

for every k, $0 \le k \le m$, since then, we let $g = h \circ \varphi$. But this is easy! Indeed, given the progressive sequence $\langle \overline{u}_1, \ldots, \overline{u}_{2m} \rangle$, we have $m + 1$ symmetric tensors $\overline{u}_{k+1} \odot \cdots \odot \overline{u}_{m+k}$, where $0 \le k \le m$. We just have to show that they form a basis of $\overset{m}{\bigodot} \widehat{\mathbf{A}}$, since then, by Lemma A.2.3, there will be a unique linear map

$$h\colon \overset{m}{\bigodot} \widehat{\mathbf{A}} \to \widehat{\mathcal{E}},$$

satisfying the conditions

$$h(\overline{u}_{k+1} \odot \cdots \odot \overline{u}_{m+k}) = b_k,$$

for every k, $0 \le k \le m$.

However, as a corollary of Lemma 11.4.1, the dimension of $\overset{m}{\bigodot} \widehat{\mathbf{A}}$ is $m + 1$ (which can also be seen directly). By the first half of Theorem 5.3.2, we know that for any sequence of $m + 1$ points $b_0, \ldots, b_m$ in $\mathcal{E}$ (which is assumed nontrivial!), there is at most one polynomial curve of degree m, whose polar form $f\colon \mathbf{A}^m \to \mathcal{E}$ satisfies the conditions

$$f(\overline{u}_{k+1}, \ldots, \overline{u}_{m+k}) = b_k,$$

for every k, $0 \le k \le m$, which implies that there is at most one linear map

$$h\colon \overset{m}{\bigodot} \widehat{\mathbf{A}} \to \widehat{\mathcal{E}},$$

satisfying the conditions

$$h(\overline{u}_{k+1} \odot \cdots \odot \overline{u}_{m+k}) = b_k,$$

for every k, $0 \le k \le m$.

By Lemma A.2.5 (1), this implies that the vectors $\overline{u}_{k+1} \odot \cdots \odot \overline{u}_{m+k}$ generate $\overset{m}{\bigodot} \widehat{\mathbf{A}}$, where $0 \le k \le m$. Since there are $m + 1$ vectors $\overline{u}_{k+1} \odot \cdots \odot \overline{u}_{m+k}$, and the dimension of $\bigodot^m \widehat{\mathbf{A}}$ is $m+1$, the symmetric tensors $\overline{u}_{k+1} \odot \cdots \odot \overline{u}_{m+k}$ form a basis of $\bigodot^m \widehat{\mathbf{A}}$, which proves the existence (and also uniqueness!) of a linear map

$$h: \overset{m}{\bigodot} \widehat{\mathbf{A}} \to \widehat{\mathcal{E}},$$

satisfying the conditions

$$h(\overline{u}_{k+1} \odot \cdots \odot \overline{u}_{m+k}) = b_k,$$

for every k, $0 \leq k \leq m$. As we already explained, the multiaffine map f, which is the restriction of $g = h \circ \varphi$ to $\mathbf{A}^m$, is the polar form of the desired curve.   ∎

Thus, judicious use of linear and multilinear algebra allowed us to prove the existence of a polynomial curve satisfying the conditions of Theorem 5.3.2, without having to go through painful calculations.

As suggested earlier, for notational simplicity, symmetric tensors $\theta_1 \odot \cdots \odot \theta_m$ will be denoted simply as $\theta_1 \cdots \theta_m$, omitting the symbol $\odot$.

The crucial point of the previous proof is that the symmetric tensors $\overline{u}_{k+1} \cdots \overline{u}_{m+k}$, where $0 \leq k \leq m$, form a basis of $\bigodot^m \widehat{\mathbf{A}}$. This leads us to investigate bases of $\bigodot^m \widehat{\mathbf{A}}$, and thus, bases of $\widehat{\mathbf{A}}$. For example, we know that $(1, \overline{0})$ is a basis for $\widehat{\mathbf{A}}$. To avoid clashes, let us denote 1 as δ (this is a vector in $\mathbf{R}$). Then, since $\theta = u\delta \mathbin{\widehat{+}} r\overline{0}$, for every $\theta \in \widehat{\mathbf{A}}$, every symmetric tensor $\theta_1 \cdots \theta_m$ can be written as

$$(u_1\delta \mathbin{\widehat{+}} r_1\overline{0}) \cdots (u_m\delta \mathbin{\widehat{+}} r_m\overline{0}) = \sum_{0 \leq i \leq m} r_1 \cdots r_m \sigma_i \left(\frac{u_1}{r_1}, \ldots, \frac{u_m}{r_m} \right) \overline{0}^{\,m-i} \delta^i,$$

where $\sigma_i(x_1, \ldots, x_m)$ is the ith elementary symmetric function in $x_1, \ldots, x_m$. For example, we have

$$\theta_1\theta_2\theta_3 = u_1u_2u_3\delta^3 + (u_1u_2r_3 + u_1u_3r_2 + u_2u_3r_1)\overline{0}\delta^2$$

$$+ (u_1r_2r_3 + u_2r_1r_3 + u_3r_1r_2)\overline{0}^{\,2}\delta + r_1r_2r_3\overline{0}^{\,3}.$$

In particular, for points $\overline{u}_1, \ldots, \overline{u}_m \in \mathbf{A}$, the symmetric tensor $\overline{u}_1 \cdots \overline{u}_m$ can be written as

$$(u_1\delta \mathbin{\widehat{+}} \overline{0}) \cdots (u_m\delta \mathbin{\widehat{+}} \overline{0}) = \sum_{0 \leq i \leq m} \sigma_i(u_1, \ldots, u_m)\overline{0}^{\,m-i} \delta^i.$$

For example, we have

$$\overline{u}_1\overline{u}_2\overline{u}_3 = u_1u_2u_3\delta^3 + (u_1u_2 + u_1u_3 + u_2u_3)\overline{0}\delta^2 + (u_1 + u_2 + u_3)\overline{0}^{\,2}\delta + \overline{0}^{\,3}.$$

The above makes it clear that the $m+1$ symmetric tensors $\overline{0}^{\,m-i} \delta^i$ generate $\bigodot^m \widehat{\mathbf{A}}$, and since $\bigodot^m \widehat{\mathbf{A}}$ is of dimension $m+1$, they form a basis of $\bigodot^m \widehat{\mathbf{A}}$. This is also a direct consequence of Lemma 11.4.1. For reasons of convenience to be revealed in a moment, we prefer the family of tensors $\binom{m}{i}\overline{0}^{m-i}\delta^i$, where $0 \leq i \leq m$, and call it the *power basis*.

We could also have used the barycentric basis $(\overline{r}, \overline{s})$, where $\overline{r}, \overline{s}$ are distinct points in **A**. Then, we can write $\theta = u\overline{r} \widehat{+} v\overline{s}$, for every $\theta \in \widehat{\mathbf{A}}$ (the condition $u + v = 1$ holding only iff θ is a point), and every symmetric tensor $\theta_1 \cdots \theta_m$ can be written as

$$(u_1\overline{r} \widehat{+} v_1\overline{s}) \cdots (u_m\overline{r} \widehat{+} v_m\overline{s}) = \sum_{\substack{I \cap J = \emptyset, |J| = k \\ I \cup J = \{1,\ldots,m\}}} \left(\prod_{i \in I} u_i\right)\left(\prod_{j \in J} v_j\right) \overline{r}^{m-k} \overline{s}^k.$$

Thus, the family of tensors $\overline{r}^{m-k}\overline{s}^k$, where $0 \leq k \leq m$, also forms a basis of $\bigodot^m \widehat{\mathbf{A}}$, which we call the *Bézier basis*.

It is easy to generalize these bases to affine spaces of larger dimensions. For example, considering the affine plane $\mathbf{A}^2$, if we use the basis $(\delta_1, \delta_2, \Omega)$ for $\widehat{\mathbf{A}^2}$, where δ_1 and δ_2 denote the unit vectors $(1, 0)$ and $(0, 1)$, and Ω the origin of $\widehat{\mathbf{A}^2}$, we have the power basis consisting of the tensors $\binom{m}{i,j,k}\delta_1^i \delta_2^j \Omega^k$, where $i + j + k = m$. If we consider a barycentric basis (r, s, t) in $\mathbf{A}^2$, then we have a Bézier basis consisting of the tensors $r^i s^j t^k$, where $i + j + k = m$. In general, if E is an affine space of dimension n, and $(\Omega, (\delta_1, \ldots, \delta_n))$ is an affine frame for E, the family of symmetric tensors

$$\delta_1^{i_1} \cdots \delta_n^{i_n} \Omega^{m-i},$$

where $i = i_1 + \cdots + i_n$, is a basis of $\bigodot^m \widehat{E}$. If $(a_0, \ldots, a_n)$ is a barycentric affine frame for E, then the family of symmetric tensors

$$a_0^{i_0} a_1^{i_1} \cdots a_n^{i_n},$$

where $i_0 + i_1 + \cdots + i_n = m$, is a Bézier basis of $\bigodot^m \widehat{E}$. It will also be useful to extend the notion of weight function defined for the homogenized version $\widehat{E}$ of an affine space E, to the symmetric tensor power $\bigodot^m \widehat{E}$. Considering any barycentric affine frame $(a_0, \ldots, a_n)$ for E, define the *weight function* (or *flavor function*) $\omega \colon \bigodot^m \widehat{E} \to K$ as the unique linear map such that

$$\omega(a_0^{i_0} a_1^{i_1} \cdots a_n^{i_n}) = 1,$$

where $i_0 + i_1 + \cdots + i_n = m$. It is immediately seen that ω is independent of the chosen affine frame. Then, it is easily seen that a tensor $\theta \in \bigodot^m \widehat{E}$ has weight 1 (flavor 1) iff it can be expressed as an affine combination of simple m-tensors of the form $b_1 \cdots b_m$, where $b_1 \cdots b_m \in E$, that is, in view of Lemma 11.3.2, iff $\theta \in \bigodot^m E$, the affine tensor power of E. It is also worth noting that $\bigodot^m \widehat{E}$ is generated by the simple m-tensors of the form $a_1 \cdots a_m$, where $a_1, \ldots, a_m \in E$, which is obvious, since for any barycentric affine basis $(a_0, \ldots, a_n)$ for E, the family of tensors

$$a_0^{i_0} a_1^{i_1} \cdots a_n^{i_n},$$

where $i_0 + i_1 + \cdots + i_n = m$, is a Bézier basis of $\bigodot^m \widehat{E}$. Actually, in view of the remark just after Lemma 11.3.2, the tensor power $\bigodot^m \widehat{E}$ is even generated by the simple m-tensors of the form a^m, where $a \in E$. This is certainly not obvious at first glance.

What Lemma A.2.5 showed is that the symmetric tensors $d_k = \overline{u}_{k+1} \cdots \overline{u}_{m+k}$ form a basis of $\bigodot^m \widehat{A}$. We call such a family of tensors a *de Casteljau basis*, or *de Casteljau pole system*. We now give another proof that these tensors are linearly independent, by computing a determinant. As earlier, using the basis $(\delta, \overline{0})$ for $\widehat{A}$, we express every point $\overline{u}$ as $u\delta \widehat{+} \overline{0}$, and we get

$$d_k = (u_{k+1}\delta \,\widehat{+}\, \overline{0}) \cdots (u_{k+m}\delta \,\widehat{+}\, \overline{0}) = \sum_{0 \leq i \leq m} \sigma_i(u_{k+1}, \ldots, u_{k+m})\overline{0}^{\,m-i}\,\delta^i.$$

The $m + 1$ tensors d_k are linearly independent iff the determinant of the $(m + 1)(m + 1)$ matrix $M = (m_{i,k}) = (\sigma_i(u_{k+1}, \ldots, u_{k+m}))$, where $0 \leq i \leq m$, and $1 \leq k \leq m + 1$,

$$\det(M) = \begin{vmatrix} 1 & \sigma_1(u_1, \ldots, u_m) & \cdots & \sigma_m(u_1, \ldots, u_m) \\ 1 & \sigma_1(u_2, \ldots, u_{m+1}) & \cdots & \sigma_m(u_2, \ldots, u_{m+1}) \\ 1 & \sigma_1(u_3, \ldots, u_{m+2}) & \cdots & \sigma_m(u_3, \ldots, u_{m+2}) \\ \vdots & \vdots & \ddots & \vdots \\ 1 & \sigma_1(u_{m+1}, \ldots, u_{2m}) & \cdots & \sigma_m(u_{m+1}, \ldots, u_{2m}) \end{vmatrix}$$

is nonnull. We claim that

$$\det(M) = \prod_{1 \leq i \leq j \leq m} (u_{m+i} - u_j).$$

We will proceed by induction. One way to compute $\det(M)$ is to imitate what we did in the computation of the Vandermonde determinant. If we subtract the mth row from the $(m + 1)$-th (the last row), then the $(m - 1)$-th row from the mth, and so on, ending by subtracting the first row from the second, we notice that the first column contains 1 in the first row, and 0 elsewhere, and that all the other entries on row i, where $2 \leq i \leq m + 1$ (counting from top down), contain the factor $(u_{m+i-1} - u_{i-1})$. Thus, we can factor

$$\prod_{2 \leq i \leq m+1} (u_{m+i-1} - u_{i-1}) = \prod_{1 \leq i \leq m} (u_{m+i} - u_i),$$

and by expanding according to the first column, we get a similar determinant, but of size $m \times m$, and involving only the $2m - 2$ elements $u_2, \ldots, u_{2m-1}$. Then, we can conclude by induction.

Of, course, we rediscover the condition for a progressive sequence, namely, $\det(M) \neq 0$ iff $u_{m+i} \neq u_j$, for all i, j, with $1 \leq i \leq j \leq m$.

It is also instructive to go through the steps of polarizing, homogenizing, and tensoring, explicitly, and we now give such an example. Consider the polynomial curve

$F: \mathbf{A} \to \mathbf{A}^3$, defined as follows (assuming the standard affine frame $(\Omega, (\vec{e_1}, \vec{e_2}, \vec{e_3}))$, for $\mathbf{A}^3$):

$$F_1(u) = 7u^3 + 6u^2 - 3u + 4,$$

$$F_2(u) = 1u^3 + 3u^2 + 9u - 5,$$

$$F_3(u) = 2u^3 - 3u^2 + 12u - 8.$$

We first polarize $F: \mathbf{A} \to \mathbf{A}^3$, getting $f: \mathbf{A} \times \mathbf{A} \times \mathbf{A} \to \mathbf{A}^3$, given by

$$f_1(u_1, u_2, u_3) = 7u_1u_2u_3 + 2u_1u_2 + 2u_1u_3 + 2u_2u_3 - 1u_1 - 1u_2 - 1u_3 + 4,$$

$$f_2(u_1, u_2, u_3) = 1u_1u_2u_3 + 1u_1u_2 + 1u_1u_3 + 1u_2u_3 + 3u_1 + 3u_2 + 3u_3 - 5,$$

$$f_3(u_1, u_2, u_3) = 2u_1u_2u_3 - 1u_1u_2 - 1u_1u_3 - 1u_2u_3 + 4u_1 + 4u_2 + 4u_3 - 8.$$

Taking the basis $(\delta, \overline{0})$ for $\widehat{\mathbf{A}}$, and $(\vec{e_1}, \vec{e_2}, \vec{e_3}, \Omega)$ for $\widehat{\mathbf{A}^3}$, the result of homogenizing $f: \mathbf{A} \times \mathbf{A} \times \mathbf{A} \to \mathbf{A}^3$ is $\widehat{f}: (\widehat{\mathbf{A}})^3 \to \widehat{\mathbf{A}^3}$, given by

$$\widehat{f_1}((u_1, r_1), (u_2, r_2), (u_3, r_3)) = 7u_1u_2u_3 + 2u_1u_2r_3 + 2u_1u_3r_2 + 2u_2u_3r_1$$
$$- 1u_1r_2r_3 - 1u_2r_1r_3 - 1u_3r_1r_2 + 4r_1r_2r_3,$$

$$\widehat{f_2}((u_1, r_1), (u_2, r_2), (u_3, r_3)) = 1u_1u_2u_3 + 1u_1u_2r_3 + 1u_1u_3r_2 + 1u_2u_3r_1$$
$$+ 3u_1r_2r_3 + 3u_2r_1r_3 + 3u_3r_1r_2 - 5r_1r_2r_3,$$

$$\widehat{f_3}((u_1, r_1), (u_2, r_2), (u_3, r_3)) = 2u_1u_2u_3 - 1u_1u_2r_3 - 1u_1u_3r_2 - 1u_2u_3r_1$$
$$+ 4u_1r_2r_3 + 4u_2r_1r_3 + 4u_3r_1r_2 - 8r_1r_2r_3,$$

$$\widehat{f_4}((u_1, r_1), (u_2, r_2), (u_3, r_3)) = 0u_1u_2u_3 + 0u_1u_2r_3 + 0u_1u_3r_2 + 0u_2u_3r_1$$
$$+ 0u_1r_2r_3 + 0u_2r_1r_3 + 0u_3r_1r_2 + 1r_1r_2r_3.$$

Note that we could have first homogenized $F: \mathbf{A} \to \mathbf{A}^3$, getting

$$\widehat{F_1}(u, r) = 7u^3 + 6u^2r - 3ur^2 + 4r^3,$$

$$\widehat{F_2}(u, r) = 1u^3 + 3u^2r + 9ur^2 - 5r^3,$$

$$\widehat{F_3}(u, r) = 2u^3 - 3u^2r + 12ur^2 - 8r^3,$$

$$\widehat{F_4}(u, r) = 0u^3 + 0u^2r + 0ur^2 + 1r^3.$$

and then polarized $\widehat{F}: \widehat{\mathbf{A}} \to \widehat{\mathbf{A}^3}$, getting the same trilinear map $\widehat{f}: (\widehat{\mathbf{A}})^3 \to \widehat{\mathbf{A}^3}$.

Finally, we compute the tensored version $(\widehat{f})_\odot: \bigodot^3 \widehat{\mathbf{A}} \to \widehat{\mathbf{A}^3}$ of $\widehat{f}: (\widehat{\mathbf{A}})^3 \to \widehat{\mathbf{A}^3}$, assuming the power basis of $\bigodot^3 \widehat{\mathbf{A}}$, that is, we write a symmetric tensor in $\bigodot^3 \widehat{\mathbf{A}}$ as

$$a\,\delta^3 + b\,\overline{0}\delta^2 + c\,\overline{0}^2\delta + d\,\overline{0}^3.$$

For example, for

$$(u_1\delta \mp r_1\overline{0})\,(u_2\delta \mp r_2\overline{0})\,(u_3\delta \mp r_3\overline{0}),$$

we have $a = u_1u_2u_3$, $b = (u_1u_2r_3 + u_1u_3r_2 + u_2u_3r_1)$, $c = (u_1r_2r_3 + u_2r_1r_3 + u_3r_1r_2)$, and $d = r_1r_2r_3$. Then, we easily see that

$$(\widehat{f_1})_{\odot}(a\,\delta^3 + b\,\overline{0}\delta^2 + c\,\overline{0}^2\delta + d\,\overline{0}^3) = 7a + 2b - 1c + 4d,$$

$$(\widehat{f_2})_{\odot}(a\,\delta^3 + b\,\overline{0}\delta^2 + c\,\overline{0}^2\delta + d\,\overline{0}^3) = 1a + 1b + 3c - 5d,$$

$$(\widehat{f_3})_{\odot}(a\,\delta^3 + b\,\overline{0}\delta^2 + c\,\overline{0}^2\delta + d\,\overline{0}^3) = 2a - 1b + 4c - 8d,$$

$$(\widehat{f_4})_{\odot}(a\,\delta^3 + b\,\overline{0}\delta^2 + c\,\overline{0}^2\delta + d\,\overline{0}^3) = 0a + 0b + 0c + 1d.$$

Note how tensoring eliminates duplicates that polarizing introduced. This is because symmetry is built in. The columns of the above matrix have a geometric significance. Note that the four columns happen to be the tensors (in the present case, vectors)

$$(\widehat{f})_{\odot}(\delta^3),\ (\widehat{f})_{\odot}(\overline{0}\delta^2),\ (\widehat{f})_{\odot}(\overline{0}^2\delta),\ (\widehat{f})_{\odot}(\overline{0}^3).$$

The first three are vectors, and the last one is a point. Now if we rescale each tensor $\overline{0}^{m-k}\delta^k$ by $\binom{m}{k}$, we arrive at a geometric interpretation for the columns of the coefficients of the homogenized map $\widehat{F}$: the coefficients of u^k in the formula for the coordinates of $F(\overline{u})$ are precisely the coordinates (except the last one) of the tensor (in this case, vector)

$$(\widehat{f})_{\odot}\left(\binom{m}{k}\overline{0}^{m-k}\delta^k\right).$$

This explains why it is interesting to rescale by $\binom{m}{k}$.

Similarly, if the affine basis $(\overline{r}, \overline{s})$ for $\mathbf{A}$ is used, it is easy to see that the tensors (in this case, points)

$$\widehat{f}_{\odot}(\overline{r}^{m-k}\overline{s}^k)$$

are the Bézier control points of the curve F. Thus, as abstract as it is, $\widehat{f}_{\odot}$ carries some very tangible geometric significance. An advantage of the Bézier basis is that the tensors $\overline{r}^{m-k}\overline{s}^k$ are really points.

Some results on osculating flats are also shown as well as a generalized version of Lemma 5.5.2 (conditions on polar forms for polynomial maps to agree to kth order). However, this material is quite technical. It can be found in Appendix B (Section B.4).

Problems

[10 pts] **1.** Fill in the details of the proof of Lemma 11.1.5.

[10 pts] **2.** Given some linear maps $f: E \to E'$, $g: F \to F'$, $f': E' \to E''$, and $g': F' \to F''$, prove that

$$(f' \circ f) \otimes (g' \circ g) = (f' \otimes g') \circ (f \otimes g).$$

[20 pts] **3.** Let E and F be two vector spaces of finite dimension. Recall that the set of linear maps from E to F is denoted as $L(E; F)$. Let $\alpha: E^* \times F \to L(E; F)$ be the map defined such that

$$\alpha(f, \vec{v})(\vec{u}) = f(\vec{u})\vec{v},$$

for all $f \in E^*$, $\vec{v} \in F$, and $\vec{u} \in E$. Prove that α is bilinear and that the unique linear map

$$\alpha_\otimes: E^* \otimes F \to L(E; F)$$

induced by α is an isomorphism.

    Hint: Show that if $\alpha(f, \vec{v})(\vec{u}) = \vec{0}$ for all $\vec{u} \in E$, then either $f = 0$ or $\vec{v} = \vec{0}$.

[20 pts] **4.** (a) Prove that the notion of an affine space freely generated by a set I makes sense (mimic the construction of the free vector space $K^{(I)}$).

    (b) Quotients of affine spaces can be defined as follows. Given an affine space E and a subspace $\vec{F}$ of $\vec{E}$, an *affine congruence on E* is defined as a relation $\equiv_{\vec{F}}$ on E, determined such that

$$a \equiv_{\vec{F}} b \quad \text{iff} \quad \vec{ab} \in \vec{F}.$$

    Prove that $E/\equiv_{\vec{F}}$ is an affine space with associated vector space $\vec{E}/\vec{F}$.

    (c) Prove that tensor products of affine spaces exist.

[10 pts] **5.** Prove Lemma 11.3.2.

[10 pts] **6.** Prove that $\widehat{\bigodot^n E}$ and $\bigodot^n \widehat{E}$ are isomorphic.

[10 pts] **7.** Prove that the number of homogeneous monomials

$$X_1^{j_1} \cdots X_p^{j_p}$$

of total degree n in p variables is $\binom{p+n-1}{n}$. Prove that this is also the number of finite sequences $(j_1, \ldots, j_p)$ such that $j_1 + \cdots + j_p = n$, $j_k \geq 0$.

[10 pts] **8.** Prove that the dimension of $\bigodot^n E$ is $\binom{p+n-1}{n}$.

[20 pts] **9.** Let E be a real vector space of dimension n. Viewing $\mathbf{C}$ as a vector space (of dimension 2) over $\mathbf{R}$, we can define the tensor product $\mathbf{C} \otimes E$, which is a real vector

space. Since every element of $C \otimes E$ is of the form $\sum_i x_i \otimes \vec{u_i}$, where $x_i \in C$ and $\vec{u_i} \in E$, we can define multiplication by a complex scalar $z \in C$ as

$$z \cdot \left(\sum_i x_i \otimes \vec{u_i} \right) = \sum_i z x_i \otimes \vec{u_i}.$$

(a) Prove that the above operation makes $C \otimes E$ into a complex vector space called the *complexification of E*. Show that every vector in $C \otimes E$ can be written as

$$\sum_i \lambda_i \otimes \vec{u_i} + \sum_i \mu_i \otimes \vec{u_i},$$

where $\lambda_i, \mu_i \in R$, that is, as $\vec{u} + i\vec{v}$, where $\vec{u}, \vec{v} \in R \otimes E$ (and recall that $R \otimes E$ is isomorphic to E).

(b) Consider the structure $E \times E$ under the addition operation

$$(\vec{u_1}, \vec{u_2}) + (\vec{v_1}, \vec{v_2}) = (\vec{u_1} + \vec{v_1}, \vec{u_2} + \vec{v_2}),$$

and the multiplication by a complex scalar $z = x + iy$ defined such that

$$(x + iy) \cdot (\vec{u}, \vec{v}) = (x\vec{u} - y\vec{v}, \ y\vec{u} + x\vec{v}).$$

Prove that the above structure is a complex vector space. Denoting the above vector space as E_C, prove that $C \otimes E$ is isomorphic to E_C.
   Hint: Note that

$$(\vec{0}, \vec{v}) = i(\vec{v}, \vec{0}),$$

and thus, identifying E with the subspace of E_C consisting of all vectors of the form $(\vec{u}, \vec{0})$, we can write

$$(\vec{u}, \vec{v}) = \vec{u} + i\vec{v}.$$

Prove that if $(\vec{e}_1, \dots, \vec{e}_n)$ is any basis of E, then $((\vec{e}_1, \vec{0}), \dots, (\vec{e}_n, \vec{0}))$ is a basis of E_C. We call such a basis a *real basis*.

(c) Prove that every linear map $f : E \to E$ can be extended to a linear map $f_C : E_C \to E_C$ defined such that

$$f_C(\vec{u} + i\vec{v}) = f(\vec{u}) + if(\vec{v}).$$

(d) Prove that every bilinear form $\varphi : E \times E \to R$ can be extended to a bilinear map $\varphi_C : E_C \times E_C \to C$ defined such that

$$\varphi_C(\vec{u_1} + i\vec{v_1}, \vec{u_2} + i\vec{v_2}) = \varphi(\vec{u_1}, \vec{u_2}) - \varphi(\vec{v_1}, \vec{v_2}) + i[\varphi(\vec{v_1}, \vec{u_2}) + \varphi(\vec{u_1}, \vec{v_2})].$$

Furthermore, if φ is symmetric, so is φ_C.

PART IV

APPENDICES

Linear Algebra

A.1   Vector Spaces

The purpose of the appendices is to gather results of linear algebra and analysis used in our treatment of the algorithmic geometry of curves and surfaces. In fact, there is probably more material than really needed, and we advise you to proceed "by need."

The appendices contain no original material, except perhaps for the presentation and the point of view. We recommend the following excellent books for an extensive treatment of linear algebra, polynomials, and geometry: *Linear Algebra and Its Applications*, by Strang [81]; *Algebra*, by Lang [47]; *Algebra*, by Artin [1]; *Algebra*, by Mac Lane and Birkhoff [52]; *Algèbre*, by Bourbaki [14, 15]; *Algebra 1*, by Van Der Waerden [84]; *Algèbre Linéaire et Géométrie Classique*, by Bertin [8]; *Géométrie 1 and 2*, by Berger [5, 6]; *Géométries Affines, Projectives, et Euclidiennes*, by Tisseron [83]; *Algèbre Linéaire et Géométrie Elémentaire*, by Dieudonné [25].

Another useful and rather complete reference is the text *Finite-Dimensional Spaces*, by Walter Noll [57]. But beware, the notation and terminology are a bit strange! The text *Geometric Concepts for Geometric Design*, by Böhm and Prautzsch [11], is also an excellent reference on geometry geared towards computer-aided geometric design.

We begin by reviewing some basic properties of vector spaces. The first two chapters of Strang [81] are highly recommended.

Given a set A, recall that a family $(a_i)_{i \in I}$ of elements of A is simply a function $a: I \to A$. If A is a ring with additive identity 0, we say that a family $(a_i)_{i \in I}$ has *finite support* iff $a_i = 0$ for all $i \in I - J$, where J is a finite subset of I (the support of the family). We can deal with an arbitrary set X by viewing it as the family $(X_x)_{x \in X}$ corresponding to the identity function id: $X \to X$. We agree that when $I = \emptyset$, $(a_i)_{i \in I} = \emptyset$. A family $(a_i)_{i \in I}$ is finite if I is finite. Given a family $(u_i)_{i \in I}$ and any element v, we denote as $(u_i)_{i \in I} \cup_k (v)$ the family $(w_i)_{i \in I \cup \{k\}}$ defined such that $w_i = u_i$ if $i \in I$, and $w_k = v$, where k is any index such that $k \notin I$. Given a family $(u_i)_{i \in I}$, a subfamily of $(u_i)_{i \in I}$ is a family $(u_j)_{j \in J}$ where J is any subset of I.

In this chapter, unless specified otherwise, it is assumed that all families of scalars have finite support. We begin by reviewing the definition of a vector space. For every $n \geq 1$, let $\mathbf{R}^n$ be the set of n-tuples $x = (x_1, \ldots, x_n)$. Addition can be extended to $\mathbf{R}^n$ as follows:

$$(x_1, \ldots, x_n) + (y_1, \ldots, y_n) = (x_1 + y_1, \ldots, x_n + y_n).$$

We can also define an operation $\cdot : \mathbf{R} \times \mathbf{R}^n \to \mathbf{R}^n$ as follows:

$$\lambda \cdot (x_1, \ldots, x_n) = (\lambda x_1, \ldots, \lambda x_n).$$

The resulting algebraic structure has some interesting properties, those of a vector space. The definition below is stated for an arbitrary field K, but you may safely assume that $K = \mathbf{R}$.

Definition A.1.1

Given a field K, a vector space over K *(or K-vector space) is a set E (of vectors) together with two operations $+ : E \times E \to E$ (called* vector addition*)[1] and $\cdot : K \times E \to E$ (called* scalar multiplication*), satisfying the following conditions:*

(V0) E is an abelian group with respect to $+$, with identity element $\vec{0}$;

(V1) $\alpha \cdot (\vec{u} + \vec{v}) = (\alpha \cdot \vec{u}) + (\alpha \cdot \vec{v})$, for all $\alpha \in K$, $\vec{u}, \vec{v} \in E$;

(V2) $(\alpha + \beta) \cdot \vec{u} = (\alpha \cdot \vec{u}) + (\beta \cdot \vec{u})$, for all $\alpha, \beta \in K$, $\vec{u} \in E$;

(V3) $(\alpha \beta) \cdot \vec{u} = \alpha \cdot (\beta \cdot \vec{u})$, for all $\alpha, \beta \in K$, $\vec{u} \in E$;

(V4) $1 \cdot \vec{u} = \vec{u}$, for all $\vec{u} \in E$.

Given $\alpha \in K$ and $\vec{v} \in E$, the element $\alpha \cdot \vec{v}$ is also denoted as $\alpha \vec{v}$. The field K is often called the field of scalars. Unless specified otherwise or unless we are dealing with several different fields, in the rest of this chapter, we assume that all K-vector spaces are defined with respect to a fixed field K. Thus, we will refer to a K-vector space simply as a vector space. For simplicity, we also assume that $K = \mathbf{R}$, the field of real numbers, although all definitions and proofs hold for any commutative field K.

From (V0), a vector space always contains the null vector $\vec{0}$, and thus is nonempty. From (V1), we get $\alpha \cdot \vec{0} = \vec{0}$, and $\alpha \cdot (-\vec{v}) = -(\alpha \cdot \vec{v})$. From (V2), we get $0 \cdot \vec{v} = \vec{0}$, and $(-\alpha) \cdot \vec{v} = -(\alpha \cdot \vec{v})$. The field K itself can be viewed as a vector space over itself, addition of vectors being addition in the field, and multiplication

---

1. The symbol $+$ is overloaded, since it denotes both addition in the field K and addition of vectors in E. However, if we write elements of E as vectors, that is, of the form $\vec{u}$, it will always be clear from the type of the arguments which $+$ is intended.

by a scalar being multiplication in the field. As noted earlier, $\mathbf{R}^n$ is a vector space over $\mathbf{R}$. Next, we review the concepts of linear combination and linear independence.

Definition A.1.2

Let E be a vector space. A vector $\vec{v} \in E$ is a linear combination *of a family $(\vec{u_i})_{i \in I}$ of elements of E iff there is a family $(\lambda_i)_{i \in I}$ of scalars in K such that*

$$\vec{v} = \sum_{i \in I} \lambda_i \vec{u_i}.$$

When $I = \emptyset$, we stipulate that $\vec{v} = \vec{0}$. We say that a family $(\vec{u_i})_{i \in I}$ is linearly inde-*pendent iff for every family $(\lambda_i)_{i \in I}$ of scalars in K,*

$$\sum_{i \in I} \lambda_i \vec{u_i} = \vec{0} \quad \text{implies that} \quad \lambda_i = 0 \text{ for all } i \in I.$$

Equivalently, a family $(\vec{u_i})_{i \in I}$ is linearly dependent *iff there is some family $(\lambda_i)_{i \in I}$ of scalars in K such that*

$$\sum_{i \in I} \lambda_i \vec{u_i} = \vec{0} \quad \text{and} \quad \lambda_j \neq 0 \text{ for some } j \in I.$$

We agree that when $I = \emptyset$, the family $\emptyset$ is linearly independent.

A family $(\vec{u_i})_{i \in I}$ is linearly dependent iff some $\vec{u_j}$ in the family can be expressed as a linear combination of the other vectors in the family. Indeed, there is some family $(\lambda_i)_{i \in I}$ of scalars in K such that

$$\sum_{i \in I} \lambda_i \vec{u_i} = \vec{0} \quad \text{and} \quad \lambda_j \neq 0 \text{ for some } j \in I,$$

which implies that

$$\vec{u_j} = \sum_{i \in (I - \{j\})} -\lambda_j^{-1} \lambda_i \vec{u_i}.$$

The notion of a subspace of a vector space is defined as follows.

Definition A.1.3

Given a vector space E, a subset F of E is a linear subspace *(or* subspace*) of E iff F is nonempty and $\lambda \vec{u} + \mu \vec{v} \in F$ for all $\vec{u}, \vec{v} \in F$, and all $\lambda, \mu \in K$.*

It is easy to see that a subspace F of E is closed under arbitrary linear combinations of vectors from F, and that any intersection of subspaces is a subspace. Letting $\lambda = \mu = 0$, we see that every subspace contains the vector $\vec{0}$. The subspace $\{\vec{0}\}$ will be denoted as 0 (with a mild abuse of notation).

Given a vector space E, given a family $(\vec{v_i})_{i \in I}$, the subset V of E consisting of the null vector $\vec{0}$ and of all linear combinations of $(\vec{v_i})_{i \in I}$ is easily seen to be a subspace of E. Subspaces having such a "generating family" play an important role and motivate the following definition.

Definition A.1.4

Given a vector space E and a subspace V of E, a family $(\vec{v}_i)_{i \in I}$ of vectors $\vec{v}_i \in V$ spans V or generates V iff for every $\vec{v} \in V$, there is some family $(\lambda_i)_{i \in I}$ of scalars in K such that

$$\vec{v} = \sum_{i \in I} \lambda_i \vec{v}_i.$$

We also say that the elements of $(\vec{v}_i)_{i \in I}$ are generators of V and that V is spanned by $(\vec{v}_i)_{i \in I}$, or generated by $(\vec{v}_i)_{i \in I}$. If a subspace V of E is generated by a finite family $(\vec{v}_i)_{i \in I}$, we say that V is finitely generated. A family $(\vec{u}_i)_{i \in I}$ that spans V and is linearly independent is called a basis of V.

It is a standard result of linear algebra that every vector space E has a basis, and that for any two bases $(\vec{u}_i)_{i \in I}$ and $(\vec{v}_j)_{j \in J}$, I and J have the same cardinality. In particular, if E has a finite basis of n elements, every basis of E has n elements, and the integer n is called the *dimension* of the vector space E. We prove the above result in the case where a vector space is generated by a finite family. We begin with a crucial lemma.

Lemma A.1.5

Given a linearly independent family $(\vec{u}_i)_{i \in I}$ of elements of a vector space E, if $\vec{v} \in E$ is not a linear combination of $(\vec{u}_i)_{i \in I}$, then the family $(\vec{u}_i)_{i \in I} \cup_k (\vec{v})$ obtained by adding $\vec{v}$ to the family $(\vec{u}_i)_{i \in I}$ is linearly independent (where $k \notin I$).

Proof: Assume that $\mu \vec{v} + \sum_{i \in I} \lambda_i \vec{u}_i = \vec{0}$, for any family $(\lambda_i)_{i \in I}$ of scalars in K. If $\mu \neq 0$, then μ has an inverse (because K is a field), and thus we have $\vec{v} = -\sum_{i \in I}(\mu^{-1}\lambda_i)\vec{u}_i$, showing that $\vec{v}$ is a linear combination of $(\vec{u}_i)_{i \in I}$ and contradicting the hypothesis. Thus, $\mu = 0$. But then, we have $\sum_{i \in I} \lambda_i \vec{u}_i = \vec{0}$, and since the family $(\vec{u}_i)_{i \in I}$ is linearly independent, we have $\lambda_i = 0$ for all $i \in I$. ∎

Note that the proof of the above lemma holds for arbitrary vector spaces, not only for finitely generated vector spaces. The next theorem also holds in general, but the proof is more sophisticated for vector spaces that do not have a finite set of generators (it uses Zorn's lemma). Thus, we only prove the theorem for finitely generated vector spaces.

Theorem A.1.6

Given any finite family $S = (\vec{u}_i)_{i \in I}$ generating a vector space E and any linearly independent subfamily $L = (\vec{u}_j)_{j \in J}$ of S (where $J \subseteq I$), there is a basis B of E such that $L \subseteq B \subseteq S$.

Proof: Consider the set of linearly independent families B such that $L \subseteq B \subseteq S$. Since this set is nonempty and finite, it has some maximal element, say, $B = (\vec{u_h})_{h \in H}$. We claim that B generates E. Indeed, if B does not generate E, then there is some $\vec{u_p} \in S$ that is not a linear combination of vectors in B (since S generates E), with $p \notin H$. Then, by Lemma A.1.5, the family $B' = (\vec{u_h})_{h \in H \cup \{p\}}$ is linearly independent, and since $L \subseteq B \subset B' \subseteq S$, this contradicts the maximality of B. Thus, B is a basis of E such that $L \subseteq B \subseteq S$.   ∎

Theorem A.1.6 also holds for vector spaces that are not finitely generated. In this case, the problem is to guarantee the existence of a maximal linearly independent family B such that $L \subseteq B \subseteq S$. The existence of such a maximal family can be shown using Zorn's lemma. To learn more about Zorn's lemma and the proof of Theorem A.1.6, consult either Lang [47], Appendix 2, §2 (pp. 878–884) and Chapter III, §5 (pp. 139–140); or Artin [1], Appendix §1 (pp. 588–589). The following lemma giving useful properties characterizing a basis is an immediate consequence of Theorem A.1.6.

Lemma A.1.7

Given a vector space E, for any family $B = (\vec{v_i})_{i \in I}$ of vectors of E, the following properties are equivalent:

1. B is a basis of E.

2. B is a maximal linearly independent family of E.

3. B is a minimal generating family of E.

The following *replacement lemma* shows the relationship between finite linearly independent families and finite families of generators of a vector space.

Lemma A.1.8

Given a vector space E, let $(\vec{u_i})_{i \in I}$ be any finite linearly independent family in E, where $|I| = m$, and let $(\vec{v_j})_{j \in J}$ be any finite family such that every $\vec{u_i}$ is a linear combination of $(\vec{v_j})_{j \in J}$, where $|J| = n$. Then, there exists a set L and an injection $\rho: L \to J$ such that $L \cap I = \emptyset$, $|L| = n - m$, and the families $(\vec{u_i})_{i \in I} \cup (\vec{v_{\rho(l)}})_{l \in L}$ and $(\vec{v_j})_{j \in J}$ generate the same subspace of E. In particular, $m \leq n$.

Proof: We proceed by induction on $|I| = m$. When $m = 0$, the family $(\vec{u_i})_{i \in I}$ is empty, and the lemma holds trivially with $L = J$ (ρ is the identity). Assume $|I| = m + 1$. Consider the linearly independent family $(\vec{u_i})_{i \in (I - \{p\})}$, where p is any member of I. By the induction hypothesis, there exists a set L and an injection $\rho: L \to J$ such that $L \cap (I - \{p\}) = \emptyset$, $|L| = n - m$, and the families $(\vec{u_i})_{i \in (I - \{p\})} \cup (\vec{v_{\rho(l)}})_{l \in L}$ and $(\vec{v_j})_{j \in J}$ generate the same subspace of E. If $p \in L$, we can replace L by $(L - \{p\}) \cup \{p'\}$ where p' does not belong to $I \cup L$, and replace ρ by the injection ρ' that agrees with ρ on $L - \{p\}$ and such that $\rho'(p') = \rho(p)$. Thus, we can always assume that $L \cap I = \emptyset$. Since $\vec{u_p}$ is a linear combination of $(\vec{v_j})_{j \in J}$ and the families $(\vec{u_i})_{i \in (I - \{p\})} \cup$

$(\overrightarrow{v_{\rho(l)}})_{l \in L}$ and $(\overrightarrow{v_j})_{j \in J}$ generate the same subspace of E, $\overrightarrow{u_p}$ is a linear combination of $(\overrightarrow{u_i})_{i \in (I-\{p\})} \cup (\overrightarrow{v_{\rho(l)}})_{l \in L}$. Let

$$\overrightarrow{u_p} = \sum_{i \in (I-\{p\})} \lambda_i \overrightarrow{u_i} + \sum_{l \in L} \lambda_l \overrightarrow{v_{\rho(l)}}. \tag{1}$$

If $\lambda_l = 0$ for all $l \in L$, we have

$$\sum_{i \in (I-\{p\})} \lambda_i \overrightarrow{u_i} - \overrightarrow{u_p} = \overrightarrow{0},$$

contradicting the fact that $(\overrightarrow{u_i})_{i \in I}$ is linearly independent. Thus, $\lambda_l \neq 0$ for some $l \in L$, say, $l = q$. Since $\lambda_q \neq 0$, we have

$$\overrightarrow{v_{\rho(q)}} = \sum_{i \in (I-\{p\})} (-\lambda_q^{-1}\lambda_i)\overrightarrow{u_i} + \lambda_q^{-1}\overrightarrow{u_p} + \sum_{l \in (L-\{q\})} (-\lambda_q^{-1}\lambda_l)\overrightarrow{v_{\rho(l)}}. \tag{2}$$

We claim that the families $(\overrightarrow{u_i})_{i \in (I-\{p\})} \cup (\overrightarrow{v_{\rho(l)}})_{l \in L}$ and $(\overrightarrow{u_i})_{i \in I} \cup (\overrightarrow{v_{\rho(l)}})_{l \in (L-\{q\})}$ generate the same subset of E. Indeed, the second family is obtained from the first by replacing $\overrightarrow{v_{\rho(q)}}$ by $\overrightarrow{u_p}$, and vice versa, and $\overrightarrow{u_p}$ is a linear combination of $(\overrightarrow{u_i})_{i \in (I-\{p\})} \cup (\overrightarrow{v_{\rho(l)}})_{l \in L}$ by (1), and $\overrightarrow{v_{\rho(q)}}$ is a linear combination of $(\overrightarrow{u_i})_{i \in I} \cup (\overrightarrow{v_{\rho(l)}})_{l \in (L-\{q\})}$ by (2). Thus, the families $(\overrightarrow{u_i})_{i \in I} \cup (\overrightarrow{v_{\rho(l)}})_{l \in (L-\{q\})}$ and $(\overrightarrow{v_j})_{j \in J}$ generate the same subspace of E, and the lemma holds for $L - \{q\}$ and the restriction of the injection $\rho: L \to J$ to $L - \{q\}$, since $L \cap I = \emptyset$ and $|L| = n - m$ imply that $(L - \{q\}) \cap I = \emptyset$ and $|L - \{q\}| = n - (m+1)$. ∎

Actually, we can prove that Lemma A.1.8 implies Theorem A.1.6 when the vector space is finitely generated. Putting Theorem A.1.6 and Lemma A.1.8 together, we obtain the following fundamental theorem.

Theorem A.1.9

Let E be a finitely generated vector space. Any family $(\overrightarrow{u_i})_{i \in I}$ generating E contains a subfamily $(\overrightarrow{u_j})_{j \in J}$ that is a basis of E. Furthermore, for every two bases $(\overrightarrow{u_i})_{i \in I}$ and $(\overrightarrow{v_j})_{j \in J}$ of E, we have $|I| = |J| = n$.

Proof: The first part follows immediately by applying Theorem A.1.6 with $L = \emptyset$ and $S = (\overrightarrow{u_i})_{i \in I}$. Assume that $(\overrightarrow{u_i})_{i \in I}$ and $(\overrightarrow{v_j})_{j \in J}$ are bases of E. Since $(\overrightarrow{u_i})_{i \in I}$ is linearly independent and $(\overrightarrow{v_j})_{j \in J}$ spans E, Lemma A.1.8 implies that $|I| \leq |J|$. A symmetric argument yields $|J| \leq |I|$. ∎

Remark: Theorem A.1.9 also holds for vector spaces that are not finitely generated. This can be shown as follows. Let $(\overrightarrow{u_i})_{i \in I}$ be a basis of E, let $(\overrightarrow{v_j})_{j \in J}$ be a generating family of E, and assume that I is infinite. For every $j \in J$, let $L_j \subseteq I$ be the finite set

$$L_j = \{i \in I \mid \overrightarrow{v_j} = \sum_{i \in I} v_i \overrightarrow{u_i}, \quad v_i \neq 0\}.$$

Let $L = \bigcup_{j \in J} L_j$. Since $(\vec{u}_i)_{i \in I}$ is a basis of E, we must have $I = L$, since otherwise $(\vec{u}_i)_{i \in L}$ would be another basis of E, and by Lemma A.1.5, this would contradict the fact that $(\vec{u}_i)_{i \in I}$ is linearly independent. Furthermore, J must be infinite, since otherwise, because the L_j are finite, I would be finite. But then, since $I = \bigcup_{j \in J} L_j$ with J infinite and the L_j finite, by a standard result of set theory, $|I| \leq |J|$. If $(\vec{v}_j)_{j \in J}$ is also a basis, by a symmetric argument, we obtain $|J| \leq |I|$, and thus, $|I| = |J|$ for any two bases $(\vec{u}_i)_{i \in I}$ and $(\vec{v}_j)_{j \in J}$ of E.

When $|I|$ is infinite, we say that E is of infinite dimension, the dimension $|I|$ being a cardinal number that depends only on the vector space E. The dimension of a vector space E is denoted as $\dim(E)$. Clearly, if the field K itself is viewed as a vector space, then every family (a) where $a \in K$ and $a \neq 0$ is a basis. Thus $\dim(K) = 1$.

Let $(\vec{u}_i)_{i \in I}$ be a basis of a vector space E. For any vector $\vec{v} \in E$, since the family $(\vec{u}_i)_{i \in I}$ generates E, there is a family $(\lambda_i)_{i \in I}$ of scalars K such that

$$\vec{v} = \sum_{i \in I} \lambda_i \vec{u}_i.$$

A very important fact is that the family $(\lambda_i)_{i \in I}$ is *unique*.

Lemma A.1.10

Given a vector space E, let $(\vec{u}_i)_{i \in I}$ be a family of vectors in E. Let $\vec{v} \in E$, and assume that $\vec{v} = \sum_{i \in I} \lambda_i \vec{u}_i$. Then, the family $(\lambda_i)_{i \in I}$ of scalars such that $\vec{v} = \sum_{i \in I} \lambda_i \vec{u}_i$ is unique iff $(\vec{u}_i)_{i \in I}$ is linearly independent.

Proof: First, assume that $(\vec{u}_i)_{i \in I}$ is linearly independent. If $(\mu_i)_{i \in I}$ is another family of scalars in K such that $\vec{v} = \sum_{i \in I} \mu_i \vec{u}_i$, then we have

$$\sum_{i \in I} (\lambda_i - \mu_i) \vec{u}_i = \vec{0},$$

and since $(\vec{u}_i)_{i \in I}$ is linearly independent, we must have $\lambda_i - \mu_i = 0$ for all $i \in I$, that is, $\lambda_i = \mu_i$ for all $i \in I$. The converse is shown by contradiction. If $(\vec{u}_i)_{i \in I}$ was linearly dependent, there would be a family $(\mu_i)_{i \in I}$ of scalars not all null such that

$$\sum_{i \in I} \mu_i \vec{u}_i = \vec{0}$$

and $\mu_j \neq 0$ for some $j \in I$. But then,

$$\vec{v} = \sum_{i \in I} \lambda_i \vec{u}_i + \vec{0} = \sum_{i \in I} \lambda_i \vec{u}_i + \sum_{i \in I} \mu_i \vec{u}_i = \sum_{i \in I} (\lambda_i + \mu_i) \vec{u}_i,$$

with $\lambda_j \neq \lambda_j + \mu_j$ since $\mu_j \neq 0$, contradicting the assumption that $(\lambda_i)_{i \in I}$ is the unique family such that $\vec{v} = \sum_{i \in I} \lambda_i \vec{u}_i$. ∎

If $(\vec{u_i})_{i \in I}$ is a basis of a vector space E, for any vector $\vec{v} \in E$, if $(v_i)_{i \in I}$ is the unique family of scalars in K such that

$$\vec{v} = \sum_{i \in I} v_i \vec{u_i},$$

each v_i is called the *component* (or *coordinate*) *of index i of* $\vec{v}$ *with respect to the basis* $(\vec{u_i})_{i \in I}$.

Given a field K and any (nonempty) set I, we can form a vector space $K^{(I)}$ that, in some sense, is the standard vector space of dimension $|I|$.

Definition A.1.11

Given a field K and any (nonempty) set I, let $K^{(I)}$ be the subset of the cartesian product K^I consisting of families $(\lambda_i)_{i \in I}$ with finite support of scalars in K.[2] We define addition and multiplication by a scalar as follows:

$$(\lambda_i)_{i \in I} + (\mu_i)_{i \in I} = (\lambda_i + \mu_i)_{i \in I},$$

and

$$\lambda \cdot (\mu_i)_{i \in I} = (\lambda \mu_i)_{i \in I}.$$

It is immediately verified that, because families with finite support are considered, addition and multiplication by a scalar are well defined. Thus, $K^{(I)}$ is a vector space. Furthermore, the family $(\vec{e_i})_{i \in I}$ of vectors $\vec{e_i}$, defined such that $\overrightarrow{(e_i)}_j = 0$ if $j \neq i$ and $\overrightarrow{(e_i)}_i = 1$, is clearly a basis of the vector space $K^{(I)}$. When $I = \{1, \ldots, n\}$, we denote $K^{(I)}$ as K^n. The function $\iota: I \to K^{(I)}$, such that $\iota(i) = \vec{e_i}$ for every $i \in I$, is clearly an injection.

When I is a finite set, $K^{(I)} = K^I$, but this is false when I is infinite. In fact, $\dim(K^{(I)}) = |I|$, but $\dim(K^I)$ is strictly greater when I is infinite.

A.2   Linear Maps

A function between two vector spaces that preserves the vector space structure is called a homomorphism of vector spaces, or linear map. Linear maps formalize the concept of linearity of a function.

Definition A.2.1

Given two vector spaces E and F, a linear map *between E and F is a function $f: E \to F$ satisfying the following two conditions:*

---

2. Where K^I denotes the set of all functions from I to K.

$$f(\vec{x} + \vec{y}) = f(\vec{x}) + f(\vec{y}) \quad \text{for all } \vec{x}, \vec{y} \in E;$$

$$f(\lambda\vec{x}) = \lambda f(\vec{x}) \quad \text{for all } \lambda \in K, \ \vec{x} \in E.$$

Setting $\vec{x} = \vec{y} = \vec{0}$ in the first identity, we get $f(\vec{0}) = \vec{0}$. The basic property of linear maps is that they transform linear combinations into linear combinations. Given a family $(\vec{u}_i)_{i \in I}$ of vectors in E, given any family $(\lambda_i)_{i \in I}$ of scalars in K, we have

$$f\left(\sum_{i \in I} \lambda_i \vec{u}_i\right) = \sum_{i \in I} \lambda_i f(\vec{u}_i).$$

The above identity is shown by induction on the size of the support of the family $(\lambda_i \vec{u}_i)_{i \in I}$, using the properties of Definition A.2.1.

Given a linear map $f \colon E \to F$, we define its *image* (or *range*) Im $f = f(E)$, as the set

$$\text{Im } f = \{\vec{y} \in F \mid f(\vec{x}) = \vec{y}, \quad \text{for some } \vec{x} \in E\},$$

and its *kernel* (or *nullspace*) Ker $f = f^{-1}(\vec{0})$ as the set

$$\text{Ker } f = \{\vec{x} \in E \mid f(\vec{x}) = \vec{0}\}.$$

Lemma A.2.2

Given a linear map $f \colon E \to F$, the set Im f *is a subspace of F, and the set* Ker f *is a subspace of E. The linear map $f \colon E \to F$ is injective iff* Ker $f = 0$ *(where 0 is the trivial subspace $\{\vec{0}\}$).*

Proof: Given any $\vec{x}, \vec{y} \in \text{Im } f$, there are some $\vec{u}, \vec{v} \in E$ such that $\vec{x} = f(\vec{u})$ and $\vec{y} = f(\vec{v})$, and for all $\lambda, \mu \in K$, we have

$$f(\lambda\vec{u} + \mu\vec{v}) = \lambda f(\vec{u}) + \mu f(\vec{v}) = \lambda\vec{x} + \mu\vec{y},$$

and thus, $\lambda\vec{x} + \mu\vec{y} \in \text{Im } f$, showing that Im f is a subspace of F. Given any $\vec{x}, \vec{y} \in$ Ker f, we have $f(\vec{x}) = \vec{0}$ and $f(\vec{y}) = \vec{0}$, and thus,

$$f(\lambda\vec{x} + \mu\vec{y}) = \lambda f(\vec{x}) + \mu f(\vec{y}) = \vec{0},$$

that is, $\lambda\vec{x} + \mu\vec{y} \in$ Ker f, showing that Ker f is a subspace of E. Note that $f(\vec{x}) = f(\vec{y})$ iff $f(\vec{x} - \vec{y}) = \vec{0}$. Thus, f is injective iff Ker $f = 0$. ∎

A fundamental property of bases in a vector space is that they allow the definition of linear maps as unique homomorphic extensions, as shown in the following lemma.

Lemma A.2.3

Given any two vector spaces E and F, given any basis $(\vec{u}_i)_{i \in I}$ of E, given any other family of vectors $(\vec{v}_i)_{i \in I}$ in F, there is a unique linear map $f \colon E \to F$ such that

$f(\vec{u_i}) = \vec{v_i}$ *for all* $i \in I$. *Furthermore,* f *is injective iff* $(\vec{v_i})_{i \in I}$ *is linearly independent, and* f *is surjective iff* $(\vec{v_i})_{i \in I}$ *generates* F.

Proof: If such a linear map $f : E \to F$ exists, since $(\vec{u_i})_{i \in I}$ is a basis of E, every vector $\vec{x} \in E$ can be written uniquely as a linear combination

$$\vec{x} = \sum_{i \in I} x_i \vec{u_i},$$

and by linearity, we must have

$$f(\vec{x}) = \sum_{i \in I} x_i f(\vec{u_i}) = \sum_{i \in I} x_i \vec{v_i}.$$

Define the function $f : E \to F$, by letting

$$f(\vec{x}) = \sum_{i \in I} x_i \vec{v_i}$$

for every $\vec{x} = \sum_{i \in I} x_i \vec{u_i}$. It is easy to verify that f is indeed linear, it is unique by the previous reasoning, and obviously, $f(\vec{u_i}) = \vec{v_i}$.

Now, assume that f is injective. Let $(\lambda_i)_{i \in I}$ be any family of scalars, and assume that

$$\sum_{i \in I} \lambda_i \vec{v_i} = \vec{0}.$$

Since $\vec{v_i} = f(\vec{u_i})$ for every $i \in I$, we have

$$f\left(\sum_{i \in I} \lambda_i \vec{u_i}\right) = \sum_{i \in I} \lambda_i f(\vec{u_i}) = \sum_{i \in I} \lambda_i \vec{v_i} = \vec{0}.$$

Since f is injective iff Ker $f = 0$, we have

$$\sum_{i \in I} \lambda_i \vec{u_i} = \vec{0},$$

and since $(\vec{u_i})_{i \in I}$ is a basis, we have $\lambda_i = 0$ for all $i \in I$, and $(\vec{v_i})_{i \in I}$ is linearly independent. Conversely, assume that $(\vec{v_i})_{i \in I}$ is linearly independent. If

$$f\left(\sum_{i \in I} \lambda_i \vec{u_i}\right) = \vec{0},$$

then

$$\sum_{i \in I} \lambda_i \vec{v_i} = \sum_{i \in I} \lambda_i f(\vec{u_i}) = f\left(\sum_{i \in I} \lambda_i \vec{u_i}\right) = \vec{0},$$

and $\lambda_i = 0$ for all $i \in I$, since $(\vec{v_i})_{i \in I}$ is linearly independent. Since $(\vec{u_i})_{i \in I}$ is a basis of E, we just showed that Ker $f = 0$, and f is injective. The part where f is surjective is left as a simple exercise. ∎

By the second part of Lemma A.2.3, an injective linear map $f: E \to F$ sends a basis $(\vec{u}_i)_{i \in I}$ to a linearly independent family $(f(\vec{u}_i))_{i \in I}$ of F, which is also a basis when f is bijective. Also, when E and F have the same finite dimension n, $(\vec{u}_i)_{i \in I}$ is a basis of E, and $f: E \to F$ is injective, then $(f(\vec{u}_i))_{i \in I}$ is a basis of F (by Lemma A.1.7).

We can now show that the vector space $K^{(I)}$ of Definition A.1.11 has a universal property that amounts to saying that $K^{(I)}$ is the vector space freely generated by I. Recall that $\iota: I \to K^{(I)}$, such that $\iota(i) = \vec{e}_i$ for every $i \in I$, is an injection from I to $K^{(I)}$.

Lemma A.2.4

Given any set I, for any vector space F, and for any function $f: I \to F$, there is a unique linear map $\overline{f}: K^{(I)} \to F$, such that

$$f = \overline{f} \circ \iota,$$

as in the following diagram:

$$
\begin{array}{ccc}
I & \xrightarrow{\iota} & K^{(I)} \\
& f \searrow & \downarrow \overline{f} \\
& & F
\end{array}
$$

Proof: If such a linear map $\overline{f}: K^{(I)} \to F$ exists, since $f = \overline{f} \circ \iota$, we must have

$$f(i) = \overline{f}(\iota(i)) = \overline{f}(\vec{e}_i),$$

for every $i \in I$. However, the family $(\vec{e}_i)_{i \in I}$ is a basis of $K^{(I)}$, and $(f(i))_{i \in I}$ is a family of vectors in F, and by Lemma A.2.3, there is a unique linear map $\overline{f}: K^{(I)} \to F$ such that $\overline{f}(\vec{e}_i) = f(i)$ for every $i \in I$, which proves the existence and uniqueness of a linear map $\overline{f}$ such that $f = \overline{f} \circ \iota$. ∎

The following simple lemma will be needed later when we study spline curves.

Lemma A.2.5

Given any two vector spaces E and F, with F nontrivial, given any family $(\vec{u}_i)_{i \in I}$ of vectors in E, the following properties hold:

1. *The family $(\vec{u}_i)_{i \in I}$ generates E iff for every family of vectors $(\vec{v}_i)_{i \in I}$ in F, there is at most one linear map $f: E \to F$ such that $f(\vec{u}_i) = \vec{v}_i$ for all $i \in I$.*

2. *The family $(\vec{u}_i)_{i \in I}$ is linearly independent iff for every family of vectors $(\vec{v}_i)_{i \in I}$ in F, there is some linear map $f: E \to F$ such that $f(\vec{u}_i) = \vec{v}_i$ for all $i \in I$.*

Proof: (1) If there is any linear map $f: E \to F$ such that $f(\vec{u}_i) = \vec{v}_i$ for all $i \in I$, since $(\vec{u}_i)_{i \in I}$ generates E, every vector $\vec{x} \in E$ can be written as some linear combination

$$\vec{x} = \sum_{i \in I} x_i \vec{u}_i,$$

and by linearity, we must have

$$f(\vec{x}) = \sum_{i \in I} x_i f(\vec{u_i}) = \sum_{i \in I} x_i \vec{v_i}.$$

This shows that f is unique if it exists. Conversely, assume that $(\vec{u_i})_{i \in I}$ does not generate E. Since F is nontrivial, there is some vector $\vec{y} \in F$ such that $\vec{y} \neq \vec{0}$. Since $(\vec{u_i})_{i \in I}$ does not generate E, there is some vector $\vec{w} \in E$ that is not in the subspace generated by $(\vec{u_i})_{i \in I}$. By Theorem A.1.6, there is a linearly independent subfamily $(\vec{u_i})_{i \in I_0}$ of $(\vec{u_i})_{i \in I}$ generating the same subspace, and by Theorem A.1.6 again, there is a basis $(\vec{e_j})_{j \in I_0 \cup J}$ of E, such that $\vec{e_i} = \vec{u_i}$, for all $i \in I_0$, and $\vec{w} = \vec{e_{j_0}}$, for some $j_0 \in J$. Letting $(\vec{v_i})_{i \in I}$ be the family in F such that $\vec{v_i} = \vec{0}$ for all $i \in I$, defining $f: E \to F$ to be the constant linear map with value $\vec{0}$, we have a linear map such that $f(\vec{u_i}) = \vec{0}$ for all $i \in I$. By Lemma A.2.3, there is a unique linear map $g: E \to F$ such that $g(\vec{w}) = \vec{y}$, and $g(\vec{e_j}) = \vec{0}$, for all $j \in (I_0 \cup J) - \{j_0\}$. By definition of the basis $(\vec{e_j})_{j \in I_0 \cup J}$ of E, we have $g(\vec{u_i}) = \vec{0}$ for all $i \in I$, and since $f \neq g$, this contradicts the fact that there is at most one such map.

(2) If the family $(\vec{u_i})_{i \in I}$ is linearly independent, then the conclusion follows by Lemma A.2.3. Conversely, assume that $(\vec{u_i})_{i \in I}$ is linearly dependent. Then, there is some family $(\lambda_i)_{i \in I}$ of scalars (not all zero) such that

$$\sum_{i \in I} \lambda_i \vec{u_i} = \vec{0}.$$

By the assumption, for every $i \in I$, there is some linear map $f_i: E \to F$, such that $f_i(\vec{u_i}) = \vec{y}$, and $f_i(\vec{u_j}) = \vec{0}$, for $j \in I - \{i\}$. Then, we would get

$$\vec{0} = f_i\left(\sum_{i \in I} \lambda_i \vec{u_i}\right) = \sum_{i \in I} \lambda_i f_i(\vec{u_i}) = \lambda_i \vec{y},$$

and since $\vec{y} \neq \vec{0}$, this implies $\lambda_i = 0$, for every $i \in I$. Thus, $(\vec{u_i})_{i \in I}$ is linearly independent. ∎

Although in this book we will not have many occasions to use quotient spaces, they are fundamental in algebra, and they are needed to define tensor products, which are useful to provide nice conceptual proofs of certain properties of splines. The next section may be omitted until needed.

A.3   Quotient Spaces

Let E be a vector space, and let M be any subspace of E. The subspace M induces a relation $\equiv_M$ on E, defined as follows: For all $\vec{u}, \vec{v} \in E$, $\vec{u} \equiv_M \vec{v}$ iff $\vec{u} - \vec{v} \in M$.

We have the following simple lemma.

Lemma A.3.1

Given any vector space E and any subspace M of E, the relation $\equiv_M$ is an equivalence relation with the following two congruential properties:

1. *If $\vec{u_1} \equiv_M \vec{v_1}$ and $\vec{u_2} \equiv_M \vec{v_2}$, then $\vec{u_1} + \vec{u_2} \equiv_M \vec{v_1} + \vec{v_2}$.*

2. *If $\vec{u} \equiv_M \vec{v}$, then $\lambda \vec{u} \equiv_M \lambda \vec{v}$.*

Proof: It is obvious that $\equiv_M$ is an equivalence relation. Note that $\vec{u_1} \equiv_M \vec{v_1}$ and $\vec{u_2} \equiv_M \vec{v_2}$ are equivalent to $\vec{u_1} - \vec{v_1} = \vec{w_1}$ and $\vec{u_2} - \vec{v_2} = \vec{w_2}$, with $\vec{w_1}, \vec{w_2} \in M$, and thus,

$$(\vec{u_1} + \vec{u_2}) - (\vec{v_1} + \vec{v_2}) = \vec{w_1} + \vec{w_2},$$

and $\vec{w_1} + \vec{w_2} \in M$, since M is a subspace of E. Thus, we have $\vec{u_1} + \vec{u_2} \equiv_M \vec{v_1} + \vec{v_2}$. If $\vec{u} - \vec{v} = \vec{w}$, with $\vec{w} \in M$, then

$$\lambda \vec{u} - \lambda \vec{v} = \lambda \vec{w},$$

and $\lambda \vec{w} \in M$, since M is a subspace of E, and thus $\lambda \vec{u} \equiv_M \lambda \vec{v}$. ∎

Lemma A.3.1 shows that we can define addition and multiplication by a scalar on the set E/M of equivalence classes of the equivalence relation $\equiv_M$.

Definition A.3.2

Given any vector space E and any subspace M of E, we define the following operations of addition and multiplication by a scalar on the set E/M of equivalence classes of the equivalence relation $\equiv_M$ as follows: For any two equivalence classes $[\vec{u}], [\vec{v}] \in E/M$, we have

$$[\vec{u}] + [\vec{v}] = [\vec{u} + \vec{v}],$$

$$\lambda[\vec{u}] = [\lambda \vec{u}].$$

By Lemma A.3.1, the above operations do not depend on the specific choice of representatives in the equivalence classes $[\vec{u}], [\vec{v}] \in E/M$. It is also immediate to verify that E/M is a vector space. The function $\pi: E \to E/F$, defined such that $\pi(\vec{u}) = [\vec{u}]$ for every $\vec{u} \in E$, is a surjective linear map called the natural projection *of E onto E/F. The vector space E/M is called the* quotient space *of E by the subspace M.*

Given any linear map $f: E \to F$, we know that Ker f is a subspace of E, and it is immediately verified that Im f is isomorphic to the quotient space $E/$ Ker f.

A.4   Direct Sums

Before considering linear forms and hyperplanes, we define the notion of direct sum and prove some simple lemmas. There is a subtle point, which is that if we attempt to define the direct sum $E \oplus F$ of two vector spaces using the cartesian product $E \times F$, we don't quite get the right notion because elements of $E \times F$ are ordered pairs, but we want $E \oplus F = F \oplus E$. Thus, we want to think of the elements of $E \oplus F$ as multisets of two elements. It is possible to do so by considering the direct sum of a *family* $(E_i)_{i \in \{1,2\}}$, and more generally of a family $(E_i)_{i \in I}$. For simplicity, we begin by considering the case where $I = \{1, 2\}$.

Definition A.4.1

Given two vector spaces E_1 and E_2, we define the (external) direct sum $E_1 \oplus E_2$ *of E_1 and E_2, as the set*

$$E_1 \oplus E_2 = \{\{\langle 1, \vec{u}\rangle, \langle 2, \vec{v}\rangle\} \mid \vec{u} \in E_1, \ \vec{v} \in E_2\},$$

with addition

$$\{\langle 1, \vec{u_1}\rangle, \langle 2, \vec{v_1}\rangle\} + \{\langle 1, \vec{u_2}\rangle, \langle 2, \vec{v_2}\rangle\} = \{\langle 1, \vec{u_1} + \vec{u_2}\rangle, \langle 2, \vec{v_1} + \vec{v_2}\rangle\},$$

and scalar multiplication

$$\lambda\{\langle 1, \vec{u}\rangle, \langle 2, \vec{v}\rangle\} = \{\langle 1, \lambda\vec{u}\rangle, \langle 2, \lambda\vec{v}\rangle\}.$$

We define the injections $in_1 \colon E_1 \to E_1 \oplus E_2$ *and* $in_2 \colon E_2 \to E_1 \oplus E_2$ *as the linear maps defined such that*

$$in_1(\vec{u}) = \{\langle 1, \vec{u}\rangle, \langle 2, \vec{0}\rangle\},$$

and

$$in_2(\vec{v}) = \{\langle 1, \vec{0}\rangle, \langle 2, \vec{v}\rangle\}.$$

Note that

$$E_2 \oplus E_1 = \{\{\langle 2, \vec{v}\rangle, \langle 1, \vec{u}\rangle\} \mid \vec{v} \in E_2, \ \vec{u} \in E_1\} = E_1 \oplus E_2.$$

Thus, every member $\{\langle 1, \vec{u}\rangle, \langle 2, \vec{v}\rangle\}$ of $E_1 \oplus E_2$ can be viewed as an *unordered pair* consisting of the two vectors $\vec{u}$ and $\vec{v}$, that is, as a *multiset* consisting of two elements.

Remark: In fact, $E_1 \oplus E_2$ is just the product $\prod_{i \in \{1,2\}} E_i$ of the family $(E_i)_{i \in \{1,2\}}$.

This is not to be confused with the cartesian product $E_1 \times E_2$. The vector space $E_1 \times E_2$ is the set of all ordered pairs $\langle \vec{u}, \vec{v}\rangle$, where $\vec{u} \in E_1$, and $\vec{v} \in E_2$, with addition and multiplication by a scalar defined such that

$$\langle \vec{u_1}, \vec{v_1}\rangle + \langle \vec{u_2}, \vec{v_2}\rangle = \langle \vec{u_1} + \vec{u_2}, \vec{v_1} + \vec{v_2}\rangle,$$

$$\lambda\langle \vec{u}, \vec{v}\rangle = \langle \lambda\vec{u}, \lambda\vec{v}\rangle.$$

There is a bijection between $\prod_{i \in \{1,2\}} E_i$ and $E_1 \times E_2$, but as we just saw, elements of $\prod_{i \in \{1,2\}} E_i$ are unordered pairs!

Of course, we can define $E_1 \times \cdots \times E_n$ for any number of vector spaces, and when $E_1 = \ldots = E_n$, we denote this product as E^n.

The following property holds.

Lemma A.4.2

Given two vector spaces E_1 and E_2, $E_1 \oplus E_2$ is a vector space. For every pair of linear maps $f \colon E_1 \to G$ and $g \colon E_2 \to G$, there is a unique linear map $f + g \colon E_1 \oplus E_2 \to G$, such that $(f + g) \circ in_1 = f$, and $(f + g) \circ in_2 = g$, as in the following diagram:

$$
\begin{array}{ccc}
E_1 & & \\
in_1 \downarrow & \searrow f & \\
E_1 \oplus E_2 & \xrightarrow{\;f+g\;} & G \\
in_2 \uparrow & \nearrow g & \\
E_2 & &
\end{array}
$$

Proof: Define

$$(f + g)(\{\langle 1, \vec{u}\rangle, \langle 2, \vec{v}\rangle\}) = f(\vec{u}) + g(\vec{v}),$$

for every $\vec{u} \in E_1$ and $\vec{v} \in E_2$. It is immediately verified that $f + g$ is the unique linear map with the required properties. ∎

We already noted that $E_1 \oplus E_2$ is in bijection with $E_1 \times E_2$. If we define the *projections* $\pi_1 \colon E_1 \oplus E_2 \to E_1$ and $\pi_2 \colon E_1 \oplus E_2 \to E_2$, such that

$$\pi_1(\{\langle 1, \vec{u}\rangle, \langle 2, \vec{v}\rangle\}) = \vec{u},$$

and

$$\pi_2(\{\langle 1, \vec{u}\rangle, \langle 2, \vec{v}\rangle\}) = \vec{v},$$

we have the following lemma.

Lemma A.4.3

Given two vector spaces E_1 and E_2, for every pair of linear maps $f \colon D \to E_1$ and $g \colon D \to E_2$, there is a unique linear map $f \times g \colon D \to E_1 \oplus E_2$, such that $\pi_1 \circ (f \times g) = f$, and $\pi_2 \circ (f \times g) = g$, as in the following diagram:

$$
\begin{array}{ccc}
 & E_1 & \\
f \nearrow & \pi_1 \uparrow & \\
D \xrightarrow{\;f \times g\;} & E_1 \oplus E_2 & \\
g \searrow & \pi_2 \downarrow & \\
 & E_2 &
\end{array}
$$

Proof: Define

$$(f \times g)(\vec{w}) = \{\langle 1, f(\vec{w})\rangle, \langle 2, g(\vec{w})\rangle\},$$

for every $\vec{w} \in D$. It is immediately verified that $f \times g$ is the unique linear map with the required properties. ∎

It is a peculiarity of linear algebra that sums and products of finite families are isomorphic. However, this is no longer true for products and sums of infinite families. When U, V are subspaces of a vector space E, letting $i_1: U \to E$ and $i_2: V \to E$ be the inclusion maps, when $U \oplus V$ is isomomorphic to E under the map $i_1 + i_2$ given by Lemma A.4.2, we say that E is a direct (internal) sum of U and V, and we write $E = U \oplus V$ (with a slight abuse of notation, since E and $U \oplus V$ are only isomorphic). It is also convenient to define the sum $U + V$ of U and V.

Definition A.4.4

Given a vector space E, let U, V be any subspaces of E. We define the sum $U + V$ of U and V as the set

$$U + V = \{\vec{w} \in E \mid \vec{w} = \vec{u} + \vec{v}, \quad \text{for some } \vec{u} \in U \text{ and some } \vec{v} \in V\}.$$

We say that E is the (internal) direct sum of U and V, denoted as $E = U \oplus V$,[3] iff for every $\vec{x} \in E$, there exist unique vectors $\vec{u} \in U$ and $\vec{v} \in V$, such that $\vec{x} = \vec{u} + \vec{v}$.

It is immediately verified that $U + V$ is the least subspace of E containing U and V. Note that by definition, $U + V = V + U$, and $U \oplus V = V \oplus U$. The following two simple lemmas hold.

Lemma A.4.5

Let E be a vector space. The following properties are equivalent:

1. $E = U \oplus V$.

2. $E = U + V$ and $U \cap V = 0$.

Proof: First, assume that E is the direct sum of U and V. If $\vec{x} \in U \cap V$ and $\vec{x} \neq \vec{0}$, since $\vec{x}$ can be written both as $\vec{x} + \vec{0}$ and $\vec{0} + \vec{x}$, we have a contradiction. Thus $U \cap V = 0$. Conversely, assume that $\vec{x} = \vec{u} + \vec{v}$ and $\vec{x} = \vec{u}' + \vec{v}'$, where $\vec{u}, \vec{u}' \in U$ and $\vec{v}, \vec{v}' \in V$. Then,

$$\vec{v}' - \vec{v} = \vec{u} - \vec{u}',$$

where $\vec{v}' - \vec{v} \in V$ and $\vec{u} - \vec{u}' \in U$. Since $U \cap V = 0$, we must have $\vec{u}' = \vec{u}$ and $\vec{v}' = \vec{v}$, and thus $E = U \oplus V$. ∎

---

3. Again, with a slight abuse of notation!

Lemma A.4.6

Let E be a vector space, and assume that $E = U \oplus V$. Then,

$$\dim(E) = \dim(U) + \dim(V).$$

Proof: Let $(\vec{u_i})_{i \in I}$ be a basis of U and let $(\vec{v_j})_{j \in J}$ be a basis of V, where I and J are disjoint. Clearly, $(\vec{u_i})_{i \in I} \cup (\vec{v_j})_{j \in J}$ is a basis of E. ∎

We now give the definition of a direct sum for any arbitrary nonempty index set I. First, let us recall the notion of the product of a family $(E_i)_{i \in I}$. Given a family of sets $(E_i)_{i \in I}$, its product $\prod_{i \in I} E_i$ is the set of all functions $f : I \to \bigcup_{i \in I} E_i$, such that $f(i) \in E_i$, for every $i \in I$. It is one of the many versions of the axiom of choice that if $E_i \neq \emptyset$ for every $i \in I$, then $\prod_{i \in I} E_i \neq \emptyset$. A member $f \in \prod_{i \in I} E_i$ is often denoted as $(f_i)_{i \in I}$. For every $i \in I$, we have the *projection* $\pi_i : \prod_{i \in I} E_i \to E_i$, defined such that $\pi_i((f_i)_{i \in I}) = f_i$. We now define direct sums.

Definition A.4.7

Let I be any nonempty set, and let $(E_i)_{i \in I}$ be a family of vector spaces. The (external) *direct sum $\bigoplus_{i \in I} E_i$ of the family $(E_i)_{i \in I}$ is defined as follows:*

$\bigoplus_{i \in I} E_i$ consists of all $f \in \prod_{i \in I} E_i$, which have finite support, and addition and multiplication by a scalar are defined as follows:

$$(f_i)_{i \in I} + (g_i)_{i \in I} = (f_i + g_i)_{i \in I},$$

$$\lambda(f_i)_{i \in I} = (\lambda f_i)_{i \in I}.$$

We also have injection maps $in_i : E_i \to \bigoplus_{i \in I} E_i$, *defined such that* $in_i(x) = (f_i)_{i \in I}$, *where $f_i = x$, and $f_j = 0$, for all $j \in (I - \{i\})$.*

The following lemma is an obvious generalization of Lemma A.4.2.

Lemma A.4.8

Let I be any nonempty set, let $(E_i)_{i \in I}$ be a family of vector spaces, and let G be any vector space. The direct sum $\bigoplus_{i \in I} E_i$ is a vector space, and for every family $(h_i)_{i \in I}$ of linear maps $h_i : E_i \to G$, there is a unique linear map

$$\left(\sum_{i \in I} h_i \right) : \bigoplus_{i \in I} E_i \to G,$$

such that $(\sum_{i \in I} h_i) \circ in_i = h_i$, for every $i \in I$.

Remark: When $E_i = E$, for all $i \in I$, we denote $\bigoplus_{i \in I} E_i$ as $E^{(I)}$. In particular, when $E_i = K$, for all $i \in I$, we find the vector space $K^{(I)}$ of Definition A.1.11.

We also have the following basic lemma about injective or surjective linear maps.

Lemma A.4.9

Let E and F be vector spaces, and let $f: E \to F$ be a linear map. If $f: E \to F$ is injective, then there is a surjective linear map $r: F \to E$ called a retraction, such that $r \circ f = \mathrm{id}_E$. If $f: E \to F$ is surjective, then there is an injective linear map $s: F \to E$ called a section, such that $f \circ s = \mathrm{id}_F$.

Proof: Let $(\vec{u}_i)_{i \in I}$ be a basis of E. Since $f: E \to F$ is an injective linear map, by Lemma A.2.3, $(f(\vec{u}_i))_{i \in I}$ is linearly independent in F. By Theorem A.1.6, there is a basis $(\vec{v}_j)_{j \in J}$ of F, where $I \subseteq J$, and where $\vec{v}_i = f(\vec{u}_i)$, for all $i \in I$. By Lemma A.2.3, a linear map $r: F \to E$ can be defined such that $r(\vec{v}_i) = \vec{u}_i$, for all $i \in I$, and $r(\vec{v}_j) = \vec{w}$ for all $j \in (J - I)$, where $\vec{w}$ is any given vector in E, say, $\vec{w} = \vec{0}$. Since $r(f(\vec{u}_i)) = \vec{u}_i$ for all $i \in I$, by Lemma A.2.3, we have $r \circ f = \mathrm{id}_E$.

Now, assume that $f: E \to F$ is surjective. Let $(\vec{v}_j)_{j \in J}$ be a basis of F. Since $f: E \to F$ is surjective, for every $\vec{v}_j \in F$, there is some $\vec{u}_j \in E$ such that $f(\vec{u}_j) = \vec{v}_j$. Since $(\vec{v}_j)_{j \in J}$ is a basis of F, by Lemma A.2.3, there is a unique linear map $s: F \to E$ such that $s(\vec{v}_j) = \vec{u}_j$. Also, since $f(s(\vec{v}_j)) = \vec{v}_j$, by Lemma A.2.3 (again), we must have $f \circ s = \mathrm{id}_F$. ∎

The converse of Lemma A.4.9 is obvious. We now have the following fundamental lemma.

Lemma A.4.10

Let E, F, and G be three vector spaces, $f: E \to F$ an injective linear map, $g: F \to G$ a surjective linear map, and assume that $\mathrm{Im}\, f = \mathrm{Ker}\, g$. Then, the following properties hold:

1. *For any section $s: G \to F$ of g, $\mathrm{Ker}\, g \oplus \mathrm{Im}\, s$ is isomorphic to F, and the linear map $f + s: E \oplus G \to F$ is an isomorphism.*[4]

2. *For any retraction $r: F \to E$ of f, $\mathrm{Im}\, f \oplus \mathrm{Ker}\, r$ is isomorphic to F.*[5]

Proof: (1) Since $s: G \to F$ is a section of g, we have $g \circ s = \mathrm{id}_G$, and for every $\vec{u} \in F$,

$$g(\vec{u} - s(g(\vec{u}))) = g(\vec{u}) - g(s(g(\vec{u}))) = g(\vec{u}) - g(\vec{u}) = \vec{0}.$$

Thus, $\vec{u} - s(g(\vec{u})) \in \mathrm{Ker}\, g$, and we have $F = \mathrm{Ker}\, g + \mathrm{Im}\, s$. On the other hand, if $\vec{u} \in \mathrm{Ker}\, g \cap \mathrm{Im}\, s$, then $\vec{u} = s(\vec{v})$ for some $\vec{v} \in G$ because $\vec{u} \in \mathrm{Im}\, s$, $g(\vec{u}) = \vec{0}$ because $\vec{u} \in \mathrm{Ker}\, g$, and so,

$$g(\vec{u}) = g(s(\vec{v})) = \vec{v} = \vec{0},$$

---

4. The existence of a section $s: G \to F$ of g follows from Lemma A.4.9.
5. The existence of a retraction $r: F \to E$ of f follows from Lemma A.4.9.

because $g \circ s = \mathrm{id}_G$, which shows that $\vec{u} = s(\vec{v}) = \vec{0}$. Thus, $F = \mathrm{Ker}\, g \oplus \mathrm{Im}\, s$, and since by assumption, $\mathrm{Im}\, f = \mathrm{Ker}\, g$, we have $F = \mathrm{Im}\, f \oplus \mathrm{Im}\, s$. But then, since f and s are injective, $f + s: E \oplus G \to F$ is an isomorphism. The proof of (2) is very similar. ∎

Given a sequence of linear maps $E \xrightarrow{f} F \xrightarrow{g} G$, when $\mathrm{Im}\, f = \mathrm{Ker}\, g$, we say that the sequence $E \xrightarrow{f} F \xrightarrow{g} G$ is *exact at F*. If in addition to being exact at F, f is injective and g is surjective, we say that we have a *short exact sequence*, and this is denoted as

$$0 \to E \xrightarrow{f} F \xrightarrow{g} G \to 0.$$

The property of a short exact sequence given by Lemma A.4.10 is often described by saying that $0 \to E \xrightarrow{f} F \xrightarrow{g} G \to 0$ is a (short) *split exact sequence*.

As a corollary of Lemma A.4.10, we have the following result.

Lemma A.4.11

Let E and F be vector spaces, and let $f: E \to F$ be a linear map. Then, E is isomorphic to $\mathrm{Ker}\, f \oplus \mathrm{Im}\, f$, and thus,

$$\dim(E) = \dim(\mathrm{Ker}\, f) + \dim(\mathrm{Im}\, f).$$

Proof: Consider

$$\mathrm{Ker}\, f \xrightarrow{i} E \xrightarrow{f'} \mathrm{Im}\, f,$$

where $\mathrm{Ker}\, f \xrightarrow{i} E$ is the inclusion map, and $E \xrightarrow{f'} \mathrm{Im}\, f$ is the surjection associated with $E \xrightarrow{f} F$. Then, we apply Lemma A.4.10 to any section $\mathrm{Im}\, f \xrightarrow{s} E$ of f' to get an isomorphism between E and $\mathrm{Ker}\, f \oplus \mathrm{Im}\, f$, and Lemma A.4.6, to get $\dim(E) = \dim(\mathrm{Ker}\, f) + \dim(\mathrm{Im}\, f)$. ∎

The following lemma will also be useful.

Lemma A.4.12

Let E be a vector space. If $E = U \oplus V$ and $E = U \oplus W$, then there is an isomorphism $f: V \to W$ between V and W.

Proof: Let R be the relation between V and W, defined such that

$$\langle \vec{v}, \vec{w} \rangle \in R \quad \text{iff} \quad \vec{w} - \vec{v} \in U.$$

We claim that R is a functional relation that defines a linear isomorphism $f: V \to W$ between V and W, where $f(\vec{v}) = \vec{w}$ iff $\langle \vec{v}, \vec{w} \rangle \in R$ (R is the graph of f). If $\vec{w} - \vec{v} \in U$ and $\vec{w'} - \vec{v} \in U$, then $\vec{w'} - \vec{w} \in U$, and since $U \oplus W$ is a direct sum, $U \cap W = 0$, and thus $\vec{w'} - \vec{w} = \vec{0}$, that is, $\vec{w'} = \vec{w}$. Thus, R is functional. Similarly, if $\vec{w} - \vec{v} \in U$ and

$\vec{w} - \vec{v'} \in U$, then $\vec{v'} - \vec{v} \in U$, and since $U \oplus V$ is a direct sum, $U \cap V = 0$, and $\vec{v'} = \vec{v}$. Thus, f is injective. Since $E = U \oplus V$, for every $\vec{w} \in W$, there exists a unique pair $\langle \vec{u}, \vec{v} \rangle \in U \times V$, such that $\vec{w} = \vec{u} + \vec{v}$. Then, $\vec{w} - \vec{v} \in U$, and f is surjective. We also need to verify that f is linear. If

$$\vec{w} - \vec{v} = \vec{u}$$

and

$$\vec{w'} - \vec{v'} = \vec{u'},$$

where $\vec{u}, \vec{u'} \in U$, then, we have

$$(\vec{w} + \vec{w'}) - (\vec{v} + \vec{v'}) = (\vec{u} + \vec{u'}),$$

where $\vec{u} + \vec{u'} \in U$. Similarly, if

$$\vec{w} - \vec{v} = \vec{u}$$

where $\vec{u} \in U$, then we have

$$\lambda \vec{w} - \lambda \vec{v} = \lambda \vec{u},$$

where $\lambda \vec{u} \in U$. Thus, f is linear. ■

Given a vector space E and any subspace U of E, Lemma A.4.12 shows that the dimension of any subspace V such that $E = U \oplus V$ depends only on U. We call $\dim(V)$ the *codimension* of U, and we denote it as $\mathrm{codim}(U)$. A subspace U of codimension 1 is called a *hyperplane*.

The notion of rank of a linear map or of a matrix is often needed.

Definition A.4.13

Given two vector spaces E and F and a linear map $f : E \to F$, the rank $\mathrm{r}(f)$ *of f is the dimension* $\dim(\mathrm{Im}\, f)$ *of the image subspace* $\mathrm{Im}\, f$ *of F.*

We have the following simple lemma.

Lemma A.4.14

Given a linear map $f : E \to F$, the following properties hold:

1. $\mathrm{r}(f) = \mathrm{codim}(\mathrm{Ker}\, f)$.

2. $\mathrm{r}(f) + \dim(\mathrm{Ker}\, f) = \dim(E)$.

3. $\mathrm{r}(f) \leq \min(\dim(E), \dim(F))$.

Proof: Since by Lemma A.4.11, $\dim(E) = \dim(\mathrm{Ker}\, f) + \dim(\mathrm{Im}\, f)$, and by definition, $\mathrm{r}(f) = \dim(\mathrm{Im}\, f)$, we have $\mathrm{r}(f) = \mathrm{codim}(\mathrm{Ker}\, f)$. Since $\mathrm{r}(f) = \dim(\mathrm{Im}\, f)$, (2) follows from $\dim(E) = \dim(\text{Ker } f) + \dim(\text{Im } f)$. As for (3), since Im f is a subspace of F, we have $\text{r}(f) \leq \dim(F)$, and since $\text{r}(f) + \dim(\text{Ker } f) = \dim(E)$, we have $\text{r}(f) \leq \dim(E)$.   ∎

The rank of a matrix is defined as follows.

Definition A.4.15

Given an $m \times n$ matrix $A = (a_{i\,j})$ over the field K, the rank $\text{r}(A)$ of the matrix A is the maximum number of linearly independent columns of A (viewed as vectors in K^m).

In view of Lemma A.1.7, the rank of a matrix A is the dimension of the subspace of K^m generated by the columns of A. Let E and F be two vector spaces, and let $(\vec{u_1}, \ldots, \vec{u_n})$ be a basis of E, and $(\vec{v_1}, \ldots, \vec{v_m})$ a basis of F. Let $f \colon E \to F$ be a linear map, and let $M(f)$ be its matrix with respect to the bases $(\vec{u_1}, \ldots, \vec{u_n})$ and $(\vec{v_1}, \ldots, \vec{v_m})$. Since the rank $\text{r}(f)$ of f is the dimension of Im f, which is generated by $(f(\vec{u_1}), \ldots, f(\vec{u_n}))$, the rank of f is the maximum number of linearly independent vectors in $(f(\vec{u_1}), \ldots, f(\vec{u_n}))$, which is equal to the number of linearly independent columns of $M(f)$, since F and K^m are isomorphic. Thus, we have $\text{r}(f) = \text{r}(M(f))$, for every matrix representing f.

It can be shown using duality that the rank of a matrix A is also equal to the maximal number of linearly independent rows of A.

If U is a hyperplane, then $E = U \oplus V$ for some subspace V of dimension 1. However, a subspace V of dimension 1 is generated by any nonzero vector $\vec{v} \in V$, and thus we denote V as $K\vec{v}$, and we write $E = U \oplus K\vec{v}$. Clearly, $\vec{v} \notin U$. Conversely, let $\vec{x} \in E$ be a vector such that $\vec{x} \notin U$ (and thus, $\vec{x} \neq \vec{0}$). We claim that $E = U \oplus K\vec{x}$. Indeed, since U is a hyperplane, we have $E = U \oplus K\vec{v}$ for some $\vec{v} \notin U$ (with $\vec{v} \neq \vec{0}$). Then, $\vec{x} \in E$ can be written in a unique way as $\vec{x} = \vec{u} + \lambda\vec{v}$, where $\vec{u} \in U$, and since $\vec{x} \notin U$, we must have $\lambda \neq 0$, and thus, $\vec{v} = -\lambda^{-1}\vec{u} + \lambda^{-1}\vec{x}$. Since $E = U \oplus K\vec{v}$, this shows that $E = U + K\vec{x}$. Since $\vec{x} \notin U$, we have $U \cap K\vec{x} = 0$, and thus $E = U \oplus K\vec{x}$. This argument shows that a hyperplane is a maximal proper subspace H of E.

In the next section, we shall see that hyperplanes are precisely the Kernels of nonnull linear maps $f \colon E \to K$, called linear forms.

A.5   Hyperplanes and Linear Forms

Given a vector space E over a field K, a linear map $f \colon E \to K$ is called a *linear form*. The set of all linear forms $f \colon E \to K$ is a vector space called the *dual space of E*, and denoted as E^*. We now prove that hyperplanes are precisely the Kernels of nonnull linear forms.

Lemma A.5.1

Let E be a vector space. The following properties hold:

1. *Given any nonnull linear form $f \in E^*$, its kernel $H = \text{Ker } f$ is a hyperplane.*

2. *For any hyperplane H in E, there is a (nonnull) linear form $f \in E^*$ such that $H = \operatorname{Ker} f$.*

3. *Given any hyperplane H in E and any (nonnull) linear form $f \in E^*$ such that $H = \operatorname{Ker} f$, for every linear form $g \in E^*$, $H = \operatorname{Ker} g$ iff $g = \lambda f$ for some $\lambda \neq 0$ in K.*

Proof: (1) If $f \in E^*$ is nonnull, there is some vector $\vec{v_0} \in E$ such that $f(\vec{v_0}) \neq 0$. Let $H = \operatorname{Ker} f$. For every $\vec{v} \in E$, we have

$$f\left(\vec{v} - \frac{f(\vec{v})}{f(\vec{v_0})}\vec{v_0}\right) = f(\vec{v}) - \frac{f(\vec{v})}{f(\vec{v_0})}f(\vec{v_0}) = f(\vec{v}) - f(\vec{v}) = 0.$$

Thus,

$$\vec{v} - \frac{f(\vec{v})}{f(\vec{v_0})}\vec{v_0} = \vec{h} \in H,$$

and

$$\vec{v} = \vec{h} + \frac{f(\vec{v})}{f(\vec{v_0})}\vec{v_0},$$

that is, $E = H + K\vec{v_0}$. Also, since $f(\vec{v_0}) \neq 0$, we have $\vec{v_0} \notin H$, that is, $H \cap K\vec{v_0} = 0$. Thus, $E = H \oplus K\vec{v_0}$, and H is a hyperplane.

(2) If H is a hyperplane, $E = H \oplus K\vec{v_0}$ for some $\vec{v_0} \notin H$. Then, every $\vec{v} \in E$ can be written in a unique way as $\vec{v} = \vec{h} + \lambda\vec{v_0}$. Thus, there is a well-defined function $f : E \to K$, such that $f(\vec{v}) = \lambda$, for every $\vec{v} = \vec{h} + \lambda\vec{v_0}$. We leave as a simple exercise the verification that f is a linear form. Since $f(\vec{v_0}) = 1$, the linear form f is nonnull. Also, by definition, it is clear that $\lambda = 0$ iff $\vec{v} \in H$, that is, $\operatorname{Ker} f = H$.

(3) Let H be a hyperplane in E, and let $f \in E^*$ be any (nonnull) linear form such that $H = \operatorname{Ker} f$. Clearly, if $g = \lambda f$ for some $\lambda \neq 0$, then $H = \operatorname{Ker} g$. Conversely, assume that $H = \operatorname{Ker} g$ for some nonnull linear form g. From (1), we have $E = H \oplus K\vec{v_0}$, for some $\vec{v_0}$ such that $f(\vec{v_0}) \neq 0$ and $g(\vec{v_0}) \neq 0$. Then, observe that

$$g - \frac{g(\vec{v_0})}{f(\vec{v_0})}f$$

is a linear form that vanishes on H, since both f and g vanish on H, but also vanishes on $K\vec{v_0}$. Thus, $g = \lambda f$, with

$$\lambda = \frac{g(\vec{v_0})}{f(\vec{v_0})}. \quad \blacksquare$$

If E is a vector space of finite dimension n and $(\vec{u_1}, \ldots, \vec{u_n})$ is a basis of E, for any linear form $f \in E^*$, for every $\vec{x} = x_1\vec{u_1} + \cdots + x_n\vec{u_n} \in E$, we have

$$f(\vec{x}) = \lambda_1 x_1 + \cdots + \lambda_n x_n,$$

where $\lambda_i = f(\vec{u_i}) \in K$, for every i, $1 \leq i \leq n$. Thus, with respect to the basis

$$(\vec{u_1}, \ldots, \vec{u_n}),$$

$f(\vec{x})$ is a linear combination of the coordinates of $\vec{x}$, as expected.

We leave as an exercise the fact that every subspace $V \neq E$ of a vector space E is the intersection of all hyperplanes that contain V.

Complements of Affine Geometry

B.1   Affine and Multiaffine Maps

This section provides missing proofs of various results stated earlier. We begin with Lemma 2.7.2.

Lemma 2.7.2

Given an affine map $f\colon E \to E'$, there is a unique linear map $\vec{f}\colon \vec{E} \to \vec{E'}$, such that

$$f(a + \vec{v}) = f(a) + \vec{f}(\vec{v}),$$

for every $a \in E$ and every $\vec{v} \in \vec{E}$.

Proof: Let $a \in E$ be any point in E. We claim that the map defined such that

$$\vec{f}(\vec{v}) = \overrightarrow{f(a)f(a + \vec{v})},$$

for every $\vec{v} \in \vec{E}$, is a linear map $\vec{f}\colon \vec{E} \to \vec{E'}$. Indeed, we can write

$$a + \lambda\vec{v} = \lambda(a + \vec{v}) + (1 - \lambda)a,$$

since

$$a + \lambda\vec{v} = a + \lambda\overrightarrow{a(a + \vec{v})} + (1 - \lambda)\overrightarrow{aa},$$

and also

$$a + \vec{u} + \vec{v} = (a + \vec{u}) + (a + \vec{v}) - a,$$

since

$$a + \vec{u} + \vec{v} = a + \overrightarrow{a(a + \vec{u})} + \overrightarrow{a(a + \vec{v})} - \overrightarrow{aa}.$$

425

Since f preserves barycenters, we get

$$f(a + \lambda \vec{v}) = \lambda f(a + \vec{v}) + (1 - \lambda)f(a).$$

If we recall that $x = \sum_{i \in I} \lambda_i a_i$ is the barycenter of a family $((a_i, \lambda_i))_{i \in I}$ of weighted points (with $\sum_{i \in I} \lambda_i = 1$) iff

$$\vec{bx} = \sum_{i \in I} \lambda_i \vec{ba_i}$$

for every $b \in E$, we get

$$\overrightarrow{f(a)f(a + \lambda \vec{v})} = \lambda \overrightarrow{f(a)f(a + \vec{v})} + (1 - \lambda)\overrightarrow{f(a)f(a)} = \lambda \overrightarrow{f(a)f(a + \vec{v})},$$

showing that $\vec{f}(\lambda \vec{v}) = \lambda \vec{f}(\vec{v})$. We also have

$$f(a + \vec{u} + \vec{v}) = f(a + \vec{u}) + f(a + \vec{v}) - f(a),$$

from which we get

$$\overrightarrow{f(a)f(a + \vec{u} + \vec{v})} = \overrightarrow{f(a)f(a + \vec{u})} + \overrightarrow{f(a)f(a + \vec{v})},$$

showing that $\vec{f}(\vec{u} + \vec{v}) = \vec{f}(\vec{u}) + \vec{f}(\vec{v})$. Consequently, $\vec{f}$ is a linear map. For any other point $b \in E$, since

$$b + \vec{v} = a + \vec{ab} + \vec{v} = a + \overrightarrow{a(a + \vec{v})} - \vec{aa} + \vec{ab},$$

$b + \vec{v} = (a + \vec{v}) - a + b$, and since f preserves barycenters, we get

$$f(b + \vec{v}) = f(a + \vec{v}) - f(a) + f(b),$$

which implies that

$$\overrightarrow{f(b)f(b + \vec{v})} = \overrightarrow{f(b)f(a + \vec{v})} - \overrightarrow{f(b)f(a)} + \overrightarrow{f(b)f(b)},$$
$$= \overrightarrow{f(a)f(b)} + \overrightarrow{f(b)f(a + \vec{v})},$$
$$= \overrightarrow{f(a)f(a + \vec{v})}.$$

Thus,

$$\overrightarrow{f(b)f(b + \vec{v})} = \overrightarrow{f(a)f(a + \vec{v})},$$

which shows that the definition of $\vec{f}$ does not depend on the choice of $a \in E$. The fact that $\vec{f}$ is unique is obvious: we must have

$$\vec{f}(\vec{v}) = \overrightarrow{f(a)f(a + \vec{v})}. \quad \blacksquare$$

Lemma 4.1.3

For every m-affine map $f: E^m \to F$, *there are* $2^m - 1$ *unique multilinear maps* $f_S: \vec{E}^k \to \vec{F}$, *where* $S \subseteq \{1, \ldots, m\}$, $k = |S|$, $S \neq \emptyset$, *such that*

$$f(a_1 + \vec{v_1}, \ldots, a_m + \vec{v_m}) = f(a_1, \ldots, a_m) + \sum_{\substack{S \subseteq \{1,\ldots,m\}, k=|S| \\ S=\{i_1,\ldots,i_k\}, k \geq 1}} f_S(\vec{v_{i_1}}, \ldots, \vec{v_{i_k}}),$$

for all $a_1 \ldots, a_m \in E$, *and all* $\vec{v_1}, \ldots, \vec{v_m} \in \vec{E}$.

Proof: First, we show that we can restrict our attention to multiaffine maps $f: E^m \to F$, where F is a vector space. Pick any $b \in F$, and define $h: E^m \to \vec{F}$, where $h(a) = \overrightarrow{bf(a)}$ for every $a = (a_1, \ldots, a_m) \in E^m$, so that $f(a) = b + h(a)$. We claim that h is multiaffine. For every i, $1 \leq i \leq m$, for every $a_1, \ldots, a_{i-1}, a_{i+1}, \ldots, a_m \in E$, let $f_i: E \to F$ be the map

$$a_i \mapsto f(a_1, \ldots, a_{i-1}, a_i, a_{i+1}, \ldots, a_m),$$

and let $h_i: E \to \vec{F}$ be the map

$$a_i \mapsto h(a_1, \ldots, a_{i-1}, a_i, a_{i+1}, \ldots, a_m).$$

Since f is multiaffine, we have

$$h_i(a_i + \vec{u}) = \overrightarrow{b(f(a) + \vec{f_i}(\vec{u}))} = \overrightarrow{bf(a)} + \vec{f_i}(\vec{u}),$$

where $a = (a_1, \ldots, a_m)$, and where $\vec{f_i}$ is the linear map associated with f_i, which shows that h_i is an affine map with associated linear map $\vec{f_i}$.

Thus, we now assume that F is a vector space. Given an m-affine map $f: E^m \to F$, for every $(\vec{v_1}, \ldots, \vec{v_m}) \in \vec{E}^m$, we define

$$\Delta_{\vec{v_m}} \Delta_{\vec{v_{m-1}}} \cdots \Delta_{\vec{v_1}} f$$

inductively as follows: For every $a = (a_1, \ldots, a_m) \in E^m$,

$$\Delta_{\vec{v_1}} f(a) = f(a_1 + \vec{v_1}, a_2, \ldots, a_m) - f(a_1, a_2, \ldots, a_m),$$

and generally, for all i, $1 \leq i \leq m$,

$$\Delta_{\vec{v_i}} f(a) = f(a_1, \ldots, a_{i-1}, a_i + \vec{v_i}, a_{i+1}, \ldots, a_m) - f(a_1, a_2, \ldots, a_m).$$

Thus, we have

$$\Delta_{\vec{v_{k+1}}} \Delta_{\vec{v_k}} \cdots \Delta_{\vec{v_1}} f(a)$$

$$= \Delta_{\vec{v_k}} \cdots \Delta_{\vec{v_1}} f(a_1, \ldots, a_{k+1} + \vec{v_{k+1}}, \ldots, a_m) - \Delta_{\vec{v_k}} \cdots \Delta_{\vec{v_1}} f(a),$$

where $1 \leq k \leq m - 1$.

We claim that the following properties hold:

1. Each $\Delta_{\vec{v_k}} \cdots \Delta_{\vec{v_1}} f(a)$ is k-linear in $\vec{v_1}, \ldots, \vec{v_k}$ and $(m-k)$-affine in $a_{k+1}, \ldots, a_m$.

2. We have

$$\Delta_{\vec{v_m}} \cdots \Delta_{\vec{v_1}} f(a)$$

$$= \sum_{k=0}^{m} (-1)^{m-k} \sum_{1 \le i_1 < \ldots < i_k \le m} f(a_1, \ldots, a_{i_1} + \vec{v_{i_1}}, \ldots, a_{i_k} + \vec{v_{i_k}}, \ldots, a_m).$$

Properties (1) and (2) are proved by induction on k. We prove (1), leaving (2) as an easy exercise. Since f is m-affine, it is affine in its first argument, and so,

$$\Delta_{\vec{v_1}} f(a) = f(a_1 + \vec{v_1}, a_2, \ldots, a_m) - f(a_1, a_2, \ldots, a_m)$$

is a linear map in $\vec{v_1}$, and since it is the difference of two multiaffine maps in $a_2, \ldots, a_m$, it is $(m-1)$-affine in $a_2, \ldots, a_m$.

Assuming that $\Delta_{\vec{v_k}} \cdots \Delta_{\vec{v_1}} f(a)$ is k-linear in $\vec{v_1}, \ldots, \vec{v_k}$ and $(m-k)$-affine in $a_{k+1}, \ldots, a_m$, since it is affine in a_{k+1},

$$\Delta_{\overrightarrow{v_{k+1}}} \Delta_{\vec{v_k}} \cdots \Delta_{\vec{v_1}} f(a)$$

$$= \Delta_{\vec{v_k}} \cdots \Delta_{\vec{v_1}} f(a_1, \ldots, a_{k+1} + \overrightarrow{v_{k+1}}, \ldots, a_m) - \Delta_{\vec{v_k}} \cdots \Delta_{\vec{v_1}} f(a)$$

is linear in $\overrightarrow{v_{k+1}}$, and since it is the difference of two k-linear maps in $\vec{v_1}, \ldots, \vec{v_k}$, it is $(k+1)$-linear in $\vec{v_1}, \ldots, \overrightarrow{v_{k+1}}$, and since it is the difference of two $(m-k-1)$-affine maps in $a_{k+2} \ldots, a_m$, it is $(m-k-1)$-affine in $a_{k+2} \ldots, a_m$. This concludes the induction.

As a consequence of (1), $\Delta_{\vec{v_m}} \cdots \Delta_{\vec{v_1}} f$ is an m-linear map. Then, in view of (2), we can write

$$f(a_1 + \vec{v_1}, \ldots, a_m + \vec{v_m})$$

$$= \Delta_{\vec{v_m}} \cdots \Delta_{\vec{v_1}} f(a)$$

$$+ \sum_{k=0}^{m-1} (-1)^{m-k-1} \sum_{1 \le i_1 < \ldots < i_k \le m} f(a_1, \ldots, a_{i_1} + \vec{v_{i_1}}, \ldots, a_{i_k} + \vec{v_{i_k}}, \ldots, a_m),$$

and since every

$$f(a_1, \ldots, a_{i_1} + \vec{v_{i_1}}, \ldots, a_{i_k} + \vec{v_{i_k}}, \ldots, a_m)$$

in the above sum contains at most $m-1$ of the $\vec{v_1}, \ldots, \vec{v_m}$, we can apply the induction hypothesis, which gives us sums of k-linear maps, for $1 \le k \le m-1$, and of $2^m - 1$ terms of the form $(-1)^{m-k-1} f(a_1, \ldots, a_m)$, which all cancel out except for a single $f(a_1, \ldots, a_m)$, which proves the existence of multilinear maps f_S such that

$$f(a_1 + \overrightarrow{v_1}, \ldots, a_m + \overrightarrow{v_m}) = f(a_1, \ldots, a_m) + \sum_{\substack{S \subseteq \{1,\ldots,m\},\, k=|S| \\ S=\{i_1,\ldots,i_k\},\, k \geq 1}} f_S(\overrightarrow{v_{i_1}}, \ldots, \overrightarrow{v_{i_k}}),$$

for all $a_1, \ldots, a_m \in E$, and all $\overrightarrow{v_1}, \ldots, \overrightarrow{v_m} \in \overrightarrow{E}$.

We still have to prove the uniqueness of the linear maps in the sum. This can be done using the $\Delta_{\overrightarrow{v_m}} \cdots \Delta_{\overrightarrow{v_1}} f$. We claim the following slightly stronger property, which can be shown by induction on m: If

$$g(a_1 + \overrightarrow{v_1}, \ldots, a_m + \overrightarrow{v_m}) = f(a_1, \ldots, a_m) + \sum_{\substack{S \subseteq \{1,\ldots,m\},\, k=|S| \\ S=\{i_1,\ldots,i_k\},\, k \geq 1}} f_S(\overrightarrow{v_{i_1}}, \ldots, \overrightarrow{v_{i_k}}),$$

for all $a_1, \ldots, a_m \in E$, and all $\overrightarrow{v_1}, \ldots, \overrightarrow{v_m} \in \overrightarrow{E}$, then

$$\Delta_{\overrightarrow{v_{j_n}}} \cdots \Delta_{\overrightarrow{v_{j_1}}} g(a) = f_{\{j_1,\ldots,j_n\}}(\overrightarrow{v_{j_1}}, \ldots, \overrightarrow{v_{j_n}}),$$

where $\{j_1, \ldots, j_n\} \subseteq \{1, \ldots, m\}$, $j_1 < \ldots < j_n$, and $a = (a_1, \ldots, a_m)$. We can now show the uniqueness of the f_S, where $S \subseteq \{1, \ldots, n\}$, $S \neq \emptyset$, by induction. Indeed, from above, we get

$$\Delta_{\overrightarrow{v_m}} \cdots \Delta_{\overrightarrow{v_1}} f = f_{\{1,\ldots,m\}}.$$

But $g - f_{\{1,\ldots,m\}}$ is also m-affine, and it is a sum of the above form, where $n = m - 1$, so we can apply the induction hypothesis and conclude the uniqueness of all the f_S.
∎

Lemma 4.4.1

Given two affine spaces E and F, for any polynomial function h of degree m, the polar form $f: E^m \to F$ of h is unique and is given by the following expression:

$$f(a_1, \ldots, a_m) = \frac{1}{m!} \left[\sum_{\substack{H \subseteq \{1,\ldots,m\} \\ k=|H|,\, k \geq 1}} (-1)^{m-k} k^m \, h \left(\frac{\sum_{i \in H} a_i}{k} \right) \right].$$

Proof: Let

$$C = \{\eta \colon \{1, \ldots, m\} \to \{0, 1\} \mid \eta(i) \neq 0 \text{ for some } i,\, 1 \leq i \leq m\}$$

be the set of characteristic functions of all nonempty subsets of $\{1, \ldots, m\}$. Then, the expression

$$E = \sum_{\substack{H \subseteq \{1,\ldots,m\} \\ k=|H|,\, k \geq 1}} (-1)^k k^m \, h \left(\frac{\sum_{i \in H} a_i}{k} \right)$$

can be written as

$$E = \sum_{\eta \in C} (-1)^{\eta(1)+\cdots+\eta(m)} \left(\eta(1) + \cdots + \eta(m)\right)^m h \left(\frac{\eta(1)a_1 + \cdots + \eta(m)a_m}{\eta(1) + \cdots + \eta(m)}\right).$$

Since

$$\frac{\eta(1)}{\eta(1) + \cdots + \eta(m)} + \cdots + \frac{\eta(m)}{\eta(1) + \cdots + \eta(m)} = 1,$$

and

$$h \left(\frac{\eta(1)a_1 + \cdots + \eta(m)a_m}{\eta(1) + \cdots + \eta(m)}\right)$$

$$= f \left(\frac{\eta(1)a_1 + \cdots + \eta(m)a_m}{\eta(1) + \cdots + \eta(m)}, \ldots, \frac{\eta(1)a_1 + \cdots + \eta(m)a_m}{\eta(1) + \cdots + \eta(m)}\right),$$

because f is multiaffine, we have

$$\left(\eta(1) + \cdots + \eta(m)\right)^m h \left(\frac{\eta(1)a_1 + \cdots + \eta(m)a_m}{\eta(1) + \cdots + \eta(m)}\right)$$

$$= \left(\eta(1) + \cdots + \eta(m)\right)^m f \left(\frac{\eta(1)a_1 + \cdots + \eta(m)a_m}{\eta(1) + \cdots + \eta(m)}, \ldots,\right.$$

$$\left.\frac{\eta(1)a_1 + \cdots + \eta(m)a_m}{\eta(1) + \cdots + \eta(m)}\right)$$

$$= \sum_{(i_1,\ldots,i_m) \in \{1,\ldots,m\}^m} \eta(i_1) \cdots \eta(i_m) f(a_{i_1}, \ldots, a_{i_m}).$$

Thus, we have

$$E = \sum_{\eta \in C} (-1)^{\eta(1)+\cdots+\eta(m)} \left(\eta(1) + \cdots + \eta(m)\right)^m h \left(\frac{\eta(1)a_1 + \cdots + \eta(m)a_m}{\eta(1) + \cdots + \eta(m)}\right)$$

$$= \sum_{\eta \in C} (-1)^{\eta(1)+\cdots+\eta(m)} \left(\sum_{(i_1,\ldots,i_m) \in \{1,\ldots,m\}^m} \eta(i_1) \cdots \eta(i_m) f(a_{i_1}, \ldots, a_{i_m})\right)$$

$$= \sum_{(i_1,\ldots,i_m) \in \{1,\ldots,m\}^m} \left(\sum_{\eta \in C} (-1)^{\eta(1)+\cdots+\eta(m)} \eta(i_1) \cdots \eta(i_m)\right) f(a_{i_1}, \ldots, a_{i_m}).$$

If $(i_1, \ldots, i_m)$ is not a permutation of $(1, \ldots, m)$, there is some $j \in \{1, \ldots, m\}$ such that $j \neq i_1, \ldots, i_m$. Let

$$J = \{\eta \in C \mid \eta(j) = 0\},$$

and for every $\eta \in J$, let η^* be defined such that $\eta^*(i) = \eta(i)$, for every $i \neq j$, and $\eta^*(j) = 1$. Note that

$$\eta^*(1) + \cdots + \eta^*(m) = \eta(1) + \cdots + \eta(m) + 1.$$

Then,

$$\sum_{\eta \in C} (-1)^{\eta(1)+\cdots+\eta(m)} \, \eta(i_1) \cdots \eta(i_m)$$

$$= \sum_{\eta \in J} (-1)^{\eta(1)+\cdots+\eta(m)} \, \eta(i_1) \cdots \eta(i_m) + \sum_{\eta \in J} (-1)^{\eta^*(1)+\cdots+\eta^*(m)} \, \eta^*(i_1) \cdots \eta^*(i_m),$$

and since

$$(-1)^{\eta^*(1)+\cdots+\eta^*(m)} \, \eta^*(i_1) \cdots \eta^*(i_m) = (-1)^{\eta(1)+\cdots+\eta(m)+1} \, \eta(i_1) \cdots \eta(i_m)$$

$$= -(-1)^{\eta(1)+\cdots+\eta(m)} \, \eta(i_1) \cdots \eta(i_m),$$

we get

$$\sum_{\eta \in C} (-1)^{\eta(1)+\cdots+\eta(m)} \, \eta(i_1) \cdots \eta(i_m) = 0.$$

If $(i_1, \ldots, i_m)$ is a permutation of $(1, \ldots, m)$, then $\eta(i_1) \cdots \eta(i_m) \neq 0$ iff $\eta(i) = 1$ for every $i \in \{1, \ldots, m\}$, in which case

$$\sum_{\eta \in C} (-1)^{\eta(1)+\cdots+\eta(m)} \, \eta(i_1) \cdots \eta(i_m) = (-1)^m.$$

Since f is symmetric, in this case

$$f(a_{i_1}, \ldots, a_{i_m}) = f(a_1, \ldots, a_m),$$

and since there are $m!$ permutations of $(1, \ldots, m)$, we get

$$(-1)^m m! f(a_1, \ldots, a_m) = \sum_{\substack{H \subseteq \{1,\ldots,m\} \\ k=|H|, k \geq 1}} (-1)^k k^m \, h \left(\frac{\sum_{i \in H} a_i}{k} \right).$$

Since $(-1)^m (-1)^m = 1$, and $(-1)^{m+k} = (-1)^{m-k}$, the above identity implies that

$$f(a_1, \ldots, a_m) = \frac{1}{m!} \left[\sum_{\substack{H \subseteq \{1,\ldots,m\} \\ k=|H|, k \geq 1}} (-1)^{m-k} k^m \, h \left(\frac{\sum_{i \in H} a_i}{k} \right) \right],$$

which concludes the proof. ∎

B.2   Homogenizing Multiaffine Maps

This section contains the proof of Lemma 10.4.1.

Lemma 10.4.1

Given any affine space E and any vector space $\vec{F}$, for any m-affine map $f: E^m \to \vec{F}$, there is a unique m-linear map $\widehat{f}: (\widehat{E})^m \to \vec{F}$ extending f, such that if

$$f(a_1 + \vec{v_1}, \ldots, a_m + \vec{v_m}) = f(a_1, \ldots, a_m) + \sum_{\substack{S \subseteq \{1, \ldots, m\}, \, k = |S| \\ S = \{i_1, \ldots, i_k\}, \, k \geq 1}} f_S(\vec{v_{i_1}}, \ldots, \vec{v_{i_k}}),$$

for all $a_1, \ldots, a_m \in E$, and all $\vec{v_1}, \ldots, \vec{v_m} \in \vec{E}$, where the f_S are uniquely determined multilinear maps (by Lemma 4.1.3), then

$$\widehat{f}(\vec{v_1} \widehat{+} \lambda_1 a_1, \ldots, \vec{v_m} \widehat{+} \lambda_m a_m)$$

$$= \lambda_1 \cdots \lambda_m f(a_1, \ldots, a_m) + \sum_{\substack{S \subseteq \{1, \ldots, m\}, \, k = |S| \\ S = \{i_1, \ldots, i_k\}, \, k \geq 1}} \left(\prod_{\substack{j \in \{1, \ldots, m\} \\ j \notin S}} \lambda_j \right) f_S(\vec{v_{i_1}}, \ldots, \vec{v_{i_k}}),$$

for all $a_1, \ldots, a_m \in E$, all $\vec{v_1}, \ldots, \vec{v_m} \in \vec{E}$, and all $\lambda_1, \ldots, \lambda_m \in \mathbf{R}$. Furthermore, for $\lambda_i \neq 0$, $1 \leq i \leq m$, we have

$$\widehat{f}(\vec{v_1} \widehat{+} \lambda_1 a_1, \ldots, \vec{v_m} \widehat{+} \lambda_m a_m) = \lambda_1 \cdots \lambda_m f(a_1 + \lambda_1^{-1} \vec{v_1}, \ldots, a_m + \lambda_m^{-1} \vec{v_m}).$$

Proof: Let us assume that $\widehat{f}$ exists. We first prove by induction on k, $1 \leq k \leq m$, that

$$\widehat{f}(a_1, \ldots, \vec{v_{i_1}}, \ldots, \vec{v_{i_k}}, \ldots, a_m) = f_S(\vec{v_{i_1}}, \ldots, \vec{v_{i_k}}),$$

for every $S \subseteq \{1, \ldots, m\}$, such that $S = \{i_1, \ldots, i_k\}$ and $k = |S|$, for all $a_1, \ldots, a_m \in E$, and all $\vec{v_1}, \ldots, \vec{v_m} \in \vec{E}$.

For $k = 1$, assuming for simplicity of notation that $i_1 = 1$, for any $a_1 \in E$, since $\widehat{f}$ is m-linear, we have

$$\widehat{f}(a_1 + \vec{v_1}, a_2, \ldots, a_m) = \widehat{f}(a_1, a_2, \ldots, a_m) + \widehat{f}(\vec{v_1}, a_2, \ldots, a_m),$$

but since $\widehat{f}$ extends f, we have

$$\widehat{f}(a_1 + \vec{v_1}, a_2, \ldots, a_m) = f(a_1 + \vec{v_1}, a_2, \ldots, a_m)$$

$$= f(a_1, a_2, \ldots, a_m) + \widehat{f}(\vec{v_1}, a_2, \ldots, a_m),$$

and using the expression of f in terms of the f_S, we also have

$$f(a_1 + \vec{v_1}, a_2, \ldots, a_m) = f(a_1, a_2, \ldots, a_m) + f_{\{1\}}(\vec{v_1}).$$

Thus, we have

$$\widehat{f}(\overrightarrow{v_1}, a_2, \ldots, a_m) = f_{\{1\}}(\overrightarrow{v_1})$$

for all $\overrightarrow{v_1} \in \overrightarrow{E}$.

Assume that the induction hypothesis holds for all $l < k + 1$, and let $S = \{i_1, \ldots, i_{k+1}\}$, with $k + 1 = |S|$. Since $\widehat{f}$ is multilinear, for any $a \in E$, we have

$$\widehat{f}(a_1, \ldots, a + \overrightarrow{v_{i_1}}, \ldots, a + \overrightarrow{v_{i_{k+1}}}, \ldots, a_m)$$

$$= \widehat{f}(a_1, \ldots, a, \ldots, a, \ldots, a_m) + \widehat{f}(a_1, \ldots, \overrightarrow{v_{i_1}}, \ldots, \overrightarrow{v_{i_{k+1}}}, \ldots, a_m)$$

$$+ \sum_{\substack{T=\{j_1,\ldots,j_l\} \\ T \subseteq S,\, 1 \le l \le k}} \widehat{f}(a_1, \ldots, \overrightarrow{v_{j_1}}, \ldots, \overrightarrow{v_{j_l}}, \ldots, a_m).$$

However, by the induction hypothesis, we have

$$\widehat{f}(a_1, \ldots, \overrightarrow{v_{j_1}}, \ldots, \overrightarrow{v_{j_l}}, \ldots, a_m) = f_T(\overrightarrow{v_{j_1}}, \ldots, \overrightarrow{v_{j_l}}),$$

for every $T = \{j_1, \ldots, j_l\}$, $1 \le l \le k$, and since $\widehat{f}$ extends f, we get

$$\widehat{f}(a_1, \ldots, a + \overrightarrow{v_{i_1}}, \ldots, a + \overrightarrow{v_{i_{k+1}}}, \ldots, a_m)$$

$$= f(a_1, \ldots, a, \ldots, a, \ldots, a_m) + \widehat{f}(a_1, \ldots, \overrightarrow{v_{i_1}}, \ldots, \overrightarrow{v_{i_{k+1}}}, \ldots, a_m)$$

$$+ \sum_{\substack{T=\{j_1,\ldots,j_l\} \\ T \subseteq S,\, 1 \le l \le k}} f_T(\overrightarrow{v_{j_1}}, \ldots, \overrightarrow{v_{j_l}}).$$

Since $\widehat{f}$ extends f, we also have

$$\widehat{f}(a_1, \ldots, a + \overrightarrow{v_{i_1}}, \ldots, a + \overrightarrow{v_{i_{k+1}}}, \ldots, a_m)$$

$$= f(a_1, \ldots, a + \overrightarrow{v_{i_1}}, \ldots, a + \overrightarrow{v_{i_{k+1}}}, \ldots, a_m),$$

and by expanding this expression in terms of the f_T, we get

$$\widehat{f}(a_1, \ldots, a + \overrightarrow{v_{i_1}}, \ldots, a + \overrightarrow{v_{i_{k+1}}}, \ldots, a_m)$$

$$= f(a_1, \ldots, a, \ldots, a, \ldots, a_m) + f_S(\overrightarrow{v_{i_1}}, \ldots, \overrightarrow{v_{i_{k+1}}})$$

$$+ \sum_{\substack{T=\{j_1,\ldots,j_l\} \\ T \subseteq S,\, 1 \le l \le k}} f_T(\overrightarrow{v_{j_1}}, \ldots, \overrightarrow{v_{j_l}}).$$

Thus, we conclude that

$$\widehat{f}(a_1, \ldots, \overrightarrow{v_{i_1}}, \ldots, \overrightarrow{v_{i_{k+1}}}, \ldots, a_m) = f_S(\overrightarrow{v_{i_1}}, \ldots, \overrightarrow{v_{i_{k+1}}}).$$

This shows that $\widehat{f}$ is uniquely defined on $\overrightarrow{E}$, and clearly, the above defines a multilinear map. Now, assume that $\lambda_i \ne 0$, $1 \le i \le m$. We get

$$\widehat{f}(\overrightarrow{v_1} \mathbin{\widehat{+}} \lambda_1 a_1, \ldots, \overrightarrow{v_m} \mathbin{\widehat{+}} \lambda_m a_m) = \widehat{f}(\lambda_1(a_1 + \lambda_1^{-1}\overrightarrow{v_1}), \ldots, \lambda_m(a_m + \lambda_m^{-1}\overrightarrow{v_m})),$$

and since $\widehat{f}$ is m-linear, we get

$$\widehat{f}(\lambda_1(a_1 + \lambda_1^{-1}\overrightarrow{v_1}), \ldots, \lambda_m(a_m + \lambda_m^{-1}\overrightarrow{v_m}))$$
$$= \lambda_1 \cdots \lambda_m \widehat{f}(a_1 + \lambda_1^{-1}\overrightarrow{v_1}, \ldots, a_m + \lambda_m^{-1}\overrightarrow{v_m}).$$

Since $\widehat{f}$ extends f, we get

$$\widehat{f}(\overrightarrow{v_1} \mathbin{\widehat{+}} \lambda_1 a_1, \ldots, \overrightarrow{v_m} \mathbin{\widehat{+}} \lambda_m a_m) = \lambda_1 \cdots \lambda_m f(a_1 + \lambda_1^{-1}\overrightarrow{v_1}, \ldots, a_m + \lambda_m^{-1}\overrightarrow{v_m}).$$

We can expand the right-hand side using the f_S, and we get

$$f(a_1 + \lambda_1^{-1}\overrightarrow{v_1}, \ldots, a_m + \lambda_m^{-1}\overrightarrow{v_m})$$
$$= f(a_1, \ldots, a_m) + \sum_{\substack{S \subseteq \{1,\ldots,m\},\, k=|S| \\ S=\{i_1,\ldots,i_k\},\, k \geq 1}} \lambda_{i_1}^{-1} \cdots \lambda_{i_k}^{-1} f_S(\overrightarrow{v_{i_1}}, \ldots, \overrightarrow{v_{i_k}}),$$

and thus, we get

$$\widehat{f}(\overrightarrow{v_1} \mathbin{\widehat{+}} \lambda_1 a_1, \ldots, \overrightarrow{v_m} \mathbin{\widehat{+}} \lambda_m a_m)$$

$$= \lambda_1 \cdots \lambda_m f(a_1, \ldots, a_m) + \sum_{\substack{S \subseteq \{1,\ldots,m\},\, k=|S| \\ S=\{i_1,\ldots,i_k\},\, k \geq 1}} \left(\prod_{\substack{j \in \{1,\ldots,m\} \\ j \notin S}} \lambda_j \right) f_S(\overrightarrow{v_{i_1}}, \ldots, \overrightarrow{v_{i_k}}).$$

This expression agrees with the previous one when $\lambda_i = 0$ for some of the λ_i, $1 \leq i \leq m$, and this shows that $\widehat{f}$ is uniquely defined. Clearly, the above expression defines an m-linear map. Thus, the lemma is proved. ∎

B.3   Intersection and Direct Sums of Affine Spaces

In this section, we take a closer look at the intersection of affine subspaces, and at the notion of direct sum of affine spaces, which will be needed in the section on differentiation.

First, we need a result of linear algebra. Given a vector space E and any two subspaces M and N, there are several interesting linear maps. We have the canonical injections $i\colon M \to M + N$ and $j\colon N \to M + N$, the canonical injections $in_1\colon M \to M \oplus N$ and $in_2\colon N \to M \oplus N$, and thus, injections $f\colon M \cap N \to M \oplus N$, and $g\colon M \cap N \to M \oplus N$, where f is the composition of the inclusion map from $M \cap N$ to M with in_1, and g is the composition of the inclusion map from $M \cap N$ to N with in_2. Then, we have the maps $f + g\colon M \cap N \to M \oplus N$, and $i - j\colon M \oplus N \to M + N$.

Lemma B.3.1

Given a vector space E and any two subspaces M and N, with the definitions above, the following is a short exact sequence:

$$0 \to M \cap N \xrightarrow{f+g} M \oplus N \xrightarrow{i-j} M + N \to 0,$$

which means that $f + g$ is injective, $i - j$ is surjective, and that Im $(f + g) =$ Ker $(i - j)$. As a consequence, we have the Grassmann relation:

$$\dim (M) + \dim (N) = \dim (M + N) + \dim (M \cap N).$$

Proof: It is obvious that $i - j$ is surjective and that $f + g$ is injective. Assume that $(i - j)(\vec{u} + \vec{v}) = \vec{0}$, where $\vec{u} \in M$, and $\vec{v} \in N$. Then, $i(\vec{u}) = j(\vec{v})$, and thus, by definition of i and j, there is some $\vec{w} \in M \cap N$, such that, $i(\vec{u}) = j(\vec{v}) = \vec{w} \in M \cap N$. By definition of f and g, $\vec{u} = f(\vec{w})$, and $\vec{v} = g(\vec{w})$, and thus, Im $(f + g) =$ Ker $(i - j)$, as desired. The second part of the lemma follows from Lemma A.4.10 and Lemma A.4.6. ∎

We now prove a simple lemma about the intersection of affine subspaces.

Lemma B.3.2

Given any affine space E, for any two nonempty affine subspaces M and N, the following facts hold:

1. *$M \cap N \neq \emptyset$ iff $\vec{ab} \in \vec{M} + \vec{N}$ for some $a \in M$ and some $b \in N$.*

2. *$M \cap N$ consists of a single point iff $\vec{ab} \in \vec{M} + \vec{N}$ for some $a \in M$ and some $b \in N$, and $\vec{M} \cap \vec{N} = \{\vec{0}\}$.*

3. *If S is the least affine subspace containing M and N, then $\vec{S} = \vec{M} + \vec{N} + \mathbf{R}\vec{ab}$.*

Proof: (1) Pick any $a \in M$ and any $b \in N$, which is possible since M and N are nonempty. Since $\vec{M} = \{\vec{ax} \mid x \in M\}$ and $\vec{N} = \{\vec{by} \mid y \in N\}$, if $M \cap N \neq \emptyset$, for any $c \in M \cap N$, we have $\vec{ab} = \vec{ac} - \vec{bc}$, with $\vec{ac} \in \vec{M}$ and $\vec{bc} \in \vec{N}$, and thus, $\vec{ab} \in \vec{M} + \vec{N}$. Conversely, assume that $\vec{ab} \in \vec{M} + \vec{N}$ for some $a \in M$ and some $b \in N$. Then, $\vec{ab} = \vec{ax} + \vec{by}$, for some $x \in M$ and some $y \in N$. But we also have

$$\vec{ab} = \vec{ax} + \vec{xy} + \vec{yb},$$

and thus, we get $\vec{0} = \vec{xy} + \vec{yb} - \vec{by}$, that is, $\vec{xy} = 2\vec{by}$. Thus, b is the middle of the segment $[x, y]$, and since $\vec{yx} = 2\vec{yb}$, $x = 2b - y$ is the barycenter of the weighted points $(b, 2)$ and $(y, -1)$. Thus x also belongs to N, since N being an affine subspace, it is closed under barycenters. Thus, $x \in M \cap N$, and $M \cap N \neq \emptyset$.

(2) Note that in general, if $M \cap N \neq \emptyset$, then

$$\overrightarrow{M \cap N} = \vec{M} \cap \vec{N},$$

because

$$\overrightarrow{M \cap N} = \{\overrightarrow{ab} \mid a, b \in M \cap N\} = \{\overrightarrow{ab} \mid a, b \in M\} \cap \{\overrightarrow{ab} \mid a, b \in N\} = \overrightarrow{M} \cap \overrightarrow{N}.$$

Since $M \cap N = c + \overrightarrow{M \cap N}$ for any $c \in M \cap N$, we have

$$M \cap N = c + \overrightarrow{M} \cap \overrightarrow{N} \quad \text{for any } c \in M \cap N.$$

From this, it follows that if $M \cap N \neq \emptyset$, then $M \cap N$ consists of a single point iff $\overrightarrow{M} \cap \overrightarrow{N} = \{\overrightarrow{0}\}$. This fact together with what we proved in (1) proves (2).

(3) It is left as an easy exercise. ∎

Remarks:

1. The proof of Lemma B.3.2 shows that if $M \cap N \neq \emptyset$, then $\overrightarrow{ab} \in \overrightarrow{M} + \overrightarrow{N}$ for all $a \in M$ and all $b \in N$.

2. Lemma B.3.2 implies that for any two nonempty affine subspaces M and N, if $\overrightarrow{E} = \overrightarrow{M} \oplus \overrightarrow{N}$, then $M \cap N$ consists of a single point. Indeed, if $\overrightarrow{E} = \overrightarrow{M} \oplus \overrightarrow{N}$, then $\overrightarrow{ab} \in \overrightarrow{E}$ for all $a \in M$ and all $b \in N$, and since $\overrightarrow{M} \cap \overrightarrow{N} = \{\overrightarrow{0}\}$, the result follows from part (2) of the lemma.

We can now state the following lemma.

Lemma B.3.3

Given an affine space E and any two nonempty affine subspaces M and N, if S is the least affine subspace containing M and N, then the following properties hold:

1. *If $M \cap N = \emptyset$, then*

$$\dim(M) + \dim(N) < \dim(E) + \dim(\overrightarrow{M} + \overrightarrow{N}),$$

and

$$\dim(S) = \dim(M) + \dim(N) + 1 - \dim(\overrightarrow{M} \cap \overrightarrow{N}).$$

2. *If $M \cap N \neq \emptyset$, then*

$$\dim(S) = \dim(M) + \dim(N) - \dim(M \cap N).$$

Proof: It is not difficult, using Lemma B.3.2 and Lemma B.3.1, but we leave it as an exercise. ∎

We now consider direct sums of affine spaces.

Given an indexed family $(E_i)_{i \in I}$ of affine spaces (where I is nonempty), where each E_i is really an affine space $\langle E_i, \overrightarrow{E_i}, +_i \rangle$, we define an affine space E whose associated vector space is the direct sum $\bigoplus_{i \in I} \overrightarrow{E_i}$ of the family $(\overrightarrow{E_i})_{i \in I}$. However, there is a difficulty if we take E to be the direct product $\prod_{i \in I} E_i$, because axiom (AF3), discussed in Chapter 2, may not hold. Thus, we define the direct sum of the family $(E_i)_{i \in I}$ of affine spaces, relative to a fixed choice of points (one point in each

E_i). When I is finite, the same affine space is obtained no matter which points are chosen. When I is infinite, we get isomorphic affine spaces.

Definition B.3.4

Let $\langle E_i, \vec{E_i}, +_i \rangle_{i \in I}$ be a family of affine spaces (where I is nonempty), where each E_i is nonempty. For each $i \in I$, let a_i be some chosen point in E_i, and let $a = (a_i)_{i \in I}$. We define the direct sum $\bigoplus_{i \in I}(E_i, a_i)$ of the family $(E_i)_{i \in I}$ relative to a as the following affine space $\langle E_a, \vec{E}, +_a \rangle$:

$$E_a = \{(x_i)_{i \in I} \in \textstyle\prod_{i \in I} E_i \mid x_i \neq a_i \text{ for finitely many } i \in I\};$$

$$\vec{E} = \bigoplus_{i \in I} \vec{E_i};$$

$+_a: E_a \times \vec{E} \to E_a$ *is defined such that*

$$(x_i)_{i \in I} + (\vec{u_i})_{i \in I} = (x_i + \vec{u_i})_{i \in I}.$$

We define the injections *$in_i^a: E_i \to \bigoplus_{i \in I}(E_i, a_i)$ such that $in_i^a(y) = (x_i)_{i \in I}$, where $x_i = y$, and $x_j = a_j$, for all $j \in I - \{i\}$. We also have functions $p_i^a: \bigoplus_{i \in I}(E_i, a_i) \to E_i$, where p_i^a is the restriction to $\bigoplus_{i \in I}(E_i, a_i)$ of the projection $\pi_i: \prod_{i \in I} E_i \to E_i$. Thus, $p_i^a((x_i)_{i \in I}) = x_i$, and we also call p_i^a a* projection.

It is easy to verify that $\bigoplus_{i \in I}(E_i, a_i)$ is an affine space. Let us check (AF3). Given any two points $x, y \in \bigoplus_{i \in I}(E_i, a_i)$, we have $x = (x_i)_{i \in I}$ and $y = (y_i)_{i \in I}$, where $x_i \neq a_i$ on a finite subset I' of I, and $y_i \neq a_i$ on a finite subset I'' of I. Then, by definition of $\bigoplus_{i \in I}(E_i, a_i)$, it is clear that the only vector $\vec{w} \in \bigoplus_{i \in I} \vec{E_i}$ such that $y = x + \vec{w}$ is $\vec{w} = (\vec{w_i})_{i \in I}$, where $\vec{w_i} = \vec{x_i y_i}$, for $i \in I' \cup I''$, and $\vec{w_i} = \vec{0}$, for all $i \in I - (I' \cup I'')$.

The injections $in_i^a: E_i \to \bigoplus_{i \in I}(E_i, a_i)$ are affine maps. This is because for every $y \in E_i$, we have $in_i^a(y) = a + \vec{in_i}(\vec{a_i y})$, where $\vec{in_i}: \vec{E_i} \to \bigoplus_{i \in I} \vec{E_i}$ is the injection from the vector space $\vec{E_i}$ into $\bigoplus_{i \in I} \vec{E_i}$. We leave as an exercise to prove the analog of Lemma A.4.8 for a direct sum of affine spaces and affine maps.

Remark: Observe that the intersection of the affine subspaces $in_i^a(E_i)$ reduces to the single point a. This is consistent with the corollary of Lemma B.3.3. When I is finite and $I = \{1, \ldots, m\}$, E_a and $+_a$ do not depend on the choice of a, but the injections in_i^a do. In this case, we write $\bigoplus_{i \in I}(E_i, a_i)$ as $(E_1, a_1) \oplus \cdots \oplus (E_m, a_m)$, and we denote each $(x_i)_{i \in I}$ as $(x_1, \ldots, x_m)$. The order of the factors (E_i, a_i) is irrelevant.

When $I = \{1, \ldots, m\}$, $m \geq 1$, if E is an affine space and $F_1, \ldots, F_m$ are m affine spaces, for any function $f: E \to (F_1, b_1) \oplus \cdots \oplus (F_m, b_m)$, letting $f_i = p_i \circ f$, we see immediately that $f(a) = (f_1(a), \ldots, f_m(a))$, for every $a \in E$. If the F_i are vector spaces, we have

$$f(a) = in_1(f_1(a)) + \cdots + in_m(f_m(a)),$$

and thus, we write $f = in_1 \circ f_1 + \cdots + in_m \circ f_m$. It is also obvious that

$$in_1 \circ \pi_1 + \cdots + in_m \circ \pi_m = \text{id}.$$

Sometimes, instead of the unordered concept of the finite direct sum of affine spaces $(E_1, a_1) \oplus \cdots \oplus (E_m, a_m)$, we have use for the finite (ordered) product of affine spaces. Given any m affine spaces $\langle E_i, \overrightarrow{E_i}, +_i \rangle$, we define the affine space $\langle E, \overrightarrow{E}, + \rangle$, called the (finite) *product* of the affine spaces $\langle E_i, \overrightarrow{E_i}, +_i \rangle$, as follows: $E = E_1 \times \cdots \times E_m$, $\overrightarrow{E} = \overrightarrow{E_1} \times \cdots \times \overrightarrow{E_m}$, and $+: E \times \overrightarrow{E} \to E$ is defined such that

$$(a_1, \ldots, a_m) + (\overrightarrow{u_1}, \ldots, \overrightarrow{u_m}) = (a_1 + \overrightarrow{u_1}, \ldots, a_m + \overrightarrow{u_m}).$$

The verification that this is an affine space is obvious. The finite product of the affine spaces $\langle E_i, \overrightarrow{E_i}, +_i \rangle$ is also denoted simply as $E_1 \times \cdots \times E_m$. Clearly, $E_1 \times \cdots \times E_m$ and $(E_1, a_1) \oplus \cdots \oplus (E_m, a_m)$ are isomorphic, except that the order of the factors in $(E_1, a_1) \oplus \cdots \oplus (E_m, a_m)$ is irrelevant, and that designated origins are picked in each E_i.

B.4   Osculating Flats Revisited

This section contains various results on osculating flats as well as a generalized version of Lemma 5.5.2 (conditions on polar forms for polynomial maps to agree to kth order). Given an affine space $\mathcal{E}$, and a subset S of $\mathcal{E}$, we denote as $\mathrm{Span}(S)$ the affine subspace (the flat) of $\mathcal{E}$ generated by S. First, given a polynomial map $F: E \to \mathcal{E}$ of degree m, we relate $\mathrm{Span}(\widehat{F}(\widehat{E}))$ to $\widehat{f}_{\odot}(\bigodot^m \widehat{E})$.

Lemma B.4.1

Given any two affine spaces E and $\mathcal{E}$, for every polynomial map $F: E \to \mathcal{E}$ of degree m with polar form $f: E^m \to \mathcal{E}$, if $\widehat{f}: (\widehat{E})^m \to \widehat{\mathcal{E}}$ is the homogenized version of f, $\widehat{F}: \widehat{E} \to \widehat{\mathcal{E}}$ is the polynomial map associated with $\widehat{f}$, and $\widehat{f}_{\odot}: \bigodot^m \widehat{E} \to \widehat{\mathcal{E}}$ is the unique linear map from the tensor product $\bigodot^m \widehat{E}$ associated with $\widehat{f}$, we have

$$\mathrm{Span}(\widehat{F}(\widehat{E})) = \widehat{f}_{\odot}\left(\overset{m}{\underset{\odot}{\bigodot}} \widehat{E} \right).$$

Proof: First, we show that

$$\mathrm{Span}(\widehat{F}(\widehat{E})) \subseteq \mathrm{Span}(\widehat{f}((\widehat{E})^m)) \subseteq \widehat{f}_{\odot}\left(\overset{m}{\underset{\odot}{\bigodot}} \widehat{E} \right).$$

The first inclusion is trivial, and since

$$\widehat{f}(\theta_1, \ldots, \theta_m) = \widehat{f}_{\odot}(\theta_1 \cdots \theta_m),$$

we have

$$\widehat{f}((\widehat{E})^m) \subseteq \widehat{f}_{\odot}\left(\overset{m}{\underset{\odot}{\bigodot}} \widehat{E} \right).$$

Since $\widehat{f}_\odot$ is a linear map, its range is a vector space, and thus

$$\text{Span}(\widehat{f}((\widehat{E})^m)) \subseteq \widehat{f}_\odot \left(\overset{m}{\bigodot} \widehat{E} \right).$$

Since the tensors of the form $\theta_1 \cdots \theta_m$, where $\theta_1, \ldots, \theta_m \in \widehat{E}$, generate $\overset{m}{\bigodot} \widehat{E}$, if we can show that $\widehat{f}_\odot(\theta_1 \cdots \theta_m) \in \text{Span}(\widehat{F}(\widehat{E}))$, the proof will be complete. Thus, we just have to show that $\widehat{f}(\theta_1, \ldots, \theta_m) \in \text{Span}(\widehat{F}(\widehat{E}))$. However, this is an immediate consequence of Lemma 4.4.1, since a multilinear map is multiaffine. ∎

Remark: We can easily prove a version of Lemma B.4.1 for the affine symmetric tensor power of E, and the affine blossom $f_\odot$ of F: we have

$$\text{Span}(F(E)) = f_\odot \left(\overset{m}{\bigodot} E \right).$$

Now, Lemma 10.5.3 can also be stated as follows in terms of $\widehat{f}_\odot$.

Lemma B.4.2

Given an affine polynomial function $F: E \to \mathcal{E}$ of polar degree m, where E and $\mathcal{E}$ are normed affine spaces, for any k nonzero vectors $\overrightarrow{u_1}, \ldots, \overrightarrow{u_k}$, where $1 \leq k \leq m$, the kth directional derivative $D_{\overrightarrow{u_1}} \ldots D_{\overrightarrow{u_k}} F(a)$ can be computed from the homogenized polar form $\widehat{f}$ of F as follows:

$$D_{\overrightarrow{u_1}} \ldots D_{\overrightarrow{u_k}} F(a) = m^{\underline{k}} \, \widehat{f}_\odot(a^{m-k} \, \overrightarrow{u_1} \cdots \overrightarrow{u_k}).$$

We can now fix the problem encountered in relating the polar form g_a^k of the polynomial map G_a^k osculating F to kth order at a, with the polar form f of F.

Lemma B.4.3

Given an affine polynomial function $F: E \to \mathcal{E}$ of polar degree m, where E and $\mathcal{E}$ are normed affine spaces, if E is of finite dimension n and $(\delta_1, \ldots, \delta_n)$ is a basis of $\overrightarrow{E}$, for any $a \in E$, for any k, with $0 \leq k \leq m$, the polar form $g: E^k \to \mathcal{E}$ of the polynomial map $G_a^k: E \to \mathcal{E}$ that osculates F to kth order at a is determined such that

$$\widehat{g}_\odot(\theta) = \widehat{f}_\odot(\kappa(\theta) \, a^{m-k}),$$

for all $\theta \in \overset{k}{\bigodot} \widehat{E}$, and where $\kappa: \overset{k}{\bigodot} \widehat{E} \to \overset{k}{\bigodot} \widehat{E}$ is a bijective weight-preserving linear map defined as follows: since the tensors

$$\delta_1^{i_1} \cdots \delta_n^{i_n} \, a^{k-i},$$

where $i = i_1 + \cdots + i_n$, form a basis of $\overset{k}{\bigodot} \widehat{E}$, κ is the unique linear map such that

$$\kappa(\delta_1^{i_1} \cdots \delta_n^{i_n} \, a^{k-i}) = \frac{m^{\underline{i}}}{k^{\underline{i}}} \delta_1^{i_1} \cdots \delta_n^{i_n} \, a^{k-i}.$$

Proof: By Lemma B.4.2, we have

$$D_{\overrightarrow{u_{j_1}}} \ldots D_{\overrightarrow{u_{j_k}}} F(a) = m^{\underline{k}} \, \widehat{f}_\odot(a^{m-k} \, \overrightarrow{u_{j_1}} \cdots \overrightarrow{u_{j_k}}),$$

and thus, we get

$$\left(\frac{\partial}{\partial x_1}\right)^{i_1} \cdots \left(\frac{\partial}{\partial x_n}\right)^{i_n} F(a) = m^{\underline{i}} \, \widehat{f}_\odot(\delta_1^{i_1} \cdots \delta_n^{i_n} \, a^{m-i}),$$

where $i_1 + \cdots + i_n = i$. Letting $b = a + h_1\delta_1 + \cdots + h_n\delta_n$, since on one hand, we have

$$G_a^k(b) = F(a) + \sum_{1 \leq i_1 + \cdots + i_n \leq k} \frac{h_1^{i_1} \cdots h_n^{i_n}}{i_1! \cdots i_n!} \left(\frac{\partial}{\partial x_1}\right)^{i_1} \cdots \left(\frac{\partial}{\partial x_n}\right)^{i_n} F(a),$$

and on the other hand, we have

$$\left(\frac{\partial}{\partial x_1}\right)^{i_1} \cdots \left(\frac{\partial}{\partial x_n}\right)^{i_n} G_a^k(a) = k^{\underline{i}} \, \widehat{g}_\odot(\delta_1^{i_1} \cdots \delta_n^{i_n} \, a^{k-i}),$$

where $i_1 + \cdots + i_n = i$, we conclude that

$$k^{\underline{i}} \, \widehat{g}_\odot(\delta_1^{i_1} \cdots \delta_n^{i_n} \, a^{k-i}) = m^{\underline{i}} \, \widehat{f}_\odot(\delta_1^{i_1} \cdots \delta_n^{i_n} \, a^{m-i}),$$

that is,

$$\widehat{g}_\odot(\delta_1^{i_1} \cdots \delta_n^{i_n} \, a^{k-i}) = \widehat{f}_\odot\left(\left(\frac{m^{\underline{i}}}{k^{\underline{i}}} \delta_1^{i_1} \cdots \delta_n^{i_n} \, a^{k-i}\right) a^{m-k}\right),$$

and thus, defining the bijective linear map $\kappa \colon \bigodot^k \widehat{E} \to \bigodot^k \widehat{E}$, such that

$$\kappa(\delta_1^{i_1} \cdots \delta_n^{i_n} \, a^{k-i}) = \frac{m^{\underline{i}}}{k^{\underline{i}}} \delta_1^{i_1} \cdots \delta_n^{i_n} \, a^{k-i},$$

we have

$$\widehat{g}_\odot(\theta) = \widehat{f}_\odot(\kappa(\theta) \, a^{m-k}),$$

for all $\theta \in \bigodot^k \widehat{E}$. Clearly, κ is weight-preserving. ∎

At last, we obtain the relationship between osculating flats and polar forms stated without proof in Section 5.4.

Lemma B.4.4

Given an affine polynomial function $F \colon E \to \mathcal{E}$ of polar degree m, where E and $\mathcal{E}$ are normed affine spaces, and E is of finite dimension n, for any k, with $0 \leq k \leq m$, and for any $a \in E$, the affine subspace spanned by the range of the multiaffine map

$$(b_1, \ldots, b_k) \mapsto f(\underbrace{a, \ldots, a}_{m-k}, b_1, \ldots, b_k)$$

is the osculating flat $\mathrm{Osc}_k F(a)$.

Proof: Let G be the polynomial map osculating F to kth order at a. From Lemma B.4.1, we know that

$$\mathrm{Span}(\widehat{G}(\widehat{E})) = \widehat{g}_\odot \left(\overset{k}{\underset{\cdot}{\bigodot}} \widehat{E} \right),$$

where g is the polar form of G. Thus, we get

$$\mathrm{Span}(G(E))$$
$$= \{\widehat{g}_\odot(\theta) \mid \theta \text{ is an affine combination of simple } k\text{-tensors of points in } E\}$$
$$= g_\odot \left(\overset{k}{\underset{\cdot}{\bigodot}} E \right).$$

From Lemma B.4.3, we have

$$\widehat{g}_\odot(\theta) = \widehat{f}_\odot(\kappa(\theta)\, a^{m-k}),$$

for all $\theta \in \overset{k}{\bigodot} \widehat{E}$, and where $\kappa \colon \overset{k}{\bigodot} \widehat{E} \to \overset{k}{\bigodot} \widehat{E}$ is a bijective weight-preserving linear map. Since κ is weight-preserving and since $\mathrm{Osc}_k F(a) = \mathrm{Span}(G(E))$, we conclude that

$$\mathrm{Osc}_k F(a)$$
$$= \{\widehat{f}_\odot(\theta\, a^{m-k}) \mid \theta \text{ is an affine combination of simple } k\text{-tensors of points in } E\}.$$

However, since $\widehat{f}$ agrees with f on E^m, the affine subspace spanned by the range of the multiaffine map

$$(b_1, \ldots, b_k) \mapsto f(\underbrace{a, \ldots, a}_{m-k}, b_1, \ldots, b_k)$$

is the osculating flat $\mathrm{Osc}_k F(a)$. ∎

We can also give a short proof of a generalized version of Lemma 5.5.2.

Lemma B.4.5

Given any two affine spaces E and $\mathcal{E}$, where E is of finite dimension, for every $a \in E$, for every $k \leq m$, two polynomial maps $F \colon E \to \mathcal{E}$ and $G \colon E \to \mathcal{E}$ of polar degree m agree to kth order at a, that is,

$$D_{\overrightarrow{u_1}} \ldots D_{\overrightarrow{u_i}} F(a) = D_{\overrightarrow{u_1}} \ldots D_{\overrightarrow{u_i}} G(a),$$

for all $\vec{u}_1, \ldots, \vec{u}_i \in \vec{E}$, *where* $0 \le i \le k$, *iff their polar forms* $f: E^m \to \mathcal{E}$ *and* $g: E^m \to \mathcal{E}$ *agree on all multisets of points that contain at least* $m - k$ *copies of* a, *that is, iff*

$$f(u_1, \ldots, u_k, \underbrace{a, \ldots, a}_{m-k}) = g(u_1, \ldots, u_k, \underbrace{a, \ldots, a}_{m-k}),$$

for all $u_1, \ldots, u_k \in E$, *iff*

$$\widehat{f}_{\odot}(u_1 \cdots u_k \, a^{m-k}) = \widehat{g}_{\odot}(u_1 \cdots u_k \, a^{m-k}),$$

for all $u_1, \ldots, u_k \in E$.

Proof: Assume that the polar forms agree as stated. This can be restated as

$$\widehat{f}_{\odot}(\theta \, a^{m-k}) = \widehat{g}_{\odot}(\theta \, a^{m-k}),$$

for all simple k-tensors $\theta \in \bigodot^k \widehat{E}$ of the form $u_1 \cdots u_k$, where $u_1, \ldots, u_k \in E$. We have shown that these tensors generate $\bigodot^k \widehat{E}$, and thus, we have

$$\widehat{f}_{\odot}(\theta \, a^{m-k}) = \widehat{g}_{\odot}(\theta \, a^{m-k}),$$

for all k-tensors $\theta \in \bigodot^k \widehat{E}$. By Lemma B.4.2, since

$$D_{\vec{u}_1} \ldots D_{\vec{u}_i} F(a) = m^{\underline{i}} \, \widehat{f}_{\odot}(a^{m-i} \, \vec{u}_1 \cdots \vec{u}_i)$$

and

$$D_{\vec{u}_1} \ldots D_{\vec{u}_i} G(a) = m^{\underline{i}} \, \widehat{g}_{\odot}(a^{m-i} \, \vec{u}_1 \cdots \vec{u}_i),$$

by letting $\theta = a^{k-i} \, \vec{u}_1 \cdots \vec{u}_i$ in

$$\widehat{f}_{\odot}(\theta \, a^{m-k}) = \widehat{g}_{\odot}(\theta \, a^{m-k}),$$

we have

$$\widehat{f}_{\odot}(a^{m-i} \, \vec{u}_1 \cdots \vec{u}_i) = \widehat{g}_{\odot}(a^{m-i} \, \vec{u}_1 \cdots \vec{u}_i),$$

and thus, we have shown that

$$D_{\vec{u}_1} \ldots D_{\vec{u}_i} F(a) = D_{\vec{u}_1} \ldots D_{\vec{u}_i} G(a).$$

Conversely, assume that F and G agree to kth order at a. Let $(\delta_1, \ldots, \delta_n)$ be a basis of $\vec{E}$. We have shown that the family of tensors

$$\delta_1^{i_1} \cdots \delta_n^{i_n} \, a^{k-i},$$

where $i = i_1 + \cdots + i_n$, forms a basis of $\bigodot^k \widehat{E}$. Letting $\theta = \delta_1^{i_1} \cdots \delta_n^{i_n} a^{k-i}$, where $i = i_1 + \cdots + i_n$, by Lemma B.4.2, since

$$D_{\overrightarrow{u_1}} \ldots D_{\overrightarrow{u_i}} F(a) = m^{\underline{i}} \, \widehat{f}_{\odot}(a^{m-i} \, \overrightarrow{u_1} \cdots \overrightarrow{u_i})$$

and

$$D_{\overrightarrow{u_1}} \ldots D_{\overrightarrow{u_i}} G(a) = m^{\underline{i}} \, \widehat{g}_{\odot}(a^{m-i} \, \overrightarrow{u_1} \cdots \overrightarrow{u_i}),$$

letting $\overrightarrow{u_1} \cdots \overrightarrow{u_i} = \delta_1^{i_1} \cdots \delta_n^{i_n}$, since by assumption these derivatives agree, and since

$$a^{m-k} \theta = \delta_1^{i_1} \cdots \delta_n^{i_n} a^{m-i} = \overrightarrow{u_1} \cdots \overrightarrow{u_i} a^{m-i},$$

we have

$$\widehat{f}_{\odot}(a^{m-k} \theta) = \widehat{g}_{\odot}(a^{m-k} \theta),$$

for all basis tensors θ of $\bigodot^k \widehat{E}$, and thus, for all $\theta \in \bigodot^k \widehat{E}$. In particular, this is true for k-tensors of the form $\theta = u_1 \cdots u_k$, where $u_1, \ldots, u_k \in E$, and thus,

$$\widehat{f}_{\odot}(u_1 \cdots u_k \, a^{m-k}) = \widehat{g}_{\odot}(u_1 \cdots u_k \, a^{m-k}),$$

for all $u_1, \ldots, u_k \in E$. ∎

For those of you who got hooked on tensors, we mention that Ramshaw's paper [65] contains a fascinating study of the algebra and geometry of the tensor powers $\bigodot^m A$ and $\bigodot^m \widehat{A}$ for $m = 2, 3$, and much more. The Möbius strip even manages to show its tail!

To close this chapter, we mention that there is a third version of the tensor product, the *exterior* (or *alternating*) *tensor product* (or *Grassmann algebra*). Roughly speaking, this tensor product has the property that

$$\overrightarrow{u_1} \wedge \cdots \wedge \overrightarrow{u_i} \wedge \cdots \wedge \overrightarrow{u_j} \wedge \cdots \wedge \overrightarrow{u_n} = \overrightarrow{0}$$

whenever $\overrightarrow{u_i} = \overrightarrow{u_j}$, for $i \neq j$. It follows that the exterior product changes sign when two factors are permuted. The corresponding algebra $\bigwedge(E)$ plays an important role in differential geometry. Determinants can also be defined in an intrinsic manner. The exterior algebra $\bigwedge(E)$ can also be obtained as the quotient of $T(E)$, by the subspace of $T(E)$ generated by all vectors in $T(E)$, of the form $\overrightarrow{u} \otimes \overrightarrow{u}$ (this requires defining a multiplication operation $(\otimes)$ on $T(E)$).

For an extensive treatment (in fact, very extensive!) of tensors, tensor algebras, and so on, see Bourbaki [14] (Chapter 3) and [15] (Chapter 4).

Topology

C.1   Metric Spaces and Normed Vector Spaces

This appendix contains a review of basic topological concepts. First, metric spaces are defined. Next, normed vector spaces are defined. Closed and open sets are defined, and their basic properties are stated. The chapter ends with the definition of a normed affine space. We recommend the following texts for a thorough treatment of topology and analysis: *Topology, a First Course*, by Munkres [54]; *Undergraduate Analysis*, by Lang [48]; and the analysis courses *Analyse I–IV*, by Schwartz [70, 71, 72, 73].

Most spaces considered in this book have a topological structure given by a metric or a norm, and we first review these notions. We begin with metric spaces. Recall that $\mathbf{R}_+ = \{x \in \mathbf{R} \mid x \geq 0\}$.

Definition C.1.1

A metric space *is a set E together with a function $d: E \times E \to \mathbf{R}_+$, called a* metric, *or distance, assigning a nonnegative real number $d(x, y)$ to any two points $x, y \in E$, and satisfying the following conditions for all $x, y, z \in E$:*

(D1) $d(x, y) = d(y, x)$.   *(symmetry)*

(D2) $d(x, y) \geq 0$, *and* $d(x, y) = 0$ *iff* $x = y$.   *(positivity)*

(D3) $d(x, z) \leq d(x, y) + d(y, z)$.   *(triangular inequality)*

Geometrically, condition (D3) expresses the fact that in a triangle with vertices x, y, z, the length of any side is bounded by the sum of the lengths of the other two sides. From (D3), we immediately get

$$|d(x, y) - d(y, z)| \leq d(x, z).$$

Let us give some examples of metric spaces. Recall that the *absolute value* $|x|$ of a real number $x \in \mathbf{R}$ is defined such that $|x| = x$ if $x \geq 0$, $|x| = -x$ if $x < 0$, and for a complex number $x = a + ib$, as $|x| = \sqrt{a^2 + b^2}$.

Example 1: Let $E = \mathbf{R}$, and $d(x, y) = |x - y|$, the absolute value of $x - y$. This is the so-called natural metric on $\mathbf{R}$.

Example 2: Let $E = \mathbf{R}^n$ (or $E = \mathbf{C}^n$). We have the Euclidean metric

$$d_2(x, y) = \left(|x_1 - y_1|^2 + \cdots + |x_n - y_n|^2 \right)^{\frac{1}{2}},$$

the distance between the points $(x_1, \ldots, x_n)$ and $(y_1, \ldots, y_n)$.

Example 3: For every set E, we can define the *discrete metric*, defined such that $d(x, y) = 1$ iff $x \neq y$, and $d(x, x) = 0$.

Example 4: For any $a, b \in \mathbf{R}$ such that $a < b$, we define the following sets:

$[a, b] = \{x \in \mathbf{R} \mid a \leq x \leq b\}$,   (closed interval)

$]a, b[= \{x \in \mathbf{R} \mid a < x < b\}$,   (open interval)

$[a, b[= \{x \in \mathbf{R} \mid a \leq x < b\}$,   (interval closed on the left, open on the right)

$]a, b] = \{x \in \mathbf{R} \mid a < x \leq b\}$,   (interval open on the left, closed on the right)

Let $E = [a, b]$, and $d(x, y) = |x - y|$. Then, $([a, b], d)$ is a metric space.

We will need to define the notion of proximity in order to define convergence of limits and continuity of functions. For this, we introduce some standard "small neighborhoods."

Definition C.1.2

Given a metric space E with metric d, for every $a \in E$, for every $\rho \in \mathbf{R}$, with $\rho > 0$, the set

$$B(a, \rho) = \{x \in E \mid d(a, x) \leq \rho\}$$

is called the closed ball *of center a and radius ρ, the set*

$$B_0(a, \rho) = \{x \in E \mid d(a, x) < \rho\}$$

is called the open ball *of center a and radius ρ, and the set*

$$S(a, \rho) = \{x \in E \mid d(a, x) = \rho\}$$

is called the sphere *of center a and radius ρ. It should be noted that ρ is finite (i.e., not $+\infty$). A subset X of a metric space E is* bounded *if there is a closed ball $B(a, \rho)$ such that $X \subseteq B(a, \rho)$.*

Clearly, $B(a, \rho) = B_0(a, \rho) \cup S(a, \rho)$.

In $E = \mathbf{R}$ with the distance $|x - y|$, an open ball of center a and radius ρ is the open interval $]a - \rho, a + \rho[$. In $E = \mathbf{R}^2$ with the Euclidean metric, an open ball of center a and radius ρ is the set of points inside the disk of center a and radius ρ, excluding the boundary points on the circle. In $E = \mathbf{R}^3$ with the Euclidean metric, an open ball of center a and radius ρ is the set of points inside the sphere of center a and radius ρ, excluding the boundary points on the sphere.

You should be aware that intuition can be misleading in forming a geometric image of a closed (or open) ball. For example, if d is the discrete metric, a closed ball of center a and radius $\rho < 1$ consists only of its center a, and a closed ball of center a and radius $\rho \geq 1$ consists of the entire space!

If $E = [a, b]$, and $d(x, y) = |x - y|$, as in Example 4, an open ball $B_0(a, \rho)$, with $\rho < b - a$, is in fact the interval $[a, a + \rho[$, which is closed on the left.

We now consider a very important special case of metric spaces, normed vector spaces.

Definition C.1.3

Let E be a vector space over a field K, where K is either the field $\mathbf{R}$ of reals, or the field $\mathbf{C}$ of complex numbers. A norm on E is a function $\| \ \| : E \to \mathbf{R}_+$, assigning a nonnegative real number $\|\vec{u}\|$ to any vector $\vec{u} \in E$, and satisfying the following conditions for all $\vec{x}, \vec{y}, \vec{z} \in E$:

(N1) $\|\vec{x}\| \geq 0$, *and* $\|\vec{x}\| = 0$ *iff* $\vec{x} = \vec{0}$. *(positivity)*

(N2) $\|\lambda \vec{x}\| = |\lambda| \ \|\vec{x}\|$. *(scaling)*

(N3) $\|\vec{x} + \vec{y}\| \leq \|\vec{x}\| + \|\vec{y}\|$. *(convexity inequality)*

A vector space E together with a norm $\| \ \|$ is called a normed vector space.

From (N3), we easily get

$$\left| \|\vec{x}\| - \|\vec{y}\| \right| \leq \|\vec{x} - \vec{y}\|.$$

Given a normed vector space E, if we define d such that

$$d(\vec{x}, \vec{y}) = \|\vec{x} - \vec{y}\|,$$

it is easily seen that d is a metric. Thus, every normed vector space is immediately a metric space. Note that the metric associated with a norm is invariant under translation, that is,

$$d(\vec{x} + \vec{u}, \vec{y} + \vec{u}) = d(\vec{x}, \vec{y}).$$

For this reason, we can restrict ourselves to open or closed balls of center $\vec{0}$.

Let us give some examples of normed vector spaces.

Example 5: Let $E = \mathbf{R}$, and $\|x\| = |x|$, the absolute value of x. The associated metric is $|x - y|$, as in Example 1.

Example 6: Let $E = \mathbf{R}^n$ (or $E = \mathbf{C}^n$). There are three standard norms. For every $(x_1, \ldots, x_n) \in E$, we have the norm $\|\vec{x}\|_1$, defined such that

$$\|\vec{x}\|_1 = |x_1| + \cdots + |x_n|,$$

we have the Euclidean norm $\|\vec{x}\|_2$, defined such that

$$\|\vec{x}\|_2 = (|x_1|^2 + \cdots + |x_n|^2)^{\frac{1}{2}}$$

and the *sup*-norm $\|\vec{x}\|_\infty$, defined such that

$$\|\vec{x}\|_\infty = \max\{|x_i| \mid 1 \le i \le n\}.$$

Some work is required to show the convexity inequality for the Euclidean norm, but this can be found in any standard text. Note that the Euclidean distance is the distance associated with the Euclidean norm. The following lemma is easy to show.

Lemma C.1.4

The following inequalities hold for all $\vec{x} \in \mathbf{R}^n$ (or $\vec{x} \in \mathbf{C}^n$):

$$\|\vec{x}\|_\infty \le \|\vec{x}\|_1 \le n \|\vec{x}\|_\infty,$$

$$\|\vec{x}\|_\infty \le \|\vec{x}\|_2 \le \sqrt{n} \|\vec{x}\|_\infty,$$

$$\|\vec{x}\|_2 \le \|\vec{x}\|_1 \le \sqrt{n} \|\vec{x}\|_2.$$

In a normed vector space, we define a closed ball or an open ball of radius ρ as a closed ball or an open ball of center $\vec{0}$. We may use the notation $B(\rho)$ and $B_0(\rho)$.

We will now define the crucial notions of open sets and closed sets, and of a topological space.

Definition C.1.5

Let E be a metric space with metric d. A subset $U \subseteq E$ is an open set *in E iff either $U = \emptyset$, or for every $a \in U$, there is some open ball $B_0(a, \rho)$ such that $B_0(a, \rho) \subseteq U$.[1] A subset $F \subseteq E$ is a* closed set *in E iff its complement $E - F$ is open in E.*

The set E itself is open, since for every $a \in E$, every open ball of center a is contained in E. In $E = \mathbf{R}^n$, given n intervals $[a_i, b_i]$, with $a_i < b_i$, it is easy to show that the open n-cube

$$\{(x_1, \ldots, x_n) \in E \mid a_i < x_i < b_i, \ 1 \le i \le n\}$$

---

1. Recall that $\rho > 0$.

is an open set. In fact, it is possible to find a metric for which such open n-cubes are open balls! Similarly, we can define the closed n-cube

$$\{(x_1, \ldots, x_n) \in E \mid a_i \le x_i \le b_i,\ 1 \le i \le n\},$$

which is a closed set.

The open sets satisfy some important properties that lead to the definition of a topological space.

Lemma C.1.6

Given a metric space E with metric d, the family $\mathcal{O}$ of open sets defined in Definition C.1.5 satisfies the following properties:

(O1) For every finite family $(U_i)_{1 \le i \le n}$ of sets $U_i \in \mathcal{O}$, we have $U_1 \cap \cdots \cap U_n \in \mathcal{O}$; that is, $\mathcal{O}$ is closed under finite intersections.

(O2) For every arbitrary family $(U_i)_{i \in I}$ of sets $U_i \in \mathcal{O}$, we have $\bigcup_{i \in I} U_i \in \mathcal{O}$; that is, $\mathcal{O}$ is closed under arbitrary unions.

(O3) $\emptyset \in \mathcal{O}$, and $E \in \mathcal{O}$; that is, $\emptyset$ and E belong to $\mathcal{O}$.

Furthermore, for any two distinct points $a \ne b$ in E, there exist two open sets U_a and U_b such that $a \in U_a$, $b \in U_b$, and $U_a \cap U_b = \emptyset$.

Proof: It is straightforward. For the last point, letting $\rho = d(a, b)/3$ (in fact, $\rho = d(a, b)/2$ works too), we can pick $U_a = B_0(a, \rho)$ and $U_b = B_0(b, \rho)$. By the triangle inequality, we must have $U_a \cap U_b = \emptyset$. ∎

The above lemma leads to the very general concept of a topological space (see standard texts on topology, such as Munkres [54]).

You should be careful that, in general, the family of open sets is not closed under infinite intersections. For example, in $\mathbf{R}$ under the metric $|x - y|$, letting $U_n =]-1/n,\ +1/n[$, each U_n is open, but $\bigcap_n U_n = \{0\}$, which is not open.

If each $(E_i, \|\ \|_i)$ is a normed vector space, there are three natural norms that can be defined on $E_1 \times \cdots \times E_n$:

$$\|(x_1, \ldots, x_n)\|_1 = \|x_1\|_1 + \cdots + \|x_n\|_n,$$

$$\|(x_1, \ldots, x_n)\|_2 = \left(\|x_1\|_1^2 + \cdots + \|x_n\|_n^2\right)^{\frac{1}{2}},$$

$$\|(x_1, \ldots, x_n)\|_\infty = \max\{\|x_1\|_1, \ldots, \|x_n\|_n\}.$$

It is easy to show that they all define the same topology, which is the product topology, that is, the same set of open sets. It can also be verified that when $E_i = \mathbf{R}$, with the standard topology induced by $|x - y|$, the topology product on $\mathbf{R}^n$ is the standard topology induced by the Euclidean norm.

C.2   Continuous Functions, Limits

If E and F are metric spaces defined by metrics d_1 and d_2, f is continuous at a iff for every $\epsilon > 0$, there is some $\eta > 0$, such that, for every $x \in E$,

if $d_1(a, x) \leq \eta$, then $d_2(f(a), f(x)) \leq \epsilon$.

Similarly, if E and F are normed vector spaces defined by norms $\| \|_1$ and $\| \|_2$, f is continuous at $\vec{a}$ iff for every $\epsilon > 0$, there is some $\eta > 0$, such that, for every $\vec{x} \in E$,

if $\left\| \vec{x} - \vec{a} \right\|_1 \leq \eta$, then $\left\| f(\vec{x}) - f(\vec{a}) \right\|_2 \leq \epsilon$.

The following lemma is useful for showing that real-valued functions are continuous.

Lemma C.2.1

If E is a topological space, and $(\mathbf{R}, |x - y|)$ the reals under the standard topology, for any two functions $f : E \to \mathbf{R}$ and $g : E \to \mathbf{R}$, for any $a \in E$, for any $\lambda \in \mathbf{R}$, if f and g are continuous at a, then $f + g$, λf, $f \cdot g$ are continuous at a, and f/g is continuous at a if $g(a) \neq 0$.

Proof: Left as an exercise. ∎

Using Lemma C.2.1, we can show easily that every real polynomial function is continuous.

When E is a metric space with metric d, *a sequence $(x_n)_{n \in \mathbf{N}}$ converges to some* $a \in E$ iff for every $\epsilon > 0$, there is some $n_0 \geq 0$, such that, $d(x_n, a) \leq \epsilon$, for all $n \geq n_0$.

When E is a normed vector space with norm $\| \|$, *a sequence $(x_n)_{n \in \mathbf{N}}$ converges to some $a \in E$* iff for every $\epsilon > 0$, there is some $n_0 \geq 0$, such that, $\left\| \vec{x_n} - \vec{a} \right\| \leq \epsilon$, for all $n \geq n_0$.

Finally, we consider normed affine spaces.

C.3   Normed Affine Spaces

For geometric applications, we will need to consider affine spaces $(E, \vec{E})$ where the associated space of translations $\vec{E}$ is a vector space equipped with a norm.

Definition C.3.1

Given an affine space $(E, \vec{E})$, where the space of translations $\vec{E}$ is a vector space over $\mathbf{R}$ or $\mathbf{C}$, we say that $(E, \vec{E})$ is a normed affine space iff $\vec{E}$ is a normed vector space with norm $\| \|$.

Given a normed affine space, there is a natural metric on E itself, defined such that

$$d(a, b) = \left\| \vec{ab} \right\|.$$

Observe that this metric is invariant under translation, that is,

$$d(a + \vec{u}, b + \vec{u}) = d(a, b).$$

Also, for every fixed $a \in E$ and $\lambda > 0$, if we consider the map $h: E \to E$, defined such that

$$h(x) = a + \lambda \overrightarrow{ax},$$

then $d(h(x), h(y)) = \lambda d(x, y)$.

Note that the map $(a, b) \mapsto \overrightarrow{ab}$ from $E \times E$ to $\vec{E}$ is continuous, and similarly for the map $a \mapsto a + \vec{u}$ from $E \times \vec{E}$ to E. In fact, the map $\vec{u} \mapsto a + \vec{u}$ is a homeomorphism from $\vec{E}$ to E_a.

Of course, $\mathbf{R}^n$ is a normed affine space under the Euclidean metric, and it is also complete.

If an affine space E is a finite direct sum $(E_1, a_1) \oplus \cdots \oplus (E_m, a_m)$, and each E_i is also a normed affine space with norm $\| \ \|_i$, we make $(E_1, a_1) \oplus \cdots \oplus (E_m, a_m)$ into a normed affine space, by giving it the norm

$$\|(x_1, \ldots, x_n)\| = \max(\|x_1\|_1, \ldots, \|x_n\|_n).$$

Similarly, the finite product $E_1 \times \cdots \times E_m$ is made into a normed affine space, under the same norm.

We are now ready to define the derivative (or differential) of a map between two normed affine spaces. This will lead to tangent spaces to curves and surfaces (in normed affine spaces).

Differential Calculus

D.1   Directional Derivatives, Total Derivatives

This appendix contains a review of basic notions of differential calculus. First, we review the definition of the derivative of a function $f: \mathbf{R} \to \mathbf{R}$. Next, we define directional derivatives and the total derivative of a function $f: E \to F$ between normed affine spaces. Basic properties of derivatives are shown, including the chain rule. We show how derivatives are represented by Jacobian matrices.

A thorough treatment of differential calculus can be found in Munkres [55], Lang [48], Schwartz [71], Cartan [16], and Avez [2]. We first review the notion of the derivative of a real-valued function whose domain is an open subset of $\mathbf{R}$.

Let $f: A \to \mathbf{R}$, where A is a nonempty open subset of $\mathbf{R}$, and consider any $a \in A$. The main idea behind the concept of the derivative of f at a, denoted as $f'(a)$, is that locally around a (that is, in some small open set $U \subseteq A$ containing a), the function f is approximated linearly by the map

$$x \mapsto f(a) + f'(a)(x - a).$$

Part of the difficulty in extending this idea to more complex spaces is to give an adequate notion of linear approximation. Of course, we will use linear maps! Let us now review the formal definition of the derivative of a real-valued function.

Definition D.1.1

Let A be any nonempty open subset of $\mathbf{R}$, and let $a \in A$. For any function $f: A \to \mathbf{R}$, the derivative of f at $a \in A$ is the limit (if it exists)

$$\lim_{h \to 0, \, h \in U} \frac{f(a + h) - f(a)}{h},$$

where $U = \{h \in \mathbf{R} \mid a + h \in A,\ h \neq 0\}$. *This limit is denoted as* $f'(a)$, *or* $\mathrm{D}f(a)$, *or* $\frac{df}{dx}(a)$. *If* $f'(a)$ *exists for every* $a \in A$, *we say that* f *is differentiable on* A. *In this case, the map* $a \mapsto f'(a)$ *is denoted as* f', *or* $\mathrm{D}f$, *or* $\frac{df}{dx}$.

Note that since A is assumed to be open, $A - \{a\}$ is also open, and since the function $h \mapsto a + h$ is continuous and U is the inverse image of $A - \{a\}$ under this function, U is indeed open and the definition makes sense. We can also define $f'(a)$ as follows: There is some function $\epsilon(h)$, such that

$$f(a + h) = f(a) + f'(a) \cdot h + \epsilon(h)h,$$

whenever $a + h \in A$, where $\epsilon(h)$ is defined for all h such that $a + h \in A$, and

$$\lim_{h \to 0,\, h \in U} \epsilon(h) = 0.$$

Remark: We can also define the notion of *derivative of f at a on the left* and *derivative of f at a on the right*. For example, we say that the *derivative of f at a on the left* is the limit $f'(a_-)$, if it exists,

$$\lim_{h \to 0,\, h \in U} \frac{f(a + h) - f(a)}{h},$$

where $U = \{h \in \mathbf{R} \mid a + h \in A,\ h < 0\}$.

If a function f as in Definition D.1.1 has a derivative $f'(a)$ at a, then it is continuous at a. If f is differentiable on A, then f is continuous on A. The composition of differentiable functions is differentiable.

Remark: A function f has a derivative $f'(a)$ at a iff the derivative of f on the left at a and the derivative of f on the right at a exist, and if they are equal. Also, if the derivative of f on the left at a exists, then f is continuous on the left at a (and similarly on the right).

We would like to extend the notion of derivative to functions $f : A \to F$, where E and F are normed affine spaces and A is some nonempty open subset of E. The first difficulty is to make sense of the quotient

$$\frac{f(a + h) - f(a)}{h}.$$

If E and F are normed affine spaces, it will be notationally convenient to assume that the vector space associated with E is denoted as $\overrightarrow{E}$, and that the vector space associated with F is denoted as $\overrightarrow{F}$.

Since F is a normed affine space, making sense of $f(a + \overrightarrow{h}) - f(a)$ is easy: we can define this as

$$\overrightarrow{f(a)f(a + \overrightarrow{h})},$$

the unique vector translating $f(a)$ to $f(a + \vec{h})$. We should note, however, that this quantity is a vector and not a point. Nevertheless, in defining derivatives, it is notationally more pleasant to denote

$$\overline{f(a)f(a + \vec{h})}$$

as $f(a + \vec{h}) - f(a)$. Thus, in the rest of this chapter, the vector $\overrightarrow{ab}$ will be denoted as $b - a$. But now, how do we define the quotient by a vector? Well, we don't!

A first possibility is to consider the *directional derivative* with respect to a vector $\vec{u} \neq \vec{0}$ in $\vec{E}$. We can consider the vector $f(a + t\vec{u}) - f(a)$, where $t \in \mathbf{R}$ (or $t \in \mathbf{C}$). Now,

$$\frac{f(a + t\vec{u}) - f(a)}{t}$$

makes sense. The idea is that in E the points of the form $a + t\vec{u}$ form a line, where $t \in \mathbf{R}$ (or $\mathbf{C}$) (more exactly, for t in some small closed interval $[r, s]$ in A containing a, the points of the form $a + t\vec{u}$ form a line segment), and that the image of this line defines a curve in F, a curve that lies on the image $f(E)$ of E under the map $f: E \to F$ (more exactly, a small curve segment on $f(A)$). This curve (segment) is defined by the map $t \mapsto f(a + t\vec{u})$, from $\mathbf{R}$ to F (more exactly from $[r, s]$ to F), and the directional derivative $\mathrm{D}_{\vec{u}} f(a)$ defines the direction of the tangent line at a to this curve. This leads us to the following definition.

Definition D.1.2

Let E and F be two normed affine spaces, let A be a nonempty open subset of E, and let $f: A \to F$ be any function. For any $a \in A$, for any $\vec{u} \neq \vec{0}$ in $\vec{E}$, the directional derivative of f at a with respect to the vector $\vec{u}$, denoted as $\mathrm{D}_{\vec{u}} f(a)$, is the limit (if it exists)

$$\lim_{t \to 0, t \in U} \frac{f(a + t\vec{u}) - f(a)}{t},$$

where $U = \{t \in \mathbf{R} \mid a + t\vec{u} \in A, \ t \neq 0\}$ (or $U = \{t \in \mathbf{C} \mid a + t\vec{u} \in A, \ t \neq 0\}$).

Since the map $t \mapsto a + t\vec{u}$ is continuous, and since $A - \{a\}$ is open, the inverse image U of $A - \{a\}$ under the above map is open, and the definition of the limit in Definition D.1.2 makes sense. Since the notion of limit is purely topological, the existence and value of a directional derivative is independent of the choice of norms in E and F, as long as they are equivalent norms. The directional derivative is sometimes called the Gâteaux derivative.

In the special case where $E = \mathbf{R}$ and $F = \mathbf{R}$, and we let $\vec{u} = \vec{1}$ (i.e., the real number 1, viewed as a vector), it is immediately verified that $\mathrm{D}_{\vec{1}} f(a) = f'(a)$, in the sense of Definition D.1.1. When $E = \mathbf{R}$ (or $E = \mathbf{C}$) and F is any normed vector space, the derivative $\mathrm{D}_{\vec{1}} f(a)$, also denoted as $f'(a)$, provides a suitable generalization of the notion of derivative.

However, when E has dimension ≥ 2, directional derivatives present a serious problem, which is that their definition is not sufficiently uniform. Indeed, there is no reason to believe that the directional derivatives with respect to all nonnull vectors $\vec{u}$ share something in common. As a consequence, a function can have all directional derivatives at a, and yet not be continuous at a. Two functions may have all directional derivatives in some open sets, and yet their composition may not. Thus, we introduce a more uniform notion.

Definition D.1.3

Let E and F be two normed affine spaces, let A be a nonempty open subset of E, and let $f: A \to F$ be any function. For any $a \in A$, we say that f is differentiable at $a \in A$ iff there is a linear continuous map $L: \vec{E} \to \vec{F}$ and a function $\epsilon(\vec{h})$, such that

$$f(a + \vec{h}) = f(a) + L(\vec{h}) + \epsilon(\vec{h}) \left\| \vec{h} \right\|$$

for every $a + \vec{h} \in A$, where $\epsilon(\vec{h})$ is defined for every $\vec{h}$ such that $a + \vec{h} \in A$ and

$$\lim_{\vec{h} \to \vec{0}, \, \vec{h} \in U} \epsilon(\vec{h}) = \vec{0},$$

where $U = \{\vec{h} \in \vec{E} \mid a + \vec{h} \in A, \, \vec{h} \neq \vec{0}\}$. The linear map L is denoted as $\mathrm{D}f(a)$, or $\mathrm{D}f_a$, or $df(a)$, or $f'(a)$, and it is called the Fréchet derivative, *or* derivative, *or* total differential, *or* differential, *of f at a.*

Since the map $\vec{h} \mapsto a + \vec{h}$ from $\vec{E}$ to E is continuous, and since A is open in E, the inverse image U of $A - \{a\}$ under the above map is open in $\vec{E}$, and it makes sense to say that

$$\lim_{\vec{h} \to \vec{0}, \, \vec{h} \in U} \epsilon(\vec{h}) = \vec{0}.$$

Note that for every $\vec{h} \in U$, since $\vec{h} \neq \vec{0}$, $\epsilon(\vec{h})$ is uniquely determined since

$$\epsilon(\vec{h}) = \frac{f(a + \vec{h}) - f(a) - L(\vec{h})}{\left\| \vec{h} \right\|},$$

and that the value $\epsilon(\vec{0})$ plays absolutely no role in this definition. The condition for f to be differentiable at a amounts to the fact that the right-hand side of the above expression approaches $\vec{0}$ as $\vec{h} \neq \vec{0}$ approaches $\vec{0}$, when $a + \vec{h} \in A$. However, it does no harm to assume that $\epsilon(\vec{0}) = \vec{0}$, and we will assume this from now on.

Again, we note that the derivative $\mathrm{D}f(a)$ of f at a provides an affine approximation of f, locally around a. Since the notion of limit is purely topological, the existence and value of a derivative is independent of the choice of norms in E and F, as long as they are equivalent norms. Note that the continuous linear map L

is unique, if it exists. In fact, the next lemma implies this as a corollary. The following lemma shows that our new definition is consistent with the definition of the directional derivative.

Lemma D.1.4

Let E and F be two normed affine spaces, let A be a nonempty open subset of E, and let $f: A \to F$ be any function. For any $a \in A$, if $\mathrm{D}f(a)$ is defined, then f is continuous at a, and f has a directional derivative $\mathrm{D}_{\vec{u}} f(a)$ for every $\vec{u} \neq \vec{0}$ in $\vec{E}$, and furthermore,

$$\mathrm{D}_{\vec{u}} f(a) = \mathrm{D}f(a)(\vec{u}).$$

Proof: If $\vec{h} \neq \vec{0}$ approaches $\vec{0}$, since L is continuous, $\epsilon(\vec{h}) \left\| \vec{h} \right\|$ approaches $\vec{0}$, and thus, f is continuous at a. For any $\vec{u} \neq \vec{0}$ in $\vec{E}$, for $|t| \in \mathbf{R}$ small enough (where $t \in \mathbf{R}$ or $t \in \mathbf{C}$), we have $a + t\vec{u} \in A$, and letting $\vec{h} = t\vec{u}$, we have

$$f(a + t\vec{u}) = f(a) + tL(\vec{u}) + \epsilon(t\vec{u})|t| \left\| \vec{u} \right\|,$$

and for $t \neq 0$,

$$\frac{f(a + t\vec{u}) - f(a)}{t} = L(\vec{u}) + \frac{|t|}{t} \epsilon(t\vec{u}) \left\| \vec{u} \right\|,$$

and the limit when $t \neq 0$ approaches 0 is indeed $\mathrm{D}_{\vec{u}} f(a)$. ∎

The uniqueness of L follows from Lemma D.1.4. Also, when E is of finite dimension, it is easily shown that every linear map is continuous, and this assumption is then redundant.

It is important to note that the derivative $\mathrm{D}f(a)$ of f at a is a continuous linear map from the *vector space* $\vec{E}$ to the *vector space* $\vec{F}$, and not a function from the affine space E to the affine space F. If $\mathrm{D}f(a)$ exists for every $a \in A$, we get a map $\mathrm{D}f: A \to \mathcal{L}(\vec{E}; \vec{F})$, called the *derivative of f on A*, and also denoted as df.

When E is of finite dimension n, for any frame $(a_0, (\vec{u_1}, \ldots, \vec{u_n}))$ of E, where $(\vec{u_1}, \ldots, \vec{u_n})$ is a basis of $\vec{E}$, we can define the directional derivatives with respect to the vectors in the basis $(\vec{u_1}, \ldots, \vec{u_n})$ (actually, we can also do it for an infinite frame). This way, we obtain the definition of partial derivatives, as follows.

Definition D.1.5

For any two normed affine spaces E and F, if E is of finite dimension n, for every frame $(a_0, (\vec{u_1}, \ldots, \vec{u_n}))$ for E, for every $a \in E$, for every function $f: E \to F$, the directional derivatives $\mathrm{D}_{\vec{u_j}} f(a)$, if they exist, are called the partial derivatives *of f with respect to the frame $(a_0, (\vec{u_1}, \ldots, \vec{u_n}))$. The partial derivative $\mathrm{D}_{\vec{u_j}} f(a)$ is also denoted as $\partial_j f(a)$, or $\frac{\partial f}{\partial x_j}(a)$.*

The notation $\frac{\partial f}{\partial x_j}(a)$ for a partial derivative, although customary and going back to Leibnitz, is a "logical obscenity." Indeed, the variable x_j really has nothing to do with the formal definition. This is just another of these situations where tradition is just too hard to overthrow!

We now consider a number of standard results about derivatives.

Lemma D.1.6

Given two normed affine spaces E and F, if $f: E \to F$ is a constant function, then $\mathrm{D}f(a) = 0$, for every $a \in E$. If $f: E \to F$ is a continuous affine map, then $\mathrm{D}f(a) = \vec{f}$, for every $a \in E$, the linear map associated with f.

Proof: Straightforward. ∎

Lemma D.1.7

Given a normed affine space E and a normed vector space F, for any two functions $f: E \to F$, for every $a \in E$, if $\mathrm{D}f(a)$ and $\mathrm{D}g(a)$ exist, then $\mathrm{D}(f+g)(a)$ and $\mathrm{D}(\lambda f)(a)$ exist, and

$$\mathrm{D}(f+g)(a) = \mathrm{D}f(a) + \mathrm{D}g(a),$$

$$\mathrm{D}(\lambda f)(a) = \lambda \mathrm{D}f(a).$$

Proof: Straightforward. ∎

Lemma D.1.8

Given three normed vector spaces E_1, E_2, and F, for any continuous bilinear map $f: E_1 \times E_2 \to F$, for every $(\vec{a}, \vec{b}) \in E_1 \times E_2$, $\mathrm{D}f(\vec{a}, \vec{b})$ exists, and for every $\vec{u} \in E_1$ and $\vec{v} \in E_2$,

$$\mathrm{D}f(\vec{a}, \vec{b})(\vec{u}, \vec{v}) = f(\vec{u}, \vec{b}) + f(\vec{a}, \vec{v}).$$

Proof: Straightforward. ∎

We now state the very useful chain rule.

Lemma D.1.9

Given three normed affine spaces E, F, and G, let A be an open set in E, and let B be an open set in F. For any functions $f: A \to F$ and $g: B \to G$, such that $f(A) \subseteq B$, for any $a \in A$, if $\mathrm{D}f(a)$ exists and $\mathrm{D}g(f(a))$ exists, then $\mathrm{D}(g \circ f)(a)$ exists, and

$$\mathrm{D}(g \circ f)(a) = \mathrm{D}g(f(a)) \circ \mathrm{D}f(a).$$

Proof: It is not difficult, but more involved than the previous two. ∎

Lemma D.1.9 has many interesting consequences. We mention two corollaries.

Lemma D.1.10

Given three normed affine spaces E, F, and G, for any open subset A in E, for any $a \in A$, let $f: A \to F$ such that $\mathrm{D}f(a)$ exists, and let $g: F \to G$ be a continuous affine map. Then, $\mathrm{D}(g \circ f)(a)$ exists, and

$$\mathrm{D}(g \circ f)(a) = \vec{g} \circ \mathrm{D}f(a),$$

where $\vec{g}$ is the linear map associated with the affine map g.

Lemma D.1.11

Given two normed affine spaces E and F, let A be some open subset in E, let B be some open subset in F, let $f: A \to B$ be a bijection from A to B, and assume that $\mathrm{D}f$ exists on A and that $\mathrm{D}f^{-1}$ exists on B. Then, for every $a \in A$,

$$\mathrm{D}f^{-1}(f(a)) = (\mathrm{D}f(a))^{-1}.$$

Lemma D.1.11 has the remarkable consequence that the two vector spaces $\vec{E}$ and $\vec{F}$ have the same dimension. In other words, a local property, the existence of a bijection f between an open set A of E and an open set B of F, such that f is differentiable on A and f^{-1} is differentiable on B, implies a global property, that the two vector spaces $\vec{E}$ and $\vec{F}$ have the same dimension.

We now consider the situation where the normed affine space F is a finite direct sum $F = (F_1, b_1) \oplus \cdots \oplus (F_m, b_m)$.

Lemma D.1.12

Given normed affine spaces E and $F = (F_1, b_1) \oplus \cdots \oplus (F_m, b_m)$, given any open subset A of E, for any $a \in A$, for any function $f: A \to F$, letting $f = (f_1, \ldots, f_m)$, $\mathrm{D}f(a)$ exists iff every $\mathrm{D}f_i(a)$ exists, and

$$\mathrm{D}f(a) = in_1 \circ \mathrm{D}f_1(a) + \cdots + in_m \circ \mathrm{D}f_m(a).$$

Proof: Observe that $f(a + \vec{h}) - f(a) = (f(a + \vec{h}) - b) - (f(a) - b)$, where $b = (b_1, \ldots, b_m)$, and thus, as far as dealing with derivatives, $\mathrm{D}f(a)$ is equal to $\mathrm{D}f_b(a)$, where $f_b: E \to \vec{F}$ is defined such that $f_b(x) = f(x) - b$, for every $x \in E$. Thus, we can work with the vector space $\vec{F}$ instead of the affine space F. The lemma is then a simple application of Lemma D.1.9. ∎

In the special case where F is a normed affine space of finite dimension m, for any frame $(b_0, (\vec{v_1}, \ldots, \vec{v_m}))$ of F, where $(\vec{v_1}, \ldots, \vec{v_m})$ is a basis of $\vec{F}$, every point $x \in F$ can be expressed uniquely as

$$x = b_0 + x_1\vec{v_1} + \cdots + x_m\vec{v_m},$$

where $(x_1, \ldots, x_m) \in K^m$, the coordinates of x in the frame $(b_0, (\vec{v_1}, \ldots, \vec{v_m}))$ (where $K = \mathbf{R}$ or $K = \mathbf{C}$). Thus, letting F_i be the standard normed affine space K with its natural structure, we note that F is isomorphic to the direct sum $F = (K, 0) \oplus \cdots \oplus (K, 0)$. Then, every function $f: E \to F$ is represented by m functions $(f_1, \ldots, f_m)$, where $f_i: E \to K$ (where $K = \mathbf{R}$ or $K = \mathbf{C}$), and

$$f(x) = b_0 + f_1(x)\overrightarrow{v_1} + \cdots + f_m(x)\overrightarrow{v_m},$$

for every $x \in E$. The following lemma is an immediate corollary of Lemma D.1.12.

Lemma D.1.13

For any two normed affine spaces E and F, if F is of finite dimension m, for any frame $(b_0, (\overrightarrow{v_1}, \ldots, \overrightarrow{v_m}))$ of F, where $(\overrightarrow{v_1}, \ldots, \overrightarrow{v_m})$ is a basis of $\vec{F}$, for every $a \in E$, a function $f: E \to F$ is differentiable at a iff each f_i is differentiable at a, and

$$\mathrm{D}f(a)(\vec{u}) = \mathrm{D}f_1(a)(\vec{u})\overrightarrow{v_1} + \cdots + \mathrm{D}f_m(a)(\vec{u})\overrightarrow{v_m},$$

for every $\vec{u} \in \vec{E}$.

We now consider the situation where E is a finite direct sum. Given a normed affine space $E = (E_1, a_1) \oplus \cdots \oplus (E_n, a_n)$ and a normed affine space F, given any open subset A of E, for any $c = (c_1, \ldots, c_n) \in A$, we define the continuous functions $i_j^c: E_j \to E$, such that

$$i_j^c(x) = (c_1, \ldots, c_{j-1}, x, c_{j+1}, \ldots, c_n).$$

For any function $f: A \to F$, we have functions $f \circ i_j^c: E_j \to F$, defined on $(i_j^c)^{-1}(A)$, which contains c_j. If $\mathrm{D}(f \circ i_j^c)(c_j)$ exists, we call it the *partial derivative of f with respect to its jth argument, at c*. We also denote this derivative as $\mathrm{D}_j f(c)$. Note that $\mathrm{D}_j f(c) \in \mathcal{L}(\vec{E_j}; \vec{F})$. This notion is a generalization of the notion defined in Definition D.1.5. In fact, when E is of dimension n, and a frame $(a_0, (\overrightarrow{u_1}, \ldots, \overrightarrow{u_n}))$ has been chosen, we can write $E = (E_1, a_1) \oplus \cdots \oplus (E_n, a_n)$, for some obvious (E_j, a_j) (as explained just after Lemma D.1.12), and then

$$\mathrm{D}_j f(c)(\lambda \overrightarrow{u_j}) = \lambda \partial_j f(c),$$

and the two notions are consistent. The definition of i_j^c and of $\mathrm{D}_j f(c)$ also makes sense for a finite product $E_1 \times \cdots \times E_n$ of affine spaces E_i. We will use freely the notation $\partial_j f(c)$ instead of $\mathrm{D}_j f(c)$.

The notion $\partial_j f(c)$ introduced in Definition D.1.5 is really that of the vector derivative, whereas $\mathrm{D}_j f(c)$ is the corresponding linear map. Although perhaps confusing, we identify the two notions. The following lemma holds.

Lemma D.1.14

Given a normed affine space $E = (E_1, a_1) \oplus \cdots \oplus (E_n, a_n)$, and a normed affine space F, given any open subset A of E, for any function $f: A \to F$, for every $c \in A$, if $\mathrm{D}f(c)$ exists, then each $\mathrm{D}_j f(c)$ exists, and

$$\mathrm{D}f(c)(\overrightarrow{u_1}, \ldots, \overrightarrow{u_n}) = \mathrm{D}_1 f(c)(\overrightarrow{u_1}) + \cdots + \mathrm{D}_n f(c)(\overrightarrow{u_n}),$$

for every $\vec{u}_i \in \vec{E}_i$, $1 \leq i \leq n$. The same result holds for the finite product $E_1 \times \cdots \times E_n$.

Proof: Since every $c \in E$ can be written as $c = a + c - a$, where $a = (a_1, \ldots, a_n)$, defining $f_a \colon \vec{E} \to F$ such that, $f_a(\vec{u}) = f(a + \vec{u})$, for every $\vec{u} \in \vec{E}$, clearly, $\mathrm{D}f(c) = \mathrm{D}f_a(c - a)$, and thus, we can work with the function f_a whose domain is the vector space $\vec{E}$. The lemma is then a simple application of Lemma D.1.9. ∎

D.2   Jacobian Matrices

If both E and F are of finite dimension, and E has a frame $(a_0, (\overrightarrow{u_1}, \ldots, \overrightarrow{u_n}))$ and F has a frame $(b_0, (\overrightarrow{v_1}, \ldots, \overrightarrow{v_m}))$, every function $f \colon E \to F$ is determined by m functions $f_i \colon E \to \mathbf{R}$ (or $f_i \colon E \to \mathbf{C}$), where

$$f(x) = b_0 + f_1(x)\overrightarrow{v_1} + \cdots + f_m(x)\overrightarrow{v_m},$$

for every $x \in E$. From Lemma D.1.4, we have

$$\mathrm{D}f(a)(\overrightarrow{u_j}) = \mathrm{D}_{\overrightarrow{u_j}}f(a) = \partial_j f(a),$$

and from Lemma D.1.13, we have

$$\mathrm{D}f(a)(\overrightarrow{u_j}) = \mathrm{D}f_1(a)(\overrightarrow{u_j})\overrightarrow{v_1} + \cdots + \mathrm{D}f_i(a)(\overrightarrow{u_j})\overrightarrow{v_i} + \cdots + \mathrm{D}f_m(a)(\overrightarrow{u_j})\overrightarrow{v_m},$$

that is,

$$\mathrm{D}f(a)(\overrightarrow{u_j}) = \partial_j f_1(a)\overrightarrow{v_1} + \cdots + \partial_j f_i(a)\overrightarrow{v_i} + \cdots + \partial_j f_m(a)\overrightarrow{v_m}.$$

Since the jth column of the $m \times n$ matrix $J(f)(a)$ with respect to the bases $(\overrightarrow{u_1}, \ldots, \overrightarrow{u_n})$ and $(\overrightarrow{v_1}, \ldots, \overrightarrow{v_m})$ representing $\mathrm{D}f(a)$ is equal to the components of the vector $\mathrm{D}f(a)(\overrightarrow{u_j})$ over the basis $(\overrightarrow{v_1}, \ldots, \overrightarrow{v_m})$, the linear map $\mathrm{D}f(a)$ is determined by the $m \times n$ matrix $J(f)(a) = (\partial_j f_i(a))$, (or $J(f)(a) = (\frac{\partial f_i}{\partial x_j}(a))$):

$$J(f)(a) = \begin{pmatrix} \partial_1 f_1(a) & \partial_2 f_1(a) & \cdots & \partial_n f_1(a) \\ \partial_1 f_2(a) & \partial_2 f_2(a) & \cdots & \partial_n f_2(a) \\ \vdots & \vdots & \ddots & \vdots \\ \partial_1 f_m(a) & \partial_2 f_m(a) & \cdots & \partial_n f_m(a) \end{pmatrix}$$

or

$$J(f)(a) = \begin{pmatrix} \frac{\partial f_1}{\partial x_1}(a) & \frac{\partial f_1}{\partial x_2}(a) & \cdots & \frac{\partial f_1}{\partial x_n}(a) \\ \frac{\partial f_2}{\partial x_1}(a) & \frac{\partial f_2}{\partial x_2}(a) & \cdots & \frac{\partial f_2}{\partial x_n}(a) \\ \vdots & \vdots & \ddots & \vdots \\ \frac{\partial f_m}{\partial x_1}(a) & \frac{\partial f_m}{\partial x_2}(a) & \cdots & \frac{\partial f_m}{\partial x_n}(a) \end{pmatrix}$$

This matrix is called the *Jacobian matrix* of Df at a. Its determinant $\det(J(f)(a))$ is called the *Jacobian* of $Df(a)$. From a previous remark, we know that this determinant in fact only depends on $Df(a)$, and not on specific bases. However, partial derivatives give a means for computing it.

When $E = \mathbf{R}^n$ and $F = \mathbf{R}^m$, for any function $f: \mathbf{R}^n \to \mathbf{R}^m$, it is easy to compute the partial derivatives $\frac{\partial f_i}{\partial x_j}(a)$. We simply treat the function $f_i: \mathbf{R}^n \to \mathbf{R}$ as a function of its jth argument, leaving the others fixed, and compute the derivative as in Definition D.1.1, that is, the usual derivative. For example, consider the function $f: \mathbf{R}^2 \to \mathbf{R}^2$, defined such that

$$f(r, \theta) = (r \cos \theta, r \sin \theta).$$

Then, we have

$$J(f)(r, \theta) = \begin{pmatrix} \cos \theta & -r \sin \theta \\ \sin \theta & r \cos \theta \end{pmatrix}$$

and the Jacobian (determinant) has value $\det(J(f)(r, \theta)) = r$.

In the case where $E = \mathbf{R}$ (or $E = \mathbf{C}$), for any function $f: \mathbf{R} \to F$ (or $f: \mathbf{C} \to F$), the Jacobian matrix of $Df(a)$ is a column vector. In fact, this column vector is just $D_{\vec{1}} f(a)$. Then, for every $\lambda \in \mathbf{R}$ (or $\lambda \in \mathbf{C}$),

$$Df(a)(\lambda) = \lambda D_{\vec{1}} f(a).$$

This case is sufficiently important to warrant a definition.

Definition D.2.1

Given a function $f: \mathbf{R} \to F$ (or $f: \mathbf{C} \to F$), where F is a normed affine space, the vector

$$Df(a)(1) = D_{\vec{1}} f(a)$$

is called the vector derivative, *or* velocity vector *(in the real case) at a. We usually identify $Df(a)$ with its Jacobian matrix $D_{\vec{1}} f(a)$, which is the column vector corresponding to $D_{\vec{1}} f(a)$. By abuse of notation, we also let $Df(a)$ denote the vector* $Df(a)(\vec{1}) = D_{\vec{1}} f(a)$.

When $E = \mathbf{R}$, the physical interpretation is that f defines a (parametric) curve that is the trajectory of some particle moving in $\mathbf{R}^m$ as a function of time, and the vector $D_{\vec{1}} f(a)$ is the *velocity* of the moving particle $f(t)$ at $t = a$. It is often useful to consider functions $f: [a, b] \to F$ from a closed interval $[a, b] \subseteq \mathbf{R}$ to a normed affine space F, and its derivative $Df(a)$ on $[a, b]$, even though $[a, b]$ is not open. In this case, as in the case of a real-valued function, we define the right derivative $D_{\vec{1}} f(a_+)$ at a, and the left derivative $D_{\vec{1}} f(b_-)$ at b, and we assume their existence. For example, when $E = [0, 1]$, and $F = \mathbf{R}^3$, a function $f: [0, 1] \to \mathbf{R}^3$ defines a (parametric) curve in $\mathbf{R}^3$. Letting $f = (f_1, f_2, f_3)$, its Jacobian matrix at $a \in \mathbf{R}$ is

$$J(f)(a) = \begin{pmatrix} \frac{\partial f_1}{\partial t}(a) \\ \frac{\partial f_2}{\partial t}(a) \\ \frac{\partial f_3}{\partial t}(a) \end{pmatrix}$$

When $E = \mathbf{R}^2$, and $F = \mathbf{R}^3$, a function $\varphi \colon \mathbf{R}^2 \to \mathbf{R}^3$ defines a parametric surface. Letting $\varphi = (f, g, h)$, its Jacobian matrix at $a \in \mathbf{R}^2$ is

$$J(\varphi)(a) = \begin{pmatrix} \frac{\partial f}{\partial u}(a) & \frac{\partial f}{\partial v}(a) \\ \frac{\partial g}{\partial u}(a) & \frac{\partial g}{\partial v}(a) \\ \frac{\partial h}{\partial u}(a) & \frac{\partial h}{\partial v}(a) \end{pmatrix}$$

When $E = \mathbf{R}^3$, and $F = \mathbf{R}$, for a function $f \colon \mathbf{R}^3 \to \mathbf{R}$, the Jacobian matrix at $a \in \mathbf{R}^3$ is

$$J(f)(a) = \begin{pmatrix} \frac{\partial f}{\partial x}(a) & \frac{\partial f}{\partial y}(a) & \frac{\partial f}{\partial z}(a) \end{pmatrix}.$$

More generally, when $f \colon \mathbf{R}^n \to \mathbf{R}$, the Jacobian matrix at $a \in \mathbf{R}^n$ is the row vector

$$J(f)(a) = \begin{pmatrix} \frac{\partial f}{\partial x_1}(a), \ldots, \frac{\partial f}{\partial x_n}(a) \end{pmatrix}.$$

Its transpose is a column vector called the *gradient* of f at a, denoted as $\operatorname{grad} f(a)$ or $\nabla f(a)$. Then, given any $\vec{v} \in \mathbf{R}^n$, note that

$$\mathrm{D}f(a)(\vec{v}) = \frac{\partial f}{\partial x_1}(a)\, v_1 + \cdots + \frac{\partial f}{\partial x_n}(a)\, v_n = \operatorname{grad} f(a) \cdot \vec{v},$$

the scalar product of $\operatorname{grad} f(a)$ and $\vec{v}$.

When E, F, and G have finite dimensions, and $(a_0, (\vec{u_1}, \ldots, \vec{u_p}))$ is an affine frame for E, $(b_0, (\vec{v_1}, \ldots, \vec{v_n}))$ is an affine frame for F, and $(c_0, (\vec{w_1}, \ldots, \vec{w_m}))$ is an affine frame for G, if A is an open subset of E, B is an open subset of F, for any functions $f \colon A \to F$ and $g \colon B \to G$, such that $f(A) \subseteq B$, for any $a \in A$, letting $b = f(a)$, and $h = g \circ f$, if $\mathrm{D}f(a)$ exists and $\mathrm{D}g(b)$ exists, by Lemma D.1.9, the Jacobian matrix $J(h)(a) = J(g \circ f)(a)$ with respect to the bases $(\vec{u_1}, \ldots, \vec{u_p})$ and $(\vec{w_1}, \ldots, \vec{w_m})$ is the product of the Jacobian matrices $J(g)(b)$ with respect to the bases $(\vec{v_1}, \ldots, \vec{v_n})$ and $(\vec{w_1}, \ldots, \vec{w_m})$, and $J(f)(a)$ with respect to the bases $(\vec{u_1}, \ldots, \vec{u_p})$ and $(\vec{v_1}, \ldots, \vec{v_n})$:

$$J(h)(a) = \begin{pmatrix} \partial_1 g_1(b) & \partial_2 g_1(b) & \cdots & \partial_n g_1(b) \\ \partial_1 g_2(b) & \partial_2 g_2(b) & \cdots & \partial_n g_2(b) \\ \vdots & \vdots & \ddots & \vdots \\ \partial_1 g_m(b) & \partial_2 g_m(b) & \cdots & \partial_n g_m(b) \end{pmatrix} \begin{pmatrix} \partial_1 f_1(a) & \partial_2 f_1(a) & \cdots & \partial_p f_1(a) \\ \partial_1 f_2(a) & \partial_2 f_2(a) & \cdots & \partial_p f_2(a) \\ \vdots & \vdots & \ddots & \vdots \\ \partial_1 f_n(a) & \partial_2 f_n(a) & \cdots & \partial_p f_n(a) \end{pmatrix}$$

or

$$
J(h)(a) = \begin{pmatrix} \frac{\partial g_1}{\partial y_1}(b) & \frac{\partial g_1}{\partial y_2}(b) & \cdots & \frac{\partial g_1}{\partial y_n}(b) \\ \frac{\partial g_2}{\partial y_1}(b) & \frac{\partial g_2}{\partial y_2}(b) & \cdots & \frac{\partial g_2}{\partial y_n}(b) \\ \vdots & \vdots & \ddots & \vdots \\ \frac{\partial g_m}{\partial y_1}(b) & \frac{\partial g_m}{\partial y_2}(b) & \cdots & \frac{\partial g_m}{\partial y_n}(b) \end{pmatrix} \begin{pmatrix} \frac{\partial f_1}{\partial x_1}(a) & \frac{\partial f_1}{\partial x_2}(a) & \cdots & \frac{\partial f_1}{\partial x_p}(a) \\ \frac{\partial f_2}{\partial x_1}(a) & \frac{\partial f_2}{\partial x_2}(a) & \cdots & \frac{\partial f_2}{\partial x_p}(a) \\ \vdots & \vdots & \ddots & \vdots \\ \frac{\partial f_n}{\partial x_1}(a) & \frac{\partial f_n}{\partial x_2}(a) & \cdots & \frac{\partial f_n}{\partial x_p}(a) \end{pmatrix}
$$

Thus, we have the familiar formula

$$
\frac{\partial h_i}{\partial x_j}(a) = \sum_{k=1}^{k=n} \frac{\partial g_i}{\partial y_k}(b) \frac{\partial f_k}{\partial x_j}(a).
$$

Given two normed affine spaces E and F of finite dimension, given an open subset A of E, if a function $f : A \to F$ is differentiable at $a \in A$, then its Jacobian matrix is well defined.

You should be warned that the converse is false. There are functions such that all the partial derivatives exist at some $a \in A$, but yet, the function is not differentiable at a, and not even continuous at a. For example, consider the function $f : \mathbf{R}^2 \to \mathbf{R}$, defined such that $f(0, 0) = 0$, and

$$
f(x, y) = \frac{x^2 y}{x^4 + y^2} \qquad \text{if } (x, y) \neq (0, 0).
$$

For any $\vec{u} \neq \vec{0}$, letting $\vec{u} = \begin{pmatrix} h \\ k \end{pmatrix}$, we have

$$
\frac{f(\vec{0} + t\vec{u}) - f(\vec{0})}{t} = \frac{h^2 k}{t^2 h^4 + k^2},
$$

so that

$$
\mathrm{D}_{\vec{u}} f(0) = \begin{cases} \frac{h^2}{k} & \text{if } k \neq 0 \\ 0 & \text{if } k = 0. \end{cases}
$$

Thus, $\mathrm{D}_{\vec{u}} f(0)$ exists for all $\vec{u} \neq \vec{0}$. On the other hand, if $\mathrm{D} f(0)$ existed, it would be a linear map $\mathrm{D} f(0) : \mathbf{R}^2 \to \mathbf{R}$ represented by a row matrix $(\alpha \ \beta)$, and we would have $\mathrm{D}_{\vec{u}} f(0) = \mathrm{D} f(0)(\vec{u}) = \alpha h + \beta k$, but the explicit formula for $\mathrm{D}_{\vec{u}} f(0)$ is not linear. As a matter of fact, the function f is not continuous at $(0, 0)$. For example, on the parabola $y = x^2$, $f(x, y) = \frac{1}{2}$, and when we approach the origin on this parabola, the limit is $\frac{1}{2}$, when in fact, $f(0, 0) = 0$.

However, there are sufficient conditions on the partial derivatives for $\mathrm{D} f(a)$ to exist, namely, continuity of the partial derivatives. If f is differentiable on A, then f defines a function $\mathrm{D} f : A \to \mathcal{L}(\vec{E}; \vec{F})$. It turns out that the continuity of the partial derivatives on A is a necessary and sufficient condition for $\mathrm{D} f$ to exist and to be continuous on A. We first state a lemma that plays an important role in the proof of several major results of differential calculus. If E is an affine space (over $\mathbf{R}$ or $\mathbf{C}$), given any two points $a, b \in E$, the *closed segment* $[a, b]$ is the set of all points $a + \lambda(b - a)$, where $0 \leq \lambda \leq 1$, $\lambda \in \mathbf{R}$, and the *open segment* $]a, b[$ is the set of all points $a + \lambda(b - a)$, where $0 < \lambda < 1$, $\lambda \in \mathbf{R}$.

Lemma D.2.2

Let E and F be two normed affine spaces, let A be an open subset of E, and let $f: A \to F$ be a continuous function on A. Given any $a \in A$ and any $\vec{h} \neq \vec{0}$ in $\vec{E}$, if the closed segment $[a, a + \vec{h}]$ is contained in A, if $f: A \to F$ is differentiable at every point of the open segment $]a, a + \vec{h}[$, and

$$\max_{x \in]a, a + \vec{h}[} \|Df(x)\| \leq M,$$

for some $M \geq 0$, then

$$\left\| f(a + \vec{h}) - f(a) \right\| \leq M \left\| \vec{h} \right\|.$$

As a corollary, if $L: \vec{E} \to \vec{F}$ is a continuous linear map, then

$$\left\| f(a + \vec{h}) - f(a) - L(\vec{h}) \right\| \leq M \left\| \vec{h} \right\|,$$

where $M = \max_{x \in]a, a + \vec{h}[} \|Df(x) - L\|$.

The above lemma is sometimes called the "mean-value theorem." Lemma D.2.2 can be used to show the following important result.

Lemma D.2.3

Given two normed affine spaces E and F, where E is of finite dimension n, and where $(a_0, (\vec{u_1}, \dots, \vec{u_n}))$ is a frame of E, given any open subset A of E, given any function $f: A \to F$, the derivative $Df: A \to \mathcal{L}(\vec{E}; \vec{F})$ is defined and continuous on A iff every partial derivative $\partial_j f$ (or $\frac{\partial f}{\partial x_j}$) is defined and continuous on A, for all j, $1 \leq j \leq n$. As a corollary, if F is of finite dimension m, and $(b_0, (\vec{v_1}, \dots, \vec{v_m}))$ is a frame of F, the derivative $Df: A \to \mathcal{L}(\vec{E}; \vec{F})$ is defined and continuous on A iff every partial derivative $\partial_j f_i$ (or $\frac{\partial f_i}{\partial x_j}$) is defined and continuous on A, for all i, j, $1 \leq i \leq m$, $1 \leq j \leq n$.

Lemma D.2.3 gives a necessary and sufficient condition for the existence and continuity of the derivative of a function on an open set. It should be noted that a more general version of Lemma D.2.3 holds, assuming that $E = (E_1, a_1) \oplus \cdots \oplus (E_n, a_n)$, or $E = E_1 \times \cdots \times E_n$, and using the more general partial derivatives $D_j f$ introduced before Lemma D.1.14.

Definition D.2.4

Given two normed affine spaces E and F, and an open subset A of E, we say that a function $f: A \to F$ is of class C^0 on A, or a C^0 function on A, iff f is continuous on A. We say that $f: A \to F$ is of class C^1 on A, or a C^1 function on A, iff Df exists and is continuous on A.

Since the existence of the derivative on an open set implies continuity, a C^1 function is of course a C^0 function. Lemma D.2.3 gives a necessary and sufficient condition for a function f to be a C^1 function (when E is of finite dimension). It is easy to show that the composition of C^1 functions (on appropriate open sets) is a C^1 function.

It is also possible to define higher-order derivatives. For a complete treatment of higher-order derivatives and of various versions of the Taylor formula, see Lang [48].

[1]   Michael Artin. *Algebra*. Prentice Hall, first edition, 1991.

[2]   A. Avez. *Calcul Différentiel*. Masson, first edition, 1991.

[3]   A.A. Ball and D.J.T. Storry. Conditions for tangent plane continuity over recursively generated B-spline surfaces. *ACM Transactions on Computer Graphics*, 7(2):83–102, 1988.

[4]   Richard H. Bartels, John C. Beatty, and Brian A. Barsky. *An Introduction to Splines for Use in Computer Graphics and Geometric Modelling*. Morgan Kaufmann, first edition, 1987.

[5]   Marcel Berger. *Géométrie 1*. Nathan, 1990. English edition: *Geometry 1*. Universitext. Springer-Verlag.

[6]   Marcel Berger. *Géométrie 2*. Nathan, 1990. English edition: *Geometry 2*. Universitext. Springer-Verlag.

[7]   Marcel Berger and Bernard Gostiaux. *Géométrie Différentielle: Variétés, Courbes et Surfaces*. Collection Mathématiques. Puf, second edition, 1992. English edition: *Differential Geometry, Manifolds, Curves, and Surfaces*. GTM No. 115, Springer-Verlag.

[8]   J.E. Bertin. *Algèbre Linéaire et Géométrie Classique*. Masson, first edition, 1981.

[9]   W. Böhm and G. Farin. Letter to the editor. *Computer Aided Design*, 15(5):260–261, 1983. Concerning subdivison of Bézier triangles.

[10] W. Böhm, G. Farin, and J. Kahman. A survey of curve and surface methods in CAGD. *Computer Aided Geometric Design*, 1:1–60, 1984.

[11] W. Böhm and H. Prautzsch. *Geometric Concepts for Geometric Design*. AK Peters, first edition, 1994.

[12] Wolfgang Böhm. Subdividing multivariate splines. *Computer Aided Design*, 15:345–352, 1983.

[13] J.-D. Boissonnat and M. Yvinec. *Géométrie Algorithmique*. Ediscience International, first edition, 1995.

[14] Nicolas Bourbaki. *Algèbre, Chapitres 1–3*. Eléments de Mathématiques. Hermann, 1970.

[15] Nicolas Bourbaki. *Algèbre, Chapitres 4–7*. Eléments de Mathématiques. Masson, 1981.

[16] Henri Cartan. *Cours de Calcul Différentiel*. Collection Méthodes. Hermann, 1990.

[17] E. Catmull and J. Clark. Recursively generated B-spline surfaces on arbitrary topological meshes. *Computer Aided Design*, 10(6):350–355, 1978.

[18] G.M. Chaikin. An algorithm for high-speed curve generation. *IEEE Computer Graphics and Image Processing*, 3:346–349, 1974.

[19] P.G. Ciarlet. *Introduction to Numerical Matrix Analysis and Optimization*. Cambridge University Press, first edition, 1989. French edition: Masson, 1994.

[20] E. Cohen, T. Lyche, and R. Riesenfeld. Discrete B-splines and subdivision techniques in computer aided geometric design and computer graphics. *Computer Graphics and Image Processing*, 14(2):87–111, 1980.

[21] Philip J. Davis. *Circulant Matrices*. AMS Chelsea Publishing, second edition, 1994.

[22] Carl de Boor. *A Practical Guide to Splines*. Springer-Verlag, first edition, 1978.

[23] Paul de Faget de Casteljau. *Shape Mathematics and CAD*. Hermes, first edition, 1986.

[24] Tony DeRose, Michael Kass, and Tien Truong. Subdivision surfaces in character animation. In *Computer Graphics (SIGGRAPH '98 Proceedings)*, pages 85–94. ACM, 1998.

[25] Jean Dieudonné. *Algèbre Linéaire et Géométrie Elémentaire*. Hermann, second edition, 1965.

[26] Manfredo P. do Carmo. *Differential Geometry of Curves and Surfaces*. Prentice Hall, 1976.

[27] D. Doo. A subdivision algorithm for smoothing down irregularly shaped polyhedrons. In *Proceedings on Interactive Techniques in Computer Aided Design, Bologna, Italy*, pages 157–165. IEEE, 1978.

[28] D. Doo and M. Sabin. Behavior of recursive division surfaces near extraordinary points. *Computer Aided Design*, 10(6):356–360, 1978.

[29] D.W.H. Doo. *A Recursive Subdivision Algorithm for Fitting Quadratic Surfaces to Irregular Polyhedrons*. Ph.D. thesis, Brunel University, Oxbridge, England, 1978.

[30] G. Farin. Triangular Bernstein-Bézier patches. *Computer Aided Geometric Design*, 3:83–127, 1986.

[31] Gerald Farin. *NURB Curves and Surfaces, from Projective Geometry to Practical Use*. AK Peters, first edition, 1995.

[32] Gerald Farin. *Curves and Surfaces for CAGD*. Academic Press, fourth edition, 1998.

[33] Olivier Faugeras. *Three-Dimensional Computer Vision, A Geometric Viewpoint*. MIT Press, first edition, 1996.

[34] D.J. Filip. Adapative subdivision algorithms for a set of Bézier triangles. *Computer Aided Design*, 18:74–78, 1986.

[35] J.-C. Fiorot and P. Jeannin. *Courbes et Surfaces Rationelles*. RMA 12. Masson, first edition, 1989.

[36] J.-C. Fiorot and P. Jeannin. *Courbes Splines Rationelles*. RMA 24. Masson, first edition, 1992.

[37] William Fulton. *Algebraic Curves*. Advanced Book Classics. Addison-Wesley, first edition, 1989.

[38] R.N. Goldman. Subdivision algorithms for Bézier triangles. *Computer Aided Design*, 15:159–166, 1983.

[39] A. Gray. *Modern Differential Geometry of Curves and Surfaces*. CRC Press, second edition, 1997.

[40] Donald T. Greenwood. *Principles of Dynamics*. Prentice Hall, second edition, 1988.

[41] Joe Harris. *Algebraic Geometry, A First Course*. GTM No. 133. Springer-Verlag, first edition, 1992.

[42] D. Hilbert and S. Cohn-Vossen. *Geometry and the Imagination*. Chelsea Publishing Co., 1952.

[43] Christoph M. Hoffman. *Geometric and Solid Modeling*. Morgan Kaufmann, first edition, 1989.

[44] H. Hoppe, T. DeRose, T. Duchamp, M. Halstead, H. Jin, J. McDonald, J. Schweitzer, and W. Stuetzle. Piecewise smooth surface reconstruction. In *Computer Graphics (SIGGRAPH '94 Proceedings)*, pages 295–302. ACM, 1994.

[45] J. Hoschek and D. Lasser. *Computer Aided Geometric Design*. AK Peters, first edition, 1993.

[46] Jan J. Koenderink. *Solid Shape*. MIT Press, first edition, 1990.

[47] Serge Lang. *Algebra*. Addison-Wesley, third edition, 1993.

[48] Serge Lang. *Undergraduate Analysis*. UTM. Springer-Verlag, second edition, 1997.

[49] Aaron Lee, Wim Sweldens, Peter Schroder, Lawrence Cowsar, and David Dobkin. MAPS: Multiresolution adaptive parameterization of surfaces. In *Computer Graphics (SIGGRAPH '98 Proceedings)*, pages 95–104. ACM, 1998.

[50] Charles Loop. *Smooth Subdivision Surfaces Based on Triangles*. Master's thesis, University of Utah, Department of Mathematics, Salt Lake City, 1987.

[51] Charles Loop. A G^1 triangular spline surface of arbitrary topological type. *Computer Aided Geometric Design*, 11:303–330, 1994.

[52] Saunders Mac Lane and Garrett Birkhoff. *Algebra*. Macmillan, first edition, 1967.

[53] Dimitris N. Metaxas. *Physics-Based Deformable Models*. Kluwer Academic Publishers, first edition, 1997.

[54] James R. Munkres. *Topology, A First Course*. Prentice Hall, first edition, 1975.

[55] James R. Munkres. *Analysis on Manifolds*. Addison-Wesley, 1991.

[56] A.H. Nasri. Polyhedral subdivision methods for free-form surfaces. *ACM Transactions on Computer Graphics*, 6(1):29–73, 1987.

[57] Walter Noll. *Finite-Dimensional Spaces*. Kluwer Academic Publishers, first edition, 1987.

[58] Joseph O'Rourke. *Computational Geometry in* C. Cambridge University Press, first edition, 1994.

[59] Dan Pedoe. *Geometry, A Comprehensive Course*. Dover, first edition, 1988.

[60] J. Peters and U. Reif. Analysis of generalized *B*-spline subdivision algorithms. *SIAM Journal of Numerical Analysis*, 35(2), 1997.

[61] J. Peters and U. Reif. The simplest subdivision scheme for smoothing polyhedra. *ACM Transactions on Graphics*, 16(4):420–431, 1997.

[62] Les Piegl and Wayne Tiller. *The NURBS Book*. Monograph in Visual Communications. Springer-Verlag, first edition, 1995.

[63] Helmut Prautzsch. *Unterteilungsalgorithmen für Multivariate Splines*. Ph.D. thesis, TU Braunschweig, Braunschweig, Germany, 1984.

[64] F.P. Preparata and M.I. Shamos. *Computational Geometry: An Introduction*. Springer-Verlag, first edition, 1988.

[65] Lyle Ramshaw. Blossoming: A connect-the-dots approach to splines. Technical report no. 19, Digital SRC, Palo Alto, California, 1987.

[66] U. Reif. A unified approach to subdivision algorithms near extraordinary vertices. *Computed Aided Geometric Design*, 12, pages 153–174, 1995.

[67] R.F. Riesenfeld. On Chaikin's algorithm. *IEEE Computer Graphics and Image Processing*, 4:304–310, 1975.

[68] J.-J. Risler. *Mathematical Methods for CAD*. Masson, first edition, 1992.

[69] Pierre Samuel. *Projective Geometry*. Undergraduate Texts in Mathematics. Springer-Verlag, first edition, 1988.

[70] Laurent Schwartz. *Analyse I. Théorie des Ensembles et Topologie*. Collection Enseignement des Sciences. Hermann, 1991.

[71] Laurent Schwartz. *Analyse II. Calcul Différentiel et Equations Différentielles*. Collection Enseignement des Sciences. Hermann, 1992.

[72] Laurent Schwartz. *Analyse III. Calcul Intégral*. Collection Enseignement des Sciences. Hermann, 1993.

[73] Laurent Schwartz. *Analyse IV. Applications à la Théorie de la Mesure*. Collection Enseignement des Sciences. Hermann, 1993.

[74] Thomas Sederberg, Jianmin Zheng, David Sewell, and Malcom Sabin. Non-uniform recursive subdivision surfaces. In *Computer Graphics (SIGGRAPH '98 Proceedings)*, pages 387–394. ACM, 1998.

[75] H.P. Seidel. A general subdivision theorem for Bézier triangles. In Tom Lyche and Larry Schumaker, editors, *Mathematical Methods in Computer Aided Geometric Design*, pages 573–581. Academic Press, 1989.

[76] J.-C. Sidler. *Géométrie Projective*. InterEditions, first edition, 1993.

[77] Ernst Snapper and Robert J. Troyer. *Metric Affine Geometry*. Dover, first edition, 1989.

[78] Jos Stam. Exact evaluation of Catmull-Clark subdivision surfaces at arbitrary parameter values. In *Computer Graphics (SIGGRAPH '98 Proceedings)*, pages 395–404. ACM, 1998.

[79] Eric J. Stollnitz, Tony D. DeRose, and David H. Salesin. *Wavelets for Computer Graphics Theory and Applications*. Morgan Kaufmann, first edition, 1996.

[80] Gilbert Strang. *Introduction to Applied Mathematics*. Wellesley-Cambridge Press, first edition, 1986.

[81] Gilbert Strang. *Linear Algebra and Its Applications*. Saunders HBJ, third edition, 1988.

[82] Gilbert Strang and Nguyen Truong. *Wavelets and Filter Banks*. Wellesley-Cambridge Press, second printing, 1997.

[83] Claude Tisseron. *Géométries Affines, Projectives, et Euclidiennes*. Hermann, first edition, 1994.

[84] B.L. Van Der Waerden. *Algebra, Vol. 1*. Ungar, seventh edition, 1973.

[85] O. Veblen and J.W. Young. *Projective Geometry, Vol. 1*. Ginn, second edition, 1938.

[86] O. Veblen and J.W. Young. *Projective Geometry, Vol. 2*. Ginn, first edition, 1946.

[87] Hermann Weyl. *The Classical Groups. Their Invariants and Representations*. Princeton Mathematical Series, No. 1. Princeton University Press, second edition, 1946.

[88] D. Zorin, P. Schroder, and W. Sweldens. Interpolation subdivision for meshes with arbitrary topology. In *Computer Graphics (SIGGRAPH '96 Proceedings)*, pages 189–192. ACM, 1996.

[89] Denis Zorin. *Subdivision and Multiresolution Surface Representation*. Ph.D. thesis, Caltech, Pasadena, California, 1997.

Jean Gallier received the degree of Civil Engineer from the Ecole Nationale des Ponts et Chaussees in 1972 and a Ph.D. in computer science from UCLA in 1978. That same year he joined the University of Pennsylvania, where he is presently a professor in CIS with a secondary appointment in mathematics. In 1983, he received the Linback Award for distinguished teaching. Gallier's research interests range from constructive logics and automated theorem proving to geometry and its applications to computer graphics, animation, computer vision, and motion planning. The author of *Logic in Computer Science*, he enjoys hiking (especially the Alps) and swimming. He also enjoys classical music (Mozart), jazz (Duke Ellington and Oscar Peterson), and wines from Burgundy, especially Volnay.